What people are saying ....

"Seals, Trumpets, bowls and beasts .... what is a layman to do? Open your Bible and follow along with Wayne Gaylord as he opens the veil on the Book that "opens the veil". From the blessing offered for reading Revelation in the first chapter to the concluding victory of our Lord Jesus Christ in the final chapters, Wayne leads us through all the details in between. Read and be encouraged, informed and blessed!"
Dr. Jimmy Pritchard, Senior Pastor, First Baptist Church, Forney, Texas

"Over the years I have read many commentaries on the Book of Revelation – across the spectrum of viewpoints and theories. Wayne Gaylord's FINALLY HOME is different. Not because he takes a clear and unapologetic Dispensational point-of-view – others do that as well. No, FINALLY HOME is different because it is delectably readable, refreshingly understandable, and best of all, eminently practical. Read it, and you will understand that God gave this amazing book to encourage Christians to live for Christ .... today."
Dr. C. Richard Wells, Chancellor, John Witherspoon College, Rapid City, South Dakota

"The Book of Revelation is cloaked in mystery, symbolism and metaphor that can make it sometimes difficult to understand. Wayne Gaylord's FINALLY HOME unfolds the mysteries, reveals the symbolism, and explains the metaphors without being dry and tedious. Filled with Wayne's down-home-humor and personal anecdotes, you will be laughing one minute and seriously riveted on the deep biblical truths in the next. What a great way to study God's Word!"
Rev. Al Gist, Senior Evangelist and Founder of Maranatha Ministries, Longville, Louisiana

"What a privilege to read about the things of Heaven – The New Earth, The New Heaven and The New Jerusalem in FINALLY HOME. It is a wonderful book with so much information for people to consider and turn to Jesus for salvation. The book is filled with love, hope and pure joy as we read about our new home in Heaven!"
Wanda Boyer, Housewife

"Finally Home is simply a book that unveils prophecy – from the birth of Christ to His ultimate reign as KING of kings and LORD of lords. Great times are ahead for the family of God!"
Shannon Petrea, R.N.

"The Book of Revelation sadly scares many people, not so much because of its many descriptions of disasters and divine judgment, but because they often consider it almost entirely beyond their ability to understand. In his wonderful commentary, FINALLY HOME, Wayne Gaylord lays it out verse by verse and concept by concept, and puts its marvelous truths within our grasp. We discovered that it really wasn't that unfathomable after all — we just needed to take it a piece at a time, and dare to believe that God means what He says. Plunge into its truths with Wayne, and you will be surely blessed!"

Dennis Pollock, Senior Evangelist to Nigeria, Kenya, Uganda and other parts of Africa

"Wayne Gaylord has thoroughly researched the subject. He uses a common sense approach to the commentary, highlighting the literal return of Jesus Christ and the literal establishment of His Kingdom on earth. This is a must read for anyone who wishes to better understand the Book of Revelation."

Rev. Gary Fisher, Founder and Senior Evangelist for Lion of Judah Ministries, Franklin, Tennessee

Finally Home

A Verse by Verse Journey Through the Book of Revelation

JOHN WAYNE GAYLORD

WESTBOW
PRESS®
A DIVISION OF THOMAS NELSON
& ZONDERVAN

WestBow Press books may be ordered through booksellers or by contacting:

WestBow Press
A Division of Thomas Nelson & Zondervan
1663 Liberty Drive
Bloomington, IN 47403
www.westbowpress.com
1 (866) 928-1240

This book is dedicated to all believers who are faithfully watching the eastern sky for the Lord's return, but specifically:

*To my friend, **Jim McConnell**, whose encouragement and persistence convinced me of the need to add this book to the field of Bible prophecy.*

*To **my wife, Arlene**, who spent many hours of proofreading and making valuable suggestions.*

*To my friend and mentor, **Dr. David R. Reagan**, who made the Book of Revelation come alive and taught me "when the plain sense makes sense, don't look for any other sense or you will wind up with nonsense."*

CONTENTS

Preface ix

Introduction xi

Chapter 1: *Introduction and God's Table of Contents*............................1

Chapter 2: *Jesus Critiques Four Churches in Asia*................................33

Chapter 3: *Jesus Critiques Three Churches in Asia* 57

Chapter 4: *The Rapture of the Church* 75

Chapter 5: *The Seven Sealed Book* 89

Chapter 6: *The Four Horsemen of the Apocalypse* 107

Chapter 7: *144,000 Jews Are Sealed for Protection* 135

Chapter 8: *The Seventh Seal is Opened* 151

Chapter 9: *The Three Woe Trumpets and The Bottomless Pit* 161

Chapter 10: *The Mighty Angel and The Little Book*............................177

Chapter 11: *Two Witnesses and the Seventh Trumpet*..........................191

Chapter 12: *War in Heaven* 217

Chapter 13: *The Two Beasts* 247

Chapter 14: *144,000 Evangelists on Mount Zion* 275

Chapter 15: *The Song of Moses and The Song of the Lamb*.................303

Chapter 16: *The Seven Bowl Judgments* 309

Chapter 17: *Mystery Babylon*..325

Chapter 18: *Babylon the Great* 347

Chapter 19: *The Second Coming of Jesus Christ*..................................369

Chapter 20: *Satan Bound, White Throne Judgment, Final Rebellion*....403

Chapter 21: *The New Heaven, The New Earth, The New Jerusalem*......435

Chapter 22: *The Eternal State*...505

References 535

PREFACE

When I was 16, I was given a book by an elderly Christian friend, Orville Mitchell Sr., who was one of the original founders of *Young Life.* The book was entitled, *Lectures on the Book of Revelation* by Dr. H. A. Ironside, and it instilled in me a lifelong love for prophecy and the study of God's Word.

In 1987, I came across a radio program that caught my attention. It was called, "Christ in Prophecy," and the speaker was Dr. David R. Reagan. It was so powerful I became a regular listener. The program was fresh, alive and challenged me to dig deeper into God's Word, especially in the area of prophecy. Not long after that, I arranged a meeting with Dr. Reagan. It was a meeting that would change the course of my life, and begin a deep friendship that would last over the years.

As a Bible teacher for many years, I do not take teaching God's Word for granted nor do I accept the task lightly. It is an awesome responsibility, and I am keenly aware that the Lord will hold me to a higher standard for teaching the truth *"once delivered to the saints"* (Jude 1:3).

This book is the outgrowth of a series of lessons I brought to the Believers Bible Class at First Baptist Church, Forney, Texas. My desire is that the Lord will take this presentation and inspire others to dig deeper into the marvelous riches of the grace and mercy of the Lord Jesus Christ.

INTRODUCTION

This is not a book to identify the Antichrist, but rather to unveil the glory and majesty of the Lord Jesus Christ. My purpose is to present a book that is not only understandable for the layman or teacher, but useful in explaining some of the more confusing aspects of the Revelation, and to harmonize some of its "seeming contradictions." It is also to show how the book can be used as an important tool for witnessing to non-believers since it stresses that the time for decisions is short.

The Book of Revelation contains material that is sometimes literal and sometimes symbolic. I have not approached the book with preconceived ideas. Instead, I have endeavored to let the Holy Spirit guide, relying on the oft quoted statement by Dr. Reagan, "If the plain sense makes sense, don't look for any other sense or you will wind up with nonsense." A literal approach to interpreting the book will be used unless common sense and the context dictate otherwise.

If Scripture says there are four angels, I believe there are four angels. But if Scripture says we see the Lamb of God as though it was slain, we know we are not looking for a four legged animal. I will attempt to set forth the various interpretations of Revelation, and when possible, direct the reader to a fuller discussion of such subjects.

The material has been gleaned from the writings, sermons and messages of scores of pastors, teachers and writers over my 60 years of Bible study. I have attempted to give credit to specific sources when they can be identified, but sometimes that information is not available. My apologies to any source that has been inadvertently omitted from the references, and trust that God will give those individuals the recognition they so richly deserve at the Bema Seat of Christ.

CHAPTER ONE

Introduction and God's Table of Contents

The best way to get the most from this study is to have your Bible open and follow along with the verses indicated. The Book of Revelation is not an impossible book to understand, but it is challenging because there are so many moving parts. Consequently, some principles or statements are repeated from time to time in order to reinforce the teaching.

Someone might ask the question, "Why study prophecy in the first place, especially the Book of Revelation?" Let me give you 5 reasons:

1) God wants us to read and understand it (Revelation 1:3).
2) Jesus told us to watch for signs of His coming (Matthew 24:42).
3) It reveals God's plan for the future of humankind (Revelation 1:19).
4) It will give us an urgency to share the gospel with all our friends and relatives for the time is short (Revelation 1:3; 22:6, 10).
5) It will call us to holy living (I John 3:2-3).

In the study of any book of this importance and magnitude, it is vitally important to make certain preparations before the actual study begins. Few people in their lifetime have dedicated the time and effort to go through the Book of Revelation verse by verse to glean what God would have them learn. To begin with let us get acquainted with some of the words that you would hear if you went to a Bible school or seminary. They are not words we generally use in everyday conversation, so they tend to be a little intimidating.

> Theology – the study of God
> Bibliology – the study of the Bible
> Angelology – the study of angels
> Anthropology – the study of man
> Soteriology – the study of salvation
> Ecclesiology – the study of the Church
> Eschatology – the study of end times or the last days

So, when someone asks what you are reading, you can say, "Oh, I am just studying Eschatology." They will either be impressed or they will think you have lost your mind. Before we actually begin to go through the Book of Revelation, I want to give you an overview along with some tips on how to get the most out of these lessons.

First, look at what the Bible, God's Word, says about itself. *"All Scripture is given by inspiration of God, and is profitable for doctrine, for reproof, for correction, for instruction in righteousness: that the man of God may be perfect, thoroughly furnished unto all good works"* (II Timothy 3:16-17). In other words, the Bible is our owner's manual – our guide to everyday living which our Creator designed so that we would get the most out of life. A little girl, when asked what the word Bible means replied, "B.I.B.L.E. stands for Basic Instructions Before Leaving Earth." As mentioned above, the Bible affirms that *"All Scripture is given by inspiration of God,"* and therefore implies that in its original transmission it is inerrant and trustworthy. But sadly, many churches ignore prophecy, particularly the Book of Revelation saying that it is too confusing or that it was fulfilled in the 1st Century, and is therefore irrelevant for us today. That is a dubious statement to make considering that 25-30% of the entire Bible is prophetic in nature and speaks of things that will happen in the future.

Dr. Tim LaHaye meticulously went through the Bible, and identified all the verses in the New Testament that have to do with prophecy.[1] Here is the percent for each Book he found related to prophecy: Matthew 26%, Mark 19%, Luke 22%, John 20%, Acts 13%, Romans 21%, I Corinthians 19%, II Corinthians 5%, Galatians 11%, Ephesians 5%, Philippians 10%, Colossians 9%, I Thessalonians 18%, II Thessalonians 40%, I Timothy 4%, II Timothy 20%, Titus 2%, Philemon 0%, Hebrews 45%, James 6%, I Peter 20%, II Peter 41%, I John 6%, II John 15%, III John 0%, Jude 40%, Revelation 95%.

Many have said that the Book of Revelation is like a Chinese puzzle. We cannot figure it out – we cannot understand it – so it is best to just leave it alone. Others say that virtually everything predicted in Revelation was fulfilled within 100 years of Christ's death. All that is left, they say, is the Great White Throne Judgment, the sentencing of Satan and our entering the Eternal State. This interpretation is embodied by what is called preterism and is the general teaching of the Roman Catholic Church and many of today's liberal Protestant churches.[2]

At the outset, let me say that I subscribe to the Biblical principle of love taught throughout the Scriptures: love your neighbor – love your enemies – and love those with whom I disagree and those who disagree with me. As I record differences of opinion with other groups and denominations, such differences have to do with varying interpretations of Biblical doctrines and teachings and are not in any way intended to impugn any individuals or churches. When the term cult is used, it is referring to those religious systems or groups that are generally considered outside the main stream of church orthodoxy. Every effort is made to fairly present their position from their own writings. It is never our intention to mislead anyone.

There are no agendas or motives other than to introduce the readers to the marvelous Person of the Lord Jesus Christ as presented in the Holy Scriptures. We praise God that our country allows freedom to debate ideas without recriminations and I expect the same from those who hold differing opinions or interpretations from me. The conclusions reached herein are strictly those of the author and do not necessarily reflect the views of any other individual or churches.

The Roman Catholic Church believes that the Rapture (which we will discuss shortly) will occur simultaneously with the Second Coming, and therefore will not precede the Tribulation Period. To say that virtually everything in the Book has been fulfilled and there is nothing left but the final judgment is an unsound interpretation of the Book. It is easily proven that most of these prophecies have not yet been fulfilled.

It takes very little effort to arrive at the conclusion that most of the events in the Book have been fulfilled in the 1st Century. You do not have to study what the signs and symbols mean. You just ignore the details, and believe that all that is left is one final event where the saved and the lost are divided into two groups with one group going to Heaven and the other to Hell. With this view, prophecy is tied up with a nice ribbon and you do not have to sweat the details.

The next time someone says to you that the prophecies in Revelation have already been fulfilled, turn to Revelation 9:18 and ask them, "When in the history of mankind (other than Noah's flood) was one-third of the world's population killed?" Earlier, we read that *"All Scripture is inspired and is profitable …."* (II Timothy 3:16), and that includes the Book of Revelation. It is mandatory that it be seriously studied.

There are at least seven keys to understanding the Book of Revelation:

1. **God wants you to understand it.** How do we know that? Turn to Revelation 1:3. *"Blessed is he that readeth, and they that hear the words of this prophecy, and keep those things which are written therein: for the time is at hand."*

This is the only Book in the entire Bible where God promises a blessing to those who read it and keep the things written therein. Consequently, God would not mock us by saying, "I am going to give a blessing to those who read this and keep the things written therein and – ha, ha, ha – the joke's on you because you cannot understand it!" God does not operate that way. When He promises to bless those who read it and keep what it says, He means it. So it goes without saying, God wants you to understand it. And if we rely on the Holy Spirit who directed John to write it in the first place, He will help us understand it, and give us new insights into its message virtually every time we read it.

Let me say a word about skeptics who read the Book with a critical attitude. They are plentiful on the internet. One such critic is Roberta Grimes, attorney, radio host and nationally known writer. In her article entitled "Apocalyptic Nonsense", she views the writings of the Apostle John in the Revelation as the "ramblings" of a confused man.[3] In the light of that comment, consider I Corinthians 2:14 (NLT), *"But people who aren't Christians can't understand these truths from God's Spirit. It all sounds foolish to them because only those who have the Spirit can understand what the Spirit means."* To non-believers, the Book of Revelation is foolishness. Bill Gothard once remarked at one of his seminars I attended, "Revelation was written to believers, so if non-believers do not understand it, that is what they get for reading other people's mail."

2. **Our second key is a common sense principle:** "If the plain sense makes sense, don't look for any other sense, or you'll wind up with nonsense." A variation of this principle has been voiced by a number of theologians, but I first heard it from Dr. David Reagan.[4] An example is found in Revelation chapter 7. God seals (or puts his protection on) 144,000 Jews – 12,000 from each of the 12 tribes of Israel. The Jehovah's Witnesses say these are 144,000 from their group. But God says these are all JEWS! "When the plain sense makes sense .... " well, you know the rest.

3. **Follow the table of contents.** Revelation 1:19 gives us the table of contents for the Book, and it is given in three tenses: past, present and future. It says: *"Write the things which thou hast seen* [past events], *and the things which are* [present events], *and the things which shall be hereafter* [future events]." When we apply this table of contents to the Book, here is how it unfolds:

> Chapter 1 is the past or the things which John has seen.
> Chapters 2-3 are the present or the things which are.
> Chapters 4-22 are the future or the things which lie ahead.

4. **Be careful as to what time frame the Scripture is in.** Is it past, present or future?

5. **Another key is to study the writings of the Old Testament prophets.** There are about 300 prophecies in the Old Testament relating to the first coming of Christ, and there are about 500 prophecies in the Old Testament relating to His Second Coming. Why are there nearly twice as many prophecies for the Second Coming? It is because at His Second Coming Jesus is coming in judgment and wrath, and God in His mercy wants to give everyone plenty of warning.

6. **Watch for flash-forwards.** This key is one of the most important ones. We are all familiar with its cousin, flashbacks. Writers use this tool all the time to bring past events to our minds. You will be reading about Billy who is 25 years old, and when you come to the next chapter it begins with "Billy – it's time to get up! Today is your birthday! You are 7 years old!" This is a flashback. But the key that really opens the Book as nothing else does is the discovery that God

also uses flash-forwards! He can do this because He knows what is going to happen in the future. *"Remember the former things of old, For I am God, and there is no other; I am God, and there is none like Me, Declaring the end from the beginning, And from ancient times things that are not yet done, Saying, 'My counsel shall stand, And I will do all My pleasure'"* (Isaiah 46:9-10 NKJV).

Few commentators have discovered this key. This understanding of flash-forwards will make this Book come alive as never before; otherwise, one will be totally confused as to the chronology of events taking place. We will cover flash-forwards in detail later. Just remember that God uses them from time to time. When the action is SO intense that we can hardly stand it, God calls time-out, and shows us a flash-forward of something that will happen in the future to encourage us, and confirm that He is in complete command of things.

7. **And finally, keep your eyes on Jesus.** The Revelation is also called the Apocalypse, which in Greek means "the unveiling." If you have an older KJV, it says the name of the Book is, "The Revelation of St. John the Divine." It is unfortunate that it is styled like that. It is not the Revelation of John; it is the Revelation to John regarding the unveiling of Jesus Christ. It will show us how the Suffering Lamb becomes the Conquering Lion. What Revelation is to the New Testament, the Book of Daniel is to the Old Testament. And though they were written over 500 years apart, they fit together like a hand in glove as we will see later in this study.

Satan does not want you to read or study the Book of Revelation because it tells how everything is going to end, including His final judgment. I have long taken the position that Satan, even though he can read his fate in the 20th chapter of Revelation, he does not believe it. He thinks that somehow, someway, he is going to overthrow God in that final encounter.

A few years ago, someone gave me this good advice: "If Satan is bugging you, and is always reminding you of your past – remind him of his future! He will leave in a hurry after that."

The Book of Revelation has incredibly good news for the believer. But it has incredibly bad news for the unbeliever. This is confirmed in the first chapter of an Old Testament Book named for the prophet, Nahum. In chapter 1, verse 7 (NLT) it says, *"The LORD is good."* But in that same chapter, verse 3 (NLT) says, *"The LORD is slow to get angry, but His power is great, and He never lets the guilty go unpunished."*

I gave you an outline earlier based on timing: the past, present and future. Let me give you another outline of the Book of Revelation based on the events as they are taking place:

Chapters 1-3 Jesus and the Church Age
Chapters 4-18 Jesus and the Tribulation Period
Chapters 19-20 Jesus and the Millennial Kingdom
Chapters 21-22 Jesus and the Eternal State

That great theologian and scientist, Dr. Henry Morris, made a brilliant observation. He said, "The Book of Revelation is not hard to understand. It is hard to believe. If you believe it, you will understand it."[5]

In preparation for this study, please do the following. Read through the entire Book of Revelation at one sitting. You can do it in about an hour. Don't be distressed if you do not understand it. Just read it straight through. But before you start, ask God for understanding just as Solomon asked God for wisdom, and God will honor your prayer. Claim the promise of Revelation 1:3 for yourself, "*Blessed is he that readeth, and they that hear the words of this prophecy, and keep those things which are written therein: for the time is at hand.*" Will you understand every detail? Probably not. But you will be amazed as to how much the Holy Spirit will help you understand, and you will begin to get a clearer picture of God's master plan for the human race.

Before we actually move into the Book, let me tell you there are 8,000 different interpretations. Just kidding, but there is a sizable number. Most of the different interpretations can be boiled down into two groups: 1) the timing of the Rapture; and 2) the timing and nature of the Millennium. But first, we need a definition of terms.

The Rapture: The sudden snatching away of the believers from the earth (whether alive or dead) to meet the Lord in the air as described in I Thessalonians 4:13-17.

The Tribulation Period: When God pours out His wrath during seven years of intense judgments that come upon the earth as described by Jesus in Matthew 24:6-24 and Revelation chapters 6-18.

The Millennium: The 1,000 year reign of Jesus Christ over His Kingdom as described in Revelation chapter 20 and by various prophets throughout the Old Testament.

The different interpretations of these events fall into several categories, generally relating to the timing of the events as shown below. It will help you to get familiar with these terms. They are not hard to learn, and when you hear them from the pulpit you can say, "I know what the pastor is talking about!"

1) **pre-Tribulation Rapture**. This means that the Rapture takes place before the Tribulation Period begins. I will be teaching from this perspective in this study because I believe the Scriptures clearly support it.

2) **mid-Tribulation Rapture**. This means that the Rapture will take place midway or 3 1/2 years into the seven year Tribulation Period.

3) **post-Tribulation Rapture**. This means that the Church – those true believers in Christ will go through the Tribulation Period just like the unbelievers, and will be raptured at the end of the Tribulation Period.

4) **pre-Wrath Rapture.** Proponents of this view of the Rapture argue that the first three quarters of the Tribulation is the wrath of man and the wrath of Satan, and not the

wrath of God. Therefore, they hold the view that the Church will suffer through the first three quarters of the Tribulation since, they say, the Church is promised protection only from the wrath of God.

5) **No Rapture**. This means that there is no such thing as the Rapture, and that the Tribulation Period has already occurred in the 1st Century. Further, that every human will be resurrected at the same time at the end of the age. The believers will go to Heaven and the unbelievers will go to Hell.

The second major category that causes controversy is the timing of the Millennium. Again, remember these terms. They are easy to understand if you will carefully consider what they are saying.

1) **pre-Millennial View**. This means that the Second Coming of Christ will occur just prior to the Millennium when Christ sets up His earthly kingdom. I will be teaching from this perspective in this study because I believe the Scriptures clearly support it.

2) **post-Millennial View**. This means that the Church will get better and better at evangelism until the entire world is converted ushering in 1,000 years of peace. Then Christ will come back and receive His Kingdom from the Church.

3) **Amillennial View.** This view holds that there will be no Millennium. "A" in Latin means no. For example, take the word moral. You might say, "He is a moral person." But if that person has no morals, you might say, "He is an amoral person." Consequently, Amillennialism simply means that there is not going to be a literal Millennium, but a spiritual Millennium, and that we are in it at the present time.

One other distinction needs to be pointed out. The Rapture and the Second Coming are two very different events. They are as different as daylight and dark. Here are the major differences:

Rapture	Second Coming
Christ comes for Church	Christ comes with Church
Christ comes in the air	Christ comes to the earth
Revealed only to Paul	Foretold to O.T. Prophets
To get Christ's Bride	To execute wrath
Happy event for believers	Wailing by non-believers
Can occur at any moment	Not imminent

Keep these two events separate in your mind as we go through this study. In summary, I will be teaching this from a pre-Tribulation standpoint (i.e., the Rapture will occur BEFORE the awful Tribulation Period) and from a pre-Millennial standpoint (i.e., Christ's Second Coming will be BEFORE the setting up of His Millennial Kingdom on the earth).

There are Biblical scholars who embrace each of the different viewpoints we discussed. So, in studying this, you should look at all pertinent Scriptures. Do not take verses out of context, and pray that the Holy Spirit will guide you into all truth. A good teacher always believes in what he or she is teaching, and I believe the things in this study with all my heart. In fact, I agree with the Bible teacher who said: "I believe the Bible from Genesis to maps."

In the Evolution vs. Creation debate, one scientist looks at the Grand Canyon and says, "This canyon was created over millions of years from a little bit of water." But another scientist looks at the same Grand Canyon and says, "This canyon was created over a short period of time from a whole lot of water." A good illustration is what happens when you direct a stream of water from a water hose into a pile of sand. A deep trench is dug. I realize that good people can look at the same set of facts and come to different conclusions and that is certainly the case when it comes to interpreting prophecy.

It is important that we study end time events or God would not have put so much prophecy in the Bible. But, as one teacher said, "We can disagree without being disagreeable." It is reported that a man went up to the great Baptist preacher, Charles Haddon Spurgeon, after one of his revival meetings and pointed out a difficult passage in Revelation. He said, "Tell me what this means." And Spurgeon, with a twinkle in his eye said, "It means exactly what it says."[6]

Dr. David Reagan had a different experience when he was about 12 years old. He was reading Zechariah chapter 14, which says that Jesus is coming back and when He does, His feet will touch the Mount of Olives in Jerusalem. Young Reagan became confused because his pastor had told the congregation over and over that, "There is not one verse in the Bible that even implies that Jesus will ever set His feet on this earth again." So he went to his pastor, pointed out the verses in Zechariah 14, and asked what it meant. The pastor stared at the passage and then finally said, "Son, I don't know what it means, but I'll guarantee you one thing: It doesn't mean what it says!"[7] We may not always understand it, but we can rest assured that the Bible means exactly what it says. Is the Book of Revelation literal or symbolic? The answer is: Yes! It is both literal and symbolic. But we will use a literal interpretation, unless common sense and context warrants otherwise.

The author of the Book is the Apostle John, the same person who wrote the Gospel of John and the epistles of I, II and III John. He is about 95 years old by this time, and the Roman Empire, under the tyrant Domitian, is so afraid of this old man that he orders him exiled to the Isle of Patmos. This is a small rocky island about 75 miles off the coast of present day Turkey in the Mediterranean Sea. The Book of Revelation was written not only to give encouragement to those living at that time who were being imprisoned and martyred daily for the cause of Christ, but also to those who suffer during the awful Tribulation Period as described in Chapters 6-18.

When I began writing this book my wife, Arlene, told me to use the "K.I.S.S." method. I asked, "What is that?" She replied, "Keep it simple, Sweetie!" I will try to follow her advice.

We have mentioned the disagreements concerning the timing of the Rapture and the nature and timing of the Millennium. But, there are also disputes regarding the relevancy of the Book for our current day. These can be categorized as follows:

The Preterist Group believes that virtually all prophecy in the Bible is really history, and the Book of Revelation is a symbolic picture of 1st Century conflicts, and not a description of what will occur in the end times. This is the official position of the Roman Catholic Church, and you will see later in our study why they take this position. They teach that virtually all of the Book of Revelation was fulfilled in 70 A.D. when the Romans attacked and destroyed Jerusalem, and God's covenant with Israel ended at that time. Preterism further teaches that every event normally associated with the end times, i.e., the Tribulation, Christ's Second Coming, the resurrection of the dead and the final judgment, is in the process of being fulfilled.[8]

Then there is the **Idealist or Spiritualist Group**. They believe that we cannot make any sense out of the details of the Book of Revelation; so therefore, it is only given to us to show that good eventually wins out over evil.

The last group is the **Futurist Group** that teaches the majority of the Revelation describes events that are yet in the future, and that Revelation is simply a picture of things to come; in other words, it is history written in advance. We will be studying from this perspective.

There are people in all countries who earn a good living by making predictions. Some of them are in legitimate occupations such as weather forecasters, stock market analysts and political consultants; but, there are others in a suspect group – fortune tellers, mystics and psychic readers.

A number of years ago, radio station KRLD in Dallas quoted *Newsweek* which said there were 50 of the nation's top psychics in 2003 who made predictions of things that would happen in 2004. The article said, "Test your skills against those of the experts." And then it gave the accuracy of these noted psychics. I thought it might be 50% or 60%, but I was shocked when I read the report. Their accuracy was ZERO. That's right. They did not get a single prediction correct! In the Old Testament, prophets who were not 100% accurate, 100% of the time, were stoned to death because it proved they were not from God! Scripture says, *"But the prophet who presumes to speak a word in my name which I have not commanded him to speak, or who speaks in the name of other gods, that same prophet shall die"* (Deuteronomy 18:20 RSV).

In 1979 a popular weekly newspaper published a list by the nation's leading psychics of what was in store for 1980. They got a few general predictions correct, like "Ted Kennedy will make a bid for the Presidency." But they missed 95% of their predictions. Here is some that they missed: President Carter will be injured in a hang gliding accident; Debbie Boone will appear in an X-rated movie; an Eskimo beauty will win the Miss World contest; the NFL will hire its first female football referee; and Ronald Reagan's wife, Nancy, will leave him. None of these things happened. But when God makes a prediction, He is 100% accurate, and it comes to pass 100% of the time. God says in Isaiah 46:10 (NLT) that there is none like Him. *"Only I can tell you what is going to happen even before it happens. Everything I plan will come to pass, for I do whatever I wish."* God's ultimate purpose is to have His will done on earth as it is in Heaven, and this is going to happen one day whether men like it or not.

Current international events seem to mirror the conditions and happenings that were predicted throughout the Bible for the last days of this age. Yet, little prophetic teaching and preaching about this emanates from the pulpits across the country. This stems from two reasons. First, many pastors have not studied prophecy to a large degree, and know little about it. And other pastors say, "The study of prophecy is divisive, and I do not want to get into it." A pastor who says this does not understand the effect of proper teaching or preaching of prophecy. Because first, it will motivate the listeners to holy living as never before; and secondly, it should put a sense of urgency within them to share the gospel with as many people as possible at every opportunity because the time is short.

As we said previously, God intends for us to study all portions of Scripture, and prophecy constitutes a significant portion of the Bible. Unfortunately, many pastors do not want to see the Lord return, at least not now, because they are enjoying the fruits of a luxurious lifestyle. You can see them on TV every day. Take for example one TV evangelist who said, "If you have bicycle faith, all you're gonna' get is a bicycle.[9] I'm trying to get you out of this malaise of thinking that Jesus and the disciples were poor .... the Bible says that He has left us an example that we should follow His steps. That's the reason why I drive a Rolls Royce. I'm following Jesus' steps."[10]

Too many people have settled down here. This is their real home. We are warned about this by the Apostle John, *"Do not love the world or the things that belong to the world. If anyone loves the world, love for the Father is not in him. Because everything that belongs to the world – the lust of the flesh, the lust of the eyes, and the pride in one's lifestyle – is not from the Father, but is from the world. And the world with its lust is passing away, but the one who does God's will remains forever"* (I John 2:15-17 Holman).

I have found that many scholars divide the Book into three main sections according to chapter content:

1) The Church Age: chapters 1-3
2) The Rapture, Tribulation and Second Coming: chapters 4-19
3) The Millennium and the Eternal State: chapters 20-22

Let me mention a pet peeve of mine. This is the Book of Revelation. Do not let anyone catch you saying, "The Book of Revelations" (plural). To me, that is like screeching your nails on a blackboard, and shows the person is not very familiar with the Book. When a preacher says, "Turn to the Book of Revelations" – I feel like hollering, "There AIN'T such a Book!" It is THE Revelation – one, continuous manifestation and unveiling of God's unique Son, the Lamb of God, the anointed Prophet, Savior, Priest and King!

I have never studied Greek, but I do have a wonderful English/Greek lexicon which I will refer to throughout this study. The New Testament was written in koine Greek which was the language spoken by the common people. In koine Greek, the word "revelation" is "apocalypse," and it means the "unveiling" or "uncovering."[11] As an example, you are familiar with a sculptor or a painter who has just finished his prize exhibit, and there is a grand unveiling. Well, the Revelation is the grand unveiling – the uncovering – the manifestation – of Jesus Christ in all His glory. It says so in chapter 1, verse 1, *"The Revelation of Jesus Christ."*

When Jesus was praying that awesome prayer in John 17:5 He said, *"And now, O Father, glorify thou Me with thine own self with the glory which I had with Thee before the world was."* That glory was veiled while He was here on earth as He voluntarily limited Himself in a number of areas, none of which involved His deity since He never was less than 100% God. His Godhead and power were hidden for the most part by His humanity (Philippians 2:7). But thank God, those limitations were completely removed at His resurrection, and He will be unveiled in all His glory at the proper time for the whole world to see.

Verse 1 tells us how the message came to us. *"The Revelation of Jesus Christ, which God gave unto Him, to shew unto His servants things which must shortly come to pass; and He sent and signified it by His angel unto His servant John"* (Revelation 1:1). Here is how this message was handed down. God gave it to Jesus Christ, who sent it by His special angel to His servant John to show unto His servants (that is you and me.) No wonder so many people stick their head in the Book and say, "I don't understand it." It could be because they are not His servants!

Notice also in verse 1 it says, *"Things which must shortly come to pass ...."* (Revelation 1:1b). Must means it is absolutely certain that these events will take place. And when it says, "shortly come to pass" in the original Greek it means, "rapidity of action once it begins."

Here is a good illustration that bears this out. I found four Kildee eggs in our backyard where Mother Kildee made a nest in pebbles on the ground. If I approached the nest when she was in the vicinity, she would run about 15 feet in the opposite direction and holler and flutter her wings like she had been hurt – anything to lure me away from her nest. She sat on the nest day in and day out, and when she would leave, I would take a quick look at the eggs. It did not look like anything was happening. Then one day the nest was empty. I had just checked it the night before. Did some varmint get them? No. My friend Ray, told me that when they hatch, it is all of a sudden – quickly – shortly to come to pass. The little birds scatter in all directions when they are born, and almost just as quickly they learn to fly away. Soon or quickly, as relates to the hatching, does not mean it would happen in the next second, but quickly as in a succession of events once they begin to unfold.

When Scripture says these end time events will shortly come to pass, it means that they will happen in a brief period of time, and when you consider all that will be pushed into a seven year time period, it tends to be amazing. And the verse says, "He signified it ….". Think of the word as "sign-i-fied" it – He made it known by signs and symbols.

Some say John did this because he was being held captive and only cryptic messages could get by his Roman guards. There is probably some truth in that. But more significant is the fact that of the 404 verses in the Book of Revelation, at least 278 of them are alluded to in the Old Testament.[12] Do you know what this means? It means that you must have a working knowledge of the entire Bible to fully understand what John is talking about!

That great old expositor, Dr. H. A. Ironside, made a statement which I have underlined in red in his commentary because it is so significant. Here is what he wrote, "It may be laid down as a principle of first importance that every symbol used in Revelation is explained or alluded to somewhere else in the Bible. Therefore, he who would get God's mind as to this portion of His Word must study with earnest and prayerful attention every other part of Holy Scripture."[13] Wow – what insight! This means that interpretation of prophecy must be done by comparing Scripture with Scripture which is what we will try to do as we go through the Book.

Verse 2:*".... who bear record of the Word of God, and of the testimony of Jesus Christ, and of all things that He saw."* John's task was to record a true account of what he saw – and what he saw was the Word of God and the testimony of Jesus Christ.

Verse 3: *"Blessed is he that readeth, and they that hear the words of this prophecy, and keep those things which are written therein: for the time is at hand."* We read in Daniel 12:4 that Daniel was to *"shut up the words and seal the book"* – it was not to be understood until the time of the end. But here in Revelation we find that it was not to be a sealed Book. It was to be understood during the Church Age, but especially as the end of the age approaches. The Book of Revelation says we are to read it, hear and keep it (Revelation 1:3). In other words, take it into our souls, and let our hearts burn with its message of urgency. Blessed means happy – take this Book into your heart, and you will experience the joy of the Lord. You will know what Paul means when he says to look expectantly for our "blessed hope" which is the Rapture.

Revelation was written around 96 A.D. and completes the 27 Books of the New Testament that the orthodox Christian community considers as inspired by God. In fact, in the last chapter of the Book, God gives a dire warning to anyone who would add to or take away from the words of this Book. It speaks of finality. In other words with this writing it completes God's written Word to mankind. It flies in the face of God to take books like the *Book of Mormon,* the Watchtower writings, or *Science & Health with Key to the Scriptures*, and elevate them to a position equal with God's Word. Jesus Himself gave a warning about this in Revelation 22:18-19. I would not take God's warning lightly!

In verse 3, God says, *"The time is at hand."* He wants every generation to be looking for Christ's return and believe that they are living in the days immediately preceding the Rapture. John was convinced that Jesus' return was imminent – meaning that He could return at any time. Paul was convinced of that and so were Charles Spurgeon, Dwight L. Moody and Billy Graham. And we too should look for His return at any time. Verse 3 promises a blessing to everyone who reads and keeps in their hearts what is in this Book. Revelation is meant to be understood!

The word Revelation in Greek is "apocalypse." It means uncovering or unveiling. It is the opposite of the word "apocrypha" which means hidden. Apocrypha is the name given to the dozen or so books which are included in the Catholic Bible, but not considered divinely inspired by the early Church Fathers or the Jewish rabbis. Consequently, the apocrypha is not found in either Protestant or Jewish Bibles.

I remember reading a statement by the late Reverend Louis Talbot, that great teacher from another generation, that said in effect, "Many people treat the Book of Revelation like the priest and Levite treated the man who was beaten and robbed in the story of the Good Samaritan – they passed by on the other side. The Devil has turned thousands of people away from this portion of God's Word. He does not want anyone to read any book that tells of his being cast out of Heaven. Nor is he anxious for us to read of the ultimate triumph of his number one enemy, Jesus Christ. The more you study the Book of Revelation, the more you understand why Satan fights so hard to keep people away from it."

Dr. Talbot was the former pastor of the Church of the Open Door in Los Angles. The church was built in 1915 with seating capacity of 4,000. It was the brainchild of its founder, Rev. R. A. Torrey. Rev. Talbot was the pastor from 1936 to 1949 and was succeeded by Dr. J. Vernon McGee who was pastor there for 21 years until 1970. In its heyday, the attendance exceeded 3,000, but by the mid-eighties attendance had dropped to 800. The church's debt was in arrears by $7.5 million and the church was facing bankruptcy. A sale for $23 million was struck with the eccentric TV preacher, Gene Scott, but quickly turned soured with both sides claiming bad faith. After many contentious lawsuits and delays, the church finally went into bankruptcy and was demolished to build an office tower. The church's last service was held June 23, 1985.[14]

Before we continue, I want to call your attention to the similarities and contrasts between the first Book of the Bible – Genesis, and the last Book – Revelation.

Genesis gives us the creation of the Heaven and the earth.

Revelation tells us of a New Heaven and a New Earth.

Genesis shows us the earthly Paradise with the Tree of Life and the river that flowed out of Eden which were lost as a result of sin.

Revelation shows us the Paradise of God with the Tree of Life and the pure river of water of life proceeding out of the throne of God.

In Genesis we see that the first man, Adam, is given dominion over all God's creation.

In Revelation we behold the Second Man, Christ and His Bride, the Church, ruling over a redeemed world.

In Genesis we are told of the first sacrificial lamb.

In Revelation we see the Lamb of God, once slain, is now in the midst of the throne.

In Genesis we learn of the beginning of sin when the serpent entered the garden and deceived Eve.

In Revelation that old serpent, called the Devil and Satan, is cast into the Lake of Fire.

In Genesis we have the first murderer, the first polygamist, the first rebel, the first drunkard and the first idolater.

In Revelation all such people who have refused to accept God's grace in Christ Jesus are banished from His presence forever.

In Genesis we view the rise of Babel or Babylon.

In Revelation we watch its destruction.

Genesis shows us how sorrow, death, pain and tears came into the world.

Revelation does not close until we see God wipe away all tears, and welcome His redeemed into a home where sin, death, pain and sorrow are no more.

These are just a few of the contrasts between the first and last Book. You can probably find many others.

Now we come to verse 4: *"John to the seven churches which are in Asia: Grace be unto you, and peace, from Him which is, and which was, and which is to come; and from the seven Spirits which are before the throne."* Let us dissect this verse. First, notice the author is John. Is this John the Apostle? Many liberal theologians say no. They compare the style of writing with the Gospel of John, and conclude that two different people wrote them.

But not so fast! Think about this for a minute. The Gospel of John was written during a relatively quiet time when John was surrounded by friends and generally ignored by the Roman officials. Revelation was written when John was a prisoner of Rome on an isolated island with no friends around, threatened with death at any time, and during the intensity of all the horrendous things he saw, probably wrote as fast as he could. No wonder these writings differ in style, plus Revelation chapters 2 and 3 were dictated to him as was much of the rest of the Book through visions from God.

I am perplexed as to why it is such a big thing with the skeptics to try to prove John did not write this. Maybe it is to try to show that the author was lying. They are wrong if they think John did not write this Book. And let me share with you my reasoning. Five times in the Book the writer says his name is John (Revelation 1:1, 4, 9; 21:2; 22:8). The author was a Jewish Christian, not a Greek Christian. It comes out in his writings. He is a man from Israel who thinks Hebrew, but writes Greek. He is saturated with the language and phraseology of the Old Testament. Secondly, he is a man of deep spiritual insight. He is allowed to look farther into the plans of God than any other mortal has been allowed to do. Third, he is a man of principle. He calls Rome *"The mother of all prostitutes"* (Revelation 17:5 NLT). John calls them as he sees them, and he is uncompromising in his beliefs.

Fourth, he is a man of authority. He tongue lashes the churches of Asia without any timidity on his part. Fifth, look at his choice of words. John is the only writer that uses the Greek term "Logos" – the Word – as a personal name for Christ. In John 1:1, he said, *"In the beginning was the Word (Logos)….."*. And in Revelation 19:11-13 he says, *"And I saw Heaven opened, and behold a white horse; and He that sat upon him was called Faithful and True …. and on His head were many crowns …. and His name is called The Word of God"* (Logos) . And he is the only writer that uses the term "Lamb of God" as a description of Christ; in fact, he uses it 28 times in the Book of Revelation alone![15]

John is the only apostle who mentions that Christ was pierced in His side during His crucifixion (John 19:34). And in Revelation 1:7, we find that John mentions that piercing again: *"Every eye shall see Him and they also which pierced Him …. "*. Also, he simply calls himself "servant John" (Revelation 1:1). No other description is given. All the churches immediately knew who wrote this letter. They knew all about this Apostle who walked alongside of Jesus, and who was called *"The disciple whom Jesus loved"* (John 13:23). And the clincher is that most of the early Church Fathers attributed the authorship of Revelation to John the Apostle.[16]

Let's continue to look closely at verse 4, *"John to the seven churches which are in Asia …."*. There were more churches in Asia than seven. For example, there was the church at Hierapolis (Colossians 4:13) and the great church at Colossae (Colossians 1:1-2). But these particular seven churches were chosen for a specific reason which we will see in a moment. The churches were all in an area that was known as Asia Minor. Today it is known as Turkey. If you have a map at the back of your Bible, take a look at Asia Minor. The seven churches formed a rough circle. These churches were located in the cities of Ephesus, Smyrna, Pergamos (also known as Pergamum), Thyatira, Sardis, Philadelphia and Laodicea. God selected these seven churches because the messages were: 1) individualized for the needs of that particular church; and 2) each church is representative of part of the period we call the "Church Age" (from the day of Pentecost to the Rapture). We will see this in great detail when we get to chapter 2.

We have mentioned previously that God loves numbers, and He uses them symbolically to stand for certain things. He especially likes the number 7, and He chose it to be the number of perfection.[17] We will see a lot of sevens as we go through the Book. Here are some of the sevens we will encounter in Revelation; you can find many others:

Angels 8:2	Mountains 17:9
Candlesticks 1:12	Seals 5:1
Churches 1:11	Spirits 1:4
Heads and Crowns 12:3	Stars 1:16
Horns and Eyes 5:6	Thunders 10:3
Kings 17:10	Trumpets 8:2
Lamps 4:5	Vials 15:7

Even the Tribulation Period in the eyes of God is perfect judgment because it lasts seven years. Seven is not just important in the Bible, but in the secular world as well. Our lives are ordered by the seven-day week (Exodus 35:2).

Continuing in verse 4, John says, *"Grace be unto you and peace …. "*. This order could not be reversed. You cannot have God's peace before He has extended His grace to you. When grace has done its part, peace follows. Romans 5:1 says, *"Therefore being justified by faith, we have peace with God through our Lord Jesus Christ."*

This is so typical of God's love for mankind. In Revelation which records the awful judgments that man has brought upon himself, God starts out by talking about grace and peace. And this grace and peace are not only coming from the Father, but the verse says they are also coming from the seven spirits before the throne. We will see later that the term seven spirits is referring to the Holy Spirit (Isaiah 11:2-3). These spirits cannot be angelic beings. Grace and peace only come from God.

And then in the rest of verse 4 and in the first line of verse 5, we have the Godhead, the Trinity, which the Jehovah's Witnesses and others say does not exist. But this Scripture is another example of the Trinity. The greeting is from the Father and Jesus Christ as both are described as *"I AM"* (The Father in Exodus 3:14 and the Son in John 8:58). The words *"I AM"* encompass the past, present and future. This is a description of the Father and the Son – " .... *from Him which is, and which was, and which is to come."* The greeting is also from the Holy Spirit – *".... and from the seven spirits which are before His throne"* (Revelation 1:4). This is a designation of the Holy Spirit in all of His fullness since seven is the number of perfection (Isaiah 11:2).

Remember, this message was given in signs and symbols, and most of these are explained for us somewhere else in the Bible. If you will turn to Isaiah 11:1-2, you will see the sevenfold description of the Holy Spirit who will rest upon the Messiah.

> The Spirit of the Lord: the nature of Jesus.
> The Spirit of wisdom: the ability to make right decisions.
> The Spirit of understanding: ability to understand everything.
> The Spirit of counsel: the ability to give sound advice.
> The Spirit of might: the power to do what God wants done.
> The Spirit of knowledge: the ability to know all things.
> The Spirit of the fear of the Lord: the proper reverence of God.

This is a picture of the Holy Spirit in His sevenfold role as the Divine Administrator. The Father and the Son make the plans and the Holy Spirit is the executor of those plans.

Verse 5 begins, *"And from Jesus Christ, who is the faithful witness .... ".* Grace and peace are also coming from Jesus Christ, the faithful witness. Jesus faithfully witnessed to the love that the Father has for us. He faithfully witnessed to the world about the one and only way to escape the awful judgment that awaits all who reject God. And above all, He is the faithful witness unto death, telling the Father, *".... not my will, but thine, be done"* (Luke 22:42). So here you have a beautiful picture of the Trinity in verses 4 and 5 – the Father, the Son and the Holy Spirit. The rest of verse 5b referring to Christ says, *"and the first begotten of the dead, and the prince of the kings of the earth. Unto Him that loved us, and washed us from our sins in His own blood."*

Someone has raised the question, "Why is Jesus called the first begotten from the dead since Lazarus and others died and were raised first?" The answer is simple. The others were raised from physical death to physical life only to eventually die a second time. Jesus Christ was raised from the dead to immortality – never to die again! He is the first to have been resurrected with a new, physical, glorified body that will never die nor ever wear out. Jesus is referred to in Scripture as "the first begotten from the dead" (Revelation 1:5) and "the firstborn from the dead" (Colossians 1:18). He is also called "the only begotten Son" (John 3:16). Do not let the cultic groups who darken your door confuse you about this. They claim this proves that Jesus is a created being.

The terms "first begotten from the dead" or "firstborn from the dead" refer to this fact that He is the first to be resurrected with this glorious body. I Corinthians 15:35-58 describes in detail our resurrected bodies, and it says clearly in verse 20 of that same chapter that Christ is the first fruits. He is the first to be resurrected in a series of resurrections which we will discuss in detail later. The phrase "first begotten from the dead" or "firstborn from the dead" is entirely different from the "only begotten son." The term "only begotten Son" refers to His incarnation when He was born in Bethlehem, whereas the terms "first begotten from the dead" or "firstborn from the dead" refer to His resurrection.

The late Dr. Robert Lightner, professor emeritus at Dallas Theological Seminary, wrote 24 books in the field of Systematic Theology. Eminently qualified to address this verse he said, "The terms 'only begotten from the dead' or 'firstborn from the dead' mean the only one of a kind, never to be repeated."[18] Cultic groups will try to convince you that Jesus is a created being – firstborn among many others. That is a fallacy. Numerous verses confirm that Jesus is divine and equal with His Father. Isaiah 9:6 states that Christ is *"The mighty God, The everlasting Father."*

Continuing our discussion of Revelation 1:5, the King James Version of the Bible has an inaccurate translation of a word in this verse. Instead of *"prince,"* the Greek actually says, *"and the ruler of kings on earth"* (ESV). That will happen when Christ becomes the King of kings and Lord of lords as described in Revelation 19:16. In Revelation 1:5 it says, *"Unto Him that loved us, and washed us from our sins in His own blood."* In the Greek, the tense of the word "loved" means that He loved us in the past, He loves us now, and He loves us in the future. But "washed" cannot be translated any other way except in the past tense. It was only done once – when we were saved. In other words, He washed us clean (position-wise) from sin when we accepted Him as our Savior. This was done once in the past, and is a done deal as far as our relationship with Him is concerned. But from a practical standpoint, when we sin from day to day, we must ask the Lord for forgiveness in accordance with I John 1:9, and He will continually "cleanse" us to restore our fellowship with Him.

One more incredible truth from Revelation 1:5 that you do not want to miss. Does it say that our sins were washed away when the waters of baptism flowed over you? No! Look at the verse carefully, and see what has washed away our sins – it was Jesus. Verse 5 says, *"And washed us from our sins in His own blood."* Will another translation say something differently when they translate verse 5? Will one mention baptism or water as washing away our sins?

Let us see if that is the case. The NIV: *"To Him who loves us, and has freed us from our sins by His blood."* The NLT: *"All glory to Him who loves us, and has freed us from our sins by shedding His blood for us."* The NASB: *"To Him who loves us, and released us from our sins by His blood."* The Holman: *"To Him who loves us, and has set us free from our sins by His blood."* The ESV:

"To Him who loves us, and has freed us from our sins by His blood." The Phillips Paraphrase: *"To Him who loves us, and has set us free from our sins through His own blood."*

I do not see how anyone can miss it – baptism does not wash away our sins, but the blood of Christ does! There is a great song written and sung by Andrae Crouch that says, *"The Blood (of Jesus) Will Never Lose Its Power."* Not only has He washed away our sins in His blood, but He has made us kings and priests unto God and the Father. Some religious groups (such as the Mormons) have a closed "priesthood" available only to a select few. The Catholics also have a closed priesthood. But every believer in Christ is deemed a priest as we will see in the next paragraph.

What is a priest supposed to do? Represent us to God. At the crucifixion, the veil entering the Holy of Holies was split from top to bottom – indicating that every believer is a priest in that he or she has access to God through prayer. The Apostle Peter confirms this: *"But you are a chosen race, a royal priesthood, a holy nation, a people for His own possession, that you may proclaim the excellences of Him who called you out of darkness into his marvelous light"* (I Peter 2:9 ESV). Accordingly, every believing Christian is priest in that he or she is an intercessor to God. What a marvelous thing God has done in setting us in places of service and honor in His kingdom. I like the J. B. Phillips paraphrase of Revelation 1:6: *"To Him …. who has made us a kingdom of priests to His God and Father, to Him be glory and power for timeless ages, Amen!"*

Chapter 1, verse 7 gives the grand theme of the Book of Revelation, and it is the unveiling of the Lord Jesus Christ. And so John in his enthusiasm breaks out with the good news of Christ's return. *"Behold, He cometh with clouds; and every eye shall see Him, and they also which pierced Him: and all kindreds of the earth shall wail because of Him. Even so, Amen."*

John could not wait until the last chapter to tell us the good news that we win! Christ is coming back in the clouds, victoriously and visibly. When Jesus left this earth, He went away in the clouds, and when He returns at His Second Coming, He is coming back in the clouds! It says *"every eye shall see Him"*. In one of the great miracles, God will make sure that every one that ever lived shall behold Him in all His glory.

In Matthew 26:63b (NLT), we see Jesus on trial before the High Priest, Caiaphas. Caiaphas smirked at Him and said, *"I demand in the name of the living God that you tell us whether you are the Messiah, the Son of God."* And then Jesus replied, *"Yes, it is as you say …. "* (Matthew 26:64a NLT). I remember when I was a teenager, Jim Rayburn, founder of *Young Life*, was talking to us about this. He said Caiaphas demanded, "I order you to tell us – are you really the Son of God?" And Jim, in his Texas drawl, said Jesus answered, "You bet I am, Buster!"

But what I really want you to see is Jesus' next words in that same verse. *"And in the future you will see Me, the Son of Man, sitting at God's right hand in the place of power and coming back on the clouds of Heaven"* (Matthew 26:64 NLT). That was more than Caiaphas could stand. He joined the boisterous crowd in slapping Him and spitting in His face. But do you know what? When Jesus returns, every eye shall see Him and that includes Caiaphas, and he will wish he could take back that slap. What will the reaction be to all these Christ-rejecters when they see Christ coming back in the clouds? All of them will wail and moan because they realize Christ is really who He said He was, and He is coming back in judgment.

When John says everyone shall see Him, he inserts a little phrase here, *"and they also which pierced Him"* (Revelation 1:7). The piercing of Jesus' side was recorded only by John in his Gospel (John 19:34). It is not in Matthew, Mark or Luke. But John was there – he saw it and he never forgot seeing that spear thrust into Jesus' side. He saw their fierce looks; he saw their wicked hearts; he saw their cruel hands and witnessed their blasphemy as they mocked and spit on the King of kings. And now, as John records that every eye shall see Him, he adds, *"And they also which pierced Him."* John never forgot it.

Remember folks, this is not the Rapture; this is the Second Coming of Christ. At the Rapture, only the Christians will see Him. We will be caught up to be with Him in the clouds in the twinkling of an eye, and the unbelievers will wonder what happened to millions of people who have disappeared.

At the end of the Tribulation Period, we will come back with Christ at the Second Coming, *"When Christ, who is our life, is revealed, then you also will be revealed with Him in glory"* (Colossians 3:4 NASB). It says that when Christ is revealed in all His glory, we will be revealed as well because we are coming back with Him.

Job looked forward to this public appearing. *"But as for me, I know that my Redeemer lives, and that He will stand upon the earth at last. And after my body has decayed, yet in my body I will see God! I will see Him for myself. Yes, I will see Him with my own eyes. I am overwhelmed at the thought!"* (Job 19:25-27 NLT). At the Second Coming every eye shall see Him just like it says in Matthew 24:27. As the lightning flashes across the sky and is seen from the east to the west, so shall the coming of the Son of Man be. And millions will wail because they did not accept Him while they had the opportunity.

Then Revelation 1:8 says, *"I am Alpha and Omega, the beginning and the ending, saith the Lord, which is, and which was, and which is to come, the Almighty."* This exact description was applied to God the Father in Revelation 1:4. Here is the dilemma that people face who deny the Trinity – those folks who claim that Jesus is not equal with the Father. This little exercise will clear up any confusion. Verse 4 says, " .... *from Him which is, which was and which is to come"*. Who is John referring to? Although this describes Jesus elsewhere, John is not talking about Jesus in verse 4 because we see in the next verse that he says this message is also from Jesus: "And from Jesus Christ .... ". So, verse 4 is talking about God the Father and the same description is in verse 5 is referring to Jesus.

Also, in verse 11, it says: *"I am Alpha and Omega ...."* and this Person keeps speaking until verse 18 when He says, *"I am He that liveth and was dead.... "*. So we know for certain that Jesus is speaking here! There is no getting around it – John uses the same words to describe the Father as he does the Son. As we learned in geometry, if things are equal to the same thing, they are equal to each other. If "A" equals "C" and "B" equals "C", then it is a fact that "A" and "B" equal each other. In other words, if the Father is described as the One *"which is, and was, and which is to come"* and the Son is described as the One *"which is, and was, and is to come"* – then the Father and the Son are equal to each other.[19]

The most precious thing in God's eyes in this universe is you – God's people. You cost the most. He made the stars and the planets with just a word. But you, the redeemed of God, cost the agony and the tears, the blood and the death of the Son of God. You, my brothers and sisters in Christ, are the pearl of great price for which He laid down His life (Matthew 13:45-46).

Then John introduces himself, but he does not brag and say, "I am John the Apostle" nor does he say, "I am John the disciple whom Jesus especially loved." No. Though John was the last of Christ's apostles, and entitled to great respect and esteem, he considered himself only one of the brethren, sharing in the common persecutions which had already claimed the lives of the other apostles as well as countless followers. In verse 9 he says, *"I, John, who also am your brother, and companion in tribulation, and in the kingdom and patience of Jesus Christ, was in the isle that is called Patmos, for the word of God, and for the testimony of Jesus Christ."* He introduces himself as a Christian brother and companion in tribulation. He is talking about the general tribulations and hardships that we as Christians go through daily, and more so in their case, as it was costing many of them their very lives from the repressive Roman government.

At the time of this writing by John, all the other apostles were dead, most having been put to death by the Roman government. I do not know this for a fact, but I suspect this is the conversation that the captain of the guard had with the Emperor Domitian. "Your Excellency. We have arrested John, one of the original followers of Jesus. Shall we crucify him or behead him?" And I can imagine the Emperor saying this, "Neither. It will look like we are weak if we kill this old man. Just put him in isolation, and maybe his followers will forget about him." So, John was imprisoned on the Isle of Patmos because of his testimony for Christ (Revelation 1:9).

But great things come out of tribulation and persecution. I think of that Baptist preacher, John Bunyan, who refused to stop preaching the Gospel of Christ and so, he was confined to the Bedford Prison in England where he remained for twelve long years. And during that time, he drew even closer to the Lord, and out of that hardship in prison, he penned one of the mightiest books in Christian literature – *Pilgrim's Progress.*[20]

I think of Hugh Latimer, Bishop of Worcester in 1555, who encouraged Bible reading and opposed doctrinal error. For his efforts, he was burned at the stake at Oxford, England by the Roman Catholic Church along with his associate, Nicholas Ridley. As he felt the flames engulfing him, Latimer's last words have lived on for centuries: "Be of good cheer, Master Ridley. By God's grace this day we shall light such a fire in England that I trust shall never be put out!"[21] And the light of such faith burned brightly for centuries. But sadly, in our day, we see the flame flickering, sputtering, and threatening to go out as it has in many of the European countries. Only six percent of England's population regularly attends a Christian church of any kind. And, according to my friend, Ken Humphries, evangelist to Northern Ireland, there are now more Islamic mosques in England than active Methodist churches – in the country where Methodism was founded!

If we are faced with persecution and threat of prison for the sake of Christ, will we deny Him? How will we answer that old hymn written by Isaac Watts nearly 300 years ago – *"Am I a soldier of the cross, a follower of the Lamb? And shall I fear to own His cause, or blush to speak His name?"* We will find in the next chapter a solemn warning: Christ will remove that candlestick – that church – that individual – that ceases to be a light for Him.

John is not referring to THE Tribulation in verse 9, that seven year period in which up to one-half of the world's population will die. Some respected Bible teachers believe that the Body of Christ will go through the Tribulation Period, but I am not one who embraces that belief. There are too many solid reasons why I believe the Church will not go through the seven year Tribulation Period, but let me just give you a few.

Jesus is coming to get His Bride which is the Church. God the Father is speaking in II Corinthians 11:2: *"For I am jealous over you with godly jealousy: for I have espoused you to one husband, that I may present you as a chaste virgin to Christ."* Jesus is the perfect husband. *"Husbands, love your wives, as Christ loved the Church and gave Himself up for her, that He might sanctify her, having cleansed her by the washing of water with the Word, so that He might present the Church to Himself in splendor, without spot or wrinkle or any such thing, that she might be holy and without blemish"* (Ephesians 5:25-28 ESV).

So I ask you this important question: Would a perfect husband-to-be allow his bride to be abused right before the wedding? Of course not! So Christ is coming for His Bride before the horrendous events of the Tribulation start to happen.

Jesus said His coming will be like it was in the days of Noah. *"When the Son of Man returns, the world will be like the people were in Noah's day"* (Luke 17:26 NLT). In other words, society will be marked by violence and immorality as was Noah. But what most people miss is that Noah and his family were taken completely out of danger. They were not asked to hang on to the side of the Ark as the waters lashed and rocked the vessel, but were safe inside the Ark, floating high above the judgment that was falling on the unbelievers. The Rapture will take the believers out of harm's way before God's judgment falls.

When God's patience has run out, and He directly and expressly sets out to let His judgment fall upon this wicked world, He makes sure that His children are out of harm's way. So John identifies with his Christian brothers in their persecution and says, "Hey, I am here on the little windswept island called Patmos in the middle of the Mediterranean, and do you know why I am here? I am here '*.... for the word of God, and for the testimony of Jesus Christ*'" (Revelation 1:9).

This could happen again. The way things are going, you and I might have to face hardships, prison and exile for our belief in the Bible and for the testimony of Jesus Christ. It is getting closer to this reality all the time. Netherlands was the first country to approve same-sex marriages, and since that time 26 other countries have followed suit.[22]

John's persecution came because of his devotion to Christ. Jesus said in John 15:18-20, *"If the world hate you, ye know that it hated Me before it hated you. If ye were of the world, the world would love his own: but because ye are not of the world, but I have chosen you out of the world, therefore the world hateth you."* So John is in exile; a prisoner on a lonely island. Is he feeling sorry for himself? Listen to what he was doing. Verse 10: *"I was in the Spirit on the Lord's day, and heard behind me a great voice, as of a trumpet."* There has been much disagreement between scholars as to whether "the Lord's day" refers to Sunday or "the Day of the Lord" which is described by the prophet, Joel (Joel 1:15). The Day of the Lord, as we will see later, encompasses a long period – from the Tribulation Period (seven years) and the Second Coming of Christ all the way through His Millennium Kingdom (1,000 years).

The view that it means the Day of the Lord was held by Joseph Seiss, a notable Lutheran scholar at the beginning of the last century. He taught that John in a vision was carried through the centuries to view the Tribulation Period. His main argument was that nowhere else in Scripture is Sunday called the Lord's day.[23] But this is an argument from silence, and does not prove anything. It is possible that John introduced it here for the first time to designate the special day that elsewhere in Scripture is called "the first day of the week" (Mark 16:9; I Corinthians 16:2).

If John had meant the "Day of the Lord," he could have easily said so. He was certainly familiar with this term in the Hebrew Scriptures (for example Joel 2:31). But John said, "*the Lord's day*" which literally means, "the day belonging to the Lord." There is no such word as "Lordian", but if there was, it would have been correct to translate it, "I was in the Spirit on the Lordian day" – the day belonging to the Lord.[24]

After Jesus rose from the dead, He appeared to His disciples on Sunday – the first day of the week. Matthew 28:1 supports this as it says, *"In the end of the Sabbath, as it began to dawn toward the first day of the week....".* This then became the Lord's day. Scripture says, *"And upon the first day of the week, when the disciples came together to break bread, Paul preached unto them ...."* (Acts 20:7). Notice it says, *"when the disciples came together"* – it was a regular meeting time for them to partake of the Lord's Supper, and hear the Word preached. The implication is that they met regularly on the first day of every week. Listen to Paul's instructions in I Corinthians 16:2 : *"Upon the first day of the week let every one of you lay by him in store, as God hath prospered him …."*. They brought their tithes and offerings on Sunday.

It was on this first day of the week, Sunday, when John was *"in the spirit"*. No doubt he was praying and reading some of the sacred scrolls his friends had been able to sneak in to him. He was alone, far away from an assembly of believers, yet he was observing the Lord's day. Many folks go on vacation, far away from their local church, and they never think of worshipping the Lord wherever they might be on the Lord's day. I have known others that always stop to worship with a local Bible-believing church wherever they may be.

I understand that going to a strange church can lead to surprising results. Several years ago, Arlene and I were driving back from Illinois. It was a Sunday morning, and in each little town we came to, we would look for a Baptist church. Finally, we found one in a little out of the way place. Probably about a hundred people gathered to worship. The time was right for the service, so we stopped in to worship with them. The young assistant pastor was preaching his first sermon. And it was from the Book of Revelation! Basically, his message was this: Revelation is so confusing, we cannot know anything about it. He said it is best to just go on to some other Book which the Lord has made plain, but he continued in Revelation. I wonder why he continued when he said we could not know anything about it.

I would never interrupt a church service, but Arlene was so afraid that I was going to stand up and say, "Excuse me, sir, but the Bible says in II Timothy 3:16-17 ALL Scripture is profitable for us. That includes the Book of Revelation, and it is the ONLY Book in the Bible in which the reader is promised a blessing for reading and keeping the things that are written therein (Revelation 1:3). It is the public unveiling of Jesus Christ in all His glory and I would like to give you a brief outline of the Book of Revelation so that you can understand it." As I said, I might inject this into a private conversation, but I would never interrupt any church service with such a comment.

If you are on vacation or visiting relatives and you just cannot make it to church, at least take time to pray and read your Bible. God will know it, and He is the only One who really counts. Many times members have told me, "We will not be in church next week; we have relatives visiting us." Wouldn't it be a better testimony to say to the relatives, "Why don't you go to church with us? We need our batteries charged for the coming week. We will only be gone a little over an hour." That is a much better testimony than leaving the impression that your church attendance is not important. Cult members sometimes put us to shame. You seldom catch them missing a service because relatives are visiting.

And in the last phrase of verse 10, John says, "…. *and* [I] *heard behind me a great voice as of a trumpet."* What John heard was not a trumpet, but a great magnificent voice "as of" a trumpet – one that gets your immediate attention. The trumpet in Scripture was often accompanied by divine manifestations and commands, and it emphasizes authority (Exodus 19:13, 16, 19). When the Rapture occurs, it will be preceded by the trump of God (I Thessalonians 4:16).

So here is John, in solitary confinement on the Isle of Patmos for his faithfulness to Christ. Is he moping? Is he blaming others for his predicament? No! John is worshipping on the Lord's day – Sunday – the first day of the week. That is when he hears a great voice that sounds with the clarity of a trumpet. What does the voice say? Verse 11: *"…. I am Alpha and Omega, the first and the last: and, What thou seest, write in a book, and send it unto the seven churches which are in Asia;* [and then He names them]: *unto Ephesus, and unto Smyrna, and unto Pergamos, and unto Thyatira, and unto Sardis, and unto Philadelphia, and unto Laodicea."*

As we studied earlier, these seven churches were located in an area we now call Asia Minor which includes a portion of modern day Turkey. There were other churches in this area besides these seven, but the Lord picked out these seven for a very special reason which we will see shortly. John was told to write what he sees, and send it to these seven churches. Verses 12-15 : *"And I turned to see the voice that spake with me. And being turned, I saw seven golden candlesticks; and in the midst of the seven candlesticks one like unto the Son of Man, clothed with a garment down to the foot, and girt about the paps* [or the breasts] *with a golden girdle. His head and His hairs were white like wool, as white as snow; and His eyes were as a flame of fire; and His feet like unto fine brass, as if they burned in a furnace; and His voice as the sound of many waters."*

What a great description by John, probably writing on a scroll as fast as he could what he was seeing and hearing. The first thing he saw was seven golden candlesticks, and in the midst of them was one who looks like the Son of Man (Revelation 1:13). It was Jesus' favorite name for Himself (Mark 2:10) as he used it 78 times in the Gospels.

John gives us a description of this Person – this Son of Man – who is none other than Jesus Himself. The language here is very symbolic and expressive. Another thing we see is that God loves numbers. He is the ultimate mathematician. Throughout the Bible, you will find that different numbers represent different things. For instance, the number seven means perfection – the ultimate. And in this description of Christ, we see that there are seven descriptions of our Lord's personal features. These are highly symbolic and include His hair, eyes, feet, voice, hands, mouth and face.

Notice that the Son of Man was clothed with a garment down to the foot. This is the robe of the priest and the judge. But here, He is not in His role as priest or intercessor, but as Judge as we will see when He addresses each individual church. The girdle or sash is mentioned in Isaiah 11:5 : *"And righteousness shall be the girdle of his loins, and faithfulness the girdle of his reins."* Jesus came as a servant the first time as evidenced by the washing of the feet of His disciples

(John 13:5). But here in verse 13 of Revelation chapter 1, the girdle is around His chest only. He is not in the capacity of a servant, but as Supreme Judge. Remember, we are told in John 5:22 that all judgment has been delegated to the Son.

In the Book of Daniel, we find a similar description as the one given by John. *"As I looked, thrones were set in place, and the Ancient of Days took His seat. His clothing was as white as snow; the hair of His head was white like wool...."*. (Daniel 7:9a NIV). The description of the Ancient of Days (which is the Father) is the same basic description we have for Jesus here in Revelation 1:13-16 as He comes as Supreme Judge of the Universe. Not only does His white hair picture wisdom and maturity, it also pictures His purity. And those eyes are like a flaming fire – nothing will be hidden from those eyes. When Jesus walked the earth, those eyes were filled with compassion. He cried over the Jewish people who rejected Him, and wished that He could gather them as a hen gathers her baby chicks (Luke 13:34). But now, those eyes are a flaming fire. It is time for justice to be carried out!

We are told in Hebrews 9:27-28 (NIV), *"Just as man is destined to die once, and after that to face judgment, so Christ was sacrificed once to take away the sins of many people; and He will appear a second time, not to bear sin, but to bring salvation to those who are waiting for Him."* This clearly states that at Christ's Second Coming, He is not coming to address the sin question, but to consummate the plan of salvation for those who are waiting for Him. As my dear mother used to say, "Salvation has three parts: past, present and future. We have been saved from the penalty of sin; we are being saved from the power of sin; and we will be saved from the presence of sin."

In Hebrews we find: *"Neither is there any creature that is not manifest in His sight: but all things are naked and opened unto the eyes of Him with whom we have to do"* (Hebrews 4:13). He sees the secret things. Someone described our true character as the way we act when there is no one else around. That is why God can render true judgment. He sees our secret things – nothing is hidden from His eyes. John says His feet were like fine brass as if they burned in a furnace. This calls to mind the brass laver and altar outside the Tabernacle (Exodus 30:18), and it speaks of judgment which leads to spiritual cleanliness.

Christ's voice was like the sound of many waters. I have had the experience of standing at Niagara Falls and listening to the water pour over the Falls. The sound is indescribable as over a million gallons of water per second cascade over the side. The Lord's voice commands even more attention.

Verse 16: *"And He had in His right hand seven stars; and out of His mouth went a sharp two-edged sword: and His countenance was as the sun shineth in His strength."* He has in His hand seven stars. We will find out what this mystery is about when we get to verse 20 of this chapter. This sword is a dramatic picture of the Word of God as we are told that, *"The Word of God is quick, and powerful, and sharper than any two-edged sword, piercing even to the dividing asunder of soul and spirit, and of the joints and marrow, and is a discerner of the thoughts and intents of the heart"* (Hebrews 4:12).

We need to use common sense to recognize when symbols are being employed. For example, when Scripture speaks of a sword coming out of Christ's mouth here and also in Revelation 19:15, it does not mean He is a sword swallower. We know that it symbolizes the Word of God as it has been described previously in Hebrews 4:12. The Bible is our manual for living, and all mankind will be judged according to the things written in this Book and in what I call the Book of Works that track our lives, motives and actions (Revelation 20:12-15). In Revelation 19 we find that this sword – His Word – is what He will ultimately use to judge the nations. This sword is two-edged. It cuts one way for the believer and one way for the unbeliever. For the believer, it calls us to holy living because the time is short. For the unbeliever, it says flee from the wrath that is to come and into the loving arms of Jesus Christ.

"And His countenance was as the sun shineth in His strength" (verse 16). John is seeing the Shekinah Glory of God. Jesus is also known as the Sun of Righteousness (Malachi 4:2) and the Light of the world (John 8:12). The sun is the most brilliant light we know anything about. You can look directly into our solar sun for just a few seconds and do irreversible damage to the pupils of your eyes. The Bible says that we cannot look upon God – upon His full glory and live. God will have to give us supernatural help in this regard during the Millennium. John saw the face of Jesus on the Mount of Transfiguration (Matthew 17:2), and His face now appears as it did that day, shining brighter than the sun. It was the same light Paul saw when he was converted on the road to Damascus and was instantly blinded (Acts 9:3, 8; Acts 22:6; Acts 26:13).

When Christ appears at His Second Coming, all other sources of light will fade away – the sun, moon and stars. Christ's glory alone will illuminate a dark and sinful world. No wonder that John falls down when he sees Jesus. Look at verse 17: *"And when I saw Him, I fell at His feet as dead. And He laid His right hand upon me, saying unto me, 'Fear not; I am the first and the last.'"* Jesus says, "John – there is nothing to fear – I am here at the beginning – I am here at the end – I have everything under control. There is nothing for you to be afraid of."

The next sentence is the most encouraging one that I know for grieving Christians. *"I am He that liveth, and was dead; and, behold, I am alive for evermore, Amen; and have the keys of Hell and of death"* (Revelation 1:18). Wow! Praise God from whom all blessings flow!

I must digress a moment because there is an insidious teaching among some TV evangelists that is a lie from the Devil himself. And what a terrible interpretation it is. They are teaching that when Jesus was on the cross and said, *"It is finished"* (John 19:30), He did not mean His redemptive work was finished. He meant that His physical life was coming to an end. I used to be reluctant to name names, but then I read in II Timothy 4:14 (ESV) where the Apostle

Paul was not hesitant in warning his fellow believers about false teachers. He said, *"Alexander the coppersmith did me great harm; the Lord will repay him according to his deeds."* He also named Demas as a deserter (II Timothy 4:10).

According to TV evangelists Kenneth Copeland, Frederick K. C. Price, the late Kenneth Hagan, the late Paul Crouch and others in the Word of Faith movement, Jesus' redemptive work on the cross was not finished, it was just beginning. It is summed up best by Frederick K. C. Price: "Do you think the punishment for our sin was to die on the cross? If that were the case, the two thieves could have paid your price. No, the punishment was to go into Hell itself and to serve time in Hell separated from God. Satan and all the demons of Hell thought that they had Him bound and they threw a net over Jesus and they dragged Him down to the very pit of Hell itself to serve our sentence."[25] These Word of Faith teachers avow that "After Jesus died on the cross, He still had to go to Hell for 3 days and nights to suffer at the hands of the Devil and his demons." Do they not remember Jesus' own words to the thief on the cross? *"And Jesus said unto him, Verily I say unto thee, Today shalt thou be with me in Paradise"* (Luke 23:43).

Before Calvary when a believer died, his soul and spirit went to a "holding place" until the penalty for sin was paid in full. This place had two compartments – one for those who had put their trust in God and one for those who had not. In the Hebrew, this place was called "Sheol." In the Greek, it was called "Hades." It was one place, but it had two compartments; one was called "Torments" and one was called "Paradise."

This is best illustrated by a parable which Jesus gave. *"Jesus said, There was a certain rich man who was splendidly clothed and who lived each day in luxury. At his door lay a diseased beggar named Lazarus. As Lazarus lay there longing for scraps from the rich man's table, the dogs would come and lick his open sores. Finally, the beggar died and was carried by the angels to be with Abraham. The rich man also died and was buried, and his soul went to the place of the dead. There, in torment, he saw Lazarus in the far distance with Abraham. The rich man shouted, 'Father Abraham- - have some pity! Send Lazarus over here to dip the tip of his finger in water and cool my tongue, because I am in anguish in these flames.' But Abraham said to him, 'Son, remember that during your lifetime you had everything you wanted, and Lazarus had nothing. So now he is here being comforted, and you are in anguish. And besides, there is a great chasm separating us. Anyone who wanted to cross over to you from here is stopped at its edge, and no one there can cross over to us'"* (Luke 16:19-26 NLT).

Right before Jesus died on the cross, He said, *"Father, I entrust my spirit into your hands!"* (Luke 23:46 NLT). He did not say, "Satan, into thy clutches I commit my being. Take Me to Hell and torture Me." When Christ said, *"It is finished"* (John 19:30), He meant just that. And then He went to Paradise, and led the souls of the believers back to Heaven with Him. Jesus literally moved the location of Paradise from Hades in the heart of the earth to Heaven. This is described in Ephesians 4:8-10: "*When He* [Christ] *ascended up on high, He led captivity captive, and gave gifts unto men. (Now that He ascended, what is it but that He also descended first into the lower parts of the earth? He that descended is the same also that ascended up far above all heavens, that He might fill all things.*)" So Paradise is now in Heaven. How do we know that? Because we find in II Corinthians 12:2, Paul talks about being caught up into the Third Heaven, and he calls it "Paradise." And we find in Revelation 2:7 that it states the Tree of Life is in the midst of Paradise. At Calvary, Paradise was moved to Heaven where it has been ever since. When Jesus left Hades, He not only took Paradise with Him and all its inhabitants, He took with Him the keys to Hell and death (Revelation 1:18). Truly, He is Conqueror!

In verse 19 of Revelation chapter 1, John is given the command to write: "*Write the things which thou hast seen, and the things which are, and the things which shall be hereafter.*" One theologian has divided the Book of Revelation into four divisions; another into five; another into seven. These are not bad, and each presents a logical case for their division. But the point is they are all man-made divisions. But here in verse 19 are the divisions for the Book as given by Christ Himself. Pastors say that every fine sermon should have three points. Well, God has divided Revelation into three divisions or parts, and He tells us what is in each part.

The things which thou has seen (that is, the past), and the things which are (that is, the present that are going on during this Church Age), and the future – the things which shall be hereafter (meta tauta in Greek) or as one translation says: "*Therefore write the things which you have seen, and the things which are, and the things which will take place after these things*" (Revelation 1:19 NASB).

After what things? Why, after the things that are going on now in the Church Age. We are currently living in the same period that John was living in, which is the Church Age or as it is sometimes called the Age of Grace.

Since Israel rejected their Messiah, Israel has been temporarily set aside while all the peoples of the world are being called by faith into the family of God. It is like there is a parenthesis of an undeterminable amount – it has already been 2,000 years between the 69th and 70th week of Daniel. The prophetic time clock has temporarily stopped until God again begins to deal with Israel as a nation. We currently live in that parenthesis between Daniel's 69th and 70th week. "*Seventy weeks are decreed about your people and your Holy City, to finish the transgression, to put an end to sin, and to atone for iniquity, to bring in everlasting righteousness, to seal both vision and prophet, and to anoint a most holy place*" (Daniel 9:24 ESV).

Later in our study, we will show conclusively that these "weeks" are weeks of years. In Hebrew each week is a "shabua" which is a generic word meaning seven, just like our English word dozen means 12. Seventy shabuas (70 x 7 = 490 years) are determined upon Israel during which specific things that Daniel mentions will be accomplished. The next verse, Daniel

9:25, accounts for 69 weeks (shabuas) or 483 years, leaving one week (of seven years) for the Tribulation. This is little hard to follow if it is new to you, but we will repeat it later in much more detail, and hopefully it will become clear to you. You and I are currently living in the age that Revelation 1:19 calls *"the things that are."* We are living in the here and now. But after the Rapture, the 70th week (Daniel 9:24) – also called The Tribulation Period will begin.

As Christians, we are just going along as usual – today – tomorrow – and suddenly, Boom! The Rapture calls us home and then a new period begins. Verse 19 calls it "meta tauta" – "the things which shall be after these things" – a future period after the Church Age that ushers in the Tribulation Period. After the Church is raptured, the pendulum on the prophetic clock starts to tick again as God begins to deal with the nation of Israel during the 70th week as detailed in the ninth chapter of Daniel, verses 24-26. These final seven years of the Tribulation Period are, according to Jesus, the worst seven years in the history of mankind and, if they were not shortened, *"no flesh would survive"* (Matthew 24:22).

If you want to relate the chapters of Revelation to the three divisions of the Book that are shown in Revelation 1:19, they can be broken down as follows:

Chapter 1 covers the things which John had just seen: primarily the magnificent vision of Jesus Christ in all His glory.

Chapters 2-3 cover the things which are: the Church Age extending from the day of Pentecost to the Rapture of the Body of Christ.

Chapter 4 through the remainder of the Book covers the things which shall be after the Church Age: The Tribulation Period, the Battle of Armageddon, the Second Coming, the Millennium and the Eternal State.

I had the privilege to sit under the ministry of that great expository preacher, Dr. W. A. Criswell, for over 20 years. He said that when he was in seminary, he heard a lecturer saying that in ancient times there was a key to the interpretation and the meaning of the Book of Revelation; but we do not possess it today. The key has been lost. But Dr. Criswell said, "The key hasn't been lost! We have it right here in the 19th verse where God shows us how to open the lock and divide the Book."[26]

Remember, we said the Bible is its own best interpreter. In Revelation 1:20, Jesus told John to write: *"The mystery of the seven stars which thou sawest in my right hand, and the seven golden candlesticks."* And then He reveals what they mean: *"The seven stars are the angels of the seven churches: and the seven candlesticks which thou sawest are the seven churches."*

Let us start with the candlesticks or lampstands. A lampstand does not originate its light. It only conveys it. If we have a lampstand, we must get light from somewhere else to shine from the lampstand. So, here is a lampstand. Verse 20 says it is a church, and it exists for the purpose of giving light. But the only light the true Church has is the light of Christ. Jesus said, *"I am the light of the world*" (John 8:12). We as the Church are to be a reflector of that light. Jesus is seen walking in the midst of the lampstands – in the midst of His churches. And that is where He should be – in the midst of His people. And what is He doing? A letter to one of the churches tells us He is trimming the candlesticks – making sure they give good light. But He was not just maintaining them. He was also evaluating them, judging their fitness for service. He had the golden snuffers with Him to snuff out the light, and remove the lampstand if necessary. And He has done that many times as we will see a little later.

Whenever a church is not what it ought to be, it arouses the indignation of Christ. We settle in – we get comfortable – we compromise – and indifference sets in. This angers Christ. We are prone to compare our local church with other churches. But that is not the test. When we are willing to bring our lives and the life of our church before Christ's eyes from which nothing is hidden, and truly ask that the Holy Spirit fill us, then true revival will come.

In Revelation 1:16, it says that Jesus is holding the stars in His right hand. There is something about the right hand that signifies strength and authority. Even in our secular society, we have to raise our right hand in a court of law. We use our right hand to honor the flag and the national anthem as we cover our hearts.

In verse 20 (ESV), we find the words,"*The mystery of the seven stars .... and the seven golden lampstands*". The Greek word for mystery is "musterion." It does not mean a riddle or a puzzle. It is not something you can figure out by using your brainpower like solving a Perry Mason mystery by deductive reasoning. Musterion means something that has been hidden since the foundation of the world, and can only be known when God decides to reveal it. The Church was a musterion to the Old Testament saints. They thought if Gentiles were ever to be saved, they would have to become Jewish, and be adopted into the Jewish culture.

The Rapture was a musterion to the Old Testament saints and even to the twelve apostles. The Old Testament prophets only knew of the coming of their Messiah, and even then did not see it clearly. They saw in the Psalms, Isaiah and Zechariah that the Messiah would come as a lowly, suffering servant with no particular attraction. We are told this by Isaiah the prophet: "*For He grew up before Him like a young plant, and like a root out of dry ground; He had no form or majesty that we should look at Him, and no beauty that we should desire Him*" (Isaiah 53:2 ESV).

But then, in visions by the same writers, they saw the Messiah coming in all His glory as a victorious ruler and King (Psalm 24:8). In fact, the descriptions were so diverse that many rabbis taught there would be two Messiahs – one who would suffer and die and another who would reign as King over all the earth. They did not see that it was the same Messiah coming first as the suffering Lamb and then returning as the conquering Lion. Someone pointed out that their view was as though they were looking at two mountain peaks lined up one after the other. The first was the suffering Messiah and the second was the conquering King; but they could not see the valley (the Church Age) in between. And they certainly did not see the Rapture of the Church with Christ coming for His Bride. It was a musterion – a mystery that man could not know until it was revealed by God to the Apostle Paul. God first revealed it in I Thessalonians 4:13-18.

Next we are introduced to the stars that were held in Jesus' right hand, and the lampstands of which He was in the midst. They are a mystery – a musterion. But then He reveals to us that the lampstands are seven churches and He names them. We can look at a map of Asia Minor and find each one. But wait. God presents these churches in such a way that He expects us to use common sense to unravel the final mystery about them. And it is this: The lampstands represent all of God's churches throughout the history of the Church Age. We will get a closer look at these churches in the next two chapters.

CHAPTER TWO

Jesus Critiques Four Churches in Asia

As we study each of these seven churches, we will not only see that their warnings and commendations fit the conditions of that local church at that particular time in John's day, but we can also see that they fit perfectly the history and description of the universal Church (true believers from all denominations) from the time it was established on the day of Pentecost to the time of the Rapture when the Church no longer appears on earth.

It is not an accident that there are seven churches mentioned. There were a number of churches throughout the area, but seven is symbolic for perfection in the Bible, and these seven churches perfectly describe the history of the universal Church as we will see.

It says that the stars are the angels of the seven churches. The Greek word for angels is "angelos." It means messenger.[1] Some commentators believe that these are actual angels assigned to oversee each church. This could be true. But from a practical sense, the pastor is the human leader of the church. He is the messenger who sets the direction for his people each week so that the church will be a beacon and a lighthouse for Christ in the local community. And when the pastor leads that church into heresy, apathy and apostasy, God says, *"I will remove thy candlestick"* (Revelation 2:5). Sadly, this has happened to thousands of churches throughout Europe. When I think of those grand old teachers and preachers in England from another generation – Charles Spurgeon, John Darby, John Wesley and Alexander Maclaren – it makes me sad.

England today is spiritually dead with only 6% of their population attending church each week. You would have to say that their lampstand is only a glimmer, and it seems that God is about to extinguish it. And liberalism is gaining more control in America as each year passes. Prayer has been taken out of the schools and any mention of Christ is being erased from public life and replaced by a tepid lukewarm religion. Few prayers in the public arena end with Jesus' name. Instead we have "in His name" or "in God's name" or simply "Amen" in no one's name. That will be addressed by Christ's messages to the seven churches in the next two chapters. I am so proud of my former pastor, Bro. Jerry Griffin who pastored at FBC, Forney for 33 years. He recently was asked to give the opening prayer for the Texas State Senate in Austin. He prayed a tremendous prayer – and closed it "in Jesus' name." Good for him!

As we begin to look at the letters to the seven churches, we must not forget the table of contents for the Book as given in chapter 1, verse 19. Jesus told John to *"Write the things which thou hast seen* [the past], *and the things which are* [the present], *and the things which shall be hereafter* [the future]." We have just seen the "past" in chapter 1. Now we are going to see the present – "the things which are" in the next two chapters.

The first letter is directed to the church at Ephesus where John was pastor prior to his arrest and imprisonment. Beginning at chapter 2, we read in verses 1-3: "*Unto the angel* [or messenger] *of the church of Ephesus write; These things saith He that holdeth the seven stars in His right hand, who walketh in the midst of the seven golden candlesticks; I know thy works, and thy labour, and thy patience, and how thou canst not bear them which are evil: and thou hast tried them which say they are apostles, and are not, and hast found them liars: And hast borne, and hast patience, and for my name's sake hast laboured, and hast not fainted.*"

Ephesus was the capital and the largest city of the province of Asia. It had a great seaport- a very wealthy and cultured city. It was also on a great highway where travelers from the east going to and from Rome would pass through it. We would describe it as "politically correct," but a very corrupt city. Politically correct because they preached "tolerance," just like our society does today. And by tolerance, I do not mean the kind we had when I was growing up – allowing freedom of worship according to the dictates of your heart so long as it did not harm anyone. I mean the tolerance such as "all religions are equal, and none are superior to any other." The only thing tolerance will not allow in today's society is "intolerance." More and more pressure is being put on Jesus' statement, "*I am the way, the truth and the life: No man cometh unto the Father except by me*" (John 14:6). Society's new tolerance does not like that statement, saying it is prejudiced and biased. The new watchword is, "My religion is just as valid as yours, and you need to acknowledge that truth."

Paul visited Ephesus and preached Christ on Mars Hill in Acts 17 as the only way to be saved. The scholars were glad to debate with him about this in the synagogue. But when Paul mentioned the resurrection, some laughed and mocked him and did not believe, but others said they wanted to hear from him again at a later time (Acts 17:32). But some believed and Paul names them in verse 34. That is generally the case whenever the Gospel is preached – "*Some believed the things which were spoken, and some believed not* (Acts 28:24). They probably wanted Paul to stay longer and debate with them, but Paul "*departed from among them*" (Acts 17:33). Had he stayed eventually his life would have been in danger as was the case in the other cities he preached in. It is amazing, but when the skeptics and unbelievers could not win their debates with Paul, they invariably turned to violence (Acts 17:2-5).

On Paul's next missionary trip, as recorded in the 19th chapter of Acts, he stayed about two years, and debated and taught in one of the rabbinical schools. As a result, many people were saved, and immediately they burned their occult books (Acts 19:19). They were also turning from their false goddess, Diana. They understood that when you are saved, it dramatically changes your lifestyle! Well, guess what? A silversmith named Demetrius was hit in the pocketbook – no one was buying his silver goddesses anymore. So he riled up the townspeople saying, "Paul is not tolerant. He is saying that Jesus is the only way to God."

The unbelievers could not stand for that. They said, "Why, Ephesus is on the map; it is the home of the great Temple of Diana. It is one of the ancient Seven Wonders of the World, and Paul is threatening what we stand for!" (Acts 19:24-29).

There is not much difference between liberal churches that turn away from the fundamentals of the Christian faith and the pagan worship at Ephesus. If we say, "Oh, Christ is not the only way, He is just one of the many ways to get to Heaven," then the world would have no problem accommodating Christianity; nor would the unbelievers in Ephesus! Some say, "Wouldn't it be just grand if all the churches could put aside their doctrinal differences and just be one, big happy family? All could agree to accept a common creed worded so that everyone could subscribe to it, and so the shame of Christendom's divisions would be ended." That sounds good on the surface, but in reality it is not. You might be caught off guard by such a grand plan, but if you follow the teachings set out in the Book of Revelation, you will be well armed against such a heresy.

You will learn later in this study that just such a religious federation is going to arise. It is designated as "Babylon the Great" in the 17th chapter of Revelation. It will be a giant, world church. We see the preparation for this being made all around us today. In contrast, God's divine order is this: separation from evil, not a fusion of diverse satanic systems.

The Greek word for Ephesus means "desirable." A Greek would apply this term to the maiden of his choice. The church at Ephesus was a desirable church. The Greek word "ecclesia", translated "church" in our Bibles, means a called-out assembly. As used in Scripture, sometimes it referred to the local church, and sometimes it referred to the "Universal Church" – that body of believers that is composed of born-again believers from all walks of life and from many different denominations.

Although the Church's mission is to faithfully take the Gospel throughout the ends of the earth, the Bible is very clear that the churches would never convert the entire world. Jesus proposed a rhetorical question in Luke 18:8. He asks when He returns, if He will find faith on the earth. It sounds like He was certain He would not, and without question the Book of Revelation confirms this.

The post-Millennialists teach that when Jesus returns, the Church will present to Him a world that has just been converted – a world without spot or blemish, but perfectly in sync with Christ's principles. But the truth of the matter is that there are not many post-Millennialists anymore. WWI and WWII and the 50-plus wars worldwide since that time have crushed those hopes and dreams. If anything, it proves that they have it backwards.

The perfect church with perfect members will never be achieved until Christ comes back, and accomplishes the things revealed in the ninth chapter of Daniel. Things that we cannot do ourselves: like putting an end to sin, and like bringing in everlasting righteousness. The Church will never convert the whole world. "Ecclesia" means a called-out group – called out from where? Called out from the evil world system. If the Church converted the whole world that would be the end of the Church because there would not be anything that it is called out from!

We find that Ephesus was a busy, achieving church – topping all the charts on the standard of excellence. Christ acknowledges their works, their labor and their patience. Lives were being touched. Works speak of actual service being rendered, while labor indicates that painful effort was required to produce the works. They were a sacrificing, ministering church. And this is not the pastor's assessment, or the deacons, or some committee – this was Jesus' evaluation as He walks among His churches and He knows their true condition. They were also standing for the truth. *"Thou canst not bear them which are evil"* (Revelation 2:2). This was a church with conviction. They stood for moral purity and sound doctrine.

Church discipline is virtually unheard of today. I was working on a church project a few years back, and I had the opportunity to look at the church minutes from nearly 100 years ago. They told of some members who were "dropped from fellowship" for their bad testimony. If a church severed someone's membership today, most likely the church would hear from the ACLU claiming some form of civil rights had been violated.

The church at Ephesus stood firm on the fundamentals of the faith. It weeded out the false teachers. The Southern Baptist Convention, headquartered in Nashville, Tennessee stood at a crossroads several years ago. Its delegates from churches across the country met to determine whether it would stand on the infallible, inerrant written word of God or whether "experience" is just as valid. In other words, the phrase "God told me so" would be just as valid as an assertion in Scripture. Praise God, the Southern Baptists voted overwhelmingly to trust 100% in the inerrancy of the Bible over someone's religious experience. If the experience (dream, vision, etc.) contradicts Scripture then Scripture would prevail. This action was led by Drs. W. A. Criswell, Paige Patterson, the late Adrian Rogers and Albert Mohler. If the Bible says something is wrong, then it is wrong. If it says it is right, then it is right.

Truth is truth and does not change according to the whims of society. The Southern Baptists remained faithful and followed the example at Ephesus: *"Thou hast tried them which say they are apostles, and are not, and hast found them liars"* (Revelation 2:2b). And do not think the church at Ephesus did not catch a lot of flak for their moral stance. You can tell that from the way Scripture describes the church. *"And hast borne, and hast patience, and for my name's sake hast labored, and hast not fainted"* (Revelation 2:3). This speaks of their posture in the face of opposition and hostility. But then we find in verses 4 and 5 that Christ was not entirely pleased with all their actions. Their work became more important than their worship. Here is a principle that runs through Scripture: how you finish is more important than how you start. *"Nevertheless I have somewhat against thee, because thou hast left thy first love. Remember therefore from whence thou art fallen, and repent, and do the first works; or else I will come unto thee quickly, and will remove thy candlestick out of his place except thou repent"* (Revelation 2:4-5).

In one simple sentence the picture changes. Here apparently is a church doing all the right things for the wrong reasons. They are doing great things. They have great programs, but they left their first love (Revelation 2:4). "Left" is a strong word. It means abandoned or forsaken. Their love for Christ has faded and they are going in the wrong direction! The term "first love" always conjures up thoughts of intense love, all-consuming – burning like a flame. Consider a newly married couple. Their life is one continuous story of affection – a delight in one another. Sharing, helping and providing is not work. It is performed with gladness.

Men, your wives like to hear from you the words, "I love you." But we men forget. Shirley in my Sunday school class asked her husband, Ray, if he still loved her. He said, "When we got married, I told you that I love you, and if anything ever changes, I'll let you know." That was not the right answer, Ray!

We need to remember that in our walk with Christ, it is not our religious rituals – it is not our "going through the motions" – it is our love for Jesus and each other as brothers and sisters in Christ that is the essence of Christianity.

I received a birthday card several years ago from a Christian teacher that had the best description of God's will that I have ever read. It simply said, "God's will is exactly what I would choose if I knew all the facts."[2] God also gave this man tremendous insights into basic principles of family life that few teachers grasped at that time or since. I have heard of Christian men or women leaving their spouse, saying, "I don't love you anymore." But that is a symptom; it is not the root problem. When a man says he no longer loves his wife, the root problem is that he does not love Jesus as much as he did before. When you say, "I do", then the spouse becomes the right one for you. He is saying that your commitment – your word in front of God and the world – should trump feelings!

I went to the wedding of a young girl in my office. To my surprise, she had re-written the wedding vows to make them more suitable to her liking. Instead of "as long as we both shall live" – it was changed to "as long as we both shall love." When we make a commitment before God at the wedding altar, it should be a commitment that is not based on fickle feelings. Rather, it is a commitment to your spouse, and that commitment should reflect the deep love that Christ Himself exhibited for His Bride as described in Ephesians 5:25 : *"Christ loved the Church and gave Himself for it."*

Husbands, do you love your wife with such a love that you will be willing without a moment's hesitation to give your life for her? That is the expectation of a Christian marriage. If every man in the country adopted that attitude, there would never have been the women's lib movement.

I heard a story of a five year old girl who became seriously ill, and her parents rushed her to the hospital. After initial tests, the doctors told the parents that she needed an immediate blood transfusion to save her life. The problem was that she had a very rare blood type, and there was little time to find a match. They quickly drew blood from both parents, but it was not a match. Time was running out. But then they thought to test her little brother who was a year older than her. Bingo – it was a match! They explained to him that his sister needed his blood in order to live. He readily agreed to the transfusion. As the medical staff began hooking him up for the procedure, he hugged and kissed his mother and father and, with tears in his eyes, told them goodbye. They were shocked. It was only then that they realized the little fellow thought he was giving all his blood to his sister and that he would die. What a great illustration of selfless love!

In verse 5, Christ says *".... repent, and do the first works."* What did we do when we first met the Lord? We repented. We confessed to Jesus that we wanted Him to be Lord of our life. We had an all-consuming love for Him. In verse 6, Jesus again commends them for standing fast. *"But this thou hast, that thou hatest the deeds of the Nicolaitans, which I also hate"* (Revelation 2:6). Many church members will be in for a big shock someday. All of our service, all of our work in the church that is not motivated by our love for Christ, will be worthless. It will be burned up as dross (I Corinthians 3:13).

Does it surprise you that Jesus commends hating? But notice He commends hating of the deeds and not the people. A number of years ago, I listened intently to the debate between Dr. W. A. Criswell and the atheist, Madalyn Murray O'Hair. It was carried live on radio station KRLD in Dallas. Ms. O'Hair said that you cannot hate the actions of a person without hating the person. Dr. Criswell explained to her that God hates sin, but loves the sinner. She scoffed at that idea. She wishes now that she had listened to the gospel since a few years after that she and her son and granddaughter were tortured and murdered by a former employee of O'Hair's atheist organization.[3]

You can despise and hate the actions of people – the terrorists – the bin Ladens of the world. And yet you can pray for them and sincerely say, "If those people come to a saving knowledge of the Lord Jesus Christ, I can forgive them and love them and welcome them into the family of God." The Bible condemns the deeds and actions of those who practice the "alternative lifestyle" as our culture calls it. But I do not hate those people. I could calmly and sanely discuss this with them, and show them from Scripture that this practice is called "an abomination" by God, and will eventually escort them down the path that leads to destruction (Leviticus 18:22; 20:13; Revelation 21:8; Romans 1:18-32). I would do everything in my power to lead them down the right path. Saul of Tarsus was a murderer. Before his name was changed to Paul, he was searching out, arresting and putting innocent Christians to death. But God changed his heart.

No one knows exactly who these Nicolaitans were, but we have a reasonable assumption. The name itself comes from two Greek words – "nikao" meaning to conquer, and "laos" meaning the people. Putting them together, you have the phrase "To rule over the people." It was the early attempts to install a system of clergy or priests who would "lord it over the people." The term may refer to the followers of an early deacon, Nicolas of Antioch, mentioned in Acts 6:5. At any rate, they were only deeds here in this passage; but when we get to the letter to the church at Pergamos later in this chapter, we find that the problem had advanced so that it was now called the doctrine of the Nicolaitans. It appears that this was the nucleus of the powerful priesthood that has ruled over millions of people for hundreds of years. When a priest or pastor tells you not to read the Bible or you will get confused and that you should leave such study to him, then you are approaching the doctrine of the Nicolaitans.

Just such a conversation was confirmed by a lady in my office. I started a small Bible study class for some of the workers during our lunch hour. It was strictly voluntary. About six or eight came including our receptionist, Anne, who was a Catholic. She thoroughly enjoyed our Bible study until she mentioned it to her priest. He told her not to attend any more meetings, stating that she would only get confused. She apologized to me for not being able to come to the classes anymore. "The doctrine of the Nicolaitans" – ruling over the people – seems to have come into play. Remember, Jesus said, *"And ye shall know the truth, and the truth shall make you free* (John 8:32).

Verse 7a: *"He that hath an ear, let him hear what the Spirit saith unto the churches ...."*. This does not mean simply to hear, but to absorb it. James 1:22- 24 says hearing without response brings fatal results. So when the Holy Spirit specifically says for you to listen, you had better listen, and respond to what He says. And here is what He says in the last part of Revelation 2:7 says, *"To him that overcometh will I give to eat of the Tree of Life, which is in the midst of the Paradise of God."*

There are those who overcome the world, and there are those who are overcome by the world. Just what is the Bible's definition of an overcomer? We find the answer in I John 5:5 (NIV): *"Who is it that overcomes the world? Only he who believes that Jesus is the Son of God."*

Look at the last phrase in verse 7b: *".... the Tree of Life, which is in the midst of the Paradise of God."* The last time we saw the Tree of Life it was in the Garden of Eden, or in Paradise you might say. It is still in Paradise as we have just seen in Revelation 2:7, but Paradise is in Heaven according to Revelation 22:2 which in context is giving us a tour of Heaven. *"In the midst of the street of it, and on either side of the river, was there the Tree of Life, which bare twelve manner of fruits, and yielded her fruit every month ...."* (Revelation 22:2). How and when was Paradise moved from the Garden of Eden to Heaven? As we explained earlier in this study, when Jesus died on the cross the penalty for sin was fully paid. He then went to Paradise which was located in Hades, and led the saved to Heaven, which in effect, transferred Paradise to Heaven when He led captivity captive (Ephesians 4:8).

Next we come to the second of these letters to the seven churches, the church at Smyrna. As we study each of these letters, we can clearly see they reflect the condition of the Body of Christ at that particular time in that specific local body as well as picturing the Universal Church at a particular time in Church history as we will see later. Revelation 2:8-9 : *"And unto the angel of the church in Smyrna write; These things saith the first and the last, which was dead, and is alive; I know thy works, and tribulation, and poverty, (but thou art rich) and I know the blasphemy of them which say they are Jews, and are not, but are the synagogue of Satan."* These letters to the church at Smyrna, and the one to Philadelphia in the next chapter, are the only ones that have no condemnation or warning. Everything that is said to them is positive and encouraging.

The city of Smyrna was founded about 1,000 B.C. and was destroyed around 600 B.C. Alexander the Great conquered the known world some 250 years later, and when he died his empire was split among four of his top generals. This was predicted several hundred years before by the prophet Daniel (Daniel 8:22). The four generals and the territories they commanded are: Lysimachus (a/k/a Antigonis) who took Asia Minor (modern Turkey); Cassander who took Macedonia (basically Greece); Seleucius Nicator who took Syria and the remainder of the Middle East and Ptolemy who took Egypt.

Smyrna was in the region ruled by Antigonis. He set out to rebuild Smyrna around 300 B.C. and rebuilt it into one of the most beautiful cities that has ever existed. Smyrna sat on a hill rising from the Mediterranean Sea so that it appeared as if the city wore a crown. It was even referred to as "the Glory of Asia" because of its breathtaking beauty. It was the birthplace of the great Grecian poet, Homer. Smyrna's main street was lined with magnificent temples in honor of all the Greek and Roman deities. Contrast that to the Christians who lived there that had to meet in homes, underground tombs, or anywhere they could find a place to gather in secret.

When Rome rose to power and crushed its opposition, namely the various warring factions of the Greeks, it put into place what it called "Pax Romana" – the peace of Rome. The people were tired of centuries of war and turmoil, and the Romans brought peace at last. The Romans were asked as we are today, "Are you better off now than you were four years ago?" And their response was a loud "yes." No wonder they began to worship the Caesars. This worship in the beginning was more political than religious; however, the Caesars soon warmed to the idea of being adored, and it became a crime against Rome if a citizen did not worship, bow down and equate the Caesar with deity.

Christianity would have been accepted if the Christians had simply put Jesus alongside of all the Roman and Greek gods who had temples dedicated to them, and had attested that Jesus was just one of many gods to worship. That was also the case in Greece. Sounds like that old record is being dusted off, and played for us again in the United States. When the Christians in Smyrna would not place Caesar on par with Christ, they were considered bad citizens and unpatriotic – a crime punishable by death. And so, Christians were tortured on the rack, and endured all manner of atrocities as they faced wild beasts as entertainment in the big coliseum. Church history tells us that as many as five million Christians may have been put to death during this period. Every Christian should read about this era in the book, *Foxe's Christian Martyrs of the World,*[4] then we would soon discover the foolishness of Christians complaining about their church accommodations in this day of luxury and comfort in which we live.

The name of the city of Symrna comes from the Greek word translated in Scripture as "myrrh." The very word means bitter and was symbolic of the fact that the church at Symrna would suffer horribly. Myrrh was a gum resin from a little scrubby tree. There were basically two uses for it. First, it could be made into a perfume, but it had to be crushed to give off its sweet fragrance. The church at Smyrna was crushed under the iron heel of Rome, but the fact is, the Church never smelled sweeter!

Myrrh was very expensive – a pint was worth a year's wages. It was one of the gifts brought at Christ's birth. It was also poured on Christ's feet by Martha's sister, Mary, and she was immediately criticized for her wastefulness. *"Then Mary took a twelve ounce jar of expensive perfume made from essence of nard, and she anointed Jesus' feet with it and wiped his feet with her hair. And the house was filled with the fragrance. But Judas Iscariot, one of His disciples – the One who would betray Him – said, 'That perfume was worth a small fortune. It should have been sold and the money given to the poor'"* (John 12:3-5 NLT). Do you think that Judas was interested in the poor? The next verse answers that question. *"Not that he cared for the poor – he was a thief who was in charge of the disciples' funds, and he often took some for his own use"* (John 12:6 NLT).

Myrrh's second use was to make embalming fluid. When Joseph of Arimathea carefully took Christ's body off the cross, the Bible says he was joined by Nicodemus and they wrapped Jesus' body with linen cloths, along with about a hundred pounds of aloes and myrrh according to Jewish burial customs (John 19:38-40). We learned that about twelve ounces of myrrh cost about a year's wages – so either they used a lot more of aloes in the mixture or else Joseph of Arimathea (whom we were told was a rich man) really stepped up to the plate!

Jesus said to the church at Smyrna, *"I know thy works, and tribulation …."* (Revelation 2:9). The word tribulation in this passage means pressure primarily from the Roman government – unrelenting pressure like having a huge boulder on your chest until you finally suffocate – a pressure that is never ending, never letting up. He also says that He knows their poverty. In Greek, there are two words for poverty. One is "penes" from which we get our word penny. It means a pittance, working for a bare minimum just enough to buy the essentials. The other word is "ptocheia" – it means destitute – abject poverty, with no resources whatsoever.

Most of the citizens of Smyrna were living in luxury in the city that was known as the "Glory of Asia." The Christians, however, had nothing; they were destitute. It was similar to the Jews in Germany during WWII. It was open season on them. You could rob them, cheat them, loot them, destroy their houses; they were all fair game. How strong would you be today if your faith was going to cost you everything that you had? How strong would your faith be if, after losing everything, you then were going to be thrown into a pit of lions?

When the Germans were killing the Jews, young Corrie ten Boom was confused and scared about all the turmoil that was in the air. Here is how Corrie described it: "But that night as Father stepped through the door I burst into tears. 'I need you!' I sobbed. 'You can't die! You can't!' Father sat down on the edge of the narrow bed. 'Corrie,' he began gently, 'When you and I go to Amsterdam, when do I give you your ticket?' I sniffed a few times, considering this. 'Why, just before we get on the train.' Father replied, 'Exactly. And our wise Father in Heaven knows when we're going to need things, too. Don't run out ahead of Him, Corrie. When the time comes that some of us will have to die, you will look into your heart, and find the strength you need – just in time.'"[5]

In verse 9, Jesus refers to those false teachers who claimed to be Jews but they were not; that is, they claimed to be circumcised inwardly of the heart and spirit as described in Romans 2:29; but they were not, because they were not true believers. They were Judaizers who wanted to bring in Jewish legalism and mix it with the grace of God. There are many in the church today that pretend outwardly to have some kind of relationship with Christ. They may have even joined their local church, but they have not been born again. They are pretenders and God says they are of the "synagogue of Satan."

Christ says that these deceivers embrace works- salvation. It is rampant in many churches today. It seems that man always wants to add to the provision that God has made. There has never been a song with a greater message than this: *Nothing But the Blood of Jesus* written by a Baptist preacher, Robert Lowry, in 1876. But mankind constantly wants to add something to the blood. They say the blood of Christ is needed, but you also have to do this and do that. Some add baptism as essential. Some say you must attend church every Sunday. Others say you must partake of the Lord's Supper every Sunday. Another says if you have not spoken in tongues, you are not saved. I heard a preacher on the radio say you can do all of these things we have mentioned, but if you do them on Sunday, you are out of luck. They must be observed on the Sabbath (Saturday) or you will be consigned to the hottest part of Hell.

So Jesus encourages the believers in Smyrna. He says, *"I KNOW thy pain – I KNOW thy suffering – I KNOW thy poverty."* In the Greek language, there were two words for "know." One means that you know something by observation. I know that if you hit your finger it will hurt because I have seen people do it. In fact, one time, to Arlene's chagrin, I was watching one of my favorite shows, the Three Stooges. I guess Arlene does not like pure genius. Moe was holding a nail in position, and he turned to Curly who was holding the hammer and said, "When I nod my head, you hit it with the hammer." You can guess what happened next.

The other Greek word means to "know" by experience. One time I was putting a stake down in the yard. My young grandson, Taylor, was helping me. I hit my finger with a hammer, causing severe pain. I thought Taylor was going to pass out. He ran in the house crying, "Gramma – Gramma – Granddaddy hit his finger." He was white as a sheet and Arlene had to make him lie down. So, I know that a hit finger hurts, not just by observation, but also by experience.

When Jesus said "I know" in verse 2, the Greek word that is used here is the one that means Jesus knew from experience. He had been there and done that. He told these believers in effect, "I know your poverty; I know your pain; I know your suffering." Hebrews 4:15 says: *"For we have not a high priest which cannot be touched with the feeling of our infirmities."* Infirmities mean weaknesses. They also can mean disease or health problems often related to old age. It is a comfort to know that our Savior and High Priest is touched by our infirmities. Jesus said, "Take heart! I know what you are going through." Scripture tells us that what we are going through in this life in the form of sickness, hurt and sorrow, is nothing compared to the joys that await us in Heaven. It is one of my favorite verses, and one we should read frequently when we suffer with a debilitating disease or have lost a loved one: *"I consider that our present sufferings are not worth comparing with the glory that will be revealed in us"* (Romans 8:18 NIV).

Jesus goes on to remind these Christians in Smyrna that false teachers who would add to His gospel are all part of the synagogue of Satan. Paul had said the same thing earlier, in his letter to the Galatians: *"I am astonished that you are so quickly deserting the One who called you by the grace of Christ and are turning to a different gospel – which is really not gospel at all. Evidently some people are throwing you into confusion and are trying to pervert the gospel of Christ. But even if we or an angel from Heaven should preach a gospel other than the one we preached to you, let him be eternally condemned!"* (Galatians 1:6-8 NIV). Paul saw that this perversion of the Scriptures would lead to a monstrous system of works-salvation and almost a complete disappearance of the doctrines of salvation by grace and justification by faith.

One group of false teachers in Ephesus wanted to continue a system of apostolic succession, while in Smyrna, another group wanted to continue the priesthood. Eventually, the two merged into a vast worldly system with an imaginary apostolic succession and an elaborate visible priesthood. So, in time, this doctrine of the Nicolaitans conquered the laity and placed them in legalistic bondage under a system of ritualistic ordinances, sacrifices and penances. We find that system has survived and is flourishing in the Roman Church today.

Revelation 2:10 says: "*Fear none of those things which thou shalt suffer: behold, the Devil shall cast some of you into prison, that ye may be tried; and ye shall have tribulation ten days: be thou faithful unto death, and I will give thee a crown of life.*" These poor Christians were not told, "Cheer up, things are going to get better." No, Jesus told them, "Cheer up. Things are going to get worse! You are going to be tried. You are going to be tested. Many of you will be killed. But do not worry because in the end I am going to give you a crown of life." This reward from the Savior Himself will be worth it all!

The pastor of the church in Smyrna was that faithful servant, Polycarp. He was a convert of the apostle John. And some fifty years after this letter to Smyrna was written, Polycarp himself was arrested along with ten other Christians, and brought before the head magistrate. Most were thrown to the lions. Polycarp was offered his freedom if he would deny Christ. If not, he would be burned at the stake. Polycarp answered, "Eighty-six years have I served Christ, and He has always been good to me. How then can I blaspheme my King and my Savior?"

The governor said he would burn Polycarp at the stake if he did not deny Christ. Polycarp said, "You threaten me with fire which burns for an hour, and after a little, is extinguished. Are you ignorant of the eternal fire of the coming judgment?" And history records that on his last day on earth, Polycarp prayed this prayer: "I thank you, God that you have graciously thought me worthy of this day and of this hour that I may be numbered with the martyrs who die for Christ."[6]

If, when you accepted Christ, you thought that the Christian life would be easy and all your problems would be solved, you are sadly mistaken. We are never told that in Scripture. Sometimes, I think in our intense desire to win people to Christ, we are reluctant to "tell them the whole story." Jesus never painted a flowery picture. He never withheld the truth. In fact, He said, "*I have told you all this so that you may have peace in Me. Here on earth you will have many trials and sorrows. But take heart, because I have overcome the world*" (John 16:33 NLT).

I wonder how many people would walk down the aisle to be baptized if the pastor said, "Now folks, before you make this decision, let us read what the Holy Spirit said through the Apostle Paul: "*Everyone who wants to live a godly life in Christ Jesus will be persecuted ....*" (II Timothy 3:12 NIV).

Jesus Himself said people will mock you and persecute you and lie about you and say all sorts of evil things against you all because you are followers of Him (Matthew 5:11). If those things were said to the people joining the church, we probably would not have near as many coming forward. But you know what? With a commitment like that, those that did come forward would most likely be in church every Sunday instead of just having their name on the church roll. They would be a force to be reckoned with! It grieves me that one day many people will discover that the book that contains the church records is not the same as the Book that contains the names of those written in the Lamb's Book of Life.

Continuing with our passage, what is meant by the ten days of tribulation? History records that there were ten great persecutions of the Church carried out by ten Roman emperors during this period.[7]

1) Nero (64-68 A.D.) burned Rome and blamed the Christians; he threw Christians to the wild beasts; he executed Paul and probably Peter.
2) Domitian (90-96 A.D.) killed thousands of Christians in Rome; he banished John to the Isle of Patmos.
3) Trajan (104-117 A.D.) decreed that Christianity was illegal; he burned Ignatius, Bishop of Antioch, at the stake.
4) Marcus Aurelius (161-180 A.D.) tortured and beheaded Christians.
5) Severus (200-211 A.D.) burned, crucified and beheaded Christians.
6) Maximinius (235-237 A.D.) executed many Christians.
7) Decius (250-253 A.D.) tried to wipe out Christianity by killing all the Christians he could find.
8) Valerian (257-260 A.D.) continued the extermination of all Christians; he killed Cyprian, the Bishop of Carthage.
9) Aurelian (270-275 A.D.) persecuted Christians in any manner that he could.
10) Diocletian (303-312 A.D.) was possibly the fiercest of the persecutors; he also burned all the Scriptures he could find.

Whether the ten days relates to these ten edicts issued against Christians or not, the clear intent of the passage is meant to prepare the Church for intense suffering, and yet to assure them it would be very brief in contrast to the endless ages of glory beyond it. Paul said, *"For our present troubles are quite small and won't last very long. Yet they will produce for us an immeasurably great glory that will last forever!"* (II Corinthians 4:17 NLT).

When we get through with these seven letters in chapters 2 and 3, we will look back briefly at what Christ has to say to each one, and we will see clearly how these churches paint a perfect picture of Church history from Pentecost to the present time.

Before we get to the third letter, look again at a verse in chapter 2. From its message, you can tell it was written not just to this one particular church in Smyrna, but to churches everywhere in every age. *"He that hath an ear, let him hear what the Spirit saith unto the churches; He that overcometh shall not be hurt of the second death"* (Revelation 2:11). It is essential that we are part of the overcomers, and that we escape the second death. There are two questions that jump out at us: who are the overcomers and what is the second death? First, let us review who the overcomers are. They are special people because they are given great promises.

Revelation 2:7 says the overcomers will eat of the Tree of Life. Revelation 2:11 says the overcomers will not be hurt by the second death. Revelation 2:26 says the overcomers will have power over the nations. Revelation 3:5 says that the overcomers will have their name forever recorded in the Book of Life, and will be clothed in white raiment. Revelation 3:12 says that the overcomers will receive a new name from Christ. Revelation 3:21 says that the overcomers will sit with Christ upon His throne. And Revelation 21:7 says that the overcomers will inherit all things. Wow! With all those benefits to look forward to, everyone should be asking how they can become overcomers. But they should be careful to get their answer from Scripture, because some teachers would tell us that we must endure, that we must keep holding on, and if we do not give out before our life ends, we will have overcome. They put the emphasis on us – we must hold on – we must endure. But I have some good news for you. If you put your trust in Christ, it will be Christ that is holding on to you! It will be His power that determines whether or not you will endure.

But just who is an overcomer? We mentioned this before but it serves us well to repeat it. The answer is given clearly in I John 5:4 (NIV): *"For everyone born of God has overcome the world. This is the victory that has overcome the world, even our faith."* So, now we know the most important answer – those who believe that Jesus is the Son of God and are born again with a new nature are the overcomers, and they have been promised great things by the Savior Himself. One of the things He says in this letter is that they will not be hurt by the second death. Death is scary. Will we have to die not only once, but twice? What is this second death? Scripture teaches there are two deaths: one is physical and one is spiritual. Neither means to cease to exist; neither means annihilation; but each means separation.

First, let us consider physical death. It does not mean that you will cease to exist. It means the separation of your body from your soul and spirit. At death, your fleshly body will turn to dust in the grave, but your soul and spirit live on. It is just separated from your body. Paul tells us that if we are believers, when we die the real "us" (our soul/spirit) goes to be with the Lord, and the body goes into the grave to wait the day of resurrection when they will be joined together in a miracle of re-creation.

It is very sad when someone says, "I am going to commit suicide. I am going to kill my body because I want to escape all my troubles." But death is not the end of life. The soul and spirit live on to face the Creator, whose sixth commandment says, "You shall not murder" (Exodus 20:13 NIV). Suicide is the murder of your own body. I understand that depression is a horrible malady, and Satan whispers, "Take the easy way out" when in reality that is far from the truth. I will admit there have been times when I have been sorely depressed, but what has helped me the most in those tough times is the verse of Scripture that says, *".… the One who is in you is greater than the one who is in the world"* (I John 4:4 NIV).

But what is this second death that Scripture speaks of? Look what John sees. He records it in Revelation chapter 20. *"And I saw the dead, small and great, stand before God; and the books were opened: and another book was opened, which is the Book of Life: and the dead were judged out of those things which were written in the books, according to their works. And the sea gave up the dead which were in it; and death and Hell delivered up the dead which were in them: and they were judged every man according to their works. And death and Hell were cast into the Lake of Fire. This is the second death. And whosoever was not found written in the Book of Life was cast into the Lake of Fire"* (Revelation 20:12-15).

It is clear that being cast into the Lake of Fire is the second death. But we were just told that the overcomers will not be hurt by the second death. And who did I John 5:5 say are the overcomers? Read it again and underline it in your Bible because it is so important: *"Who is he that overcometh the world, but he that believeth that Jesus is the Son of God?"*

Jesus said, "You must be born again." A Christian is born twice. You became a child of your parents by being born physically the first time. You become saved by being born again, so you are born the second time into the family of God as you accept Christ as your personal savior. If you are in the family of God, the second death which is eternal separation from God will never affect you. So here is a nugget of truth my mother told me many years ago. If you are born twice, you will never die but once. If are born once, you will die twice. If you are born twice – physically and spiritually – you will only die once: physically. If you are born only once – physically – you will die twice: physically and spiritually. Think about it.

Let us now go on to the third letter that was written to the church at Pergamos. *"And to the angel of the church in Pergamos write; These things saith He which hath the sharp sword with two edges"* (Revelation 2:12). This church needs to look to the Word of God for its authority, not to men. That is why the sharp two-edged sword is mentioned. It is a symbol of the Word of God. Here is what the writer of Hebrews has to say, *"For the Word of God is quick, and powerful, and sharper than any two-edged sword …."* (Hebrews 4:12a).

"I know thy works, and where thou dwellest, even where Satan's seat is: and thou holdest fast my name, and hast not denied my faith, even in those days wherein Antipas was my faithful martyr, who was slain among you, where Satan dwelleth" (Revelation 2:13). Christ says, *"I know where thou dwellest, even where Satan's seat is …."*. The NIV says, *"even where Satan's throne is."* Where is Satan's throne? If you had asked this question to any of those early Christian martyrs who had been put to death for their witness for Christ, without hesitation they would have pointed to the Emperor's throne in Rome.

The church in Pergamos is commended for not denying the faith. The great Arian controversy was raging at this time in church history. An early Church father by the name of Arius, a priest in Egypt, vehemently denied the divinity of Jesus. Arius claimed that Jesus was

100% man and zero percent divine. He also taught that Jesus was not eternal, and that He was a created being. That is what the Mormons believe; that is what the Jehovah's Witnesses believe. And a fellow by the name of Athanasius, a bishop in Alexandria, upheld the deity of Christ. Athanasius quoted John the Apostle who said, *"In the beginning was the Word, and the Word was with God, and the Word was God"* (John 1:1): It was the most important issue the Church had ever been called on to face, and for over a century it was the burning question of the day. Was Jesus really God?

The Church was wracked by controversy over two Greek words: "homoiosian" and "homoousian." The first means "like substance"; the second means "of the same substance." "Like substance" was the battle-cry of Arius who said Jesus was only a man. "Same substance" was the battle cry of Athanasius who said Jesus was 100% man, but at the same time, 100% God. So irreconcilable was this issue that Emperor Constantine himself got in the middle of it and called a great Church Council in Nicea in 325 A.D. to settle the matter once and for all. The result of that debate was a document which served as the basis for what is now known as the Nicean Creed which confirmed the belief of Athanasius.

When the debate was hotly contested and a brilliant Arian was swaying the people, a pastor from the deserts of Africa sprang to his feet. Clad chiefly in tiger's skin, he ripped it from his back disclosing great scars from having been thrown to the lions in the great coliseum. He cried, "These are the marks of the Lord Jesus Christ, and I cannot bear to hear this blasphemy any longer ….". He then proceeded to give a stirring address setting forth so clearly the truth of the deity of Christ that the majority of the Council realized in a moment that this was indeed the Spirit of Almighty God speaking.[8] The result was that this august Church Council put itself on record as confessing the true deity of our Lord Jesus Christ. If they had not done so, then today the Unitarians would be orthodox, and you and I would be members of a cult. But God did not let that happen.

It is recorded that a number of years later, Emperor Theodosius, leaned toward embracing Arianism that taught Christ was not divine. He wanted Athanasius to accept the Arians with open arms at the Lord's Table. It would be like Christians saying today, "The Muslims believe in God; so let us invite them to join us in the Lord's Supper." But Athanasius refused to invite the Arians to join him at the Lord's Table. The Emperor said to him, "Do you not realize that the entire world is against you?" And Athanasius, that old champion of truth, drew himself up and answered the Emperor bravely with words that have echoed down through the corridors of time – "Then I am against all the world!"[9] What a Braveheart!

In verse 13, the word Antipas in Greek means "against all." I believe this verse was speaking not only of Athanasius, but to all those faithful servants down through the years who have not, and will not deny the name and deity of Jesus Christ. John continues: *"But I have a few things against thee, because thou hast there them that hold the doctrine of Balaam, who taught Balak to cast a stumbling block before the children of Israel, to eat things sacrificed unto idols, and to commit fornication"* (Revelation 2:14). What in the world is this talking about – this doctrine of Balaam?

In the Book of Numbers, we find that Balak was king of the Moabites. He was afraid of the Israelite army because it had been wiping out everything that opposed it. So, King Balak offered a huge amount of money to Balaam, a Midianite priest, to place a curse upon Israel. Balaam was unable to do that, but he offered the king a suggestion that would accomplish the same purpose. He said, "Have the Moabite women flirt with and seduce the men of Israel. Encourage them to intermarry, and soon Israel will be compromised and will be no threat to any of you." Here is what this is saying. In the early persecuted Church, pictured by the letter to the church at Smyrna, Satan threw everything possible in the way of suffering at those poor Christians. But what was the result? They prospered; their ranks grew under intense hardship.

So Satan changed tactics. In this period, pictured by the letter to the church at Pergamos, Satan began to have the world entice the Church, bow to her, seek her favors, and introduce false doctrines from within. The result was what Diocletian's persecution could not do, Emperor Constantine's patronage did. It corrupted the Church, and she forgot her calling as a chaste virgin espoused to an absent Lord. She gave her hand in marriage to the world that had crucified her Bridegroom.

Now we come to the next verse: *"So hast thou also them that hold the doctrine of the Nicolaitans, which thing I hate"* (Revelation 2:15). Earlier in this chapter, the church at Ephesus was told that they hated the deeds of the Nicolaitans. But now, the Nicolaitans have progressed in the wrong direction so that it is no longer the deeds of the Nicolaitans, but it is the doctrine of the Nicolaitans. The word Nicolaitans comes from two Greek words: one meaning to "rule over" and the other meaning "the laity" or the common people.

My Catholic friends would disagree with me, but I think that clearly this is the beginning of the mastery of the priests over the lay people of the Church. Consequently, today instead of what Baptists call the priesthood of every believer (I Peter 2:5) that entitles a believer to go to the very throne of God in prayer and supplication, the Roman Catholic Church has firmly put into place a hierarchy of priests, bishops, and archbishops. They are now the mediators between God and man instead of Christ Jesus (I Timothy 2:5). In plain language, the doctrine of the Nicolaitans is lording over the common people. So Christ issues a solemn warning: *"Repent; or else I will come unto thee quickly, and will fight against them with the sword of my mouth"* (Revelation 2:16). Notice the way Christ fights against these false teachers – with the sword of His mouth. He uses the Word of God.

And then the final promise in verse 17 is to all the churches: *"He that hath an ear, let him hear what the Spirit saith unto the churches; To him that overcometh will I give to eat of the hidden manna, and will give him a white stone, and in the stone a new name written, which no man knoweth saving he that receiveth it."* He promises two things for the believers. First, that He will give them to eat of the hidden manna. Manna was the name of the food that God provided the children of Israel when they wandered in the wilderness (Exodus 16:15). The promise of manna means that God will provide all our needs.

The second thing He promises to believers is that He will give them a white stone that contains a new name that only the recipient knows what it is. In the courts of John's day, if a man was found guilty, he was given a black stone. If he was found innocent, he would be given a white stone. Jesus is saying, "I will give you a white stone, and because you are trusting in Me for your redemption, you will be found innocent."

And what is this new name? Some think we will be given a new name that will reflect our life on earth. We may be called "generous" or "loyal" or "lazy." Abram's name was changed by God to Abraham which in Hebrew means "the father of many." Jacob's name was changed by God to Israel. It is not a Hebrew name, but a Biblical name that means "God perseveres." So our name will quite probably reflect our character in this life.

Acts 13:9, Saul's name is changed to Paul. "Then Saul (who was also called Paul ....)." From that time on, the Apostle was called Paul, a Roman name which means "humble." Paul certainly deserved that name because he was God's instrument in writing 13 Books of the New Testament according to most Bible scholars; however, it was probably 14 Books because he most likely wrote the Book of Hebrews. Dr. C. R. Stam presents an airtight case for Paul's authorship of Hebrews in his book, *The Epistle to the Hebrews.*[10] And God says He is going to give us a new name. But look carefully at this verse. It implies that Jesus will give us a new name that will only be known between you and Him. That name will remind us that we will have a special intimate relationship with Him. Let us make sure our character is clean – we do not want a name that will embarrass us!

Jesus Himself has been called by many names: Alpha and Omega, the Bread of Life, the Good Shepherd, etc. At least fifty names are used for Him and by Him throughout Scripture. And Jeremiah tells us that during the Millennium Jesus will have a new name. Why is it going to be changed? We have a hint in Hebrews 9:28: *"So Christ was once offered to bear the sins of many; and unto them that look for Him shall He appear the second time without sin unto salvation."* This says that Christ is going to come a second time, but this Coming will be apart from the sin question. In other words, this second time He will not be coming to bear the sins of the world. The Age of Grace will have passed. He will not be coming to save souls. And so, His name is going to be changed from Yeshua meaning *"the Salvation of God"* to Tsidkenu meaning *"THE LORD OUR RIGHTEOUSNESS"* (Jeremiah 23:6). So never forget this: your name is important! And when you accepted Christ as your Savior, your name was written in the Lamb's Book of Life.

We have now covered three of the seven letters that Christ told John to write. We have four more to go, and then we can look back to see how they fit into the big picture. It is almost like putting a jigsaw puzzle together. When finished, you can stand back and take in the entire picture and you will have a good grasp of 2,000 years of Church history.

Now we come to the fourth letter that John was told to write. It is to the church at Thyatira. The city of Thyatira was not known for its grandeur, its culture nor its excellence in learning as was Ephesus. However, it did have a pretty good economy. Lydia, a seller of purple dye, was from Thyatira as mentioned in chapter 16 of Acts.

I have already pointed out that the names of these churches are significant. In summary, the first letter was to the church at Ephesus which meant desirable, but remember she left her first love. The second letter was to the suffering church at Smyrna. Smyrna comes from the word myrrh which has to be crushed to give off its fragrance. The church at Smyrna was crushed under the iron heel of Rome, but the church never gave a sweeter fragrance. The third letter was to the church at Pergamos. The name comes from two Greek words meaning marriage and elevation. This church was elevated to a prestigious position, and in effect married to the world.

Now we have the fourth letter, and it is to the church at Thyatira. Many of you have relatives or friends as I do that are Roman Catholics. I love them immensely, and I do not mean to offend them, but the Bible has some direct things to say about Catholicism. God lets the chips fall where they may. He never shies away from the truth. Thyatira comes from two Greek words, one meaning "a sacrifice or incense offering" and the other meaning "that which goes on continually." So putting them together, the word Thyatira means a continual sacrifice.

It is the outgrowth of the church of Pergamos which was elevated and given a prestigious position on the world scene. It was in the 7th Century that the Bishop of Rome was first regularly recognized as the visible head of the church on earth. Most historians agree that this was the beginning of the papacy. Previously there was no Roman Catholic Church in the full sense of the term until the pope was declared the head of Christendom. It is important to bear this in mind because you will often hear Catholics say, "The original church was the Roman Catholic Church, and all the different branches of the Protestant churches have simply broken off from Rome." That is an absolute fallacy. There was no such thing as the papacy until the 7th Century. For six centuries before that, the church was becoming more and more corrupt, drifting further and further away from the Word of God.

We said that the word Thyatira comes from two Greek words meaning a continual sacrifice. Does that ring a bell? The great fundamental error of the Roman Catholic Church is called "the sacrifice of the mass" and it is continual. The Roman Catholic priests declare that in the mass they offer a continual sacrifice for the sins of the living and the dead. This is the central blasphemy of the church at Rome, denying the finished work of Christ on the cross.

Christ Himself on the cross declared, *"It is finished"* (Luke 19:30). That truth is confirmed by Hebrews 9:24-26 (NLT): *"For Christ has entered into Heaven itself to appear now before God as our Advocate. He did not go into the earthly place of worship, for that was merely a copy of the real Temple in Heaven. Nor did He enter Heaven to offer Himself again and again, like the earthly high priest who enters the Most Holy Place year after year to offer the blood of an animal. If that had been necessary, He would have had to die again and again, ever since the world began. But no! He came once for all time, at the end of the age, to remove the power of sin forever by His sacrificial death for us."* Then in Hebrews 10:18 (NLT), the Holy Spirit testifies: *"Now when sins have been forgiven, there is no need to offer any more sacrifices."*

One of my favorite Bible teachers from a generation past is the late Dr. Harry A. Ironside, 20 years pastor of the famed Moody Memorial Church in Chicago. His books are long out of print, but they are wonderful commentaries. Dr. Ironside met a Roman Catholic priest while traveling by train across the country. They had great discussions, and vowed to continue with letters when they got back home. And continue they did. They exchanged incisive letters for quite some time until the priest was transferred to Ireland.

The letters were not argumentative. They were civil and instructive, but they clearly reflected the heresy that has attached itself to many of the Catholic doctrines. You can sense the heartfelt concern that Dr. Ironside had for this priest from his closing letter: "Read carefully, dear sir, and note it well – '*I commend you to God, and to the Word of His grace, which is able to build you up, and to give you an inheritance among all them which are sanctified*' (Acts 20:32). How is it that so many since have ignored instruction so clearly? And turning from the patient, persistent study of the Holy Scriptures, have sought instead unto tradition, church and councils, all fallible, all manifestly having erred and reversed one another again and again! Am I wrong in seeking to cleave alone to God and to the word of His grace? Will you not seek henceforth to do the same? With kindest greeting and earnest prayers for your blessing, I remain, dear sir, your sincere friend, H. A. Ironside."[11]

Dr. Ironside had many opportunities to discuss these issues with many priests over the years. Here is a telling conversation that gets to the meat of the matter. Dr. Ironside to the priest: "What is your function as a sacrificing priest?" The priest answered: "It is my privilege to offer up the Lord Jesus from time to time (as) a continual sacrifice for the sins of the living and the dead." Dr. Ironside: "Well, Christ has to be slain that He may be offered up, doesn't He?" The priest: "Yes." Dr. Ironside: "You claim then that every time you offer the sacrifice of the mass, you are sacrificing Christ for the sins of the living and the dead?" The priest: "Yes." Dr. Ironside: "Well, then, you kill Christ afresh every time you offer that sacrifice!"[12]

The conclusion is inescapable. The only way that Christ can be a sacrifice is to be put to death; therefore, the priest kills Him afresh every time he offers the mass. They cannot get away from this. Peter said on the day of Pentecost, *"Jesus .... ye have taken, and by wicked hands have crucified and slain"* (Acts 2:23). I Peter 3:18 says that Christ died ONCE for our sins – not to die over and over. Hebrews 6:5-6 confirms this: that if it were possible for one to ever fall from grace and become "unsaved" then Christ would have to be crucified again for that person to be saved. But that is never going to happen!

Now we come to Revelation 2:18-19. *"And unto the angel of the church in Thyatira write; These things saith the Son of God, who hath His eyes like unto a flame of fire, and His feet are like fine brass; I know thy works, and charity, and service, and faith, and thy patience, and thy works; and the last to be more than the first."*

Concerning the Roman Catholic Church, there have been good works done by them throughout the last several hundred years that cannot be overlooked. Before Martin Luther came on the scene, every hospital throughout Europe was a Catholic hospital. Every orphanage was a Catholic orphanage. There have been nuns and monks who have laid down their lives for Christ. Stories abound about their good works. The Lord does not forget that. If there are hearts in the Church of Rome that, amid the superstition, liturgy and ritual, that reach out to the Lord Himself, He meets them in grace and mercy.

Even though they have done good works, God puts His finger on a sore spot. *"Notwithstanding I have a few things against thee, because thou sufferest that woman Jezebel, which calleth herself a prophetess, to teach and to seduce my servants to commit fornication, and to eat things sacrificed unto idols. And I gave her space to repent of her fornication; and she repented not"* (Revelation 2:20-21). Undoubtedly, there was an actual woman in the city who was trying to lead believers into a life of fornication, sexual excesses and paying homage to false gods. But, as a picture, it also shows exactly what was happening to the professing church at that time in history. But, since Revelation is given to us in signs and symbols and pictures, we should take note of the original Jezebel in the Book of I Kings. She was the epitome of corruption, immorality and idolatry; a perfect picture of the professing church during the dark ages. Notice that God says He gave her space to repent. When did He do that? Have you ever heard of John Wickliffe in England? Or John Knox in Scotland? Or Martin Luther in Germany? Or John Calvin in France?

This was an awful time in the history of the Roman Church – burning dissenters at the stake and selling indulgences to the masses. If you wanted to commit a certain sin of gratification, you just needed to pay the priest a certain amount of money, and you could commit the sin without any penalty or guilt associated with it.

You could not reverse or change the order of these seven letters and have them make any sense as to the history of how things were in the Roman Church. It just would not fit the outline of history. And during this dark period of church history, God raised up reformer after reformer. He says, *"I gave her* [the church] *space to repent .... and she repented not"* (Revelation 2:21). In fact, instead of repenting, she added to her blasphemy by declaring on December 8, 1854 that Mary, the mother of Jesus, was born sinless.[13] And then Mary was elevated to the position of a female God stating that she was caught up into Heaven without dying.[14] And then Mary was crowned as Queen of Heaven.[15] Sixteen years later, at the Vatican Council of 1870, the Church of Rome came out with an unbelievable dogma – the infallibility of her popes.[16] We will address this later in more detail.

A move has been underway in the Roman Catholic Church during the last few years to elevate Mary to "co-redemptrix," that is co-redeemer, and then you can either be saved by trusting in Jesus or trusting in Mary.[17] Many have argued that some people, especially women, would be more comfortable coming to a female Savior. Sounds like salvation by convenience rather than following Scripture which requires a perfect blood sacrifice and a resurrection. So far, this blasphemous doctrine has not been adopted, but it could easily be done. All it would take would be for the pope to declare it, and it would become doctrine. And it would have to be accepted by the Catholic community because what the pope declares is without error in accordance with the doctrine of the pope's infallibility.

But God reminds them in Revelation 2:22-23 that judgment is coming. *"Behold, I will cast her into a bed, and them that commit adultery with her into great tribulation, except they repent of their deeds. And I will kill her children with death; and all the churches shall know that I am He which searcheth the reins and hearts: and I give unto every one of you according to your works."* Thyatira and her followers will be in bed together, experiencing great tribulation except for those who repent. Her offspring that follow her teachings will suffer the same fate as Jezebel's, hence the phrase *"and I will kill her children ...."*. We have seen great judgment come upon the Church of Rome during our lifetime as millions have been paid out due to sexual abuse by various priests in the United States. And National Public Radio reports that worldwide sexual abuse has cost the Roman Church over $3 billion.[18]

Jesus said He will judge and punish every one of them according to their works. Did you know there will be degrees of punishment in Hell, just as there will be degrees of reward in Heaven? You will find this principle in Luke 12:47-48 as Jesus tells the parable of the unfaithful servant.

But there is always a remnant – a few in every generation, in every church, in every organization that remain faithful to the Lord. He addresses them in Revelation 2:24-25: *"But unto you I say, and unto the rest in Thyatira, as many as have not this doctrine, and which have not known the depths of Satan, as they speak; I will put upon you none other burden. But that which ye have already hold fast till I come."* He says, "Those of you who have not held to this false doctrine, you have been through enough. I will not put any other burden on you. But stand fast and hold on until I come."

And then in closing, He addresses the overcomers as in previous letters. Revelation 2:26-29 (NLT): "*To all who are victorious, who obey Me to the very end, I will give authority over all the nations. They will rule the nations with an iron rod and smash them like clay pots. They will have the same authority I received from My Father, and I will also give them the morning star! Anyone who is willing to hear should listen to the Spirit and understand what the Spirit is saying to the churches.*"

There are two promises given to the overcomers in this verse. I hope you remember from our previous comments as to who these overcomers are. We find in I John 5:4-5, the overcomers are those who have placed their faith in the Lord Jesus Christ. What are these two promises given here to the overcomers? One: the overcomers are given power over the nations. They will rule jointly with Christ over the kingdoms of the world. And two: they are promised to have the morning star. In the secular world, Venus is called the morning star because it is the brightest object in the sky just before the sun rises and sets. The "Bright and Morning Star" is also one of the names of Jesus (Revelation 22:16).

So in effect, He promises to give the morning star to each overcomer (believer) – it is the gift of Himself. This is a promise today and a reminder that Jesus will indwell the believer through the Holy Spirit. He will never leave us no matter how tough or dark the times become.

CHAPTER THREE

Jesus Critiques Three Churches in Asia

Each of these seven letters closes with the admonition, *"He who has an ear, let him hear what the Spirit says to the churches."* Next, we will be looking at the fifth letter to the church at Sardis. Sardis was a thriving, but unusual city. The Greeks referred to it as the greatest of all cities. It was built at the base of a large valley. On three sides of the city, natural rock formations extended vertically so that it was impossible to enter the city except through the one passage into the valley. It was virtually an unconquerable fortress. As a result, the city was easily fortified and defended.

Sardis was conquered by invading forces only twice in its history. Once when an enemy scout was studying the massive sheer walls when he saw a soldier on top of the wall drop his helmet. It was not very long until the soldier appeared at the bottom, retrieving his dropped helmet. This aroused the enemy's interest. How did he get down so fast? He secretly watched the soldier make his way back up the face of the wall to the top, using small cut outs in the rock for his feet. The entrance was only known to the leaders of the city and a few soldiers. This enemy soldier reported the findings to his captain, and that night a scouting party secretly searched for these hidden steps. And it wasn't long until they found them. The next evening under cover of darkness the enemy soldiers climbed the wall and made it into the city, easily overpowering the forces within who were so confident of their security, they did not even bother to have any guards on duty.[1]

The city was defeated because the entrance was discovered by the enemy, and had been left unattended by the guards. The citizens of Sardis were so smug in believing in their security that it resulted in their downfall. That is the reason this letter to Sardis emphasizes *"be watchful"* (Revelation 3:2).

These seven letters have three distinct applications. First, they were instructions to each particular individual church. These were real churches that existed at the end of the 1st Century, and Jesus had a specific word that fit their particular church. Secondly, these letters, when looked at as a whole, continue to paint a clear panoramic picture of Church history. You cannot change the order of these churches and say they picture the chronological history of the Church for they would not. Third, the messages are instructive to every church and to every believer in every age. The commendations and warnings given are just as valid in today's churches as they have been throughout the last two thousand years.

Let us look at the content of this letter to the church at Sardis. *"And unto the angel of the church in Sardis write; These things saith He that hath the seven spirits of God, and the seven stars; I know thy works, that thou hast a name that thou livest, and art dead"* (Revelation 3:1). Christ is speaking. The seven spirits of God is a reference to the Holy Spirit in His sevenfold completeness (Isaiah 11:1-2). The Jews for the most part today do not realize that their Menorah, the seven-branched candlestick, clearly pictures the third person of the Trinity.

The Spirit of God is represented by the central shaft of the Menorah. He is called the Spirit of Wisdom: this tells of His ability to judge fairly and rightly. He is the Spirit of Understanding: He has the ability to comprehend. He is the Spirit of Counsel: He can help us with our every need. He is the Spirit of Might: He is all powerful and nothing can stop Him. He is the Spirit of Knowledge: He knows all facets of the truth. And finally, He is the Spirit of the Fear of the Lord: He reproduces in us the kind of reverence that we should have toward God.

Just as Pergamos and Thyatira represented the period in which the Church was sinking deeper and deeper into the pit of despair, the church at Sardis represents the time of the great Reformation when the Church came out of the dark ages. This period of Church history had great reformers: Martin Luther, John and Charles Wesley, John Knox, John Calvin and many others. These reformers discovered that the just shall live by faith, but in only two generations they were again bogged down by man-made creeds, liturgies and rituals that were dead as doornails.

The Reformation began in 1517 when Martin Luther nailed his famous "95 Theses" to the door of the Wittenberg Castle Church in Wittenberg, Germany. These were 95 unscriptural things that he vehemently objected to that were going on in the Roman Catholic Church of which Luther was a bishop. He challenged the Catholic Church to show where these are sanctioned in Scripture.[2]

Martin Luther had been questioning his own personal salvation for some time. He struggled with the idea that doing penance, which was inflicting personal hurt upon his body, would assure his salvation. This drove him into a deep study of what God's Word said about salvation. In Romans 1:17 he read, *"The just shall live by faith,"* and this lit the spark that started the fires of revival throughout Europe, eventually resulting in what is known as the Reformation.[3] But sadly, over the next two generations the people lost sight of the One they were worshiping, and Christianity became a dead organization of creeds and ritualism.

The Protestant churches made some of the same errors that the Catholic Church did. It formed state churches in Germany and other countries just as the Catholics had done throughout Europe for the previous 1,000 years. Whole countries were declared to be Christian just by issuing an edict. You were automatically a Christian if you were born into a Christian home; hence infant baptism spread rapidly. The result was that in a few years the Protestant churches were in a mess. Their members, having no clue that they had to be born from above, bore little difference from the Catholic Church. About the only difference was that the Protestants did not recognize the pope as Christ's personal representative on earth.

Christ said this church at Sardis was dead, and when the Great Physician said you were dead, you did not need a second opinion! Have you ever seen a tree with the heart decayed and eaten out? Even though a hole is there, and there is emptiness inside that tree, it may have green leaves. It may appear to flourish long after its heart is gone, but it is doomed. A church can be like that; Sardis was. It gave every evidence of growing and doing works, but Jesus said, *"you are dead"* (Revelation 3:1b NLT). Here was a church that was a corpse, and did not even know it.

A living church will have growth. Its members will be increasing in number and in maturity. Its members will have compassion for each other, love for each other and a heart for soul winning. Christ said we are one body. When a physical body starts to die, the various organs of the body cease to function and begin to shut down.

When you are at the hospital anxiously awaiting word on a relative or loved one, it is devastating when the doctor comes out and says, "I am sorry, but the bodily functions are beginning to shut down." The organs begin to stop functioning, stop coordinating and stop fulfilling their job in the body. And the body begins to die. A church dies in the same manner.

Another evidence of life is emotion, excitement and feeling. Do not be afraid to let your faith out. If you feel like saying "Amen", say it. It will not hurt you. Emotions are good. I weep, I sing, I laugh, I mourn. That is a sign that life is present. A dead church does not do this; it just goes through the motions. When a church lives only in the past on its reputation and history, it is a dead church.

I am reminded of that great structure in England, Westminster Abbey. A tour group was going through there a few years ago, and the tour guide said, "Folks, gaze on this magnificent church. Why, it has the most beautiful marble walls in all the earth. It has the most beautiful chandeliers that have ever been crafted. It is a prestigious church. The coronation services of all the great kings are held right here. It is the burial place of all the royalty of England. Does anyone have any questions?" A little old lady in tennis shoes with a Bible under her arm asked, "How long has it been since anyone was saved here?" The tour guide looked her over, and said with a frown to the group, "We've got to move along." I think Jesus might have asked the same question.

Someone who is about to freeze to death usually is not even aware of his or her condition because the symptoms often begin gradually. They may even begin to feel warm and comfortable right before they go to sleep.[4] The church at Sardis was so cold and satisfied, it was about to freeze to death without realizing it.

"Be watchful, and strengthen the things which remain, that are ready to die: for I have not found thy works perfect before God" (Revelation 3:2). In every one of the previous letters to the churches, Christ has a word for something good that they are doing. But to the church at Sardis

He has nothing but condemnation. He tells them to strengthen the things which remain that were ready to die. What remained? Well, they probably had praying, preaching and teaching. But these things were watered down, tepid and needed to be strengthened. They needed to have life breathed into them by renewing their love for Jesus Christ.

Someone might say, "Does God expect us to be perfect?" The word perfect does not mean without flaws; it connotes maturity. It means being complete or satisfactory. In other words, Christ is saying to this church, "You do not meet God's requirements." The outward observance of religion may have looked good in the eyes of men, but remember, God looks on the heart and this church was coming up short.

"Remember therefore how thou hast received and heard, and hold fast, and repent. If therefore thou shalt not watch, I will come on thee as a thief, and thou shalt not know what hour I will come upon thee" (Revelation 3:3). Christ exhorts them to remember all the great preaching and teaching they had heard, and to repent of things that had made them grow cold. Otherwise, He would come and remove their lampstand. He would take away their testimony, and the light of truth provided by the Holy Spirit. This He eventually had to do, and when it happened, they did not even know the Spirit had left them!

It reminds me of the fellow who visited one of these prestigious but cold liberal churches. After saying "Amen" several times, the fellow was tapped on the shoulder by an usher, who said, "Shhhhhh ....". The man said, "Well I have the Spirit" whereas the usher said, "Well you didn't get Him here!"

"Thou hast a few names even in Sardis which have not defiled their garments; and they shall walk with Me in white: for they are worthy" (Revelation 3:4). A few were faithful; Jesus knows their names. He does not overlook a single one who is faithful to Him. In Scripture, garments depict a person's character. Isaiah 64:6 says that our righteousness is as filthy rags – that is, our bad character. But believers have been promised that we will be clothed with Jesus' righteousness. A few in Sardis were true believers, and these few had not defiled their garments.

Sardis in Greek means "remnant." A few had remained true and faithful to their Lord as we see in the next verse. Christ is going to clothe His true followers in white raiment signifying His righteousness and purity. *"He that overcometh, the same shall be clothed in white raiment; and I will not blot out his name out of the Book of Life, but I will confess his name before my Father, and before his angels"* (Revelation 3:5).

Remember who the overcomers are? I am going to keep reminding you of I John 5:5: *"Who is he that overcometh the world, but he that believeth that Jesus is the Son of God?"* Jesus says that these overcomers – these saved ones – will have clothes of white.

Some teachers point to this verse and say, "See, you can lose your salvation, because only the overcomers will not be blotted out of the Book of Life." But folks, that is my point! The overcomers according to I John 5:5 are all those who believe and trust in Jesus – the saved ones – those who have been born again. And Christ says He will NOT blot them out of the Book of Life. That is called eternal security. It goes by other names: perseverance of the saints or "once saved, always saved." That is a core doctrine of the Baptists. There are a few denominations that stand with Baptists on this, notably, the Presbyterians. Many other denominations believe that you can lose your salvation – the Methodists, the Churches of Christ, the Assemblies of God, the Roman Catholics and the Pentecostals. They believe that Jesus endured everything on the cross for you so you could become one of His children. But He still might let go of your hand and let you fall away if you prove to be unworthy. However, I find too many verses in Scripture that teach otherwise. Jesus says He gives us eternal life. Just how long is that? 100 years? 10,000 years? No, it is eternal!

I read recently that the average age of a member of the Presbyterian Church is 62. One commentator estimates that if the Rapture does not occur in the meantime this church will be dead and gone within 50 years. The Episcopal Church has lost over one-third of its members in the last 40 years, and will probably lose many more due to its approval of same-sex marriages and homosexuals in its pulpits. And it is reported that the United Methodist Church is losing more than 1,500 members a week. There are a lot of good people in these denominations, but their national leaders are leading them down the road to liberalism, and Jesus said to such churches, *"I will remove thy candlestick"* (Revelation 2:5). Even Baptist churches are baptizing fewer each year, so it is imperative that sound doctrine be preached and taught in all the pulpits.

All the people who have ever lived will have their name written in God's Book of Life. Those who have reached the age of accountability, and who have never trusted Christ as their Savior will appear at the Great White Throne Judgment and find that their name has been blotted out of the Book of Life. The Bible calls this the second death (Revelation chapter 20).

Let me say a word about several books that God keeps. Among all His other names, I like to say that He is the Ultimate Accountant. There is a Book of Life, there is the Lamb's Book of Life, and there is the Book of Works. There are many, many interpretations as to how these books interact. Let us look at some Scriptures that pertain to this, and see if we can obtain some clarity.

Exodus 32:33: *"And the Lord said unto Moses, Whosoever hath sinned against Me, him will I blot out of My book."*

Revelation 3:5a: *"He that overcometh, the same shall be clothed in white raiment; and I will not blot out his name out of the Book of Life ....".*

Revelation 22:19a: *"And if any man shall take away from the words of the book of this prophecy, God shall take away his part out of the Book of Life ....".*

Psalm 69:28: *"Let them be blotted out of the book of the living, and not be written with the righteous."*

Revelation 20:12: *"And I saw the dead, small and great, stand before God; and the books were opened: and another book was opened, which is the Book of Life: and the dead were judged out of those things which were written in the books, according to their works."*

Revelation 20:15: *"And whosoever was not found written in the Book of Life was cast into the Lake of Fire."*

At this point, because of the blotting out, the names in the Book of Life and the Lamb's Book of Life are identical. Let me explain. When every human soul is conceived, even if there is an abortion, his or her name is written into the Book of Life. They become part of the human race. Throughout their life, entries are made regarding their works and motives, whether these works are good or bad.

At the end of their life, if they have reached the age of accountability and have not trusted Jesus Christ as their personal Savior, their names are blotted out of the Book of Life. The reason is, no matter how good some of them may be, their nature will always reflect sin against God. They need a Savior to wipe the slate clean. It is not a balancing act between good works and bad works. Romans 3:23 tells us: *"For all have sinned, and come short of the glory of God."*

In the case of an abortion that baby has not had the opportunity to choose to sin; however, that baby was conceived in sin (Psalms 51:5) and has inherited a sin nature. It goes without saying that all such persons whether aborted or born who have never reach the age of accountability either through actual maturity or from being mentally challenged, are covered by the blood of Jesus. These children of God will be ushered into the heavenly portals.

However, Scripture says that a lost person's good works may mitigate his punishment. In other words, a good moral man who never accepts Christ will be punished less severely than someone of Hitler's caliber who has murdered millions. You will find this principle of varying degrees of punishment in the parable of the unfaithful servant in Luke 12:47-48.

There is another book that God keeps. It is called, "The Lamb's Book of Life." In it are recorded only the names of those persons who are saved – those who have been washed by the blood of the Lamb. As previously mentioned, this book also lists the names of those millions of infants who were aborted and those mentally challenged who never understood right from wrong.

One thing is certain however. If your name is recorded in the Lamb's Book of Life, you are secure forever – your name will never be blotted out! At the end of a person's life, if he or she has not trusted Christ as their Lord and Savior, their name will be blotted out of the Book of Life, which is the book of the living. At this point, those names which have not been blotted out of the Book of Life and the Lamb's Book of Life will be identical. Each one will contain the names of those who are God's children for eternity.

Hal Lindsey agrees: "When God opens this book at the Great White Throne Judgment, the only names left in it will be the names of those who have believed in Christ as Savior and Lord. That is why the name of the book is changed from the "Book of Life" to the "Lamb's Book of Life."[5]

But one of the most exciting truths is contained in the last part of verse 5. If one does not deny Him before men, He says, *"I will confess his name before my Father and before His angels"* (Revelation 3:5b). When you stand in Heaven, Jesus will take you by the hand, usher you past the angels, past the waiting throngs, and take you to the very throne of God where He will personally say your name to the Father. That, my friend, is awesome!

"He that hath an ear, let him hear what the Spirit saith unto the churches" (Revelation 3:6). The church at Sardis was dead. It ceased being a beacon for the Gospel, and instead embraced a form of cold ritualism. But there were a few in Sardis that had not defiled their garments, and who had stayed true to their calling.

Now we come to John's sixth letter. It is to the church at Philadelphia. It was chosen for a specific purpose. Its name, Philadelphia, is the same name as the city in Pennsylvania. It means "brotherly love." This should be a characteristic of all churches, but unfortunately it is not.

The general format of these letters thus far is that Christ would commend the church for something positive, and then He would put His finger on their weaknesses. Only two churches escaped His condemnation – the suffering church at Smyrna that stayed faithful while enduring great persecution, and the church at Philadelphia that maintained a true witness in the midst of unbelief and apostasy.

"And to the angel of the church in Philadelphia write; These things saith He that is holy, He that is true, He that hath the key of David, He that openeth, and no man shutteth; and shutteth, and no man openeth" (Revelation 3:7). It is Jesus who saying this, and Scripture says He is holy and true. These are attributes of God the Father, proving again that Jesus is God.

The reference to Christ having the key of David goes back to a reference in the Old Testament to King David's treasurer, Eliakim. Referring to Eliakim, Isaiah 22:22 says, *"And the key of the house of David will I lay upon his shoulders; so he shall open, and none shall shut; and he shall shut, and none shall open."* In David's time, Eliakim was the key holder in the royal palace. His office gave him full authority to act on behalf of the king. If he locked a palace door, it remained locked. If he unlocked it, it remained unlocked. Eliakim was a picture of the ultimate key holder, Jesus Christ.

Revelation 1:18 tells us that Jesus possesses the keys of death and Hades. He took them away from Satan during the three days His body was in the grave. Jesus can be called the

Master Locksmith because He now has all the keys. He decides what doors will remain open and what doors will stay closed! *"I know thy works: behold, I have set before thee an open door, and no man can shut it: for thou hast a little strength, and hast kept my word, and hast not denied my name"* (Revelation 3:8). An open door in Scripture is an opportunity for ministry that God sets before us.

The previous letter was to the church at Sardis, a picture of the Church during the time of the Reformation. It had a great start, but then a cold, formal, liturgical cloud settled over all the Protestant churches in the 16th and 17th Centuries. But God, through His grace and mercy, opened some doors of opportunity.

When we study the history of the Church, we find that this Philadelphian church was the church of the open door. It began with the spirit filled revivals of the 19th Century followed by the great missionary outreach around the world by men like Hudson Taylor, William Carey, Adoniram Judson, and David Livingstone. These are not household names to today's average church member, but I guarantee you they are in God's Hall of Fame. Of such people, and other missionaries who came later like Lottie Moon, God said, *"The world was not worthy of them"* (Hebrews 11:38a Holman).

A spiritual revival followed and spread through the churches, led by such men as George Whitefield, Dwight L. Moody, Billy Sunday, and in our generation, Billy Graham. It was a revival spurred by the Church getting back to the basics of true prayer and worship. It was returning to its first love.

In the mid-eighteen hundreds, people were being converted by the thousands in New York City alone. The movement spread up and down the New England states. The Baptists had so many converts they had to start baptizing them in the local rivers. In 1857 alone, it is estimated that there were up to one million new converts. Then it swept through Ireland, Scotland and England, moved along by such evangelists as Charles Spurgeon, and the Wesley Brothers.[6]

The church at Philadelphia is a perfect picture of the true believers inside the professing Church of the end times, just as the seventh letter to the church at Laodicea is a perfect picture of the unsaved inside the professing Church of the end times. Both Churches – the true and the false – will continue together to the end of the age. This is pictured in Matthew 13:24-30 by the wheat and the tares growing together.

But then abruptly, God closed the door of opportunity almost as fast as it opened. The Soviet Union pulled down its Iron Curtain. China persecuted and barred Christian missionaries. Peter and Mary Stam for many years were missionaries to China. They were taken and shot by the Chinese Communists for refusing to deny Christ. In chapel at Wheaton College, we often heard firsthand accounts of their faithfulness in the face of death.[7]

Revelation 3:8b says, *"Thou hast a little strength."* This does not mean they have a little strength left. It means they are in the minority; the world no longer listens and is closing in on them. But that is when the Lord says, *"My strength is made perfect in weakness"* (II Corinthians 12:9). Big opportunities and little strength on our part is God's recipe for victory. Just ask David about his encounter with Goliath! Some folks say that David lacked faith because he picked up five smooth stones (I Samuel 17:40). I love Dr. Criswell's answer to that. He said Goliath had four brothers who were giants (II Samuel 21:18-22), and David was going to be ready for them if they came for revenge![8]

There are two characteristics of the church at Philadelphia. His Word is kept and His name is confessed. There is obedience to His Word and the preaching of His name. Christianity once held sway over the United States. The country listened when its Christian leaders spoke out. Sadly, that is no longer the case.

Several years ago, when Disney began promoting the homosexual lifestyle, Southern Baptists voted to boycott Disney's products until they cleaned up their act.[9] Disney's CEO at the time, Michael Eisner, sort of pooh-poohed the idea that Baptists will listen to their leaders on matters such as this. Ellen DeGeneres, the outspoken lesbian, quickly came to Eisner's defense against the Baptists.[10] But Sandra, in charge of our church's program for children, removed all Disney movies and products from its program and prohibited future purchases. Our pastor and staff fully supported her action. American Family Association led by Don Wildmon hastened to aid greatly in the boycott.[11]

The boycott began to gain momentum over the next few years. Richard Land, President of the Southern Baptist Morals and Ethics Division, and Michael Eisner, Chairman of Disney, continued to trade barbs as the boycott began to gain momentum over the next few years.[12]

Disney's annual report in 1999 contained a letter to the stockholders by Chairman Eisner that was seven pages long trying to explain why Disney was doing well in spite of its earnings being down 25% from the previous year.[13] He never mentioned the boycott as having any impact on the company's earnings. The next few years were volatile as Disney continued to move away from its G-rating image. Eventually Eisner was fired in 2005, but not until he walked away with millions in accordance with his employment contract.

Southern Baptists can display large numbers – sixteen million or more. A number of Baptist churches can boast an attendance of 10,000 or more on a given Sunday. Impressive! But too much of the time their members are AWOL from Christ's army when it comes to social issues. In recent elections, I had Christian friends who voted for and defended candidates who strongly advocated abortion, homosexual lifestyles and same-sex marriages. I can never understand their reasoning, and someday they will have to explain to God why they vote for candidates who openly support things that God calls an abomination.

Millions of others are simply apathetic to societal ills. They just do not care. And it is best illustrated by their lack of faithfulness to church attendance. The average Baptist church has an attendance of between 25-30% of those members on the church roll. Of course, many are homebound and can no longer attend, but there are just as many who had rather go to the lake and pursue other worldly pleasures. But they do not have to answer to me. However, they will have to answer to Christ in view of Scripture's clear directive in Hebrews 10:25 (NLT): *"And let us not neglect our meeting together, as some people do, but encourage and warn each other, especially now that the day of His coming back again is drawing near."*

The Philadelphia church is a picture of Christ's true followers in the closing hours of Christ's Church upon the earth. And it includes you if you have trusted Christ as Savior. Praise God for those who are obedient to His Word, and have not denied His Name – men like Drs. W. A. Criswell, Charles Stanley, Adrian Rogers, Paige Patterson, Albert Moehler, David Jeremiah, David Reagan, and my own pastors, Jimmy Pritchard and Jerry Griffin. Such men stood strong and were instrumental in making sure that the Southern Baptist denomination did not join the camp of liberal denominations that played fast and loose with Biblical doctrines. Just like the church in Philadelphia, Southern Baptists chose to stay the course and remain faithful to God's inerrant Word.

"Behold, I will make them of the synagogue of Satan, which say they are Jews, and are not, but do lie; behold, I will make them to come and worship before thy feet, and to know that I have loved thee" (Revelation 3:9). Every age is marked by counterfeit religions. It was the same in the 1st Century with teachers claiming to be Jews, and wanting to lead the Church back into the bondage of Jewish law and legalism.

It is the same today. The majority of churches have no use for the grace of God. They want to burden you with works-salvation. But God continues to work through His faithful remnant. Maybe I should not feel this way, but there is a little bit of "I told you so" in me that wants to be vindicated. Jesus says that there is coming a time when they will have to worship Christ. He is going to do this for Himself and for us – publicly! Romans 14:11: *"For it is written, AS I LIVE, SAITH THE LORD, EVERY KNEE SHALL BOW TO ME, AND EVERY TONGUE SHALL CONFESS TO GOD."*

Those true believers at the end of the age are represented by the church at Philadelphia and they will escape the horrors of the Tribulation. *"Because thou hast kept the word of my patience, I also will keep thee from the hour of temptation, which shall come upon all the world, to try them that dwell upon the earth"* (Revelation 3:10). Without question, this testing period is the seven year Tribulation Period and the Church will be kept from it, not through it. It will literally be a time of Hell on earth, complete with famines, earthquakes, epidemic diseases running wild, wars, natural disasters and unparalleled horror.

This promise to the Philadelphian church that God will *"keep them from the hour of temptation"* or testing has great importance as to how one views the timing of the Rapture. As mentioned previously, there are three major views regarding this. The pre-Tribulation view is that all true believers are raptured before the Tribulation begins, and therefore they avoid the entire seven year period of judgment. The mid-Tribulation view is that the Church will endure three and one-half years, but is raptured midway through the Tribulation Period. The post-Tribulation view is that all believers will go through this awful judgment, and the Rapture will occur at the end of this seven year period. I am solidly in the camp of the pre-Tribulation view because I believe the Scriptures clearly teach this. It is the only view that provides for the imminent return of Christ – the only view that provides that He can come back at any moment!

We share this view with some of the most outstanding Bible scholars of our time. Here are a few of them that you will recognize. They all have earned doctorates or other advanced theological degrees: John Ankerberg, Kay Arthur, David Breese, W. A. Criswell, M. R. DeHaan, Jimmy Draper, Gary Fisher, Gary Frazier, Al Gist, Norman Geisler, Billy Graham, H. A. Ironside, Grant Jeffrey, David Jeremiah, Woodrow W. Kroll, Zola Levitt, Hal Lindsay, J. Vernon McGee, Paige Patterson, J. Dwight Pentecost, David R. Reagan, Charles Ryrie, Chuck Swindoll, John Walvoord and Jack Van Impe.

There are dozens of reasons to support the pre-Tribulation view. Revelation 3:10 which we read a few moments ago is just one of the passages we are studying that confirms this. Notice that this "hour of temptation," or as the NASB says, this "hour of testing" is not a local or regional testing. It is going to affect the entire world. And the purpose of it is to test or try those that dwell upon the earth. In other words, judgment will be for the earth dwellers only – those who have settled down here. They have become comfortable with the world system that Satan is running. Our real citizenship is in Heaven according to Philippians 3:20.

Some point out that Christians for generations have not been shielded from general tribulation. But there is a BIG difference here. The tribulations that Christians have been enduring during our lifetime have been instigated at the hand of Satan. He is called the "god of this world" (II Corinthians 4:4). The Tribulation described in Revelation 3:10 will be instigated and directed by God as judgment on a sinful and rejecting world.

So what is going to happen to the true followers of Christ? Answer: They will be raptured before this awful Tribulation Period begins. There is a little word in Greek that will substantiate this. The Greek preposition "ek" means out of something. It is the very opposite of the Greek preposition "eis" which means through or in the midst of something. In other words, Noah was saved "eis" through the flood, but the true Christians will be saved "ek" – from or out of the Tribulation.

It is interesting to note that the Church is referred to 19 times in the first three chapters of Revelation. But from Revelation chapters 4 through 18 which cover the entire Tribulation

Period, the Church on earth is never mentioned! And when the Church is mentioned in chapter 19, it is already in Heaven and is coming back with Jesus! Wouldn't Christ have given the Church a word of encouragement during this terrible Tribulation Period if the Church was going to be on earth? Such as "Hang on – I am with you – do not be discouraged" or words to that effect. But He says nothing of the sort. He never even mentions the Church. And the reason no word is given is because the Church is in Heaven. It has been raptured (Revelation 4:1) prior to this time of Tribulation on the earth! We will cover this more thoroughly when we study chapter 4.

"Behold, I come quickly: hold that fast which thou hast, that no man take thy crown" (Revelation 3:11). When Jesus says He is coming quickly, He does not necessarily mean "soon" as we think of "right away", though it could be. We are to live expecting Him to come back at any time. But in the original Greek, He is saying, "When I come back, it will be quickly." The Rapture will be fast – in the *"twinkling of an eye"* (I Corinthians 15:52). And the Second Coming will be just as fast: *"For as the lightning comes from the east and flashes to the west, so will be the coming of the Son of Man"* (Matthew 24:27 NIV).

Jesus warns us not to let anyone take our crown. This is not referring to our salvation as we can never lose that. A crown is part of our rewards. We can lose our rewards if we are not diligent. I cringe to think of the Christians who have attended church faithfully for years, and yet in later life, their love grew cold and they quit coming to God's house of worship. Jesus said do not do that! You have come this far, do not let any man steal your crown; do not abandon your doctrines! Keep holding on to them. Keep on being true to the Word; keep on praying, witnessing and attending church so long as your health permits.

"Him that overcometh will I make a pillar in the Temple of my God, and he shall go no more out: and I will write upon him the name of my God, and the name of the city of my God, which is New Jerusalem, which cometh down out of Heaven from my God: and I will write upon him my new name" (Revelation 3:12). I keep stressing not to forget I John 5:5. If you have trusted Christ, you are one of the overcomers, and this verse says you will be a pillar in the Temple of God in the New Jerusalem.

Scripture says that you will *"no more go out"* – in other words, Christ will satisfy your every need, and you will feel secure. And in verse 13, the message is for all of us: *"He that hath an ear, let him hear what the Spirit saith unto the churches."* Are you an earth dweller? Are you comfortable with this world system? Or do you long every day for the soon return of Christ? I hope you are yearning to go "home" and saying to this world, "I don't belong here!"

Now we come to the seventh and last letter. It was to the church at Laodicea, the church that made God vomit. The city of Laodicea was very wealthy. It enjoyed a thriving wool industry. It felt it did not need anything from anybody, including God. Reminds me of America today.

The word "Laodicea" comes from two Greek words – "laos" meaning the people, and "dikao" meaning to rule. In other words, "the people ruling" or "the rights of the people." It speaks of a time when the Church becomes enamored with its own importance, its own power, and a time when the authority of God and His Word are ignored and the rights of the individual are magnified.

Can you believe that the following statement was written in 1920?! "Laodicea is a compound word and means the rights of the people. The masses of the people are realizing their power as never before – "vox populi, vox Dei – the voice of the people is the voice of God – ringing through the world with clarion-like distinctness."[14] Imagine my surprise when right after reading those words, I turned on the news and there was Hillary Clinton giving a speech to the Democratic National Convention, July 28, 2016, in which she said, "We will defend all our rights – civil rights, human rights, voting rights, women's rights, workers' rights, LGBT rights and the rights of people with disabilities!"[15]

Let me say something about the Roman Catholic Church. We may disagree with its doctrines, but one thing it staunchly defends: the authority of the pope and the authority of the Catholic Church. But the new crop of priests that are currently coming on the scene are a different breed. Many do not accept this pope's teaching that priests should not marry; that priests should be celibate. And since Pope John Paul II's death, hundreds of new liberal priests are pushing for sweeping changes. High on the agenda is a pope who will allow them to marry.[16] Also, look for a push to make Mary "co-redemptrix" with Christ. Many others want to see women, as well as homosexuals, ordained into the priesthood. In other words, "the rights of the people" – the same meaning of the word "Laodicea."

In every letter to the previous six churches, Christ had something positive to say about each church. Though many were chastised, there was something that each was doing right. But do not look for a commendation for Laodicea for you will not find it. I have heard of Sunday school classes being named "the Berean Class" or the "Lydia Class" or the "Philadelphia Class," but I have never heard of one being called "The Laodicean Class."

"And unto the angel of the church of the Laodiceans write; These things saith the Amen, the faithful and true witness, the beginning of the creation of God" (Revelation 3:14). This tells us four things about Christ. First, He is the Amen. "Amen" is the last word. When everything else has been said, the only thing left to be said is "Amen." It is a word of finality, certainty and authority. Second, He is the Faithful One. He says, *"I will never leave thee, nor forsake thee"* (Hebrews 13:5b). He is always with us. Third, He is the True Witness.

I read about all these folks to whom God has supposedly given a new vision – a new direction from what the Bible tells us. Joseph Smith claimed it happened to him; Mary Baker Eddy said it happened to her; Charles Taze Russell said it happened to him; Herbert W. Armstrong said it happened to him; Reverend Sun Myung Moon said it happened to him. When I think of these people, I always remind myself to re-read Hebrews 1:1-3. Here is my paraphrase: "God, who in the past spoke to the prophets by various means, has spoken to us in these last days by His Son, and you are not to listen to others with new revelations that contradict God's Word. And now that He has atoned for sin, Christ is seated on the right hand of His Father." Unmistakably clear. God has spoken to us by His Son, and His directions and commandments are recorded in God's Word. We have no need for prophets today preaching what Paul calls "another gospel" (Galatians 1:8).

Though the church at Laodicea is not paying any attention to Him, Christ tells them He is the True Witness. I wish the churches today all across the nation would listen to Him. Fourth, He is the Creator. In this age when evolutionists are attempting to build their philosophies on mere theory or chance, we know that Christ was totally involved in this world's creation (Colossians 1:16-17).

Revelation 3:14 says, *"And unto the angel of the church of the Laodiceans write; These things saith the Amen, the faithful and true witness, the beginning of the creation of God."* This does not mean, as the Jehovah's Witnesses teach, that Christ was the first thing that God created. On the contrary, God the Father appointed Christ as His building foreman, so to speak. This is confirmed by Colossians 1:16-17. *"For by Him were all things created, that are in Heaven, and that are in earth, visible and invisible, whether they be thrones, or dominions, or principalities, or powers: all things were created by Him, and for Him: and He is before all things, and by Him all things consist."* Everything in creation has Christ's mark on it. He is the beginning of all creation.

Then we come to the real indictment against the church of Laodicea. *"I know thy works, that thou art neither cold nor hot: I would thou wert cold or hot. So then because thou art lukewarm, and neither cold nor hot, I will spew thee out of my mouth"* (Revelation 3:15-16). There were hot mineral springs in nearby Hierapolis and there were cold water springs in Colossae. An aqueduct and pipes had been built to bring the water to Laodicea. But when it got there, it was neither hot nor cold. It was lukewarm, highly distasteful to drink.

Jesus wanted this church to be committed, to be cold or hot, but not wishy-washy, not lukewarm. A hot drink on a cold day or a cold drink on a hot day is refreshing, but lukewarm is disgusting. It makes Jesus nauseated, and so He says to such a church, *"I will spew thee out of my mouth."* This lukewarm church is like so many churches today – the emphasis is on church programs rather than upon Christ and His Gospel. Dr. Theodore Epp calls it "Churchianity" rather than Christianity.[17] They relegated their Christianity to Sunday rather than to every day of the week. It was not like the church mentioned in Acts 2:47 in which the Lord added to the church daily.

A lukewarm Christian is really a contradiction – an oxymoron – if that person is truly a

Christian. It is like saying "dry water" or "clean germs." It just does not make any sense. Vance Havner once said, "People can be as straight as a gun barrel theologically, but as empty as a gun barrel spiritually."[18]

A church can be lukewarm in its commitment, and it can also be lukewarm in its doctrine. A church may ask, "Why do we have to believe in the virgin birth?" Well, this is the answer. If Jesus was not born of a virgin, He inherits the sin nature of Adam, and has His own sins to worry about let alone ours! And I always thought this was neat: that God has a sense of humor because He chose a medical doctor, Dr. Luke, to tell us about the virgin birth!

"Because thou sayest, I am rich, and increased with goods, and have need of nothing; and knowest not that thou art wretched, and miserable, and poor, and blind, and naked" (Revelation 3:17). Jesus told the church at Smyrna, *"I know thy works, and tribulation, and poverty, (but thou art rich)"* (Revelation 2:9a). But while He is spitting the Laodicean church out of His mouth, they are saying, "I am rich, and have need of nothing." They did not even know they were poor, and naked!

"I counsel thee to buy of me gold tried in the fire, that thou mayest be rich; and white raiment, that thou mayest be clothed, and that the shame of thy nakedness do not appear; and anoint thine eyes with eye salve, that thou mayest see" (Revelation 3:18). Gold, when it is mined, is put into a red hot furnace, not to destroy it, but to purify it. The ore is melted, the impurities are drawn out, and the remaining residue is pure gold.

God wants us to be rich, not in this world's goods as some TV preachers claim, but rich in purity. A bride wants to look her best at the wedding. And Jesus wants His Bride to be clothed in beautiful white raiment at the Marriage Supper of the Lamb, which in fact, is the righteousness of Christ. And He wants to anoint us with the eye salve of the Holy Spirit so that we will see things the way that God sees them. *"As many as I love, I rebuke and chasten: be zealous therefore, and repent"* (Revelation 3:19). If you have been spanked by God, and have wondered why God has disciplined you, it is because He loves you. There is nothing worse than a child without discipline.

The late Freddie Gage stood about 5'5". They say that dynamite comes in small packages and he was a powerful Baptist evangelist for over 60 years.[19]

I was in one of his revivals at Trinity Baptist Church in Lawton, Oklahoma. He said that he was eating dinner at a couple's home when their young son who was about seven years of age came in from outdoors and left the door open. Since it was somewhat chilly, the father said, "Son, will you close the door?" The boy replied, "Close it yourself old man." Freddie said, "If that had been my son, he'd have gone into the door-closing business!"

It is good to be disciplined now and then. It keeps us on the right track. *"My son, do not regard lightly the discipline of the Lord, nor be weary when reproved by Him. For the Lord disciplines the one He loves, and chastises every son whom He receives"* (Hebrews 12:5b-6 ESV). God disciplines those He loves. One fellow told me, "God must love me an awful lot because He spanks me so often."

"Behold, I stand at the door, and knock: if any man hear my voice, and open the door, I will come in to him, and will sup with him, and he with me" (Revelation 3:20). When John was given the command to write these letters, do you remember where Jesus was? He was walking among the candlesticks – walking in the midst of His churches. When we come to the end of Church history as pictured by the church at Laodicea, Jesus has been excluded. He is on the outside knocking to get in to His Church. The tense of the verb here indicates that this is not a onetime knocking. Jesus continually stands at the door knocking. He continually knocks at your heart's door. He knocks through His Word – He knocks through the Holy Spirit – He knocks through the witness of His people.[20]

There is a famous painting that you have probably seen by the artist Holman Hunt. It depicts Jesus standing at the door knocking. After Hunt painted it, he asked friends to come by and tell him their opinion of it. They said, "Why, Holman, you left out something very important. You forgot to put a door handle on it." And Holman Hunt said, "That was no mistake. The door is a picture of the human heart. Jesus is knocking, and the door must be opened from the inside."[21]

"To him that overcometh will I grant to sit with me in my throne, even as I also overcame, and am set down with my Father in His throne" (Revelation 3:21). As we said earlier, according to I John 5:5, an overcomer is one who believes that Christ is the Son of God. Our Lord is not currently on His own throne. He is at the Father's right hand on the Father's throne, and is now the Great High Priest and our Advocate against the enemy. When He comes back, Jesus will be given His own throne, and we will rule and reign as joint heirs with Him.

"He that hath an ear, let him hear what the Spirit saith unto the churches" (Revelation 3:22). Now that we have come to the end of chapter 3, I want to briefly review these letters to the seven churches. Keep in mind that John was told he would be given these messages in signs and symbols. And even though each of these letters benefited the church to which it was written, it is obvious that, as a sign or symbol, these letters carry a deeper meaning. I suggest they are a picture of Church history through the entire Church Age from the day of Pentecost to the Rapture.

We start with the first letter to the church at Ephesus (Revelation 2:1-7). Ephesus means desirable. It was the early church – the spiritually powerful apostolic Church of the 1st Century when Christ was the center of its interest. It would not tolerate hypocrites in its midst. But then, they left their first love. They took their eyes off Christ, and He removed their candlestick. This period of Church history ended around 100 A.D.

The second letter was to the church at Smyrna (Revelation 2:8-11). This was the suffering church. Smyrna comes from the word myrrh, a perfume that had to be crushed to give out its aroma. This church was crushed under the iron heel of Rome. Thousands of Christians were martyred for their testimony of Christ, but never has the Church given off such a sweet fragrance. This period of Church history lasted from about 100 A.D. to 300 A.D. under various pagan Roman emperors.

The third letter was to the church at Pergamos (Revelation 2:12-17). Pergamos is composed of two words meaning elevation and marriage. It was during this time that the Church was no longer being persecuted. It was the darling of the State; it was elevated to a prominent position and married to the world. This came to fruition under the leadership of Constantine who completed uniting the Church and State throughout Europe.

Jesus said that they dwell where Satan's seat is located. If you had asked any true believer at that time where Satan's seat was located, they would point immediately to Rome. It was during this time that the doctrine of the Nicolaitans began to take hold in the Church (Revelation 2:15). And the teaching was that the clergy were to rule over the people. It was the early stages of what would later develop in the Roman Church as a religious hierarchy that would grow stronger and stronger until it enslaved the common people. This period of Church history runs from about 300 A.D. to 500 A.D.

The fourth letter was to the church at Thyatira (Revelation 2:18-29). Thyatira is a compound word meaning continual sacrifice. This is exactly what the sacrifice of the Mass is, and covers the next 1,000 years from about 500 A.D. to 1,500 A.D. when the Catholic Church ruled with an iron fist, burning at the stake all who would disagreed with its doctrines.

The fifth letter was to the church at Sardis (Revelation 3:1-6). This was the dead church. It made a good start at attempting to reform the teachings of the Catholic Church. Under the fiery leadership of such preachers as Martin Luther, John Calvin, John Knox and others, what is known as the Reformation held great promise that the Church would return to the sound doctrines of the 1st Century. But, it never really shed many of the heretical and ritualistic forms of worship that had been ingrained in it for so many centuries. And so, it lapsed into a cold, dead worship interested more in the form of worship rather than in the One who is to be worshipped. This covers Church history from about 1,500 A.D. to 1,700 A.D.

There are two churches left: the church at Philadelphia and the church at Laodicea. In many ways, these two depict the "true" and the "false" churches of the last days. And just like the wheat and tares that Jesus mentioned, they will grow side by side until the end of the age.

The church at Philadelphia is described in Revelation 3:7-13. The word means brotherly love. This church has an open door, and pictures the great revival and missionary movement of the past couple of hundred years when the world has been literally blanketed with the message of the Gospel. It is of this Church that Christ said He would keep it from the hour of temptation that will come upon the entire world to try them that dwell on the face of the earth. I take this to mean that the Philadelphian church – the true believers of the end times – will be taken out of the world at the Rapture before the start of the Tribulation Period. So, the period of Church history depicted by the Philadelphian church is from 1700 A.D. right up to the time Christ comes back for His Bride at the Rapture.

The seventh and last church is that of Laodicea (Revelation 3:14-22). Just as the Philadelphian church represents the true believers of the end times, the Laodicean church represents the false believers of the end times. This church is indifferent and apathetic. It stands for nothing, but will compromise at anything. It nauseates Christ who is ready to spit them out of His mouth. The Laodicean Church period begins with the age of apostasy helped along by "the German School of Higher Criticism." It ushered in theological liberalism that threw out virtually everything that was supernatural in the Bible.[22] This period began around 1,800 A.D. and will continue to the end of the age.

At the very end of the Church Age, in spite of gross rebellion, Christ is not willing that any should perish; and so, He stands at the door and knocks, and offers another opportunity for anyone to open the door to eternal life. He is doing that even today. The Church Age ends with this chapter and the Rapture is just ahead!

CHAPTER FOUR

The Rapture of the Church

I am convinced that Christ will take His Church out of the world before the Tribulation Period begins. This is called the pre-Tribulationist view. There are many, many reasons I believe this, but since we are beginning chapter 4 of Revelation, let me give you one more solid reason. From chapter 6 through chapter 18, we have more details of what the Tribulation will be like than any other place in the Bible. In Daniel, we have hints; in Amos we have hints; in Joel we have hints. And Jesus told us a little more about it in the 24th chapter of Matthew. But in Revelation chapters 6-18, the curtain is drawn back and we have detail after detail of what the Tribulation will be like.

And this is significant: after we leave the seven letters to the churches at the close of chapter 3, the Church is never mentioned again on earth during this intense description of the Tribulation Period. Never! In fact, the next time we see the Church, it is in chapter 19 and it is already in Heaven! How and when did the Church get to Heaven? Right here at the beginning of chapter 4!

Look at Revelation 4:1: *"After this I looked, and, behold, a door was opened in Heaven: and the first voice which I heard was as it were of a trumpet talking with me; which said, 'Come up hither, and I will show thee things which must be hereafter'"* – or as the NASB says, *"after these things."* After what things? We should keep in mind our table of contents in chapter 1, verse 19, *"Write the things which thou hast seen* [the past – chapter 1] *and the things which are* [the present – chapters 2 and 3] *and the things which shall be hereafter"* [the future – chapter 4 through the rest of the Book].

The Book of Revelation was not written to satisfy the curiosity of natural men concerning future events. In fact, I Corinthians 2:14 says: *"But the natural man receiveth not the things of the Spirit of God: for they are foolishness unto him: neither can he know them, because they are spiritually discerned."* That is, the Scriptures are spiritually understood. Christ promised all believers that the Holy Spirit would come and guide them into all truth. Without the help of the Holy Spirit, the natural man in his own abilities is either not going to understand the Bible, or he is going to think it is all a bunch of foolishness.

The Book of Revelation is divided for us by Christ Himself into three parts. We have already looked at parts one and two (the things John has seen and the things which are in the Church Age). So now we begin to look at part three – *"the things hereafter"*. "Hereafter"– the word in

Greek is "meta tauta" – meaning "after these things." After what things? After the completion of the history of the Church on earth as pictured by the letters to the seven churches. And what does chapter 4 begin with? "Meta tauta" – the same word used in chapter 1, *"The things which must be hereafter."* So we know that we are beginning the third division of the Book.

The Book of Revelation quotes from the Old Testament 485 times, more than any other Book in the New Testament. John has just been shown the history of the Church Age as represented by the seven churches. The next thing that is said to him is, *"Come up here"* (Revelation 4:1b NLT). This is the Rapture! We do not see the Church mentioned again until chapter 19 when it is already in Heaven. How did the Church get to Heaven? It was transported to Heaven by way of the Rapture when a voice like a trumpet gives this command to John, *"Come up here."*

The Rapture could occur at any time, but do not ever set a date for it like many have done to their detriment. Jesus says only the Father knows the exact time. Many cultic groups such as the Jehovah's Witnesses, the Seventh Day Adventists, and others have set many, many dates over the years for the Lord's return. Finally the Jehovah's Witnesses, after the embarrassment of being wrong every time, decided to do something about it when their prediction for Christ's return in 1914 did not come true. So they said, "Christ DID come back in 1914, only it was not a physical, visible coming; it was an invisible, spiritual coming."[1]

At Christ's ascension, two angels said, " *…. this same Jesus, which is taken up from you into Heaven, shall so come in like manner as ye have seen him go into Heaven"* (Acts 1:11b). The Lord will return exactly as He left – bodily, physically and in plain sight of His believers.

What if someone asks you, "Where is the word Rapture mentioned in the Bible?" The critics are quick to tell you it is not there. And they are right. The word Rapture is never mentioned in our English translation, but the concept is! Just as the word Trinity is never mentioned in the Bible, the concept of the Triune God is mentioned – the Father, the Son and the Holy Spirit. The term substitutionary death is not mentioned in the Bible, but Jesus died in our place and that is certainly a substitutionary death, so we know the concept is there.

A great illustration of how the Rapture will occur can be seen in the eighth chapter of the Book of Acts. Here the Lord spoke to the evangelist Philip and told him to go south from Jerusalem to the Gaza area which was desert. It is the same Gaza Strip that the Palestinians and the Israelis are fighting over today.

So Philip went there as the Lord commanded. On his way, he met a man who turned out to be an Ethiopian eunuch. He was a man of great authority under Candace, the queen of Ethiopia. This eunuch – this holy man – was reading a scroll from the Bible. The Lord told Philip to run and catch the man's caravan. So Philip caught up with them, and he could hear that the Ethiopian was reading aloud from the 53rd chapter of Isaiah. And, according to Acts

8:32-35 (ESV), here is what he was reading: *"He was led as a sheep to the slaughter; and like a lamb dumb before his shearer, so opened He not His mouth: In His humiliation His judgment was taken away: and who shall declare His generation? For His life is taken from the earth." "And the eunuch said to Philip, 'About whom, I ask you, does the prophet say this, about himself or about someone else?' Then Philip opened his mouth, and beginning with this Scripture he told him the good news about Jesus."* After the eunuch accepted Christ as his Savior, they came to a body of water and Philip baptized him.

It should be noted that the first convert from the continent of Africa was converted using prophecy while Philip showed him from the Scriptures how this prophecy was fulfilled in the life of Christ. And after being baptized, this new convert went on his way rejoicing. But what happened to Philip? The Bible says that when they had come up out of the baptismal waters, *"the Spirit of the Lord caught away Philip, that the eunuch saw him no more ...."* (Acts 8:39b).

The Greek word used here for "caught away" is "harpazo." It means to be suddenly snatched up and transported from one place to another. Philip was snatched up and transported in an instant to another location which is exactly what will happen to the believers when Jesus comes back at the Rapture. In the early Greek manuscripts of I Thessalonians 4:17, Paul uses the same Greek word "harpazo" to describe the events of Christ's coming for His children at the Rapture. The same word is used in Acts 8:39 to describe Philip being instantly caught away to another location.

Around 400 A.D., 350 years later, the Bible was translated from Greek into Latin (called the Vulgate). And in I Thessalonians 4:17 where it says we are caught up to meet the Lord in the air, the Greek word "harpazo" was translated into the Latin word "rapere" from which comes the English word "rapture" – a sudden departure to be instantly and forcefully snatched away from one location to another.

Critics say that the pre-Tribulation Rapture is a recent teaching developed in the last 200 years, but this is not true. It has been around since this mystery was revealed to the Apostle Paul in the 1st Century. For a thorough discussion of the allegation that the pre-Tribulation view is a late development, I would refer you to Dr. Tim LaHaye's excellent book, *The Rapture*, which totally debunks such a notion.[2]

It is true that the emphasis of the imminent return of Jesus was generally lost during the Dark Ages (as were many other critical doctrines such as "the just shall live by faith" (Hebrews 10:38). But Christ's imminent return was revived in the 19th Century by Rev. John Nelson Darby, founder of the Plymouth Brethren denomination. In much the same way that Martin Luther revived the doctrine of salvation by faith, Darby revived the truth of the Rapture. His clear teaching on the Rapture greatly influenced Dwight L. Moody, as well as Dr. C. I. Scofield who later published his popular *Scofield Reference Bible*.[3] Rather than embracing a new end time theory, Darby simply rediscovered a solid biblical truth that had been there since the Apostle Paul revealed it in I Thessalonians 4:13-17, that Jesus could come at any moment without any other events having to be fulfilled.

Jesus emphasized this when He taught, *"And when these things begin to come to pass, then look up, and lift up your heads; for your redemption draweth nigh"* (Luke 21:28). The Apostle Paul certainly taught this throughout his epistles. A respected prophecy teacher, Grant Jeffrey, points out that an early Christian writer, Ephraem the Syrian, who lived from 306 to 373 A.D., was a pre-Tribulationist without defining it as such. Dr. Jeffrey says, "Ephraem's text revealed a very clear statement about the pre-Tribulation return of Christ to take his saints home to heaven to escape the coming Tribulation."[4]

At the end of the Church Age, as is seen at the end of chapter 3, Christ is on the outside, knocking on our heart's door to come in. In Revelation 4:1, there is a door opened in Heaven, and a voice like a trumpet that says, *"Come up hither!"* This is the Rapture of the Church! Here is how Paul describes it in I Thessalonians 4:16-17 : *"For the Lord Himself shall descend from Heaven with a shout, with the voice of the archangel, and with the trump of God: and the dead in Christ shall rise first: then we which are alive and remain shall be caught up* [harpazo in Greek and rapere in Latin and rapture in English] *together with them in the clouds, to meet the Lord in the air: and so shall we ever be with the Lord."*

Paul says: *"Wherefore comfort one another with these words"* (I Thessalonians 4:18). Now I ask you this. Would Paul say, *"Wherefore comfort one another with these words"* if they were going to go into the worst period of horror and destruction and tribulation this world has ever known? Of course not! He said, *"Comfort one another with these words"* because the believers are going to be kept from the hour of trial which is to come upon all those "earth dwellers" who have no interest in Christ nor do they look forward to an eternal home in Heaven (Revelation 3:10).

So, in Revelation 4:1, we see the Church, and when I say "the Church" I do not mean everyone that is on the church roll. I mean those true believers that form the Body of Christ from the day of Pentecost to the time of the Rapture. We see that a door in Heaven is opened, and the Church is called home. And when the Church departs this earth at the Rapture, the Holy Spirit, who resides in every true believer, departs also.

In II Thessalonians 2:6-8, Paul says that the "departure" (the Rapture) cannot occur until the Restrainer is removed. Some say this Restrainer is the Holy Spirit, and some say this Restrainer is Christ's believers. I say it is both. The Holy Spirit restrains evil in this world by thwarting Satan's plans at every level. And God's children restrains evil to the best of their ability by promoting good, and attempting to elect officials who adhere to God's principles. And because of the indwelling of the Holy Spirit in every believer, when the Christians depart, the Holy Spirit departs.

I should point out that the Rapture does not mark the immediate beginning of the Tribulation Period although it cannot be far behind. The Tribulation Period begins when the Antichrist signs a seven year peace agreement with the Jews to enable them to rebuild their Temple in Jerusalem as recorded in the ninth chapter of the Book of Daniel.

Notice in verse 1 of this fourth chapter, John said that the voice was "like a trumpet." When Paul described the Rapture in I Thessalonians 4:16, he says there was the *"trump of God."* In both descriptions, there is a message. In Revelation 4:1a, the message is from Christ because He is identified in the same verse as being the One who would show John *"things which must be hereafter."* But in I Thessalonians 4:16, there seems to be two sounds. First there is a shout from the archangel, and then there is the sound of the trump of God. Listen to the parable Jesus gave about this in Matthew 25:6: *"And at midnight there was a cry made, Behold the Bridegroom cometh!"*

It appears the following will happen. In accordance with the imagery of a Jewish wedding, a trumpet will sound and the archangel will cry, *"Behold, the Bridegroom cometh!"* (Matthew 25:6). And then Christ will suddenly appear in the air with a shout, and that shout will be what John heard in Revelation 4:1b, (ESV): *"Come up here."* That shout will be so loud it will wake up the dead, and we will see I Thessalonians 4:16-17 literally fulfilled: *"For the Lord Himself shall descend from Heaven with a shout, with the voice of the archangel, and with the trump of God: and the dead in Christ shall rise first: Then we which are alive and remain shall be caught up together with them in the clouds, to meet the Lord in the air: and so shall we ever be with the Lord."*

I pray that none of you, dear readers, will miss one of the greatest events in human history. And you will not miss it if you have trusted Christ as your Savior! Someone asked me, "If a person meets that requirement and are saved, then do they have to go to church?" My answer is, "Technically, they do not." But it is like a man saying, "I love my wife, but I prefer not to be with her." Because if you truly love her, you will want to be with her at every opportunity. And if that person does not want to go to the Lord's house, he needs to re-examine his relationship with the Lord to see if it is real.

That is the way it is with Christ. If you really love Him, you will want to go to His house as often as possible, and spend time with Him in prayer. You will also want to be with your brothers and sisters in Christ. *"We know that we have passed from death unto life, because we love the brethren ...."* (I John 3:14).

Revelation 4:2-3: *"And immediately I was in the spirit: and, behold, a throne was set in Heaven, and one sat on the throne. And He that sat was to look upon like a jasper and a sardine stone: and there was a rainbow round about the throne, in sight like unto an emerald."* John was immediately transported in the spirit into Heaven's throne room itself. The word "throne" is used 45 times in Revelation compared to only 15 times in the rest of the New Testament. This indeed is a glimpse into the very throne room of Heaven. And there is God sitting on the throne. He is so awesome. He is so majestic that the only way John can describe Him is that He is like two beautiful gems: the jasper and the sardine stone.

In Exodus 28:17-20, we find a description of the breastplate of the High Priest. It was adorned with twelve precious stones, each stone representing one of the twelve tribes of the children of Israel. The first and last of these two stones were the sardine (also called the sardius, carnelian or ruby) and the jasper. This is another picture of our High Priest, Christ, being the Alpha and Omega – the first and the last – as He said of Himself in Revelation 1:11.

The sardine stone is fiery red and is symbolic of Jesus' shed blood. The other stone, the jasper, is clear and sparkling. It is the equivalent of our diamond. It is described in the 21st chapter, verse 11 of this Book as being "clear as crystal." It represents the purity, the holiness and the beauty of Jesus.

The diamond is also the hardest of all precious stones. It speaks of the firmness, the permanence and the certainty of God's judgment. And around the throne was a rainbow "like unto an emerald" (Revelation 4:3). An emerald is green, which is the color of life, and is a stone in the High Priest's breastplate. Exodus 28:17-18 prescribes that the gems will be placed in the breastplate, three across and four rows down. The emerald in listed as number four in the breastplate – in the first position on the second row. Scripture does not directly state which gem had a particular Israelite tribal name attached to it, however, 1st Century Jewish historian Josephus states that the names were placed in the High Priest's breastplate according to the tribe's birth order. That would mean that the emerald would represent Judah, the fourth born son of Jacob, who is also in the lineage of Jesus. [5] Hence, Jesus is referred to in Revelation 5:5 as the "Lion of the Tribe of Judah."

Scripture tells us that a Savior was promised who would come through the descendants of Abraham (Genesis 12:3). Abraham had two sons, but God told him that the Son of Promise would come from the line of Isaac (Genesis 17:21). But Isaac also had two sons, Esau and Jacob. But God narrowed the Son of Promise as coming through the line of Jacob (Genesis 35:11-12). But Jacob had TWELVE sons! So, from which line would the Messiah come? Comparing Scripture with Scripture, we find that the Messiah would come from the line of Judah. We are told in Genesis 49:10a that *"The scepter shall not depart from Judah …. "*. The scepter is the king's staff and represents the ruling authority.

Jesus' lineage is given in the first chapter of Matthew. In verse 2, it says, *"Abraham begat Isaac, and Isaac begat Jacob, and Jacob begat Judah …. "*. There it is: Jesus is from the tribe of Judah. And here in Revelation 4:3, the rainbow around the throne looks like an emerald which is the stone for Judah in the High Priest's breastplate.

It is amazing how Scripture continues to tie all of this together. And as we will see in the coming chapters, there is judgment prophesied, but the rainbow reminds John of God's faithfulness in keeping the righteous from that judgment. When God delivered judgment on the earth in Noah's day, God said, *"I establish my covenant with you: Never again will all life be cut off by the waters of a flood; never again will there be a flood to destroy the earth"* (Genesis 9:11 NIV). The rainbow came out after the storm; and for Christ's body of believers which is now in Heaven, the storm of the Tribulation Period that is hammering the earth can never touch them.

Then John describes what he sees around the throne. *"And round about the throne were four and twenty seats: and upon the seats I saw four and twenty elders sitting, clothed in white raiment; and they had on their heads crowns of gold"* (Revelation 4:4). Instead of seats around the throne as the KJV says, most modern translations such as the ESV render the translation as thrones. So you have the throne of God surrounded by 24 smaller thrones. And seated on these smaller thrones are 24 people whom the Scriptures call elders. Who are these people? Some believe these are angels. But are they? Angels do not have children; they do not procreate as humans do (Mark 12:25); and they were all created at the same time (Genesis 1:1). Consequently, they are all the same age, so there cannot be elders among them. In addition, angels are never depicted in Scripture as wearing crowns. The evidence supports the fact that these are not angels.

Some people think that these elders are the redeemed from all ages, represented by the twelve children of Israel and the twelve apostles. This sounds intriguing, but it is more logical to conclude that this is a picture of the Church in Heaven which has just been raptured. Here are my reasons to support that conclusion. These elders represent the Church because the Old Testament saints have not yet been resurrected. Their resurrection will be discussed later. Remember, the Rapture is a specific promise to the Church, and that, at the Rapture, Paul says the "dead in Christ" (I Thessalonians 4:16-17) are resurrected. The dead in Christ is the Church – the Bride of Christ – also called the Body of Christ, and consists of every believer from the day of Pentecost to the Rapture.

Note that these elders are wearing crowns. There are two words in Greek for crowns. One is "diadema." It means in English a "diadem" like a crown a king would wear. That is not the word used here. The other word for crown in Greek is "stephanos." It is the crown that the victor wears. It is a wreath signifying victory and is the crown mentioned here. It is the crown depicted in the early Olympics. It is the stephanos crown used in the letter to the church at Smyrna in Revelation 2:10b (ESV): *"Be faithful unto death, and I will give you the crown of life."* It is also the same crown used in the letter to the church at Philadelphia in Revelation 3:11b (NIV): *"Hold on to what you have, so that no one will take your crown."*

You might wonder how 24 people can represent the millions that compose the true Church. In I Chronicles 24:3-18, we read of King David appointing 24 elders to represent the entire Levitical priesthood. He divided the priests into 24 courses – each course was to serve for eight days at a time (from Sabbath to Sabbath) in the Temple that Solomon built. After six months, the courses started over.

Specifically, look at I Chronicles chapter 24. I want you to see the eighth course in these 24 courses of priests. I Chronicles 24:10 (ESV): *"The seventh* [course] *to Hakkoz, the eighth to Abijah."* Notice the eighth course was to the family and descendants of Abijah. Now look at Luke chapter 1, where Scripture is speaking about the birth of Christ. This same arrangement of courses was in effect when Christ was born. Luke 1:5a. *"There was in the days of Herod, the king of Judea, a certain priest named Zechariah, of the course of Abijah ...."*.

These courses of twenty-four were established for one reason. The priests were many thousands in number. They could not all come together in one place at one time, but when the twenty-four priests met in the Temple in Jerusalem, the whole priesthood was represented.[6] In the secular world of politics, we call it a "representative democracy." For example, take the U.S. House of Representatives. All the citizens of the U.S. cannot come together at one time in Washington, D.C., so when the 435 Representatives meet in the Capitol Building in Washington, it is as though all the Americans are there in person. Texas has 36 individuals in the House of Representatives in Washington. When those 36 meet, it is like all the people in Texas are there. All Texans are represented.

These 24 elders picture the entire Body of Christ, represented around the throne. And do not forget, Peter said in the second chapter of his epistle, *"But ye are a chosen generation, a royal priesthood .... "* (I Peter 2:9a). The clincher that confirms that these twenty-four elders are not angels is confirmed in Revelation 5:7-9. They are singing a song that angels cannot sing. It says, *"And they sung a new song, saying, Thou art worthy to take the book, and to open the seals thereof; for thou wast slain, and hast redeemed us to God by thy blood out of every kindred, and tongue, and people, and nation."* (Revelation 5:9). The angels cannot sing the song of redemption. Only humans who have been redeemed by the blood of the Lamb can sing this song!

One other point before we leave this verse in chapter 4. If these 24 elders represent the Church, as I think they do, why are they wearing crowns, and where did they get them? Scripture says that these crowns are the victors' crowns – "stephanos" – and they are rewards for Christian service that are given out as described in the third chapter of I Corinthians.

There are five different crowns mentioned in Scripture.
Incorruptible Crown – I Corinthians 9:25-27
Crown of Rejoicing – I Thessalonians 2:19
Crown of Righteousness – II Timothy 4:7-8
Crown of Glory – I Peter 5:2-4
Crown of Life – James 1:12

We looked at these five crowns in great detail earlier in this chapter. These crowns will be given to all true believers at the "Bema Seat" – Christ's judgment seat for believers. *"For we must all appear before the judgment seat of Christ; that every one may receive the things done in his body, according to that he hath done, whether it be good or bad"* (II Corinthians 5:10). Paul said that he is looking forward to the crown that will be given to him at *"that day"* – and then he adds, *"and not only to me, but also to all who have loved His appearing"* (II Timothy 4:8b NASB).

All rewards will be given out at the same ceremony. Meanwhile on earth, those who were left behind at the Rapture will be experiencing the first phase of the awful Tribulation Period. The phrase at a funeral "He has gone on to his reward" is nice to say, but it is not quite accurate as all Christians will receive their rewards on *"that day"* when they are all given out. We are given the details of this reward ceremony in I Corinthians 3:13-15. Our work will be tested by fire. If our work is done for the Lord with the right motives, a reward will be given; otherwise, those works will be burned up, but his or her salvation is not in jeopardy.

As far as your rewards are concerned, it does not matter how smart you are, but it does matter how you use your gifts and abilities that God has given you. This is a principle we find throughout the Bible: *"Everyone to whom much was given, of him much will be required"* (Luke 12:48b ESV). Another reason that a person does not receive their rewards (or judgments) immediately after their death is that their influence lives on – whether good or bad.

Robert Ingersoll was a distinguished attorney. He was also an atheist. Not just an ordinary run-of-the-mill atheist, but he wore it on his sleeve and never missed an opportunity to demean Christianity. He rented auditoriums across the country to rant and rave about Christianity and to make fun of the Scriptures. He would often invite local ministers to debate the merits of Christianity with him. A favorite trick of his was to pull out his watch, and say, "If there is a God in the heavens, I dare him to strike me dead within 60 seconds. If I'm still alive after 60 seconds, it will prove once and for all that there is no God!"

One night after pulling this stunt, one of the ministers at the time (some believe it may have been that great preacher, Dwight L. Moody) showed up at his meeting and said, "Sir, on the way over here, a small boy with dirty hair and mud on his face came up to me and said, 'Mister, do you want to fight? If you don't fight me it will prove that you are a dirty, little coward.'" The minister continued, "I felt sorry for the poor little urchin. I tried to reason with him, but he just cursed me all the more. I could have hauled off and knocked him into the next county, but I didn't. I loved him and felt sorry for him. Finally, I just walked around him and kept going. Imagine my surprise when I got here, and saw you saying the same thing to God!"

Yes, Robert Ingersoll was devious. He could trap the unsuspecting. I read his books in high school and became quite intrigued with his arguments. Thank God I was rescued from his clutches by the most persuasive book I have ever read outside the Bible, entitled *Basis of Christian*

Faith by Dr. Floyd E. Hamilton.[7] It is a great apologetic book that has been in my library for over 60 years. I have personally used it to turn around one of my relatives who was going down the path of atheism at a secular college. He has been a Christian now for nearly 40 years.

Robert Ingersoll is dead and gone, but his writings are still in the public libraries. Madalyn Murray O'Hair read his books, and they led her down a gloomy and unhappy pathway that ended in tragedy. His negative influence in affecting the lives of others continues to live on, and consequently, his ultimate punishment continues to mount up.

On the other hand, look at the thief on the cross. He said, *"Jesus, Lord, remember me when thou cometh into thy kingdom"* (Luke 23:42). That thief did not have much time to accumulate rewards. The guards did not allow him to come down from the cross and do some good deeds so that when the rewards are given out, he would get his share. Do you think he has any rewards?

Consider this: how many sermons have been preached about the faith of the thief on the cross? How many people trusted Christ as their Savior because of his testimony? His influence lives on, and he will not want for rewards when they are given out *"on that day"*. That is why we are told: *"Therefore judge nothing before the time, until the Lord come, who both will bring to light the hidden things of darkness, and will make manifest the counsels of the heart: and then shall every man have praise of God"* (I Corinthians 4:5). That day of rewards will probably not be very long after the Rapture occurs. Jesus said, *"Behold, I come quickly; and my reward is with me, to give every man according as his work shall be"* (Revelation 22:12).

Dr. H. A. Ironside said, "It follows then that no rewards are given out till Jesus returns for His saints. Therefore, there can be no crowned elders in Heaven until after the Rapture."[8] This is another clear indication of a pre-Tribulation Rapture. At that great rewards ceremony it says your work will be made known. And not just your work, your motives as well, because *"People judge by outward appearance, but the LORD looks at a person's thoughts and intentions"* (I Samuel 16:7b NLT).

Jesus said motives are important. When you make a big show of giving, such as if you wave a $100 bill for all to see before you put it in the offering plate, or some millionaire announces in the newspaper that he is giving $10 million dollars to some hospital or charity, even though these are worthy causes, Jesus said, *"They have their reward"* (Matthew 6:2b). In other words, they have the praise of men and that is all the reward they are going to get.

Many of you have witnessed to people or invited them to church; you have taught in Sunday School; you have comforted those in sorrow; you have visited the sick or the homebound; you have worked in Vacation Bible School; you have given to missions so the Word could be preached around the world; you have planted the seed of the Gospel in someone's heart; and have done hundreds of other things in the name of Christ that you do not even remember. But God says He will never forget even a cup of cold water given in His name. One day around the throne, you will be surprised when those people, in the presence of everyone including the Lord, will look at you and say, "Thank you for what you did in the name of Christ."

Before we go any farther, let me tell you about what is called, "The 7,000 year theory of mankind."[9] I do not put much stock in it, but I want you to be aware of this theory that some subscribe to. It is one of the oldest theories dating from the earliest days of the Church. It begins with God creating the heavens and the earth in six days, and resting on the seventh. In theory, it pictures the history of mankind. In other words, God will deal with mankind for six days and rest on the seventh, and it defines God's days as being 1,000 years each. According to this theory, three different scriptures come into play. II Peter 3:8 says: *"But, beloved, be not ignorant of this one thing, that one day is with the Lord as a thousand years, and a thousand years as one day."* Hebrews 4:4-11 says that there remains a day of rest for the people of God, and it hints that this will be the 1,000 year Millennium promised by God.

Revelation 20:1-9 goes into detail about this 1,000 year Millennium. The 7,000 year theory goes on to say that God will deal with mankind for six of His days (that is, 6,000 of our years) and rest on the seventh day (the 1,000 year Millennium). According to the Jewish calendar, man first appeared on the scene about 4,000 B.C. We know for certain that approximately 2,000 years have passed since the time of Christ. Consequently, the theory says that 6,000 years (or six of God's days) have just about passed, and we are fast approaching the final day, that is, the Millennium, which is preceded by the Rapture and the Tribulation Period. I do not subscribe to this theory, but it is intriguing and I want you to be aware of it.

"And out of the throne proceeded lightnings and thunderings and voices: and there were seven lamps of fire burning before the throne, which are the seven spirits of God" (Revelation 4:5). In the town in which we live, we are used to seeing spectacular lightning and thunder that precede heavy storms. In the same way, the lightning and thunder from the throne of God is also a signal that a terrific storm is not far behind. God's patience with those earth dwellers is wearing thin. God said in Genesis, *"My Spirit shall not always strive with man"* (Genesis 6:3a); and so, judgment in the form of the Tribulation, is drawing near.

Before the Rapture, while the Church is still on earth, the throne of God is referred to as "the throne of Grace" (Hebrews 4:16). We regularly approach it in prayer. But once the Church is called home at the Rapture, the throne emanates "lightnings and thunderings" and becomes a throne of judgment for those who have rejected Christ (Revelation 4:5). The seven lamps of fire burning before the throne, which are described as the seven spirits of God, picture the Holy Spirit in all His perfection, for the number seven always denotes fullness or completeness. The seven characteristics of the Holy Spirit are given to us in Isaiah 11:2 which we have mentioned earlier in this study: the Spirit of the Lord; the Spirit of wisdom; the Spirit of understanding; the Spirit of counsel; the Spirit of might; the Spirit of knowledge; and the Spirit of the fear of the Lord.

The Holy Spirit has full and complete knowledge of every thought, every word and every deed for every human being. And He will lay it out as evidence for those who have rejected Christ. There will be no false evidence presented; the perfect Spirit of God will reveal the whole truth. And as we read of the *"seven lamps of fire burning before the throne"*, we remember that the Holy Spirit has been associated with fire before. On the day of Pentecost, He appeared as cloven tongues of fire resting on each of the Apostles (Acts 2:3).

What else did John see? *"And before the throne there was a sea of glass like unto crystal: and in the midst of the throne, and round about the throne, were four beasts full of eyes before and behind"* (Revelation 4:6). He saw a sea of glass like crystal. In the 30th chapter of Exodus, verses 17-21, precise directions were given for the building of a laver for the Tabernacle. The purpose of this laver or basin was for the priests to wash their hands and feet while performing their priestly duties. In Exodus 38:8, the Hebrew women contributed their mirrors. The King James Version says "looking glasses." These were probably inlaid into the basin so that a reflection was made to assure someone that they had indeed experienced complete cleansing.

Many years later, when the permanent Temple was erected in Jerusalem, they built ten smaller lavers and one large one (I Kings 7:38). The smaller ones were primarily for the purpose of washing the sacrifices, and the larger one was for the priests to wash their hands and feet prior to their ministering in the Temple. The large laver was about 15 feet in diameter and about 7 ½ feet deep. In II Chronicles chapter 4, this large laver is referred to as a sea. It is also called a sea in I Kings 7:23. This sea symbolized the Word of God because it contained water used for priestly cleansing. We are told in the New Testament that the Church is sanctified and cleansed by the *"washing of water by the Word"* (Ephesians 5:26).

John describes what is in front of him as *"a sea of glass like unto crystal .... "* (Revelation 4:6). But this sea is not for cleansing, therefore it is solid as crystal. Later in the Book, we find that the martyred Tribulation saints are standing on it! (Revelation 15:2). It is still the Word of God, but it is no longer needed cleansing. Why? Here is what the Holy Spirit directed the Apostle Paul to say about the Church: *"That He [Christ] might present it to Himself, a glorious Church, not having spot, or wrinkle, or any such thing; but that it should be holy and without blemish"* (Ephesians 5:27).

Do you long for a perfect church? When we are raptured and arrive in Heaven and get our new white garments, we will be a perfect Church without spot or blemish – a perfect Bride because the garments we have put on are the righteousness of Christ. Jesus Christ has perfectly cleansed us in His blood, and those who are around the throne will no longer need to wash in the water of the laver. Our cleansing does not have to be repeated and so, the water is firm, solid and clear as crystal. This sea which symbolizes the Word of God abides forevermore – a glassy sea, yet solid like crystal. It is firm and glorious on which the people of God can stand eternally.

Now we come to the last half of verse 6, chapter 4: *".... and in the midst of the throne, and round about the throne, were four beasts full of eyes before and behind."* Who are or what are these beasts? Well, it is certain there is one thing they are not. They are not beasts!

The King James Version made an error in translating this word as "beasts," and it has caused untold confusion over the years – especially since there are two "beasts" that arise in chapter 13, and they are real brutes! The Greek word in chapter 13 that is rendered "beasts" is "theria." It means wild animals. But the Greek word here in verse 6 is entirely different. It is "zoa." Singular is "zoon". It simply means "living ones."

To illustrate what a colossal translation error that the King James made in verse 6 rendering the word "zoa" as "beasts" – 10 other reputable translations either say, "living ones" or "living beings" or "living creatures." And the NKJV which generally just corrects English grammar and sentence structure has changed this from "four beasts" to "four living creatures."

So, back to our question: "Who are these four "living ones?" Take note of their description. It says they were full of eyes, picturing that nothing escapes their attention. They are aware of everything. What other features are subscribed to these living ones? *"And the first beast was like a lion, and the second beast like a calf, and the third beast had a face as a man, and the fourth beast was like a flying eagle"* (Revelation 4:7). Remember, we said previously the symbols in Revelation are almost always alluded to in some other portion of Scripture. Ezekiel was given a glimpse into God's throne room in Ezekiel chapter 1:5-10. His description is almost identical to that of John's. Same type faces – same number of wings.

Ezekiel calls them cherubim in chapter 10:1 of his Book, which is a classification of angels. The prophet, Isaiah, was also privileged to glimpse into the throne room of Heaven, and in chapter 6 of Isaiah, verses 1-3, he says: *"I saw also the Lord sitting upon a throne, high and lifted up, and His train filled the temple. Above it stood the seraphim: each one had six wings; with twain he covered his face, and with twain he covered his feet, and with twain he did fly. And one cried unto another, and said, 'Holy, holy, holy, is the Lord of host: the whole earth is full of His glory.'"*

We know from Genesis and Isaiah that there are at least two classifications of angels: the cherubim (Genesis 3:24) and the seraphim (Isaiah 6:6). Bible scholars are split down the middle as to whether these "living ones" in Revelation are cherubim or seraphim. What complicates the issue is that the description of these two classifications of angels is almost identical. In other words, you cannot look at their description and tell whether they are cherubim or seraphim. I believe the key is that you must look at their duties. Though their features are very similar, it appears that their duties are distinctly different. Generally, the cherubim have to do with protection and security. For instance, they were placed as guards at the entrance to the Garden of Eden after Adam and Eve were banished from the Garden (Genesis 3:24). The seraphim on the other hand seem to be involved in worship, praise and adoration. Therefore, as we will see in Revelation 4:8, it appears that these four living ones are seraphim as they cry day and night, *"Holy, holy, holy."* That fits the primary duty of the seraphim, that of praise and adoration.

Dr. J. Vernon McGee came up with an interesting interpretation. He believes that these living ones are simply a picture of Christ in the four Gospels.[10] Here is what he says, "The first living creature was like a lion, (the king of beasts) and the first Gospel represents the Lord Jesus as the King. The second living creature was like an ox (or bullock). This is a beast of burden, the servant animal domesticated. In the Gospel of Mark, Christ is presented as a Servant. The third living creature had a face as a man. The Gospel of Luke presents the Lord Jesus Christ as the Son of Man. It is His humanity that is emphasized in Luke. The fourth living creature was like a flying eagle. He communicates the deity of Jesus as seen throughout the Gospel of John."

Other commentators have noted that these living creatures also represent the animal world. The lion represents the wild animals; the ox, the domesticated animals; the eagle, the birds; and man, the head of all creation.

These are all interesting analogies, but we must stick with our premise that says generally Scripture will interpret Scripture. So, in accordance with what Ezekiel (chapter 10) and Isaiah (chapter 6) said, it appears these living ones are angels, and when we look at what they are doing, they must be seraphim.

"And the four beasts had each of them six wings about him; and they were full of eyes within: and they rest not day and night, saying, 'HOLY, HOLY, HOLY, LORD GOD ALMIGHTY, WHICH WAS, AND IS, AND IS TO COME.' And when those beasts [living ones] *give glory and honor and thanks to Him that sat on the throne, who liveth for ever and ever, The four and twenty elders fall down before Him that sat on the throne, and worship Him that liveth for ever and ever, and cast their crowns before the throne, saying, 'Thou art worthy, O Lord, to receive glory and honor and power: for thou hast created all things, and for Thy pleasure they are and were created'"* (Revelation 4:8-11).

CHAPTER FIVE

The Seven Sealed Book

As you may know, chapter headings, verses and punctuation in the Bible were added some 500 years ago. The first person to divide New Testament chapters into verses was Italian Dominican biblical scholar, Santi Pagnini (1470–1541), but his system was never widely adopted.[1] The first Bible in English to use both chapters and verses was the Geneva Bible published in 1560. These divisions soon gained acceptance, and have since been used in nearly all English Bibles and the vast majority of those in other languages.

The chapters and verses are not part of the original Scriptures and consequently, are not inspired but are very effective in helping to find specific sections of the Bible. With that in mind, let me say that there should not be a break between Revelation chapters 4 and 5. They are designed to be read together.

A door was opened in Heaven, and the Church is pictured in the throne room of God. It is a glorious sight – the beauty and majesty of the throne itself is enough to take your breath away. Now, continuing in chapter 5, the Church and the entire heavenly host are praising God. And in the midst of all of this, our attention is drawn to the One sitting on the throne. It is God the Father, and He is holding a book.

There are several books mentioned in Revelation that we discussed earlier. There is a variety of interpretations among commentators on the meaning and purposes of these books. Should you want to explore this further, here are some specific passages in Scripture that refer to various books: Exodus 32:32; Psalm 69:28; Luke 10:20; Philippians 4:3; Revelation 3:5; 13:8; 20:12; 20:15; and 21:27.

The Bible also describes a different kind of book that is sealed which we will see as we go through this 5th chapter, and it is an important key to understanding the rest of Revelation. "*And I saw in the right hand of Him that sat on the throne a book written within and on the backside, sealed with seven seals*" (Revelation 5:1). The Greek word "epi" is used here. It means the book was resting upon God's hand and not being grasped. He was waiting for someone to take it. When it says the book, it does not mean a bound book that we normally see in a library; rather it means a scroll, a roll of parchment, probably made of sheepskin. This scroll was written on each side, and was sealed with seven seals. In the Greek, the first verse actually says it was sealed down with seven seals. It could not be said any stronger. It was sealed shut!

Picture a roll of parchment written on each side and spread out on a table. Roll it up partially and put a seal on it; roll it up some more, and put another seal on it. Continue until the scroll is completely rolled up with seven seals attached to it. When a seal is broken, the scroll is unrolled up to the next seal, showing what was written up to that point. When the seventh seal has been broken, the entire scroll is unrolled and lay bare, and the entire message can be read.

"And I saw a strong angel proclaiming with a loud voice, 'Who is worthy to open the book, and to loose the seals thereof?' And no man in Heaven, nor in earth, neither under the earth, was able to open the book, neither to look thereon" (Revelation 5:2-3).

What is written on this scroll and why is it so important? Very simply, the scroll represents the title deed to the earth – the right to rule this earth. God originally gave this right to Adam. *"And God said, 'Let us make man in our image, after our likeness: and let them have dominion over the fish of the sea, and over the fowl of the air, and over the cattle, and over all the earth'"* (Genesis 1:26a). But Adam lost his God-given dominion over the earth when he sinned. He was cheated out of his inheritance by Satan himself. But we must remember that the earth is permanently God's possession by right of His creation. *"The earth is the LORD'S, and the fullness thereof; the world, and they that dwell therein"* (Psalm 24:1). And a promise is made in Matthew 5:5: *"Blessed are the meek: for they shall inherit the earth."* But an imposter is now on the throne – a usurper. Satan is presently the *"the god of this world"* (II Corinthians 4:4). And in I John 5:19b we find, *"the whole world lieth in wickedness"*, that is, it is in bondage to the Evil One. But praise God it is only temporary!

A strong angel asks, "Who is worthy to open the book? Who is qualified to step up and rightfully claim dominion over the earth and all who are therein?" There is silence. No one steps up. No one is found worthy! Not in Heaven – not in earth – nor anyone who has died and is *"under the earth"* (Revelation 5:3b). Of the billions of people that have ever lived, saved or unsaved, none can qualify as a Redeemer because their own souls must be redeemed (Revelation 5:4).

Since man's sin was the reason or cause that the world was lost, no man who is a sinner can buy it back because the price is a life of perfect holiness – a life of perfection! In all of the world's history, there has been *"none righteous, no not one"* (Romans 3:10). No one around the throne could even bring themselves to look at the book, let alone pick it up. They knew they did not qualify.

"Adam, what about you? Wasn't dominion over the earth given to you? Why don't you come forward and claim your property rights?" And Adam must reply, "I forfeited my inheritance because of sin. It was mine, but I sinned and lost it. The Devil cheated me out of it, and I no longer have title to it." "Is there any angel who can step up and claim it? No, not an angel among the hosts of Heaven who is worthy to say, 'I am qualified to redeem the title to this world.'"

No man can claim it. Not Abraham – not Moses – not David – not Job who was one of the three most righteous men who ever lived (Ezekiel 14:14). Not even John who is watching this because John would have to say, "I am a sinner; I am part of the problem." And so it appears that no one is worthy because it had to be opened by someone with the lawful right to do so, a rightful heir who could legally open the book.

This is confirmed by John: *"And I wept much, because no man was found worthy to open and to read the book, neither to look thereon"* (Revelation 5:4). John breaks down and weeps uncontrollably because he knows that as long as the title remains sealed, Satan will be in control of this planet. He knows that this scroll spells out the complete, final redemption of man and of Israel and of the earth. And he knows that so long as Satan controls the title deed, God's plan for the earth can never be consummated. John weeps because there seems to be no future for the earth, for mankind or for the nation of Israel. And he weeps because, momentarily, he takes his eyes off of Jesus. And that is what happens to us. We know better, but in our weakness and frailty we forget and we take our eyes off of Jesus.

John lost sight of the victory of the Lamb, and this always results in hopelessness and tears. When we get to Heaven, it will not be because we are righteous nor because we are worthy, but because we have been redeemed by the grace of God. But then, the problem is solved! *"And one of the elders saith unto me, 'Weep not: behold, the Lion of the tribe of Judah, the Root of David, hath prevailed to open the book, and to loose the seven seals thereof'"* (Revelation 5:5). Here again, Old Testament imagery comes into play. There was such a thing known as "the Kinsman-Redeemer."

The law of redemption in the Old Testament was very simple. When property was confiscated or lost through death or other means, a scroll was prepared, and on the inside of this scroll was written all the details that were required to redeem or purchase back the asset. On the outside, or backside of the scroll, was listed family names and other conditions so that a kinsman could look at it and quickly determine whether he was legally qualified to open the scroll. Then the scroll was sealed and placed in the hands of the priest for safekeeping.

There were three conditions that absolutely had to be met in order to legally qualify as a Kinsman-Redeemer. First, he had to be a close relative. Second, he had to be willing to act. And third, he had to be able to pay the price of redemption. In the story of Ruth and Boaz, we find the finest Biblical illustration of this law of redemption of the Kinsman-Redeemer.

In the book of Ruth, we read that Elimelech, his wife Naomi, and family, left Bethlehem because of a severe famine. They moved to the neighboring country of Moab. While there, Naomi's husband, Elimelech, died. They had two sons; they each had married Moabite women, Orpah and Ruth. After ten years, the region's economic situation had improved so that Naomi could return to her home in the land of Judah. Ruth chose to go with Naomi, saying, *"Entreat me not to leave thee, or to return from following after thee: for whither thou goest, I will go; and where thou lodgest, I will lodge: thy people shall be my people, and thy God my God"* (Ruth 1:16). So they returned home only to discover that the ownership of their land had passed to someone else.

They set about trying to legally get their home and land back. They found a near-kinsman, a man by the name of Boaz. He eventually fell in love with Ruth and wanted to help her get her property back. But Boaz had to admit to Ruth that there was another kinsman, a relative that was nearer kin than he (Ruth 3:12). But, when given the opportunity, the other kinsman refused to redeem the property (Ruth 4:6). So even though he technically qualified as a near-kinsman, he was not willing or able to act. This permitted Boaz to become the Kinsman-Redeemer next in line. He was a close relative, he was willing to act, and he was able to pay the price.

What a beautiful picture of our Kinsman-Redeemer, the Lord Jesus Christ. He is our relative by becoming a man (Hebrews 2:11); He was willing to act by going to the cross (John 10:18); and He was able to pay the full price (Ephesians 1:7): *"In whom we have redemption through His blood, the forgiveness of sins, according to the riches of His grace."* And again in I Peter 1:18-19 (NLT), *"For you know that God paid a ransom to save you from the empty life you inherited from your ancestors. And the ransom He paid was not mere gold or silver. He paid for you with the precious lifeblood of Christ, the sinless, spotless Lamb of God."*

On the back side of this scroll is written the legal qualifications of the Redeemer. Jesus, who was the perfect sacrifice in that He never sinned, qualified in every respect (I Peter 2:22; Hebrews 10:14). What the first Adam lost, the second Adam, Jesus Christ, regained. Hebrews chapter 2 tells us that this has not yet fully taken place. Consequently, there are some benefits of the cross that were immediate, and some that have been deferred. Upon conversion, believers are immediately indwelt by the Holy Spirit, and given the assurance that their salvation is eternally secure (Philippians 1:6).

As far as delayed benefits, a good example is that of our physical healing. The physical healing of our bodies was included in the benefits of the cross. However, our bodies are not always healed permanently; otherwise we would never die. But one day, we will get glorified bodies that will be perfect – bodies that are immune to pain and suffering, and bodies that are designed to last forever (I Corinthians 15:53). Receiving our perfect bodies is one of the delayed benefits of the cross.

Another delayed benefit is that all creation, including animal and plant life, will be redeemed from the curse that sin has placed upon it. One day, Christ will be crowned King of kings and Lord of lords as He assumes complete dominion over all the earth. Some people have scoffed at the idea that the plant kingdom and the animal kingdom will be redeemed from the curse that fell on mankind. I say not so fast. We need to see what the Scriptures say about it.

A report on the internet said an advertisement in the personal column of a Georgia newspaper read: "Single female seeks male companionship. I'm a very exciting girl who loves to play. I will go camping and fishing with you and I just love cozy winter nights lying by the fire. Candlelight dinners will have me eating out of your hand. I'll meet you at the front door when you come in from work – wearing only what nature gave me. If interested, call 404-875-6420 and ask for Annie." The phone lines lit up, and over 150 men found themselves talking to the Atlanta SPCA. Whether true or not, it makes a good story.

Most of us have always been devoted pet lovers. For many of you, your choice of a pet is a cat and that is fine. I have had a dog as long as I can remember. But other pets are just as worthy, and you love them just as much.

As a teenager, when I would get home from school I would grab my rifle, call my dog Pris, and we would go hunting in the woods behind our house. Pris, a mixed yellow lab, was not afraid of anything. One day we headed into the woods and Pris was trotting in front of me when suddenly she stopped and began barking furiously. There in front of her was a snake all coiled up in the path. I put my .20 gauge shotgun to good use, and we continued on our way.

As far as other animals are concerned, we always had a cow, a couple of hogs and a dozen or so chickens. Our barn was about 200 feet behind our house, and Dad had rigged a light in the barn that could be turned on from our house. He would turn it on after dark when he would go out to the barn to feed the hogs. Pris would always go with him. One night he turned on the light and headed to the barn. When he got about ten feet from the barn, the light went out. Was someone in the barn? It was a pretty spooky feeling. What would you do? Dad slipped up to the barn door, opened it a crack, and said, "Sic 'em Pris." She bolted into the dark, and he heard nothing but silence so he was not afraid to step into the dark. The light had a pull chain on it, so Dad stepped inside and pulled the chain. No light came on and he was relieved to find out that the light bulb simply decided to burn out when he was just ten feet from the barn.

We cannot fathom the love that God has for us, but in small way, we see the reflection of God's love in the relationship we have with our pets. Howie Hendricks, longtime chaplain at Dallas Theological Seminary, succinctly captures this in his book. "To me my dog means somebody nice and quiet to be with. He does not say 'do' like my mother, or 'don't' like my father, or 'stop' like my big brother. My dog Spot and I just sit together quietly – and I like him and he likes me."[2]

One day my wife, Arlene, called me from the SPCA. She had stopped by there on a whim, and fell in love with a black, mixed female cocker. She called me at work. I was much too busy to talk at that time, so I told her "no dog." That night I could tell that she was really upset because she gave me the silent treatment. I catch on fast. She wanted me to see the dog, so I gave in. The next morning being Saturday, we were at the SPCA when it opened.

So Hanna went home with us, and it began fourteen years of pure love. She learned a total of 44 tricks and entertained all our friends and relatives. Hanna became the pride and joy of our family. Arlene was with her when she died while I was on a business trip in Columbus, Ohio. Arlene had made Hanna a silk pillow, and I made her a wooden box in which to bury her. She was buried in the garden area of our backyard.

I went through that extensive explanation so you will understand why I gave serious thought to the question, "Will our pets be in Heaven?" One member of my Sunday school class said the question was silly. Others thought it was just wishful thinking, but hoping it to be true. However, our opinions do not count. What do the Scriptures say? Do they give us any clues? We know from Revelation 19:11 there will be horses in Heaven, but the question is, will our pets be in Heaven? The Bible has more to say about the animals God created than you probably realize.

First, it tells us that God loves all His creatures. Revelation 4:11b says: "*for thou hast created all things, and for thy pleasure they are and were created.*" And Luke 12:6 (ESV) says, "*Are not five sparrows sold for two pennies? And not one of them is forgotten before God.*" In the 10th chapter of Matthew, Jesus is stressing how important you are. He says even the hairs on your head are numbered. In other words, He knows you down to the smallest detail. He even says that a sparrow cannot fall to the ground without the Father knowing it (Matthew 10:29-31). God loves ALL His creation. Proverbs 12:10a tells us that the godly are concerned with the welfare of their animals. Where did we get this inbred notion to be kind to animals?

I was doing yard work one day when a large white dog came wandering into the yard. I do not know where he came from, but his tongue was hanging out about a foot. It was a hot day, so I immediately retrieved a small bowl from the garage and filled it with cool water. When I set it down, the dog came over and drank and drank and drank, constantly wagging his tail. What possessed me to give the dog a drink? I was busy, and could have easily ignored him. I was not even aware of the verse in Proverbs until later. It says, "*The godly are concerned for the welfare of their animals*" (Proverbs 12:10a NLT).

Most people have a love for God's creation and do not like to see animals mistreated. Recently, there was a news story about a football team in the East which was playing a rival school whose mascot was a goat. Some calloused students captured a goat, killed it, and left it on the campus of the rival school. I wondered how anyone could be that heartless. But then, I finished reading the rest of the verse in Proverbs 12:10b, "*But even the mercies of the wicked are cruel.*"

In jest, I was thinking about how your dog reacts to you as compared to how your wife reacts to you in certain situations. For example, the later you come home from work, the more excited your dog is to see you. And another thing; dogs do not notice if you call them by another dog's name. And dogs do not mind if you leave your clothes lying around the house.

How about this one – your dog's parents never come over. And when you get ready to go somewhere, your dog is never late – he is always ready to go. Dogs just love to go camping in the woods. Dogs never wake you up and ask, "If I died, would you get another dog?"

If your dog has babies, you can put an ad in the paper and sell 'em. And finally, if a dog runs off and leaves you, he will not take half your stuff with him. I heard about a little test to prove that my statements are true. Lock your wife and dog in the trunk of your car for an hour. Then open the trunk and see who is happy to see you!

Will Rogers said, "If there are no dogs in Heaven, then I want to go where they are."[3] And Mark Twain added, "Heaven goes by favor. If it went by merit, we'd stay out, and our dogs would go in."[4] And in the world of politics, President Harry Truman said, "If you want a friend in Washington, get a dog."[5] It is interesting to read what famous people have to say about animals; but in the final analysis, the important thing is what the Bible says about it.

In reading the Scriptures, I find there is ample evidence that God loves all of His creation, including the animals. In Revelation 4:11, we find that all things were created for God's pleasure. Matthew 10:29 says that even when a little sparrow falls to the ground, God is aware of it. Luke 12:6 and 12:24 tells us that God never forgets about the animals. Psalm 104:21-30 and Matthew 6:26 describe how God Himself feeds the animals. Proverbs 12:10 declares that a righteous man cares for the needs of his animals. And Job 12:10a assures us that *"In whose hand is the soul of every living thing ...."*.

Man's sin brought death and suffering to all the animals just as it did to mankind. God in Genesis 1:29-30 decreed that green plants and fruit were to be the diet for all creatures. People and animals alike were to be strictly vegetarians. Carnivorous or meat eating activity necessitates death and suffering which, in the beginning, would have had no part in the beautiful creation that God called good (Genesis 1:25).

Man was given the responsibility of serving as overseer of the animals. In fact, it was not until after Noah's flood that animals became afraid of people (Genesis 9:2). When man chose to rebel against God, man brought a curse not only on himself, but also on all those for whom he was responsible.

In Genesis 3:17b (NIV), God told Adam, *"Cursed is the ground because of you ...."*. The ground has a curse on it. That is why it is so easy to grow weeds and thorns. You do not even have to cultivate them to keep them healthy! According to Hosea 4:3 (ESV), this curse affected animals, too. Because of the sins of man, *"Therefore the land mourns, and all who dwell in it languish, and also the beasts of the field and the birds of the heavens, and even the fish of the sea are taken away."*

Romans chapter 8 tells us that the "whole" of creation suffers because of the curse of sin, and that includes the plant and animal kingdoms. But, I have some good news for you. The Bible says that after the awful seven years of Tribulation when the earth is purged of its filth and impurities, God is going to set up His Millennial Kingdom for 1,000 years (Revelation 20).[6]

One of the main purposes of the Millennium is to show the world what it would have been like if man had chosen to follow God's rules and commandments instead of rebelling and disobeying. Can you imagine how great this earth would be without the curse of sin; without thorns or weeds; without chiggers or mosquitos or fire ants? And if there are any, then they will be friendly and will have been rendered harmless. There will be no tornadoes or hurricanes – just a perfect world as God originally created it.

During the Millennium we find that, *"The wolf and the lamb will graze together, and the lion will eat straw like the ox; and dust will be the serpent's food. They will do no evil or harm in all my holy mountain, says the LORD"* (Isaiah 65:25 NASB). Scripture even tells us that the animal kingdom looks forward to the redemption of mankind that was accomplished by Jesus' death on the cross because all creation will share in this redemption!

This is confirmed by the action of the Jewish High Priest. Once a year the High Priest would enter the Holy of Holies in the Tabernacle, and sprinkle the blood of an innocent lamb on the Mercy Seat of the Ark of the Covenant as a picture of the future redemption of mankind. But then, notice something in Scripture that many people overlook. After sprinkling the blood of an innocent lamb on the Mercy Seat, the High Priest would step back and sprinkle blood on the ground in front of the Ark (Leviticus 16:14-15). Why did He do this? Because the blood on the ground was a sign that the sacrifice of the Messiah would make it possible for God to lift the curse that rests on all creation and redeem it to its original perfection!

A further word about the floor of the Tabernacle is necessary. It would seem that with all the elaborate and painstaking instructions given to construct the tabernacle, it would have a floor consistent with the beauty of the rest of the structure. Not so. The floor was simply dirt or dust from the desert where the Israelites camped. As incongruous as this may seem to us, it was no oversight on God's part; it has a specific application. The dust which was to be the serpent's food was a picture of the barren and broken world in which we live. And yet, as the High Priest sprinkles the blood on the ground, it reminds us that the earth will be renewed to its original glory.[7]

As a reminder that God has promised to redeem all of His creation, every time one of our pets died I would make them a wooden casket. On the lid of the box, I would write Romans 8:19-21 (NLT): *"For all creation is waiting eagerly for that future day when God will reveal who His children really are. Against its will, everything on earth was subjected to God's curse. All creation anticipates the day when it will join God's children in glorious freedom from death and decay."* It is clear that God loves all His creation!

I am reminded of one of my favorite stories – a bit of fiction, but a great story nonetheless with an important moral. An old man was along a dusty road enjoying the scenery when it suddenly became clear to him that he had died. He remembered dying, and that his faithful dog that had been dead for many years was walking beside him. He wondered where the road was leading them.

After a while, they came to a high white stone wall along one side of the road. It looked like fine marble. As he reached the wall he saw a magnificent gate, and the street that led to the gate was made of pure gold. The man and his dog walked toward the gate, and as he got closer he saw a man at a desk to one side of the gate. He called out, "Excuse me, Sir, where are we?" "This is Heaven," the man replied. "Great, would you happen to have some water? We have been traveling for quite a while on this road, and we are so thirsty." "Of course, Sir. Come right in, and I will have some cool water brought right up." The gate slowly swung open and the old man and his dog started in. "I am sorry, Sir, but we do not allow pets to come in. But you are welcome; here comes the water right now." The old man thought a moment, remembering all the years his faithful companion had been with him, and said, "I'm sorry, Sir. If my dog can't come in, we'll just continue on."

They turned and continued to walk down the dusty road. After a while, they came to a dirt road which led through a narrow gate that looked like it had never been closed. As the two approached the gate, the old man saw a gentleman leaning against a tree reading a book. "Excuse me, Sir," he called to the reader. "Do you have any water? My dog and I have traveled a long way, and we are so thirsty." "Sure – there is a faucet over there." The man pointed to a place that could not be seen from outside the gate. "Come on in and help yourself. There is a large cup from which to drink." How about my friend here?" The traveler gestured to his dog. "There should be a bowl by the faucet; he is welcome to share."

They went through the gate, and sure enough, there was an old-fashioned faucet with a bowl beside it. The traveler filled the bowl and set it down for the dog. He then took a long drink from the cup. When they were fully refreshed, he and his dog walked back toward the man who was standing by the tree waiting for them. "What do you call this place?" the traveler asked. "This is Heaven," was the answer. "Well, that's confusing. The man down the road said that was Heaven, too." "Oh, you mean the place with the gold looking street and the fake pearly gates? That is Hell." The old man asked, "Doesn't that make you angry for them to use your name like that?" "No," the man replied. "We are just happy that they screen out the folks who would leave their best friends behind."[8]

That is a powerful principle, and it carries over to our relatives and friends. If they need to hear about Jesus, let us make sure we do not leave any of them behind. Now, do I think that animals have a living soul? No. However, some theologians define soul as having emotions: love, anger, will, etc. Animals certainly have those. But the difference is that Man not only has a soul, but according to Scripture, God breathed the spirit of life into him giving him immortality. But that does not mean that Heaven will not have some of God's most lovable and precious creations. After all, God is sovereign and can do as He chooses.

I Corinthians 2:9 says: *"But as it is written, eye hath not seen, nor ear heard, neither have entered into the heart of man, the things which God hath prepared for them that love him."* And Matthew 7:11 says that if a sinful father knows how to give good gifts to his children, how much more does our heavenly Father know how to give fantastic gifts to us? I think one of those fantastic gifts – one of those indescribable surprises that He will delight in overwhelming us with – is that we will see our pets again. After all, Scripture tells us, *"Delight yourself in the LORD, and He will give you the desires of your heart"* (Psalm 37:4 ESV).

Some of us prefer dogs – some of us prefer cats – some of us prefer horses. God loves them all. Have you ever ridden a horse? The Bible indicates that one day you will be an expert horseman because there will be horses in Heaven! Listen to Revelation 19:11 (NLT): *"Then I saw Heaven open, and a white horse was standing there. And the One sitting on the horse was named Faithful and True. For He judges fairly and then goes to war."* And then in Revelation 19:14 (NLT) it says, *"The armies of Heaven, dressed in pure white linen, followed Him on white horses."* That is you and me, folks, if you are a follower of Christ – we will be riding in the Lord's cavalry!

But back to Revelation 5:5., where we see Jesus as the Lion of the tribe of Judah. In Genesis 49, when the patriarch Jacob was blessing his twelve sons shortly before his death, he indicates that the Messiah would come from the tribe of Judah. He prophesied this as follows: *"The scepter will not depart from Judah, nor the ruler's staff from His descendants, until the coming of the One to whom it belongs, the One whom all nations will obey"* (Genesis 49:10 NLT).

Jacob's prophecy meant that from the tribe of Judah would come the Messiah of Israel. King David was from the tribe of Judah, as was Joseph, Jesus' earthly father. Also notice in Revelation 5:5, Jesus is called the "Root of David," not a "branch of David." The Pharisees challenged Jesus on this very point. They wondered how Jesus could be the root of David, when David had died hundreds of years before. And Jesus explained to them that He existed before David was born. In fact, He even said, *"Before Abraham was, I am"* (John 8:58b). And so, He could rightly be called the "Root of David." Putting it another way, in Jesus' humanity, He was a descendant of David; in His divinity, He was the ancestor or Root of David.

This scroll which we have been describing contains God's plan as to how He is going to bring judgment on the earth to renovate it, cleanse it of everything evil, and regain that which was lost by Adam. In the end, the truth of Revelation 11:15b will be revealed: *"THE KINGDOMS OF THIS WORLD ARE BECOME THE KINGDOMS OF OUR LORD, AND OF HIS CHRIST; AND HE SHALL REIGN FOR EVER AND EVER."* We are going to see the exciting details as to how this is to be accomplished over the next few chapters as each seal is broken, and God's wrath is poured out on a godless world to rid it of sin and everything ugly.

Chapter 5 opens with God holding a book – a scroll – in His right hand. He was not "grasping" it, but as the Greek word "epi" means, it was resting in His open hand. The scroll was written on the inside and the outside, and it had been sealed with seven seals. John is waiting expectantly to see what is going to happen next. It does not take him long to realize that this scroll is the title deed to the earth. God had given to Adam dominion over the earth and everything therein. But Adam lost it. He let Satan trick him out of it by bringing sin into the world, and since that time Satan has been in the driver's seat. But it is only temporary. The scroll details how God is going to redeem the earth, and it also spells out the fate of Satan and all those who oppose Almighty God.

But there is a problem. It would take a Kinsman-Redeemer who met the three Old Testament requirements as discussed earlier in this chapter. Those requirements are: 1) a close relative; 2) one who is willing to act; and 3) one who is able to meet the redemption price. The price in this case was a sinless life whose blood would be shed for the remission of sin. So an angel calls for someone worthy, someone who would fit the Kinsman-Redeemer requirements. Initially no one stepped forward who qualified to take the book and open it.

It is like Jesus is waiting in the wings, letting the suspense build. John realizes the importance of the moment. Will the earth be redeemed? Will Israel be saved? Will the redemption of the saints finally be accomplished, or will Satan triumph after all? John can stand it no longer, and he begins to weep, thinking that Satan has won at last. But then one of the elders tells him to stop weeping. The Lion of the tribe of Judah has been found worthy to open the book, loose the seals, and begin the final countdown for the full plan of redemption.

Dr. Wim Malgo, a Dutch theologian, had this to say: "Why was it necessary for one of the elders to comfort John, who already knew that Jesus had overcome? It was because John did that which we so easily do. He lost sight of the victory of the Lamb and this always results in hopelessness and tears. How very often we insult the Lord with our weeping and discouragement. We are often ready to resign in spite of the fact that He has achieved the great and wonderful victory."[9]

Jesus is the only one who could meet these requirements. He took on humanity so that He could be a close Kinsman. *"For both He who sanctifies and those who are sanctified are all from one Father; for which reason He is not ashamed to call them brethren* (Hebrews 2:11 NASB)." He was willing to act because He said, *"No one can take my life from me. I lay down my life voluntarily …."* (John 10:18a NLT). And thirdly, He could pay the required price for redemption. *"Because by one sacrifice He has made perfect forever those who are being made holy"* (Hebrews 10:14 NIV). Now we come to Revelation, chapter 5, verse 6. *"And I beheld, and, lo, in the midst of the throne and of the four beasts, and in the midst of the elders, stood a Lamb as it had been slain, having seven horns and seven eyes, which are the seven spirits of God sent forth into all the earth."* Right after John is told to stop weeping, we are told that the Lion of the tribe of Judah is worthy to break the seals of the scroll.

John turns to look and what does he see? He does not see a Lion – he sees a Lamb! There are two words in Greek for lamb. The first is "amnos." It is a generic term for lamb. That is not the word used here. The word here is "arnios."It means a little pet lamb – one the entire family loves. In the midst of the throne – in the midst of the seraphim – in the midst of all of God's redeemed saints, John sees an arnios – a little pet lamb.

When it came time to prepare for the Jewish Passover, the Jews were not to go out and select just any lamb to be slain. The lamb was to be carefully chosen from the firstlings of the flock for its beauty and perfection (Exodus 12:5). It could have no defects. But this breaks your heart: the chosen lamb was to be placed in the bosom of the family for four days. During this time, the children and family would pet it, love it, and look upon it as a member of the family.[10] John saw this pet Lamb as "sphazo" slain. The word in Greek means violently slain. It is the word used for the sacrifice and suffering of the victim on the altar. In Jesus' body were the marks of suffering. In His hands, the print of the nails, in His side the scar from the terrible spear, and on His body the scars from the lashes of the whip. There is a powerful Southern Gospel song sung by the Florida Boys that says the only things in Heaven that are made by man are the scars in the hands of Jesus.

Yes, Jesus will still bear the marks from Calvary. That is why John said He looked like a Lamb who was slain. John the Baptist had introduced Him on earth as *"The Lamb of God, who takes away the sin of the world!"* (John 1:29 ESV). Isaiah described Him 700 years before, as a lamb led to the slaughter. And now John sees a little pet Lamb as if it had been violently slain. It is as though the curtain is drawn back as we are all holding our breath and there He is – Jesus Christ. THE LION IS THE LAMB!

And we find that He has seven horns and seven eyes, which are the seven spirits of God. You remember that seven is the number God always uses to indicate perfection or completeness. And we have seen previously in Isaiah 11:2-3 the sevenfold ministry of the Holy Spirit. The seven horns speak of perfect power, and the seven eyes indicate He knows all that is going on in the world. In other words, the seven horns and seven eyes depict two of God's important attributes: He is omnipotent which means all-powerful; and He is omniscient which means all-knowing.

One other point before we leave verse 6. It says that the Lamb is standing. Do you know what that means? Five times in the Book of Hebrews it pictures Jesus sitting on the right hand of the throne of God (Hebrews 1:3; 1:13; 8:1; 10:12; 12:2). But now, this Kinsman-Redeemer will shortly reclaim His inheritance and commence His final plan for the destruction of Satan and his evil empire. Christ is getting ready for action. He is standing!

"And He came and took the book out of the right hand of Him that sat upon the throne" (Revelation 5:7). We said that one of the legal requirements of the Kinsman-Redeemer was that He had to be willing to act. Here we see that He is willing to act. He takes the initiative. He takes the book – the scroll – from the Father who is seated on the throne. And when He takes

the book, look what happens in verse 8 (ESV): *"And when He had taken the scroll, the four living creatures and the twenty-four elders fell down before the Lamb, each holding a harp, and golden bowls full of incense, which are the prayers of the saints."* Jesus takes the book and immediately it sets off another round of worship and praise by the host of Heaven – the angels and the Church!

As they fall down to praise Him, John notices that each one of them has a harp. For worshipful music, a harp is hard to beat. There is just something heavenly about its sound. There is a certain denomination which does not condone musical instruments in the church. They claim they are the one true Church and everyone else is dead wrong. But this group that claims to be the one true Church has split many times over the years. One says that Sunday school is biblical; another says it is not.

There have been at least seventeen factions or divisions from this one so-called "true Church" – each claiming that it is correct and all the others are wrong! One group says it is a mortal sin to have any kind of musical instrument in church worship, including harps. And if you play these in church, you will not be going to heaven. And yet, here in the 5th chapter we see a scene in Heaven around the very throne of God, the most awesome worship scene that has ever been described. And guess what? The angels are playing harps! All the saints are playing harps! And God is loving it!

These worshipers have something else besides harps. Look at the last part of verse 8 (ESV). They also have *"golden bowls, full of incense, which are the prayers of the saints."* What are these prayers? These are prayers of the saints that have not yet been answered, such as prayers for loved ones on earth who are being persecuted by the forces of the Antichrist. But I think most of the prayers will express a yearning for the Second Coming of Christ which will usher in Christ's Kingdom and result in the defeat of the satanic trinity which is Satan, the Antichrist and the False Prophet. Satan will try to replace God, the Antichrist will try to replace Christ, and the False Prophet will try to replace the Holy Spirit.

Think of how many millions of times people have prayed, *"Thy kingdom come. Thy will be done in earth, as it is in Heaven"* (Matthew 6:10). Those are not empty words. That prayer will literally be answered one day. Verse 9 is a powerful verse. *"And they sang a new song, saying, 'Thou art worthy to take the book, and to open the seals thereof: for thou wast slain, and hath redeemed us to God by thy blood out of every kindred, and tongue, and people, and nation.'"*

Here is what the little scroll is all about: the redemption of that which was lost, not just mankind and the earth, but all that is in the earth. Ephesians 1:6-7a says: *"To the praise of the glory of His grace, wherein He hath made us accepted in the beloved. In whom we have redemption through His blood …."*.

A great worship scene follows with the harps expressing deepest joy and praise. Verse 9 says they sang a "new song." Probably one of the first songs they sang is found in Job 38:6-7 (NLT):

"What supports its foundations, and who laid its cornerstone as the morning stars sang together and all the angels shouted for joy?" This was a song praising God as Creator for all the things He had made.

Dr. W. A. Criswell said that the angels never sing.[11] I had never heard anyone say that before. This verse in Job says they *"shouted for joy."* I thought, "Surely, the angels sang at Christ's birth." I hear them singing at all the Christmas programs. I quickly turned to Luke, chapter 2, the familiar passage in which the angels appeared to the shepherds in the field. And I looked at verse 13: *"And suddenly there was with the angel a multitude of the heavenly host praising God, and saying, 'Glory to God in the highest, and on earth peace, good will toward men.'"* Scripture records that the angels were saying, not singing. I discovered that never in the Bible do the angels sing. Never! They always say something. They are in a doxology, in a chorus, reciting praises together, but never singing. Isn't that amazing?

I discovered something else. God's children sing! God has taken us out of the miry clay. He has set our feet upon the solid rock, and He has put a song in our hearts. Those redeemed by the blood of the Lamb just have to sing! Somehow, it is the disappointment and sorrow in life that make people sing, either in the blackness of its hour, or in the joyful deliverance when a burden has been lifted.

That is why the redeemed sing and the angels just speak about it. The angels only know redemption from observation, not experience. An angel has never been saved from sin. An angel has never fallen, and been brought back to God. The reason is that they sinned individually, whereas the sin of Adam as our formal head of the human race infected every human with a sin nature. Sometimes I forget and say, "She sings like an angel." No, it takes a lost soul who is at the end of themselves, who has been brought back to God and experienced the forgiveness of sin, to sing praises unto Him who bought us with His own blood.

But here in Revelation 5:9, a new song is sung. It is being sung by the saints who have been raptured at the beginning of the Tribulation. This song declares the worthiness of the Lord Jesus Christ, and proclaims His authority to take and open the seven-sealed book because He has been slain and His death brought redemption to people of all nations.

Some churches teach that only their particular denomination is going to Heaven. However, this verse is directed to people of all nations. It is individuals who are saved, not churches. There will be saved ones from the Baptists, Methodists, Churches of Christ, Presbyterians, Catholics and all others who have accepted Christ as their personal Savior and Lord. I am a Baptist, not because I trust the church to get me to Heaven, but because I find that their teachings and doctrines more closely align with those of the Scriptures than any other denomination.

Notice especially that Christ has redeemed these people from all nations "by His blood". It is a characteristic of our time that there is an attempt in some religious circles to remove any reference to the blood of Christ, even in church hymnals. A noted Methodist spokeswoman, Dr. Petera, at one of their large convention gatherings in Kansas City a number of years ago said (paraphrasing), "We have got to get away from mentioning a blood sacrifice. We need to get away from a barbaric bloody Christianity – such as from Abraham's bloody knife, and a doctrine which teaches that an abusive Father-God delights in the killing of His Son." I think most Methodist laypersons would disagree with this view. I wrote to the Methodist hierarchy at the time expressing my outrage, but I never received a reply. That is blasphemy and a distortion of the Gospel. Let us never forget Hebrews 9:22b (NLT): *"Without the shedding of blood, there is no forgiveness of sin."*

The redeemed continue singing that song as we look at Revelation 5:10, *"And hast made us unto our God kings and priests: and we shall reign on the earth."* The punctuation in the Bible is not inspired. It was added 500 years ago to make it read more smoothly and efficiently. So, I would instruct you to put a comma after "us" and a comma after "God". It makes the sentence easier to understand. So now we have, *"And hast made us, unto our God, kings and priests, and we shall reign on the earth."* Some translations such as the NIV say, *"And hast made them"* [instead of us]. That is permissible because it refers back to those who are singing – the redeemed. So it says that God has made the redeemed, that is you and me, to be kings and priests, and we shall reign on the earth.

II Timothy 2:12 (ESV) says that if endure, we will reign with Christ. What does that mean? Well, Christ is going to receive His Kingdom at the end of the Tribulation Period, and you and I are going to rule and reign with Him over all the nations of the world. This promise was first given to the prophet Daniel in Daniel 7:27 (NASB): *"Then the sovereignty, the dominion and the greatness of all the kingdoms under the whole Heaven will be given to the people of the saints of the Highest One; His Kingdom will be an everlasting kingdom, and all the dominions will serve and obey Him."*

This same promise is repeated in the New Testament in Revelation 2:26-27: *"And he that overcometh and keepth my works unto the end, to him will I give power over the nations. And He shall rule them with a rod of iron; as the vessels of a potter shall they be broken to shivers: even as I received of my Father."* Yes, Jesus will reign as King from Mount Zion in Jerusalem over all the earth (Isaiah 24:23 and Zechariah 14:9). And the redeemed in their glorified bodies will help with His reign. Some will be judges, but most will be teachers and administrators. There will be millions born during the 1,000 year millennial period because the survivors of the Tribulation Period will go into the Millennium in their human bodies as they have not yet received their glorified bodies, and they will have children who will need to be taught about Christ and His glorious redemptive plan.[12]

And then, in verse 11, we hear from the angels: *"And I beheld, and I heard the voice of many angels round about the throne and the beasts and the elders: and the number of them was ten thousand times ten thousand, and thousands of thousands."* John is not attempting to number them; he is just illustrating an innumerable number. In verse 12, we see what these angels are reciting: *"Saying with a loud voice, 'Worthy is the Lamb that was slain to receive power, and riches, and wisdom, and strength, and honor, and glory, and blessing.'"* Seven is the number of perfection in the Bible. And the angels named seven characteristics that the Lamb is worthy to receive: power, riches, wisdom, strength, honor, glory and blessing. Let us consider each one of these.

1) The first is Power [Gr. Dunamis]. "Dunamis" is the word from which we get our word dynamite. I am reminded of that verse in Revelation 1:16b describing Christ. *"And His countenance was as the sun shineth in His strength"* [Dunamis].

2) Riches [Gr. Ploutos] Philippians 4:19: *"But my God shall supply all your need according to His riches* [ploutos] *in glory by Christ Jesus."*

3) Wisdom [Gr. Sophia] I Corinthians 3:19 (NLT): *"For the wisdom* [sophia] *of this world is foolishness to God."*

4) Strength [Gr. Iskus] Mark 12:30: *"And thou shalt love the Lord thy God .... with all thy strength* [iskus]."

5) Honor [Gr. Timee] Hebrews 2:9: *"But we see Jesus .... crowned with glory and honor* [timee]....".

6) Glory [Gr. Doxa] Romans 11:36b: *".... to whom be glory* [doxa] *forever. Amen."* That is where we get our word "doxology," meaning a praise song. 7) Blessing [Gr. Eulogia] Romans 15:29b: *".... the fullness of the blessing* [eulogia] *of the gospel of Christ."*

These are the seven characteristics proving that Christ is worthy to receive praise and glory; and millions and millions of angels are chanting this in unison. Verse 13 says: *"And every creature which is in Heaven, and on the earth, and under the earth, and such as are in the sea, and all that are in them, heard I saying, Blessing, and honor, and glory, and power, be unto Him that sitteth upon the throne, and unto the Lamb forever and ever."* And as this chorus of voices continues to build, it is as though all creation joins in worship to the Lamb! They are praising the Lamb because the redemption price was sufficient, the title deed to the earth was reclaimed, and the Kinsman-Redeemer, Jesus Christ, has met all the legal requirements to take the book and break the seals. So the whole creation praises and rejoices in song together when the Lamb receives the scroll.

In verse 13 when John says, *"on the earth, and under the earth, and such as are in the sea"* – he is including the animal creation because the believers are already represented around the throne. There is a hint of this in Psalm 148 where it is talking about all creatures praising God, and in verse 10 of that same chapter, it specifically says, *"Wild animals and all cattle, small creatures and flying birds"* (NIV).

All creation is under the curse and bondage of sin. This not only includes the animal kingdom, but also the plant kingdom as well. That is why your plants must battle diseases such as brown spot and mold. If you are not careful, a nice little green plant will give you poison ivy. The curse touches all parts of God's creation.

Here is how the curse of the plant kingdom affected me. It was the last of July 1954, a week before Arlene and I were to be married. I was at boot camp at Ft. Campbell, Kentucky, being harassed by the 101st Airborne Division, the paratroopers they call "The Screaming Eagles".[13] It was close to 100 degrees, and we were on an eleven mile hike with full back packs ordered by Major Cardoza. He took our drinking water away at the five mile marker. The reason? He said, "You guys drink more water than a herd of pregnant water buffalo!" That was OK. We were having so much fun, running and falling in the red dust every time Sergeant Schroeder yelled for us to hit the ground to avoid make-believe enemy planes. He said it was good training for us. I noticed he didn't do it.

Among the vegetation we were falling down in, was a pretty little leafy plant. I learned it was poison ivy soon after that. I was afraid that at the wedding I would not be saying, "I do, but I itch." My fellow cadets were making all kinds of suggestions to try to clear up the rash. Fortunately, the old army G. I. (lye) soap did the trick just in time.

The Bible says in Isaiah 11:6-8 that when this curse is removed from the earth and all creation is redeemed, the wolf will dwell with the lamb, the leopard will lie down with the young goat, and the lion will eat straw like an ox. A child will play next to a cobra, and not be harmed.

That brings us to the last verse in this chapter, verse 14. *"And the four beasts* [living creatures] *said, 'Amen.' And the four and twenty elders fell down and worshiped Him that liveth for ever and ever.'"* The details of how all of this will be accomplished are recorded on the scroll that is in the hand of the Lamb, Jesus Christ. No wonder all creation is joyfully praising Him!

CHAPTER SIX

The Four Horsemen of the Apocalypse

In chapters 4 and 5, we have been witnessing scenes in Heaven. But now, as we begin chapter 6, the scene shifts back to the earth because the Tribulation Period, that time when God pours His wrath out upon the earth, is about to begin! Did you notice an important fact from the last couple of chapters? It is this: the breaking of the seals does not begin until God's saints are safely gathered around the throne in glory. Judgment does not fall until God's children are safely home.

Let us look at an incident in the life of Christ that is recorded in chapter 4 of the Book of Luke. Jesus went into the synagogue on that Sabbath day, and those in charge handed Him the scroll to read aloud the Scripture reading for that day. The Jews had a portion of Scripture designated to read each Sabbath just as we might have a portion of Scripture designated in our daily Bible readings.

When Jesus went into the synagogue, the reading for that particular Sabbath was from Isaiah 61:1-2. It was a tradition that the Jewish leaders always allowed the senior and most prestigious rabbi to read the Scripture. It is simply astonishing that they chose this young Jewish rebel named Jesus to read it. He must have had such a look of authority that they just naturally handed Him the scroll. Secondly, it was amazing that the verses scheduled for that day so closely tracked what Jesus' earthly ministry was all about.

Now for the real shocker. Compare Isaiah 61:1-2 with the words Jesus actually read as recorded in Luke 4:18-19. Here is the verse in Isaiah: *"The Spirit of the Lord God is upon me; because the LORD hath anointed me to preach good tidings unto the meek; He hath sent me to bind up the broken-hearted, to proclaim liberty to the captives, and the opening of the prison to them that are bound; To proclaim the acceptable year of the LORD, and the day of vengeance of our God; to comfort all that mourn."*

However, in Luke 4:18-19 we find what Jesus actually quoted: *"THE SPIRIT OF THE LORD IS UPON ME; BECAUSE HE HATH ANOINTED ME TO PREACH THE GOSPEL TO THE POOR; HE HATH SENT ME TO HEAL THE BROKEN-HEARTED, TO PREACH DELIVERANCE TO THE CAPTIVES, AND RECOVERING OF SIGHT TO THE BLIND, TO SET AT LIBERTY THEM THAT ARE BRUISED, TO PREACH THE ACCEPTABLE YEAR OF THE LORD."* And then He closed the book. Do you see anything that Jesus left out when He read those verses? Absolutely! He stopped when He read, *"to preach the acceptable year of the LORD."* Why did He not read, *"and the day of vengeance of our God"*? Here is why.

At the time He was reading this, it was a day of mercy; it was a day for acknowledging Christ as King. It was not a day for God's vengeance to be poured out. And it has been a day of mercy and grace since that time – and will be until the Rapture occurs and the "day of vengeance" (Tribulation Period) begins.

When God's children are gathered home at the Rapture, the acceptable year of the Lord ends. So does the Church Age. The day of grace is over. The door will be shut and the day of vengeance will begin. It is called the Tribulation Period – the 70th week of Daniel. It is what Jesus calls "the beginning of sorrows" in Matthew 24:8. Jesus said it will be a time such as there never has been on the face of the earth, nor will there ever be another like it. He said that if those days were not shortened (to seven years) no flesh would survive (Matthew 24:22).

The seven seals of judgment are opened one at a time, but when the seventh seal is opened, it contains seven trumpets; and when the seventh trumpet sounds, it contains seven bowls of judgment. Thank God that He has told us as members of the true Church in Revelation 3:10 (NIV): *"Since you have kept my command to endure patiently, I will also keep you from the hour of trial that is going to come upon the whole world to test those who live on the earth."* This verse not only tells us that we will be kept from these judgments, but it also tells us to whom these judgments are directed – "those who live on the earth – the earth dwellers" who have settled down here where their heart's treasure is.

"And I saw when the Lamb opened one of the seals, and I heard, as it were the noise of thunder, one of the four beasts saying, 'Come and see'" (Revelation 6:1). Jesus called the events that are about to be described as signs. They are signs of His Second Coming because He will come back to earth after these judgments have purified the earth.

As we said earlier, the Christians will not be present on the earth when these judgments are poured out. We will be in Heaven, receiving our crowns and rewards around the Bema Seat of Christ, and attending the Marriage and the Marriage Supper of the Lamb. That is the reason the Bible calls His Body the Bride of Christ. Just as the husband and wife are to be one in spirit, one in love and one in purpose, so we shall be one with Christ. And we can see the evidence that these signs are fast approaching. They are casting shadows, and are beginning to be fulfilled. Jesus said, *"When these things begin to take place, stand up and lift up your heads, because your redemption is drawing near"* (Luke 21:28 NIV).

In the meantime, there is a "Restrainer" or "Hinderer" who is holding back or resisting evil. We are told this in the second chapter of II Thessalonians. Who is this Restrainer? Some believe the Restrainer is the Holy Spirit; some believe the Restrainer is the Body of Christ (Christians). I believe it is both. The Holy Spirit attempts to block Satan's plans at every opportunity, and the Christians elect candidates who have pledged to follow Christian principles. However, when they get in office they often do not do that.

We indicated previously that prophecy comprises about one fourth of the Bible. It is an important doctrine that theologians call "eschatology" – the study of end time events. It is sad that you can mention the Rapture to most Christians – even mature Christians – and they hardly know anything about it, if they have even heard of it at all. It is one of the best kept secrets in most of our churches, yet Paul devotes most of the fourth chapter of I Thessalonians and much of the second chapter of II Thessalonians and the fifteenth chapter of I Corinthians to the realities of Christ's return for His Bride at the Rapture. This doctrine is so important that Paul wasted no time in imparting this truth to these young Christians at Thessalonica.

II Thessalonians 2:1, *"Now we beseech you, brethren, by the coming of our Lord Jesus Christ, and by our gathering together unto Him …."*. I read one commentary that said Christ is not really coming back. Instead, the Second Coming is when you die, and go to be with Jesus. If that is true, it should be called the "First Going" instead of the "Second Coming." Verse 1 does not sound like death has anything to do with it. Listen again: *"Now we beseech you, brethren, by the coming of our Lord Jesus Christ, and our gathering together to Him…."*. That is not death! That is the Rapture – our gathering together to meet Him in the air!

This may be a shock to you, but most theologians in the world today are liberals. They do not believe in the inerrancy of the Bible. They believe that the Bible "contains" the Word of God, but first we must toss out all the myths, legends and superstitions. And as a general rule, they do not take the Bible literally. They had rather spiritualize it so they can make it say whatever they want it to say.

Let us continue. *"Please don't be so easily shaken and troubled by those who say that the Day of the Lord has already begun. Even if they claim to have had a vision, a revelation, or a letter supposedly from us …."*. (II Thessalonians 2:2 NLT). Paul wrote his first letter to these young converts (I Thessalonians) only a few months after leaving them. This second letter was probably written a few months after that. It did not take very long for false teachers to slip into the assembly of believers, probably men who had big egos and wanted everyone to flock after them. And so, they twisted Paul's teachings as we will see shortly.

In his first letter to these young Christians at Thessalonica, Paul said that at God's appointed time, the Rapture would occur suddenly. The dead in Christ, not all the dead, but the dead in Christ would come up out of their graves, and their bodies would be changed in a moment into new, incorruptible bodies designed to last forever. And then, a nano-second after them, those Christians who are living at that time will be caught up to meet the Lord in the air. And after that, "The Day of the Lord" will be ushered in – a day of darkness and gloom that we call The Tribulation.

The believers in Thessalonica understood all of this, but they were not yet firmly grounded in their belief. At the same time, the Roman government decided to accelerate its efforts of wiping out Christianity with its teaching that a man named Jesus was going to come as a king and set up an earthly kingdom. That was certainly a threat to Caesar! So when the Romans heard about the revival that had taken place in Thessalonica, and that many Thessalonians had become converts, they sent troops there and intensified their violence against anyone naming the name of Christ. They threatened prison and death for anyone who would not disavow their newly found faith.

With that backdrop, it was easy for the false teachers with inflated egos to stand up in their assemblies and say, "I have a new revelation from God; something that the Apostle Paul didn't even know. And it is this: the Day of the Lord (The Tribulation) is already upon us. That is the reason for all these persecutions!" The believers reasoned, "If that is the case, then we have missed the Rapture, and we have been left behind! We were not saved after all!" That would shake your faith to the core. When Paul heard about this he wrote to them immediately: "Don't be shook up when you hear that the Day of the Lord has already begun. This is not true!"

At the same time, there were fraudulent letters being circulated purporting to be from Paul, and teaching false doctrine. Paul alludes to this when he said in II Thessalonians 2:2 (NLT), *"Please don't be so easily shaken or troubled by those who say that the Day of the Lord has already begun. Even if they claim to have had a vision, a revelation, or a letter supposedly from us, don't believe them."*

Pastor Paul Sadler asks a crucial question. "If Paul had taught that the Body of Christ will go through the Tribulation as some claim, then why were these saints shaken and troubled? They were shaken because Paul had taught them that they would NOT go through any part of it. The apostle warns, *'Let no man deceive you by any means ....'* (II Thessalonians 2:3 NLT). Consequently, anyone who came to them proclaiming that the Church of this age would suffer through the time of Jacob's trouble (i.e., The Tribulation) was either misinformed or a deceiver."[1]

Then Paul tells them how they can know whether the Day of the Lord has begun or not. And his advice is very pertinent to us today in determining the arrival of the Day of the Lord. He writes, *"Don't be fooled by what they say. For that day will not come until there is a great rebellion against God and the man of lawlessness is revealed – the one who brings destruction"* (II Thessalonians 2:3 NLT). Keep the word rebellion in mind. The King James Version says it a little differently: *"Let no man deceive you by any means: for that day shall not come, except there come a falling away first, and that man of sin be revealed, the son of perdition"* (II Thessalonians 2:3).

The King James Version indicates that the Day of the Lord cannot come until two things happen: 1) an apostasy – a falling away – a rebellion; and 2) the man of lawlessness – son of perdition is revealed. There is no disagreement among Bible scholars as to who this man of lawlessness is, this son of perdition. It is the Antichrist.

So, one thing is clear: the Day of the Lord cannot come until the Antichrist is revealed. But Scripture indicates that the Antichrist is not revealed until after the Tribulation has begun, and most likely that will not be until 3½ years into the Tribulation when he stands in the Temple in Jerusalem and declares himself to be God. I am convinced that the Scriptures teach that the Church has been raptured long before that. So Paul tells these Thessalonian believers, "Don't worry that someone has told you the Day of the Lord is upon you." He goes on to say, "Remember, two things must come to pass before the Day of the Lord can begin, and those two things are: 1) There is an "apostasia" (apostasy), and 2) The Man of Sin (the Antichrist) must be revealed." As long as I can remember, well-meaning prophecy teachers have taught this very thing – that these two things must take place before the Tribulation Period begins.

I have no problem with the second sign mentioned. There will be no mistaking the Antichrist. He will quickly rise to the status of world leader; he will stand in the Temple and declare himself to be God. And he will negotiate a seven year treaty between the Jews and the Arabs. He will proclaim loud and clear: "Peace in the Middle East at last."

But I do have a problem with the first requirement that Paul mentions. This falling away – this apostasy is harder to recognize. Why? Because there have always been false teachers who have fizzled out and defected from the fold. In other words, there has been apostasy in every generation. How can anyone tell which one is the apostasy that precedes the revealing of the Antichrist? These Thessalonians are experiencing apostasy in their midst at that very time. And Paul is having to caution them, "Don't believe these false teachers!" So, how can apostasy be a clear sign to look for when it exists in EVERY generation? It cannot. Paul is trying to impart to them two things they will clearly recognize – two things that cannot be misunderstood so they will know beyond a shadow of a doubt that the Day of the Lord has not yet begun.

One of the requirements is the revealing of the Antichrist. That is a definite phenomenon that everyone will recognize. He stands up in the Temple and says, "I am God." It is a legitimate sign that tells everyone that the Day of the Lord has not previously begun. But what about the other requirement – the apostasy? A closer look at this verse yields all kinds of hidden secrets. Several modern translations acknowledge that in the Greek there is a definite article preceding the word apostasy. The New American Standard Bible renders II Thessalonians 2:3 correctly in that the Day of the Lord cannot come until the apostasy occurs first.

So, here is the problem. How can any generation recognize "THE APOSTASY" if there is apostasy with people leaving the faith in every generation? This requirement is so vague it must mean something else because Paul was giving a sign to these Thessalonians that they would know for sure that the Day of the Lord has not arrived, not something at which they would have to guess.

In II Thessalonians 2:3, the King James translators used the primary meaning of this Greek term "apostasia" – and translated it "a falling away." But in this case, Scripture used a definite article – "hee apostasia" which is the apostasy – a specific one. Consider this carefully because this is very important to the conclusions drawn in this matter.

In any good dictionary, you will find that it gives you words that have a primary meaning, and then a secondary meaning; maybe even a third or a fourth meaning. I even found a word with 17 different meanings. Let me give you an example. Take the word fine for instance: f-i-n-e. Its primary meaning is "a very high grade or quality." Like a fine diamond. But it also has several secondary meanings. It can mean minute as in a very fine grain of sand. It can mean delicate as in a fine piece of linen. It can also mean accomplished as in "Ian is a fine musician." It can also mean a penalty as in "The judge assessed Carrie a fine of $100 for speeding." So, the word fine has a primary meaning, but it also has a number of secondary meanings depending on the context.

Take one more word: dash, d-a-s-h. It can mean to run quickly as in "It was raining, so Merle decided to dash to the car." It can be a punctuation mark when you are reading as in "Edwin opens our class each week with announcements – (dash), and he often entertains us with funny stories." Dash can also mean a small quantity such as "When Joyce is cooking, she often adds a dash of salt." You get the point.

When the translators came to this word "apostasia" in II Thessalonians 2:3, they gave it the primary meaning of falling away. They assumed it meant a falling away or departure from the faith. And so, they translated it in various versions as "to fall away" – "the apostasy" – "the rebellion", etc. As a result of this rendering, commentators have long taught that verse 3 means that the Rapture cannot take place until there first comes a departure from the faith – the apostasy.

I contend that this "falling away" is too vague. It cannot be identified specifically as a clear sign to look for by the Thessalonians or for anyone in any generation for that matter. It cannot be measured. You can look at the newspaper and say, "Here is where Bishop John Spong of the Episcopal Church is promoting gay marriage; and here is where he denies the virgin birth; and here where he denies Jesus' deity." This is apostasy all right, but you cannot say with certainty that this is the great apostasy. That is because apostasy is going on around us all the time. It is clear that Paul was trying to give them a definite sign that they or anyone else would immediately recognize that proves the Day of the Lord has not begun. And the Apostle Paul gave the Thessalonians just such a sign!

As we noted, "apostasia" generally means defection, a falling away, a revolt or rebellion. But not always. You must consider the context! Just as the word fine in Webster has several secondary meanings, the word apostasia has a secondary meaning namely departure or disappearance. Apostasia, which is a noun, comes from the older root verb "Aphisteemi" which is used fifteen times in the New Testament and only three have any reference to departing from the faith.

The other twelve times relate simply to a departure from one place to another. In Acts 12:10 the angel delivered Peter from prison and then – "aphisteemi" – the angel departed from him.[2]

Which rendering makes more sense in the context of what Paul is saying? If Paul tells the Thessalonians that the Day of the Lord cannot take place before the departure, he must have assumed they would know what he is referring to. What departure would they think of in the light of what he has been teaching them? Consider this: Paul spent a good portion of his previous letter to them (I Thessalonians 4:13-18) explaining the Rapture. This mystery was revealed to him by God and indicates that the Church will suddenly depart this earth. In the "twinkling of any eye" (I Corinthians 52:15) the Church will be snatched away to meet the Lord in the air (I Thessalonians 4:16-17). These Thessalonians immediately knew what Paul was referring to when he says "THE departure!" He was referring to the Rapture, the sudden departure that he had explained in his first letter to them.

In summary, why is Paul writing this second letter to these believers in Thessalonica? The answer is pure and simple. They were scared and confused. They thought they had been left behind and were about to experience the dreadful Day of the Lord, because they had been receiving false teaching to that effect. So Paul writes this second letter telling them, "Don't worry! Stay calm! The Day of the Lord – that awful Tribulation Period – cannot take place before two specific things occur. First, the Rapture must take place – that sudden departure of the Christians. Then second, after the Rapture the Antichrist will be revealed which will signal the beginning of the Day of the Lord. Bingo! Two clear recognizable signs!

Scripture continues to describe this Man of Sin: "*Who opposeth and exalteth himself above all that is called God, or that is worshipped; so that he as God sitteth in the Temple of God, showing himself that he is God*" (II Thessalonians 2:4). The Antichrist will magnify himself above all gods by falsely declaring himself to be God in the rebuilt Jewish Temple in Jerusalem in the middle of the seven year Tribulation Period. Jesus calls this the Abomination of Desolation. He said, "*The time will come when you will see what Daniel the prophet spoke about; the sacrilegious object that causes desecration standing in the Holy Place – reader, pay attention!*" (Matthew 24:15 NLT). Jesus said when this occurs, the Jews should flee immediately to the mountains because the Antichrist will try to exterminate them from the face of the earth. These will be dark days on the earth.

Jesus said it will be so bad that when it does come, there was never a time like it in the annals of mankind nor will there ever be a time like it afterwards (Matthew 24:21).But God is still available for those who will turn to Him. The seven-sealed book is about to be opened. Who breaks these seals and opens the book? We see who it is in the first verse of chapter 6. It is Jesus! We will see in the verses following that He delegates the execution of these judgments to the four mighty living ones who are before the throne. But Jesus is the One who breaks the seals and commences the judgments in accordance with John 5:22-23a (NIV): "*Moreover, the*

Father judges no one, but has entrusted all judgment to the Son, that all may honor the Son just as they honor the Father ….".

Notice that when the first seal is opened, John hears thunder. What does thunder mean? It means a storm is coming. John can actually hear the approaching wrath of God – fierce, foreboding things are about to happen. The four living ones stand before the throne of God and continually cry, "Holy, Holy, Holy" (Revelation 4:8). They signal the beginning of these judgments because God's holiness is about to be vindicated. No longer will men shake their fists in God's face and get away with it. The day of grace is past.

In Revelation 6:1 we read that one of these mighty warriors says, "Come." In the Greek, this word "erchomai" can mean either come or go. In some places in Scripture, the word is translated come and in other places it is translated go. I think in this case it means both come and go. All creation has been holding its collective breath for this momentous time in history. It is as though this mighty angel is saying, "The first seal has been broken, and it is time for the first judgment to come forth." Given this authority by God, this angel says "Come" and then he signals, "Go" as each horse is waiting in its stall, ready to ride upon the pages of history. It is time to begin the redemption of the earth!

"And I saw, and behold a white horse: and he that sat on him had a bow; and a crown was given unto him: and he went forth conquering, and to conquer" (Revelation 6:2). This is the first of what theologians call, "The four horsemen of the Apocalypse." In the mid-1920s, Notre Dame had a great football team. They were undefeated during the 1924 football season, and went on to win the national championship when they played in the Rose Bowl on New Year's Day defeating Stanford 27-10. In the backfield, they had a fantastic quarterback and three incredible running backs. Their names were Stuhldreher, Crowley, Miller and Layden. Grantland Rice, a sportswriter, called them the "four horsemen of the Apocalypse" and the name stuck.[3]

If you ask the average person on the street today, "Who are the four horsemen of the apocalypse?" they would probably not think of the Book of Revelation. Instead they would most likely say, "Weren't they the famous football players from Notre Dame?" But when the real horsemen of the apocalypse ride on to the world scene, no one will ever forget their bloody trail! Many expositors say this rider on the white horse is the Lord Jesus Christ. Not so! They get this from the fact that in the 19th chapter, we do see Jesus riding a white horse, but it is under entirely different circumstances. The rider here in chapter 6 is a great counterfeit leader, a picture of the Antichrist himself.

Christ mentions in Matthew 24 that false christs will characterize the end times. Look at Matthew 24:4-5: *"And Jesus answered and said unto them, Take heed that no man deceive you. For many shall come in my name, saying, I am Christ; and shall deceive many."*

This rider on a white horse is a false christ. Notice what he is carrying – a bow. It does not say anything about arrows. He is all bluff at this point. He intimidates, harasses and threatens. He makes great strides through negotiation without having to exhort to war. But it is a false and short-lived peace. It is the world's last great effort after the Church has been raptured to bring in a peaceful Millennium without Christ. Hitler tried it. He predicted that the Third Reich would rule for 1,000 years. It barely lasted six.

But the Antichrist will be smooth; he will be slick, almost nauseating. He will peacefully take over those nations who are convinced that he brings peace to the world. Daniel tells us, "*He shall come in peaceably, and obtain the kingdom by flatteries*" (Daniel 11:21b). This false christ will be armed with a bow. In chapter 19, Christ is armed with a sword, which is the sword of the Spirit – the Word of God. The white horse in chapter 6 signals the beginning of judgment, whereas the white horse in chapter 19 signals the end of judgment.

It says that a crown is given to the rider in chapter 6 – he did not earn it nor inherit it. It was probably given to him by the nations of the world who would sell their soul to anyone who promised, as Prime Minister Neville Chamberlin of England did when he proclaimed to Hitler and to the world, "peace in our time." God who is sovereign and who is unfolding these events allowed this to happen in accordance with His eternal plan. The Greek word used here for crown is "stephanos," and means a victor's crown or laurel of one going forth to conquer. It could be worn by anyone, whereas in chapter 19, the rider on the white horse is Christ wearing a diadem (Greek "diadema") that only Jesus can wear as King of kings and Lord of lords. Another reason we know this rider in chapter 6 is not Christ, is that He is one of four riders who come on the scene shortly. Christ is not one of four of anything – He is everything!

But many nations do not buy into this false peace. They do not readily give up their sovereignty and allegiance to this new leader who would absorb them into a one-world government. There are few things that the United States treasures more than freedom. It was founded on freedom, and will initially resist the Antichrist and his forces. And you know what happens when they resist. "*And when he had opened the second seal, I heard the second beast* [living one] *say, "Come and see"* (Revelation 6:3). The Antichrist has barely put his peace initiative in place when Jesus breaks the second seal. "*And there went out another horse that was red: and power was given to him that sat thereon to take peace from the earth, and that they should kill one another: and there was given unto him a great sword*" (Revelation 6:4).

The red horse signifies war and bloodshed. This is the result of many nations not accepting the rule of the Antichrist. And so, his true character is revealed. He is not a man of peace, but a man of violence! It says, "*power was given to him to take peace from the earth.*" I Thessalonians 5:2-3a had this very time in mind. Paul writes: "*For yourselves know perfectly that the Day of the Lord so cometh as a thief in the night. For when they shall say, Peace and safety; then sudden destruction cometh upon them …*". Millions of people have died in wars since the beginning of time. But in this awful scene, billions will die according to the Scriptures. It is beyond our comprehension.

Some of the nations did not rally around the Antichrist, and so he must bring them into submission. Is America one of them? I cannot help but wonder. I am not a prophet of doom, but there is one thing that we must consider. The United States is not mentioned in end time prophecy. There could be several reasons for this:

1) It is possible the United States has already fallen at this point, and is not in existence in the final days as a super power. This could happen overnight if the enormous debt bubble of the U.S. were to burst.
2) With the bellicose tyrants around the world threatening a nuclear holocaust, any country can be brought to their knees rather quickly.
3) The United States voluntarily gives up its sovereignty to one central authority as most of the nations of Europe are now doing, an authority that eventually will be headed up by the Antichrist.
4) The United States, weakened at the Rapture and the disappearance of most of its rock solid leadership, is therefore subdued and whipped into submission by the Antichrist.

Some religious leaders tell their congregations that Israel as a nation has been abandoned by God, and that the United States is now the "new Israel," and is therefore the recipient of all of the promises that were made in the Old Testament to Israel. This is known as "Replacement Theology."[4]

In II Timothy 4:3 (ESV), it says: *"For the time is coming when people will not endure sound teaching, but having itching ears they will accumulate for themselves teachers who suit their own passions."* These messages are popular, especially among TV evangelists, as they preach a shallow message that sounds good but has no substance. Sin is never mentioned, the blood of Jesus is never mentioned, and the need for repentance is never mentioned.

There is one other thing I want to point out before we leave the second seal. It says that the rider on the red horse has a sword. The Greek word for sword is "romphaia." When the Roman army was marching off to war, they carried a romphaia, a sword at their side. But here, the Greek word for sword that this rider is carrying is "machaira." It is the kind of weapon that can be hidden, concealed beneath the coat. It is the kind of weapon that would be used by an assassin to slit someone's throat. So this warfare will not only be armies going against each other, but also, there will be murder and assassination everywhere, just the type of warfare that is so popular in the Middle East today. The red horseman will bathe the earth in blood!

Now we come to the opening of the third seal as we begin with verse 5, chapter 6 of the

Revelation: *"And when he had opened the third seal, I heard the third beast* [living one] *say, Come and see."* The words "and see" are not in the earliest manuscripts. *"And I beheld, and lo a black horse; and he that sat on him had a pair of balances in his hand."* What usually follows a devastating war? Famine, starvation and run-away prices! This horse will be black, the color of grief and mourning and devastation.

The first horseman had a bow; the second a sword; and this one has a pair of balances or scales. But, believe it or not, this symbolizes a great weapon! We will see later that the Antichrist controls the food system so that no one can buy or sell without his permission. But here, coming off of a devastating war, the black horse and the scales are a picture of worldwide famine and starvation.

The Great Depression of the 1930's is the closest thing the United States has ever come to starvation. I have heard my Dad talk about it: the soup lines and the bread lines. In the middle of the Depression, comedians tried to make America laugh and forget their troubles. One of comedian Eddie Cantor's famous lines was this: when someone wanted a room on the top floor of a hotel, the clerk would always ask, "For sleeping or jumping?"

The closest I relate to this is the ration stamps we had during WW II for meat and other staples. We have not known starvation in this country. But today we have severe famine in Angola, Ethiopia, Rwanda, Somalia, North Korea and many others. UNICEF says that now 11% of the world's population is facing hunger and starvation and this is on the rise.[5] But as bad as that is, it does not hold a candle to the conditions that will exist when the third seal is broken. How bad will it be? *"And I heard a voice in the midst of the four beasts say, a measure of wheat for a penny, and three measures of barley for a penny; and see thou hurt not the oil and the wine"* (Revelation 6:6).

The word translated measure means just enough wheat to make one meal. A measure would equal sixteen of our American ounces. The penny or "denarius" was a full day's wages. In other words, it will take a full day's wages for one meal. And this meal must be shared by the whole family! A full day's wages for one meal, that is, if you are going to eat wheat. Now, if you will settle for barley, the food usually reserved for animals, you can get three meals for a day's work. We think that prices are exorbitant now. Prices will be unprecedented in the days of the Tribulation.

"But see thou hurt not the oil and the wine" (verse 6b). The oil and the wine are put in contrast with the wheat and the barley. The wheat and the barley are the food of the poor, almost out of reach; but the food and luxuries of the rich, are not even touched. The poor can barely get by; the rich are no better off. Ezekiel says of this period: "[The rich] *shall cast their silver in the streets, and their gold shall be removed: their silver and their gold shall not be able to deliver them in*

the day of the wrath of the LORD: they shall not satisfy their souls, neither fill their bowels: because it is the stumbling block of their iniquity" (Ezekiel 7:19).

Scripture says, *"Go to now, ye rich men, weep and howl for your miseries that shall come upon you. Your riches are corrupted, and your garments are moth-eaten. Your gold and silver is cankered; and the rust of them shall be a witness against you, and shall eat your flesh as it were fire. Ye have heaped treasure together for the last days"* (James 5:1-3). No wonder Jesus said, *"Lay not up for yourselves treasures on earth, where moth and rust doth corrupt, and where thieves break through and steal: But lay up for yourselves treasures in Heaven, where neither moth nor rust doth corrupt, and where thieves do not break through nor steal: For where your treasure is, there will your heart be also"* (Matthew 6:19-21). And all this devastation and all this worldwide famine, plays right into the hands of the Antichrist. We will see that when we get to the 13th chapter of Revelation. It says, *"And no one could buy or sell anything without that mark, which was either the name of the Beast or the number representing his name"* (Revelation 13:17 NLT). Hunger is the basic human need, and the Antichrist will use it to his advantage as a means of motivating people to give him absolute allegiance.

This brings us to the fourth seal. *"And when he had opened the fourth seal, I heard the voice of the fourth beast say, Come and see. And I looked, and behold a pale horse: and his name that sat on him was Death, and Hell followed with him. And power was given unto them over the fourth part of the earth, to kill with the sword, and with hunger, and with death, and with the beasts of the earth"* (Revelation 6:7-8). Let me clear up a technicality here. It says that the fourth rider is named Death, and Hell followed him. Actually, the correct translation is that Hades followed the rider, not Hell. We mentioned earlier that the Old Testament place of the dead was called in the Hebrew, "Sheol" and in the Greek, "Hades." That is where the people's souls went when they died whether they were a child of God or not. The believers did not go to Heaven immediately because the penalty or remission of their sins by the blood of Christ had not yet taken place. Their bodies went into the ground, and their spirits went to a holding place of the dead called Sheol. My mother used to say, "They were saved on credit." The payment for their sins was to be made later at the cross.

In verse 8, we see that the fourth seal brings forth this rider whose name is Death, and he is followed closely behind by Hades – which since the cross only has one compartment that contains the souls of the damned. Death will claim the body, and for the unsaved Hades will claim the soul. And this rider, Death, is given the power to kill one-fourth of the inhabitants of the earth with four judgments: war (or the sword), hunger (or famine), death (or disease) and wild beasts (violence).

In Matthew 24:7, Jesus said this period will be characterized by war, famine and pestilences. In Ezekiel 14:21, the prophet mentions these same plagues: sword, hunger, pestilence and beasts.

People say peace, but the sword is coming. People cry prosperity, but famine is coming. People boast of advances in medical science, but pestilence is coming. These beasts or wild creatures will help to rapidly spread diseases. Aids or the "green-monkey virus" has already killed millions of people worldwide. The rat flea virus spread the Bubonic Plague all across Europe in the 1300's. It was called the Black Death, and before it ran its course, 25 million people lay dead in its path.[6] The head of the World Health Organization said two decades ago, "We are standing on the brink of a global crisis of infectious diseases. During the past 20 years at least 30 new diseases have emerged to threaten the lives of millions of people, and for many of these diseases, there are no treatments, no cure and no vaccine."[7] Dark days are ahead for the earth dwellers.

Notice that even the color of the horse that Death is riding is pale. The Greek word is "chloros" from which we get our word chloroform. It is the pale green color of a rotting corpse. My mission is to warn you of this impending danger, and to urge you to make sure that you have put your trust in Jesus. If so, you will be in that group that the Lord refers to when He says, *"Because you have kept my word about patient endurance, I will keep you from the hour of trial that is coming on the whole world, to try those who dwell on the earth"* (Revelation 3:10 ESV).

Let us look at a summary of the seals as they are opened. The scene is in Heaven. Jesus is opening a seven-sealed book that contains the judgments that will redeem the earth. As each seal is broken, a specific judgment is loosed. The first seal brought forth a rider with a bow, and he is on a white horse. This pictures the Antichrist and the false peace he will bring upon the earth. The peace is short-lived. Jesus opens the second seal and a rider comes forth on a red horse. He is brandishing a sword, and this pictures the bloody and violent war that will engulf the entire world. The third seal is opened. A rider with scales in his hand, riding on a black horse comes forth. This pictures the famine and starvation that follows such a world war. The fourth seal is broken, and coming on the scene is a rider on a pale horse. His name is Death, and he is followed closely by Hades. What a terrible time to be on the earth. Thank God, as believers, we will have been transported to Heaven before this calamity strikes. In other words, these judgments are for the earth dwellers – those who have settled down here and want no part of Heaven.

Before we get into the breaking of the fifth seal, I want to give you a summary of how we got to this point in time. For 1,500 years before the Cross, God was dealing in a covenant relationship with his chosen people Israel. He first made this known to Abraham (Genesis 12:1-3). This promise was repeated to Abraham no less than 6 times. (Genesis 12:7; 13:14-17; 15:1-6; 15:18-21; 17:1-8; 22:17-18).

Later God reconfirmed this covenant through Abraham's son, Isaac (Genesis 26:1-5), and his son, Jacob (Genesis 28:10-17). Jacob's name was subsequently changed to Israel (Genesis 35:10). He had 12 sons that later became known as the "children of Israel." God gave His chosen people

His holy law, and declared that if they obeyed it, they would be blessed beyond imagination. But if they did not, if they were disobedient and turned to the false gods of the surrounding nations, He would no longer protect them and disaster would come their way. Further He would scatter them across the nations (Deuteronomy 4:27-31), and then one day, He would restore them to their land, and fulfill every promise He had made to them (Jeremiah 16:14-15). Israel completely broke down under every test. And in accordance to His word, ten tribes were defeated and carried away by the monarchs of Assyria led by Tiglath-Pileser III and Shalmaneser in 722 B.C. In 586 B.C., the remaining two tribes were conquered by Babylon under King Nebuchadnezzar, and carried away as slaves to the land of Babylon which is present-day Iraq.

After 70 years of captivity, a remnant returned to Jerusalem, and rebuilt the walls and the Temple as predicted by Daniel the Prophet (Daniel 9:25). It was their descendants who were living in Israel when Jesus was born in Bethlehem. The prophet Daniel said there would be seventy "sevens" that would occur before God's plan to redeem the earth and accomplish all the events listed therein. The "seventy sevens" (490) as described in Daniel chapter 9 were like a lock on the treasure chest of history. If one can determine if this number 490 is weeks, months or years, he will find the key to open this treasure chest of information.

If I had to pick out one verse in all of Daniel that is key to understanding the end times, it would be chapter 9, verse 24. At first, it looks difficult to understand, but if you will take it slowly step by step, and absorb what it is saying, you will have an understanding of the time frame of end time events that will exceed 99% of what the average Christian knows about it. And when you see it clearly, you will agree it fits like a glove!

Because it is so important that I am going to present Daniel 9:24 in three different versions. First, the King James Version: "*Seventy weeks are determined upon thy people and upon the Holy City, to finish the transgression, and to make an end of sins, and to make reconciliation for iniquity, and to bring in everlasting righteousness, and to seal up the vision and prophecy, and to anoint the most Holy.*" Next, the New International Version: "*Seventy sevens are decreed for your people and your Holy City to finish transgression, to put an end to sin, to atone for wickedness, to bring in everlasting righteousness, to seal up vision and prophecy and to anoint the most holy.*" And finally, the New Living Translation: "*A period of seventy sets of seven has been decreed for your people and your Holy City to put down rebellion, to bring an end to sin, to atone for guilt, to bring in everlasting righteousness, to confirm the prophetic vision, and to anoint the Most Holy place.*"

So, the KJV says "seventy weeks," the NIV says "seventy sevens," and the NLT says "seventy sets of seven." To understand this, one must look at the word for seven in Hebrew. It is "shabua." It is a generic term that means seven – like our word dozen means twelve.

The "70 weeks" in the KJV is very confusing because the original Hebrew is NOT saying 70 weeks. It is saying 70 sevens or 70 sets of 7. What are these sevens? Are they days? Are they weeks? Are they years? We will come back to that in a minute. But first notice that, whatever amount of time it turns out to be, this is the amount of time that is "determined upon thy people" (Daniel 9:24). "Thy people" of course is Daniel's people – Israel. So, a certain amount of time was decreed by God in which certain things are to be accomplished relating to Israel or putting it another way, things that must come to pass relating to God's chosen people.

What does Gabriel say that is going to happen during this specific period of time during these mysterious 70 sets of seven? There are six things that will be accomplished (Daniel 9:24). You can readily see that these things cannot be accomplished without Christ's return.

1) **"To finish the transgression."** Israel had been transgressing God's law since the days of Moses – and this transgression will stop.

2) **"To make an end of sin."** Not only is Israel going to stop sinning, God is going to put an end to sin, period! Romans 11:26-27 says: *"And so all Israel shall be saved: as it is written, There shall come out of Zion the Deliverer, and shall turn away ungodliness from Jacob* (Israel): *For this is my covenant unto them, when I shall take away their sins."*

3) **"To make reconciliation for iniquity."** God is not just going to put an end to sin; He is going to provide a payment for sin that makes reconciliation with Him possible.

4) **"To bring in everlasting righteousness."** He is going to bring in a Kingdom in which righteousness prevails.

5) **"To seal up the vision and prophecy."** That is, to bring all these prophesies to their sure and complete fulfillment.

6) **"To anoint the most holy,"** or as the NLT correctly says, **"To anoint the Most Holy Place."** With the end of sinning among Daniel's people, and the bringing in of righteousness, a new Jewish Temple will be built and anointed. This Temple will be set aside for worship in the place where it has always been – on Mt. Zion in Jerusalem.

So we find that all six of these prophecies will be fulfilled when Israel receives and accepts its Messiah, and it will happen during this time period of 70 sets of 7. Now that we see WHAT is going to happen, we want to look at the time frame in which it happens. We have already said that in Daniel 9:24, the Hebrew word for week is shabua, and it simply means 7 like our word dozen means 12. So seventy sets of sevens is the time frame. It could be talking about days, weeks, or years. So seventy sets of seven is 490 of something (70 x 7 = 490).

If my pastor, Bro. Jim, announced plans for our new multimillion dollar sanctuary, and all he said was, "It will be finished in the time frame of 2 dozen, did he mean 24 days? 24 weeks? 24 months? or 24 years? You would have to use common sense. You would rule out 24 days and 24 weeks and 24 years. They would be improbable. But 24 months would be reasonable.

Let me give you a different illustration. If you had an old treasure chest with a big lock on it, and you had a handful of keys, and you tried each one without success, but then you tried one funny shaped key and presto – the lock opened. You would therefore conclude that the key was made for that lock. So let us try various amounts of time with these shabuas or sevens – and see if the lock opens. To save time, I will tell you, I have already tried 490 days – 490 weeks – 490 months – and I did not find anything in Israel's history that remotely comes close to what Gabriel said would be accomplished during these 70 sets of seven. But, when you use years, you come to an astonishing conclusion. And remember, Daniel has just been thinking about years since Israel's 70 years of captivity was running out (Daniel 9:20). Let me show you an Old Testament passage where the word shabua (translated "week" by the KJV) means 7 years, and it will confirm our premise.

In Genesis 29, we read that Laban had two daughters. Jacob wanted to marry the youngest, Rachel. He worked for Laban seven years for the right to marry her. But Laban pulled a fast one. He switched daughters on Jacob at the last minute. Jacob was furious when he found out. "You tricked me!" he yelled. Laban said, "Hold on – our custom is that we never marry off the youngest daughter (Rachel) first." Now listen to the words of Laban: *"Fulfill her week, and we will give thee this also for the service which thou shalt serve with me yet seven other years"* (Genesis 29: 27). In other words, "work seven more years and Rachel is yours." Genesis 29:28-29 says that Jacob worked seven more years in order to marry Rachel. So there is a precedent that a shabua was seven years. So let us proceed on the basis that we have 70 sets of 7 – or 490 years in which God is going to accomplish those six things we mentioned earlier, including providing a full penalty for sin and putting an end to it, and bringing in everlasting righteousness.

First, I would call attention to the fact that in Daniel 9:25 these 490 years are divided into three groups: the first is 49 years, the second is 334 years, and the third is 7 years. Look at verse 25 (NLT): *"Now listen and understand! Seven sets of seven (49 years) plus sixty-two sets of seven (434 years) will pass from the time the command is given to rebuild Jerusalem until the Anointed One comes. Jerusalem will be rebuilt with streets and strong defenses, despite the perilous times."* Notice that this leaves one week of seven years remaining of the original 490 years.

The grammatical structure in Hebrew is a little difficult to follow, but here is what it is saying: during the first 49 years, the city and the wall of Jerusalem will be rebuilt. Then after the next 434 years, the Messiah will come and be killed; 49 years and 434 years total 483 years, so we still have seven years remaining which we will talk about in a moment.

We are going to use years for this time frame, and see if that key opens the lock. But when do these years begin? When do we begin counting the 490 years? That question is crucial! You must begin counting at the right place. Verse 25 of Daniel 9 tells us when these 490 years begin. It says, *"From the time the command is given to rebuild Jerusalem ...."*. These 490 years begin to run when the decree is given to rebuild Jerusalem. Searching the Scriptures, we find there were 4 decrees in the Bible that relate to the rebuilding of the Holy City, and if you start from the wrong one, you will wind up totally confused.

In 536 B.C., King Cyrus of Persia issued a decree that would allow the Jews to go back to Jerusalem and rebuild their Temple. It did not authorize the rebuilding of the walls and the city (Ezra 1:1-2). In Ezra 5: 9-13, we find that a question arose as to whether the Jews really had the authority or not to rebuild their Temple. So the king at the time, Darius the Mede, issued the second decree reaffirming what King Cyrus had decreed earlier. It did not authorize the rebuilding of the walls or the city – only the Temple. We find a third decree was issued in 477 B.C. by King Artaxerxes of Persia in Ezra 7:16-24, but it was only to pay for accessories in the Temple and for related priestly services. Nothing was authorized regarding the building of the city or the walls.

However, look at Nehemiah 2:1. It nails down the exact time: in the month of Nisan in the 20th year of the reign of Artaxerxes. Historians are generally in agreement that the year was 445 B.C. Nehemiah enters the king's presence, and the king asks Nehemiah, "Why the long face?" And Nehemiah replies, "And [Nehemiah] *said unto the king, Let the king live forever: why should not my countenance be sad, when the city, the place of my fathers' sepulchers, lieth waste, and the gates thereof are consumed with fire?"* (Nehemiah 2:3).

The king asked Nehemiah (verse 4), "What are you requesting?" And Nehemiah answered the king, *"If it please Your Majesty, and if you are pleased with me, your servant, send me to Judah to rebuild the city where my ancestors are buried"* (Nehemiah 2:5 NLT). So Nehemiah requested from the king that he be permitted to return and rebuild his ancestral home, Jerusalem.

The king empathized with Nehemiah so much so that he immediately signed a decree authorizing this request, and also sent a letter to the keeper of the king's forest that says the Jews may have all the timber and supplies they need to rebuild the walls and the gates to the city (Nehemiah 2:6-8 NLT). So we have our starting point for the 490 years! Scripture is always accurate because the ultimate author is God and not man!

You might not catch the significance of Nehemiah 2:10 (ESV): *"But when Sanballat the Horonite and Tobiah the Ammonite servant heard this, it displeased them greatly that someone had come to seek the welfare of the people of Israel."* And just as the terrorists today want to disrupt the peace proceedings in the Middle East, the Ammonites planned to halt the rebuilding of Jerusalem's wall. Why? Because it would put a stop to their terrorist raids on innocent Jews inside the city.

Remember what Daniel said about the rebuilding of the wall? Look again at the last phrase in Daniel 9:25: " .... *the street shall be built again, and the wall, even in troublous times."* Nehemiah recorded the exciting story of how he and his men built the wall with their weapons at their side to defend against surprise attacks (Nehemiah 4:13). The historian Josephus wrote that when the Ammonites, Moabites and Samaritans heard that the building was proceeding, they lay snares to disrupt the building process. They slew many of the Jews, and sought how to kill Nehemiah as well.[8]

Nehemiah made the workmen labor with their armor on – with a sword at their side and a shield nearby, and a watchman with a trumpeters stationed around the city to sound an alarm when the enemy attacked (Nehemiah 4:18-20). It is no wonder that Daniel wrote in Daniel 9:25: " *…. the street and wall will be built in troublous times.*" So the Temple and walls and the city were rebuilt during the first 49 years of the 490 years.

For the next roughly 400 years, there was no prophet in the land – no voice from Heaven. Only silence. Theologians have called this period "the 400 silent years." But then, in the fullness of time (Galatians 4:4), and in accordance with over 100 prophecies in the Old Testament, the Messiah was born as a baby in Bethlehem. We call it the Incarnation – when God became Man! He laid aside His royal robes of glory, and entered the human race, though He was 100% Divine and 100% Man. Why did He do this? He did it to save as many as would trust Him as their Savior. Scripture says that *"For God so loved the world, that He gave His only begotten Son, that whosoever believeth in Him should not perish, but have everlasting life"* (John 3:16). Truly, " *…. the Son of Man came to seek and to save the lost"* (Luke 19:10 ESV).

Now look at verse 26 of Daniel chapter 9 (NLT): *"After this period of sixty-two sets of seven, the Anointed One will be killed, appearing to have accomplished nothing, and a ruler will arise whose armies will destroy the city and the Temple. The end will come with a flood, and war and its miseries are decreed from that time to the very end."* Scripture said that during the first 49 years from the decree in 445 B.C., the streets and wall would be rebuilt in troublesome times. And it was. Then it says after another 62 sets of 7s – or 434 years – the Messiah would be "cut off" or killed; but not for Himself. And He did not die for Himself!

If you go forward on the calendar this 49 years plus 434 years from the king's decree to rebuild the city, you will come to the date of about 38 A.D. But all the encyclopedias tell us that the Romans made an error in calculating their calendar. That is why Bible scholars tell us that Jesus was really born in 4 B.C. based on our calendar. So, this moves our calculation on the calendar back to 34 A.D. Finally, we need to make an adjustment for the fact that the Jews use a 360 day lunar calendar instead of the 365 day calendar we inherited from the Romans.

Sir Robert Anderson was Assistant Commissioner of Scotland Yard, and a devout Christian scholar in his own right. Using the calculations based on Scripture passages from Daniel 9 and Nehemiah 2, he concluded that when Jesus rode into Jerusalem on Palm Sunday, it had been exactly 483 years from the time that King Artaxerxes issued the decree to rebuild Jerusalem![9]

Verse 26 of Daniel chapter 9 says that after these 69 weeks, i.e., after the 483 years, the Anointed One, literally meaning the Messiah, shall be cut off (killed). As the KJV says, "*but not for Himself."* So within a week of Jesus' entry into Jerusalem as recorded in Matthew 21, Jesus was crucified – killed – cut off – but not for Himself! It was for our sins. And the last part of verse 26 says that the people of the prince who is to come will destroy the city and the Temple. Here is the key: it says the people of the prince who is to come will destroy the city and the Temple. We know from secular history that the Romans destroyed the city and the Temple in 70 A.D.[10] Consequently, it is the Romans who are the people of the prince (Antichrist) who is yet to come that gives credence to the view that the Antichrist will head up a revived Roman Empire.

At this point we have covered 69 weeks of Daniel's 70 weeks or shabuas. There is one week left – one seven year period remaining of the original 490 years. And we have shown that these 490 years relate to a time when God is dealing directly with the nation of Israel. Those liberal churches who claim that God has washed his hands of Israel, and therefore the Church is the recipient of all the Old Testament prophecies given to Israel, will not understand or agree with my next statement.

When the Jewish people rejected Jesus as their Messiah, God temporarily set them aside and directed His evangelistic program toward the Gentiles (Romans 11:25). This was initially done through the Apostle Paul who was known as the "Apostle to the Gentiles" (Romans 11:13). As a result of the Jews' rejection of their Messiah, the pendulum on God's prophetic time clock for the Jewish nation was temporarily stopped. The Church was founded on the day of Pentecost which many theologians call the beginning of "The Church Age" or the "Age of Grace." This period has effectively run for the last 2,000 years.

This Church Age will come to a close when the Rapture occurs, when Christ suddenly returns in the air to gather His Church unto Himself (I Thessalonians 4:13-18). At this point the pendulum on God's prophetic time clock will again be set in motion to count down the final seven years remaining of Daniel's 490 years as God again begins to deal directly with His chosen people, Israel.

Scripture indicates that this seven year period will not begin to run until the Jews are back in their homeland – which they are now – and the prophetic clock will not start until the *"....complete number of Gentiles comes to Christ"* (Romans 11:25 NLT). This could occur at any time. When the last person in the Church Age (from the day of Pentecost to the Rapture) accepts Jesus, the Rapture will occur, and the last "week" of the seven years of Daniel's 70 weeks will begin to run. Shortly thereafter, the Antichrist will rise to power and will sign a seven year peace treaty between the Jews and Arabs. This appears to be the starting point of the seven year Tribulation Period, which also corresponds to the infamous 70th week of Daniel.

Verse 27 of Daniel 9 tells us what the Antichrist is going to do. *"And he shall confirm the covenant with many for one week* [that is, he will make a peace treaty between the Jews and Arabs for seven years so the Jews can rebuild their Temple], *and in the midst of the week* [that is, after 3½ years] *he* [the Antichrist] *shall cause the sacrifice and the oblation to cease* [the

Antichrist is going to break his covenant, and stop their Temple worship and sacrifices] *and for the overspreading of abominations he shall make it desolate, even until the consummation, and that determined shall be poured upon the desolate."*

The last part of this passage is best understood by Jesus' comments in Matthew 24:15: *"When ye therefore shall see the ABOMINATION OF DESOLATION, spoken of by Daniel the Prophet, stand in the holy place (whoso readeth, let him understand)."* The Antichrist himself will stand in the holy Temple in Jerusalem, and proclaim that he is the true Messiah, the Holy One of God, and that will be the greatest abomination ever committed in the earth. But praise God, Jesus said, *"And when these things begin to come to pass, then look up, and lift up your heads; for your redemption draweth nigh* (Luke 21:28).

Because the Rapture could happen at any time, think for a minute of all the chaos that will be going on if suddenly all the Christians are removed from this earth. This is really going to happen one day. Are you prepared? You say, "Yes, I am ready to meet the Lord." But that is not what I have in mind. Is your house prepared? When the unbelievers take over your house, will there be any materials to help them find the truth? Do you have Bibles in prominent places? Someone else will be using your house, because if you are a Christian, it will be empty. So leave a guide for them. On our coffee table in the living room, there is a Bible. Next to it there is a DVD entitled, *Did Many People Disappear?* It is about an hour long, and it gives precise instructions to those left behind as to what has happened and how they can survive the Tribulation and get to Heaven.[11]

Just inside the entry way in our house, we have a beautifully framed message on the wall. It reads:

"To Whom It May Concern ~ This Household is looking for the imminent return of our Lord. When it occurs ~ as it surely will ~ that in a day, in a night, or in an hour, it is discovered that millions of people are missing and this home is found empty, then know that there has taken place that which the Apostle Paul wrote about in I Thessalonians 4:14-17 [Reference is in the Christian's Holy Bible]. It will mean that Christ has called out of this world all the saved, which were we of this household. Do not search for us. We will be back in seven years when Christ comes with His saints to destroy the Antichrist and the World Governments and set up His kingdom. Beware of the Antichrist who will come with lying wonders. Do not be deceived by the Antichrist and do not let the Antichrist put his mark on your forehead or hand. Read carefully these passages of Holy Scripture and pray and understand: Revelation, 13th Chapter and the chapters following. Also the prophecies in the book of Daniel ~ God is right now willing to help you. Pray and ask God to forgive you of your sins. Know that Jesus Christ is the Son of God who died on the cross to pay for your sins. Ask Jesus to be your Lord and Savior. Believe, confess and accept in faith that you are now a child of God. May God bless you and give you the courage to defend your decision that Jesus Christ is Lord. We will be Rejoicing and waiting for you in Heaven."[12]

We have already seen four judgments hit the earth as the four seals are broken. Now the fifth seal is about to be opened. The scene shifts from earth to Heaven. *"And when he had opened the fifth seal, I saw under the altar the souls of them that were slain for the Word of God, and for the testimony which they held: And they cried with a loud voice, saying, How long, O Lord, holy and true, dost thou not judge and avenge our blood on them that dwell on the earth?"* (Revelation 6:9-10). Who are these martyred saints who are crying out? They cannot be the Church for they are already in Heaven, represented by the crowned elders before the first seal is broken (Revelation 4:4).

The 11th chapter of Romans makes it clear who these martyrs are. It says that after the fullness of the Gentiles has come in, that is, after the Age of Grace is passed and the Church is removed to Heaven at the Rapture, the blindness will pass away from Israel, and they will realize that Jesus is truly their Messiah. They will mourn for Him and for themselves as they realize their true condition for rejecting their Messiah, the Lord Jesus Christ (Revelation 1:7).

Thousands will be saved during this first part of the Tribulation, but most of them will be martyred – killed for their belief in Jesus Christ. It will cost the life of most who name the name of Christ during the Tribulation Period, and this horrible intensity will increase during the last 3½ years which Jesus calls the Great Tribulation.

Someone might ask, "Will anyone be saved during the Tribulation Period?" The answer is an emphatic yes! A great multitude will be saved, but those who do place their faith in Christ will pay a severe price for doing so, generally with their life. If people will not give their hearts to Christ now while it is relatively easy, when the Tribulation judgment sets in it will be extremely difficult to do this. There will be great pressure to deny Christ. In Matthew 24, Jesus was giving many details about the end times, and He said, *"Then shall they deliver you up to be afflicted, and shall kill you: and ye shall be hated of all nations for My name's sake"* (Matthew 24:9). And those souls who prove faithful unto death are pictured here under the altar. The Bible says of them *".... slain for the Word of God, and for the testimony which they held"* (Revelation 6:9b).

Perhaps you have heard of "soul sleep." This is the belief that the body and soul stay in the grave until Christ returns. Scripture does not confirm this. When a believer dies, his or her body goes into the grave to await the resurrection, but their spirit goes to be with the Lord. Paul tells us *".... to be absent from the body and to be present with the Lord"* (II Corinthians 5:8b). The saints mentioned in verses 9 and 10 were killed during the first part of the Tribulation, and their souls are not sleeping – they are in Heaven under the altar. They are conscious, and are pleading with God to avenge their death.

A question is often raised, "In Heaven, will we remember things that happened on earth?"

Probably not everything, but in a limited sense, we will. Here is a case where these martyred saints remembered what happened to them on earth, and they want justice for the Antichrist and his henchmen! Another question is, "How will these on earth who are saved during this Tribulation hear the Gospel with all the Christians gone?" Some will read Bibles that have been left in the houses. Some will hear tapes or watch Christian videos which were left behind in prominent places. The vast majority will hear the Gospel preached by 144,000 evangelists and two special witnesses who the Lord will send to preach the Gospel (Revelation chapters 7 and 11). We will hear more about them in the following chapters.

Notice that these souls in verse 10 do not pray as Stephen did when he was being stoned in the seventh chapter of Acts, *"Lord, lay not this sin to their charge"* (Acts 7:60). John did not see these saints tortured and murdered by the Antichrist and his followers. He only sees the results – thousands of souls under the altar crying out to God, " .... *how long, Oh, Lord, holy and true, dost thou not judge and avenge our blood on them that dwell on the earth?"* (Revelation 6:10). The Age of Grace has passed, and they wonder when God is going to give those God-haters what is coming to them.

How does God answer their question as to when He is going to avenge their deaths? His reply is somewhat surprising. The Book of Job teaches us that God wants us to trust Him, not ask a bunch of questions. He does not reply with a direct answer to these martyred saints. Nor does He rebuke them for asking for retribution. He simply ignores their question, and tells them to rest. In a polite way, He implies it is none of their business. Their enemies will be taken care of at the proper time.

"And white robes were given unto every one of them; and it was said unto them, that they should rest yet for a little season, until their fellow servants also and their brethren, that should be killed as they were, should be fulfilled" (Revelation 6:11). God responds by giving them white robes, which are symbolic of their righteous acts (Revelation 19:8). Unlike the raptured believers who have their glorified bodies, these martyred saints have to wait until the end of the Tribulation before their bodies are resurrected. So critics ask, "How can a soul wear a white robe?" Well, it does not say these robes are nylon, or cotton or polyester. I think it would be easy for God to create a "soul-robe" if He wants to. That is no problem! So God gives them white robes and He says, "Just rest a little while. The Tribulation must run its course, and there are still several years to go. Your brethren – your friends and fellow believers must be killed and will join you here. Trust me. I will take care of your enemies at the proper time!"

Why were these martyrs slain? The Greek word used for slain here is "sphazo." It is the slaying – the cutting – the terrible slaughter of a sacrifice. That is the word used here describing the death of these martyrs. To the world they were murdered, but to God they were offered as a sacrifice unto Him. They gave their lives for the Lord, and the Lord looked upon them as His martyrs, and they will be amply rewarded for all eternity.

II Thessalonians 1:7-8 says the Lord Jesus will be revealed from Heaven in flaming fire, taking vengeance on those that know not God. Why doesn't God stamp out evil immediately? He operates on a different level than we do. His ways are higher than our ways. We cannot understand the problem of suffering and pain and evil, but it is all part of His plan and He does not make mistakes.

The Book of Revelation follows in broad outline the 24th chapter of Matthew in which Jesus talks about events of the end times. He called the first 3½ years of the Tribulation "the beginning of sorrows," and the last 3½ years "the Great Tribulation." Previously in this sixth chapter, we saw four seals opened by Jesus, each one bringing judgments upon the unbelievers who live on the earth.

Up to now, basically the judgments have been for God to remove His hedge of protection, step back and let mankind inflict hurt upon one another under the direction of the Antichrist. The world has seen many false saviors who promised to deliver the world from sorrow. The Greek word for savior is "Soter" from whence comes the term "Soteriology" which is the study of things related to salvation. The lives of these so-called saviors throughout history – Napoleon, Hitler, Stalin, etc., without exception are written in blood, tears, war and death. The Antichrist will be no different except that his devastation will be far greater than those who have gone before him. In fact, Jesus said this period will be worse than anything before or after in the history of mankind.

With the opening of the next seal, the devastating action is going to accelerate. Man will not just be left to his own destructive devices. The action is going to pick up from now on as we see God take a more direct role in sending judgment after judgment upon the earth.

Remember, the souls who had been killed by the Antichrist are before the throne, and are pleading and crying to God: *".... O Sovereign Lord, holy and true, how long before you will judge and avenge our blood on those who dwell on the earth?"* (Revelation 6:10 ESV). What they are really saying is, "Oh God, we have just endured a terrible time. When are you going to triumph over evil, and bring in your everlasting Kingdom? We are ready for some divine action, O God!" And what does God do? God gives them white robes, and tells them to be patient because He will act at the proper time.

Then the Lamb breaks open the sixth seal and we see the results: *"And I beheld when He had opened the sixth seal, and, lo, there was a great earthquake; and the sun became black as sackcloth of hair, and the moon became as blood; and the stars of Heaven fell unto the earth, even as a fig tree casteth her untimely figs, when she is shaken of a mighty wind. And the Heaven departed as a scroll when it is rolled together; and every mountain and island were moved out of their places"* (Revelation 6:12-14).

An earthquake is a scary phenomenon. People are helpless. There are no places to run or hide. In recent years we have seen massive earthquakes in Salvador, Turkey and India which have resulted in the loss of thousands of lives. A pregnant woman knows that as she approaches the time of delivery, birth pangs increase in two ways: in frequency and intensity. Jesus said as we approach the end of the age, earthquakes will be like birth pangs – the closer we get to the return of Christ, earthquakes will increase in frequency and intensity.[13]

The Greek word for earthquake is seismos. Hal Lindsey says it literally means "a violent, catastrophic shaking." From it, we get our word seismograph – an instrument for recording earth tremors. David Jeremiah says this: "It is as if God has reached down to planet earth with His hands, and is shaking the earth, causing everything that is not tied down to become loose." The writer to the Hebrews says the day is coming when God is going to shake the earth and the earth will know it has been shook! (Hebrews 12:26).

God often uses an earthquake in connection with a momentous event. There was an earthquake when Moses was given the Ten Commandments. There was an earthquake when Jesus was crucified on the cross. And the Second Coming of Christ will be accompanied by a mighty earthquake. Here in Chapter 6, it appears that this earthquake will be the "granddaddy" of them all. Many commentators point out that the Book of Revelation was given in symbols, and there is truth in that. They say this earthquake is a symbol, and it pictures the complete breakdown of law and order in the society – and certainly that will happen. However, by the actions of the victims, this appears to be an actual earthquake. The sun becomes dark and the moon becomes as red as blood. Most crimes are committed at night. It is a known fact that darkness contributes to depression, and Satan and sin are often associated with darkness. The Greek word "aster", translated here as stars, can also be translated meteors. This could easily be a horrendous meteor shower that produces devastating results on the earth. No wonder, as we will see in a moment, men cry out for the rocks to fall on them.

Others think that John is recording this exactly as he sees it, not realizing that he is describing the results of a nuclear holocaust. The shaking of the earth – the resulting debris in the air causing the sunlight to be shut out – the fires burning all over the earth giving the moon a reddish effect – the mountains and islands moved out of their places – and the atmospheric heaven disappearing like a rolled-up scroll. Sounds like an apt description of a nuclear holocaust.

This is also described by Joel the prophet: *"I will cause wonders in the heavens and on the earth – blood and fire and pillars of smoke. The sun will be turned into darkness, and the moon will turn blood red before that great and terrible Day of the Lord arrives"* (Joel 2:30-31 NLT). The earthquake will scare the daylights out of them. *"Then the kings of the earth and the great ones and the generals and the rich and the powerful, and everyone, slave and free, hid themselves in the caves and among the rocks of the mountains"* (Revelation 6:15 ESV). No matter what a person's status is, they all will be so afraid they will hide in caves and among the rocks.

It is a strange phenomenon but a fact – when everything is going smoothly in life, most people have little regard for religion. But when a catastrophe strikes, such as happened on 9-11 in New York City, churches across the country are filled to capacity for several weeks. After America's tragedy in 2001, Ed Young, Senior Pastor of the Second Baptist Church in Houston said, "After 9-11 we had about twenty thousand people show up – the largest crowd in the history of our church. And when I walked on stage I looked around and said, 'Where have you guys been? Does it take something like this for you to show up at church?'"[14] And as these judgments were unleashed here in Chapter 6, the people reacted with one of the largest prayer meetings ever recorded. There is a problem, however. They are praying to the dumb rocks instead of to the Creator who made those rocks!

It is interesting to note that these people know where this judgment is coming from. They did not blame climate change; they did not blame creatures from outer space. They cried out to the rocks, *"Fall on us and hide us from the face of the One who sits on the throne* [the Father] *and from the wrath of the Lamb* [Jesus Christ]. *For the great day of their wrath has come, and who will be able to survive?"* (Revelation 6:16-17 NLT). They know they are being warned, but they do nothing about it. There is an old saying, "There are no atheists in foxholes." And during the Tribulation there will be no atheists when the time of God's wrath is turned loose as they will know who is behind this judgment!

Think about this paradox. A lamb is the most gentle of all animals on the face of the earth. This has led some people to think of Jesus as One who could never punish the ungodly. They conclude that eventually everyone will be saved, and there are several denominations that actually teach this very thing. A lady told me one time, "I just love that preacher on TV from Houston. He never mentions sin. He never mentions judgment. He only speaks of the love of God, and it makes me feel good." I gently reminded her that love is great because Scripture says God is love, and we would not be saved without the love of God. But that is just one side of the coin. That is just one side of His nature. Jesus had far more to say about judgment than He did about love. That is because He does not want anyone to experience the wrath of God.

We are reminded of this by the Apostle Peter, *"The Lord is not slow in keeping His promise, as some understand slowness. He is patient with you, not wanting anyone to perish, but everyone to come to repentance"* (II Peter 3:9 NIV). But everyone will not do that. We all have an awesome responsibility to warn people of these terrible judgments that lie ahead, and tell them that God's great love has provided a way of escape for them.

These people in chapter 6 know the score. You would think that they would fall on their faces and repent. Instead, they would rather curse God and die. Even John is astounded by this. After things heat up in the 9th chapter of this Book, John records, " *.... and yet they did not repent*" (Revelation 9:21). So sad! They are hard-hearted just like Pharaoh of Egypt. That story really used to bother me as to the fairness of it. God would send a plague, and Pharaoh would call Moses in and say, "I have had enough. I will let your people go." The KJV says, "*But the LORD hardened Pharaoh's heart, so that he would not let the children of Israel go*" (Exodus 10:20). I used to think, "Wait a minute. It is not right that Pharaoh wanted to do the right thing, but God hardened his heart, and the plagues kept coming!" But a close study of the original Hebrew according to Pastor Carey Daniel reveals this: the first several times, Pharaoh hardened his own heart. He went so far down the road and his heart was so hard, that God simply finished the job when it was evident that he was not going to repent.[15]

It is the same when a non-believer hears the Gospel for the first time. The Holy Spirit nudges them and woos them toward Christ. If the person says no, something happens inside their heart. The next time, it is easier for them to say no. If he or she does not break through that mindset and come to Christ, eventually the Holy Spirit does not come calling anymore. God says His Spirit will not always strive with man (Genesis 6:3). There comes a time when the Spirit will no longer tug at a person's heart. My pastor, Bro. Jim, said he stood by the bedside of a dying man, pleading with him to come to Christ. But the man's response was, "I want to, but I just can't." One would think that men under the judgment of God would be the first to cry out to God for mercy; but sadly that is not always the case.

The most notorious killer of a previous generation was John Dillinger. The FBI hunted him down like a rat. His picture was everywhere: public enemy No. 1. It is reported that he cut off the ends of his fingers to destroy any fingerprints, and he went through painful surgery to change the appearance of his face. But every noise, every door that opened, reminded him that justice was coming after him. It eventually caught up with him, and at age, 31 he was riddled with bullets by FBI agents.[16]

You would think that all this judgment and hopelessness would drive men to God, but only the grace of God can change a human heart, and save a human soul. Here is an awesome, but true statement by H. A. Ironside (paraphrased): "If the love of Calvary does not draw a man to God, no amount of punishment will ever do it."[17]

In the midst of this great day of wrath, the unbelievers cry out, "*For the great day of their wrath has come, and who will be able to survive?*" (Revelation 6:17 NLT). And the truth is, outside of Christ, no one! In fact, Jesus Himself said in Matthew 24:22a: "*And except those days should be shortened, there should no flesh be saved ....*". If the Tribulation Period lasted any longer than its prescribed time, no one would survive. But the period mercifully comes to an end when Christ comes back and announces that the kingdoms of this world have become the Kingdom of Christ.

This has been a busy chapter. We have seen the rider on the white horse, the red horse, the black horse and the pale green horse representing respectively a false peace, war, famine and death (Revelation 6:2-8). We have seen the souls under the altar who were martyred during this period for their faithfulness to Christ and for their testimony. They cry out to God, "Oh Lord, how much longer are you going to wait before you exact justice upon the earth?" (Revelation 6:9-10). Then God said, "Time Out – I am going to show you what awaits those infidels." And then God gives us a panoramic view of how He is going to literally shake the entire planet, affecting even the sun, the moon and the stars (Revelation 6:12-17). But a remnant will be protected by God until their mission is complete as we will see in the next chapter.

CHAPTER SEVEN

144,000 Jews Are Sealed for Protection

———————

Close to one-half of the Tribulation Period (3½ years) has run its course. The last half of the Tribulation is just around the corner. Things are about to get much worse – fast! The Antichrist is going to get more treacherous and belligerent. The judgments are about to become more intense. Persecutions and death are going to accelerate. And so, before this terrible period picks up steam and becomes even more terrible than it has been, God says, "Time out." There are some important things that He wants to do before these judgments increase and the Antichrist's persecutions get worse.

Consequently, Chapter 7 is like a parenthesis. God is stopping the action so that He can put in place certain things before the Tribulation begins. Verse 1 says: *"And after these things I saw four angels standing on the four corners of the earth, holding the four winds of the earth, that the wind should not blow on the earth, nor on the sea, nor on any tree."* This verse has long been derided as reflecting an ignorant concept of earth's structure – one that viewed the earth as flat and having four corners.

The charge is silly. God knows what He created.

Listen to Isaiah 40:22a (NLT): *"It is God who sits above the circle of the earth."* That was written thousands of years before people accepted the fact that the earth is round. That is, some people. Believe it or not, there is still in existence "The Flat Earth Society" that will argue with you till you are blue in the face that the earth is flat. Much of their arguments come from taking Biblical quotes out of context rather than drawing from science. This society was organized in the 1800's, and has had a checkered past. Recently it has fallen on hard times, and it is reported that it now has only a few thousand members.[1]

I think sensible people recognize that the quote "four corners of the earth" is simply an oft used expression of speech. It is still used today; people realize what it is. It is the same expression that a sailor or meteorologist would call the four quadrants of the compass or the four directions on a map. The expression "four winds of the earth" is common usage for north, south, east and west. The important thing is that this verse tells us that the angels were located in four different key positions on the earth, and it pictures a calming effect on the earth before judgment breaks forth.

God often uses angels to carry out His assignments. The Bible has a lot to say about angels, and this would be a good place to cover some of the highlights about them. Here is a good Bible trivia question that will stump the average Christian. The Bible gives the name of three angels. Who are they? Most people can answer one – Gabriel. A few more can name the second one – Michael. But the third angel's name will probably not come to mind – Lucifer.

People tend to put Lucifer opposite of Jesus, and forget that Lucifer is an angel. Jesus is deity, and as such, He is far superior to Lucifer. Lucifer (also known as Satan and the Devil) is a created being, albeit a powerful one. He might have been an archangel though Scripture does not call him one. An archangel appears to be one of great importance, but we are not told how many have this title. The word archangel occurs only twice in the Bible (I Thessalonians 4:16 and Jude 6) and only one angel (Michael) is specifically called an archangel. One noted theologian, Dr. Henry C. Thiessen, believes that Gabriel was probably an archangel. He wrote: "The archangels appear to have the specific responsibilities of protecting Israel (Daniel 10:13, 21; 12:1); of announcing the birth of the Savior (Luke 1:26-38); of defeating Satan and his angels in their attempt to kill the Man Child and the woman (Revelation 12:7-12); and of heralding the return of Christ for His own" (I Thessalonians 4:16-18).[2]

The creation of angels is included in Genesis 1:1: *"In the beginning God created the Heaven and the earth."* That includes the creation of everything. We also have the verse in Colossians 1:16 (NIV) which leaves no doubt about this: *"For by Him* [Christ] *all things were created: things in Heaven and on earth, visible and invisible, whether thrones or powers or rulers or authorities; all things were created by Him and for Him."* So, it is clear that angels are created beings. When were they created? We are not told specifically, but they were already present when God created the earth.

In case you did not know it, Genesis is not the oldest book in the Bible. The first five books of the Bible – Genesis, Exodus, Leviticus, Numbers and Deuteronomy, sometimes called "The Pentateuch" by Bible scholars, were recorded by Moses. God instructed and guided Moses in this process as he describes things and events that go back to the beginning of creation. But the oldest written manuscript is actually the Book of Job. In chapter 38, verses 4-7 of Job, it states that the sons of God (angels) shouted for joy when the foundations of the earth were laid. This is poetic language, but the picture is clear – the angels were present when the earth was formed.

How many angels are there? We are not for sure, but the Bible states that angels do not marry; they do not procreate. There are no indications that God ever created any more angels than He did originally. So we surmise that however many He created in the beginning, there is the same number today – thousands upon thousands. Hebrews 12:22 (NIV) states, *"But you have come to Mount Zion, to the heavenly Jerusalem, the city of the living God. You have come to thousands upon thousands of angels in joyful assembly."*

When the Romans came to arrest Jesus in the Garden of Gethsemane, Peter pulled his sword to protect his Master. But Jesus told him to put away his weapon. *"Do you think I cannot call on my Father, and He will at once put at my disposal more than twelve legions of angels?"*

(Matthew 26:53 NIV). That is about the number of fans that gather in the stadium to watch the Cowboys each week.

And Jesus did not say that was all the angels. That is just the number that was standing by in case He needed them. Daniel had a vision of God's throne, and here is what he saw: "…. *thousands upon thousands attended Him; ten thousand times ten thousand stood before Him*" (Daniel 7:10b NIV). That is 100 million! Anyway you figure it – that's a bunch of angels!

What about the nature of angels? What do they look like? Do they have wings, and are they dressed in white apparel? Realize that angels are spirits, and spirits are invisible to the human eye. They are not tied to a material body though sometimes God allows them to take on visible form. They are immortal, so they are not subject to illnesses.

It is common to see angels pictured as females in the movies and in advertisements. However, in the Bible, they are referred to as "sons of God" (Job 38:7). And almost every time they took on visible form, it was in the form of a man. The only exception is mentioned in Zechariah 5:7 which refers to a woman in a basket, and a few verses later, two women with wings. Most commentators agree that these were angels. In Isaiah 6:2 when Isaiah had his vision of the Temple, he saw seraphim. This is a type of angel which we will discuss later. They each had 6 wings. On another occasion, Ezekiel saw angels with four wings (Ezekiel 1:5). It is interesting to note that although angels have wings, they do not need wings to travel. They are spirit beings, and are not limited to time or space as we are. But God has made them visible at times for the encouragement and protection of His children to show that God is indeed looking out for our well-being.

Another phenomenon is that angels often appear as beings of dazzling light. When Mary Magdalene and the other Mary came to the empty tomb, they saw an angel. Here is their description: "*His appearance was like lightning, and his clothes were white as snow*" (Matthew 28:3 NIV).

What do the angels do for a living? What is their occupation? Well, they have 3 duties: 1) they keep the halos polished; 2) they keep the clouds fluffed up; and 3) they practice constantly on their harps. I am being facetious. Their first duty is to give praise and worship to God. That is what they were doing in the Christmas story, "*Suddenly a great company of the heavenly host appeared …. praising God and saying, "Glory to God in the highest …."* (Luke 2:13-14a NIV). In Revelation 19:6 (NIV), John describes a host of angels this way: "*Then I heard what sounded like a great multitude, like the roar of rushing waters and like the loud peals of thunder, shouting: 'Hallelujah! For our Lord God Almighty reigns.'*"

The second duty of angels is just as their name implies – God's messengers to bring announcements or to bring answers to our prayers. The angel Gabriel told Zechariah, the priest, that God had heard his prayers, and that a son would be born to Elizabeth who would be John the Baptist, the forerunner of the Christ (Luke 1:13). One of the most enlightening passages in the Bible regarding how God sometimes sends angels to answer our prayers is in the 10th chapter of Daniel. It also tells how that sometimes our answers are delayed, thanks to the evil angels (Daniel 10:12-13).

Another important duty of the angels is that of protection for God's children. The Apostle Peter was miraculously delivered from prison by an angel of the Lord in Acts 12 as a direct result of the Church coming together, and fervently praying for Peter's deliverance. We are told in Psalm 91:11 (ESV): *"For He will command His angels concerning you to guard you in all your ways."*

One of the most dramatic rescues in Scripture was when Daniel was facing a group of hungry lions. We are told how he was kept from harm by an angel sent by the Lord (Daniel 6:22). Comedians Amos & Andy in their popular radio show of a previous generation were discussing this, and Andy said, "The lions didn't hurt Daniel because they were old circus lions."Amos said, "Naw – it was B. C. – before circuses!"

Hebrews 1:14 says, *"Are they* [angels] *not all ministering spirits, sent forth to minister for them who shall be heirs of salvation?"* Sometimes, we use the word angels as a term of endearment – "You have been such an angel to me." One fellow said his wife is an angel. "She's always up in the air about something, she's always harping about the least little thing, and she never has an earthly thing to wear."

The Greek word for angel (angelos) means messenger. Most of the time when this word is used it is speaking about those heavenly created beings. From Isaiah 14:12 and Ezekiel 28:14, we find that Lucifer once held a prominent place among the angels. But pride entered his heart and he had designs on replacing God Himself. The result was that he was cast out of Heaven as well as one-third of the angels who pledged their allegiance to him (Revelation 12:4). Consequently, there are "good angels" and "evil angels." There are a few instances in Scripture where the writer is speaking about a human as a messenger (angelos), but for our purposes, we will be concentrating not on humans, but on those heavenly beings called "good angels", whose primary duties are to carry out the purposes of God.

In our current society, it seems like people around the world are obsessed with angels as never before. They are on lapel pins, necklaces, key chains and in your flower garden as statuettes. Go to any bookstore, be it Christian or not, and you will normally find whole shelves full of books on the topic of angels. The movies that come out of Hollywood are saturated with angels, though most of them showcase evil angels. In the last generation, it was *Rosemary's Baby,* and then *The Exorcist, Exorcist II, The Omen,* and today they are coming out faster than you can keep up with them. The New Age gurus have really zeroed in on angels. New Agers do not think much of God, but they love angels.

A popular book by Karen Goldman, a New Ager, says that you, too, can be an angel. Here is her quote: "We are all angels in training. You don't have to die to become an angel."[3] We are not angels. Hebrews 1:14 tells us that angels are ministering spirits sent to help those who are saved. Other New Agers have written self-help books that will enable you to control and manipulate angels so that they work to your benefit. I remember reading a book by a New Ager who wrote, "Angels are friendly, tame little deities, not the enflamed beings of the Bible." He went on to say, "We are all capable of walking down a street, and having a conversation with our angels. When you ask your angel for something, you can be sure that your prayers will be answered. Most people think that God is directing the angels, but it is WE that are giving them their assignments." Weird! Where do people come up with this nonsense?

God Himself is the one to whom we should pray – the One to whom we should look to for answers. Our trust and confidence should be only in Him! We are reminded in I Timothy 2:5 that there is only one Mediator between God and man, and that man is Jesus Christ.

Several times in Scripture we are privileged to see what happens when someone tries to attribute worship to an angel. This is forcibly brought out in Revelation 19:10a (NIV) when the Apostle John says, *"At this* [awesome vision] *I fell at the feet* [of this angel] *to worship him. But he said to me, 'Do not do it! I am a fellow servant with you .... Worship God!'"*

Many times we see little statuettes hanging in cars to protect the occupants from accidents like some kind of magic doll to ward off evil. God had a word for this in the Old Testament. He said, "You are praying to sticks and stones that are dead as a doornail instead of to the Creator who made those sticks and stones" (paraphrase of Deuteronomy 4:28).

We cannot go very far in the study of angels without asking, "Were all angels created to serve God?" Again, we refer back to Colossians 1:16b): *".... all things were created by Him* [Christ] *and for Him."* If this is true, what happened in the case of Satan? His name, Lucifer, means "morning star." He was beautiful; he was what we would call scintillating – and he was powerful. He had great authority. But, pride entered his heart. He decided he wanted God's job, but that job was already taken! Satan wanted to be top boss. He did not want anyone telling him what to do. He had a problem with authority! And so do a lot of people. Haven't we seen kids that have a problem with authority? Like one parent told me, their rebellious son did not want anyone telling him what to do, so he ran away from home and joined the Marines!

I am reminded of the time I was interviewing a nice looking young lady (at least, I thought she was a lady) for the job of secretary. The interview went really well, and I was quite impressed with her. In bringing the interview to a close, I said, "Is there anything else we should know about you?" And she replied with an expletive to the effect that she didn't allow anyone to tell her what to do. I was shocked at the language she used – especially in a job interview. Here was a person who had problems with authority. You will not be surprised to learn that she did not get the job. That was Satan's problem. He said, "I am not going to take anything off of anyone – not even You, God!" No doubt it grieved God to have His most trusted angel betray Him. God gave Isaiah an insight into what happened, and Isaiah recorded it so that all mankind would know.

In its historical context, the following passage in Isaiah is a prophetic judgment against the king of Babylon. Yet, like many passages of prophecy, it has a broader meaning, and there is no question that this is talking about the fall of Satan. It is recorded for us in Isaiah 14:12-13a: *"How art thou fallen from Heaven, O Lucifer, son of the morning! How art thou cut down to the ground, which didst weaken the nations! For thou hast said in thine heart, I will ascend into Heaven, I will exalt my throne above the stars of God ...."*. Lucifer goes on to say in Isaiah 14:14: *"I will ascend above the heights of the clouds; I will be like the most high."* And then God responds in the next verse, *"Yet thou shalt be brought down to Hell, to the sides* [depths] *of the pit"* (Isaiah 14:15).

Lucifer and his minions seek to make life miserable for every person. By contrast, we are told that the primary mission of the good angels is to help God's children. Revelation 7:1 shows us the power of the good angels. They are not omnipotent nor are they all-powerful like God, but as Psalm 103:20 says, they do excel in power.

These angels in 7:1 are engaged in the job of restraining the great wind systems. The tremendous power involved in this operation becomes especially remarkable when we consider the awesome strength of blizzards, cyclones, hurricanes and tornados. Yet four angels – only four of them – have turned off this mighty wind machine. And now a great calm has come over the earth – no breezes across the land – no leaves rustling in the forests – no waves are breaking on the seashore. The earth is waiting in anticipation for what will happen next!

In the seventh chapter of the Book of Daniel, Daniel has a vision. He sees four winds striving over the mighty sea, and out of that turbulence arose four beasts (Daniel 7:1-3). These beasts represent the four great empires (Babylonian, Medo-Persian, Grecian and Roman) that are in existence from Daniel's time to the time of Christ's return to set up His Kingdom (Daniel 7:14).

In Revelation 7:1, the picture comes into focus. The winds are striving to be turned loose – to deliver their judgments upon the earth, but the angels are holding them back at the command of God. God could have held back these four winds Himself, but He likes to delegate duties to servants who are faithful and devoted. That is why you will never get bored in Heaven. You may want to rest for a thousand years, but when you are refreshed, God will have plenty of enjoyable things for you to do and you will love it!

In chapter 7 of Revelation, we are seeing an intermission, a parenthesis, between the "beginning of sorrows" (Matthew 24:8-13) as Jesus calls the first half of the Tribulation, and the "Great Tribulation" (Matthew 24:21) as He calls the last half. We will see other parentheses as we go through this book. Each is like a short period of God's grace in the midst of judgment.

Revelation 7:2-3: *"And I saw another angel ascending from the east, having the seal of the living God: and he cried with a loud voice to the four angels, to whom it was given to hurt the earth and the sea, saying, Hurt not the earth, neither the sea, nor the trees, till we have sealed the servants of our God in their foreheads."* Another mighty angel appears in the east. Some have even suggested this angel could be Christ Himself. Though Christ is not an "angel" – which is a created being – yet the name, angel, simply means a messenger. At any rate, his voice is strong enough to reach the four angels stationed at the four quadrants of the earth. He tells them to hold their position because he has a special assignment in mind. He has the seal of God with him. His assignment is to seal a specific number of God's children so that they will be protected from the Antichrist and from the intense judgments that are yet to come. This seal of protection will be effective until their mission on earth is finished.

This is not the first time God has protected His chosen ones. In Noah's day, as recorded in chapter 6 of Genesis, God protected everyone who put their trust in Him. Had there been ten righteous men found in Sodom, fire would never have fallen on the city (Genesis 18:32).

In Egypt, the children of Israel were protected against all the plagues that were sent. And on the last night of the plagues, the death angel passed over those who had applied the blood on the doorposts according to their instructions as recorded in Exodus chapter 12. God sealed or protected His children from the death angel. And here in Revelation, the judgments are about to become more intense so God said, "Wait until I make sure that my evangelists will be protected against harm until their mission is accomplished." And guess what? The Antichrist is going to be a copycat. In chapter 13, we find that he is going to put a mark on his followers so that they cannot buy or sell without having that mark. Not to have it, will mean being hunted down and killed.

The purpose of this special sealing by God here in the 7th chapter of Revelation is to protect His servants from physical death. But also notice that they are sealed in their foreheads. Could this be a special protection of their minds? Listen to what Jesus said in Matthew 24:24: *"For there shall arise false christs, and false prophets, and shall show great signs and wonders; insomuch that, if it were possible they shall deceive the very elect."*

These believers will be sealed in their minds so that they cannot be deceived by the Antichrist! Remember, even in the Age of Grace in which we are now living, the Holy Spirit seals all believers so that they will not experience spiritual death. Look at the last part of Ephesians 4:30 (NASB): *"Do not grieve the Holy Spirit of God, by whom you were sealed for the day of redemption."* You can backslide, you can become a carnal Christian, but you cannot fall out of the family of God if you are a true believer any more than you can fall out of your own earthly family. Why can't you fall out of the family of God? Because you are sealed by the Holy Spirit until the day of redemption. What great assurance every believer has!

In Tim LaHaye's Left Behind series, when a person became a believer, an undefined "mark" – possibly a cross – appeared on the believer's forehead. But, it could only be seen by other believers. So if you were a believer and were arrested and taken before a judge, you might look up and see the mark of Christ on the judge's head, and you knew he would secretly try to help you. The authors have come into a lot of criticism over this Christian "mark" as it is not supported by Scripture.[4] This Christian mark is speculative by Tim LaHaye and Jerry Jenkins, but it makes for an exciting storyline. We will hear more about the mark of the Antichrist later.

You would think that anyone reading this work by Tim LaHaye and Jerry Jenkins would know that it is fiction and not try to formulate Bible doctrines from it. The front cover of the first book in the Left Behind series says, *"A Novel of the Earth's Last Days."* But on the other hand, it would get criticism by those not sharing a pre-Tribulational view no matter how it was written; a post-Tribulationist would consider the book unreliable because of the Christians being taken out at the Rapture before the Tribulation begins.

We live in a society where almost every statement made by anyone is challenged and comes under fire. On second thought, it is not only our society. The only perfect Man to ever walk the earth 2,000 years ago, was highly criticized and eventually crucified!

"And I heard the number of them which were sealed: and there were sealed a hundred and forty and four thousand of all the tribes of the children of Israel" (Revelation 7:4). Who are these 144,000 and where did they come from? There have been scores of different opinions. The Jehovah's Witnesses say that these 144,000 will all be Jehovah's Witnesses. When this group was first founded around 1900, their slogan was "join the Jehovah's Witnesses and be one of the 144,000 who will live in Heaven." Then, as their membership grew and exceeded 144,000, they had a problem. It was hard to attract new members if the spaces in Heaven were already taken, so they changed their teaching. They originally said that only those alive in 1914 would go to Heaven – everyone else would live on the New Earth.

But all those folks are now dead, so it is rumored that the plan will be changed again – only the best of the Jehovah's Witnesses will be part of the 144,000 that will go to Heaven; the remainder will live on the New Earth. That is one of the reasons their members are so faithful in walking the neighborhoods, knocking on doors and distributing their *Watchtower* magazine. They are working to become one of the "anointed" i.e., one of the 144,000 and thus achieve a place in Heaven. The Jehovah's Witnesses understand Jesus' words in John 3:3, *"Except a man be born again, he cannot see the kingdom of God,"* to apply to the 144,000 who are "born again" as "anointed" sons of God in Heaven.[5]

But another group would take issue with them: The Seventh Day Adventists. They say that these 144,000 are from their denominations who are found observing the Jewish Sabbath when the Lord comes back.

Probably the largest number of theologians is from the school that says these 144,000 represent the Church. But these 144,000 cannot be the Church. We have seen that the Church has already been raptured, and is around the throne in Heaven while this is taking place on the earth. Dr. Harry Ironside said whenever he meets individuals who insist they are part of the 144,000 – be it Jehovah's Witnesses or otherwise – he always asks them, "Which tribe are you from?" He asks this because the Bible is clear – every one of these 144,000 is Jewish![6] Every one of these difficulties can be cleared up if we will keep one principle firmly in mind from Dr. David Reagan: "When the plain sense makes sense, don't look for any other sense, or you will wind up with nonsense."[7]

Verses 5-8 even names them! "*Of the tribe of Judah were sealed twelve thousand, of the tribe of Reuben were sealed twelve thousand, of the tribe of Gad were sealed twelve thousand, of the tribe of Asher were sealed twelve thousand, of the tribe of Naphtali were sealed twelve thousand, of the tribe of Manasseh were sealed twelve thousand, of the tribe of Simeon were sealed twelve thousand, of the tribe of Levi were sealed twelve thousand, of the tribe of Issachar were sealed twelve thousand, of the tribe of Zebulun were sealed twelve thousand, of the tribe of Joseph were sealed twelve thousand, of the tribe of Benjamin were sealed twelve thousand.*"

What else must God do to convince us that these are Jews?! Someone asked, "Haven't you heard of the ten lost tribes of Israel? How will they be identified?" Listen! They are not lost to God. He knows the tribe to which every Jew belongs. Dr. Reagan asked the late Jewish evangelist, Zola Levitt, if he believed that the 144,000 of Revelation chapter 7 were Jews, and if they would serve as evangelists trying to convert the world to Jesus. Zola said, "Of course! Why do you think the Lord has given us the kind of personality that we have? Haven't you ever noticed that Jews are very pushy people? God has given us that kind of personality so that we can be the world's greatest salesmen. And one day, during the Tribulation, 144,000 believing Jews are going to use those skills to convert a great host of Gentiles to Jesus. We are going to push people up against the wall and hold them by the throat until they say, 'Jesus'. Before the Tribulation is over, we are going to convert more people to Jesus than you Gentiles have done in the past 2,000 years."[8]

Dr. W. A. Criswell, the late pastor of the First Baptist Church, Dallas, said, "I have never seen one genuinely devout converted Jew who did not put most Gentile Christians to shame when it comes to evangelism. When Jews are truly converted, they are converted totally and completely, just like the Apostle Paul. If twelve Jews turned the world upside down in the 1st Century, just think what 144,000 will do!"[9]

There will be scores of converts during the Tribulation in spite of two strong deterrents. First, the Antichrist will use demonic power to influence the masses; and second, Scripture reveals a somber truth: most of the converts will pay with their very life as the Antichrist will seek to annihilate them. In addition, the Antichrist will take his fury out on the Jews during this time. Zechariah chapter 13 states that he will kill two-thirds of the Jewish people, but these 144,000 evangelists will be supernaturally protected until their mission is completed.

These twelve tribes are not listed in any particular order, but we do see that Judah is listed first. He is not the oldest son, but remember Jesus was from the tribe and lineage of Judah, hence the preeminence. The twelve tribes of Israel are mentioned elsewhere in the Bible, but this is a slightly different list than has ever been presented before. The most significant change is that Dan and Ephraim have been omitted completely. Why these omissions? Because both of these tribes were the very picture of idolatry – and God hates idolatry. J. I. Packer says it this way, "It is impossible to worship nothing; we humans are worshipping creatures, and if we do not worship the God who made us, we shall inevitably worship someone or something else."[10] It appears that the tribes of Dan and Ephraim forfeited their opportunity to be evangelists during the Tribulation Period because of their susceptibility to idolatry.

The Jewish rabbis for centuries have taught that the False Prophet would come from the tribe of Dan. They glean this in part from the prophecy that Jacob made regarding each of his sons just before he died. These prophecies by Jacob are recorded in the 49th chapter of Genesis. In verse 17 (ESV), we read: *"Dan shall be a serpent in the way, a viper by the path, that bites the horse's heels so that his rider falls backward."* And from the historical record in the 18th chapter of the Book of Judges, we find that Dan was the first tribe to go into idolatry, and it would not surprise me if the tribe of Dan would be the leader of any Jews who wanted to worship the Antichrist and his idolatrous image that he will build.

When we study the Book of Hosea, we find that the name of Ephraim was almost synonymous with idolatry. So because of gross idolatry, God has replaced these two tribes. The first is Levi who replaces Dan. Levi is the priestly tribe which never was given land rights, so they were not in previous lists that had to do with inheritance. The second is Joseph, Ephraim's father, who is elevated to take his son's place.

There are so many little jewels in the Book of Revelation that we find new ones every time we dig into it. For instance, in chapter 7 verse 3 it says, *".... till we have sealed the servants ...."*. In Greek, the word for servants is "doulos" – bond slaves. The same word is used in Revelation 1:1 where God says this Book is being written to show His servants – His bond slaves – what soon must come to pass.

If you read between the lines, you will discern that this Book will be a survival manual for God's people during the Tribulation Period. And they will understand far more than we do because they will see the realities taking place all around them, and we are only seeing the shadows. It will be as fresh as their daily newspaper. And while these faithful servants are preaching the Gospel to the lost, we will be cheering for them in Heaven, encouraging them to finish the race!

Do you think these 144,000 evangelists had any results? Were they successful? If you were a preacher, and you told your listeners, "Come and accept Christ and you will live forever, but in the meantime, you will probably be martyred by the Antichrist" – do you think you would have many takers? We will find out in the following verse. Chapter 7, verse 9: *"After this I beheld, and, lo, a great multitude, which no man could number, of all nations, and kindreds, and people, and tongues, stood before the throne, and before the Lamb, clothed with white robes, and palms in their hands."* Just who is this multitude of people? I have never seen so many different ideas as to who these people are! Here is just a few of them:

1) This is a scene here on earth of the different nationalities that have trusted Christ. (But this scene obviously is NOT on earth – it is taking place before the throne of God in Heaven!)
2) Another commentator said that these are Christians who were martyred under the reign of Constantine some 1600 years ago.
3) Still others say these are the 144,000 who were sealed earlier in this chapter. (Not so; 144,000 is a large number, but it is not a multitude that no man can number!)
4) And then there are the liberal theologians who say that the mention of this great multitude has no specific significance – it is just an illustration to show that good will far outweigh evil.

This is amazing! It is so clear to me. God has just commissioned 144,000 Jewish preachers earlier in this chapter for the purpose of preaching the Gospel. As a result, this multitude of people that no man can number is now standing in front of the throne of God. It is obvious that these people accepted Christ through the preaching of these 144,000 evangelists, and the Antichrist killed these converts for not worshipping him. Nothing could be clearer than that.

What a harvest by these Jewish evangelists! But they are not just preaching to the Jews. Responding to their message is a great multitude that no man can number from every nation and language on the face of the earth. You can be assured that the Antichrist and the False Prophet will be furious, and will try every means at their disposal to stop this great revival.

The Antichrist will deny people without his mark to buy food or medicine, and when that does not work he vows to behead them. As you can see from verses 9 and 10, these believers mean business. No wishy-washy commitments from them. "I am going to serve Jesus" – whop – their lives are ended. These people are clothed in white robes (which we learned earlier is the righteousness of Christ) that these saints are wearing.

I have searched the Scriptures, and do not find any comfort for anyone after the Rapture who had heard the Gospel message during the Age of Grace, and had said no to Christ. Hopefully, I am wrong. Once you have heard the Gospel and have turned it down, II Thessalonians 2:10-12, strongly implies that you will be drawn like a magnet to the Antichrist. There is good reason to believe that these converts during the Tribulation are those who have never clearly heard or understood the Gospel previously. It will be more difficult to trust Christ after the Rapture because the Holy Spirit will not be here on earth in residence. You see, He was present before Pentecost in Old Testament times, but He was not a resident until Pentecost when He came to live within every believer. And after the Rapture, when the Christians are taken out of the world, the Holy Spirit leaves also to take up residence again in Heaven. This is not to say that the Holy Spirit will not act during the Tribulation Period, but His operations will be similar to those in Old Testament times.

Jimmy Draper, that fiery preacher who was at First Baptist Church, Euless, said this: "65% of this country's people say they are church members, yet never more than 15% of them attend church. If we could be saved and not changed, then we could lose our salvation and never miss it. No change equals no salvation!"[11] According to II Corinthians 5:17, when you become a Christian, old things are passed away – you are a new creation. That is what is meant by the new birth.

One church I heard about instituted the following policy. After a member had missed five years without ever attending church or Sunday school, and without showing the slightest interest in the church or supporting it whatsoever, the pastor and two deacons would go out to visit them to find out their intentions and see if the church could minister to them. If they were not interested in continuing the relationship, they would be removed from the church roll. Of course many would be excused for health reasons, as would the aged and the homebound. But the question should be put to every able-bodied member, "Are you with us or are you against us?" As the Bible says, *"Choose this day whom you will serve …."* (Joshua 24:15a ESV). I have no doubt that Jesus would take as much time as necessary if they were truly wanting to follow Him, but if they snubbed the Gospel or His Church, or showed no interest, He would not waste His breath on them.

In earlier times, the "church letter" meant something. When someone moved their membership from one church to another, a letter was written recommending the person along with comments such as, "This individual served the Lord faithfully for many years as a member in good standing of our church." What if their church letter said, "These people were members for 10 years and they never came to our services, and never contributed anything to the support of the Kingdom." Such a church letter would be very beneficial in deciding whether to accept them as new members. At least they would have an opportunity to explain their intentions. The vote on their membership would really be meaningful instead of just being a rubber stamp. Now you know why they will never put me in charge of membership!

Baptists have been criticized over the years, especially by the Churches of Christ, for "voting on folks becoming church members." I had this discussion with a Church of Christ minister who visited me when I was in the army at Ft. Sill, Oklahoma. I explained that this vote by the congregation is predicated on the validity of the prospective member's statement of faith. I said that the Churches of Christ minister essentially "votes" on their prospective members or at least approves or disapproves them. To prove this, I asked, "What if I came forward in one of your services and wanted to join your church, but I made it clear that I did not believe that baptism is essential to salvation. You would not accept me for membership, correct?" He agreed. "So I contend that a democratic vote by the church body is just as valid as a vote by the minister."

At any rate, these converts who are gathered around the throne of God are joyously worshipping, celebrating and waving palm branches to the Lord. This calls to mind the throng that was waving palm branches when Jesus made His entry into Jerusalem a week before He was crucified. Only this time, He will be vindicated in history instead of being crucified. *"And cried with a loud voice, saying: 'SALVATION TO OUR GOD, WHICH SITTETH UPON THE THRONE, AND UNTO THE LAMB'"* (Revelation 7:10). There is no question in the minds of these believers as to who is responsible for their salvation and victory. It is not due to their good works; it is not their improved self-esteem. What they are saying is this: "Our salvation is due to God Almighty and to His Son, Jesus Christ!"

"And all the angels stood round about the throne, and about the elders and the four beasts, and fell before the throne on their faces, and worshipped God, saying, Amen: Blessing and glory, and wisdom, and thanksgiving, and honor, and power, and might, be unto our God for ever and ever. Amen!" (Revelation 7:11-12). What a time Heaven is having praising and worshipping God!

"And one of the elders answered, saying unto me, 'What are these which are arrayed in white robes? And whence came they?' I said unto him, 'Sir, thou knowest.' And he said to me, 'These are they which came out of great tribulation, and have washed their robes, and made them white in the blood of the Lamb'" (Revelation 7:13-14). Putting this in conversational English, the elder said, "John, who are these people you see in white robes?" And John says, "Beats me – I have never seen them before. There is not a face in that vast throng that I recognize." That is astonishing! If this multitude represents the Church as some liberals teach, John would have recognized some of them just as you would today if you were to see the redeemed of Christ's Church in Heaven – your family, your loved ones, your friends. But John says, "I have never seen them before. I have no idea who they are." And then the elder tells John why he does not know them. "No wonder you don't recognize them. They lived over 2,000 years after you did. These are the ones who came out of the Great Tribulation. They are the Tribulation saints, and they have washed their robes and made them white in the blood of the Lamb."

Even in these dark, dark days of the Tribulation, God displays His mercy and grace. He chooses 144,000 Jews. He seals them. He empowers them to preach the Gospel. And those who will listen to them and turn in faith to Christ, their souls will be saved by the blood of the Lamb. *"Therefore are they before the throne of God, and serve Him day and night in His Temple: and He that sitteth on the throne shall dwell among them"* (Revelation 7:15). The expression, *"serve Him day and night"* simply means that they serve Him all the time. They are busy doing enjoyable things, and carrying out the will of the Father.

"They shall hunger no more, neither thirst anymore; neither shall the sun light on them, nor any

heat" (Revelation 7:16). Remember, these souls have just come out of the Great Tribulation. They did not have the mark of the Beast, and so, it was illegal for them to buy food or drink, and they were slain whenever they could be apprehended.

We would love to know the individual stories that take place for these Tribulation saints as they try to stay a step ahead of the Antichrist. No doubt, many a kind person will offer them shelter and help, putting their own lives in danger. I think we will hear many of these courageous stories when we get to the other side. This is the context in which Jesus is speaking in Matthew 25:35-36: *"For I was an hungered, and ye gave me meat: I was thirsty, and ye gave me drink: I was a stranger, and ye took me in: Naked, and ye clothed me: I was sick, and ye visited me: I was in prison, and ye came unto me."*

And they asked, "When did we do this, Lord?" *"And the King shall answer and say unto them, 'Verily I say unto you, inasmuch as ye have done it unto one of the least of these my brethren, ye have done it unto me'"* (Matthew 25:40). These will be comforting words to them!

"For the Lamb which is in the midst of the throne shall feed them, and shall lead them unto living fountains of waters: and God shall wipe away all tears from their eyes" (Revelation 7:17). The Lamb now becomes their Shepherd. Tears had been a way of life for these poor souls. Under the Antichrist's regime, they had known nothing but sorrow, pain and heartache. They had been oppressed and persecuted. They had seen many of their loved ones and friends tortured and beheaded. God may have delegated these judgments on earth to be poured out by an angel, but notice, He does not delegate comfort – God Himself will wipe away their tears!

Dr. M. R. DeHaan says: "What a picture of peace, joy and quietness! Contrast this with the chapter that follows when the opening of the seals is resumed and we study the judgments of the seven trumpets when the seventh seal is opened. Here we have a resumption of the awful judgments of the Tribulation, but far, far removed from them are His redeemed saints who because of their faith in the Lord Jesus Christ are in the place of eternal bliss and peace."[12] Praise the Lord as He is always caring for His children! The Book of Revelation mentions twice that God will wipe away tears. And both come after judgment. The first time is here – the second is at the end of the Tribulation.

The activities that will be going on in Heaven during the Tribulation are the rewards for service that will be given out to all believers at the "Bema" seat – the judgment seat of Christ. Not only are they weeping for the rewards they receive for service that they have probably long forgotten, but from the words of commendation they receive from their Lord and Master that are overwhelming to them.

The second time that tears are wiped away is after the Great White Throne Judgment in Revelation 21:4 when the unsaved are consigned to Hell. Many Christians will be weeping not only for these souls that must endure eternal punishment, but also because of missed opportunities to present the Gospel to them. In each case, we are consoled by God as He wipes away all our tears.

Verse 17 also mentions *"living fountains of waters."* This is one of the most gracious promises in the Word of God. There will be an abundance of refreshing water in the New Jerusalem, and its inhabitants will never thirst again. A river of pure water will flow in plentiful supply from the very throne of the Lamb becoming, as we find in Revelation 22, a great river that will water the entire earth. This verse says that the Lamb will feed them, and lead them to living fountains of waters. This brings to mind a familiar passage to all of us. *"The LORD is my shepherd; I shall not want. He maketh me to lie down in green pastures: He leadeth me beside the still waters. He restoreth my soul ...."* (Psalm 23:1-3a).

Let us summarize this chapter. God has temporarily stopped the judgments that have been falling upon the earth. During this lull, He has sealed for special protection 144,000 Jews – 12,000 from each of the twelve tribes of Israel. They will carry the Gospel to the ends of the earth and as a result, multitudes will give their lives to Christ. Most of the converts are killed by the Antichrist and his henchmen. But, immediately they find themselves before the throne of God, worshipping Him and praising Him for their salvation that was made possible through the blood of the Lamb. And God comforts them and wipes away all their tears.

The martyrs who had been killed by the Antichrist ask God how long before He avenges their blood. In chapter 8 and the one following, God begins to do just that. Just when it seems that the judgments could not get any worse, they do – more intense and more horrendous. God has warned over and over that judgment is coming.

Why are the fields and the trees rejoicing? We will see in a moment, but it is because these judgments are hard on them as well. And when God is through judging the earth, ALL creation – even the animals and plants and trees – will be redeemed from the curse that holds them in its grip (Romans 8:22-23). This judgment upon the earth is confirmed by Paul in Romans 1:18 when he mentions a time when the *"Wrath of God is revealed from Heaven against all ungodliness and unrighteousness of men ...."*

In Psalm 96, verses 11-13 (NLT), the people sang:
"Let the heavens be glad, and let the earth rejoice!
Let the sea and everything in it shout His praise!
Let the fields and their crops burst forth with joy!
Let the trees of the forest rustle with praise before The LORD!
For the LORD is coming! He is coming
To judge the earth. He will judge the world with
Righteousness and all the nations with His truth."
Amen!

CHAPTER EIGHT

The Seventh Seal is Opened

———————

There is a great silence in Heaven before the final seal is opened and judgment breaks forth as we read in Revelation 8:1: *"And when He had opened the seventh seal, there was silence in Heaven about the space of half an hour."* This is very unusual because Heaven is seldom silent. It is generally filled day and night with worship and praise by the living ones, while the saints sing to God and to their Savior, Jesus Christ (Revelation 4:8).

The judgments that are coming are so terrible, so intense, that all of Heaven is silent. Moments before, there was majestic praise and worship going on around the throne by millions of angels, the elders, the saints, the living creatures – all singing and shouting praises to God. But now, nothing but silence. One hardly dares to breathe. All motion is stopped! The four living creatures will cease their talk about the holiness of God. The twenty-four elders will suspend their declarations about the worthiness of the Lamb. The heavenly hosts will stop their praise, and the Tribulation saints will cease their singing. An eerie silence moves across Heaven.

You have been outside before a storm hits and heard thunder reverberating in the distance. You saw flashes of lightning that illuminate the sky. Then suddenly everything becomes still. It seems there is not a breath of wind to move the leaves. Even the birds seek a hiding place. Absolute, terrifying, foreboding silence. It is the calm before the storm – the most awful storm that will ever break over this poor orb we call earth. Dr. David Jeremiah is reported to say it is like the anticipation that the symphony orchestra feels when it is holding its breath and waiting expectantly while the maestro has his baton poised in midair. Silence in Heaven for half an hour. If our radios, televisions or computers go off for ten seconds we start getting antsy. Does half an hour seem like a short time? It does unless you see a child drowning, and then even one minute seems like forever; or if you are waiting to see if your child survives a traumatic operation; or unless you are on the 84th floor of the Twin Towers while rescuers are frantically trying to reach you. In such devastating cases, half an hour can seem like an eternity.

After the last seal is broken, the scroll is fully unrolled. We have heard the cries of pain and sorrow emanating from the earth as the other seals were broken – four dreaded riders on horses have decimated the world. One-fourth of all humanity has been killed. At the end of chapter 6, the earth dwellers had assumed that the great day of God's wrath had come and was about to end. But what has gone before is but a prelude – it is minor compared to what is about to happen.

The great hosts of Heaven have watched the Lamb of God open the seals one by one. They have seen that each judgment is worse than the previous one. This seventh seal when opened unleashes more fury than all that has gone on before. Is there any wonder that every living thing awaits in silence? This silence also gives the world a short breather. It gives the earth dwellers time to begin explaining things away on a natural basis. After all, they reason all this turmoil was only nature reacting and not really God at all. Just as there will be plenty of explanations around the world when millions and millions of Christians disappeared at the Rapture, so there will be plenty of natural explanations for these judgments upon the earth.

"And I saw the seven angels which stood before God; and to them were given seven trumpets" (Revelation 8:2). As we have previously mentioned, the number seven in Scripture represents perfection. Here the judgments are perfect, and the angels selected are the perfect ones to carry out these judgments. In Jewish tradition, the trumpet ("shofar") was made from a ram's horn and was used for many things. It was used to call soldiers to battle. It was used to call the people to worship. It was used to make an important announcement and to announce a festival or feast. The trumpet held a very important place in the life of Israel. In this case, the sounding of each trumpet will announce a specific judgment of God upon the earth. The first four trumpets deal with natural disasters or catastrophes. I say natural, but God is directing them. The last three deal with specific judgments poured out upon the people of the earth.

Here is how these judgments unfold. First, there were six seals and each represented a specific judgment. But when the seventh seal is broken, we find there are seven trumpets. And when we get to the seventh trumpet, it sounds and produces seven bowl judgments. And when the bowl judgments are concluded, that will be the end of the age as we know it, and it will usher in the Second Coming of Jesus Christ (Revelation 10:7). In other words, the seventh seal has within it the rest of the events in the Book of Revelation, and God's plan for redeeming planet earth.

When we read about these seven trumpets, we immediately think of the seven trumpets in connection with the fall of Jericho. The priests of Israel were given trumpets, and they were told to march around the pagan city for seven days blowing their trumpets (Joshua 6:2-5).

Seven times on the seventh day they did so, and at the seventh blast, the walls fell down flat. Jericho is a type of this evil world which has rejected Christ and, just like Jericho, this world will collapse after these seven trumpets have sounded.

Here are the solemn words of the prophet, Zephaniah, as he describes this very period of time at the close of the history of mankind: *"The great day of the Lord is near, it is near, and hasteth greatly, even the voice of the Day of the Lord: the mighty man shall cry there bitterly. That day is a day of wrath, a day of trouble and distress, a day of wasteness and desolation, a day of darkness and gloominess, a day of clouds and thick darkness, a day of the trumpet ...."* (Zephaniah 1:14-16a).

"And another angel came and stood at the altar, having a golden censer; and there was given unto him much incense, that he should offer it with the prayers of all saints upon the golden altar which was before the throne" (Revelation 8:3). Some commentators say this cannot be Jesus because He is seated on the throne and this angel is standing at the altar. This is where common sense comes in. Jesus' normal place is seated at the right hand of God. But that does not mean He cannot move around to fulfill other obligations. Bear in mind that this angel ministers to both God and man. Who can this be? I Timothy 2:5 tells us: *"For there is one God, and one mediator between God and men, the man Christ Jesus."* Christ appeared in the Old Testament many times, and was usually called, "The Angel of the Lord" (Genesis 22:11-15). He wrestled with Jacob (Genesis 32:22-31). He walked with Shadrack, Meshach and Abednego in the fiery furnace (Daniel 3:25). Hebrews 7:25b says that *"He ever liveth to make intercession for them."* And that is what He is doing.

Some people think that God does not always answer our prayers. But He does! Sometimes He says "yes" – sometimes He says "no" – and sometimes He says "not yet" as these prayers are to be answered in God's time. Millions of Christians have prayed over the years, *"Thy kingdom come. Thy will be done in earth, as it is in Heaven"* (Matthew 6:10). His direct will is not always being carried out on earth at this time, but such prayers have been collected and at the proper time will be offered up to God the Father.

Another indication that this angel is Jesus is the fact that Scripture never speaks of any created being, angel or otherwise, offering incense with the prayers of saints to make them acceptable to God. The Roman Church does. Its followers pray to Mary, to Peter and to various saints in hopes they will curry favor with God. But the Bible tells us as individual believers to come directly to the throne of God with our requests, praying in Jesus' name (John 16:23).

Often we pray sincerely, but we might not use the right words. We clumsily and awkwardly send our prayers skyward. The English language seems so inadequate at times. Consequently, these prayers have to be refined, and purified by the Holy Spirit to reflect the desires of our heart. I am reminded of Romans 8:26: *"Likewise the Spirit also helpeth our infirmities* [our weaknesses]: *for we know not what we should pray for as we ought: but the Spirit itself maketh intercession for us with groanings which cannot be uttered."* In other words, the Holy Spirit takes our feeble prayers, refines them, and mixes them with the sweet fragrance of incense before they are offered up to the very throne of God.

And what is the result? Look at verse 4 of Revelation 8: *"And the smoke of the incense, which came with the prayers of the saints, ascended up before God out of the angel's hand."* Were the Tribulation martyrs praying to forgive those who had just killed, persecuted and tortured the Jews and Gentile believers? No! The time of grace and mercy had past. They prayed for divine retribution – for the fire of judgment to come down as did Elijah in his day (II Kings 1:10, 12).

Back in chapter 6, the Tribulation martyrs were praying to God, *"How long, O Lord, holy and true, dost thou not judge and avenge our blood on them that dwell on the earth? (Revelation 6:10).* Now we are about to see the prayers of these saints answered. *"And the angel took the censer, and filled it with fire of the altar, and cast it into the earth: and there were voices, and thunderings, and lightnings, and an earthquake"* (Revelation 8:5). Try to visualize this awesome scene. On earth, the Antichrist and False Prophet are rising to power, and telling the earth dwellers to worship Satan, while at the same time the Antichrist's henchmen are hunting down and killing God's people.

These martyred saints have gone to Heaven, and are praying to be avenged. At first, they are told to wait until the number of saved is increased (Revelation 6:11), but then after a brief time, God responded by having His angel hurl the burning censer to earth. This is a clear indication of God's wrath. It will be followed by loud thunderclaps, flashes of lightning and an earthquake. What a contrast this is to the silence that began this chapter!

The fire represents God's judgment upon sin in the earth. The same golden censer from which the prayers of the saints are offered to God now becomes a fiery weapon releasing judgment earthward. All who reject Christ must endure His righteous vengeance. Hebrews 10:26-27 tells us: *"For if we sin willfully after that we have received the knowledge of the truth, there remaineth no more sacrifice for sins, but a certain fearful looking for of judgment and fiery indignation, which shall devour the adversaries."* I hear this frequently on television: "God would never punish anyone – God is Love." Let me remind you of Hebrews 10:28-29 (NLT): *"Anyone who refused to obey the law of Moses was put to death without mercy on the testimony of two or three witnesses. Think how much more terrible the punishment will be for those who have trampled on the Son of God and have treated the blood of the covenant as if it were common and unholy. Such people have insulted and enraged the Holy Spirit who brings God's mercy to his people."*

God is love, but He is also a God of holiness and His holiness demands that sin be punished. Again in the tenth chapter of Hebrews it says, *"It is a fearful thing to fall into the hands of the living God* (Hebrews 10:31). We are also told, *"For our God is a consuming fire"* (Hebrews 12:29).

Then the seven angels prepare to get into the act. *"And the seven angels which had the seven trumpets prepared themselves to sound"* (Revelation 8:6). As these tremendous events are about to take place, we are reminded that there are several things we are told in Scripture that lead up to the establishment of Christ's Kingdom on earth.

First is peace, or at least, everyone is saying peace. Then an ambitious leader presents himself as the savior of the world – one who says he will bring peace to the earth. He claims to have all the answers to all the problems of the world. This pattern has continued over and over again throughout history. The leader promises to deliver the people from all their woes. And then the inevitable happens – blood and warfare breakout followed by famine and pestilence. We have seen that happen in Cuba. We have seen it happen in China. We have seen it happen in Russia, and in Iraq and Iran. Whether it is past or present history, it always follows the same pattern. These men come with their schemes and their programs and promise to bring Utopia with them. But what follows is bloodshed, execution squads, severe food shortages, and eventually dreaded disease and pestilence. And then, of course, comes the persecution of God's people. Always – always – there comes the slaughter of God's people. Then warnings from God, and then judgment.

No nation, dictator or tyrant has ever yet defied God and lived. Every time a nation turns in those directions, there invariably follows God's warning and judgment. And the seals we have seen opened in our previous study follow this to a tee. First, a talk of peace; second, war; third, famine; fourth, pestilence; fifth, persecution of God's people; sixth, warnings from God; and seventh, judgment from above. We cannot be dogmatic as to the nature of these judgments. Are these verses to be taken literally, or are they symbols of something else? We have been wading in waist deep water so far, so let us pray that the Holy Spirit will keep us from going under as we venture farther into the deep water of prophecy.

Look at the next few verses, and then we will see how the different camps of interpreters approach the question as to what all this means. *"The first angel blew his trumpet, and hail and fire mixed with blood were thrown down upon the earth, and one-third of the earth was set on fire. One-third of the trees were burned, and all the grass was burned"* (Revelation 8:7 NLT).

A liberal teacher would spiritualize this verse, and would say that the hail and fire mixed with blood and the destruction are simply symbols of divine wrath; and are not necessarily literal. Hal Lindsay who interprets this verse literally sees this differently. He points out that most of the lumber for the building of houses will be gone, along with much of the grain which means that food will be scarce. With this massive loss of vegetation it will cause soil erosion, floods and mudslides. Air pollution will be immense, and the ecology will be thrown chaotically out of balance.[1]

"The second angel sounded, and something like a great mountain burning with fire was thrown into the sea; and a third of the sea became blood, and a third of the creatures which were in the sea and had life, died; and a third of the ships were destroyed" (Revelation 8:8-9 NASB). The second angel's trumpet will signal judgment upon the sea. It reminds me of the first plague on Egypt in the days of Moses that turned the waters into blood. It was not symbolic – it was literal. It was a plague against Egypt's false goddess of the sea, and it killed the fish and frogs, and made the water unfit to drink.

Liberal teachers would say that the mountain in verse 8 represents kingdoms, the sea pictures the nations, and the burning mountain means that one of the kingdoms is having an internal revolution. But Theodore Epp, a respected prophecy teacher who sticks with a literal interpretation whenever possible, says: "Imagine the great catastrophe when this large burning mass is hurled into the sea and a third part of the sea life dies. A third of the ships are also destroyed. Perhaps the death of a third of the sea life and the destruction of a third of the ships are the result of some chemical reaction in the water such as radioactivity following an atomic explosion."[2]

I do not think this is a real mountain going into the sea. You say, "Ah ha – wait a minute. You are spiritualizing when you said before it should be a literal interpretation." Remember, my rule of interpretation says to take things literally unless you have valid reasons from Scripture for giving them a symbolic meaning. The reason here is that Scripture never says this was a huge mountain thrown into the sea as verified by the following six translations from the Greek.

> The KJV says – "as it were a great mountain."
> The NIV says – "something like a huge mountain."
> The ESV says – "something like a great mountain."
> The RSV says – "something like a great mountain."
> The NASB says – "something like a great mountain."

John is describing this as he sees it. He does not say it is a huge mountain. He says it is like a huge mountain. It appears that it will either be a nuclear missile or a giant burning meteor that crashes into the sea. In the last decade, scientists have become aware of the dangers should one of these large meteorites crash into the earth. Congress has directed NASA to implement plans to avoid such a disaster and scientists have been working toward that end.[3]

Would we survive if such a meteorite hit the earth? Such an event would be a rarity, but here is how a graduate student in the Astronomy Department at Cornell University describes it. "The impact with the earth's crust will finally stop the asteroid. The energy of the impact will vaporize the asteroid and a large amount of the earth's crust, creating a crater more than one hundred kilometers across, throwing all that rock into the air. Some of this debris will be going so fast that it will fly right out of the earth's atmosphere and go into orbit around the earth. Most of the debris will rain back down on the earth – every part of the earth, not just near the impact site – heating the atmosphere until it is like the inside of an oven, triggering forest fires and cooking anything that is not sheltered underground. The combination of dust from the impact and soot from the forest fires will remain in the earth's atmosphere for a year or so, blocking the light of the sun. Without sunlight, much of the earth's plant life, on land and in the sea, will die. Many species of animals as well as the human race will die out, either in the initial catastrophe, or in the ensuing years due to lack of food and the general devastation of the environment."[4]

A Pulitzer prize winning writer for the *New York Times* reported this: "If a huge asteroid should crash into the middle of the Atlantic Ocean, say goodbye to Broadway, the beach houses on Long Island and just about everything else on the East Coast as far inland as the foothills of the Appalachians. The coastal lands would be devastated not by the actual impact, some 1,500 miles away, but by a relentless succession of colossal waves traveling at the speed of jet aircraft and towering much higher than the Empire State Building. In the aftermath, a few hours later, the receding water from these tsunami waves would leave almost nothing standing."[5] Whatever this judgment is, it will cause a great portion of the sea to turn to blood, probably from all the sea creatures that are killed. As a result of this huge mass hitting the sea, tidal waves will cause a third of the ships to be destroyed.

"Then the third angel blew his trumpet, and a great flaming star fell out of the sky, burning like a torch. It fell upon one-third of the rivers and on the springs of water. The name of the star was Bitterness (Wormwood). It made one-third of the water bitter, and many people died because the water was so bitter. Then the fourth angel blew his trumpet, and one-third of the sun was struck, and one-third of the moon, and one-third of the stars, and they became dark. And one-third of the day was dark and one-third of the night also" (Revelation 8:10-12 NLT). The third angel sounds his trumpet and another great star blazing like a torch falls from the sky. It is called Wormwood. It contaminates the rivers and springs. We have already seen that a great portion of the sea has been turned into blood, and now the drinking water is polluted. Wormwood is mentioned several times in Scripture. It is one of the bitterest of all vegetation known to man and is sometimes fatal.[6]

This huge missile or meteor or whatever it is, is named Wormwood because it hits the fresh water outlets and turns them so bitter and poisonous that many people die. Some die from drinking it and no doubt, many others die from thirst. Hal Lindsey said, "Man can live about forty days without food, about three days without water, about eight minutes without air, but only for one second without hope."[7] The weak and sick among us have much less time than that before they succumb to these catastrophes.

Some teachers say that when this flaming star falls from Heaven, it means that some highly respected religious authority denounces Christ; he becomes an apostate and his influence produces the awful results pictured by the poisoning of the waters, that is, the poisoning and contamination of religious doctrines. At least one commentator, Dr. H. A. Ironside, asks this question: "Who is this star?" He goes on to say, "While I do not want to try to prophesy, let me give you a suggestion. Who occupies the highest place in the Church in the minds of millions of professing Christians? Can you imagine what might be the effect on a vast number of people if tomorrow the newspapers carried this lead story: "The Pope declares that Christianity is all a sham and religion is a fraud"?

Further, what if he said, 'The only true God and Savior

of the world is our glorious leader' and then he names the Antichrist!? Don't you think that the waters of truth would be contaminated, and that many people would die because of it?"[8] This is an interesting theory and it is certainly possible, but I still lean toward the interpretation that this great burning falling star, is either a missile or a meteorite that will traumatize the earth dwellers.

I am not dogmatic as to whether these judgments are literal or not; however, I am inclined to believe that they are literal. Why do I believe these descriptions should be taken literally? Because, first, we have precedents for this – it has happened before. In Exodus, when Moses confronted the Pharaoh to "let my people go" – the seventh plague on Egypt was a rain of grievous hail mixed with fire that smote the cattle, the plants and the trees (Exodus 9:18-20). God also rained hail, fire and brimstone on Sodom and Gomorrah (Genesis 19:24). There is no reason to believe that God will not do it again, only this time, it will be a worldwide calamity.

Keep in mind this is the Book of Revelation which means it is the unveiling of what we are reading. Unlike the Book of Daniel (Daniel 12:9) which was closed to our understanding until the end times, this Book according to Revelation 22:10 is unsealed for all to see and understand. Consequently, we have just read an exact description of what is going to take place. Some commentators, particularly Catholic scholars, say these trumpet judgments have already taken place in the 1st Century, but John wrote that these things would come to pass after the Church is raptured (Revelation 4:1). If this judgment has already taken place, when exactly was one-third of the earth burned up so that the grass and trees were destroyed? It has not happened! But God says that it will happen during the Tribulation Period.

In verse 12, there is no doubt that the earth is being hit by one disaster after another. The fourth angel sounds and a third of the sun, moon and stars turn dark. In other words, earth's light is diminished by a third. Some think that the explosion of a nuclear device would hurl smoke, dirt and debris into the upper atmosphere. This would not only contaminate the waters and make them bitter, but it would also greatly reduce the light of the sun, moon and stars that would normally reach the earth.

If this were to happen, in all probability fires would break out all around the globe, and large amounts of smoke and debris from these fires could cover at least half the earth's surface, preventing most of the sunlight from reaching the earth's surface. With greatly reduced sunlight, less rain and lower temperatures, farming would virtually come to a standstill. The result would be worldwide famine. The reality is always far worse than any description can depict.

These four trumpet judgments that have just been described affect: 1) the earth; 2) the sea; 3) the fresh waters; and 4) the heavenly bodies including the sun, moon and stars. Theologians who like to spiritualize these events will say, "This doesn't really mean that something will happen to the sun, moon and stars. It just means that our light – our understanding – will be darkened." But let us not forget what Jesus Christ Himself said about these times, *"There will be signs in the sun, moon and stars. On the earth, nations will be in anguish and perplexity at the roaring and tossing of the sea"* (Luke 21:25 NIV).

The nations are going to be in anguish and perplexity because the scientists and meteorologists will be unable to come up with a reasonable explanation. But there will be a remnant of believers on earth – those who have not yet been caught and put to death by the Antichrist and his forces. These believers will be strengthened in their faith by such passages as Psalm 46:1-3: *"God is our refuge and strength, a very present help in trouble. Therefore will we not fear, though the earth be removed, and though the mountains be carried into the midst of the sea; though the waters thereof roar and be troubled, though the mountains shake with the swelling thereof."* For these believers, it will be an encouragement to read these words when this exact event is taking place!

While the earth and its inhabitants are reeling under these severe judgments, they receive a strange and eerie message. *"And I beheld, and heard an angel flying through the midst of Heaven, saying with a loud voice, 'Woe, woe, woe, to the inhabiters of the earth by reason of the other voices of the trumpet of the three angels, which are yet to sound!'"* (Revelation 8:13). Some translations say an eagle was flying through the midst of Heaven with this message. But it makes little difference as to whom or what the messenger is. The point is that God has chosen a message to go out to the inhabitants of the earth in loud and clear terms. In vernacular Greek, here is what it is saying – "You ain't seen nothin' yet!"

There are three more trumpets to be blown by three more angels. And verse 13 in effect is saying, "Oh, we feel sorry for you earth dwellers because these last trumpets are going to usher in judgments the likes of which no one has ever seen before." In fact, they have become known as the "woe" trumpets because these angels cry, "Woe, woe, woe" to the inhabitants of the earth because of what lies ahead for them. It is no wonder that Jesus called the first half of the Tribulation, "the beginning of sorrows" (Matthew 24:8) and the last half, "The Great Tribulation" (Matthew 24:21). When God offered these unbelievers full and free salvation through the death of His beloved Son, they turned away from Him, and are now referred to as *"those who dwell upon the earth"* (Revelation 3:10), commonly called earth dwellers.

Jesus said in Matthew 24:14: *"And this gospel of the kingdom shall be preached in all the world for a witness unto all nations; and then shall the end come."* We have long associated this verse to missionaries going all over the world preaching the Gospel, and this certainly has merit. But, in a more literal sense, this happens just before the final disastrous woe trumpets bring in the most horrible judgments this world has ever known.

J. H. Melton, former teacher at Baptist Bible College, Springfield, Missouri, says, "When these trumpets once give out their ringing sounds, the vibrations will run through the universe, and everything created for human blessedness shall turn into a source of disaster and trouble to them that know not God and nor obey the Gospel of Christ."[9]

This angel will fly across the sky, preaching to the whole world in their own native tongue, the Gospel of the Kingdom, just as the Holy Spirit did at Pentecost. And as Jesus said, *"And then shall the end come"* (Matthew 24:14b). The first three and one-half years are bad, but not as bad as the last three and one-half years. As we said previously, Jesus in Matthew 24:8 described the first half of the Tribulation as "the beginning of sorrows", but the last half as "the Great Tribulation"(Matthew 24:21). As more judgments come down the pike, we will see that they become more severe and the loss of life is greater. Jack Van Impe points out that only two verses cover the scope of each of the first four trumpets, but trumpet five requires twelve verses and trumpet six requires nine verses.[10]

CHAPTER NINE

The Three Woe Trumpets and The Bottomless Pit

In this chapter we will see what happens when the three remaining trumpets are blown. It is considered one of the most difficult chapters in Revelation to understand because of the symbols to be interpreted. Unlike other chapters where many of the symbols are explained, this chapter offers few explanations for the symbols used. For example, here is how the symbolic language is explained in Revelation 1:20: "*The mystery of the seven stars which thou sawest in my right hand, and the seven golden candlesticks. The seven stars are the angels of the seven churches; and the seven candlesticks which thou sawest are the seven churches.*" However, the symbolism in chapter 9 is not that specific, so we must lean heavily on the Holy Spirit to guide us as we go through this.

"*And the fifth angel sounded, and I saw a star fall from Heaven unto the earth: and to him was given the key of the Bottomless Pit*" (Revelation 9:1). First, let us correct the tense of a word here. The Greek word translated "fall" is "peptokota." It is in the perfect tense which means it has already happened. The KJV translates peptokota as "fall" as though John had just seen this star fall. However, this is a faulty translation.

Modern translations have corrected this.
The NIV: "*I saw a star that had fallen from Heaven.*"
The NLT: "*I saw a star that had fallen from Heaven.*"
The RSV: "*I saw a star fallen from Heaven.*"
Phillips Paraphrase: "*I saw a star that had fallen from Heaven.*"
The NASB: "*I saw a star from Heaven which had fallen.*"

It is clear that this was an event that had taken place in ages past. John was not seeing the star fall at the time he was writing this. Also, notice that this is more than a star or a planet. It says, "*to him was given the key ….*". This is a person. We have seen this analogy before. The stars in Revelation chapter 1 turned out to be the seven pastors of those particular seven churches.

Who is this person? But first, let us see what is given to him. "*And to him was given the key to the Bottomless Pit.*" What is this *Bottomless Pit*? In the Greek it is "abussos" – which means "pit of the abyss." It has a connection with Hades which, according to Matthew 12:40, is located in the heart of the earth. To understand more about the Bottomless Pit, we need to explore the whole region that houses demonic beings. There are a number of names that many times are mistakenly used interchangeably. For example – Hades, Sheol, Gehenna, Hell, Torments, Lake of Fire, the Second Death, Tartarus and the Bottomless Pit.

Basically, these can be categorized into four distinct groups: Sheol and Hades into one group; Gehenna and Torments into another; the Bottomless Pit and Tartarus into another; and Hell, Lake of Fire and the Second Death into another. Here is a concise definition of these groups. Sheol (Hebrew) and Hades (Greek) simply mean "a place of the dead." People who were saved prior to the cross could not go directly to Heaven. They had to wait until Christ paid the penalty for their sins on Calvary because nothing that defiles can ever enter Heaven (Revelation 21:27). Therefore, Sheol/Hades can be viewed as a "holding place" before the cross for the souls of both Christians and non-believers. After the cross the believers are escorted by Christ to Heaven while the unsaved continue to be held in Sheol/Hades awaiting the Great White Throne Judgment. Drastic changes occurred when Christ arose from the dead that first Easter morning. His blood was presented to and accepted by God the Father (John 20:17) proving for all time that His sacrifice satisfied the holiness and justice of God.

Jesus went to Sheol/Hades, took the keys of death from Satan (Revelation 1:18), unlocked the doors of Paradise so to speak, and transferred Paradise housing the souls of the believers to Heaven (Ephesians 4:8). This left Sheol/Hades with only one compartment, which from then on is referred to as Hell, containing the souls of the unbelievers who are awaiting their appearance at the Great White Throne Judgment (Revelation 20:11-15). After this judgment, death and Hades (Hell) are cast into the Lake of Fire which is known as the Second Death (Revelation 20:14). This is the end of the road. Alighieri Dante wrote so aptly in *The Divine Comedy* published in 1472 that there is a sign over Hell – "Abandon hope all ye who enter in."[1]

Few sermons are preached on Hell in our current society since most preachers tend to shy away because it is so unpleasant. They had rather discuss the brighter things of Scripture. Many liberal theologians go so far as denying the literal existence of Hell, and instead spiritualize these truths as being simply a state of mind. They say there is not a literal place called Hell, but rather Hell is the life we create for ourselves while on this earth. However, Jesus had more to say about the aspects of Hell than He did about Heaven. When you read the description of Hell from the lips of Jesus, it is such a picture of reality, it is hard to think of it as an illusion (Mark 9:44-48). Truth cannot become a non-truth simply by denying it.

Though it is not pleasant to talk about, chapter 9 gives us a startling glimpse into the horrors of Hell. The word "Gehenna" also served as an illustration of Hell and the Lake of Fire. Gehenna was located near the southeast corner of the old city of Jerusalem, and was where the city garbage was taken. Hence, it was a stinking, burning trash heap, and provided a visual picture of the fires of Hell.

The last of these horrendous locations is known as the Bottomless Pit or Tartarus. Some teachers have given it the name of "Tartarus" although this name is not found in most Bible translations. This is where "the worst of the worst" evil angels were locked away awaiting their ultimate fate (II Peter 2:4). In today's legal system, it would be like a defendant being convicted of a capital crime, sentenced to death, and is now waiting in solitary confinement until the sentence is carried out. The angels held in Tartarus are probably the instigators along with Satan of the rebellion against God as opposed to just followers.

When this evil one is given the key to the Bottomless Pit, we see what happens when he opens it. "*When he opened it, smoke poured out as though from a huge furnace, and the sunlight and air were darkened by the smoke. Then locusts came from the smoke and descended on the earth, and they were given power to sting like scorpions*" (Revelation 9:2-3 NLT). These demonic creatures have been locked away for eons, and have been bitterly resenting their confinement. They have been chafing to take vengeance on mankind whom they regard as the cause for their unhappy circumstances.

Scripture says that smoke along with swarms of locusts darken the sun. Recently, there was a newspaper headline that read, "Biblical Plague of Locusts Block Out the Sun."[2] How large are these swarms? *National Geographic* reports, "A desert locust swarm can be 460 square miles in size and between 40 and 80 million locusts packed into less than half a mile square," confirming that locusts can effectively block out the sun.[3]

Pure evil in the form of these locusts poured out of the Pit, and they were given power to sting like scorpions. When I was growing up, we lived in an old frame house close to a wooded area. We never lacked for scorpions and, once stung by one you never forget it. Many times as a teenager I prepared to take a bath when a glance in the bathtub revealed a scorpion which had fallen in the tub and could not climb out. Needless to say, he got the bath first – with an abundance of hot water!

"*And there came out of the smoke locusts upon the earth: and unto them was given power, as the scorpions of the earth have power*" (Revelation 9:3). The day is coming when all Hell will be loosed on this earth. The Bottomless Pit will be opened, and all the evil, hellish things that have been locked away will be temporarily set free causing a strange darkness to blot out the sun. "*And it was commanded them that they should not hurt the grass of the earth, neither any green thing, neither any tree; but only those men which have not the seal of God in their foreheads*" (Revelation 9:4). But God limited what they could do. They could hurt people, but only those who did not have the seal of God on their foreheads. And the demons were more than willing to get on with their grizzly assignment.

Someone asked, "What about the great multitude that had been won to Christ through the witness of the 144,000 sealed evangelists? Will they be tormented as well?" It would hardly seem likely that God would allow these to be so grievously injured. I believe the vast majority, if not all of them, have already been martyred at the hand of the Antichrist. If any are still alive, there is no doubt that God will protect them from this judgment that is designed for the Christ rejecters.

"And to them it was given that they should not kill them, but that they should be tormented five months: and their torment was as the torment of a scorpion, when he striketh a man" (Revelation 9:5). Why are they limited to five months? It is unclear, but one commentator, William R. Newell, says that five months is the natural life period of the locust.[4] It is also interesting to note that five months – 150 days – was the duration of the rising flood waters in the days of Noah (Genesis 8:3). The unbelievers suffered, and all died during this five month judgment in Genesis. During the Tribulation, as in the days of Noah, men will again suffer for five months; however, this time they wanted to die but death eluded them.

Bible scholar David Hocking has this to say: "While a scorpion sting is usually not fatal, it is extremely painful. The venom affects the veins and nervous system. Normally the pain and discomfort last for several days, but the torment of this judgment in Revelation 9 lasts for five months!"[5] *"And in those days shall men seek death, and shall not find it; and shall desire to die, and death shall flee from them"* (Revelation 9:6). Five months is a long time for men to experience this awful judgment. No doubt they will flee to the mountains, the seas, the deserts. They will lock their doors, bar their windows, cringe in their cellars. But there is no escape. This plague is so fearful and so painful men will seek death but cannot find it.

We live in a day when we do everything we can to keep from dying. We want the medical technicians to hook up all kinds of equipment, machines and tubes that will preserve our life just a little while longer. But these poor men who find themselves under the judgment of the fifth trumpet of woe will want to die but they cannot. I can envision their guns jamming; I can envision their poison having no effect. Men may injure themselves trying to end their life, but that will only increase their suffering. This affirms the depravity of man. These men had rather die than turn to God. How very sad!

Dr. J. Vernon McGee says, "It is not a laughing matter to reject Jesus. People say there are many important things in this life. I am willing to grant that many things take second, third and fourth place, but the most important decision you can ever make is the one concerning the Lord Jesus Christ."[6] What a true statement! God controls life and death. When He deems it is time for people to die, they die. When He says the time to die is not yet, they will not die.

Did you know that God has determined the exact day you will die? Some scientists even say that your death date is encoded in your DNA![7] It is human nature to want to live as long as possible; however, God decided how long we will live long before we were born. We often fret about why a good person is taken from the earth so soon while some reprobate lives to a ripe old age. But in my study, I discovered something that gives me peace with this. I do not fret about it anymore because I realize that God whose wisdom is perfect has laid out the best plan for His children as to when they will leave this earth.

We have heard it said, "Our days are numbered." But did you know this is actually true? Scripture indicates that when a person is conceived, that person's name is recorded in the Book of Life. And in the same book, God records how long that person is allotted to live. Someone might say, "How can that be?" God is all-knowing and therefore knows when each person will die. But there is more to it than that. Psalm 139:16 (NLT) says, *"You saw me before I was born. Every day of my life was recorded in your book. Every moment was laid out before a single day had passed."*

In God's Book of Life, it is recorded the day and the hour that you and I will breathe our last breath. But because of our freewill that God has granted us, we have input into our longevity – an input into this formula of life.

For example, God's fifth commandment says that we should honor our parents so that we will live a long life. If you honor and respect them, that is factored into our longevity. I Corinthians 11:30 says that if you partake of the Lord's Supper in a frivolous and disrespectful manner, your days will be cut short. That is factored into the outcome. If you tempt God by intentionally walking in front of a train or jumping out of a ten story building, that is factored in. Proverbs 3:1-2 says that if a person keeps God's laws and follow His commandments, that will prolong your life and is factored in. Otherwise, if you live a quiet life, serving God to the best of your abilities, there will come a time when God says, "Welcome home my good and faithful servant."

Someone might ask, "But what about a young person who loves the Lord but is cut down in the prime of life, or a middle aged believer who dies from a deadly disease? Why does God allow that to happen?" This is a mystery known only to God, but we are given a hint. In Isaiah 57:1-2 (NLT), God says that sometimes a godly man or woman dies early because of God in His mercy wants to spare them the pain and heartache that He sees waiting for them if they continue in this life. And so, especially during the Tribulation, God's sovereignty is clearly manifest as He allows many believers to be put to death by the Antichrist while many non-believers are left to suffer severely as the various judgments pound the earth.

"The locusts looked like horses armed for battle. They had gold crowns on their heads, and they had human faces. Their hair was long like the hair of a woman, and their teeth were like the teeth of a lion. They wore armor made of iron, and their wings roared like an army of chariots rushing into battle. They had tails that stung like scorpions, with power to torture people. This power was given to them for five months. Their king is the angel from the Bottomless Pit; his name in Hebrew is Abaddon, and in Greek, Apollyon – the Destroyer" (Revelation 9:7-11 NLT). The fact that they are prepared for battle is an indication of the swiftness with which these locusts attack. The

crowns they are wearing are not diadems. They are stephanos – the victors' crowns, signifying that they will conquer everything in their path.

Their faces are like the faces of men, signifying purpose, drive and intelligence with which they operate. John is describing this scene as best that he knows how. The resemblance of a locust to a horse, especially to a horse equipped with armor, is so striking that the word locust in German is "Heupferd" meaning "hay-horse", and in Italian, "Cavaletta" – meaning "little horse". The reference to the hair of women means they will be beguiling and seductive, while at the same time, they will be ready to tear and bite with the viciousness of a lion. Their armor was like iron meaning it was indestructible. These demons cannot be stopped by human forces alone. They are only vulnerable to the name and power of Jesus Christ.

Some commentators say that these locusts are simply armored tanks, and this is a 1st Century description of them through the eyes of John. We have always had wars and scary weapons of destruction, like the invention of the nuclear bomb, to come out of these wars. But here the Bottomless Pit is opened, the vilest angels are temporarily released, and dreadful judgments are carried out. This passage appears to be highly symbolic. We cannot be dogmatic that this description is to be taken literally though it certainly could. However, whatever turns out to be the case, you can rest assured that the reality will be much worse than words can describe. One should do everything possible to avoid such a traumatic event, and the only sure way is to become a child of God by believing and trusting in Jesus Christ.

Think of the fifth trumpet this way – as if every prison in the world threw open its doors, and set free the vilest offenders known to man. It will be this, but many times worse. This is what the fifth trumpet releases – only the doors are the doors to Hell, and the offenders are the worst demonic angels to ever go up against God. Saying it another way: the worst of the angels are locked away in the Bottomless Pit, where the other angels sympathetic to Satan are out on bond so to speak, assisting Satan in his demonic activities. I get this from two verses. The first is Jude 6, which states, *"And the angels which kept not their first estate, but left their own habitation, He hath reserved in everlasting chains under darkness unto the judgment of the great day."*

The second reference to certain angels being kept in chains is in II Peter 2:4 (NLT): *"For God did not spare even the angels when they sinned; He threw them into Hell, in gloomy caves and darkness until the judgment day."*

So, after Christ was crucified, He went to Hades for three days, NOT to suffer at the hands of Satan as some TV evangelists teach, but to forcibly obtain the keys to death and Hades (Revelation 1:18).[8] When Jesus said on the cross, "It is finished"– He meant it! Jesus went to Hades immediately after His crucifixion to set free those believers who were being held there until their penalty was paid, and to take them back to Heaven with Him (Ephesians 4:8).

In the eighth chapter of Luke, we find the story of the madman in the area of the Gadarenes on the eastern shore of the Sea of Galilee. He was possessed and tormented by a legion of demons; that is more than 6,000. Demons are simply another name for the evil angels who are not locked away in the Bottomless Pit. They are under the direction of their master, Satan. Just as Jesus began to cast these demons out of the poor man, the demons begged Jesus to send them into the nearby herd of swine, but not to the abyss. It is a terrible place; even the demons detest going there. Jesus sent them into the swine that promptly ran over the cliff, and committed suicide rather than be possessed by these demons (Luke 8:33). A jokester said that is where we first learned of "deviled ham."

We find in Revelation 9:1 that Jesus gives the key to the Bottomless Pit to this fallen star – this fallen angel. Who is this fallen angel that Jesus gives this key to? Can there be any doubt? Listen to a portion of Isaiah 14:12-14: *"How art thou fallen from Heaven, O Lucifer, son of the morning – for thou hast said in thine heart, I will ascend into Heaven, I will exalt my throne above the stars of God – I will ascend above the heights of the clouds; I will be like the most High."* Jesus remembers this well. In Luke 10:18, Jesus tells his disciples that He saw Satan fall like lightning from Heaven. Satan was literally cast out of the third Heaven – the abode of God the Father. Originally, before Satan sinned, he had access to the third Heaven, but after sinning, he was denied further access. However, from the Book of Job, we learn that Satan was called "the accuser of the brethren." He had access to what we might call the "outer chambers of heaven" – the second heaven – which we will discuss shortly.

Here are the three realms of heaven: 1) our immediate atmosphere; 2) outer space – the sun, moon and stars; and 3) the home of God. Hebrews 4:14 (NASB) says, *"Therefore, since we have a great High Priest who has passed through the heavens, Jesus the Son of God, let us hold fast our confession."* The fact that Jesus passed through the heavens gives evidence that there is more than one heaven. The Apostle Paul refers to the "third Heaven" in II Corinthians 12:2.

Common sense tells us if there is a third Heaven, there must be a first and second heaven. Although Scripture does not specifically make such a designation, we can infer this from certain passages. For example in Genesis 6:7a, *"And the LORD said, 'I will destroy man whom I have created from the face of the earth; both man, and beast, and the creeping thing, and the fowls of the air ....'".* When the word translated air is used in Scripture, it generally is the Greek word "ouranos" which is our atmosphere. We have a good example of this in James 5:18: *"And he [Elijah] prayed again, and the heaven gave rain and the earth brought forth her fruit."* This is the first heaven. We refer to it as the atmospheric heaven or the terrestrial heaven, and includes the air that we breathe, and the space that immediately surrounds the earth which extends approximately 20 miles above the earth.

The space above the terrestrial heaven is the celestial heaven also called the second heaven. Its scientific name is the stratosphere, and includes the realm of the astronaut as well as the sun, moon and stars. It is referred to in Matthew 24:29 (NASB): *"But immediately after the tribulation of those days, THE SUN WILL BE DARKENED, AND THE MOON WILL NOT GIVE ITS LIGHT, AND THE STARS WILL FALL FROM THE SKY, AND THE POWERS OF THE HEAVENS WILL BE SHAKEN."* Again in Deuteronomy 4:19a (NASB): *"And beware not to lift up your eyes to heaven and see the sun and the moon and the stars, all the host of Heaven, and be drawn away and worship them and serve them …."*.

And then there is the third Heaven – or the "Heaven of Heavens" which is where God dwells. Of course, God is everywhere since He is omnipresent. I Kings 8:27 (NASB) tells us, *"But will God indeed dwell on the earth? Behold, heaven and the highest Heaven cannot contain you, how much less this house which I have built!"* But the third Heaven is special because that is where His throne is located. Deuteronomy 10:14 reminds us, *"Behold, the heaven and the Heaven of Heavens is the LORD'S thy God, the earth also, with all that therein is."* Again in Hebrews 9:24 (NASB) we are told, *"For Christ did not enter a holy place made with hands, a mere copy of the true one, but into Heaven itself, now to appear in the presence of God for us."* Hebrews 8:1 (NLT) says, *"Here is the main point: Our High Priest sat down in the place of highest honor in Heaven, at God's right hand."*

In verse 1 of this ninth chapter of Revelation which we referred to earlier, John sees this angel – Satan – who had fallen from Heaven like a great star. Some commentators think that this is one of Satan's strongest angels that is given the key to the Bottomless Pit. But with Satan's huge ego, it is doubtful that he would share this moment with anyone else. Jesus gives Satan the key to the Bottomless Pit, and Satan can hardly wait to turn loose his evil minions in the world to cause more pain and suffering upon mankind.

There is no greater contrast in Scripture than God's love and God's wrath. This great contrast is presented over and over, but none pictures it as well as John 3:36: *"He that believeth on the Son hath everlasting life: and He that believeth not the Son shall not see life; but the wrath of God abideth on him."* This is the most important choice for every human being. There are some very scary things revealed in the Book of Revelation, but be assured, if you have received Jesus Christ as your personal Savior, you have nothing to fear; in fact, just the opposite. The end of the age is pictured for the believer as joyful beyond your wildest imagination.

When the first six seals were broken, we had for the most part, man inflicting his evil will upon other men with God's permissive will in effect. But in the seventh seal, we have something much more devastating. God takes the initiative, and is giving Satan and his angels much more leeway in carrying out their diabolical plans. *"And they had tails like unto scorpions, and there were stings in their tails: and their power was to hurt men five months"* (Revelation 9:10).

Notice four things that describe the damage inflicted by these creatures from Hell:

1) They are painful – it will be like a constant scorpion sting.
2) They are protracted – their hurt will continue for five months.
3) They are personal – they will inflict excruciating pain on every person on earth, except those who are sealed and protected by the power of God.
4) They are perpetual – men will try to kill themselves to escape the torment, but death will elude them.

There seems to be no escaping the conclusion that these locusts from Hell are, indeed, demonic spirits. They have been long confined in the Pit of the Abyss, but are now released for a little season perhaps so men will understand the fearful consequences of continuing to reject God's great salvation. These demonic invaders can fly like locusts, run like horses, and sting like scorpions. Their sounds are deafening. The terror which such creatures generate can be easily imagined. No wonder that men seek death as a way to escape!

Men surely know by now that Christ is in Heaven, the raptured saints are in Heaven, the holy angels have been seen flying through the sky by the earth dwellers, and it is evident that the wrath of the Lamb is being visited on the earth. Yet these earth dwellers persist in their hatred of God, choosing Satan instead, and so God allows them to experience a little direct fellowship with their future co-inhabitants of the Lake of Fire!

The big question is, "Why don't these people turn to God?" We get a hint in II Thessalonians chapter 2. Paul describes these end time Christ rejecters as those who give themselves up to unclean spirits, to blasphemy and to unbelief. *"And for this cause God shall send them strong delusion, that they should believe a lie"* (II Thessalonians 2:11). Actually, there is a definite article in the Greek so that this should read, as the NIV correctly translates it, *"that they should believe the lie"* (author's emphasis). And what lie is that? It is the lie of the Antichrist when he tells these people, "I AM GOD! Things are going to get better. That false god, Jehovah, is causing all of this, but I will soon correct that. I have our top scientists working on this, and we will soon have some relief for you. Our armies will soon be able to destroy these locust-like creatures."

Someone says, "Why did God send them this strong delusion so that they would believe this lie? This seems to be unfair." Listen closely: God never pours out His judgment without warning. Every instance in the Bible when He meted out His judgment upon the earth, He gave warning after warning after warning. He did this in Noah's time before the flood. He had Noah warn the people for 120 years. He warned the residents of Sodom and Gomorrah to flee from the wrath that was to come. He warned Nineveh through the prophet, Jonah (Jonah 1:1-2). He sent prophet after prophet to warn the children of Israel to repent, and to forsake the false gods of their neighboring countries. He warned Pharaoh over and over. After each plague, Pharaoh would waver but, as things got better, Pharaoh would then harden his heart. He would resolve that, "I can get through this – I don't need to turn to God. And I certainly don't need to release thousands of slaves resulting in the loss of free labor." But it is a losing battle when you go up against the God of the universe.

Throughout the Bible, the result has always been the same when the Gospel is preached, and a decision is required. The result is best described in Acts 28:24 (NIV) after Paul preached to them: *"Some were convinced by what he said, but others would not believe."* Jesus reminded the people that Isaiah the prophet was ignored, and therefore God hardened their hearts. *"HE HATH BLINDED THEIR EYES, AND HARDENED THEIR HEART; THAT THEY SHOULD NOT SEE WITH THEIR EYES, NOR UNDERSTAND WITH THEIR HEART, AND BE CONVERTED, AND I SHOULD HEAL THEM"* (John 12:40). The unbelieving Israelites referred to by Isaiah had been given ample opportunity to repent, but time and again they had deliberately closed their eyes to the light. Since light rejected produces night, they had in effect blinded themselves until the Lord finally withdrew the light they had been offered.

People have often asked, "What about the savages in Africa who have never heard the Gospel? Will they be lost forever? That used to bother me a lot. Is God unfair? Then I learned a principle that is true throughout the Bible: "God gives every individual some spiritual light. If they follow that light, they will be given more light."

Missionaries who have gone to the darkest part of Africa and confronted savages who had never seen a white man and never heard the Gospel, have reported that when they encountered the natives, they would often hear them say, "We have been praying that the Great Spirit would send someone to tell us about Him." Anyone who follows the light they are given – be it in America or the jungles of Africa – will be given more light until they finally arrive at the feet of Jesus.

Isaiah said, *"The Lord has blinded their eyes and hardened their hearts ...."* (John 12:40-41 NLT). Is that fair? Did they have a choice if God was the one who hardened their hearts? Here is another Biblical principle. God never "hardens" the heart of a person until that person has steeled himself against the Lord so persistently that there is no longer any hope. Then God closes the door of opportunity.

This is not to say that God is no longer willing to save a person, but rather that God foresees that he or she will never turn around. God's grand invitation to "whosoever will" has no exceptions. We also know that Scripture says in II Peter 3:9 that God is longsuffering, not willing that any should perish. Nevertheless, there is a point of no return when God's patience runs out, and He sees that the person will never repent. God says in Genesis 6:3a, *"My Spirit shall not always strive [plead] with man ...."*.

In other words, God seals the doom of a man who has already permanently closed his ears to the Lord's appeal. This same truth is revealed by the Apostle Paul in the first chapter of the Book of Romans. After describing the sins of the type of civilization that God pours His wrath upon, Paul says, *"For this cause God gave them up …."* (Romans 1:26a).

There is an important principle here. When people persist in iniquity, when people choose to be vile and continually turn their back on God and His Church, God lowers the hedge of protection around them, and lets sin run its course. And God eventually will let them experience what it is to be a servant of the Devil, and they are rewarded with horrendous suffering as we find in Revelation 9:10. But it is of man's own choosing!

"And they had a king over them, which is the angel of the Bottomless Pit, whose name in the Hebrew tongue is Abaddon, but in the Greek tongue hath his name Apollyon" (Revelation 9:11). I do not think this is Satan because this angel lives in the Bottomless Pit, and he will be locked up until the Pit is opened as described in Revelation 9:2. Instead, this sounds like a strong, evil angel – maybe the counterpart of that mighty angel, Michael. He is even elected king over these misfits. His name in both Greek and Hebrew means "Destroyer", and he is tickled to death to lead his band of misfits to vent their rage on these earth dwellers.

"One woe is past; and, behold, there come two woes more hereafter" (Revelation 9:12). This should motivate each of us to win people to Christ as we do not want anyone to experience these horrible judgments.

As a quick summary: When the seventh and final seal of the all-important scroll was opened, it revealed seven angels with seven trumpets. When the first four trumpets sounded, specific judgments were poured out upon the earth and its inhabitants. Then an angel flies across the heavens telling the people on earth that three more trumpets would sound, bringing three judgments more terrible than has gone on before. They are called the "woe trumpets" or the "woe judgments".

Chapter 9 opens with the first of these woes as the fifth angel sounds his trumpet. The Bottomless Pit is unlocked, and all the demons of Hell pour out causing the sun to be darkened (Revelation 9:1-2). They were compared to a locust swarm, except they look like horses with heavy armor. They have long, flowing hair and faces like men. The worst part is they have stings in their tails that feel like scorpion stings. Their torment will last five months, and their victims will seek death, but it will evade them (Revelation 9:7-10). No one on earth is immune to these painful attacks except the 144,000 evangelists who previously in chapter 7 were sealed by God for special protection against the Antichrist and his forces, and the Tribulation believers.

We now come to the second woe. *"And the sixth angel sounded, and I heard a voice from the four horns of the golden altar which is before God, saying to the sixth angel which had the trumpet, 'Loose the four angels which are bound in the great river Euphrates'"* (Revelation 9:13-14).

Before we continue, I have something new for you to consider. In Exodus, Moses was given the pattern to build the Tabernacle (Exodus 26). This is clarified in Hebrews 8:5 where we are told that this pattern of the Tabernacle was an exact duplicate of what exists in Heaven. In connection with the Tabernacle, there were two altars. One was the Brazen Altar or Altar of Burnt Sacrifices. It was located outside the sanctuary in the Court, and was the altar for the blood sacrifice (Exodus 27:1-5). The other altar was small, made out of gold, and stood before the veil of the Holy Place. It was called the Golden Altar (Exodus 40:26). It was the altar of worship, of prayer, mediation and intercession.

There was a gold censer – a utensil with a handle in which fire was taken from the Altar of Sacrifice and carried to the Golden Altar where incense was burned unto God. Blood was taken from the Altar of Sacrifice on the Day of Atonement, and sprinkled on the four golden horns (or corners) of the altar. The purpose of this ritual was to teach the people that prayer and worship are based upon sacrifice and the shedding of blood, without which there is no remission of sins, and without which no man can come into the presence of God.

A cry comes from the four horns of the Golden Altar to *"loose the four terrible angels bound in the river Euphrates"* (Revelation 9:14). What an amazing thing! Up to this point, the blood of the sacrifice and the prayers of intercession had always been for mercy – and God would forgive and God would save. But here in the Tribulation Period, the blood that cries and the voice that is raised is no longer for forgiveness or for God's mercy. The Age of Grace is past! This is the voice of judgment and damnation! How could such a thing be? It is this: God's way for a man to be saved is in the pure, undefiled blood of Jesus Christ. This is the only way that a man can ever see God's face and live. When a man turns down this offer, when a man treads underfoot the blood of the Covenant, then the very altar cries out against that man's unbelief and rejection.

"For whatsoever a man soweth, that shall he also reap" (Galatians 6:7b). With the judgment of the sixth trumpet, the time for reaping is come. And in chapter 9:13 we see that this cry is coming from the four horns of the altar calling for judgment to be loosed.

The Euphrates River is a very historic place. That is the area where the Garden of Eden was located (Genesis 2:14- 15). That is the area where the first murder was committed. And that is the area where the first promise was given of a coming Savior (Genesis 3:15). It was here that Nimrod founded the city of Babel eventually resulting in the disastrous Tower of Babel (Genesis 10:10-11:9). This is the area where Abraham received his call from God. And this is the area where years later Nebuchadnezzar built the mighty city of Babylon to which Daniel was carried as a slave. The Euphrates has long been a fountainhead of idolatry. It was also both the boundary line of the old Roman Empire and the land of Israel. It served as a natural barrier to keep the Asian hordes from overrunning the tiny nation of Israel.

Now look at chapter 9:15, *"And the four angels were loosed, which were prepared for an hour, and a day, and a month, and a year, for to slay the third part of men."*

In the Greek, there are definite articles – these angels were prepared by God for the hour, the day, the month and the year. In other words, this is no accident that they are loosed. The time has been decreed by God in ages past for just this particular time. And these imprisoned spirits had been waiting a long time for their chance to wreak havoc on mankind.

"And the number of the army of the horsemen were two hundred thousand thousand: and I heard the number of them" (Revelation 9:16). This is an army of two hundred thousand thousand – 200 million soldiers! I wonder what John thought when he heard this. By some estimates, there were not 200 million people in the world when this was written let alone an army of that number. Ezekiel predicted this time when he wrote, *"And thou shalt come up against my people of Israel, as a cloud to cover the land; it shall be in the latter days, and I will bring thee against my land, that the heathen may know Me, when I shall be sanctified in thee, O Gog, before their eyes"* (Ezekiel 38:16). Then in Revelation 9:17, John is shown a description of these soldiers: *"And thus I saw the horses in the vision, and them that sat on them, having breastplates of fire, and of jacinth, and brimstone: and the heads of the horses were as the heads of lions; and out of their mouths issued fire and smoke and brimstone."*

There is a big disagreement between commentators on the meaning of this. Each has good points. One group believes that these are supernatural creatures, prepared by God, hideous in their description, ready to slay one-third of mankind. Another group sees these as humans, and I lean toward this interpretation. One nation – China – could mount an army of 200 million men. I think these oriental hoards have detested the Antichrist from the beginning, and they see a way to come against him in the Battle of Armageddon. The NIV translates this verse (9:17a) as follows: *"The horses and riders I saw in my vision looked like this: Their breastplates were fiery red, dark blue and yellow as sulfur …."*. It is interesting to note that China's flag is red and yellow, and its men wear dark blue uniforms. Just an observation. And we find a little later in the Book that this giant army engages the Antichrist and his armies on the plains of Jezreel. This description by John could be what it looked like to a 1ˢᵗ Century observer. He could easily be seeing a scene of modern weapons and warfare with its machine guns, helicopters, armored tanks, heavy artillery and flamethrowers.

Dr. David Reagan collects church signs on marquees. One church's marquee had the pastor's sermon listed on the sign in front of the church. It said, "When will life's final battle be fought?" Underneath it said, "First Baptist Church, Sunday at 7 PM."

"By these three was the third part of men killed, by the fire, and by the smoke, and by the brimstone, which issued out of their mouths" (Revelation 9:18). Men will be consumed in the flames, suffocated by the smoke, and poisoned by the sulphur gases. In the judgment connected with the sounding of the fifth trumpet, the horrible creatures that were released from Hell were restrained from killing anyone, but they could inflict terrible pain for five months. Now, with

this sixth trumpet judgment, we find that one out of every three people is going to be killed. Putting this into perspective, look what is going to happen to the earth's population:

1) A few hundred million will leave the earth at the Rapture.
2) One-fourth of the remaining population will die from wars, natural disasters, starvation, diseases and poisoned water when the fourth seal is opened (Revelation 6:8).
3) One-third of those still alive will die when the four angels at the Euphrates are released (Revelation 9:15).

In other words, more than 50% of the world population will die by the time the sixth trumpet woe is finished. By today's population, that would be more than 3 billion people. The first woe was painful – the second is lethal. There will be a cry and wail go up from this earth like has never been heard in all of history. Oh, what sorrow!

And to think, that the official teaching of the Catholic Church is that the Tribulation Period was fulfilled during the 1st Century. But Jesus said in Matthew 24:21, "*For then shall be great tribulation, such as was not since the beginning of the world to this time, no, nor ever shall be.*

An official Catholic website says this: "The Catholic Church believes in preterism."[9] Preterism is a name of a system for the interpretation of the Book of Revelation. Its strange name comes from a Latin word meaning past tense. The word is appropriate because this view holds that either all or most of the Book of Revelation was fulfilled in the 1st Century! Remember, Jesus said as quoted above, more people will die in the Tribulation Period than at any time in the entire history of mankind. So, for one to hold to the position that the Tribulation Period was fulfilled in the 1st Century, one would have to say that more people died in the 1st Century than the 25 million that died from the Black Plague that swept through Europe in the 14th Century – and that did not happen.[10]

"*For their power is in their mouth, and in their tails: for their tails were like unto serpents, and had heads, and with them they do hurt*" (Revelation 9:19). Again, this could be some supernatural creatures that are inflicting pain upon the earth, or it could be a picture of new weapons spitting fire and destruction on every hand. It will be understood when the time comes. It really does not make a lot of difference. The main point is that massive devastation will cover the earth and you do not want to be here as a part of it!

"*And the rest of the men which were not killed by these plagues yet repented not of the works of their hands, that they should not worship devils, and idols of gold, and silver, and brass, and stone, and of wood: which neither can see, nor hear, nor walk*" (Revelation 9:20). By this time, millions have been saved by the preaching of the 144,000 evangelists and by the two witnesses which we will study in chapter 11, and by the great wealth of Christian literature and videos that believers leave behind at the Rapture.

Do the unbelievers who were not killed by this awful judgment turn to God? No! Instead, there is a revival of idolatry. They continue to worship Satan and gods made with their hands out of gold, silver, brass, stone and wood. In the end, these people line up on Satan's team believing that with Satan's leadership, they can eventually overthrow God and the hosts of Heaven.

"Neither repented they of their murders, nor of their sorceries, nor of their fornication, nor of their thefts" (Revelation 9:21). It mentions four major sins: murders, sorceries, fornication and theft. All of these plague our modern society, but they will get worse during this traumatic time. In 2017 in the U.S. alone there were over 1,250,000 violent crimes[11] and they will accelerate in the end times when people harden their hearts and return to idol worship. Remember the rider on the red horse from chapter 6? It says the rider is sent to *"take away peace from the earth, and that they should kill one another"* (Revelation 6:4). And that will happen in the extreme.

The next major sin mentioned is sorcery. It comes from the Greek word, "pharmakeia", which is the source of our English word pharmacy. It means "drugs" in the sense that the end times will be characterized by rampant substance abuse. In a few places, this word pharmakeia is translated "witchcraft". It speaks to me of the fact that as people get hooked on drugs, they open their minds to all sorts of demon possession and control. No wonder they will believe the Antichrist will amply provide whatever drugs they desire, and he will certainly do that.

Bob Woodward is a Washington reporter who broke the Watergate story which resulted in the resignation of President Richard Nixon. Reporter Bob Woodward wrote, "Hillary Clinton has brought witchcraft into the White House in the form of her friend, Psycho-spiritist, Jean Houston. Hillary and Mrs. Houston met together on numerous occasions in the White House. Mrs. Houston led Hillary into conversations with the dead, including several with Eleanor Roosevelt and Mahatma Ghandi.[12]

This was common knowledge among the White House staff. Even the FDR Foundation reported that Hillary received the following information from the (deceased) Mrs. Roosevelt: "Buck up and grow skin as thick as a rhinoceros."[13]

Fornication is mentioned as the third major sin. The word means a flagrant disregard for marriage. Even though divorce and infidelity seem rampant today and we wonder how it can get any worse, it is nothing compared to what it will be like when all restraints are removed. With the acceptance of same-sex marriages, along with their motto "we have a right to marry anyone we choose," there is no feasible or moral argument against someone being married to two or three people at the same time, or even marrying their pet animal. It seems farfetched, but so did the movement in 2016 to allow boys and girls to shower together. Christians have fought this ungodly provision tooth and nail, but it has not gone away. Remember, during the Tribulation, the Antichrist will promote the breakdown of all such moral restraints.

Finally, the last major sin listed is thievery, which is directly linked to all the other sins. God has given us a glimpse as to what this awful time will be like. In eternity, God will not permit open defiance of His will. Our Lord Jesus tells us that, in Hell, there will not only be weeping because of suffering, but there will be gnashing of teeth which expresses continued rebellion and hatred in the heart of man against God (Luke 13:28).

We should avail ourselves of every opportunity to keep people from experiencing these dreadful events. Ninety years ago, Dr. Harry Ironside, long time pastor of Moody Bible Church in Chicago, wrote a great statement in his commentary on the Book of Revelation. It is so powerful, I have written it in my Bible. It explains why most of these poor souls in the Tribulation Period refuse to turn to Christ. "If the cross of Christ, with its marvelous exhibition of holy love, will not reconcile men to God, then punishment will never avail to win their hearts."[14]

In our study thus far, we have seen six of the seven seals opened. The judgments seem to get worse with the opening of each new seal. Millions are killed, but those remaining still do not repent. Instead they choose to continue to serve dead gods made of gold, silver, brass and wood – gods that can neither hear nor see nor are able to rescue them from their terrible plight.

When the seventh seal is opened, it will reveal seven angels with seven trumpets. As each angel sounds his trumpet, we find that a particular judgment is released upon the earth. The seventh angel is poised to sound the seventh trumpet. But things on earth have become so bad, it appears that all hope is lost, and that Satan is going to win this battle after all.

It is at this point that God says, "Wait a minute. My followers need some encouragement. They need to know that I am still on the throne and in control. They need to know that in just a little while, Satan will be crushed."

And so, God calls another "time out." Some might call it a "flash-forward." God inserts a parenthesis before He goes on with the details of the terrible things that lie ahead. This parenthesis, as we will see, extends from Revelation chapter 10 verse 1 through chapter 11 verse 14. This parenthesis tells us something between the sixth and seventh trumpets that we need to know about grace and mercy and love. We will see this in chapter 10.

CHAPTER TEN

The Mighty Angel and The Little Book

———————

In Chapter 10, a detailed description is given of a mighty Angel who comes down from Heaven. This is no ordinary angel as you can tell from His description. Who is He?

It is amazing to me how these astute commentators line up in one of two groups. One group says that this mighty Angel is probably Michael, the archangel. This group of teachers includes Drs. William R. Newell, Jimmy Draper, Theodore Epp, J. Vernon McGee, John Walvoord, Charles Ryrie and W. A. Criswell. What an impressive group of Bible scholars!

But there is another group of theologians who are just as impressive. This second group believes that this mighty Angel described by John is none other than the Lord Jesus Christ. These scholars include Drs. Arno C. Gaebelein, Henry M. Morris, David Jeremiah, Gary Fisher, Jack Van Impe, H. A. Ironside, Hal Lindsey and David Reagan.

I am in the latter camp. To me, the description given cannot be anyone other than the Lord Jesus Christ Himself. If you think otherwise, that is fine – you have a lot of good company. But when you read the description given by John, can you come to any other conclusion than this is someone other than the incomparable Jesus Christ? I think not. Look closely at the description, and then make up your own mind as the Holy Spirit guides you.

The term angel, which actually means messenger, is used in three different ways in Scripture. Sometimes the Bible simply says "angels". This refers to the heavenly host. Sometimes it says, "An angel of the Lord," and it is referring to a particular angel out of the host of angels who might be carrying out a specific service at that time. The identity of "The Angel of the Lord" is not precisely spelled out in the Bible; however, there are many important clues as to His identity. There are Old and New Testament references to "angels of the Lord," "an angel of the Lord," and "The Angel of the Lord."

It seems when the definite article "the" is used, it is specifying a unique being, separate from the other angels. The Angel of the Lord speaks as God, identifies Himself with God and exercises the responsibilities of God (Genesis 16:7-12; 21:17-18; 22:11-18; Exodus 3:2-6; Judges 2:1-4; 6:11-24; 13:3-22; II Samuel 24:16; Zechariah 3:1; 12:8). In several of these appearances, those who saw the Angel of the Lord feared for their lives because they had seen the Lord. Therefore, it is clear that in at least some instances, the Angel of the Lord is a theophany, an appearance of God in physical form. And it is worthy to note that the appearances of "the Angel of the Lord" cease after the incarnation of Christ. Angels are mentioned numerous times in the New Testament, but "The Angel of the Lord" is never mentioned in the New Testament after the birth of Christ.[1]

Before Christ came to earth, He was known as the Word of God. And when Jacob wrestled with a messenger from God and his name was changed to Israel, Jacob said later, *"I have seen God face to face, and my life is preserved"* (Genesis 32:30b). As The Angel of the Lord – or as some translations say, The Angel of Jehovah – Christ often appeared in the Old Testament. In Exodus 3:2-9, The Angel of the Lord appeared to Moses, and commissioned him to go to Egypt to rescue the Israelites. Because The Angel of the Lord appeared frequently to Israel, it is not unusual that we would find Him appearing again in the last days, in the period called "the time of Jacob's trouble" (Jeremiah 30:7).

Look closely at this Angel's description in verse 1. He was wrapped in a cloud. A cloud always surrounds deity, and a cloud has always been associated with two things: 1) the presence of God; and 2) the return of Jesus. On Mount Sinai, when God delivered the Ten Commandments, He came down in a thick cloud (Exodus 19:9). In a cloud, God led the Israelites through the desert (Exodus 16:10). When God spoke to Moses in Exodus 24:15, it was in a cloud. When Solomon built and dedicated the magnificent Temple in Jerusalem, God came in a cloud, dwelling in the Temple as His house (II Chronicles 6:1-2). When Ezekiel was called on 500 years later to declare the desolation of that holy Temple, he saw the cloud lift up from the most Holy Place, hover a moment over the door of the sanctuary, and then move over the city. It hung above the city wall and then slowly moved over to the adjoining mountain on the east (the Mount of Olives) as though He was reluctant to leave, and then went up into the heavens (Ezekiel chapters 9-11). It is the same place that Zechariah says the Lord's feet will touch down when He comes back at the Second Coming or as Tim LaHaye likes to call it, "The Glorious Appearing." When Christ ascended into Heaven, a cloud received Him out of their sight (Acts 1:9); and when He returns it will be in a cloud (Revelation 1:7).

This Angel had a rainbow over His head. It is the rainbow providing a canopy for the very throne of God (Revelation 4:3). It also brings to mind God's mercy in the midst of judgment. He promised in Noah's time never to destroy again the earth by water, and He used the rainbow as an eternal sign of this promise.

His face was like the sun. Remember, Jesus is the light of the world. Malachi 4:2 refers to the Lord as the *"Sun of Righteousness."* This brightness reflects the very Shekinah Glory of God Himself. Saul of Tarsus looked into that brightness on the road to Damascus, and he was blinded for three days and nights. The voice out of that brightness said, *"Saul, Saul, why do you persecute Me?"* (Acts 9:4 NIV). In Revelation 1:16, John described Jesus' face as bright as the sun at midday. If you were to look directly into the sun for a few seconds, the light is so bright it could permanently damage the retinas of your eyes. And finally, Scripture says this mighty

Angel's legs were like pillars of fire. And again, in Revelation chapter 1, verse 15 John says that the feet of the Son of Man were like unto fine brass as if they burned in a furnace. This is a picture of divine judgment.

In summary, let us look one more time at this mighty Angel's description. *"And I saw another mighty Angel come down from Heaven, clothed with a cloud: and a rainbow was upon His head, and His face was as it were the sun, and His feet as pillars of fire* (Revelation 10:1). Of no created angel could such glorious things be said, because God said, *"I am the LORD: that is My name: and My glory will I not give to another ...."* (Isaiah 42:8a).

This is the third time in the Book of Revelation that we have seen a "special Angel" that is set apart from the other angels. And each time, I am convinced that it is the Lord Jesus Christ Himself. The first time was in chapter 7, verses 2-3, when He was commanding the four angels to withhold their judgments upon the earth until the 144,000 witnesses were sealed. The second time was in chapter 8, verse 5, when He combined the prayers of the saints with incense before the throne, and then mixed the bowl with fire and poured it out upon the earth. The third time is here in chapter 10, where we will see that He is about to possess His everlasting Kingdom. And what is striking about these three appearances? In the first, He is a Prophet; in the second, a Priest; and in the third, a King. So, Christ is pictured in these first ten chapters of the Revelation in His 3-fold office of Prophet, Priest and King!

Now that we have a good idea who this angel is, let us see what He is doing. *"And He had in His hand a little book open: and He set His right foot upon the sea, and His left foot on the earth"* (Revelation 10:2). This is the same book or scroll that we saw in chapter 5, only then, it was rolled up and sealed with seven seals. It was the title deed to the earth, and everyone was crying because no one was worthy to open it and reclaim what Satan had stolen. No one, that is, until the Lord Jesus Christ stepped forward and proved that He is worthy.

Then, as each seal is broken, specific judgments are unleashed upon the earth and its inhabitants. When the seventh and last seal was broken, seven angels with seven trumpets were revealed. Six trumpets have sounded with their respective judgments and plagues, and now we have a "time out" before the seventh angel sounds the seventh trumpet. So, all the seals have been broken and, as verse 2 says, the book is now fully opened. In the Greek, it is very emphatic. It is like writing it with all caps. The book is now OPENED!

On the Christian Science official website, it says that this little book is in effect synonymous with *Science and Health with Key to the Scriptures* by Mary Baker Eddy.[2]

In her writings, she constantly shows little regard for the inspiration of the Scriptures as she believed her revelations were superior to the Bible. Here is a typical example: "The material record of the Bible is no more important to our well-being than the history of Europe and America."[3] Throughout her writings, Mrs. Eddy had no problem simply contradicting

Scripture at any point. As an example, "One sacrifice, however great, is insufficient to pay the debt of sin."[4]

You can look at what most cults believe and simply say, "That is wrong." But with Christian Science, it is like trying to nail Jell-O to the wall. It is mumbo-jumbo. Most of the time you can read what Mrs. Eddy wrote and, when you get through, you wonder what she said.

Here is a case in point: "The belief that man has existence or mind separate from God is a dying error. This error Jesus met with divine Science and proved its nothingness. Because of the wondrous glory which God bestowed on His anointed, temptation, sin, sickness and death had no terror for Jesus. Let men think they had killed [His] body. Afterwards He would show it to them unchanged."[5] Did He let men think they had killed His body when they hadn't really killed Him? I guess Peter was fooled too, because on the day of Pentecost he preached, *"this Jesus …. you crucified and killed by the hands of lawless men …."* (Acts 2:23 ESV). And if "killed" is not clear enough, the NIV says He was "put to death."

What do you suppose is meant by Christ planting one foot on the earth and one foot on the sea? That is a sign of authority – that is a sign of possession! When a man sets his foot on something that means he possesses it. For example, God says to His people: *"Wherever you set your feet, the land will be yours. Your frontiers will stretch from the wilderness in the south to Lebanon in the north, and from the Euphrates River in the east to the Mediterranean Sea in the west"* (Deuteronomy 11:24 NASB). The same declaration was given to Joshua in the first chapter of Joshua: *"Every place on which the sole of your foot treads, I have given it to you, just as I spoke to Moses"* (Joshua 1:3 NASB). When Christopher Columbus landed in the Americas, the first thing he did was put his foot on the soil, and claim the land in the name of the King of Spain. By planting His foot on the land and the other foot on the sea, Christ is officially saying, "I am the legal heir, and I am hereby claiming the right to the earth and all that is therein." He is re-affirming Psalm 95:5 which says, *"The sea is His, and He made it: and His hands formed the dry land."*

He not only made it, He has redeemed it with His blood. Scripture further says*, "For God was pleased to have all His fullness dwell in Him* [Christ], *and through Him to reconcile to Himself all things, whether things on earth or things in Heaven, by making peace through His blood, shed on the cross"* (Colossians 1:19-20 NIV). As Psalm 24:1 (ESV) says, *"The earth is the LORD'S and the fullness thereof."* Are you not in awe of the majesty of Christ? Listen again to the way John describes Him. He was *"clothed with a cloud: and a rainbow was upon His head, and His face was as it were the sun, and His feet as pillars of fire"* (Revelation 10:1b). What an awesome God who deserves all our praise and worship!

We are in the midst of a parenthesis between the sounding of the sixth and seventh trumpets. Jesus is holding the scroll – the little book – except this time, it is open. All the seals have been broken, and the scroll is completely exposed for everyone to see. We see Christ standing with one foot on the earth and the other on the sea indicating that He has the power and authority, and is reclaiming the earth and all that is therein. *"And* [He] *cried with a loud voice, as when a lion roareth"* (Revelation 10:3a). Folks, this is exciting – the suffering servant, the Lamb of God who uttered not a word, but went like a sheep to the slaughter to give His life for us. This Lamb is now the Lion – the Lion of the Tribe of Judah! And when He speaks, it is with a loud voice and it strikes terror into His enemies!

A lion roars just before he completes whatever action he is contemplating. And when this lion roars, God expresses His right to rule the earth. Joel 3:16 says, *"The LORD also shall roar out of Zion, and utter His voice from Jerusalem; and the heavens and the earth shall shake: but the LORD will be the hope of His people, and the strength of the children of Israel."* And in Hosea 11:10 we find, *"He shall roar like a lion: when He shall roar, then the children shall tremble…."*. Continuing with Revelation 10:3: *"When He had cried, seven thunders uttered their voice."* Remember, the number seven means completeness – perfection. The seven thunders is a symbol for the voice of God. Job 37:5 (NLT) says: *"God's voice is glorious in the thunder. We cannot comprehend the greatness of His power."*

So Jesus is standing with one foot on the earth and one foot on the sea, and He roars with a loud voice. And when He does, God the Father thunders from the throne. In Job chapters 26 and 27, we find that thunder is a symbol of God's wrath. Something awesome, and maybe something awful, is about to happen. Let us see what it is.

"And when the seven thunders had uttered their voices, I was about to write: and I heard a voice from Heaven saying unto me, 'Seal up those things which the seven thunders uttered, and write them not'" (Revelation 10:4). Did you notice something strange? John is writing the Apocalypse which means the unveiling. It means the revealing of many mysteries; but suddenly, John is told not to write what he has just heard from the seven thunders. What do you suppose he heard?

William Miller, an early preacher with Seventh-day Adventists' leanings, claimed that he had figured out what the seven thunders had uttered. It was that Christ was returning between March 21, 1843 and March 21, 1844. When the objection was raised that no one knows the day nor the hour when Jesus would come back (Mark 13:32) Miller said, "I'm not claiming to know the day or the hour, only the year." His prediction proved to be wrong and his prestige never really recovered from this fiasco. He died a few years later a "broken and disillusioned man."[6]

Ellen White, another early leader of what became known as the Seventh-day Adventists, implied that God imparted to her what He would not tell John, and it also had to do with the exact date of Christ's Second Coming.

This of course, proved false. Her inaccurate prophecies are well documented. She endorsed William Miller's prophecy that Jesus would return in 1844. When He did not, she proclaimed that Jesus supposedly entered the heavenly sanctuary and the door to salvation was closed. No one was saved after that time until this "shut door doctrine" was rescinded in 1850.[7]

Another minister on the internet said that the message of the seven thunders foretold seven of God's strongest preachers who would share their messages with the world, such as: Enoch would preach the Second Coming; Jeremiah would pronounce judgment on Israel; James would preach about God's grace; Peter and Paul would present the Gospel to the Jews and the Gentiles; Martin Luther would thunder the necessity of faith; and Charles Finney would stress holiness. This is pure speculation.

It is interesting the number of religious leaders whom God let in on this secret, and singled them out to know what the seven thunders said though He would not tell John. I am being facetious. The fact is, if God had intended for us to know what this message was, He would have had John write it down. But He specifically told John not to record it, so I conclude that it is not for us to speculate. We know from the verses preceding it, that it has to do with judgment. John has already seen warfare, blood, famine, heartache, hail, fire and men begging to die but unable to do so. We can only conclude that whatever John was instructed not to record must have been beyond human imagination and understanding.[8] God says we are not supposed to know, and that is good enough for me.

And then this mighty one whom I am convinced is Christ Himself prepares to utter an important message. But before He does, He raises His hand to Heaven and swears an oath. *"And the Angel which I saw stand upon the sea and upon the earth lifted up His hand to Heaven, and sware by Him that liveth for ever and ever, who created Heaven, and the things that therein are, and the earth, and the things that therein are, and the sea, and the things which are therein, that there should be time no longer"* (Revelation 10:5-6). Always in the Bible, the lifted hand is the sign of authority, and He calls for everyone to listen to this important announcement.

Then He heightens the suspense by making an oath. He swears that there will be no further delay in carrying out this announcement. Some commentators have made a lot to do about this oath. Some say that it proves that this angel is not Jesus because He is swearing an oath to someone in higher authority than He is. Really? Look closely at the verse. He is swearing an oath to the One who is eternal – who lives forever and ever, and who created the heavens, the earth, the sea and all the things in them.

He is swearing an oath to the Creator of all that we see. Who is the Creator? Listen to Colossians 1:16-17 (ESV): *"For by Him* [Christ] *were all things created, that are in Heaven, and that are in earth, visible and invisible, whether they be thrones, or dominions, or principalities, or powers: all things were created by Him, and for Him: And He is before all things, and by Him all things consist"* – or saying it another way, *"in Him all things hold together."* Is it possible that Christ is swearing an oath to Himself, saying in effect, "I swear by My power and I will carry this out?" Absolutely! There is precedent for this. We see this when God was confirming the Abrahamic Covenant in Genesis 22 that He swore by Himself. You and I are instructed not to swear an oath because we do not have the power to guarantee the result; but God does. He can promise a thing, and He has the power to bring it to pass. We are told this in Hebrews 6:13 (ESV), *"For when God made a promise to Abraham, because He could swear by no greater, He swore by Himself."* This is what Christ does here in verse 6. Since there is no one greater than God, He swears by Himself.

What is this momentous announcement He swears to carry out? Well, the King James is a little confusing here. It says in Revelation 10:6b, *"that there should be time no longer."* Some commentators say this means that there is not going to be such a thing as "time" after this. But, the Bible says there is yet to be a 1,000 year Millennium, and there are other references that show time will be around for a while longer. Time was created for man. Time does not affect God. He is outside of time so to speak. That is why Jesus could say, *"Before Abraham was, I AM"* (John 8:58b). But verse 6 is not talking about doing away with time. In the Greek, it literally means, "there will be no further delay." It means, "Let's get on with it." As Todd Beamer said on 9-11 as the terrorist plane sailed over Pennsylvania heading for the White House, "Let's roll."[9]

God has indeed been longsuffering. He has accomplished a wonderful plan of redemption and has been very patient, not willing that any should perish, but that all should come to a saving knowledge of Jesus Christ (II Peter 3:9b). He has waited year after year, century after century for lost men to accept His Son as their Savior, but He will not compel them against their will. Finally, He has reluctantly initiated the terrible judgments during the Day of the Lord. Even during the awful Tribulation Period, some accept Him, and He joyfully welcomes them into His presence (Revelation 7:9). But those who have persisted in hardening their hearts throughout these harsh judgments have extended the Lord's patience to the end.

You will remember the souls around the altar in chapter 6 who were martyred by the Antichrist. *"They cried out with a loud voice, 'O Sovereign Lord, holy and true, how long before you will judge and avenge our blood on those who dwell on the earth?'"* (Revelation 6:10 ESV). God heard their prayers, and said they should rest for a little while. He was being longsuffering, but now, time has run out and He declares, *"that there will be delay no longer"* (Revelation 10:6b NASB).

Now we come to one of the most profound verses in the entire Bible. You have been waiting for this all your life whether you realize it or not! *"But in the days of the voice of the seventh angel, when he shall begin to sound, the mystery of God should be finished, as He hath declared to his servants the prophets"* (Revelation 10:7). This mystery of God is the long delay of our Lord in taking the Kingdom unto Himself and establishing righteousness in the earth! For centuries we have been praying, *"Thy kingdom come. Thy will be done in earth as it is in Heaven* (Matthew

6:10). We have seen time after time God's permissive will being carried out in the earth – but not always His direct will. Nothing happens without God's ultimate approval, but why has He waited so long in stamping out pain, heartache and evil?

The mystery of God is seen in these thousands of years in which sin and death run rampant. There is no village – no neighborhood – no human heart that has not felt the sting of death and heartache. We see good people suffer while seemingly bad people suffer no loss.

This was the perplexing problem facing Asaph when he penned the 73rd Psalm. Most of us have had these emotions at some time during our life. Asaph said, *"Truly God is good to Israel, to those whose hearts are pure. But as for me, I came so close to the edge of the cliff! My feet were slipping, and I was almost gone. For I envied the proud when I saw them prosper despite their wickedness. They seem to live such a painless life; their bodies are so healthy and strong. They aren't troubled like other people or plagued with problems like everyone else. They wear pride like a jeweled necklace, and their clothing is woven of cruelty. These fat cats have everything their hearts could ever wish for! They scoff and speak only evil; in their pride they seek to crush others. They boast against the very heavens, and their words strut throughout the earth. And so the people are dismayed and confused, drinking in all their words. 'Does God realize what is going on?' they ask. 'Is the Most High even aware of what is happening?' Look at these arrogant people – enjoying a life of ease while their riches multiply. Was it for nothing that I kept my heart pure and kept myself from doing wrong? All I get is trouble all day long; every morning brings me pain. If I had really spoken this way, I would have been a traitor to your people. So I tried to understand why the wicked prosper. But what a difficult task it is!"* (Psalm 73:1-16 NLT)

Asaph was totally frustrated trying to serve God, and yet it seemed the wicked sailed by without any troubles. But then something happened to open his eyes! He went to church! *"Then one day I went into your sanctuary, O God, and I thought about the destiny of the wicked"* (Psalm 73:17 NLT). He realized that the wicked have as many problems as believers do; he just was not seeing clearly because of his pity party. He gained an eternal perspective, and saw the ultimate fate of the unsaved and it was not a pretty picture.

There is no life without tears. No matter how great your home is – no matter how great your life is – no matter how great the relationship with your spouse is – there is no home that does not eventually feel the sting of the death angel. The pages of history from the time of the very first murder in the Garden of Eden until this present hour are written in blood, tears and death. The mystery of God is the delay in taking the Kingdom unto Himself. This is the most inexplicable mystery the mind can imagine – the mystery of evil. For thousands of years God has allowed Satan to wrap his slimy, cruel tentacles around human life and around this earth. Is God indifferent to this? Is He aware of it? Oh, the mystery of the delay of God!

This mystery has been a stumbling block to more people than anything you can imagine.

The infidel, the atheist, the agnostic – they all laugh and mock and ask where God is. Every generation receives from the next generation these awful inheritances of iniquity. We pass its judgments on to our children and to our children's children. Will this flood tide go on forever? Will sin and death reign forever? Is the grave to be filled forever? No!! God says there is a barrier – a boundary – beyond which and over which the flood tides of sin and death cannot and will not roll. Our missionaries are slain, our churches burned and vandalized, and uncounted millions are oppressed and living in despair. And God just looks on. He does not intervene. He seemingly does not care. Oh the mystery of the delay of the Lord God in taking His Kingdom.

These things that seemingly work so tragically against us, things that we do not understand and seemingly cannot cope with God says that for His people in a mysterious way are for the development of our souls and the strengthening of our lives. They are intended to grow great spirits and great hearts and great people. In the battles and the challenges and the losses that we do not understand, God one day will show us how *"all things work together for good to them that love God, to them who are called according to His purpose"* (Romans 8:28b).

Why God chooses that our ultimate and final victory is wrought in tears, why God chooses that it be wrought in conflict, why God chooses that it be wrought in death and heartache – I cannot understand. It belongs to the mystery of God. But folks, here is the encouraging news, and I believe this with all my heart and soul. Somewhere beyond the starry sky, there stands a herald angel with a trumpet in his hand. And by the decree of Almighty God, there is a day, there is an hour, there is an elected time – an appointed time – when that angel shall sound his trumpet and the kingdoms of this world shall become the Kingdom of our Lord and His Christ! (Revelation 11:15).

Then Scripture says, *"But when the seventh angel blows his trumpet, God's mysterious plan will be fulfilled. It will happen just as He announced it to his servants the prophets"* (Revelation 10:7 NLT). Hallelujah! The forbearance will be over. God will say to death, "This is your last victim." He will say to Satan, "This is your last destruction."

When the Lord closed His apocalyptic sermon in the 24th chapter of Matthew, He closed it with a parable concerning this delay. The parable is about a servant who said in his heart that his master has delayed his coming. The servant said it may be a long time before he comes back (Luke 12:45-46). We are also told about a parable involving ten maidens who were going to meet the bridegroom, and subsequently, participate in the wedding festival. But the bridegroom delayed his coming and all of the maidens went to sleep. Five had oil in their lamps and were prepared while five foolish ones were unprepared and had no oil. When the cry came, *"Behold, the bridegroom cometh; go ye out to meet him"* (Matthew 25:6b), the five wise maidens went in to the wedding party, while the five foolish ones went about searching for oil. As a result the door was shut, and the five foolish ones were left out. Oil in Scripture is a symbol of the Holy Spirit. This parable shows the importance of not delaying your acceptance of Christ as Savior. We are warned in Scripture to always be ready for Christ's return because the door of opportunity will then be closed.

When I enumerated the many "signs of the times" to a friend, and told him that the Lord is coming back soon, he replied, "Oh, they said that when my mother was a child." And that is true. Every generation has felt that his or her generation was the time when God would intervene. Eve thought that the great promise to her would shortly come to pass (Genesis 3:15). John the Baptist thought Christ's Kingdom was at hand (Matthew 3:2). The Apostles thought it would be in their day. When the Apostle Paul was discussing the Rapture, he said, "*we which are alive and remain*" (I Thessalonians 4:17) – clearly indicating he thought he would be alive at the Rapture. Martin Luther and other great reformers thought it would not be long before Christ's coming.

We look to the heavens with expectancy and say, "Surely He will come soon." I have a note on the wall by my desk: "Maybe Today!" But no one knows the time of His return for His saints at the Rapture. We do have some general guidelines about His Second Coming with His saints. So next on the calendar is the Rapture and then, shortly after that, seven years of Tribulation, then Christ's Second Coming when He will set up His Millennial Kingdom.

A great man of faith and a noted author was Sir Walter Scott, who died nearly 150 years ago. Regarding this mystery of God that will be finished at the sounding of the trumpet of the seventh angel, Scott wrote: "Does it not seem strange that Satan has been allowed for six thousand years to wrap and twist his coils around the world, to work evil and spoil and mar the work of God?

Is it not a mystery why God, the God of righteousness and holiness, allows evil to go unpunished, and His own people to be crushed and broken on every hand? Truly, this is the mystery of God. God bears with evil till the hour of judgment arrives, when He will avenge the cry of His elect, and come out of His place to punish the wicked. Evil, now tolerated and allowed, will be openly punished. The mystery is at an end. Christ is about to reign."[10]

"*And the voice which I heard from Heaven spake unto me again, and said, 'Go and take the little book which is open in the hand of the Angel which standeth upon the sea and upon the earth'*" (Revelation 10:8). John, for the first time, is no longer a spectator. Instead, he is asked to play a part in one of the visions that is unfolding before him. And what a strange part it is!

We must remember who is holding the little book. Here is John's description of that One: He is "*clothed with a cloud: and a rainbow was upon His head, and His face was as it were the sun, and His feet as pillars of fire*" (Revelation 10:1b). There is no doubt in my mind that this is a description of the Lord Jesus Christ. God would not stand for any created being to be described in these terms. Never!

John is instructed to go take this little book from the hand of this mighty Angel [Christ]. Let us see what happens next. *"And I went unto the Angel, and said unto Him, 'Give me the little book.' And He said unto me, 'Take it, and eat it up; and it shall make thy belly bitter, but it shall be in thy mouth sweet as honey.' And I took the little book out of the Angel's hand, and ate it up; and it was in my mouth sweet as honey: and as soon as I had eaten it, my belly was bitter"* (Revelation 10:9). When John asks for the book, he is told to eat it. I have had to eat my words before, but I do not think that is what it is talking about!

Almost the exact thing happened when God was speaking to Ezekiel: *"'But thou, son of man, hear what I say unto thee; Be not thou rebellious like that rebellious house: open thy mouth, and eat that I give thee.' And when I looked, behold, a hand was sent unto me; and, lo, a roll of a book* [in other words, a scroll] *was therein; And he spread it before me; and it was written within and without: and there was written therein lamentations, and mourning, and woe. Moreover he said unto me, 'Son of man, eat that thou findest; eat this roll, and go speak unto the house of Israel.' So I opened my mouth, and he caused me to eat that roll. And he said unto me, 'Son of man, cause thy belly to eat, and fill thy bowels with this roll that I give thee.' Then did I eat it; and it was in my mouth as honey for sweetness. And he said unto me, 'Son of man, go, get thee unto the house of Israel, and speak with my words unto them'"* (Ezekiel 2:8-3:4).

Ezekiel saw a scroll in God's hand, and it was written on the front and the back like the one John is seeing. And it contained lamentations, and mourning and woe just like the judgments we have been reading about during the breaking of the seals! Ezekiel would soon find that these words were bitter in his stomach as he had to tell the house of Israel about their impending destruction at the hands of the Babylonians under King Nebuchadnezzar. And that is exactly John's experience. *"It was in my mouth sweet as honey: and as soon as I had eaten it, my belly was bitter"* (Revelation 10:10b).

This strange command is not really strange at all. We are very familiar with this expression, "I bought that book and devoured it in one sitting." To devour it, to eat it up, is to assimilate it; to digest it; to take it into your being. As Jeremiah said, *"Thy words were found, and I did eat them …."* (Jeremiah 15:16a). We are to take in God's words and then testify. We are to study, learn, meditate and then we can speak out for the Lord. We must really take in the Word of God before we can give it out. Second-hand truth is never very convincing. Teaching, studying and sharing the Word of God is the most important thing we do apart from worship. When we have properly studied and digested the Word of God, we have something real to share with others.

What is all this bitterness and sweetness talking about? Here is a picture of one of the most profound truths in all of Scripture. The Book of Revelation pictures this truth perfectly. The sweetness of this Book as it unveils the redemptive plan of God, as we see all our tears wiped away, as we see death conquered, it has sweetness beyond compare. It is a magnificent thing, full of interest, and it has captured the hearts of men ever since it was revealed. But, there is no student of the Word, and there is no scholar who has ever sought to understand these prophetic messages, but that learns in them the terrible violence of the storm that is coming.

The Gospel itself is like that. The same Gospel that guarantees salvation to those who receive it, guarantees judgment to those who reject it. This is also true for the Christian. The Word of God is sweet if we obey it; it is bitter if we disobey it. Jesus said, *"I am come that they might have life, and that they might have it more abundantly"* (John 10:10b). And then He gave us an owner's manual to follow [the Bible], yet most people ignore it. Just like the lines of Frank Sinatra's famous song, "I planned each charted course, Each careful step along the byway, And more, much more than this –I did it my way." It became his signature song. However, the other side of the story is that his daughter said that her father came to hate the song – he said it sounded "self-serving."[11] When he died, someone asked me, "How much did he leave?" I sadly replied, "He left it all."

The Apocalypse unveils a bitter future for many people. I am convinced that any teacher who diligently studies this Book will see the awful hand of judgment that is being prophesied. And that is the reason for the urgent message that men everywhere ought to repent so that they might escape the wrath that is to come. To have a word from Heaven is sweet like honey, to sift eternal truths from God's Word is like sugar in the cane, but there is bitterness ahead for those who ignore the warnings.

That is exactly what John is experiencing here. All the blessings of God – how sweet they are! But to a people who refuse God's warnings, the words are as bitter as gall. This has always been the case.

When Isaiah saw in a vision the Lord high and lifted up (Isaiah 6:1), it was glorious. But in the light of God's glory when Isaiah came to examine himself, he cried, *"Woe is me for I am a man of unclean lips"* (Isaiah 6:5a). And then Isaiah listened to the message that God wanted him to deliver to the people. It was filled with warnings and judgments because the people had turned their backs on Him.

One of the main reasons I love to study prophecy is because of what it does for us on the inside. The Apostle John, writing about the Lord's return, said: *"And every man that hath this hope in him purifieth himself, even as He is pure"* (I John 3:3). The vision God gave to Isaiah was sweet, but the words of impending destruction were bitter.

That should be our message today. Every message of hope and glory – every message of liberty and God's blessing – every message of salvation and goodness – every promise made to us by God – these things are sweet beyond compare. But every faithful teacher of the Word who understands God's complete message can always see underneath that sweetness and blessedness the bitter side of things that are there for those who reject Christ. That is why we need dedicated preachers and teachers who can discern the times that we live in – the faithful preacher who will speak out on these things that are sweet and dear to our hearts, but also warn us to be diligent lest we fall.

At a family Christmas celebration, one of my relatives stood up and said, "I propose a toast to the Christ child, who came to set an example of love and forgiveness." Well, that sounded sweet like honey, but I happened to know that this individual did not believe that a good God could ever punish someone for sin, and He certainly would not send anyone to Hell. Of course Jesus loves sinners! Of course Jesus forgives sin! He tells us, *"For God so loved the world, that He gave His only begotten Son, that whosoever believeth in Him should not perish, but have everlasting life"* (John 3:16). But most people ignore what Jesus said in the last verse of that same chapter: *"and he that believeth not the Son shall not see life; but the wrath of God abideth on him"* (John 3:36b).

If I have an indictment against the liberal pulpits today, it is the preacher who tells about the love of God, but never mentions the warnings that are faithfully recorded in Scripture. Pastor Joel Osteen, of the Lakewood Church in Houston, has been very clear many times that he does not talk about hell, sin or damnation because he does not want people going on a guilt trip. He says it is bad for their self-esteem. A few years ago, this same preacher was being interviewed by Larry King. King asked him about who is going to Heaven: "What if you are Jewish or Muslim and you don't accept Christ at all?" Osteen answered: "You know, I'm very careful about saying who would or wouldn't go to Heaven. I don't know ….".[12] John MacArthur calls him a "pagan religionist".[13]

In that same vein, others have said that God is love and goes by many names including Allah. However, the Holy Spirit did not say, "It does not matter what name God goes by ….". Instead God directed Peter to tell the High Priest about Jesus saying, *"Neither is there salvation in any other: for there is none other name under Heaven given among men, whereby we must be saved"* (Acts 4:12). He could have said, "There is no other person" – and then we could have argued today that He could be called by any name. But he did not. He said, "There is no other name whereby we must be saved!"

In our society, you can invoke the name of God at most gatherings without anyone getting too upset. But when you invoke the name of Jesus, it is a whole different story. It is true that God is a God of love, but He is also a God of justice and holiness. Several years ago, I heard that great Negro preacher, E. V. Hill, say that their telephone rang at home. His wife answered it and said to him that the White House was calling. He took the phone and listened intently as they invited him to pray at the upcoming Presidential inauguration. What an honor! Everything went smoothly until they asked him not to pray in Jesus' name. It took a lot of willpower, but he graciously declined the offer, saying, "If I can't pray in Jesus' name, there ain't gonna be no prayer." What a man of God! The White House relented and Rev. Hill gave the invocation in 1973 at President Nixon's inauguration.[14]

Now we come to the last verse in this chapter. *"And He said unto me, 'Thou must prophesy again before many peoples, and nations, and tongues, and kings'"* (Revelation 10:11). The KJV has one faulty word in this verse. The NIV, NASB and all the other modern translations have translated it correctly. It is the Greek word "epi". It is not "before many peoples." It is "about" or "concerning many peoples." The verse should read, *"Then he said to me, 'You must prophesy again about many peoples, nations, languages, and kings'"* (Revelation 10:11 NLT). And John is going to do just that in the following chapters, as he describes in detail for us the Antichrist and his domination over all of the peoples of the earth.

CHAPTER ELEVEN

Two Witnesses and the Seventh Trumpet

As we come to chapter 11, please be reminded that we are still in that parenthesis, that interim period between the sounding of the sixth and seventh trumpets. Things got so hectic and so bleak in chapter 9 that God said in chapter 10, "Time out. I have got to show my people some things that are going to take place shortly so they will not get discouraged."

At this time in Scripture, Christ is not actually merging His Kingdom with the kingdoms of the world which is still in the future at the end of the seventh trumpet. Instead, God is showing John (and his readers) what is going to take place at the blowing of the seventh trumpet. In fact, this interim period continues through verse 14. We know this because in verse 15 the seventh angel blows his trumpet.

One of the most able Biblical scholars of the last century was a man by the name of Dean Alford, who died in 1871. He was an English expositor and contributor to many famous Bible commentaries. Dean Alford said that the 11th chapter was the most difficult to understand than any chapter in the Book of Revelation.[1] We cannot maneuver around it, so let us pray the Lord will give us insights into His Word.

"And there was given me a reed like unto a rod: and the angel stood, saying, 'Rise, and measure the temple of God, and the altar, and them that worship therein'" (Revelation 11:1). I have never seen so many varying interpretations of any one verse. One teacher says the Temple is used figuratively as a picture of the faithful people of the Church. Another says the command to measure the Temple is simply calling attention to the size of the Church. Another one believes the altar stands for the Church. Another says that the words "Holy City" when used in Revelation means the Church. Another says that the two witnesses, whom we will see in verse 3, simply represent a picture of the Church. To these interpreters, every expression here – every symbol – every pattern – every presentation describes the Church. But to force everything in this chapter to mean the Church is to lose all opportunity to listen to the mind of the Holy Spirit in the matter.

We saw strong evidence that the Church was called to Heaven in Revelation 4:1, and from that time until the Church comes back with Christ at the Second Coming (Revelation 19:11), the Church is never seen or mentioned on earth during this entire period. In fact, when you look at this closely, you will see that we are unmistakably on Jewish ground. The physical Temple never had anything to do with the Church. The Temple of God during the Age of Grace which we are living in now is our bodies. That is where the Holy Spirit abides until the Rapture of the Church (I Corinthians 6:19).

There are five Temples mentioned in the Bible in addition to our bodies being called a Temple. First, there was Solomon's Temple. King David's dream was to build it, but because of his adulterous sin with Bathsheba, he was not allowed to do so (I Chronicles 28:3). David's son, Solomon, was appointed by God to build the first Temple (I Chronicles 28:6). It was unbelievably beautiful, adorned with gold, silver and precious stones. Later, when the Babylonian army came under the leadership of King Nebuchadnezzar, it left the city of Jerusalem in complete ruins including the Holy Temple. And of course, King Nebuchadnezzar looted the Temple treasury and carried all the gold and silver vessels back to Babylon (II Kings 24:13).

Finally, when their captivity had come to an end, the Jews were allowed to go back and rebuild the city of Jerusalem, and build the second Temple under the direction of Zerubbabel (Ezra 3:2-3, 8). It eventually fell into disrepair and lay desolate for 150 years. It became an eyesore for Herod the Great, and he totally rebuilt it and enlarged it shortly after Jesus' birth. It became known as Herod's Temple. Herod the Great was called great – not because he was a great man, but because he was a master builder.

This third Temple was the Temple that Jesus was referring to when He said, *"Do you see all these buildings? I assure you, they will be so completely demolished that not one stone will be left on top of another!"* (Matthew 24:2 NLT). His prediction was fulfilled in 70 A.D. when the Roman army, under the direction of General Titus, completely destroyed it.[2]

For the last 2,000 years, the Jews have not had a Temple in Jerusalem which is why animal sacrifices have ceased since that time. The fourth Temple is the one that will be built during the seven year Tribulation Period. It will be built where it has always stood -- on the Temple Mount in Jerusalem. The Temple Mount is the most contested, fought over, piece of real estate in the entire world, and it does not contain but about 35 acres. It is the most Holy site of the Jews. It also houses the "Dome of the Rock" – that gold dome that is prominent in every picture of Jerusalem, and where Muhammad is said to have ascended into Heaven. It also houses the Al-Aqsa Mosque.[3]

The city of Mecca where Muhammad was born and the city of Medina where Muhammad is buried are the two most holy sites of Islam. However, because the Jews so revere Jerusalem, the Muslims have named it their third most holy city just to intimidate the Jews. There is no other reason since there is no historical record that Muhammad ever went to Jerusalem nor was it ever a significant city in the annals of Islam.[4]

The Palestinian Authority has control of the Temple Mount at the current time, and many people say there is no way the Muslims will ever let the Jews build their next Temple on this site. However, Scripture says it will happen, and that settles it. There is at least one scenario whereby this could happen. Daniel discusses the seven year Tribulation Period in the 9th chapter of Daniel. There it says the Antichrist will make a seven year agreement with the Jews who will waste no time in building their new Temple on the Temple Mount.

Daniel also predicts that "in the midst of that week" – that is, after 3½ years – the Antichrist will break the covenant and begin to slaughter the Jews unmercifully.

There is room on the Temple Mount for the Jews to construct their Temple. But the question still remains, "Why would the Muslims allow the Jews to do this?" Here is a possible scenario. The Antichrist and the Muslims both hate the Jews. However, the Antichrist could go to the Muslims with this secret message: "I will sign a seven year peace agreement with Israel to allow them to rebuild their Temple and you can agree that it can be built on the Temple Mount. We have heard for centuries that the Jews have gold, silver and precious jewels hidden away so they will bring it out and adorn their new Temple when it is built. Then, when the Temple is finished and is embellished with these precious metals, I will break the covenant in the midst of it, seize the wealth of the Jews, and exterminate them forever!" The Muslims will happily go along with this devious plan.

The Jews are ready right now to start construction on their Temple just as soon as permission is granted by the Palestinians. There is an organization in Israel called "The Temple Institute." They have all the furniture, the table of shew bread, the altar of incense, the brazen altar, the large solid gold seven-branched candlestick and the rest of the accouterments ready to go into the new Temple as soon as it is completed. They are currently training a number of priests in the art and methods of offering animal sacrifices so that they can reinstitute the sacrificial offerings when the time comes. From chapter 9 in the Book of Daniel, we know that the Antichrist is going to negotiate a seven year peace agreement between the Jews and the Arabs in the guise of allowing the Jews to rebuild their Temple.

The 8th chapter of Daniel gives us a strong hint that the Antichrist will come from the region of the kings of Seleucus, that is, from Syria. The perfect picture or type of the Antichrist is Antiochus who was of Syrian origin, and who gave himself the surname "Epiphanes" which means "the visible god". He acted as though he really was a god, but the people used a play on words and called him "Epimanes" meaning "the madman". He was violently bitter against the Jews, as will be the Antichrist, and was determined to exterminate them and their religion. He devastated Jerusalem in 168 B.C., defiled the Temple by erecting an altar to Jupiter, prohibited Temple worship, forbid circumcision on penalty of death, sold thousands of Jewish families into slavery, destroyed all copies of Scripture that could be found and resorted to every conceivable torture in order to force the Jews to renounce their religion. He desecrated the Jewish Temple by sacrificing a pig on its altar.[5] This is a picture of what the Antichrist will do, and is what Jesus referred to as the "Abomination of Desolation" (Matthew 24:15).

The Antichrist will eventually go into this fourth Temple, and will declare to the world that he is the true God. Though the Antichrist will arise in Europe and for a time will have Rome as his headquarters, I am convinced he will have some Syrian blood flowing through his veins.[6]

His cohort will be the False Prophet who quite possibly will be of Jewish ancestry. Jesus, when referring to a future Messiah to the Jews, said, *"I am come in my Father's name, and ye receive Me not: if another shall come in his own name, him ye will receive"* (John 5:43). There is a good possibility that many Jews will accept the Antichrist's cohort, the False Prophet, because he looks and talks "Jewish," and will possibly have traces of Jewish blood in his veins.

The fifth Temple will be the most glorious one ever built. It will be the Millennial Temple, and we will look at it in detail a little later. What is this business about measuring the Temple mentioned in verse 1? Does God want to know how large it is? No. Any time God commands something to be measured, He is conveying two thoughts.

First, He is conveying the thought of ownership. If you go to buy a house or a lot, one of the very first things you do is measure the property. God says, "Measure this – it belongs to Me." The second thing God has in mind when He directs a measurement is the preparation for judgment or destruction.

Amos the prophet saw a plumb line and was commanded to measure Israel for destruction (Amos 7:8-9). So each of those ideas, ownership and judgment, are signified in Revelation chapter 11 verse 1, and it relates to God's anger toward His chosen people. Let me say a word about God's judgment of His own people. When we studied the civil war of Israel, and the eventual splitting of the kingdom into the North and the South, we did not see a return to God but a pursuit of gross idolatry.

Consequently, God's judgment fell just as He had warned through His prophets. God used the treacherous heathen from the North – that barbaric nation of Assyria led by such fierce infidels such as Ashurbanipal, Sargon, Sennacherib, and Tiglath-pileser. They destroyed Israel like wiping a plate clean. The Southern Kingdom fared a little better because they had a few good kings that tried to bring in spiritual revival, but usually it was short-lived. It survived another 135 years before God used the evil Babylonians (Chaldeans) to punish Judah.

The Jews constantly wondered how God could punish an evil nation with another nation which was more sinful.

Basically, that is what the entire Book of Habakkuk is all about. Habakkuk was given a prophecy about Judah that predicted those wicked Babylonians (Chaldeans) would come and utterly destroy Judah. This left Habakkuk in tears. He answered the Lord in effect, "We may be sinful and we may have profaned your Temple, but we are not as vile as those Chaldeans. Lord, how can you punish someone who is evil with someone who is more evil?" And the Lord's answer is shocking. He said, *"But the LORD is in His holy Temple: let all the earth keep silence before Him"* (Habakkuk 2:20). You may have sung that line in a chorus and never knew the context of it. The Lord in effect said, "Habakkuk, shut up! I am sovereign, and I know what I am doing!"

A somber thought is that America is not above being judged. I believe that God has held back judgment thus far because of the number of committed Christians who are trying to serve Him and do the right thing. But the majority is thumbing their noses at God. They have kicked Him out of our schools – they have booted Him out of our public life – they have mandated generic public prayers that could just as well have been directed to gods of wood and stone.

They have supported a corrupt entertainment venue that comes out of Hollywood. We turn our dollars over to this corrupt industry, and they laugh all the way to the bank, not caring one iota if they destroy the morals of our children. Parents close their eyes to their kids idolizing the punk-rock and rap crowd whose God is vulgarity. In fact the late, great comedian, Steve Allen was dismayed at all the filth masquerading as comedy. He said, "In America today, we have 'vulgarians' entertaining barbarians."[7] They are attempting to erase God's name from our coins, from our Pledge of Allegiance, and eventually from our National Anthem. If America does not think that God can judge this country by using Muslim terrorists or violent storms to do it, America is sadly mistaken. We need to get on our knees and ask God to forgive us for taking our liberties for granted and for worshiping God whenever we feel the mood is right.

Jesus is coming back soon and I hope you will get serious about your desire for holy living. I have been guilty in the past of saying, "That was a good movie if you can overlook the foul language." I do not say that anymore. God has convicted me of this, and I cannot sit still and watch garbage like that. It is like saying, "That was a great milkshake if you can ignore the septic tank water that was added."

We have been discussing the building of the fourth Temple. But more importantly, you and I are helping to build a structure in Heaven. Jesus said, *"I go to prepare a place for you …."* (John 14:3a). I am looking forward to going there, but I believe that the materials He will be using are the materials that you and I send on ahead (Matthew 6:19).

In summary, there will be a total of five Temples:

1) The magnificent Temple that King Solomon built;
2) The Temple that Zerubbabel built after the Jews returned from exile;
3) The Temple in existence during Jesus' lifetime, called Herod's Temple;
4) The Temple to be built during the Tribulation Period; and
5) The Millennial Temple.

Several hundred years ago, on top of Mt. Moriah in Jerusalem, the Muslims built a large shrine which is called the "Dome of the Rock." It is located on top of what is known as the Temple Mount. It is the gold dome building that you see in most pictures of Jerusalem, and it is very close to the Western Wall where the Jews go to pray. The Jews refer to the wall as the "Western Wall," but the Arabs call it the "Wailing Wall" probably to remind the Jews at every opportunity of all the pain and suffering that Israel has endured throughout the centuries.

Why does Israel consider the Temple Mount one of its most holy places? Because this is the exact area where the Temple and the Holy of Holies was located throughout Old Testament times. Israel has control of and provides the security for the city of Jerusalem, except for the Temple Mount area. The Palestinian Authority controls the Temple Mount, and this is a constant irritation to the Jews. In fact, not only do the Muslims control the Temple Mount, they have gone to great lengths to remove any archaeological evidence that a Jewish Temple ever stood there! Just about any dispute can be negotiated, but if you were charged with settling this dispute between these two parties, how would you do it? The Muslims say, "This is one of our most holy places; we are not giving it up." The Jews say, "This is one of our most holy places, and we are not giving it up." Each side is willing to fight and die for this disputed plot of real estate. How can it be resolved?

Presidents Carter, Reagan and Bush (the first) tried their best, but they could not resolve it. President Clinton got both sides to the table, but then it fell apart. President George W. Bush with his "land for peace" agreement, tried to negotiate peace, but he was not successful. President Obama was sure he could bring both sides together with his two-state solution, but again his effort was unsuccessful.[8] Not to be discouraged, President Trump has tackled the job with new energy and new enthusiasm with a hope that lasting peace can be achieved. It will fail as well. But there will be one who will be successful – at least in the short run. The Antichrist will temporarily resolve the problem.

When Jesus was arrested that night in the Garden of Gethsemane, He was taken a short way into the heart of Jerusalem to the house of Caiaphas, the High Priest, to discuss the charges against Him. They were joined by a number of high ranking Jewish officials constituting the Sanhedrin – the Jewish high court. The full court consisted of 70 members, plus the incumbent high priest, bringing the total membership to 71. It generally met in one of the rooms of the Temple, but after the Temple was destroyed by the Romans in 70 A.D., it was moved to other locations, finally settling in Tiberius on the shore of the Sea of Galilee until it was disbanded around 425 A.D. So for nearly 1,600 years, there has been no official Sanhedrin, and no meetings by the group.

History was made in October 2004 when orthodox Jewish leaders embarked on an effort to re-establish this ancient court. These religious authorities believe it is necessary to re-establish the Sanhedrin because only this properly ordained body can authenticate the Messiah when He comes. This statement is so ridiculous, it is worth repeating. These religious authorities believe it is necessary to re-establish the Sanhedrin because only this properly ordained body can authenticate the Messiah when He comes.

Doesn't this make you almost laugh out loud? Jesus said in Matthew 24:26, *"Wherefore if they shall say unto you, Behold, He is in the desert; go not forth: behold, He is in the secret chambers; believe it not. For as the lightening cometh out of the east, and shineth even unto the west, so also shall the coming of the Son of Man be."* These fellows at the Sanhedrin are in for a big surprise! The people on earth are not going to need a group of 71 religious dignitaries to authenticate the authenticity of the Messiah! They are not going to get together and say, "We have an announcement – this is the real Messiah; you can take our word for it." This is how Revelation 1:7 describes His coming: *"Behold, He cometh with clouds; and every eye shall see Him, and they also which pierced Him; and all kindreds of the earth shall wail because of Him."* He will not need a stamp of approval by any third party, let alone the Sanhedrin before whom He stood trial some 2,000 years ago.

The first meeting of this new Sanhedrin was held in February 2005, and one of the first orders of business was to discuss the moving of the location to Jerusalem to one of the rooms in the Temple where historically it had always been. But, they had two problems with this. First, there is no Temple in Jerusalem in which to move to. And second, the Muslims control the spot where the Temple is supposed to be built. I would say that is a problem. So, quite naturally, their discussion centered around the exact location where the old Temple stood. This is the spot where the Jews want the new Temple to be built. Does this mean the "Dome of the Rock" would have to be torn down? Not unless you want to start World War III with the Muslims!

The Sanhedrin examined ancient documents, and listened to expert testimony as to the exact location of where the Temple stood. Two separate opinions surfaced. One opinion said, "The exact location of the original Temple is directly on the spot where the Dome of the Rock now stands." In other words, load your weapons; we are going to have to blast the Muslims out of the area. If that happens, it will be one of the bloodiest battles this world has ever known. But I do not think it will come to that.

Here is where the other theory comes into play as to where the original Temple stood. This theory, advanced by Dr. Asher Kaufman, a Hebrew physicist and scholar, says that the original Temple was built north of where the Dome of the Rock now stands, approximately 26 meters from the Dome of the Rock. This seems to agree with Revelation 11:1-2 in which John is told to measure the Temple, but to leave out the outer court *"for it is given to the Gentiles."*

Dr. Kaufman developed this theory in part after studying certain archaeological evidences before the Muslims destroyed such evidence. But Dr. Kaufman asserts there is another important fact that must be considered. He says that according to ancient accounts of the Temple, its east-west centerline passed through the center of the Eastern Gate. If you follow this straight line through the Eastern Gate, it would go directly to a place on the Mount of Olives where the innocent lambs without spot or blemish were prepared for sacrifice on the prescribed altar. In this manner, the sacrificing priest stood with the lamb portraying the Perfect Lamb who would take away the sins of the world. He could look directly from his place on the Mount of Olives through the Eastern Gate to the Holy of Holies as he sprinkled the sacrificial blood.

Dr. Kaufman also determined that if you would draw a straight east-west line from the Mount of Olives through the Eastern Gate, it would bisect a small shrine called the "Dome of the Spirits." This little shrine sits on the only bedrock appearing on the Temple Mount. The rest of the Mount has been paved. Dr. Kaufman is sure that this foundation stone was the floor of the ancient Holy of Holies.[10] So, what does all this mean? Here is what it might mean: the new Temple could be rebuilt on its original site on the Temple Mount without disturbing the Dome of the Rock! We previously read in Revelation 11:2 that the "outer court" will be given to the Gentiles before the Messiah returns; consequently, it sounds like a perfect prophecy because not only is the outer court "given to the Gentiles," but a Gentile building (the Dome of the Rock) is standing there!

Revelation 11:2 continues to say that the holy city (Jerusalem) *"shall they tread under foot forty and two months."* That is 3½ years which is the last half of the Tribulation when the False Prophet will make Jerusalem his headquarters, and will literally tread underfoot the Holy City for 42 months. This further fits what Daniel was told 2,500 years ago in Daniel 9:26-27 (NLT) referring to this very time: *"After this period of sixty-two sets of seven, the Anointed One will be killed, appearing to have accomplished nothing, and a ruler will arise whose armies will destroy the city and the Temple. The end will come with a flood, and war and its miseries are decreed from that time to the very end. He will make a treaty with the people for a period of one set of seven, but after half this time, he will put an end to the sacrifices and offerings. Then as a climax to all his terrible deeds, he will set up a sacrilegious object that causes desecration, until the end that has been decreed is poured out on this defiler."*

Instead of "one set of seven," the KJV translates this as "one week." We thoroughly aired this out previously in chapter 6, but it will serve us well to revisit it here. "One week" in Hebrew is "shabua" and means seven like our English word dozen means 12. So, the treaty is for seven years, but the Antichrist breaks the treaty in the midst of the week, i.e. after 3½ years. The ruler in Daniel 9:27 is the Antichrist. We know this from Daniel 9:26 because it says he is the prince of the people who destroyed the city of Jerusalem and the Temple. What people did this? History confirms that the city and the Temple were destroyed in 70 A.D. by the Romans.[11]

Let me simplify this in my own words that will make it a little clearer. The Antichrist will sign a peace treaty between Israel and the Arab nations for seven years; and in the midst of the term, that is after 3½ years, the new Temple will have been completed; it will have been adorned with gold, silver and precious jewels. The Antichrist shall then violate the agreement, confiscate all the wealth of Israel, and put a stop to Israel's sacrifices. Then the Antichrist will stand in the new Temple and declare himself to be God, which Jesus in Matthew 24:15 calls the Abomination of Desolation.

Continuing with verse 2: *"But the court which is without the Temple leave out, and measure it not; for it is given unto the Gentiles: and the Holy City shall they tread under foot forty and two months."* The Jews have always been very strict as to who could enter the Temple proper. Gentiles were restricted to the outer court under penalty of death.[12] In the latter verses of the 21st chapter of Acts, Paul almost got himself killed when he brought into the Temple four Jewish converts from Greece who were mistook by the Jewish leaders as being Gentiles.

In Ephesians, Paul reminds the Gentiles that Christ has broken down this wall of separation and we are now one in Christ: *"Wherefore remember, that ye being in time past Gentiles in the flesh, who are called Uncircumcision by that which is called the Circumcision in the flesh made by hands; that at that time ye were without Christ being aliens from the commonwealth of Israel, and strangers from the covenants of promise having no hope, and without God in the world; but not in Christ Jesus ye who sometimes were far off are made nigh by the blood of Christ. For He is our peace, who hath made both one, and hath broken down the middle wall of partition between us"* (Ephesians 2:11-14).

So God tells John, "Measure the Temple – I am going to judge Israel. But do not measure the outer Court – do not fool with the Gentiles – I will take care of them later." Verse 2 tells us that the (unbelieving) Gentiles will control or will *"tread under foot"* the outer court as well as the rest of the Holy City. One commentator wrote, "We don't know what city that is." Excuse me, but duh! The only city in the Bible that is ever called "holy" is none other than the city of the great King – Jerusalem (Nehemiah 11:1; Matthew 4:5; Matthew 27:53).

There is a disagreement among Bible scholars as to what part of the Tribulation these verses are referring to. It seems clear to me that these 42 months have to be the last half of the Tribulation Period. Remember, the Antichrist outwardly, but deceitfully, works with the Jews during the first half of his peace treaty though he is playing havoc with the rest of the world.

It is during this last 3½ years that the Gentiles tread underfoot the outer court and the Holy City (Revelation 11:2). And if it were not for the two mighty men to whom we are about to be introduced, the poor Jews would probably be wiped out completely. The Antichrist will try to hunt down all the Jews he possibly can in order to kill them; nonetheless, he will keep a wary eye on these two mighty men who are supernaturally protected from any harm. *"And I will give power unto my two witnesses, and they shall prophesy a thousand two hundred and threescore days, clothed in sackcloth"* (Revelation 11:3). The two witnesses will be preaching during the same time frame as the Great Tribulation. We are told that the Gentiles would trample the Holy City for 42 months and the two witnesses will prophecy 1,260 days. It is the same amount of time – 3½ years. The prophets' duration is given in days probably to emphasize that they are not weekend preachers. Every single day for 3½ years they faithfully preach the Word, and it nearly drives the Antichrist crazy with rage because he cannot stop them.

The question has been hotly debated, "Who are these two witnesses?" There are two major schools of thought that break down like this. One group believes these two witnesses are Elijah and Enoch. Their reasoning is that Elijah, a Jew, preaches to the Jews, and Enoch, a Gentile, preaches to the Gentiles. They also say that these two witnesses are later killed, and they point to the verse in Hebrews that says, *"It is appointed unto men ONCE to die ...."* (Hebrews 9:27a). They reason, therefore, that Elijah and Enoch are the only two men in the Bible that did not die physically. Elijah was taken to Heaven in a whirlwind and with chariots of fire (II Kings 2:11), and Enoch *"walked with God: and he was not; for God took him"* (Genesis 5:24).

This school of thought may be correct, however it is somewhat of a weak argument just to pick out the two men that had not tasted death simply because the Bible says, *"It is appointed unto men once to die ...."*. Remember, those alive at the Rapture will never see physical death. God can certainly make exceptions, and I think this verse in Hebrews is simply stating a general principle.

Here is why I think that these two witnesses will be Elijah and Moses. Remember, we said that whenever possible we should look at the Old Testament Scriptures to determine what God is trying to tell us in Revelation. Malachi, the last Book of the Old Testament, gives us a hint: *"Remember ye the law of Moses my servant, which I commanded unto him in Horeb for all Israel, with the statutes and judgments. Behold, I will send you Elijah the prophet before the coming of the great and dreadful day of the Lord"* (Malachi 4:4-5).

It is ironic that Scripture mentions these two prophets in the same breath – Moses and Elijah – and then goes on to say that Elijah will come right before that great and terrible day of the Lord. Some believe that this "Elijah" will really be John the Baptist. I do not because in the first chapter of John, the Jews who knew the Scriptures, asked John the Baptist if he was Elijah who was to come before the Day of the Lord, and John the Baptist replied, "I am not" (John 1:19-21).

Another reason that supports that these two will be Moses and Elijah is because they performed the very same miracles in the Old Testament as they perform here in the 11th chapter of Revelation. We will look at this in more detail a little later in this chapter. The last part of verse 3 says that they are clothed in sackcloth. Sackcloth is a heavy, coarse garment woven out of camel hair or goat hair. It was worn by ancients as a sign of sorrow and great mourning.

When these two witnesses stand clothed in sackcloth, they become a symbol of national, worldwide mourning. The day is evil, and the times are filled with sorrow calling for sackcloth and personal mourning. We have a number of instances when sackcloth represented intense sorrow.

Jacob is a case in point. His son, Joseph, had a "coat of many colors" that his father had made for him (Genesis 37:3). Joseph's brothers were jealous of him. They threw him in a pit, killed a goat and smeared its blood on the coat to make it appear he had been slain.

The brothers took it to their father, Jacob. They acted as though they were innocent and let their father make up his own mind as to what had happened to Joseph. They said, "This looks like Joseph's coat, but we do not know for sure." They lied. Jacob said, "Oh, yes, this is Joseph's coat, and there is blood on it. Oh, a wild animal must have killed him" (Genesis 37:33). So Jacob put on sackcloth, and mourned for his son for a number of days (Genesis 37:34).

Another example where sackcloth was related to mourning is when David heard of the cruel murder of Abner, his longtime Chief of Staff. David tore his clothes and put on sackcloth to mourn his loss (II Samuel 3:31).

That great Assyrian general, Sennacherib, who ruled Assyria from 705 B.C. to 681 B.C., swept across Israel after the kingdom had divided, utterly destroying everything in his path. Then his armies marched into the heart of the Southern Kingdom, Judah, and surrounded its capital, Jerusalem. The walls were the only thing keeping out those murderous hoards. It would have been only a matter of time before the walls were breached.[13]

In the most coarse and blasphemous language, Sennacherib called on good King Hezekiah to surrender. He reminded Hezekiah of the awful things that would happen to him and his subjects if their surrender was not immediate. Scripture says that Hezekiah put on sackcloth, and prayed for the deliverance of his people. The Lord heard his prayer, and what an astounding deliverance the Lord sent as the Angel of Death slew 185,000 of Sennacherib's soldiers in one night (II Kings 19:14-35). In writing their own history, kings seldom mentioned their defeats. In secular history, King Sennacherib never mentioned this disastrous defeat. He simply recorded that he withdrew from his siege of Jerusalem due to "pressing problems at home." He was assassinated in 681 B.C. by his own sons.[14]

"These are the two olive trees, and the two candlesticks standing before the God of the earth" (Revelation 11:4). What do these olive trees and the candlesticks have to do with anything? Well, as usual, we have to go back to other parts of Scripture. This time to the third chapter of the Book of Zechariah. Zechariah is God's prophet of the restoration – of a new hope – of a new day for Israel.

In the third chapter of Zechariah, we find the High Priest, Joshua, standing before the Angel of the Lord (who is none other than the pre-incarnate Christ). Satan is at his right hand to cause trouble. Joshua is clothed in filthy garments – a clear picture of a mortal being beset with sin and unrighteousness. Satan is quick to point out to God how sinful and unworthy Joshua is. Elsewhere in Scripture Satan is called the "accuser of the brethren," and he is living up to his reputation (Revelation 12:10). And God the Father says to His Son (the Angel of the Lord), *"Take away his filthy garments …. I will clothe thee with a change of raiment"* (Zechariah 3:4). In other words, "Son, take away his sin, and give him a clean heart."

In the next chapter of Zechariah, the angel asks, "What do you see?" And Zechariah says, "I see a candelabra – a seven-branched lampstand, and I see olive trees." An olive tree on one side and an olive tree on the other side. The oil pours from the olive trees into the lampstands into the candelabra. And the prophet asks what this means, and the Lord says, *"Not by might, nor by power, but by my Spirit, saith the Lord of hosts"* (Zechariah 4:6). Oil in Scripture has always been a picture of the Spirit of God. And a lampstand has always been a symbol of a shining witness – the reflection of God's truth. In other words, the lampstands represent His witnesses giving out the light of truth to the world as they are empowered by the Holy Spirit to carry out their assignment.

God sends these two witnesses pictured by the two olive trees and the lampstands to warn the earth of the judgments by which He shall clear this whole planet of unrighteousness and sin. In His infinite mercy, God always warns before He pours out judgment. Two seems to be the number of confirmation in Scripture. In the law, and reconfirmed in the 18th chapter of Matthew, there must always be two witnesses to establish the truth. In the mouths of two witnesses, a person was deemed guilty or innocent (Matthew 18:16). There were two angels who testified to the resurrection of our Savior. There were two angels who testified to our Lord's ascension into Heaven.

Many times our Lord sent His witnesses out two by two. There were Moses and Aaron, Joshua and Caleb, Peter and John, Paul and Silas, Timothy and Titus. And here in Revelation, we find that His two witnesses, who are most likely Elijah and Moses, will be a thorn in the side of the Antichrist and the False Prophet as the two witnesses faithfully preach God's Word.

At any rate, God protects these two witnesses during this last half of the Tribulation Period until their mission is complete. They drive the Antichrist bonkers! No doubt, he is telling all his subjects that he is the true god and that everyone must obey him. And then these two preachers come along and defy him and preach the Gospel, inviting people to turn their lives over to the true God. I am sure the Antichrist screams at his generals, "Those two preachers near the wall in Jerusalem carry on from daylight to dark. They blaspheme my name, and say all sorts of evil things against me. Therefore, if you do not present me with their heads, I will make sure that I have yours!"

I can see the tanks, the bazookas, the flamethrowers – all the modern weapons of war assembled to take out these two upstarts dressed in their weird sackcloth clothing. The nightly news adds to the frustration everyone is feeling: "Two prophets appear in Jerusalem daily wearing old burlap and declaring judgment is at hand." And the newspaper subtitle will be, "His Most Excellency vows to rid the city of these intruders before sundown." But, what happens when anyone tries to thwart their mission? *"And if any man will hurt them, fire proceedeth out of their mouth and devoureth their enemies; and if any man will hurt them, he must in this manner be killed"* (Revelation 11:5). It probably will not take the Antichrist's henchmen very long to figure out that these guys are here to stay. They probably have a message on their sackcloth, but it does not say, "Don't mess with Texas." It says, "Don't mess with Israel!"

Just like the 144,000 Israelite evangelists who were sealed and protected during the first 3½ years of the Tribulation (Revelation 7:4), these two witnesses will be protected during the last 3½ years until their mission is accomplished at which time they will be killed by the Antichrist. Look at verse 6: *"These have power to shut Heaven, that it rain not in the days of their prophecy: and have power over waters to turn them to blood, and to smite the earth with all plagues, as often as they will."*

Previously we gave some reasons why we think that these two witnesses will be Moses and Elijah. They are given power by God to perform the same miracles that were associated with Moses and Elijah in the Old Testament. First, let us consider Elijah. In I Kings 18:37-38, Elijah had his famous duel on the top of Mount Carmel with the prophets of Baal calling down fire from Heaven.

Several years ago, I stood on the top of Mount Carmel overlooking the Valley of Armageddon. My pastor, Jim Pritchard, was leading tour group. He was preaching a stirring message about Elijah's confrontation with the followers of Baal. Just as his message was reaching the most climactic point, there was a BOOM that shook the ground and reverberated through the sky! We found out later it was the sonic boom of an Israeli air force jet that was on the way to drop its payload a few miles from us, just across the Lebanese border. But it sure put an exclamation point to Jim's message! But the point is, Elijah's ministry was associated with fire and judgment falling from Heaven.

There was another time involving Elijah and fire. The king of Israel, Ahaziah (son of Ahab and Jezebel) was walking out on the balcony of his palace in Samaria when he fell through the latticework down to the ground (II Kings 1:2-16). The king knew he was critically injured from the fall, so he called in his servants and said, "Go inquire of Baalzebub (the infamous god of the Philistines) to see if I am going to recover or not."

The Lord instructed Elijah to go meet these servants, and to tell them, "Don't waste your time going to inquire from a false god. Jehovah, the true God, has told me that your king will not recover." Of course, the king was furious when he heard that, especially coming from some old man wearing a goat hair garment. So the king ordered three of his captains to take 50 men each with them and bring Elijah back by force. The first captain brought his 50 men to seize Elijah. But at Elijah's command, fire came down and devoured the squadron of 50 men (II Kings 1:10). Another captain with his 50 men was ordered to go and seize Elijah. Again, at Elijah's command, fire came down and devoured this squadron of 50 men (II Kings 1:12).

The third captain of 50 men had seen what had happened to the other squadrons, so what did he do? He fell on his face before Elijah and in effect said, "I know you are a true prophet of God and our king wants to talk with you. Will you please come with me?" (II Kings 1:13-14). This captain was no dummy. He decided that civility was the best approach. The point is that Elijah's ministry was marked by fire from Heaven!

Elijah's ministry was also associated with drought. In the 17th chapter of I Kings, Elijah told King Ahab that there would be no rain for the next few years, until he (Elijah) prayed for it to rain (I Kings 1:1). How many years do you suppose it was before Elijah prayed again, and rain returned to Israel? Our answer is found in the New Testament. *"Elijah was a man subject to like passions as we are, and he prayed earnestly that it might not rain: and it rained not on the earth by the space of three years and six months"* (James 5:17).

The two witnesses have the power to *"shut up heaven that it rain not in the days of their prophecy …."*. How long was their prophecy? We have the answer a few verses earlier, in verse 3. *"And I will give power unto my two witnesses, and they shall prophesy a thousand, two hundred and threescore days …."* – in other words, 1,260 days. That is 3½ years, the exact time that these two witnesses were preaching, and prophesying during the last half of the Tribulation Period!

As we conclude looking at verse 6, we note that these two prophets have the power to do something else miraculous. They have the power *"over waters to turn them to blood, and to smite the earth with all plagues, as often as they will"* (Revelation 11:6b). We have already seen that Elijah's ministry was associated with fire from Heaven as well as the power to stop the rain. Who comes to mind when you think of turning the waters to blood, and smiting the earth with all sorts of plagues and diseases? Of course! Moses! Listen to Exodus 7:20: *"And Moses …. lifted up the rod, and smote the waters that were in the river, in the sight of Pharaoh …. and all the waters that were in the river were turned to blood."*

Again, in Exodus 8, God told Moses to warn Pharaoh that he would have a judgment of frogs if he did not free the Israelites from being slaves. When Pharaoh refused, listen to verse 3 as to how bad the judgment was. *"And the river shall bring forth frogs abundantly, which shall go up and come into thine house, and into thy bedchamber, and upon thy bed, and into the house of thy servants, and upon thy people, and into thine ovens"* (Exodus 8:3).

After promising to free the Israelites if the frogs went away, Pharaoh reneged on his promise; and so, we see in Exodus 8:16, Moses called down a plague of lice. The lice were everywhere – both man and beast were scratching!

Pharaoh said, "Kings X." I will let those Israelites go if you will remove the lice!" The lice were removed and Pharaoh reneged again. Next, a plague of flies visited him (Exodus 8:21). They were everywhere. Pharaoh reneged again. You think he would have learned, but he was the most stubborn guy you ever heard of.

This time, God promised to strike the livestock of the Egyptians if Pharaoh did not release the Israelites. Pharaoh again promised to release them, but later changed his mind. And so, God did as He had promised. All the cattle, the oxen, the horses and the sheep of the Egyptians died, but none of the livestock belonging to the Israelites was injured (Exodus 9:6).

The next plague that was sent was boils after Pharaoh failed to live up to his promise (Exodus 9:10). Have you ever had a boil? Very painful! Imagine boils all over you. Pharaoh called in his magicians, what someone might call today, "TV faith healers." But they had so many boils on themselves, they could not help the king.

Pharaoh continued to break his promises to release the children of Israel, and God followed with grievous hailstones. It was not just ordinary hail. Exodus 9:24 says that it was hail mixed with fire! Nor was it hail the size of marbles. It was so big that, if you got caught out in it, both man and beast would die. God was trying His best to get Pharaoh's attention, but Pharaoh continued in his stubbornness. You have known people like that. I run into them every day.

And then Exodus chapter 10 tells us that Pharaoh again broke his promise to release the Israelites. This time, God sent a plague of locusts. They covered the earth; they stripped bare every green thing; they filled the houses. You would have thought Pharaoh would surrender. But he did not. After telling Moses to call off the locusts because he had had enough, he reneged again! He was thinking how much it was going to cost him if he released all of his free laborers.

Then there was a plague of darkness over the land of Egypt for three days (Exodus 10:22). When God orders it to be dark, it is DARK! I remember being in Carlsbad Caverns, some 800 feet below the surface. When they turned out all the lights, it was pitch black! But the guide eventually turned on the lights – which Pharaoh could not do.

When Pharaoh lied again regarding the release of the Israelites, God's patience ran out. He sent to most grievous plague of them all - - the death of the first born in all the families throughout Egypt (Exodus 11:5). Only the families of the Israelites would be spared if they applied the blood from an innocent lamb to their doorposts as instructed in Exodus 12:1-12. This plague was so painful throughout the land that, this time, Pharaoh relented and allowed the Israelites to leave Egypt. This fateful night was labeled "The Passover" – and is one of the celebrated feasts observed by the Jewish people to this very day – when the death angel passed over, slaying the firstborn in every Egyptian family throughout the land, and paving the way for the Israelites to throw off their bondage of slavery. It is a beautiful picture of Christ as the sacrificial Lamb who took away our sins.

So, back to where we studied about the two witnesses in this chapter. They have the power to call down fire on anyone who tries to attack them. They have the power to dry up the skies so that it does not rain. The people do not mind as long as they have water to drink. But then, these two witnesses cause the waters to turn to blood. Can you imagine the stench? And then all kinds of plagues and diseases come upon mankind. No wonder the ungodly men and women on earth had come to fear and hate these witnesses with such intensity. Right from the beginning they had been told that the plagues had been sent as punishment from God for their wickedness and continuing rebellion against Christ.

We are now going to get a real introduction to the Beast, that diabolic figure called the Antichrist who has turned over his very will to Satan during the last days. This Beast is wreaking havoc upon the world, but especially on the Christians and the Jews. He is beside himself with rage because he cannot stop these two witnesses from preaching the truth of God.

This Beast will not claim to be Christ, but he will openly blaspheme and oppose Christ, boasting that he has received his authority from Satan, and that he and his master will soon depose of Jehovah God. We will see a lot more of his diabolical schemes in the next few chapters, but here, he commissions his forces to wipe out these two prophets. However, God has put a special hedge of protection around them until their mission is complete.

This reminds me of an awesome statement made by Lottie Moon, that faithful missionary to China in the early 20th Century. It was unbelievable all the hardships that Lottie Moon had to endure, being threatened with death on every hand. Her quote should be memorized or at least written in every Christian's Bible. Paraphrasing, it says "If you are in the Lord's will, then you are immortal until you have completed the mission God has for you."[15] That is powerful! You do not need to worry about being a victim in a tsunami, a tornado, a fatal automobile accident or whatever. If you are in the Lord's will, then you are immortal until you have completed the mission God has for you.

That was the way it was with these two witnesses. Their mission was complete, and God brought them home. *"And when they shall have finished their testimony, the Beast that ascended out of the Bottomless Pit shall make war against them, and shall overcome them, and kill them"* (Revelation 11:7). Scripture describes the Beast as "ascending out of the Bottomless Pit," that is, this Beast will have a satanic character. He is a man all right, but he has turned his heart and soul and will over to Satan himself.

Webster's Dictionary defines the word perdition as "eternal damnation." There are only two people in Scripture that are referred to as "the son of perdition." One was Judas (John 17:12) and the other is the Antichrist (II Thessalonians 2:3). Scripture says that these two mighty witnesses finished their testimony. The last person who was going to turn to God under their preaching has done so. Therefore, in the eyes of God, it is Mission Accomplished!

Even though the witnesses have now been killed, the Antichrist hated them so much he refuses to allow them to have a decent burial. *"And their dead bodies shall lie in the street of the great city, which spiritually is called Sodom and Egypt, where also our Lord was crucified"* (Revelation 11:8). The Antichrist left their bodies lying in the street on public display. He hated every day that they preached to the people so now it is his turn! And so he commands their bodies to lie in the street as a grizzly reminder of what will happen to anyone who opposes him.

Notice that the city was spiritually called "Sodom and Egypt" (Revelation 11:8). That is because Sodom was the most immoral city one could think of. That is the city that Abraham could not even find ten righteous men! And, of course, Egypt was known for its idolatry – chasing after false gods. But if you look closely, the verse will tell you the city where these two witnesses had been preaching. It is not the literal city of Sodom; it is not any city in Egypt. It is in the city "where our Lord was crucified." It is Jerusalem! The city called holy is desecrated by the Antichrist.

How long will their bodies lie in the streets? Verse 9 tells us: *"And they of the people and kindreds and tongues and nations shall see their dead bodies three days and a half, and shall not suffer their dead bodies to be put in graves."* It is ironic but there is some kind of message here – they preached for 3½ years and their visible witness to the unbelievers continued for 3½ days after they were dead. Not only is the Antichrist overjoyed at their deaths, but all the followers of the Antichrist participate in this gross celebration. All the peoples of the earth – every tongue – every tribe – shall look upon these dead bodies and rejoice.

It is interesting to note that God could in some miraculous way supernaturally allow all the peoples of the world at the same time to see these two bodies lying there. Critics who deny miracles have gleefully pointed out for 2,000 years how utterly ridiculous such a statement is – that the whole world would see these bodies at the same time. They said, "Boy, it takes a lot of faith to believe such idiotic nonsense." But Bible believing Christians remained faithful and said, "We do not know how it will be done, but we believe God's Word cannot lie."

God could easily perform a miracle to accomplish this, but most of the time He works through existing means and existing technologies to accomplish His purposes. Before our generation, this viewing of the two bodies worldwide would be impossible apart from a direct miracle by God. But in our generation, we know how easily it could be accomplished. Simply point a camera at these two dead bodies, send a signal up to a satellite and presto! – the whole world is able to look upon the bodies of these two men.

John faithfully wrote down what the Lord told him to write though John never had a clue as to how the whole world could look at the streets of Jerusalem at the same time! When God's Word issues a prophecy, no matter how impossible it may seem at the moment, you can be assured that it will be faithfully fulfilled.

Verse 10: *"And they that dwell upon the earth shall rejoice over them, and make merry, and shall send gifts one to another; because these two prophets tormented them that dwelt on the earth."* I do not know what the temperature will be when this happens, but most of the time it is warm in Jerusalem. A corpse would decompose very quickly. Can you imagine the insult? The indescribable shame as these two prophets of God lay in the streets of Jerusalem, and their bodies begin to decay right before the eyes of the crowd. Were the people outraged and horrified over such a deplorable act? No! They were so happy they gave gifts to each other. We have an Antichrist – and now we have an Anti-Christmas! They stop where they are, and give gifts to each other – not because of LOVE, but because of HATE! They are thrilled that their tormentors are dead!

Two times verse 10 refers to those who dwell on the earth. They are mentioned eleven times in the Book of Revelation (3:10; 6:10; 8:13; 11:10 twice; 13:8, 12, 14 twice; 14:6; 17:8). This is referring to those Christ-rejecters who have settled down on earth, and embraced its worldly values.

These two prophets, like Christ, had returned to Jerusalem to do their preaching, and the resulting plagues they invoked had affected nations everywhere. They had been regarded for nearly 3½ years as the greatest enemies of the human race, and had been feared and hated the world over. The news of their conquest and execution spread immediately throughout the world, probably carried by satellite to media outlets everywhere.

Believers who wanted to give them a decent burial were driven away. The gloating of the macabre spectators knew no bounds, and the Beast who had killed them quickly became an international hero. No doubt he led the chorus: "Joy to the world – the Lord is dead!"

The Antichrist will certainly go on international TV or other outlets with his own "State of the Union" message. No more would angels fly across the sky proclaiming the Gospel of Christ. No more would the people be tormented by stinging scorpion-like locusts. No more would they see frightful horse-demons charging down on them. And the greatest of the human enemies, the two prophets of God, are lying dead in the streets of Jerusalem. The Antichrist is preparing to declare to the world that his triumph is complete. But God has a big surprise waiting for him and his followers! Look at the next two verses: *"And after three days and a half the spirit of life from God entered into them, and they stood upon their feet; and great fear fell upon them which saw them. And they heard a great voice from Heaven saying unto them, 'Come up hither.' And they ascended up to Heaven in a cloud, and their enemies beheld them"* (Revelation 11:11-12).

Their resurrection is not unusual – at least not to Christians. Our Lord was resurrected, and Christians will be resurrected at the Rapture in the twinkling of an eye! But what is unusual, is that this is the only instance where the enemies of God saw a resurrection. His enemies did not witness the Lord's resurrection. The only evidence was the empty tomb and the grave clothes which were left behind.

The Rapture will be in secret as far as the world is concerned. The unbelievers will not witness it. The only evidence of it is the millions of people who disappear. My friend, Evangelist Jack Hollingsworth, said: "We're not going to see it – we are going to be it!" Even when Elijah was taken up in God's chariot only faithful Elisha was allowed to witness it. But here, in the case of these two witnesses, the resurrection and ascension occur openly and boldly. As they were going up, Scripture says, *"their enemies beheld them"* (Revelation 11:12). Wow! Wonder what their enemies thought about that! Rejoicing quickly turned into great fear!

All the news networks no doubt had their cameras pointed at them, and before their director could yell "cut," the world saw "the news as it is." These spectators are fully described in Philippians: *"For I have told you often before, and I say it again with tears in my eyes, that there are many whose conduct shows they are really enemies of the cross of Christ. Their future is eternal destruction. Their god is their appetite, they brag about shameful things, and all they think about is this life here on earth"* (Philippians 3:18-19 NLT). Woe to the earth dwellers! And lest you get the wrong idea, we are not rejoicing over the judgment that awaits these earth dwellers. We are sad. Sad because, except for their pride, they could come into the family of God and experience the joy that awaits the followers of Christ.

Before we leave these two mighty men, let me say this. Many of the respectable commentators are divided on when these witnesses appear on the scene. One thing we know, however, is that their ministry covers 3½ years or half of the Tribulation Period. But which half? One group says they preach during the first 3½ years and one group says they preach during the last 3½ years. There are some very good arguments on both sides of the fence. I have studied this, prayed about it, and looked at this as carefully as I could, and it seems to me that these two witnesses appear during the "Great Tribulation" – the last 3½ years of the Tribulation.

Satan has had more than his share of disappointments. He has been like a yoyo; up one minute and down the next. You'd think he would have learned by now. He was exuberant when he announced he was taking over the leadership of Heaven. But then he was banished along with his pitiful misfits. He rejoiced when Adam and Eve fell, apparently marring the wonderful plans God had for the human race. But then, he was outmaneuvered again as a Savior was promised. When the Savior was born into the world, Satan worked through King Herod to slay all the babies, thus thinking he had spoiled the plans for the Savior of the world. Foiled again! Mary and Joseph escaped to Egypt with the young child.

Satan's greatest success was within reach that day on the Cross. He watched Jesus die. He watched Him being placed in a tomb. He watched the Roman Guard shut Him away with a huge boulder. Satan's crowning achievement had finally been realized – he thought.

No doubt Satan was as exuberant as those earth dwellers, as they watched God's prophets lie in the streets of Jerusalem for 3½ days. And as that great Easter song says, *Then Came the*

Morning.[16] Praise the Lord! What a surprise God had in store for Satan and the Antichrist and the spectators who were watching the two witnesses. The Spirit of the Living God entered their bodies and they stood upon their feet. Mayhem broke out as people scrambled to get out of their way! The Perrys have a great song that relates to Jesus' miracles – the water into wine – the raising of Lazarus – the empty tomb. They sing, *I Wish I Could Have Been There!*[17] Truly, I wish I could have been there to see these two witnesses raised from the dead!

There is another fascinating aspect connected with the witnesses' ascension. It says they *"ascended up to Heaven in a cloud"* (Revelation 11:12). The Greek is very emphatic here concerning that cloud. The NASB translates it correctly: *"They ascended up to Heaven in THE cloud."* I can envision the Lord sending His golden chariot down for them, the Shekinah glory of Heaven, and they were caught up before the astonishing gaze of these earth dwellers.

"And the same hour was there a great earthquake, and the tenth part of the city fell, and in the earthquake were slain of men seven thousand: and the remnant were affrighted, and gave glory to the God of Heaven" (Revelation 11:13). There was an earthquake when Christ was crucified; there was an earthquake at the time of His resurrection. God often speaks through earthquakes. They are sobering reminders that man must face ultimate judgment. After the amazing ascension of these two prophets, that same hour a great earthquake destroys a tenth of the city and seven thousand men are killed.

Commentator John Gill says that in the original Greek of Revelation 11:13, it carries the connotation that these seven thousand men were men of distinction – men of renown – men of prominence. Men that you would recognize their names if you lived on the planet. We often have the mistaken notion that celebrities and men of prominence are immune to tragedy, but when 7,000 are killed in one hour, and the aftershocks wipe out a tenth of the city, reality sets in. It will be quite a jolt to those who survive this latest judgment. In fact, they are so traumatized they acknowledge the God of Heaven. This does not mean they are converted – it simply means they are so scared they acknowledge the power of Almighty God.

In the next chapter, we see these unbelievers blaspheming the Lord again. There is no real change in their lives – not the change that accompanies true conversion. They are like the atheists in foxholes who call out to God when the bullets are flying, then forget Him once peace is restored.

Pastors have told me that they have seen scores of men and women who, when the doctor tells them they only have a short time to live, cry, "Oh, I've wasted my life; if I could just get well, I'd be a different person." But, if he or she does get well, the promise is usually forgotten. A change of heart must come from within your heart and soul, not just from the surface because you are afraid of dying. Real change and a personal devotion to Christ will last forever. It will make a new man – a new woman – a new home. Not because they are fearful or terrified of dying, but because they truly love Jesus in their hearts. That is what it means to be saved. If people could only realize what lies ahead, they would see that now is the time to place their faith in Him while there is still an opportunity.

Then there is a somber message: *"The second woe is past, and behold, the third woe cometh quickly"* (Revelation 11:14). At the end of chapter 8 an angel said, *"woe, woe, woe"* to the inhabitants of the earth because of the three angels who were yet to sound their trumpets. In chapter 9, the fifth angel sounded his trumpet, and terrible scorpion-like locusts inflicted great pain. Then the sixth angel sounded and a demon army from Hell killed one-third of the world's population.

In Revelation 11:15 we come to the third woe ushered in by the seventh and last trumpet. It is not one shrill blast over a moment of time, but some type of continuation. The third woe is actually the consummation of the age, and brings about the final judgment of mankind. We know this from Revelation 10:7 which says: *"in the days of the voice of the seventh angel, when he shall begin to sound, the mystery shall be finished."* The seventh angel and his sounding, and all the repercussions that follow thereafter, constitute the final judgment of God encompassing the complete redemption of mankind and planet earth, and the unveiling of the New Heaven and New Earth.

The days of the voice of the seventh angel will also include the seven bowl judgments that we will study when we come to chapter 16. Chapters 12-22 are a detailed description of what we find in Revelation 11:13-18. This passage covers everything involved (in just 6 verses) in the completion of the whole mystery of God – the pouring out of the last seven bowls of wrath upon the earth; the battle of Armageddon; the Second Coming of Christ; the establishment of the Millennial Kingdom; the Great White Throne Judgment; and the New Heaven and the New Earth.

All of this will take place during the *"days of the voice of the seventh angel"* (Revelation 10:7). The kingdom is not actually established until the 19th chapter, but here in verse 15 of chapter 11, we have a preview: *"And the seventh angel sounded; and there were great voices in Heaven, saying, 'THE KINGDOMS OF THIS WORLD ARE BECOME THE KINGDOMS OF OUR LORD, AND OF HIS CHRIST; AND HE SHALL REIGN FOR EVER AND EVER.'"*

This is the prayer that Christians down through the ages have been praying: *"Thy Kingdom come. Thy will be done, in earth as it is in Heaven"* (Matthew 6:10). Those prayers are finally answered: *"And He shall reign for ever and ever"* (Revelation 11:15). This is the line that is repeated many times in George Frederick Handel's famous anthem, the *Hallelujah Chorus*.

Verse 15 is actually a flash-forward to the end of the age. In the next few chapters, we are going to see some of the details of the vile and devastating results that happen because of the reign of the Antichrist. And so, in order to keep from being depressed about the awful things coming down the pike, John is given a view as to what happens at the end of the Tribulation when Christ's victory becomes a reality. This is the event for which all Christendom has been waiting.

The whole question of sovereignty will now be settled. Who controls the universe – God or Satan? The issue has raged in the minds of people throughout the ages. Now the issue will be settled once and for all. Believers everywhere look forward to the time when evil will be eradicated, and Christ will reign supreme over all the earth. The plant and animal life groan in travail, waiting the time for that awful curse to be removed so that things will return to what they were before man's Fall in the Garden of Eden (Romans 8:19-21).

In the original Greek, the word "kingdom" – "*he hasileia*" is singular. The verse should read, as modern translations correctly render it, "*The kingdom of the world has become the Kingdom of our Lord and of His Christ; and He will reign forever and ever*" (Revelation 11:15 NASB). As humans we label various man-made kingdoms of the world, but as God sees it, there is really only one kingdom down here and it belongs to Satan.

During Jesus' temptation, Satan carried Him to a high mountain, and showed Him all the man-made kingdoms of the world. He said, "*All this I will give thee if thou wilt bow down and worship me*" (Matthew 4:9). Satan offered Christ all the kingdoms of this world. If Satan did not possess this to offer, it was no real temptation to Jesus. But the temptation was real. In II Corinthians 4:4, Paul refers to Satan as the god of this world. When God is portraying the kingdoms of the world as He did in Daniel 7, He sees them all as beasts: a lion, a bear, a leopard, and the fourth was so dreadful it defied description.

It seems our society is going downhill. One of my favorite preachers, Adrian Rogers, described it perfectly: "Our world is getting gloriously dark." Violence is on the upswing. Sometimes it seems that the whole planet is simply an endless cemetery – the earth is full of death and the dead. Russia is just as vile today as it was under the Soviet dictators. China is just as repressive today as it was under any of its former dynasties. North Korea is being run by a power hungry rogue. All the kingdoms on earth are really just one kingdom presided over by the powers of darkness. The brutalities we see in the Middle East in the name of religion are unbelievable. But God says that sin will not always rule in this earth. Satan will not always go unchallenged. The grave will not always open up to receive God's people. There is coming a day when death will be no more, sin will be no more, and Satan will be no more. All this will happen "*in the days of the voice of the seventh angel*" when "*THE KINGDOMS OF THIS WORLD ARE BECOME THE KINGDOMS OF OUR LORD AND HIS CHRIST*" (Revelation 11:15).

What happens in Heaven after this great announcement in verse 15? The Church which is in Heaven at this time, represented by the 24 Elders, falls down and worships God. Look at verses 16-17: "*And the four and twenty elders, which sat before God on their seats, fell upon their faces, and worshiped God, Saying, We give thee thanks, O Lord God Almighty, which art, and wast, and art to come; because thou hast taken to thee thy great power, and hast reigned."* Take note! This verse contains one of the greatest affirmations that this is the Word of God. Look at the verse closely. In the KJV, it says, *"We give thee thanks, O Lord God Almighty, which art and wast, and art to come."* That is the exact same description we had in Revelation 1:4 and Revelation 1:8. But John left out the phrase *"and art to come"* here in Revelation 11:17 (as we see it correctly omitted in the NASB, ESV, NLT, NIV).

An early scribe, remembering John's description in Revelation 1:4 and 1:8, simply thought, "John made an omission. I'll help him out by putting in the phrase *'and art to come.'"* But John left it out for a reason. You see, in verse 17, Christ has already come in the mind of God! The kingdom of this world has already become the kingdom of God and His Christ in the time frame that this is being described! The modern translations all have it right, and if you look at verse 17 the NKJV, it has a little footnote that says the phrase *"and art to come"* is not in the earliest manuscripts.

"And the nations were angry, and thy wrath is come, and the time of the dead, that they should be judged, and that thou shouldest give reward unto thy servants the prophets, and to the saints, and them that fear thy name, small and great: and shouldest destroy them which destroy the earth" (Revelation 11:18). Isn't it strange, but true – the things that cause rejoicing in Heaven, causes anger and hatred on earth? And in the general panoramic statement, it says that everyone will get their just desserts. The *"time of the dead"* in verse 18a refers to the Great White Throne Judgment when all unbelievers will be judged and cast into Hell. But then in verse 18b, there are rewards for God's children. *"Thy servants the prophets and the saints"* – all those Old Testament believers, will get their just rewards.

"Them that fear thy name" mentioned in verse 18b are those Tribulation martyrs who were beheaded by the Antichrist rather than take his mark and worship him. They will be justly rewarded. But what does it really mean about fearing God's name? When anyone hears His name, are they to be afraid? No! The context refers to respecting and revering God's name. I detest hearing God's name used as a curse word. I have known people who use God's name in vain so often they are not even aware of what they are saying. Somewhat better, but not much better, are those people who seem to be embarrassed to say the name of God, and so they refer to Him as the "Man upstairs" or the "Magic Man in the Sky." What Scripture is saying here is that He will reward those who have a healthy respect for His name. The Church age saints are not mentioned among the group here that is receiving rewards because they are already in Heaven (Revelation 4:1), and they have already received their rewards (I Corinthians 3) as shown by the crowns on their heads (Revelation 4:4).

In Heaven, the Church is praising God, but on earth, the nations are angry, and God's wrath will not be withheld any longer. Evil men will be judged. Believers will have already been judged at the Bema Seat of Christ (I Corinthians chapter 3). This is not to judge believers for their sins. That judgment was satisfied by Christ on the Cross. This is to judge believers for their works, their motives and their opportunities to determine rewards. But the unsaved will be judged at the Great White Throne Judgment. There will be no believers there, only Christ rejecters. An important lesson we have seen throughout this Book is that people who have not accepted Christ will not be welcome in God's presence. Earth dwellers are in love with this world, interested only in material things, and self-centered pursuits. Heaven dwellers love to worship and adore God. The two have nothing in common.

The last phrase of verse 18 says that God will destroy those that destroy the earth. This includes the Antichrist, the False Prophet, and their followers. In fact, one of the names of Satan is "Destroyer" (Revelation 9:11 NIV). Instead of protecting and enjoying this beautiful world that God created for us, we have allowed sin to rob us of most of the world's benefits. We have squandered our natural resources. Instead of caring for the animals and the plants which are committed to our dominion, we have become their enemy, and many are now extinct. Wars have devastated our forests and scorched the lands. Greed has polluted the waters and poisoned the air. Nutrients have been leached from the soils, and lands have been over-cultivated and over-grazed. In the Greek, the word for "destroy" is the same as the word for "corrupt." Man has destroyed the earth by corrupting it. And lest we become too discouraged by the violence and horror of these terrible days, there is a vision described in the next verse to cheer our hearts.

"And the Temple of God was opened in Heaven, and there was seen in His Temple the Ark of His Testament: and there were lightnings, and voices, and thunderings, and an earthquake, and great hail" (Revelation 11:19). The Temple on earth has been corrupted by the Antichrist, so God directs John's attention to God's Temple in Heaven.

It is open to John's view, and the only object John sees is the Ark of the Covenant. It formerly resided in the Holy of Holies in the Temple, but the contents of the Ark may have been lost when the Ark was captured by Israel's enemies (I Samuel 4:11) - - but you can be assured their precious treasures will be residing in the Ark in Heaven: a pot of manna signifying that God will always supply every need; Aaron's budding rod signifying that God is the giver of life; and two stone tablets that contain God's laws signifying His Holiness and Justice.

The Ark was a rectangular shaped box made of acacia wood and overlaid with gold. It had a gold lid called the mercy seat. On the gold lid were two cherubim with their wings spread over the mercy seat, and they were looking down at the box (Exodus 25:10-22). In Heaven, the Ark was not shut up in the Holy of Holies. It was open and available to all God's children. What is so significant about John's seeing the Ark? It is this. The Ark was located in the Holy of Holies in the Temple; nobody saw it but the High Priest, and then only once a year. But after the cross, the Ark is open for all to see as a reminder that God's glory and innermost secrets will be revealed to His people. It is also a reminder that our High Priest, Jesus Christ, offered the ultimate sacrifice, and in doing so, tore down the veil separating us from the presence of God in the Holy of Holies.

The last verse of chapter 11 indicates that the final judgments of The Great Tribulation are about to begin. Most people today believe that God is either 1) too loving to ever pour out His wrath on the world, or 2) incapable of doing so. The prominent Jewish Rabbi, Harold Kushner, said there is evil in this world for one of two reasons. Either God does not care – or He cares and is not powerful enough to do anything about it.[18] But we know from Scripture that He is indeed powerful enough, but it is his mercy and patience that is all that has stayed His hand up to this point (II Peter 3:9).

Men through the centuries have searched for the lost Ark of the Covenant. Hollywood has made movies about it, but it isn't lost. God knows where the Ark is, and has it safely secured for display in the heavenly Temple. Then, at the end of the verse, the scene shifts from Heaven to earth where there are lightnings, thunderings, an earthquake and great hail. It is preparing us for the horrific scenes that will take place during the last 3½ years of the Tribulation Period – the period that Jesus called "*The Great Tribulation*" (Matthew 24:21).

Anyone who has ever played in the snow understands the "snowball effect." Take a snowball the size of a baseball, plop it down in some wet snow, and begin to roll it along. It gets larger and larger. This is a perfect way to describe what happens during the last 3½ years of the Tribulation. It will be the most horrifying and traumatic period the world has ever seen. And when the Antichrist begins his persecution in earnest, disasters increase at such a pace that Jesus Himself said that if those days were not shortened, no life would survive; but God does shorten this period to only 3½ years, and then He intervenes to bring all this madness to a halt (Matthew 24:22).

We have reached a milestone! Revelation has 22 chapters and we have finished eleven of them – halfway home! Amazing, exciting events are waiting, so let's not tarry!

CHAPTER TWELVE

War in Heaven

———————

God is going to step back, let us catch our breath, and in the next few chapters fill in the details of the last 3½ years of the Tribulation Period. This is the time Jesus referred to as "The *Great Tribulation*" because the Antichrist will be orchestrating evil on the earth as never before in the history of mankind (Matthew 24:21).

However, the remarkable vision seen by John in this chapter looks back to the beginning of history then races forward to the time of Christ, and finally to the events still to be consummated in this final period. An understanding of chapter 12 is essential to comprehend the full significance of the great signs about to be unveiled. Dr. Paige Patterson, past president of the Southern Baptist Convention, said, "If you are confused about the meaning of the 12th chapter, you will likely be confused about the rest of the Book."[1] As we go through this chapter, you will notice that the Church is not mentioned. That is because this chapter only deals with God's chosen people, Israel.

In this 12th chapter, we are introduced to five important personages. They are introduced in this order: first, the radiant woman clothed with the sun (verse 1); second, the great red dragon (verse 3); third, the Man-child who will rule the world (verse 5); fourth, Michael the Archangel (verse 7), and fifth, the remnant of the Seed of the woman (verse 17). Dr. Theodore Epp had this to say about this chapter: "Some interpreters have entitled Revelation 12 by this one word – war. This involves war on earth, war in Heaven, and war on earth again. Others divide Revelation 12 as 'The conflict of the woman with the dragon in the past, the conflict of the woman with the dragon in the heavens, and the conflict of the woman with the dragon in the future.'"[2]

Let us begin our reading at chapter 12, verses 1-2: *"And there appeared a great wonder in Heaven; a woman clothed with the sun, and the moon under her feet, and upon her head a crown of twelve stars. And she being with child cried, travailing in birth, and pained to be delivered."*

Who is this woman who is so marvelously described? If you are wrong as to the identification of this woman, you are going to be wrong in your interpretation of many, many events in the next several chapters. As we try to determine who this woman is, let me point out an important fact. The word wonder in Greek is "semeion" – the same word that is normally translated sign. In fact, the Greek word semeion is found 51 times in the New Testament, and in 48 of them it is translated sign. Most modern translations render this verse in this manner: *"And there appeared a great sign in Heaven"*. So, let us be clear: it does not say a woman appeared in Heaven. It is a sign or a symbol; it is not a real woman.

Verse 1 says a great sign appeared in Heaven, and then gives a description of this sign. The sign is a woman *"clothed with the sun, and the moon under her feet, and upon her head a crown of twelve stars"* (Revelation 12:1). Let us look at who this woman (sign) is not. In spite of what the Roman Catholic Church teaches, she is not the Virgin Mary. Look at verse 6 for a moment. After she gives birth to the male child, it says she *"fled into the wilderness, where she hath a place prepared of God, that they should feed her there a thousand two hundred and threescore days."* And again in verse 14: *"And to the woman were given two wings of a great eagle, that she might fly into the wilderness, into her place, where she is nourished for a time, and times, and half a time, from the face of the serpent."* Finally, verse 17: *"And the dragon was wroth with the woman, and went to make war with the remnant of her seed, which keep the commandments of God, and have the testimony of Jesus Christ."*

First, nothing like this ever happened to the Virgin Mary. According to Dr. J. Dwight Pentecost, "Mary was never persecuted, never fled into the wilderness, and was never protected for 1,280 days."[3] It also says in verse 17 that Satan was angry, and went after the woman (Israel) and the remnant (believing Jews) of her Seed. Second, according to Catholic doctrine and confirmed by their website, Mary had no other children before or after Jesus was born,[4] so how could there be a remnant of her Seed? Third, though Mary was highly favored by God and blessed among women, she was never worshiped in the Scriptures nor did her description even come close to her being clothed with the sun, moon and stars.

Then there are those who say that this radiant woman represents the Church. This is called "Replacement Theology." They go as far as to say that the Jews forfeited all their promises throughout the Old Testament because they rejected the Messiah, and the Church is now the recipient of all those Old Testament promises. Unfortunately, they do not understand the promises made by God to the Jews as relates to the land of Israel. What many people do not know is that there are two Old Testament covenants pertaining to the land of Israel. The Abrahamic Covenant gives the title of the land to the Jews in perpetuity – forever (Genesis 13:15). A later covenant, "the Mosaic Land Covenant" of Deuteronomy chapters 28-30, defines the conditions for possession and enjoyment of the land. This later covenant is often referred to as the "Palestinian Covenant," but that is a misnomer since the land was never called Palestine until after the second Jewish revolt in 132-135 A.D. At that time the Romans dubbed it Palestine to erase the memory of its Jewish heritage, and to insult the Jews since Palestine is the Latin word for Philistine, the ancient enemy of Israel. I prefer to call it the "Land Covenant".

The following is an illustration by Dr. David Reagan that clearly shows the role and relationship of these two covenants. Suppose you buy a car for your teenage son and put the title in the son's name. But you explain to the son that there are conditions for using the car – such as no speeding. And you warn your son that a speeding ticket will result in the loss of the privilege of driving the car for a period of two weeks or more. If the son gets a ticket, and you lock the car in the garage for two weeks, the car still belongs to the son because the son's name is on the title; but the son has temporarily lost possession of the vehicle. In like manner, the Abrahamic Covenant gave the title of the land to the Jews in perpetuity. The Mosaic Land Covenant defined the terms for possession and use of the land. Having possession of something is not the same thing as having the title or ownership to it. The Jews have lost possession (or use) of the land from time to time because of their disobedience, but they have never lost their God-given title to the land.[5]

When these misguided teachers say that the woman in verse 1 is the Church, that means the Church gave birth to the Messiah and consequently, they have the picture reversed! The Scripture is very clear. This woman, whoever she is or whoever she represents gives birth to the Messiah. To say that the Church gave birth to Jesus is to speak diametrically opposite to what the Scriptures avow. It is Christ who gave birth to the Church. The Church was instituted on the day of Pentecost when 120 of Jesus' followers were fasting and praying in the Upper Room, waiting for the power of the Holy Spirit as they had been directed. Later, Peter delivered his powerful message to the crowds gathered that day, at the end of which, he gave an invitation to accept Jesus as their Messiah. About three thousand people responded, and they were added to the original 120 believers (Acts 2:41).

Jesus had promised in Matthew 16:18 that He would build His Church, and the gates of Hell would not prevail against it. Look at Ephesians 5, verse 31: *"For this cause shall a man leave his father and mother, and shall be joined unto his wife, and they two shall be one flesh."* But then most of us quit reading and miss the next verse as it is very important. It says, *"This is a great mystery: but I speak concerning Christ and the Church."* What is this great mystery about Christ and the Church? Here is what Paul is trying to tell us. As Eve was taken out of the side of Adam, so the Church was born out of the pierced, open, bleeding side of our Lord.

The Church is always referred to as a chaste virgin – a Bride who is some day to be presented to Christ (II Corinthians 11:2). For the Bride of Christ is to be found in labor, travailing to give birth to Christ before the Marriage of the Lamb even takes place, is scandalous. In Scripture the Church is never referred to as a mother, but always as a chaste Bride. The clear fact is that Christ gave birth to the Church; the Church did not give birth to Christ. If this woman is a picture of the Church, and the Church gave birth to Christ, then you cannot escape the conclusion that Christ would marry His mother (the Church) at the Marriage of the Lamb, and then He would be known as the Son of His Bride. Sort of like, "I'm my own Grandpa." Any interpretation that tries to make the Church the mother of Christ is just plain foolish.

There is one more person that this woman does not represent. She is not Mary Baker Eddy, the founder of Christian Science. Some have said that Mrs. Eddy modestly admits that she is the woman clothed with the sun, moon and stars. Others say she never made that claim. Whether she did or not, we know that she did not disclaim it – and she readily accepted such admiration when given by her followers.

Victoria Sargent, CSD (Doctor of Christian Science), said to Mrs. Eddy, "My students recognize you to be God's witness and mouthpiece. They are convinced that God is guiding you in this work which you are carrying on for the cause of Christian Science. They feel that you fulfill the prophecies of the Scriptures – that you represent the God-crowned woman mentioned in the Apocalypse." Mrs. Eddy was quick to respond to these sentiments.

Pointing her finger upward, she said, "That is from above." Caroline D. Noyes, CSD, wrote, "There is one distinguishing feature in Mrs. Eddy's students and loyal followers or of her faithful teachers – they always recognized and have always done so, the fact that Mrs. Eddy was the woman St. John prophesies about in Revelation XII ....".[6]

Some of Mrs. Eddy's followers put her on par with Jesus Christ and, rather than disavow such blasphemy, she seemed to actually enjoy it. Judge Septimus Hanna, a close friend of Mrs. Eddy and a loyal Christian Science follower, wrote the following letter which was received with Mrs. Eddy's admiration and approval. "By common belief of all Christians, Christ Jesus represented the male-hood of God. Is it not reasonable to assume that a full or completed revelation includes God's female-hood? If God is male only, it seems that He would embrace within Himself but a half of Being or Individuality; and it would be impossible to reconcile such a conception with His own declaration in Genesis that out of His self-hood He created 'male and female.'

Must the Woman of the Apocalypse be personalized or individualized to mankind? By every principle of logical sequence in Biblical prophecy, Yes. In so far as these evidences are being now brought into view through Christian Science, may it not be consistently claimed that the second-coming is here; and in so far as a single woman has been the instrument of bringing these evidences into view, may it not be consistently claimed that she is the personal representative of that second-coming?"[7]

If you understood this gobble-dee-goop, please explain it to me. This is very typical of most of the Christian Science writings including those by Mary Baker Eddy; they make no sense. So, if this woman in Revelation 12 is not the Virgin Mary, if she is not the Church, and if she is not Mary Baker Eddy, then just who is she or what does she represent? The fact is, she is plainly identified in the Holy Scriptures.

In Romans 9:5 (NLT), Paul is talking about his kinsmen, the Israelites. It says, *"Their ancestors were great people of God, and Christ Himself was a Jew as far as His human nature is concerned"* (Also see Hebrews 7:14). The beloved Apostle Paul said that the one who gave birth to the Messiah is the nation and family of Israel. That nation is likened to a woman who bore in her womb the great Savior of the world who is destined to rule over all men in earth and all hosts in Heaven. Humanly speaking, Jesus is a kinsman from the nation of Israel.

It is clear that this woman, who is giving birth to the Messiah, refers to the nation of Israel. That identification can also be seen in her description. Look at Genesis 37. It tells of the dream that Joseph had in which the sun and the moon and the 11 stars bowed down to him. This story goes on to make it clear that the sun was picturing Jacob (whose name was later changed to Israel), the moon was picturing Rachel, and the 11 stars were the brothers of Joseph – with Joseph being the 12th star. He and all his brothers comprise the 12 children or tribes of Israel.

When you look at the passage in Revelation 12 in this light, everything fits together perfectly. So the first sign in chapter 12 is the nation Israel, symbolized by a woman trying to give birth to a child – the Messiah, the Lord Jesus Christ. And then, we are introduced to another sign in Heaven as we read verse 3: *"And there appeared another wonder in Heaven; and behold a great red dragon, having seven heads and ten horns, and seven crowns upon his heads."* We do not have to speculate as to who this is – we are told. Look at verse 9: *"The great dragon .... called the Devil ....".* So this new sign is a red dragon. Remember, this is a sign or symbol depicting Satan. But it is probably where people get the absurd idea that the Devil, has horns and carries a pitchfork. In reality, he is slick, manipulative and cunning. Red signifies violence, murder and mayhem. Christ said in John 8:44 that Satan was a murderer from the beginning.

Satan is also called a dragon in Revelation 12:9. A dragon conjures up images of a dreadful, awful creature. It is a picture of the ugliness and horribleness that always accompanies sin. Its seven heads all wore crowns, indicating kingly power, and the number seven tells us that this pictures complete satanic control. These crowns are not the victors' crown that represents rewards for the saints. These are the diadem – the imperial crowns worn by kings and heads of State. These heads are later interpreted in Revelation chapter 17 as the kingdoms of this world that Satan controls.

There have been six Gentile world governments to date with inferences in Scripture that the seventh will be the final Gentile kingdom in the last days.[8]

They are:

1) Assyrian
2) Egyptian
3) Babylonian
4) Medo-Persian
5) Greek
6) Roman

   7) The Revised Roman Empire which the Antichrist will rule over during the Great Tribulation

The ten horns are interpreted in Revelation chapter 17 as ten kings or rulers during the end times. This same vision was seen in Daniel chapter 7. However, in Daniel's vision the dreadful beast had swallowed up all the other kingdoms and so, he only saw one beast with horns.

The ten horns also relate to the Antichrist, as we will see later. He, too, has ten horns in connection with the ten nation Empire over which he will rule. It is a sobering thought to realize that all governments of men are ultimately controlled by the Devil through God's permissive will; however we are told that God Himself ordains the powers that be (Romans 13:1). The best that Christians can do in this regard is to elect godly men in positions of political power so they will be a restraining force against evil. However, II Thessalonians 2:7 (NASB) reminds us that all these restraining forces will be removed at the Rapture, and evil will run its course during the Tribulation. Everything points to the fact that this symbol – this radiantly clothed woman – is the nation of Israel.

We were also introduced to another sign or symbol, that of a red dragon with seven heads and ten horns. Look at verse 4: *"And his tail drew the third part of the stars of heaven, and did cast them to the earth: and the dragon stood before the woman which was ready to be delivered, for to devour her child as soon as it was born."* We do not have to speculate who this dragon represents. Verse 9 tells us it is Satan himself. The scene we are about to witness speaks of the entire age long conflict of good versus evil. Its details are squeezed into these few verses before us. As John witnesses this amazing scene, he no doubt recalls the Lord's words recorded for us in Luke 10:18. *"And he said unto them, I beheld Satan as lightning fall from heaven."*

Satan was not originally what his evil titles indicate. God created him, and honored him above all the other angelic creatures. His name was Lucifer, meaning light bearer, or torch bearer. God established him as a trusted Archangel and surrounded him with splendor. Ezekiel says, *"Thou wast perfect in thy ways from the day that thou wast created, till iniquity was found in thee"* (Ezekiel 28:15). He forgot that he was just a created being, and began to picture himself as a mighty ruler – mightier in fact than God Himself. His pride caused him to aspire to the sovereignty that belongs only to God. Lucifer said, "I will" – instead of "Thy will." As a result, God cast him out of Heaven (Ezekiel 28:16-17). We have the best description of Satan's rebellion and expulsion from Heaven in Isaiah 14:12: *"How art thou fallen from Heaven, O Lucifer, son of the morning!"*

When Satan rebelled, and was kicked out of Heaven, a large number of angels were persuaded to follow him. Jesus in Matthew 25:41 spoke of *"the Devil and his angels."* We do not know exactly how many angels were cast out of Heaven with Satan, however, when Satan was cast out he drew one-third of the stars with him according to verse 4. In context, it is saying that one-third of the angels chose to follow Satan. I like those odds – one-third in Satan's favor and two-thirds in God's favor. Because Satan is not omnipresent, he must rely on these evil angels to carry out his bidding throughout the world. We are also told that the worst of the angels – the instigators – are locked in chains awaiting their final judgment (Jude 6). They are freed from their prison for a short time during the Tribulation Period to harass the unbelievers living on the earth (Revelation 9:2-4).

What else did this dragon do? It says he stood before the woman, which was ready to be delivered, to devour her child as soon as it was born. Hold that thought as we will come back to it. The fact of the matter is that Satan did everything he could to keep this child from being born. The first prophecy of a coming Savior who would crush the head of the serpent (Satan) was given in Genesis 3:15.

As soon as Satan digested that first prophecy that spelled his doom, Satan set about to thwart God's plans at every turn. He noted that Cain was a man of the earth – worldly – unlike his brother, Abel. So Satan reasoned, "I will put anger in Cain's heart, and if he kills Abel, that might end the godly line that God had planned." But he did not count on Eve having another child, Seth, who was godly in all respects, and who eventually was an ancestor in Christ's lineage (Luke 3:38). There are many, many other examples of how Satan tried to disrupt God's plan to bring a Savior into the world such as trying to break the lineage when Moses was born (Exodus 1:22); trying to influence Saul to kill David (I Samuel 19:1-2); and trying to exterminate the Jews during the life of Esther (Esther 4:14). Satan never lets up.

But let us move forward to Christ's actual birth. The wise men from the East (probably in the area of Babylon which is modern-day Iraq) saw a brilliant star – a super nova – as they were studying and charting the heavens. Daniel spent most of his life in this region, and these men undoubtedly had portions of the scroll Daniel had written which gives an accurate timetable for the birth of the promised Messiah (Daniel 9: 25). These wise men knew that the time for the Messiah was at hand. They were also privy to the writings of the prophet Micah so they could even pinpoint that the birthplace of the Messiah was to be in Bethlehem (Micah 5:2; Matthew 2:2-6). So they made their journey westward to find and worship this newborn King.

On one of my tours to the Holy Land, we were visiting the Church of the Nativity in Bethlehem which was built around 330 A.D. over the traditional site of the birthplace of Jesus. Bethlehem was under the control of the Palestinians, and therefore when we went in, the Arabs made our Jewish guide get off the bus and wait outside the city until we came back. We had to hire an Arab guide for our visit into Bethlehem. No Jews are allowed in Bethlehem.

When we entered the Church of the Nativity, the Arab guide was saying what he thought we wanted to hear. "The baby Jesus was born right here at this spot. The manger was here on this slab. The moonlight came right in that window over there, and shined in the baby's face, so that Mary and Joseph had to move him right over here. When the wise men arrived, they tied their camels to a hitching post outside that door, and came in to see him."

That description would be comical if it was not so ridiculous. The fact of the matter is that the wise men saw the star. By the time they made preparations, raised finances, outfitted their camels, hired their servants and guides, and made the long journey to Bethlehem, it took them about two years to arrive at their destination. Jesus was no longer a baby. How do we know this? We infer this in Scripture in two places. First, the wise men arrived in Jerusalem, and began to inquire where the young King of the Jews lived. Word made its way to Herod, and he was quite upset at the thought he might be dethroned. So, he called a private meeting with the wise men and said, *"Go to Bethlehem and search carefully for the child. And when you find him, come back and tell me so that I can go and worship him, too"* (Matthew 2:8 NLT).

The wise men departed, saw the star again, and it led them to where Jesus was in Bethlehem. But notice in Matthew 2:11, baby Jesus was long gone from the manger. It says, *"And when they were come into the house, they saw the young child* (not a baby) *and worshipped Him."* So, by the time the wise men arrived in Bethlehem to see this baby Messiah, He was now living in a house with his parents.

The second indication is that when Herod realized the wise men were not coming back to squeal on the new King, he did some quick math and decided that if he killed all the babies two years old and under, he would surely get this new upstart claiming to be king.

Satan was busy behind the scenes trying to spoil God's plan of bringing the Messiah into the world or, as the Bible says in Revelation 12, verse 4, *"to devour her child as soon as it was born."* Satan was foiled again as Mary and Joseph were warned in a dream about Herod, and made an escape to Egypt (Matthew 2:12). As Jesus grew into manhood, Satan tried a different approach. He tempted Jesus with the promise of wealth and power if He would join forces with him (Matthew 4:9), but Satan was rebuffed again when Jesus answered him by quoting Scripture (Matthew 4:10).

Satan thought he had won again when Jesus was crucified. But, His subsequent resurrection and ascension sealed Satan's fate once more. In prophecy, there is such a thing as "telescoping" where great events are pictured to look as though they occur one after another, but often they are separated by a valley or a great span of time. Revelation 12:5 is a case in point. *"And she brought forth a Man-child, who was to rule all nations with a rod of iron: and her child was caught up unto God, and to His throne."*

If anyone is in doubt as to whom this Man-child is, just turn over to the Psalms. In chapter 2, God the Father is speaking to His Son, the coming Messiah. And He says this: *"Thou shalt break them with a rod of iron; thou shalt dash them in pieces like a potter's vessel"* (Psalm 2:9).

And, as we said earlier, the woman is a symbol of Israel, as our Lord was born a Jew from the tribe of Judah. As far as telescoping is concerned, the verse says He was born, and in the next breath He ascended into Heaven, leaving the details of His life on earth to other Scriptures.

Let us breakdown verse 5. *"She brought forth a Man-child …. who was to rule all nations with a rod of iron."* It has been 2,000 years, and it has not happened yet. It is still in the future; *"and her child was caught up unto God and to His throne"* (Revelation 12:5). This passage skips over Christ's entire life from His birth to His ascension. But that is the way prophecy is usually presented. Only the major topic is highlighted. This Man-child was "caught up" – in Greek the word is "Harpazo." It is the same word used when describing the Rapture in I Thessalonians 4:17. We, in the Body of Christ, will also experience "harpazo" – caught up to meet the Lord in the air at the Rapture.

"And the woman fled into the wilderness, where she hath a place prepared of God, that they should feed her there a thousand two hundred and threescore days" (Revelation 12:6). Most prophecy teachers believe that this place prepared for Israel is a mountainous area in the Jordanian desert called "Petra." In Greek, the name Petra means a large, immovable rock. Petra is like a rock fortress. There are sheer rock ledges rising hundreds of feet into the air, with only one pass leading into it – excellent for protection purposes. A portion of Petra has been opened to tourism the last several years, and many are awed by its impregnability. It could well be that this is the very place that the Jews will escape to when the Antichrist pours out his fury against them during the last 3½ years the Tribulation.

Remember, in the 16th chapter of Matthew, Peter had just made his assertion, *"Thou art the Christ, the Son of the living God"* (Matthew 16:16). And Jesus says, "Peter, you could not have figured this out by yourself – God had to reveal it to you" (Matthew 16:17). And then Christ makes that awesome statement: *"Thou art Peter* (Gk. Petros – a small stone), *and upon this rock* (Gk. Petra – a large, immoveable rock) *I will build my Church"* (Matthew 16:18).

Some, like the Catholic Church, think that this Petra – this immoveable rock – was Peter upon which Christ would build His Church. How immoveable was Peter? Not very; Jesus just told him he was a small, movable stone. And only four verses later, Peter unwittingly is trying to stop Christ from going to the cross! (Matthew 16:22). And Christ tells him, *"Get thee behind me, Satan"* (Matthew 16:23). In other words, Christ is telling Peter, "Your plan is exactly the plan Satan is trying to put into effect to keep me from going to the cross!" It is clear to me that Jesus was referring to Himself as the immovable stone on which His Church will be built (Matthew 16:18; Ephesians 2:20).

There are others who think that this Petra – this immoveable rock upon which Christ will build His Church – is the "confession" that Peter had just made, that Christ is the Son of the Living God. I do not quibble with that interpretation because it certainly contains the truth.

However, we do not have the benefit of hand gestures when we read the written Word, and so, I believe that Jesus is saying this: "You are Petros – a small, moveable stone (thumping Peter on his chest), but upon this Petra – (patting His own chest) – this large, immoveable rock ledge, I will build My Church, and the gates of Hell shall not prevail against it." This certainly is compatible with Paul's statement: *"For other foundation can no man lay than that is laid, which is Jesus Christ"* (I Corinthians 3:11).

Before we leave this passage, consider this: "The gates of Hell will not prevail against the Church" (Matthew 16:18b). Folks, the Church (that's you and me) is not supposed to be hunkered down behind Petra – this large rock – waiting for the enemy to attack. We are supposed to be on the offense. We are to take the battle to Satan. Do not sit back in the church, and just take what comes each week – ho hum, same old thing. Take the battle to Satan – take the battle to the very gates of Hell and those gates will not hold up. We are in a battle! Do something to help us win. If you can't fight, then carry bullets, but get involved!

Look at verse 6. God says He will protect the woman (Israel) for 1,260 days – the exact time frame of the last half of the Tribulation Period when this dragon (Satan) is trying to exterminate the Jews. Some commentators believe that these 3½ years refer to the first half of the Tribulation. This is not a big problem to quibble over. Personally, I think that during the first 3½ years the Jews harassed, but will not be hunted down – because there will be a seven year peace treaty in effect between the Antichrist and the Jews as they will be rebuilding their Temple (Daniel 9:27). Then in the middle of these 7 years, the Antichrist will break his covenant with the Jews (Daniel 9 says he breaks it in the midst of the seven years – that is, 3½ years into the 7- year term of the agreement), and is empowered by Satan to try to exterminate the Jews.

This sudden breaking of the agreement will surely generate intense anger by the Jews against the Beast (Antichrist), who at first had seemed like their friend, but has now turned on them with a vengeance. This is when the Jews will really need God's protection. God directs them to a place prepared by Him, possibly the natural rock fortress Petra in Jordan. How can anyone say that the Bible just contains random thoughts of men who wrote down their own ideas about things? It is incredible how all these pieces fit together!

You could not round up 40 diverse writers over a 1,000 year period – some kings – some farmers – some highly educated – some fishermen – and have each of them write a portion of a book, writing history and prophecy independently of each other – and have it all fit together perfectly without any inconsistencies or inaccuracies. It is absurd to think that the Bible happened by accident. There is no other explanation except that God was directing the entire process!

"And there was war in Heaven: Michael and his angels fought against the dragon; and the dragon fought and his angels, and prevailed not; neither was their place found any more in Heaven.

And the great dragon was cast out, that old serpent, called the Devil, and Satan, which deceiveth the whole world: he was cast out into the earth, and his angels were cast out with him" (Revelation 12:7). What a startling revelation – war in Heaven! This may come as a shock to you, but Satan has had access to Heaven from the beginning – at least to the outer court. It is interesting that the Great Tribulation begins with a war in Heaven and ends with a war on earth – the Battle of Armageddon when God intervenes in human history, and Christ comes back to put a stop to all the world's madness.

The Archangel Michael and Satan know each other well. They have been antagonists for a long time. For example, we find a confrontation between them that is recorded in a perplexing verse in Jude. It says they were battling over the body of Moses. *"Yet Michael the Archangel, when contending with the Devil he disputed about the body of Moses, durst not bring against him a railing accusation, but said, 'The Lord rebuke thee'"* (Jude 9). What is this strange argument over the disposition of the dead body of Moses? The real point here is this: Satan IS powerful. Michael was not allowed to pronounce judgment on Satan at this time. No doubt, there was a timing element here – it was not yet time for the "beginning of the end." So Michael said, *"The Lord rebuke thee"* (verse 9). In effect, Michael said, "Satan, the Lord will take care of you at the proper time."

We do not know exactly why Michael and Satan had a dispute over the body of Moses, but I do have an educated guess. Moses was one of the greatest prophets in Israel. *"And there arose not a prophet since in Israel like unto Moses, whom the Lord knew face to face"* (Deuteronomy 34:10). Moses was so highly revered by the Israelites, that Satan wanted the body of Moses to use it as an instrument of idolatry. Even the brazen serpent that Moses raised in the wilderness was kept and used as an instrument of idolatry until it was destroyed by the good king, Hezekiah (II Kings 18:4).

That same kind of idolatry exists today in our world. If you go to Red Square in Moscow, you will find a vast mausoleum. Inside of it, there is a glass casket containing the body of Nikolai Lenin. His body is nearing 150 years old, but he looks no older than 53. The Russian government spends about $220,000 annually for various treatments to keep the body looking fresh for the 2½ million visitors who file by his open casket each year to pay homage and obeisance to the memory and life of the father of Communism.[9] If that isn't idolatry, it is certainly very close to it. I think that is what Satan envisioned – the children of Israel worshiping the remains of Moses.

Listen to Deuteronomy 34:5-6: *"So Moses the servant of the LORD died there in the land of Moab, according to the Word of the LORD. And He buried him in a valley in the land of Moab, over against Bethpeor: but no man knoweth of his sepulcher unto this day."* Did you know that no man buried Moses? God did! And only God knows where he was buried, and will raise him up at the proper time!

"And I heard a loud voice saying in Heaven, 'Now is come salvation, and strength, and the kingdom of our God, and the power of his Christ: for the accuser of our brethren is cast down, which accused them before our God day and night'" (Revelation 12:10). Satan is mysteriously in the outer courts of Heaven, constantly throwing up insults to God, and pointing out our miserable failures. When Heaven is finally cleansed of demonic power, and Satan himself has been banished, this will be a signal for a glad cry of victory from all the redeemed in Heaven.

There are at least 4 reasons for this great rejoicing.

1) Satan is kicked out of his access to the outer court of Heaven;
2) God's strength has crushed Satan's might;
3) God's kingdom is about to arrive; and
4) the power of Christ will be seen as He comes to set up His Kingdom. We have already seen a number of celebrations around the throne, but this time the celebration is more exciting than ever since it demonstrates that Satan is a defeated foe, and that the beginning of the end is rapidly unfolding.

Satan will no longer be in shouting distance to God as he was when he accused Job, which privilege he has abused for ages by continually hurling accusations against God's redeemed. Now, we comprehend more fully the meaning of Ephesians 6:12 where Paul tells us that we wrestle not with flesh and blood, but with principalities and powers, with spiritual wickedness in high places, literally, in the heavens. Hence, Satan is called *"the prince of the power of the air"* (Eph. 2:2).

Though Satan has considerable power, he is certainly not omnipotent. That is proven by the fact than when he set out to make life miserable for Job, he could only operate in the bounds and restrictions that God allowed him (Job 1:12). And yet, the saints overwhelmed Satan, and were victorious during the Tribulation Period when Satan was in control. How did they do this? It is astonishing that men made out of dust could triumph over this seven-headed serpent, crowned with seven diadems, and with an agenda to eradicate the Jews as well as others who would not pledge allegiance to him. Was it because they were more numerous? No. The fact is they were few in number, comparatively speaking. Was it because they were men of prestige and wealth? Hardly. They had little. Was it because they wielded great influence? Why, they did not even have enough influence to stay out of the jails, dungeons and the guillotines. How did they do it? Look at Revelation 12:11: *"And they overcame him by the blood of the Lamb, and by the word of their testimony; and they loved not their lives unto the death."* What an amazing verse! There were three essentials involved in their victory. First, they overcame Satan by the blood of the Lamb. Not only does the blood wash them clean, it gives them access by prayer to the very throne of Almighty God.

An old Jewish tradition says that Satan accuses the saints day and night except on the Day of Atonement. I wish the Jews could understand that, for the Christian who looks to the blood of Jesus, every day is a Day of Atonement!

The Bible is so clear about this; it is a mystery to me as to why some denominations are trying to delete the mention of blood from every song in their hymnal. One of their liberal spokesmen said, "We need to get away from the bloody cross, and the abusive heavenly father." What blasphemy! Hebrews 9:22b (NASB) says, *"without shedding of blood there is no forgiveness* [of sin]." So, not only these saints overcame Satan by the blood of the Lamb, but also *"by the word of their testimony"* (Revelation 12:11). I cannot help but think of Stephen whose face shone like that of an angel as he was making his defense of the faith (Acts 6:15). Or, Paul and Silas, beaten, thrown into a dungeon, yet who prayed, and sang praises to God (Acts 16:25). How could you overcome men like that? Satan couldn't!

Finally, the verse says, *".... and they loved not their lives unto the death"* (Revelation 12:11). But, we see as always, victory over sin is achieved by the two-edged sword of God's Word. The blood of the Lamb was the necessary price for their forgiveness and redemption. This same Savior had also said that they must openly confess Him on earth, thus proving their genuine faith before He would confess them as His own to His Father in Heaven (Matt.10:32-33). This is the testimony of many Scriptures. *"If thou shalt confess with thy mouth .... and believe in thine heart ... . thou shalt be saved"* (Romans 10:9). Again, in Psalm 19:14, we find: *"Let the words of my mouth, and the meditation of my heart, be acceptable in thy sight, O LORD, my strength and my redeemer."* Show me someone who is timid and afraid to speak out as a follower of Jesus Christ, and I will show you someone who may simply be a "profess-er" and not a "possess-er" of eternal life.

Please understand this. These saints were overcomers by the blood of the Lamb and by the word of their testimony. That was their confession, and they loved not their lives unto the death. That was their commitment!

But let's come back to our burning question. Why is Satan allowed in Heaven at all? Satan has been permitted by God to act as the great prosecuting attorney, so to speak, in the High Court of the Universe. But no charge that he has brought against a child of God has ever succeeded thanks to our Advocate and defense attorney, the Lord Jesus Christ whose blood cleanses us from all sin.

One of the greatest encouragements I have discovered in my study through Revelation is what we covered in chapter 10, verse 7. When the seventh angel begins to sound, *".... The mystery of God should be finished ...."*. Why does God allow Satan to carry on for so long? That and a hundred other mysteries will be revealed to us when the seventh angel begins to sound, and God's mysteries shall be fully known.

It is evident that Satan would never voluntarily withdraw from Heaven. He must be thrown out, and it takes a war in Heaven to do so. And the time is ripe in the middle of the Tribulation, and so Michael leads his troops against Satan and his minions. Some liberal theologians believe that this is simply a picture – sort of a parable – depicting the eternal battle of good versus evil. But this is more than that. We were told in verse 3 of this chapter that the dragon is the symbol of the Devil. And we know through Scripture, that the Devil and the Archangel Michael are real angels. This war will be fought between the armies of Satan and the armies of Michael, the Archangel. It is real; it is not symbolic.

We do not know definitively how many angels there are. The Bible says there are "myriads" of them – thousands upon thousands. But however many there are, Michael commands two-thirds of them, and the Devil commands one-third of them. It never hurts to have superior numbers on your side in a war. However, if the numbers were reversed, it wouldn't matter. Michael has the ultimate secret weapon. His weapon is Almighty God.

Antichrist is making his play to control the earth, while at the same time, Satan is making his bid to control Heaven. And while the Antichrist appears to be successful at least in the early stages, Satan's all-out war against the Archangel Michael for control of Heaven results in disastrous defeat. But Satan does have considerable power. In John 12:31, he is called, "*the prince of this world.*" In Ephesians 2:2, he is called "*the prince of the power of the air.*" And in II Corinthians 4:4, he is called, "*the god of this world.*"

In Daniel chapter 10 we know that Daniel prayed, and his answer was delayed for 21 days while the forces of evil tried to block the answer coming to him. We pray on earth and God answers from Heaven. Between Heaven and earth a spiritual battle is taking place. When we persevere in prayer, we are the ultimate winners. Jesus told a parable in Luke 18:1-8 that depicts an unjust judge who denied the wishes of a poor woman. But she persisted, and kept pleading and pleading with the judge until he finally relented. Jesus compared this with persistence in prayer. The moral of the story is "don't give up." When I was in college, we had a president who was a wonderful Christian. His name was V. Raymond Edman. Billy Graham conducted his funeral, and said that he never made a major decision without checking with Dr. Edman.[10] Dr. Edman was famous for a quote he would say regularly and it is repeated often in various books and articles: "It's always too soon to quit!"[11] Paul would agree with that – he tells us to "*pray without ceasing*" (I Thessalonians 5:17).

It is amazing how even the verb tense of the Greek tells us exactly what is taking place in this conflict in Heaven. In verse 4, the Greek verb "ebalen" refers to past action. However, the Greek word "surei," translated "drew" by the KJV, the tense is present indicative. What does this mean? Simply this: the word "ebalen," in one definite action, indicates that Satan and his followers were cast to the earth in ages past. But "surei" means that Satan continues to battle to this very day (present tense) to draw those evil demons closer to him. Ephesians 2:2 says that Satan is the *"prince of the power of the air"* and as such, we must pray consistently to overcome *"spiritual wickedness in high places"* (Ephesians 6:12).

Jesus was referring to the first time Satan was cast out (Luke 10:18) when he told His disciples, *"I beheld Satan as lightning fall from Heaven."* The Greek translated by the KJV is actually the past tense – *"fallen from Heaven."* But here in Revelation 12:9, this is a future casting out. Satan and his followers lose this battle with Michael and his angels, and Satan is cast out of the outer court of Heaven never to gain access again. This happens at the beginning of the last 3½ years of the Tribulation, and Satan is so upset that he directs all his power and energy to wiping out anything and anyone who is not for him and his Antichrist, especially Israel. The Antichrist's forces will track down and slaughter every Jew he can find. Zechariah 13:8 says that two-thirds of the Jewish people will die in this holocaust.

Some teach that Satan was cast out of the outer court of Heaven at the beginning of the Tribulation as opposed to the teaching that he was cast out at the midway point. This is not to be confused with his being cast out eons earlier when he rebelled against God. Satan's judgment is in four stages. First, he was cast down from Heaven when iniquity was first found in him (Isaiah 14:12-14; Ezekiel 28:15-16). Then, here in Revelation 12, he is forever denied access to even the outer portals of Heaven. As a rebellious prisoner, he is confined for 1,000 years in the Bottomless Pit during the Millennium (Revelation 20:3). And, finally, in Revelation 20:10, he is judged and consigned to the Lake of Fire forever.

Midway through the Tribulation, at the beginning of the last 3½ years, the Antichrist is taking control of the earth while Satan attempts to take control of Heaven. Some teachers believe that this casting out of Satan in Revelation 12 refers to the original casting out of Satan from Heaven as recorded in Isaiah 14:12-14 and Ezekiel 28:12-18. My position is that in Satan's original rebellion, he was cast out of the third Heaven where God resides, but was still allowed access to the first heaven (the atmosphere) and the second heaven (the stratosphere) where he could come close to the outer court of Heaven, and hurl accusations to God against His believers as he did with Job. But the casting out of Satan in Revelation 12:7-9 barred him further access to the second heaven (the stratosphere), and thereafter his activities are confined to the earth.

My research among 18 Bible prophecy scholars regarding these two "casting outs" confirmed my position. Here is a summary of their teaching on the subject.

Dr. Jack Van Impe, popular TV evangelist, in his commentary on Revelation states that Satan is a magnificent creature to behold. In fact, his beauty brought his ruin (Ezekiel 28:17). Satan has never been in Hell, but he has been to Hades because it was in Hades that Jesus took from him the keys of death and Hades. He is the god of this world system, the prince of the power of the air, and the prince of this world. He has been in heavens one and two (the aerial and stellar heavens) since his fall out of the third Heaven, and he will remain there until he is cast to earth in Revelation 12:9. Satan's demise began when he was cast out of the third Heaven (Isaiah 14:12-14), continues until Revelation 12:9 when he is cast out of the first and second heavens, and is completed when he is cast into the Lake of Fire (Revelation 20:10).

The Apostle John foresaw this hour by the Spirit and wrote, "Now shall the prince of this world be cast out" (John 12:31). Satan and his angels prevailed not, and Satan's place where he has existed for centuries is found no longer. Instead, the dragon (Satan) which deceiveth the whole world is cast out into the earth, and this signals the end of Satan's rule in the aerial and stellar heavens, and the victory celebration begins. At this point, Satan unleashes all his fury (primarily against the Jews) *"because he knoweth that he hath but a short time"* (Revelation 12:12) – 42 MONTHS TO BE EXACT! Thus the great anti-Semetic purge now begins in earnest. And we see in the next few verses, the Jews have to run for their lives (maybe to Petra) to try to escape from the Antichrist who by this time is indwelt by Satan himself.[12]

Dr. David Jeremiah, pastor of Shadow Mountain Church, writes: "Satan and his angels are kicked out of Heaven (Revelation 12:9) and his downward path begins. From Heaven to earth – from earth to the Bottomless Pit – from the Bottomless Pit to the Lake of Fire. When this maniac of many disguises is hurled to the earth, there is praise in Heaven. Satan can no longer accuse the believers before God. Satan's ouster from Heaven will take place on a future day at the halfway point in the Tribulation."[13]

Dr. Jim Richards, Executive Director, Southern Baptists of Texas, speaking of this war in Heaven writes, "The first casting out of Satan was positional; this second casting out is geographical. He no longer has access to Heaven where he has been able to *'accuse the brethren before God.'* The inhabitants of Heaven rejoice at the removal of the adversary. This indicates that the events which take place on earth can be known by those in Heaven. Praise to Jesus erupts because of the victory over Satan."[14]

Dr. M. R. DeHaan, Founder of the Radio Bible Class, in his commentary on Revelation indicates that the casting out of Satan in Revelation 12:9 takes place at the midpoint of the Tribulation.[15]

Dr. H. A. Ironside, former pastor of Moody Memorial Church in Chicago, writes: "Satan and his host have been permitted to maintain their hold (of the airways) during the past five thousand years. Satan is called the prince of the power of the air. Believers are told that their conflict is with wicked spirits in heavenly places. But when the Church is caught up at the Rapture, these evil forces will be ignominiously driven from what we might call the outer court of Heaven and cast down to the earth. Satan's casting down will be the signal for great rejoicing in Heaven where the raptured saints now live, and it will be the signal for great sorrow upon the earth because the Devil will have come down in great wrath knowing that his time is short. And Satan will at once turn all his energies against Israel, but God has pledged Himself to preserve her through the Great Tribulation."[16]

Dr. John Hagee, pastor of the Cornerstone Church, San Antonio, writes, "At the midpoint of the Tribulation, the Antichrist makes his play to control the earth. Simultaneously, Satan makes his play to control Heaven. But while the Antichrist appears to be successful at first, Satan's all-out war against the archangel Michael for control of Heaven not only ends in stunning defeat, but in banishment from Heaven as well."[17]

Dr. Charles H. Dyer, former Professor at Large of Bible, at Moody Bible Institute, writes, "There was no war in Heaven when Satan first rebelled; God simply booted him and his angels out of Heaven itself. But in Revelation 12, there was a war – Michael prevailed and Satan and his evil forces could no longer "accuse the brethren" in the proximity to the outer courts of Heaven."[18]

Dr. Daymond R. Duck, popular author and prophecy teacher, says that as soon as Israel flees to a place of safety (Revelation 12:6) Satan is cast out of the second heaven (the stratosphere).[19]

Dr. Adrian Rogers, former President of the Southern Baptist Convention, writes: "There are two battles taking place in this passage – one in Heaven and one on earth. The purpose of this war is to cast Satan out of Heaven. On one side are the dreadful dragon and his demons; on the other side are Michael and his angels. Satan is also called the accuser. You may say, 'I thought Satan was already cast out of Heaven?' Yes, but he still has access to the third Heaven. Job 1:6 says, *'Now there was a day when the sons of God came to present themselves before the Lord, and Satan came also among them.'"* Adrian Rogers continues: "In the mystery, providence and plan of God, Satan has still been allowed access to Heaven. Although Satan has been severely limited, God has still allowed him to come and accuse all the saints before God (Revelation 12:10). But now, Michael and his angels are making sure that Satan does not have access any longer, and his abode from now on will be on earth through his empowerment of the Antichrist."[20]

Mordecai F. Ham, the evangelist who led Billy Graham to the Lord, said in his book: "In his vision, John sees Michael and his angels drive Satan and his angels out of their realm 'in the air' and force them down to earth as an army is driven into a trap prior to annihilation. No longer established in the air, Satan will be the more enraged for he will see that his end is near."[21]

Dr. W. A. Criswell, former Pastor of the First Baptist Church, Dallas, taught that this casting out of Satan occurs midway through the Tribulation. He says: "But there is a dark side to this heavenly victory – woe to the inhabiters of the earth for the Devil is come down to you having great wrath." He goes on to show how Satan is the accuser of the brethren, and has been a thorn in the side of Christians throughout the Age of Grace, but after this battle, he is cast to the earth where no one can overcome him except through the blood of the Lamb.[22]

Dr. Theodore E. Epp, founder of Back to the Bible radio broadcast, states: "In Revelation 12:7, the Apostle John records that *'there was war in Heaven. Michael and his angels fought against the dragon, and the dragon fought and his angels.'* The events in this verse are yet future. What a startling revelation – war in Heaven! But we must realize that Satan has had and still has today, access to the outer courts of Heaven. He is the accuser of the brethren. The Apostle John emphasizes this description when he says, *'For the accuser of our brethren is cast down.'* Michael is referred to in Scriptures as 'the archangel'. From other descriptions he seems especially commissioned to be the guardian of Israel. Previously, Michael and the Devil disputed about the body of Moses, and Michael was not allowed to pronounce judgment on Satan. But now the timing and the circumstances are ripe, and Michael is granted that power."[23]

Dr. Arno C. Gaebelein, prominent Methodist preacher and conference speaker, says this about Revelation 12:9: "As we saw in the message to Pergamos, his (Satan's) throne is on earth; he is the god of this age. His dominion is the air, and he is prince of the power of the air (Ephesians 2:2). Satan as the accuser of the brethren even has access into the presence of God. Satan is then cast out into the earth along with his evil angels. Then there is joy in Heaven because the accuser is cast down and his accusations are forever silenced."[24]

Dr. Henry Morris, founder of the Creation Research Institute, writes: "This casting out of Satan occurs in the very middle of the Book of Revelation, and the event it describes marks the middle of the Tribulation Period. The Rapture of the two witnesses, the breaking of the Jewish Temple treaty by the Beast, the flight of Israel (to Petra), the casting out of Satan and the appropriation of world power by the Beast all occur within a few days of each other at this midpoint of the Tribulation."[25]

Dr. Jimmy Draper, past president of the Southern Baptist Convention, had this to say: "At the signal of God, Satan is cast upon the earth. We cannot imagine the effect this is going to have. Satan maintains access to the throne of God, but suddenly halfway through the Tribulation, he is cast down and confined to the earth."[26]

Dr. Clarence Larkin, prominent Baptist pastor and author, wrote: "That the dragon and his angels were not cast out of Heaven at the time of his rebellion (which antedates the present earth) and confined in some 'prison house', is clear; for he was at liberty to visit the Garden of Eden and tempt Adam and Eve; and he had access to God in Heaven in the days of Job, 2000 years before Christ (Job 1:1). He is the god of this world system, not the God of this earth for that belongs to its Maker – God. When the dragon is cast out of the heavenlies there will be great rejoicing in Heaven because the accuser of Christ's brethren is cast down, but there will be 'woe' for the inhabitants of the earth for the dragon will be filled with great wrath because he knows that he will have but a short time to vent his wrath on the inhabitants of the earth before he is chained and cast into the Bottomless Pit."[27]

Dr. John Walvoord, former President of Dallas Theological Seminary, says: "Of course it seems strange that Satan should have access to the very throne of God, yet this is precisely the picture of Job 1, where Satan presents himself before God and accuses Job of fearing God because of God's goodness to him. Thus, early in biblical revelation, Satan is cast in the role of the accuser of the brethren, the title given him in Revelation 12:10. At this point in Revelation, Satan and his hosts are excluded from the third Heaven, (even) though their temporary dominion over the second heaven and the first heaven continues. Satan's defeat in Heaven, however, is the occasion for him to be cast into the earth and explains the particular virulence of the great tribulation time."[28]

Dr. David Reagan, founder and Senior Evangelist of Lamb & Lion Ministries, traces Satan's origin to his casting out of the third heaven in Ezekiel 28 and finally his banishment out of the outer courts of heaven in Revelation 12. Dr. Reagan has one of the most comprehensive and clearest explanations of Revelation 12 than any I have ever seen .[29]

The official website of the Roman Catholic Church is the only site I found that says that Revelation 12:9 refers to the same time frame that is described in Isaiah 14 and Ezekiel 28. They must take this position because chapters 17 and 18 are so devastating to the Roman Church in the end times, they must teach all of this was fulfilled in the 1st Century. The Churches of Christ are autonomous and teachings about the end times vary from church to church. However, for the most part, their ministers have agreed with the official position of the Catholic Church concerning Satan's expulsion from Heaven.[30]

The Antichrist has temporary success on earth while Satan's battle with Michael is a disaster with the result that Satan and his angels are cast to earth. You have probably seen cartoons where Satan has a pitchfork and is roaming around Hell, making people suffer. However, Satan is not in charge of Hell. That's some artist's imagination. Scripture says that Hell was made for the Devil and his demons. When he is cast into the Lake of Fire (Hell), Satan will suffer, not reign, as the most degraded of all God's subjects. And in the ultimate humiliation for Satan, people will look at him, shake their heads and ask, "Can this be the one who shook the earth and made the kingdoms of the world tremble? Is this the one who destroyed the world and made it into a wasteland? Is this the king who demolished the world's greatest cities and had no mercy on his prisoners?" (Isaiah 14:16-17 NLT).

It seems to me the following important events take place in the middle of the Tribulation, probably within a few days of each other: they are – the commissioning of the two witnesses to preach the Gospel (Revelation 11:3); the breaking of the covenant with the Jews by the Antichrist (Daniel 9:27); the casting out of Satan and his demons from the outer regions of

Heaven onto the earth (Revelation 12:9); the declaration by the Antichrist that he is God (II Thessalonians 2:4); the increased persecution of Israel (Revelation 12:12); and the flight of a remnant into a prepared place of safety (Revelation 12:14).

Notice, tucked away in this verse 9 is the little phrase, "*Satan …. which deceiveth the whole world*". All the world's fancy philosophies, conceived by profound humanistic thinkers who have come up with idealism, humanism, Gnosticism, hedonism, materialism, deism – and a hundred more – are all man-centered and man- honoring. None are honoring God; they all help to carry out Satan's attempt to dethrone God from His rightful place in the universe. And the one thing that all these "isms" have in common is that they all deny that God's Word is supreme. Sandy Gist says, "When they meet God, all isms will be was-isms."[31]

In the early seventies, we were in the Sheafor Bible Class at First Baptist Church Dallas, and the teacher that day was that great motivational speaker, Zig Ziglar. He was stressing the trustworthiness of the Bible and He gave a little verbal test to the class. "How many of you read the Bible every day?" A few hands went up. "How many of you read the newspaper every day?" Nearly every hand went up. "How many of you believe everything you read in the newspaper is true?" A few hands went up. "How many of you believe everything you read in the Bible is true?" Nearly every hand went up. Then he said, "I just have one more question for you. Why do you spend so much time reading something you know contains untruths, and very little time reading the Bible which contains all truth?" An important question for everyone to consider!

Voltaire, the philosopher was a skeptic – a scoffer. So was Robert Ingersoll, the proclaimed atheist. The Bible has always had its skeptics and scoffers. It draws them like a magnet. They relish pointing out all the so-called errors in the Bible. God knew there would be scoffers, and so He addressed the issue in II Peter 3:3: "*Knowing this first, that there shall come in the last days scoffers, walking after their own lusts.*" This not only tells us there will be scoffers, but the reason WHY they are scoffers. They want to tear down the Bible because they do not want any rules. They want to walk after their own lusts.

There is no scientific reason to reject the Bible. I heard about a scoffer who happened to be a school teacher. He was so proud of the fact that he was an atheist. He worn it on his sleeve and he liked to intimidate the kids. One day he asked the Christians to hold up their hands. Only one terrified little girl did. "So you are a Christian!" he boomed. "And I suppose that your father and mother are Christians, too." "Yes, sir," she managed to say. Warming up, he snickered, "And if your father was a moron, and your mother was a moron, what would you be?" She said meekly, "I guess I'd be an atheist."

Satan's first deception was in the Garden of Eden when he persuaded Eve to doubt God. And that is the same method Satan has been using ever since. If he can persuade you to question, to doubt, to compromise God's Word, then you are well on your way to being forever entrapped by him. Paul alludes to this deception by Satan in II Corinthians 4:3-4: *"But if our gospel be hid, it is hid to them that are lost; in whom the god of this world hath blinded the minds of them which believe not …."*.

Some have asked whether any one will be saved during the Tribulation. No doubt they were concerned about loved ones who have not accepted Christ and would be left here if the Rapture occurs before they are converted. This is a difficult question to answer with any degree of assurance, but let me tell you what I do know. I know that someone will not come to Christ without the Holy Spirit wooing them and playing a major role in their spiritual conversion and without the Father drawing them unto Himself (John 6:44). Secondly, I know when the Church is raptured, the Holy Spirit (the Restrainer as He is called in II Thessalonians 2:6 ESV) will leave this earth with the Church because His Temple on earth during the Church Age is in the hearts of the believers! Therefore, when the believers leave the earth at the Rapture, the Holy Spirit leaves with them because He lives within the believers!

Does this mean no one will be saved during the Tribulation? No! We know that there will be the 144,000 sealed servants of God that will be preaching the Gospel and, as a result of their preaching, multitudes are saved. But it will cost them their lives (Revelation 7:9-14). We also know that two mighty witnesses will be raised up (Revelation 11:3), and they will be preaching the Gospel. But we also know that millions of earth dwellers who had just witnessed God's awesome judgments, *"Neither* (they) *repented they of their murders, nor of their sorceries, nor of their fornication, nor of their thefts"* (Revelation 9:21). The Greek word translated here for sorceries is "pharmakon" which means "drugs." Need I say more about our generation?

Someone raised a good question: "Should anyone have the opportunity to hear the Gospel a second time before another has heard it the first time?" In other words, they are intimating that the ones saved during the Tribulation will be only those souls who have never heard the Gospel before. I don't know if this is true, but I do know that most of us were given a second, third, or more chances before we accepted Christ. And I do know that we should witness and evangelize as though there are no future opportunities for the unsaved to accept Christ!

Notice in verse 9 it says that Satan deceives the entire world. There is not a government on the face of the earth today that is not, to one extent or another, being deceived by Satan. And speaking of Satan, he has numerous names and descriptions throughout the Bible, and they certainly reflect his nature and character (you might even find more):

Abaddon – Revelation 9:11
Accuser of our Brethren – Revelation 12:10
Adversary – I Peter 5:8
Angel of the Bottomless Pit – Revelation 9:11
Apollyon – Revelation 9:11

Beelzebub – Matthew 12:24
Belial – II Corinthians 6:15
Crooked Serpent – Isaiah 27:1
Devil – Revelation 20:2
Dragon – Revelation 20:2
Enemy – Matthew 13:39
Evil Spirit – I Samuel 16:14
Father of Lies – John 8:44
Leviathan – Isaiah 27:1
Liar – John 8:44
Lucifer – Isaiah 14:12
Lying Spirit – I Kings 22:22
Man of Sin – II Thessalonians 2:3
Murderer – John 8:44
Old Serpent –Revelation 12:9
Piercing Serpent – Isaiah 27:1
Prince of Darkness – Colossians 1:13
Prince of this World – John14:30
Prince of the devils – Matthew 12:24
Prince of the Power of the Air – Ephesians 2:2
Ruler of the Darkness of this World – Ephesians 6:12
Satan – Job 1:6; Revelation 20:2
Serpent – Genesis 3:4
Son of Perdition – II Thessalonians 2:3
Son of the Morning – Isaiah 14:12
Spirit of Disobedience – Ephesians 2:2
Tempter – Matthew 4:3
The God of this World – II Corinthians 4:4
Wicked One – Matthew 13:19

Not one of his names is inspiring or uplifting, but each describes him as being lower than low. Truly, he is the worst of the worst. Right before Jesus begins to reign over His Millennial Kingdom He makes sure that Satan will cause no trouble during this period.

"And I saw an angel come down from Heaven, having the key of the Bottomless Pit and a great chain in his hand. And he laid hold on the dragon, that old serpent, which is the Devil, and Satan, and bound him a thousand years, and cast him into the Bottomless Pit, and shut him up, and set a

seal upon him, that he should deceive the nations no more, till the thousand years should be fulfilled: and after that he must be loosed a little season (Revelation 20:1-3).

Notice the phrase, *"and cast him* [Satan] *into the Bottomless Pit .... that he should deceive the nations no more."* Hallelujah! The single most important point that this passage tells us is that we are not living in the Millennium now as some cult groups and misguided teachers believe. How do we know that? Because during the Millennium, Satan will be locked up – *"that he should deceive the nations no more"* (Revelation 20:3). Can anyone in their right mind say that the nations are not currently being deceived by Satan? It is amazing to me how many people do not believe in a literal, personal Devil. Some say, "Yes, evil exists, but it's some kind of force or power, not a person."

It has been said that tragedies follow a pattern. First there is a natural disaster – either an earthquake, a tsunami, or a tornado. People die – people suffer – churches send help – aid rolls in – and then, so do the predators! Statistics show that women are much more vulnerable when a natural disaster occurs.[32] A news article reported that one man rescued a young woman by pulling her from the waters of a tsunami only to rape her moments later.[33] And no evil exists? Give me a break!

To explain these evil actions, some psychologists say people act this way when they are under extreme stress or their needs are not being met. But in the end, the psychologists were unable to come up with any root problem. They could only conclude, "It raises questions about the nature of humanity, and its capacity for evil." It raises questions?! If they would look in the Bible, they would find the answers pretty quickly. Jeremiah 17:9 says: *"The heart is deceitful above all things, and desperately wicked: who can know it?"*

Dennis Rader, the BTK serial killer in Wichita, Kansas turned out to be a city code inspector, an active member of a local church, and a well-respected family man. The "BTK" stands for "bind, torture, kill".[34] And someone says there is no such thing as evil? Everyone one of us is born with a sin nature. We have the capacity to be very cruel and very hurtful. Theologians call it "the depravity of man."[35]

Everyone can relate to what John Bradford, English evangelist, said in the 1500's after watching criminals go to the gallows, "There, but for the Grace of God, goes John Bradford."[36] And every person on planet earth could put their name in place of Bradford. However, God promises to give us a new nature if we will let Him (II Corinthians 5:17). Does this mean we will lose our old nature? Not yet. Our good and bad natures live side by side within us until we either die, or Christ comes back and our redemption is made complete. There is a story about a wise old Indian chief. He told his son that inside of us we have a good wolf and a bad wolf. His son wanted to know which one is the strongest, and the chief replied, "The one that you feed."

On January 31, 1555, John Bradford was tried by the Roman Catholic Church and condemned to death. He was taken to Newgate Prison to be burned at the stake on July 1, 1555. A large crowd delayed the execution, which had been scheduled for 4 a.m., as many who admired Bradford came to witness his death. He was chained to the stake at Smithfield with a young man, John Leaf. Before the fire was lit, Bradford begged forgiveness of anyone he had wronged, and offered forgiveness to those who had wronged him. He then turned to Leaf and said, "Be of good comfort brother; for we shall have a merry supper with the Lord this night!"[37]

Satan tries to influence us so that our evil nature directs our actions, but remember this: He that is within us, the Holy Spirit, is greater than he that is within the world, Satan (I John 4:4). One of Satan's names is "accuser." He constantly points out to God our sins and shortcomings, and no doubt says we are not worth saving. Eventually, God tires of hearing such dribble, and at the proper time, midway through the Tribulation Period, Michael and his force of good angels toss Satan out of the outer court of Heaven. This permanently bars him and his evil demons any future access. *"And I heard a loud voice saying in Heaven, 'Now is come salvation, and strength, and the kingdom of our God, and the power of His Christ: for the accuser of our brethren is cast down, which accused them before our God day and night. And they overcame him by the blood of the Lamb, and by the word of their testimony; and they loved not their lives unto the death. Therefore, rejoice, ye heavens, and ye that dwell in them. Woe to the inhabiters of the earth and of the sea! For the Devil is come down unto you, having great wrath, because he knoweth that he hath but a short time'"* (Revelation 12:10-12). Now we begin to see the dark consequence of this victory against Satan. It is those earth dwellers who were left behind at the Rapture who are affected. The angelic host warns, *"Woe to the inhabiters of the earth .... for the Devil has come down to you"* (Revelation 12:12).

While all those in Heaven are rejoicing over the expulsion of Satan from the realms of Heaven, a great woe awaits those who dwell on the earth. Satan has been thwarted at every angle by God; every plan of his has been deflected. And so, that seven-headed serpent is red with anger and malice. Stopped at every turn, Satan now has one last shot at God's chosen ones who are still on earth. No wonder he has *"great wrath"* as the Bible says. And knowing that his time is short, he turns all his fury upon those Jews and Gentiles alike who do not accept their new "Unholy Trinity": Satan, the Antichrist and the False Prophet.

These events come together so rapidly and in perfect sequence, that it is sometimes hard to visualize all that is taking place. I remember how fast that James Bond would get in and out of scrapes. In my early years, I was a big James Bond fan. Author Ian Fleming knew how to create excitement. Fleming would have James Bond in the thick of trouble, and you did not know from one minute to the next if he was going to get out of the current jam or not. And suddenly, you were transported to another place, where someone else's life hung in the balance. Things were happening so fast, you could hardly catch your breath. The same is true in the 12th chapter of

Revelation – war in Heaven – war on earth – the children of God being pursued on earth by the Antichrist and his henchmen. But in the end, the saints achieved victory over the "Unholy Trinity" by the blood of the Lamb and by their confession of Christ.

I read a great quote recently by Dr. David Jeremiah that said, "When Satan hits the earth, he is in a blaze of fury because he knows that his time is short (Revelation 12:12). He does not have much time left to destroy the believing remnant in Israel, so he unleashes every weapon he has against the Jews *'who obey God's commandments and hold to the testimony of Jesus'* (Revelation 12:17 NIV). This is the last wave of anti-Semitism that will roll over the world."[38]

We know who inhabits the earth, but what is meant in verse 12 by the inhabitors of the sea? I take it to mean the large number of people who spend most of their time on the waters – the houseboat dwellers, the fishermen, the merchant seamen and the Antichrist's navy. In other words, those who live on the water are going to feel the sting of Satan along with those who live on the land. We have had war in Heaven, and we have had Satan turning his wrath upon the inhabitants of the earth and sea. Turmoil after turmoil hits the earth!

That brings us to verses 13-14): *"And when the dragon saw that he was cast unto the earth, he persecuted the woman which brought forth the Man-child. And to the woman were given two wings of a great eagle, that she might fly into the wilderness, into her place, where she is nourished for a time, and times, and half a time, from the face of the serpent."* Remember, this woman that Satan is pursuing is not the Church. The Church didn't bring forth the Man-child; the Man-child brought forth the Church. This woman is Israel, and Satan hates Israel because she is the vehicle God used to give us our Savior, and secondly, to transmit and preserve the Bible for us.

And so, Satan sets out to eradicate Israel in the greatest ethnic cleansing campaign this world has ever known. But God has other plans for His chosen people. Scripture makes it plain that Israel should waste no time in fleeing to the place God has prepared for her safety.

Picture for a minute these various things coming to a head at the same time. In Jerusalem, the Antichrist, after 3½ years, breaks his peace agreement with the Jews (Daniel 9:27). He then enters the Temple in Jerusalem, stops the daily sacrifices, and declares himself to be God (Daniel 9:27; Matthew 24:15). At the time this is happening on earth, Satan is battling with Michael in the heavenlies, and Satan is kicked out of the outer court of Heaven and cast to the earth where he empowers the Antichrist in his quest to exterminate the Jews. Is it any wonder that Jesus says when you see these things begin to take place, run as fast as you can.

Listen to His words in Matthew 24:15-21: *"When ye therefore shall see the ABOMINATION OF DESOLATION, spoken of by Daniel the Prophet, stand in the holy place, [this is the Antichrist declaring himself to be God] (whoso readeth, let him understand:) Then let them which be in Judea flee into the mountains: let him which is on the housetop not come down to take any thing out of his house: Neither let him which is in the field return back to take his clothes. And woe unto them that are with child, and to them that give suck in those days! But pray ye that your flight be not in the winter, neither on the sabbath day: for then shall be great tribulation, such as was not since the beginning of the world to this time, no, nor ever shall be."*

For several years, the Jews have been returning to Israel at the rate of 10,000 per month. At the turn of the last century, there were only 40,000 Jews in all of Israel. Sixty years ago, there were only 400,000. Today there are over 6.7 million.[39] And just as the Bible teaches, they are returning to Israel today in unbelief (Ezekiel 36:22-28; Deuteronomy 30:1-9). In their Knesset – their parliament – it has been reported that there is not a single member who is a practicing orthodox Jew.

I dearly love the Jewish people, and it breaks my heart that they believe they are returning for the great Millennium when in reality they are returning for the Great Tribulation – the greatest bloodbath the world has ever known! Midway through the Tribulation Period, when the Antichrist stands in the Temple and declares to the world, "I am God," Jesus tells the Jews to run for all they are worth (Luke 21:21). If you are just "playing church," and find yourself left behind at the Rapture, I pray that you will fall on your face, and cry out for the mercies of God to save your soul.

There are times ahead that are so horrible that no one on earth has ever gone through such a time. An unbeliever living at this time will have two obstacles to overcome. First, converting to Christianity will put a target on you as a candidate for beheading by the Antichrist; and secondly, the inclination is strong for you to support the Antichrist. This is brought out in II Thessalonians 2:11. *"And for this cause God shall send them strong delusion, that they should believe a lie."* But those who have been raptured will be around the throne in Heaven at this time, interceding for those poor souls who are trying to elude the Antichrist and his henchmen.

This symbolic woman, Israel, in verse 14, is given the wings of a great eagle that she might escape from Satan and the Antichrist. One commentator sees in this great eagle a picture of the United States, and that the wings represent 747s that will airlift them to safety.[40] However, the U. S. is not mentioned in end time prophecy probably because it has been reduced to a third rate country as a result of its massive debt and the removal of millions of Christians at the Rapture.

It appears that verse 14 is picturing God's care and protection of his children. Most Israelites will immediately recall their miraculous escape in Pharaoh's day at the hands of the Egyptians when God said, *"Ye have seen what I did unto the Egyptians, and how I bare you on eagles' wings, and brought you unto Myself"* (Exodus 19:4). God says He is going to lead Israel to a place prepared for her where she will be nourished for *"a time, and times, and half a time."* Earlier, we discussed that this place may be Petra – a fortified city in the Jordanian desert, southeast of Jerusalem, across the Jordan River. It is a natural rock city with only one entrance surrounded by sheer rock cliffs extending hundreds of feet into the air. But wherever it is, God has promised to protect them and nourish them like He did when they wandered in the wilderness after fleeing Pharaoh's armies. God provided manna for them to eat and fresh water to drink.

God promises to protect and care for them for *"a time, and times, and half a time"* (Revelation 12:14b). What in the world does this mean? We have already established that the Hebrew word "shabua" means seven exactly like our English word dozen means twelve. We looked at this in great detail in chapter 6, but it would probably serve us well to hit the high points again at this time. The King James Version translated Daniel 9:24 as "70 weeks" that were determined upon Israel. This is really "70 sevens" or 490 of something. You will recall that we tried 70 weeks and 70 months, and nothing of significance happened to Israel during those time periods. But when we tried years, it fit perfectly (70 shabuas or 70 x 7 = 490 years). God said these 490 years were determined upon Daniel's people – Israel – and did not pertain to the Gentiles.

During the first 49 years, Israel returned from captivity and rebuilt the walls and the city of Jerusalem (which Babylon had destroyed). At the end of the next 434 years, the Messiah was cut off (killed). This is found in the 9th chapter of Daniel. That leaves 7 years yet to be fulfilled as relates to the nation of Israel. However, when the Jews rejected Jesus as their Messiah, God temporarily set aside the Jewish people, and began taking the Gospel to the Gentiles during the Church Age (Romans 11:25). These believers are referred to as Jesus' Bride.

The prophetic time clock is stopped with seven years out of the 490 years still remaining; they will start up again when God begins to deal with His chosen people, the Jews after the Rapture. When Christ comes back at the Rapture, and gathers His Church unto Himself the prophetic time clock begins to run again to fulfill the final seven years which basically runs concurrently with the Tribulation Period. So prior to the last 7 years of the 490 years, there is a parenthesis – a time out – while God turns to the Gentiles during the Church Age before He again deals with the Jewish people. This time out has now run for 2,000 years. The remaining years (that are left out of the original 490 years) constitute the Tribulation Period, and it has been divided by scripture into two parts: first half (the beginnings of sorrows) (Matthew 24:8), and the second half (the Great Tribulation) (Matthew 24:21).

The Tribulation Period has been variously referred to in Scripture as "Daniel's 70th week" (7 years – Daniel 9); "the time of Jacob's trouble" (7 years – Jeremiah 30:7); 42 months (3½ years – Revelation 11:2); and 1,260 days (3½ years – Revelation 11:3). Using that calculation, a "time" would be one year, "times" would be two years, and "half a time" would be six months – for a total of 3½ years. This calculation is confirmed in the 4th chapter of Daniel. God literally put King Nebuchadnezzar out to pasture because he had lost his mind. The Pharmaceutical Journal cites this incident in Daniel 4, and classifies the King's illness as "boanthropy."[41]

Daniel 4:16 says: *"Let his heart be changed from man's, and let a beast's heart be given unto him; and let seven times pass over him."* Verses 23, 25 and 32 all say the same thing: that the king will live like a beast in the field *"until seven times pass over him."* The context of these verses shows conclusively that a "time" was the same thing as a "year." "Until seven times pass over him" meant that Nebuchadnezzar would live in the fields for seven years. So, let us try our key of interpretation and see if it fits. If a "time" is one year, "times" should be 2 years, and "half a time" should be 6 months. "Time, times and half a time" is 1+ 2+½ equals 3½ years – exactly the way the Tribulation Period is divided. If you still wonder in Revelation 12:14 if a "time, times and half a time" is 3½ years, look back at verse 6 of this same chapter to see how long this woman, Israel, is to be protected: *"a thousand two hundred and threescore days"* – 1,260 days or 3½ years! Also, related verses are Daniel 7:25, *" And he shall speak great words against the most High, and shall wear out the saints of the most High, and think to change times and laws: and they shall be given into his hand until a time and times and the dividing of time."* And Daniel 12:7, *"And I heard the man clothed in linen, which was upon the waters of the river, when he held up his right hand and his left hand unto Heaven, and sware by Him that liveth for ever that it shall be for a time, times, and an half; and when He shall have accomplished to scatter the power of the holy people, all these things shall be finished."* It is wonderful that God is the Master Mathematician and is always 100% correct.

Continuing with Revelation 12:15-16: *"And the serpent cast out of his mouth water as a flood after the woman, that he might cause her to be carried away of the flood. And the earth helped the woman, and the earth opened her mouth, and swallowed up the flood which the dragon cast out of his mouth."* What is this water that spews out toward the woman? Some see it literally, suggesting that it will be a great flood that will seek to drown the fleeing Israelites. That is possible, but I think it is more likely a symbolic reference to the aggressive assault that Satan is going to unleash against the Jewish nation as he works through the efforts of the Antichrist. He wants to destroy every single Jew on the face of the earth. The concept of a flood is often used in Scripture to describe an onslaught of the enemy. *"When the enemy shall come in like a flood, the Spirit of the Lord shall lift up a standard against him"* (Isaiah 59:19b).

In Isaiah 8, God uses the flood waters to symbolize an attack by the King of Assyria on Judah. This is why the Jews should not go back after anything when they see the Antichrist defile the Temple. They should flee from the enemy troops, and stay ahead of the great earthquake. And we find the same reference to God's protection when the earth swallowed up Israel's enemies in Exodus 15:9-10, *"The enemy said, I will pursue, I will overtake, I will divide the spoil; my lust shall be satisfied upon them; I will draw my sword, my hand shall destroy them. Thou didst blow with thy wind, the sea covered them: they sank as lead in the mighty waters."*

Revelation 12, verse 17 says: *"And the dragon was wroth with the woman, and went to make war with the remnant of her seed, which keep the commandments of God, and have the testimony of Jesus Christ."* When I read this verse, it reminded me of when Dr. David Reagan was preaching in England a few years ago. He said: "The Day of the Lord is fast approaching when God will pour out His "wrath" upon all the world." The people in the audience looked puzzled. They whispered to each other. Dr. Reagan repeated his statement: "God's wrath is coming." They again looked puzzled and whispered to each other. Finally, Dr. Reagan asked the local pastor what was the problem. He said, "The people don't know what you are saying." Then the pastor turned to the audience and said, "Dr. Reagan means the "wroth of God." They all smiled, and nodded their heads in approval.[42]

Since Satan's plan to kill the woman's Man-child (Jesus) had failed due to the mercy and provision of God, Satan turns his fury upon the woman (Israel) and the remnant of her Seed. The remnant is the believing Jews who have kept God's commandments and accepted Jesus as their Messiah. One thing we know for certain – God will protect all of his children until their mission has been accomplished.

CHAPTER THIRTEEN

The Two Beasts

_____

We now come to chapter 13, and things are about to change in a big way. When Satan is cast out of Heaven and hurled back to earth, he finds the Antichrist a willing person to yield his mind, soul and spirit to be totally possessed by Satan. The Antichrist becomes Satan incarnate so to speak. We will now be introduced to the Unholy Trinity. We have not said much about the False Prophet, but we will be introduced to him in a big way before we finish chapter 13. *"And I stood upon the sand of the sea, and saw a Beast rise up out of the sea, having seven heads and ten horns, and upon his horns, ten crowns, and upon his heads the name of blasphemy"* (Revelation 13:1). We have talked a lot about the Antichrist, but today I want you to get a clear picture of the empire that he will head – the federation that will be his base as he is gathering all the countries of the world under his authority and control.

Some commentators say that in verse 1, John is standing on the beach and is seeing this Beast come up out of the sea. However, chapter headings and verse numbers were not in the original manuscripts. They were added during the 16th Century simply to make the verses easier to find. Consequently, the oldest manuscripts read, *"And he stood on the sand of the sea ...."* and this verse 1 should be the last verse in chapter 12.

Chapter 12, verse 17 tells us that the dragon (Satan) was beside himself. He had not been able to eradicate Israel so he turns his focus upon the remnant of her Seed and upon all who keep the commandments of God. Satan has been cast out of the heavens and is going to wreak havoc on the earth. But here is where he needs two accomplices and we will meet them shortly.

The New American Standard Bible (NASB) is generally regarded as the most accurate, word-for-word translation. I use it as my primary study Bible along with the old standby, the King James Version. I use the New Living Translation for easy reading and for obscure or difficult passages. *"And the dragon stood on the sand of the seashore ...."* (Revelation 13:1a NASB). The NASB corrects a faulty translation by the KJV, as it is Satan who is standing on the seashore (not John). Satan is looking – he is watching. He is beckoning – he is calling. Who is he calling? He is calling the one who will serve him unconditionally – the Beast – who will also be known as the Antichrist.

Common sense tells us that this scene and the following verses are highly symbolic. The dragon is Satan (Revelation 12:9), and the Beast is a man (Revelation 13:4). Scripture pictures the mass of humanity as a great sea in a state of unrest, in turmoil, raging back and forth. Now, as concerning the Beast, the lines of clarity begin to emerge. It seems that the Beast pictures a two-fold phenomenon. First, it is a picture of the final human kingdom in the last days. But, there is no kingdom without a king. There is no empire without an emperor. There is no such thing as dominion and power without someone to wield that power. And so, the Beast not only represents the final kingdom, but the Beast also represents the one who will head up that final kingdom – none other than the Antichrist himself! And Satan is standing on the sand of the sea, beckoning the Beast to come forth so that Satan can fully possess him. As Jesus was God incarnate, the Antichrist will be Satan incarnate. If you see one, you see the other. In II Thessalonians 2:3, Paul describes this Beast who is before us as *"that man of sin."*

The Jews were warned that he is coming. Listen to what the Apostle John says in I John 2:18a, *"Little children …. ye have heard that Antichrist shall come"*. When did they hear this? It was common doctrine; it was common knowledge. Whenever the Word of God was preached, wherever Scripture was taught, the message included the fact that Antichrist is coming. This final kingdom appears to be that of the Revised Roman Empire – the same one that was in control of the world when our Lord was crucified. And in the last days, it is rising from the ashes of history to again confront the King of kings and Lord of lords.

Bible scholars of past generations, deeply committed men of God, have seen this coming for a long time. Here is a quote from Walter Scott, a renowned preacher who lived in the 19th Century: "This Beast is without doubt the ancient Roman empire reappearing upon the prophetic scene."[1] Remember, we said that the Beast pictures a two-fold phenomenon – the Antichrist and his kingdom.

Folks, this is incredible! This statement was written almost two hundred years ago, and it is talking about Europe coming together to dominate the world when Europe had about as much chance of doing that as the city of Forney has of becoming the State Capitol of Texas!

And here is a quote from Bible scholar, William E. Blackstone, written nearly 150 years ago: "Perhaps you say, 'I don't believe the (Jews) are to be restored in Jerusalem'. Dear Reader, have you not read the declarations of God's word about it? Surely nothing is more plainly stated in the Scriptures."[2] I do not know if this overwhelms you like it does me, but here are two entities – Europe as an empire and Israel as a nation – both of which have been buried in the dust bowl of history for more than 2,000 years, and the Bible says they will come to life in the end times! One entitiy has already come to life. We saw it happen on May 14, 1948, when the Israeli flag was raised over Jerusalem and it again became a nation. And the other, the Revised Roman Empire, comes closer to being a reality as every day passes. The European Union could be the embryo, but lately it seems to be having some problems. Of course it could be the blueprint to help the Antichrist pull Europe together when the time is ripe.

Daniel said some 2,500 years ago that the Roman Empire would come back together in the end times. "The Treaty of Rome" was signed in 1957 when 15 countries banded together as a way to enhance their economic muscle and be able to compete with the U.S.[3] Early in the 1990s that all changed when "The Maastricht Treaty" was signed on February 7, 1992. Those 15 countries that signed it without fully realizing what they were getting into basically gave up most of their sovereignty and independence.[4] Since that time, the European Union has become bigger and stronger and, by 2019, boasted a membership of 28 countries. If you were a citizen of Germany (or any other European country), you became a citizen of the European Union without even voting on it. Your passport would now say you are a citizen of the EU. Your driver's license and your car plates would now indicate you are a citizen of the EU – not Germany, not France, not Italy, but the European Union. They were truly countries "without borders" since you could travel from one country to another European country like we can go from Texas to Oklahoma.

The 12 star flag of the EU is rapidly replacing the national flags of the various countries. And this is scary: 70% of the laws passed by the English Parliament are simply ratification of laws that have come to them from Brussels, the headquarters of the European Union.

Individual citizens are finding out every day what Article 52 of the EU Charter means. It says the EU, if they wish, can suspend the right of free speech, the right to life, liberty and the pursuit of happiness, and other basic human rights. All these rights can be suspended if the EU feels it is in their best interests to do so.[5] No wonder that some of its members such as England are moving closer to withdrawing from the Union.[6] The Revived Roman Empire, which the Antichrist will head, is coming folks, just as the Bible prophesies. And the U.S. is caving in to it, although it seems that has been slowed by the election of a staunch nationalist, Donald J. Trump.

Our own Supreme Court in striking down the death penalty for criminals under 18 said, "It is proper that we acknowledge the overwhelming weight of international legal opinions." Whether this was a good ruling or not, the point is, the U.S. Supreme Court is looking more and more for guidance from the international legal community rather than looking solely to the U.S. Constitution.[7]

I wish I could say to you that the United States will not stand for this, but the scary part is that the United States is not mentioned in end time prophecy. We just are not there. It could be for several reasons. Our country has so much debt that is held by other countries that if it went into default and payment of that debt was demanded in gold or other sound assets, the U.S. would be bankrupt overnight. Our country is so politically divided, it seems that nationalism is giving way to globalism, and conservativism is giving way to socialism as its citizens demand more and more "freebies." Several states are all but bankrupt as welfare payments and benefits skyrocket. However, I think the real reason for our demise will be that, when the Rapture occurs and the Christians are all taken out of this world, the country will utterly collapse from the inside. Dark days are coming for those outside of Christ. But for the believers, praise God, *We'll Soon Be Done With Troubles And Trials!*[8]

This vision of John represents the final form of political dominion – the same that Daniel saw in Daniel chapter 7. So you see, the Beast rising out of the sea is not the same as the dragon, even though their appearances are similar. The dragon is Satan (Revelation 12:9) and the Beast is a man (Revelation 13:4-8). *"And the dragon stood on the shore of the sea. And I saw a Beast coming out of the sea. He had ten horns and seven heads, with ten crowns on his horns, and on each head a blasphemous name"* (Revelation 13:1 NIV). What a monstrosity! What are all these multiple heads and horns and crowns? We do not want to get ahead of ourselves, but I must refer you to chapter 17 of Revelation which throws some light on this mystery, and we will stay there for a little while. Chapter 17, verse 3b says *"I saw a woman sit upon a scarlet colored Beast, full of names of blasphemy, having seven heads and ten horns."*

In verse 7 of chapter 17 the angel tells John that he will tell him what the mystery is. Then, two verses later in Revelation 17: 9, the angel says, *"the seven heads are seven mountains on which the woman sitteth."* The Greek word *"oros"* just like its counterpoint *"har"* in Hebrew can mean either a mountain or a hill. This is an acceptable translation: *"the seven heads are the seven hills on which the woman sitteth."* In fact, the following versions translate this verse exactly in this manner: The Revised Standard Version; The NIV; The New Living Translation; and the Phillips Paraphrase – they all say, *"the seven heads are seven hills on which the woman sitteth."* Now folks, it doesn't take Perry Mason to figure out this mystery. Do you know what city is nicknamed, "The City Built on Seven Hills?" Of course! Listen to what the *Catholic Encyclopedia* says: "The entire Vatican is now confined within the city of Rome, which is called the City of Seven Hills."[9]

There have been other cities claiming to have been built on seven hills such as Rio de Janeiro, but ask most anyone, "What is the name of the city that is built on seven hills?" and they will answer Rome. The names of the hills are: Palatinus, Capitoline, Quirinal, Viminal, Esquiline, Caelian and Aventine.[10] The identity of this city is very important because in the 17th chapter this "City of Seven Hills" is called "Mystery Babylon" and the "Mother of Harlots." It is here that the Antichrist has his headquarters.

Daniel gives us the best indication as to what city this is. Look at Daniel 9:26: *"And after threescore and two weeks shall Messiah be cut off, but not for Himself."* We have gone over this previously, and explained how this was 483 years from our beginning point (Nehemiah 2:1-8) to the time Jesus was crucified. But what I want you to see is the next phrase in Daniel 9:26: *"and the people of the prince that shall come shall destroy the city and the sanctuary."* The prophecy in Daniel 9:26 says that the people of the prince who shall come (this devious ruler described in Daniel 7 whom we now call the Antichrist) will be the ones who will destroy the city of Jerusalem and the Temple. After Christ was crucified, "cut off" as Daniel says, I ask you who destroyed the city of Jerusalem and the Temple? The Romans![11]

The Romans had been having a lot of trouble with the rebellious Jews, and Nero was preparing to come down hard on them; however, he died in 68 A.D. before his plan was implemented. Vespasian was declared Emperor to succeed him, and it fell to his son, Titus, to deal with the Jews since he had gained quite a reputation as a military strategist. In 70 A.D. General Titus and his forces marched to Jerusalem, sacked and burned it, and completely demolished the Jewish Temple. Jesus had sadly predicted the Temple's destruction when he told his disciples, *"See ye not all these things? Verily I say unto you, There shall not be left here one stone upon another, that shall not be thrown down"* (Matthew 24:2). So, history is clear that the city of Jerusalem and the Jewish Temple were destroyed in 70 A.D. by the Romans – who are the people of the prince (Antichrist) who is to come. In the interest of clarity, let me paraphrase Daniel 9:26, but this time filling in these mysteries that we now know. "And after 483 years shall the coming Messiah be killed, but He is not killed for Himself, but for others; and the Romans, who are the same peoples from which the Antichrist will arise, shall destroy the city and the Temple."

So, the seven heads are the seven hills, describing the city of Rome (Revelation 17:9). But, they also represent seven kings. We do not have to guess about this. We are told in Revelation 17:10: *"And there are seven kings: five are fallen, and one is, and the other is not yet come; and when he cometh, he must continue a short space."* This sounds cryptic and mysterious, and I am sure it was to Daniel and John when these visions were given to them. In fact, after Daniel was told of these world empires to come, he said in Daniel 12:8-9 (paraphrasing): "Lord, I don't understand what this means." And the Lord said, "Do not worry about it Daniel. It will be understood at the proper time." God told Daniel, *"Keep this prophecy a secret; seal up the Book until the time of the end"* (Daniel 12:4 NLT).

As we approach the time of the end, more and more of these prophecies will become clear as they are unsealed. *"Then he instructed me, 'Do not seal up the prophetic words you have written, for the time is near'"* (Revelation 22:10 NLT). The Greek word for king is "basileu," and the Greek word for kingdom is "basilea." You can see how closely related these words are. Several commentators said that this could easily be translated seven kingdoms.

Revelation 17:10 says that of these seven kings or kingdoms, five are fallen – they do not exist anymore. But "one is," that is, one is still in existence, and that is the one in power as John is recording this. And the Bible says one is yet to come. Historians generally agree that there have really only been six world empires who have dominated the world in the history of mankind. Though we refer to the British Empire and the Japanese Empire, they never really conquered the known world. But there are six who have: the Egyptian Empire, the Assyrian Empire, the Babylonian Empire, the Medo-Persian Empire, the Grecian Empire and the Roman Empire.

The Bible says that five kingdoms have fallen. Those kingdoms would be the Egyptian, Assyrian, Babylonian, Medo-Persian, and Grecian. Scripture continues: *"and one is"*. That would be the one in existence when John was writing this – the Roman Empire. And then, the Bible says, *"and the other is not yet come."* Folks, the one that has *"not yet come"* is the kingdom of the Antichrist – the Revived Roman Empire.

We are also told in the 17th chapter, verse 12, that the ten horns represent *"ten kings which have received no kingdom as yet."* In other words, these rulers are still in the future. This seventh kingdom that is to come will, in its early stages, have ten kings who will share authority. They will probably be rulers over ten distinct provinces within the kingdom. This is just prior to the time that the Antichrist comes on the scene and shoves them out of the way.

Now returning to Revelation 13:1, it says that upon the Beast's heads was the name of blasphemy. How does this Beast blaspheme? This is best revealed in II Thessalonians 2:4. There it describes the Beast as one *"Who opposeth and exalteth himself above all that is called God, or that is worshipped; so that he as God sitteth in the temple of God, shewing himself that he is God."* Folks, that is blasphemy!

Much time has been spent by some teachers trying to figure out who the Antichrist is. Is it Hassan Rouhani of Iran? Is it Ayman Mohammed Rabie al-Zawahiri, leader of al-Qaeda? Is the Antichrist alive today? He may be alive and well today, but it is foolishness on our part to speculate as to who he might be. The world will not know who he is for sure, until he stands up in the Temple in Jerusalem, and declares himself to be God. Nor do I know whether he will be Jewish or not. Many teachers say that he will be. They draw this conclusion basically from two sources. First, in Daniel the 11th chapter, verse 37, it states, *"Neither shall he regard the God of his fathers, nor the desire of women, nor regard any god: for he shall magnify himself above all."*

The expression *"God of his fathers"* sounds like it refers to the God of Abraham, Isaac and Jacob. And if the Antichrist does not regard the *"God of his fathers,"* it sounds like he is Jewish. Secondly, Jesus said, *"I am come in my Father's name, and ye receive me not: if another shall come in his own name, him ye will receive"* (John 5:43). Jesus is talking about Israel accepting its Messiah, and if they accept someone else who comes in his own name, you would expect that he must be Jewish or he would not be accepted. But I have my own idea of this. I will mention it, but realize that no one knows for sure until the time comes, and he is revealed as that "man of sin." In this chapter, we will be introduced to two beasts. The first (the Antichrist) will head up the political world; the second (the False Prophet) will head up the religious world. They will work hand in hand with each other.

One will have his headquarters in Rome, the other in Jerusalem. I believe that the second

Beast in Jerusalem, also called the False Prophet, will be at least part Jewish and he will help the first Beast to negotiate a treaty with Israel to rebuild their Temple. As to the phrase "nor the desire of women," some commentators say that the verse says that he is not attracted to women and therefore the Antichrist will possibly be a homosexual, however, Commentator Kermit Zarley says this is a spurious interpretation.

"And the Beast which I saw was like unto a leopard, and his feet were as the feet of a bear, and his mouth as the mouth of a lion: and the dragon gave him his power, and his seat, and great authority" (Revelation 13:2). In Daniel chapter 7, Daniel described the beasts he saw as a lion, as a bear, as a leopard, and the fourth beast was too horrible to describe. Here, in chapter 13, John sees these first three beasts, but they were in reverse order. That is because Daniel was looking forward at the kingdoms that were yet to come, while John was looking backwards through history at the kingdoms that had already passed. Daniel, looking forward, saw Babylon, Medo-Persia and Greece. John, looking backward, saw Greece, Medo-Persia and Babylon.

Rome has always made the claim that when the Romans conquered a people, they absorbed all the good characteristics of prior cultures. So they retained the best of the lion (Babylon), the bear (Persia), the leopard (Greece), and mixed them together with the best of Rome.

Contrast this with the Muslims. When they conquer a country, and this has always been the case, they preserve nothing. They try to wipe out every building, every evidence and every vestige of those conquered people. This has happened time and again in Israel. The Muslims literally try to tear down and destroy all of its enemies' artifacts. The Romans on the other hand tried to preserve, and assimilate them into its culture. That is why we have such marvelous Greek structures still standing today because of this attitude on the part of the Romans.

"And I saw one of his heads as it were wounded to death; and his deadly wound was healed: and all the world wondered after the Beast" (Revelation 13:3). The wounding of the Beast is mentioned three times in this chapter, verses 3, 12 and 14. The wound appears to produce death, but restoration to life follows. Some commentators think that this statement represents the fall of the old Roman Empire, and its restoration through the ten nation confederacy spoken of in verse one. But throughout these descriptions, we find that the Beast not only refers to the Antichrist, but to the Empire that he presides over as well. We have already said that the seven heads mentioned in verse one refers to seven empires that will rule the world before the end of the age.

Five have already come and gone as we said. The sixth was in existence when John was writing this. The seventh is still yet to come. The head that was wounded as it were unto death was the old Roman Empire that collapsed in 476 A.D. It was not conquered by enemies from without, but it collapsed from within as documented by the noted historian, Edward Gibbon. Its moral degeneration from within was like that of a giant tree, its heart and core rotting away until it utterly collapsed.[13]

It had a wound – seemingly unto death. But 1,600+ years later, it is revived. It becomes viable again, and the entire world is amazed and follows after it. The European Union is possibly the embryo of this last world empire. However, I believe there is a double interpretation – one that also includes the leader of the empire. There will be an attempt on the Antichrist's life midway through the Tribulation, perhaps in retaliation for overthrowing three members of the original ten nation federation which we will come to later.

Such an event would give Satan the opportunity to perform a counterfeit resurrection. I do not think Satan has the power to resurrect anyone from the dead. Christ is the one who has the keys of death and the grave (Revelation 1:18). So it appears that the Antichrist is not really killed, but the wound looks real enough to be fatal. That is why Scripture says, *"One of its heads seemed to have a mortal wound "*(Revelation 13:3a ESV). It does not say "wounded unto death" but, *"seemed to have a mortal wound."* It appears that the world will believe he died, and has come back to life. Isn't it strange that Jesus Christ died and was resurrected and, though the evidence is overwhelming, the world is skeptical?

The Antichrist seemingly dies and comes back to life and, *"the whole earth marveled as they followed the Beast"* (Revelation 13:3b ESV). Everyone will follow the Beast except one group we are told about in verse 8 – the true believers in Christ. This will give the Antichrist much prestige in the eyes of the world. No wonder the world takes him seriously when he stands in the Temple in Jerusalem and declares himself to be God! He says, "After all, I've come back from the dead!" And millions, who had not previously worshipped the Antichrist, will begin to worship him because of this imitation resurrection.

"And they worshipped the dragon which gave power unto the Beast: and they worshiped the Beast, saying, Who is like unto the Beast? Who is able to make war with him?" (Revelation 13:4). And they will believe this big lie, just as II Thessalonians 2:11 says they will. The Beast appears triumphant, and the whole world rushes after him for guidance and deliverance. The plagues have stopped, and the two all-powerful witnesses are dead. Satan is hurled to the earth, and intends to help the Antichrist eradicate the Jews. The Antichrist has recovered from a seemingly fatal wound to the head. No wonder the people cry out, *"Who is like unto the Beast? Who is able to make war with him?"* (Revelation 13:4).

Thus a counterfeit resurrection will assure the world that the Antichrist is all he claims to be. The true followers of Christ, however, will not be taken in by this ruse. Instead, they will look forward to possessing the land that God has promised them. But the followers of the Antichrist are literally overwhelmed by his power and authority as he promises they will rule the land under his one-world government.

Consider for a moment the global organizations which have come into being in our generation: 1) The International Atomic Energy Agency; 2) The World Bank; 3) The United

Nations; 4) The UN Educational, Scientific and Cultural Organization (UNESCO); 5) The International Monetary Fund; 6) The World Court; and many, many others. A one-world government is coming, and it is not good news because it will be the government of the Antichrist. I can remember the hair on the back of my neck standing up when George H. W. Bush stated at the beginning of his presidency that there is a new world order coming.[14] Ironically, he did not realize that it will be headed by the Antichrist. And his speech was given on September 11, 1991 – just 20 years to the day that America got a taste of this new world order as terrorists crashed their planes into the Twin Towers.

Satan is ever the counterfeiter. There has never been an Abel without a Cain. There has never been a Jerusalem without a Babylon. There has never been a John the Baptist without a Herod. There has never been an Apostle Paul without a Nero. Satan always has his counterpart to oppose the plans of Almighty God. What a difference between Christ and the Antichrist: one willing to die to save mankind; the other willing to kill mankind.

This brings us to chapter 13, verse 5, as Scripture continues to tell us about this Beast – the Antichrist. *"And there was given unto him a mouth speaking great things and blasphemies; and power was given unto him to continue forty and two months."* This Beast will make long, spellbinding speeches filled with passion and the vilest of blasphemies.

The King James Version says he will be speaking "great things." One translation says he will be speaking marvelous things. This does not mean great or marvelous as in wonderful. In old English, great or marvelous can mean incredible or bewildering, and this is obviously the meaning as we find he is speaking blasphemies. You wonder, "How can people be so gullible as to believe the Antichrist?" The Bible teaches that the "spirit of Antichrist" has already gone out and is at work in the world today (I John 2:18; 4:3).

These "little Antichrists" have been evident in almost every generation. They seem to rise to the top during tumultuous times. Out of the bloody French revolution, Napoleon was born. Out of the chaotic Russian turmoil, Lenin and then Stalin were born. I have a video of the madman, Adolph Hitler, speaking "great things" as the KJV might say. He stirred the crowds with his speeches as to how Germany under his leadership would take its rightful place as the world leader. The masses were completely mesmerized by Hitler's promises. Eagerly, they cried, "Seig Heil – Seig Heil" (hail to victory) – as they swore to him their undivided allegiance. It will be the same with the Antichrist, only more intense. So, in a day of revolution – in a day of chaos – in a day of turbulence and fury – comes this great and final ruler.

Think of the past empires that the Romans conquered and absorbed: the majesty of Babylon; the richness of Persia; the intellect and beauty of Greece. And to that, the Romans added their respected judicial system. And each had a great leader: Nebuchadnezzar; Cyrus; Alexander the

Great; and Julius Caesar. So, you see how powerful and elegant all these kingdoms rolled into one will be when headed up by a master of deceit.

Paul Henri Spaak, former head of the Society for Worldwide Interbank Financial Telecommunications ("SWIFT") made a profound statement about the EU several years ago. "We do not want another committee. We have too many already. What we want is a man of sufficient stature to hold the allegiance of the people, and lift us out of the economic morass into which we are sinking. Send us such a man, and be he God or Devil, we will accept him."[15] WOW!! Mr. Spaak, your wish may come about sooner than you expect, and someday, the world will regret it.

One of the reasons God hates idolatry is that He wants and deserves no rivals. In Exodus 20, where He sets forth the Ten Commandments, God commands in verses 4-5 that man should not make any graven image, nor bow down or worship them because He says, " [I] *the Lord thy God am a jealous God."* In Isaiah 42:8, God says, *"I am the LORD: that is my name: and my glory will I not give to another, neither my praise to graven images."* And you can be assured that He will not share it with the Antichrist!

"And he opened his mouth in blasphemy against God, to blaspheme His name, and His tabernacle, and them that dwell in Heaven" (Revelation 13:6). Here the Beast blasphemes and curses four things. First, he hates God and curses Him. Second, he blasphemes God's name. When someone uses God's name as a curse word, he is doing the same thing that Satan and the Antichrist will do. Third, he curses the Tabernacle – the place where God dwells. Finally, this garbage spewing out of his mouth is directed at you and me – God's children – *"them that dwell in Heaven."*

Satan has been kicked out of the heavenlies, and so, he cannot hurl his insults in the halls of Heaven anymore. The Church has been raptured, and it is beyond Satan's power and influence to harm those raptured saints. All Satan can do is rant and rave and attack those believers living on the earth. *"And it was given unto him to make war with the saints, and to overcome them: and power was given him over all kindreds, and tongues, and nations"* (Revelation 13:7). The Beast makes war *"with the saints …."*.

Remember, these saints are not the Church. The Church has been raptured, and is around the throne in Heaven. These are the Tribulation saints – those believers who were converted after the Rapture and will not bow down and worship the Beast. God has always had a remnant who are true to Him. And the Beast is given the power by God to overcome them – to kill them. But remember, we were told in chapter 12, verse 11: *"And they* [the saints] *overcame him by the blood of the Lamb and by the word of their testimony; and they loved not their lives unto the death."*

The Beast has power over all the kindreds, tongues and nations. They will worship him all right, but many will do it grudgingly, because we will see before the Book is over, a number of people (and these are not Christians) will rebel against him. *"All who dwell on the earth will worship him, everyone whose name has not been written from the foundation of the world in the Book of Life of the Lamb who has been slain"* (Revelation 13:8 NASB). Here we find the expression again, *"all who dwell on the earth"* – that is, the earth dwellers. They are the ones who have decided to settle down here; they want no part of Heaven, and they will all worship the Beast.

As we mentioned previously, God is the ultimate Accountant. He keeps several sets of books, but one thing is certain: if you are listed in the Lamb's Book of Life, you are secure forever – your name will never be blotted out!

"If any man have an ear, let him hear" (Revelation 13:9). Read this verse carefully. Hold your finger there and turn back to Revelation 2. Look at verse 7: *"He that hath an ear, let him hear what the Spirit saith unto the churches."* Now look at Revelation 2, verse 11: *"He that hath an ear, let him hear what the Spirit saith unto the churches".* Now look at Revelation 2, verse 17: *"He that hath an ear, let him hear what the Spirit saith unto the churches."* Now look at Revelation 2, verse 29: *"He that hath an ear, let him hear what the Spirit sayeth unto the churches."* Now look at Revelation 3, verse 6: *"He that hath an ear, let him hear what the Spirit sayeth unto the churches."* Now look at Revelation 3, verse 13: *"He that hath an ear, let him hear what the Spirit sayeth unto the churches."* Finally, Revelation 3, verse 22: *"He that hath an ear, let him hear what the Spirit sayeth unto the churches."*

Now read Revelation 13:9 once more: *"If any man have an ear, let him hear."* I put you through that little exercise to impress on you an important point. Do you see any difference? Of course! Those admonitions in Revelation 2 and 3, all say: *".... let him hear what the Spirit sayeth unto the churches."* But in Revelation 13:9, it says, *"If any man have an ear, let him hear."* Period. No mention of the churches. Why is that? Because the Rapture takes place at Chapter 4:1, and the Church is no longer on earth but in Heaven.

So, the Holy Spirit is not speaking to the churches in Revelation 13! This causes severe problems for the post-Tribulationists who teach that the Church will go through the 7 year Tribulation Period. The Church on earth is mentioned prominently in chapters 2 and 3 of Revelation, but from chapter 4 through the end of the Tribulation, the Church is never seen or mentioned on the earth because it is in Heaven!

The life and death matter of verses 1 through 8 is so important that God repeats this somber message in verse nine: *"If any man have an ear, let him hear."* And that is what I would say to you today. If you have an ear, take heed of what this says as your eternal future depends on it. The most important thing you could ever do in this life is to make certain you are not left here on earth – moaning, "It's over." The Bible says, "Now is the day of salvation" (II Corinthians 6:2).

"He that leadeth into captivity shall go into captivity: he that killeth with sword must be killed with the sword. Here is the patience and the faith of the saints" (Revelation 13:10). Does all this

killing and bloodshed make you think of a particular religious group – a religious group that claims it is peaceful, when its very name (Islam) means submission?

Satan is depicted in Scripture as the *"god of this world"* (II Corinthians 4:4). However, I am always amazed when a tornado kills hundreds of people, and does millions of dollars in damages, and the news carries the catastrophe as an "act of God." Why don't the insurance companies call it like it is – an act of Satan? Of course, God is ultimately in control, but in His permissive will, He allows Satan leeway in wreaking havoc in this earth.

Much of this havoc is not just natural catastrophes as we would call them, but just old fashioned heartaches and suffering. Satan has demon helpers as well as human helpers. Jeremiah 17:9 says that man's heart is desperately wicked above all things. So Satan has many allies in the form of secular humanists that he can work through. And make no mistake about it: our society would be a lot worse if it was not for two restraining forces.

1) The Holy Spirit who works through the consciences of men everywhere.
2) The believers who apply Christian principles in their daily lives.

This is even reflected in the laws that society has drawn up covering how people should deal with each other. Have you ever thought what it will be like during the Tribulation Period when these two restraining forces are not here? And they will not be here. Look at II Thessalonians 2:7: *"For the mystery of iniquity doth already work: only he who now letteth will let, until he be taken out of the way."* We think of the word "let" to mean unhindered or "to allow." But in proper English 400 years ago, "let" was the opposite of unhindered. The word "let" meant to hinder or restrain. Who is retraining evil in our day? The Holy Spirit who lives in the believers, and the believers themselves who seek to impose God's principles on society. So the KJV is saying that the one who now restrains (the Holy Spirit and the believers) will continue to restrain until this restraining force is removed; that is, the Restrainer (Holy Spirit and the believers) will depart at the Rapture. Then there will be virtually no restraining force to hold back the Antichrist. Woe to those who are left behind at the Rapture!

"For this lawlessness is already at work secretly" – in other words, violence and disorderly conduct is at work today, secretly, behind-the-scenes in spite of the restraint of the Holy Spirit and Christians. *"For this lawlessness is already at work secretly, and it will remain secret until the one who is holding it back steps out of the way"* (II Thessalonians 2:7 (NLT). The One who is retraining or holding back evil is the Holy Spirit and He leaves at the Rapture along with the true believers.

Satan and the Antichrist will be overjoyed to find millions of subjects who are willing to pledge allegiance and lay down their lives to fight against God. And if you do not understand how people will be willing to do this, you do not have to look far to see examples of them today. For instance, look at Islam for a moment. Is Islam a peaceful religion? We have been told "yes" by the Muslim leaders themselves. We have been told this by the media. And we have even been told this by our government officials.

Is Islam a peaceful religion? Before we answer this, I want you to look at some statistics that relate to the Israeli-Palestinian conflict because there is no question that Islam is the driving force behind this conflict. Look at these statistics compiled by nationally known and highly respected news analyst Dennis Prager. The number of times Jerusalem is mentioned in the Old Testament is over 700. The number of times Jerusalem is mentioned in the Koran zero. The number of Jewish states that have existed on the land called Palestine is three – three different Jewish states at various times in history. The number of Arab states that have existed on the land called Palestine is zero. Never has there ever existed a Muslim state in the land called Palestine.

- How many terrorist attacks by Jews on Muslims since 1967? One.
- How many terrorist attacks by Muslims on Jews since 1967? Thousands and thousands.
- Number of Arab countries in the Middle East? 19.
- Number of Israeli countries in the Middle East? One.
- Number of Israeli democracies? One.
- Number of Arab democracies? None, although Iraq is struggling to introduce democracy, but it is a losing battle.
- Number of Arab women killed annually by their fathers or brothers in so-called honor killings – thousands.
- Number of Jewish women killed annually by their fathers or brothers in honor killings – none.
- Number of Christian or Jewish worship services allowed in Saudi Arabia – zero.
- Number of Muslim worship services allowed in Israel – unlimited.
- Number of United Nations Security Council's resolutions on the Middle East between 1948 and 1991 – 175.
- Number of these resolutions against Israel – 97.
- Number of these resolutions against an Arab state – 4.
- Number of Arab states who have been allowed to be a member of the UN Security Council – 16.
- Number of times Israel has been allowed to be a member of the UN Security Council – zero.
- Number of UN General Assembly Resolutions condemning Israel – 322.
- Number of UN General Assembly Resolutions condemning an Arab country – zero.

- In the year 2002, the Arab countries voted in the UN with the United States – 16% of the time.
- The percent that Israel voted with the United States during this same period – 92% of the time.[16]

It doesn't take a genius to realize something is wrong with this picture. If Islam is a peaceful religion, why are these statistics so out of balance? The news media says, "Well, both sides are mean to each other, and they deserve what they get." The fact is, Israel is not trying to wipe out the Arab states. It is fighting for its life. But the Arab countries over and over again have demonstrated that they will not rest until they have eradicated the nation of Israel. But, as an old country boy said, "It ain't gonna' happen." God gave this land to Abraham and his seed forever! You will find this in Genesis chapters 17:7-8; 26:3; 28:4; I Chronicles 16:16-17; and Psalm 105:8. This promise of the title to the land by Almighty God to the Jewish people was everlasting, and it was unconditional. But their effective use of the land was dependent upon their obedience.

On May 14, 1948, after nearly 2,000 years, God allowed the Jews to repossess their land, and the Arabs have been trying to get it back ever since. But they had better get used to it because here is what God says about Israel being in the land, *"I will firmly plant them there in the land I have given them, says the Lord your God. Then they will never be uprooted again"* (Amos 9:15 NLT).

Islam holds itself out as a peaceful religion, however, it is common knowledge that the Muslims want to exterminate the Jews. Iran has called America, "Big Satan" and Israel, "Little Satan." One of Iran's chief terrorist groups which is funded in part by Iran is Hamas. In the official Hamas charter, it specifically calls for the annihilation of Israel.[17]

Throughout its 1,400 year history Islam has been closely linked with fanaticism, terrorism, mass murder and conversion by the sword. The sword has been its chief weapon of evangelism. This is the history of its growth. It was not spread like Christianity through great evangelistic preaching of the Gospel, and then letting the people make their choice. Islam was spread through great military men like Saladin and Suleiman the Magnificent. And in our generation, there are treacherous men like Yasser Arafat and Osama bin Laden who left bloody trails wherever they went.

Long before the mindless age of political correctness that astute old observer, Winston Churchill, wrote "Indeed it is evident that Christianity however degraded and distorted by cruelty and intolerance, must always exert a modifying influence on men's passions, and protect them from the more violent forms of fanatical fever, as we are protected from smallpox by vaccination. But the Mahommedan religion increases, instead of lessening, the fury of intolerance. It was originally propagated by the sword, and ever since its votaries have been subject, above the people of all other creeds, to this form of madness."[18]

Some teachers say that the Koran teaches that 72 virgins will be waiting in Heaven for each Muslim killed in combat for Islam. Muslims say that was a faulty translation, and that the Koran says nothing of the sort. Whether the flack about the 72 virgins is true or not, I enjoyed a cartoon I saw recently. Bin Laden died and was standing at the pearly gates. His entrance was being blocked by 72 burly men with scowls on their faces. Such men as Thomas Jefferson, Patrick Henry, James Madison and George Washington. And St. Peter was saying to Bin Laden, "You must have misunderstood. God said you would be met by 72 Virginians!"

As we pick up the paper each day and see the death toll mounting, and the terrorist activities becoming more and more bizarre, we ask ourselves, "Is Islam a religion of peace? Is it a religion of charity and tolerance? Is it a religion of compassion?" In the children's classic, *Through the Looking Glass,* Alice was trying to believe an impossible thing. She finally told the White Queen, "One can't believe impossible things." And the White Queen answered, "I daresay you haven't had much practice. When I was younger, I always did it for half an hour a day. Why, sometimes I've believed as many as six impossible things before breakfast."[19] So, with a little practice, you can believe anything!

At times, it seems like the White Queen must be advising the leaders in Washington on Islam. Why do they insist on telling us such soothing lies about Islam? And why does a gullible public believe them? There are 3 reasons. The first is oil. The Western world, hampered by the actions of environmentalists, is heavily dependent upon Middle East oil, although the U.S. seems to be making progress and some in Washington even say we are now "energy independent." Our leaders surmise that to tell the truth about Islam would offend our suppliers. The second reason we go on believing this nonsense about Islam being a peaceful religion is our sense of tolerance and fair play. America was founded on the principle of tolerance – we have it built into our Constitution.

From our beginning there has been no religious test for public office. We even have two Muslim congressmen in Washington. The one from Minnesota, Keith Ellison, recently said on the news that Kim Jong Un of North Korea is acting more responsible than our own president![20] Unbelievable! There is no government-sanctioned Church in our country; there is no persecution of religious minorities. So, to declare that Islam is not a religion of peace seems like bigotry. It seems like religious intolerance because of the way we were raised. But the fact of the matter is that today's phenomenon is unique. America has never experienced anything like Islam before. How do you tolerate a creed that elevates homicide to a religious obligation – a religion which, if it could, would remake America into the image of Saudi Arabia or Afghanistan, carrying us back to the 7th Century where our main products would be rocks and bombs.

The third reason we go on insisting that Islam is a peaceful religion is fear. If Islam is not a religion of peace, what is the implication for the West? It is that we are in deep trouble. Islam is the fastest growing religion in the world. We live in a world with more than 1.8 billion Muslims – roughly 24% of the world's population.[21] And they have armies, ballistic missiles, and millions and millions of young people ready to blow themselves up for the glory of Allah and his prophet, Mohammed. Muslims are pouring into Europe at an alarming rate. There are more than 25.8 million Muslims living in the European Union – roughly 5% of the population,[22] and about 3.5 million Muslims living in the U.S. It is estimated that by 2040, Muslims will constitute the second largest religious group in the U.S.[23] Assuming that every religion has its share of extreme fundamentalists, nonetheless you do not find orthodox rabbis hijacking airliners in response to "Jews for Jesus."

Jesuits do not shoot up Protestant seminaries to protest the Reformation. Members of the Mormon Church do not threaten to cut your throat if you do not accept Joseph Smith as God's latter-day prophet. Buddhists do not put out contracts on those who offend them. Hindus do not call members of other religions "dogs". And still our leaders insist that Islam is a religion of peace. It is more soothing to believe that Islam is a peaceful religion than to confront the unpleasant truth. Maybe our national bird, the eagle, should be replaced by an ostrich that sticks its head in the sand, and you don't have to guess what part of the anatomy is a target.

You can call Islam a peaceful religion, but words do not alter its true nature. Hiding from the truth does not change it. Abraham Lincoln once asked his cabinet members, "How many legs does a calf have if you call its tail a leg?" They paused for a moment, and then said, "Why, five of course." And President Lincoln, brilliant as always said, "No. A calf only has four legs. Calling a tail a leg doesn't make it one."[24] And you can say that Islam is peaceful, and that it is a tolerant religion, but like the calf's tail, calling it something it isn't does not make it so. I don't know how Islam will work into the plans of Satan, but if I were a betting man, I would bet my last dollar on the fact that Islam will be in bed with the Antichrist.

Here in chapter 13, describing this Beast, six times these words occur: *"it was given unto him."* The Antichrist has no authority or power unless it is given to him by God. God holds this world and its destiny in His hands. Why the permissive will of God allows them to plunge this world into darkness and gloom, I do not understand; but as we saw in chapter 10, verse 7 (J. B. Phillips paraphrase), *"In the days which shall soon be announced by the trumpet blast of the seventh angel, the Mysterious Purpose of God shall be completed…."*. In other words, in the days of the seventh trumpet, all the mysteries of good and evil and why God has allowed things to happen the way they did will be cleared up, and we will praise God for His perfect plan.

In Revelation 13:10, we have the principle that is presented over and over throughout scripture and is reaffirmed in Galatians 6:7b: *"For whatsoever a man soweth, that shall he also reap."* Here, we find that violence begets violence. The saints are going to be overpowered by the Beast. But those that do the overpowering will themselves die by the sword. Our nature when faced with danger is to fight. But God says these saints are not to resist. Their weapons are not physical, but spiritual. Helpless and hopeless, their resource is God Himself. It is this promise and confidence that will help to sustain the saints through such a bitter persecution. Their names are written in the Lamb's Book of Life, and no power in Hell or on earth can ever erase their names. As Revelation 12:11 says: *"They overcame him by the blood of the Lamb, and by the word of their testimony; and they loved not their lives unto the death."* Daniel saw this same endtime event, and he records it in Daniel 7:2: *"I beheld, and the same horn* [the Beast] *made war with the saints, and prevailed against them."*

We now will be introduced to a second Beast who is known as The False Prophet. *"And I beheld another Beast coming up out of the earth; and he had two horns like a lamb, and he spake as a dragon"* (Revelation 13:11). Remember, the first Beast in verse 1 of this chapter came up out of the sea – out of the turbulent mass and unrest of humanity. This Beast in verse 11 comes up out of the earth. The Greek word here for earth is "ge" and many commentators, including Hal Lindsay, say this word for earth can just as easily be translated "land."[25] Whenever the Bible speaks of the land, it invariably is referring to the land of Israel. So, the first Beast arises from the sea, while the second Beast arises from the land. The sea is a symbol of unrest in the masses of humanity, while it appears the land is referring to Israel. The sea could also be referring to the Mediterranean which touches the European continent.

It appears this second Beast will arise from Israel, and will be a Jew or at least have some Jewish blood running through his veins. He will cleverly manipulate and mislead the Jews into trusting the Antichrist. He will be a Benedict Arnold – a traitor – who will help the Antichrist in his efforts to wipe out the Jews. No doubt this False Prophet will be very instrumental in talking the Jews into signing a seven year peace agreement with the Arabs, negotiated by the Antichrist, which will enable the Jews to rebuild their Temple in Jerusalem. The Antichrist will love this plan, and will proceed to put the seven year treaty into effect, knowing all along that at the proper time, he will break the treaty and seek to destroy Israel. There is no question that Satan will be gleefully orchestrating these events.

It is important to keep in mind that the focus of world events will be centered in two places during the Tribulation: Rome with its one-world government, Jerusalem with its Temple, its 144,000 Jewish evangelists and its two mighty witnesses. It is hard to imagine that masses of people will worship these two emissaries of Satan. However, you must realize that the society that upholds the Antichrist and the False Prophet will be one characterized by violence and immorality. It is exactly the same type of society that was prevalent when God was fed up with it, and sent a flood to destroy mankind in Noah's day. In fact, Jesus said that the same type of society that was in existence when God destroyed the earth by a flood will be in existence in the last days. He said, *"But as the days of Noah were, so shall also the coming of the Son of Man be"* (Matthew 24:37). And we know that the people of Noah's day suffered from the same thing our society suffers with today: violence and immorality.

Murders have doubled in the last 25 years in the U.S., but what is so striking about that is that if it was not for great strides in medical science, murders would have increased tenfold. The violence has mushroomed, but through medical advances we are able to keep people alive longer.

Our movies are some of the most violent and immoral found anywhere in the world. This is fueled by what is being taught in many of our colleges today. Professors are telling us that most young people are coming into the colleges with no moral standards. All moral choices are relevant and depend on the situation. Some have called it "situational ethics." They say it might be OK here, but wrong there. But God does not operate that way. He is the same yesterday, today and forever, and He has told us in His Word what is right and what is wrong. It is called "The Ten Commandments." God gave those for mankind to live by, not "The eleven voluntary initiatives" that Ted Turner put forth.[26]

On June 26, 1948, subscribers to *The New Yorker* received a new issue of the magazine in the mail. There was nothing to outwardly indicate that it would be any different than any other issue. But inside there was a fictional story that editors at the magazine would call "perhaps the most controversial short story" *The New Yorker* had ever published. It was Shirley Jackson's *The Lottery.* Thousands were outraged by it and cancelled their subscriptions to the magazine. Over the years, it became a classic. I remember I had to read it in my college literature class. It was about a small New England village whose residents followed an annual rite in which they drew slips of paper until finally one of them was selected to be stoned to death to appease the gods. This rite was held annually by the 300 or so residents of this small village to insure that they had a good harvest.[27] In the story, a young woman dubiously "won" the lottery. Her husband and 12 year old son had to join the others in throwing rocks at her until she died. They did this for the sake of the community.

Kay Haugaard, a teacher at Pasadena City College in California, had taught *The Lottery* to her literature classes for a number of years, and her students had universally condemned such violence as total foolishness and wickedness. But she says that lately in her classes she has students that are afraid to condemn even such totally wicked actions.[28] Is this an outgrowth of political correctness? One student said, "This killing almost seems that it is needed to insure food and crops." The teacher asked, "Do you condone human sacrifices?" The student said, "Well, I don't know – I guess – if it was a religion of long standing ....". Unbelievable! If they had lived in ancient times, I guess they would have condoned parents tossing their babies into the Nile River to appease the river gods since that was part of their culture. The teacher was shocked. This was the same student who marched so passionately to save the whales a few weeks before. Another girl in the class said, "I am taking a nursing course on tolerance and multi-culturalism at a local hospital, and we are being taught that if something is part of a patient's religion and culture, we are not to be judgmental about it."

Young people today have a different mindset than when I was in school. My generation supported real tolerance – a tolerance that said, "We may not agree with you, but we allow your worship of whatever god you choose, so long as you do not hurt innocent people in the process." The new tolerance today says, "All religions and all cultures are just as valid as any other, and you need to acknowledge this." If you teach that your way to God is superior to other ways, or is exclusive, such as Christ's teaching, *"I am THE way, THE truth and THE life: no man cometh unto the Father but by Me"* (John 14:6) – then you are mean and intolerant.

Getting back to the Antichrist, some Biblical scholars such as Dr. A. C. Gaebelein believe that the second Beast is the real Antichrist.[29] I disagree, although it does not make a lot of difference since both are inspired and possessed by Satan. Jesus said in Matthew 24:24: *"For there shall arise false Christs, and false prophets, and shall show great signs and wonders; insomuch that, if it were possible, they shall deceive the very elect."* I love that phrase, *"if it were possible"*. That is another confirmation that true believers in Christ cannot fall away. They cannot lose their salvation. Praise God that it will not be possible to deceive the elect – those true believers! But this second Beast, though just as devious as the first, will act in his position to pave the way for the Antichrist in much the same way that John the Baptist paved the way for Jesus Christ.

This second Beast may indeed claim to be Israel's Messiah, and therefore, he would have to be a Jew or his claim of being Israel's true Messiah would never be taken seriously by the Jews. At no time during his mission does this False Prophet promote himself. He is only concerned about promoting the Antichrist. There could not be a clearer imitation or counterfeit of the Holy Spirit who promotes Jesus at every opportunity. In John 16:13-14a, Jesus gives the mission of the Holy Spirit. *"Howbeit when He, the Spirit of truth, is come, He will guide you unto all truth: for He shall not speak of Himself; but whatsoever He shall hear, that shall He speak: and He will shew you things to come. He shall glorify Me ...."*.

Satan tries to counterfeit everything that God does. Both the Antichrist and the False Prophet have opened their hearts and souls to Satan, and allowed him to come in and control them completely. Revelation 13:11 says, *"And I beheld another Beast coming up out of the earth; and he had two horns like a lamb, and he spake as a dragon."* Notice Scripture says *"another Beast"*. There are two words in the Greek language for "another." One means another of a different kind, and one means another of the same kind. The word used here means another of the same kind. Verse 11 goes on to say the False Prophet has two horns like a lamb, but speaks like a dragon. This is a mixed metaphor. Have you ever heard of a lamb having horns? Jesus Himself said in Matthew 7:15, *"Beware of false prophets, which come to you in sheep's clothing, but inwardly they are ravenous wolves."* This lamb deceives the people into thinking he is gentle and meek, when all the time he has two horns indicating power, and speaks like a dragon. Praise God that our Lamb is not a fake. He is the wonderful, merciful, genuine Lamb of God!

Revelation 13:12 tells us more about the second Beast. *"And he exerciseth all the power of the first Beast before him, and causeth the earth and them which dwell therein to worship the first Beast, whose deadly wound was healed."* These two Satan empowered men have special assets to support the other – the king enforcing the religious authority of the False Prophet, and the False Prophet persuading the world's superstitious masses that the Antichrist should be worshipped and obeyed as a god.

We were told in verse 11 that the False Prophet was masquerading as a lamb, but he was a fake, because he spoke like the dragon, the Devil. Just as Jesus was the Good Shepherd, we have been warned about the worthless shepherd. Look at Zechariah 11:15-16a (NLT). *"Then the Lord said to me, Go again and play the part of a worthless shepherd. This will illustrate how I will give this nation a shepherd who will not care for the sheep that are threatened by death, nor look after the young, nor heal the injured, nor feed the healthy."* Scripture goes on to prophesy the utter doom of this false shepherd.

The False Prophet has the same power of the Antichrist, but remember, the Antichrist is described as one *"Even him, whose coming is after the working of Satan with all power and signs and lying wonders"* (II Thessalonians 2:9). But as we learn more about this second Beast, we find that he is clearly subordinate to the first Beast.

The first Beast's headquarters is in Rome, and is the head of all political government activities; the second Beast's headquarters is in Jerusalem, and is the head of all religious activities. Phillip Goodman strongly argues that most likely the first Beast is a Gentile with Syrian blood.[30] The second Beast most likely has at least some Jewish blood in his veins. But you will not find in all the earth a monster as vile as this first Beast (Antichrist) – looking like a lamb, but on the inside, as evil as Satan himself. The real Lamb of God has seven horns (Revelation 5:6) signifying complete power, while this imitation lamb has only two horns, signifying limited power.

"And he doeth great wonders, so that he maketh fire come down from Heaven on the earth in the sight of men" (Revelation 13:13). Elijah called fire down from Heaven on Mount Carmel. God's two witnesses in chapter 11 were able to shoot fire out of their mouths to destroy their enemies. And here in verse 13, Satan allows the False Prophet to perform another imitation act (the first being the imitation resurrection of the Beast) this time using fire. Never be fooled into thinking that anyone who can do miraculous things must be of God. Satan is not impotent,

but he has been granted limited powers by God. Miraculous signs do not automatically mean that someone is holy!

"And deceiveth them that dwell on the earth by the means of those miracles which he had power to do in the sight of the Beast; saying to them that dwell on the earth, that they should make an image to the Beast, which had the wound by a sword, and did live" (Revelation 13:14). Thirteen times in Revelation we read about those who "dwell on the earth" – twice in this verse. We have said before that, *"For where your treasure is, there will your heart be also"* (Matthew 6:21). These earth dwellers have settled down on this earth – it is their real home, and they are not interested in a home in Heaven. And these two great deceivers will be welcomed with open arms by those who have no use for the things of God.

Max Nordau, a reformed Jew who long ago gave up the notion that Israel's Messiah would ever come, said at a Zionist Congress, "We are ready to welcome any man as our Messiah who will lead us back to our own land, and establish us there in prosperity."[31] And Dr. Mosinsohn of the Hebrew College of Jaffa was speaking a number of years ago at the University of California. He said, "Think of all the great religious leaders who have come out of the East. Moses arose in the East; also, Buddha, Confucius, Jesus and Mohammed. And we say, with confidence, to you people of the West that if you will restore the Jew to his ancestral home it will not be long until we will give you another great religious leader who will perhaps transcend all who have gone before."[32] Think False Prophet!

Again, Scripture mentions here, that the Beast had a mortal wound, yet came back to life. We said previously that in a broad sense, this meant the old Roman Empire that was seemingly dead, but came back to life 2,000 years later; however, it has to mean more than that. The Roman Empire coming back together after 2,000 years is amazing all right, but it would not excite the people to "wonder after it." They probably would not say, "Wow, I'm going to follow this Empire no matter what because it was revived after all these years." No, there is more to it than that. It has to picture the leader of this Roman Empire – the Antichrist – who apparently received some kind of violent wound that seemingly killed him. The Bible says, *"which had the wound by the sword, and did live"* (Revelation 13:14).

This would certainly cause the people to worship him. In the first step to require everyone on the face of the earth to worship the Antichrist, this False Prophet directs the construction of an image, a statue. As a type of this, so that we can get a clear illustration, we find the same thing happening in Daniel chapter 3. King Nebuchadnezzar made a giant image to be worshipped. It was set up on the plains of Dura about six miles southeast of Babylon which is in modern day Iraq.

This image of Nebuchadnezzar was sixty cubits tall and six cubits wide. There were six musical instruments that would signal the time for worship. King Nebuchadnezzar ordered everyone, at the sound of the musical instruments, to bow down and worship him. Not to bow down and worship this image of King Nebuchadnezzar, meant that those individuals would be put to death. And we will see that those who do not worship the Antichrist or his image will be beheaded.

We are not told specifically, but I tend to believe that King Nebuchadnezzar had this statue made in his likeness just as I believe here in the 13th chapter the False Prophet had this image made in the likeness of the Antichrist. This image of the Antichrist will be placed in the Temple in Jerusalem probably shortly after the Great Tribulation begins. Jesus warned of this in Matthew 24:15-16: *"When ye therefore shall see the ABOMINATION OF DESOLATION, spoken of by Daniel the prophet, stand in the holy place (whoso readeth, let him understand) then let them which be in Judea flee into the mountains."* When the image is set up in the holy place, the Temple is soon emptied of its worshipers, and the Israelite remnant will flee into the wilderness (Revelation 12:6); but most of the earth dwellers will quickly be obedient by worshipping the Man of Sin and the Devil himself.

See how the timing of all this comes together? Satan is hurled to the earth, and denied further access to the outer regions of Heaven (Revelation 12:9). He is furious and directs his anger toward those on the earth (Revelation 12:12), and empowers his two henchmen, the Antichrist and the False Prophet, to carry out his satanic plans as revealed in chapter 13. Then a concerted effort is especially directed at Israel (Revelation 12:13), but she is given a place of protection to which she is to flee where she is protected for 3½ years (Revelation 12:14).

"And he had power to give life unto the image of the Beast, that the image of the Beast should both speak, and cause that as many as would not worship the image of the Beast should be killed" (Revelation 13:15). Only God can create life. I do not believe for a moment that the False Prophet gave life to this image. Actually, the word translated life in the Greek means breath or wind or spirit. By some act of deception, the False Prophet gives the appearance of life to this image. Whether this will be an act of ventriloquism, demonic possession, high tech computers, or something else, we know it will be a convincing performance. Those who observe this, whether in person in Jerusalem or via satellite around the world, will be convinced that the image is really speaking of its own volition.

We have seen in our day, where scientists have been able to give speeches and movements via computers to various robots, seemingly giving them life. Years ago at Disney World in Florida, I saw Abraham Lincoln walk out on stage in the Epcott Center, and deliver the Gettysburg address. It was so real that you would have thought Old Abe was there in person, but it was all done with computers, lights and robotics. And look how much farther we have come in the last few years in this field![33]

Personally, I believe that Satan will be right in the middle of all this. That is why I am in doubt that this image speaks by way of a ventriloquist, or even by the use of computers. It will be more demonic than that. I believe that Satan will send a demon from the abyss to enter the image and speak for it. We have seen evil spirits take control and operate from the body of a human, so they can certainly speak through this image.

People will be glued to their news media each evening to see what marvelous things that the image has to say. Whether this is the exact means Satan will use to get his message across remains to be seen, but the prophecy will come true in any case. The edict will be conveyed around the world that it will be considered a capital offense not to worship the Beast via his image. It is also probable that monitors will be installed in every home to feed information back to a centralized network of computers recording whether or not such worship is actually being carried out by those family members. DirecTV can already monitor which programs you are watching – a great way for an evil dictator to track down traitors!

Robotic scientist Hans Moravec, with the Carnegie Mellon University, says that by 2040 computers will enable mankind to build a freely moving robot with the intellectual capabilities of a human being.[34] It is probable that the Antichrist will use such a system to have all the facts on every member of the human race at his fingertips. He will be able to know in a moment who has received his mark, who obeys his commands, and who honors his laws. There is no doubt that the image will impress and woo many into worshipping and pledging their allegiance to it, coupled with the severe penalties for those who resist.

"And he causeth all, both small and great, rich and poor, free and bond, to receive a mark in their right hand, or in their foreheads" (Revelation 13:16). Everyone must have this mark. It does not make any difference if you are rich as a Wall Street investor, or you are as poor as the fellow on skid row. You must receive the mark or face death. It will show that you are a loyal citizen of the one-world kingdom. The Greek word translated mark is "charagma." It is used nine times, all in the Book of Revelation. One time it refers to graven images made by man's devices. Eight times it refers to something like an etching or tattoo which, once inscribed, cannot be removed. It provides a permanent eternal mark, identifying the person as a follower of the Antichrist and Satan.

No doubt registration centers will be set up in every community, and people will be instructed to report for their "marking" on or before a certain date. Merchants must have the mark in order to purchase their inventory. Customers must have it to buy anything. If you visit a doctor or specialist, you will need the mark to get treatment.

Today, governments around the world are working to bring about a "cashless" society. This will eliminate all coins and paper money so that all transactions can be easily tracked electronically. Most banks today offer a debit card that can be scanned at any retail store, and the money is taken instantly out of the purchaser's account. In 2011 in the U.S., cash purchases amounted to 36%. By 2021, U.S. purchases with cash is estimated to be only about 11%.[35] The Antichrist's mark will either be placed in the person's right hand or in the forehead. There is a symbolism connected with this. If the mark is taken in the hand then when the hand is bent, it covers your heart, and you have pledged your allegiance to the Antichrist. If the mark is taken in the forehead, it signifies that your mind is given over to the Antichrist.

In Deuteronomy 11:18, we read that the children of Israel were instructed to wear Scripture carried in little pouches (called phylacteries) on their wrists and on their foreheads. Again, Satan has tried to duplicate what God had His children do a long time ago. And remember, we discovered in the seventh chapter of Revelation, God sealed or protected his 144,000 witnesses against the Antichrist and his forces of evil by placing a seal, a mark on their foreheads.

"And that no man might buy or sell, save he that had the mark, or the name of the Beast, or the number of his name" (Revelation 13:17). In other words, "You worship the Antichrist or you do not eat!" There will undoubtedly be many who survive for a while by living off the land, growing their own food and setting up secret communes to help one another. But it will be extremely difficult to survive at all without the Mark of the Beast. From other passages in Revelation we know that thousands upon thousands of believers will be martyred during the Tribulation Period. We find this in Revelation 6:9 and again in Revelation 7:14. And this intense massacre picks up during the last 3½ years, and they are either killed outright for refusing to take the Mark of the Beast, or they starve to death because they cannot buy or sell without having the mark.

Just what is this Mark of the Beast? It will not be a card such as a credit card we are used to carrying in a purse or wallet. The Greek word indicates that it will be some sort of impressed mark or engraving. It may be something like a brand than we put on animals, but it will be an indelible mark that cannot be erased. I can remember a number of years ago reading about some people who refused to accept a personal Social Security number because they thought they were being tricked into accepting what would eventually become the Mark of the Beast.

What would be your reaction today if the government made this announcement: "Thousands and thousands of our citizens are being ripped off each year by having their credit cards stolen and their personal identities stolen. This is costing taxpayers billions of dollars. Beginning next month, each citizen will be required to have their Social Security number tattooed in a bar code on their wrist. Then, whenever anything is bought or sold or one goes to the doctor or the hospital, the transaction will be legitimately recorded. Everyone will be certain with whom they are dealing. Plus, for our senior citizens who get disoriented and wander off, we will know immediately who and where they are. There will be no more kidnapping or switching of babies because their identity will be certain." Doesn't that sound great? Would you have a problem with that? What if the government decided to put into place a "national I.D." system whereby everyone would have to have an identifying number engraved on their hand? There is serious talk about this from time to time in Congress. The technology for this is already available. A microchip can now be implanted in a dog's ear so that it can be found in case the dog becomes missing.

Is this the forerunner of this infamous mark? I used to worry about this question: "What if I were tricked – what if I were duped into taking this mark quite innocently? What if the government said, "From now on, you have to have this bar code tattooed on your wrist or you cannot buy food?" Would you do it? It is a little scary because the Bible is very clear: anyone who takes the Mark of the Beast will be cast into the Lake of Fire with no chance of reversal (Revelation 19:20). As I said, I used to worry about unwittingly taking the mark by accident.

First, let me say that the Church (true believers) will not even be here; we will have been raptured into Heaven before this time. Secondly, I believe that those who have become followers of Christ during the Tribulation cannot be tricked into receiving this mark. Matthew 24:24 says the Antichrist will be very deceitful, but the elect of God cannot and will not be deceived. Further, notice that the Bible says, "THE Mark of THE Beast." In other words, the people taking this mark will know exactly what they are doing, and to whom they are pledging allegiance. It will be a choice of the will to give allegiance to the Antichrist – they will not be tricked into it.

The ones following the Antichrist will consciously and willfully say, "By taking this mark I pledge my allegiance and my life to the Beast and his image." And by doing this, it will seal their doom forever. Such people will know there is a God, and in spite of such knowledge, they will deliberately blaspheme Him, worship the Beast, and take his mark so that they can temporarily escape physical death.

There are many details about the Mark of the Beast that we do not know at this time, but these matters will be fully known when it becomes time for the mark to be required. I know of only one exception, and it is in the field of fiction. It is conjecture by Tim LaHaye in the Left Behind series, but the following story does make sense. The 8th book of the series is entitled, *"The Mark: The Beast Rules the World."* In it, there is a new Christian, an 18 year old Chinese boy by the name of Chang Wong. His father and mother, who have already taken the mark, do not know of their son's recent conversion to Christianity. Chang made one excuse after another for not going to receive the mark at one of the government's loyalty stations. His parents were after him each day to go and get the mark. Chang would either feign sickness and could not go, or have some other excuse.

It was beginning to be an embarrassment to his family. So, his father contacted the Beast's security forces who were in charge of the loyalty station, and basically said, "My son is too timid to come in and have his mark applied. I want you to visit with him and in the course of the visit, get him to drink some tea which will be drugged. While he is asleep, you can apply the mark."

It happened just as planned. Chang was mortified and scared when he woke up to find the Mark of the Beast on his forehead. He was in terrible mental anguish while his family was rejoicing. But in the next book of the series, Chang looked at his forehead and the mark simply faded away before his very eyes.[36] As I said, this story is fiction, but I think the point is valid. The mark must be taken voluntarily and with full knowledge that the individual is pledging his or her allegiance to the Beast.

"Here is wisdom. Let him that hath understanding count the number of the Beast: for it is the number of a man; and his number is six hundred threescore and six" (Revelation 13:18). The Lord frequently uses numbers to stand for certain things throughout the Bible. For example, the number one is only divisible by itself. It is independent of any of the other numerals yet is included in all of them. It symbolizes in the Bible the unity and primacy, and the oneness of the Godhead. The number five symbolizes God's grace, goodness and favor toward humans, and is mentioned 318 times in Scripture. The Ten Commandments contains two sets of five commandments. The first five commandments are related to our relationship with God, and the last five concern our relationship with mankind.

Six is the number of Man – he was created on the sixth day. He is to work six out of the seven days. A Hebrew slave could not be a slave more than six years. The fields were not to be sown more than six years in a row, and then they had to lay unworked for a year. And ultimately, the number of Man carried to the nth degree is the number of the Antichrist – 666. This number emphasizes man's inability to solve his own problems – it is humanity fallen, filled with pride and wanting to be like God but coming up short.

For a long time people have been making calculations and trying to figure out who the Antichrist is. When I was growing up in the 1940's, I can remember reading reports where the writers were absolutely certain that the Antichrist was Hitler. After all, he pursued the Jews unmercifully, and ordered the death of over 6 million of them. And Hitler rose to power in Germany right in the middle of the old Roman Empire just as Daniel prophesied.

An assassination attempt was made on Hitler's life on July 20, 1944.[37] Colonel Claus von Stauffenberg and other German conspirators planned the assassination. A bomb was left under the table in the room in which Hitler and other officers were having a meeting. Unfortunately, the bomb was placed on the wrong side of a heavy table support which somewhat muted the effects of the blast.

Nevertheless, the room was nearly destroyed, and Hitler was badly injured but survived. Nearly 5,000 people were executed by the Nazis in retaliation for the attempt – even if you were a distant cousin of Stauffenberg you were executed. Because it seemed like a mortal wound to Hitler from which he survived, many people were sure that he was resurrected and was the Antichrist. But there was one important piece of the puzzle that was missing. The Antichrist will not be revealed according to II Thessalonians 2:1- 8 until after the Rapture – after Christ's Bride has been called home. If you need to review this, we fully aired it out in chapter 6. The Bible is full of types, examples and "pre-fulfillments," and it appears that Hitler was one of these types.

In writing, the English language uses two sets of characters – an alphabet and numbers. They are distinct from each other. A letter is a letter and a number is a number. For example, the number 5 is a 5 – it is not an "M." But the ancient world used a single set of characters to represent both letters and numbers. Such a system is called an "alphanumeric" system. In an alphanumeric system, every word has a numeric value, every sentence has a numeric value, and every paragraph has a numeric value. The same is true of every name. Every name has a numeric value. In the English language, such an instruction would seem absurd, but not in the Hebrew, Greek or even Latin. In Latin, they use Roman numerals. "V" means 5; "X" means 10; "C" means 100 and so forth.

By using the alphanumeric system as was in use during the 1st Century in Rome, a number can be calculated for every name. Would you believe me if I told you I know who the Antichrist is? Listen to my evidence because I have decided to reveal who the Antichrist is! Using my brainpower I was able to crack the code and figure it out. There are 3 keys that unlocked this mystery for me.

- Key #1 – we know that the Antichrist will be strong – he will stomp on his enemies, and he will be massive in power.
- Key #2 – the Antichrist will be charismatic – many will be strangely attracted to him, and he will be loved and adored among many groups of people.
- Key #3 – the Antichrist will be a master of the media. He will know how to be on TV all the time, charming his audience.

Those 3 keys unlock the mystery: #1 – massive in power; #2 – extremely popular with many people; #3 – master of the media. There is a character, one you know well, that fits this description. Here is a clue: he is known as the cute purple dinosaur. Some of you have figured it out by now. Now, let's see if he fits the clue given in the Bible. We are told that the number of the Antichrist's name is 666.

So let's take the name "Cute Purple Dinosaur," and change all the U's to V's as it would be properly written in Latin: CVTE PVRPLE DINOSAVR. C =100; V = 5 ;V = 5; L = 50; D = 500; I = 1; V = 5. Add these up and the total is 666! So, the Antichrist is none other than that popular, lovable, purple dinosaur character, Barney the Dinosaur that the kids all love. I owe this clever exercise to my good friend, Dennis Pollock, who came up with it to illustrate how useless it is to speculate as to who the Antichrist is.

Through another different type of calculation, Henry Kissinger's name adds up to 666. So does Jane Fonda's. In fact, statistics show that one name out of every 10,000 adds up to 666! Aside from all the speculation, let us just say that six is the number of man (short of perfection) – and seven is the number of God (perfection). And 666 is man's effort to become seven, just like Satan fallaciously said in the Garden of Eden: *"For God doth know that in the day ye eat thereof, then your eyes shall be opened, and ye shall be as gods, knowing good and evil"* (Genesis 3:5).

Here is another interesting point. Since six is one number short of the perfect seven – the three sixes together may suggest the Unholy Trinity – Satan, the Antichrist and the False Prophet. This number 666 is not something that can be figured out, or solved like you would one of the TV mysteries. It cannot be known until the proper time, and then this mystery will make complete sense to those believers who will be facing this madman.

This information to identify the Antichrist is of no practical value to us since we will be watching from the balcony of glory. But it will be of great information for those on earth to confirm someone they already suspect is the Antichrist. Once the Tribulation begins, it will be pretty evident who the Antichrist is because he will sign a seven year peace agreement with Israel. Then, to verify your suspicions, simply calculate the number of his name by using the alphanumeric system – it will then add up to 666. The final confirmation will be when he stands in the Temple, and declares himself to be Almighty God!

Someone asked me one time, if there is an all-knowing God why does He talk in riddles? Instead of saying the Antichrist's number will be 666 if God knows the future, why didn't He simply say, "The Antichrist will be Alexander Johnson or whatever his name will be? I refer the question to Jesus. Once His disciples asked Him, *"Why speaketh thou unto them in parables?"* (Matthew 13:10). Here is the Lord's reply: *"Because it is given unto you to know the mysteries of the kingdom of Heaven, but to them* [who do not believe in Me] *it is not given"* (Matthew 13:11). Thus, the only ones who will know the Antichrist for who he is, will be the ones to whom the Lord has given the wisdom to understand, i.e. the believers.

Many people stick their head into the Book of Revelation and say, "This doesn't make sense to me; it is too hard to understand." It is certainly not the place for new believers to start studying; they should begin in the Gospel of John. Jesus was never clearer when He said in John 3:36 (NASB): *"He who believes in the Son has eternal life; but he who does not obey the Son will not see life, but the wrath of God abides on him."* And then we are told: *"Seek the Lord while He may be found."* (Isaiah 55:6a). Do not seek that imperfect Beast whose number is 666, but seek the Lamb of God – a perfect 777!

CHAPTER FOURTEEN

144,000 Evangelists on Mount Zion

In the last chapter, we were introduced to two of the vilest creatures who will ever walk on this earth. You might call them Beast 1 and Beast 2 or, as they are better known, the Antichrist and the False Prophet respectively. Both get their power, authority and energy from Satan. If you have a heart for people, the Book of Revelation can get pretty heavy at times. The amount of judgment and death and suffering is overwhelming. Our hearts break when we realize that what we are reading is going to impact real people someday, maybe our friends and relatives if they are without Christ.

We also know that there are consistent breaks in the reading of these judgments where God gives a message and assurance and refreshment to the reader. That is why at the beginning of Chapter 14, God says, "Time Out" – and graciously gives John a vision of the wonderful things waiting just around the corner. In fact, Revelation 14 is somewhat a table of contents for the rest of the Revelation. It tells us what is soon to happen after evil has been abolished.

Here are some of the events we will see in this chapter.

1) Christ and the 144,000 evangelists on Mt. Zion;
2) The angel with the everlasting Gospel;
3) The fall of Babylon;
4) Judgment for those who took the Mark of the Beast;
5) A blessing upon those who die in the Lord;
6) A preview of Armageddon – the last battle.

The Apostle John has been seeing all the things that are going to take place. As he views all the vicious things that are described in chapter 13, he probably is about to be overcome with dispair when the Lord says, "Wait a minute. Let me show you the glories that await you."

And so, we have a "flash-forward" in chapter 14. And some teachers, trying to interpret these chapters in chronological order, get totally confused if they do not understand this is a view of events about to take place.

They will see the Beast and False Prophet making war on the earth dwellers; then they see Christ on Mt. Zion in Jerusalem with all His followers; then they see in chapters 15 and 16 more judgment and plagues being poured out upon the earth. And they say, "Christ must be going to come back to earth in chapter 14, and then the plagues will resume in chapters 15 and 16." Nothing of the sort! If you interpret it in chronological order, you will have nothing but mass confusion.

Chapter 14 is a flash-forward to the end of the Tribulation. It is the answer to the oft-repeated question of the Jewish remnant that is being hammered by the Antichrist: *"How long wilt thou forget me, O LORD?"* (Psalm 13:1a). David also cries out to God in Psalm 10:1 *"Why standest thou afar off, O LORD? Why hidest thou thyself in times of trouble?"* And then David answers his own question in the following psalms: *"I have seen the wicked in great power, and spreading himself like a green bay tree"* (Psalm 37:35).

"But the salvation of the righteous is of the LORD: He is their strength in the time of trouble. And the LORD shall help them, and deliver them: He shall deliver them from the wicked, and save them, because they trust in Him" (Psalm 37:39-40). Chapter 14 confirms that God will protect Israel and it also gives us a look at God's grace that awaits us.

Here is a short comparison of Chapter 13 with Chapter 14:

Chapter 13	Chapter 14
Satan's lamb, the False Prophet	God's Lamb, Jesus
Beasts from the sea and earth	Lamb on Mt. Zion
False religion	True religion
Idolatry rampant	Worship everywhere
Mark of the Beast	God's mark
666 is important	144,000 witnesses

Before we go any further, let me say that some of my friends will not use anything except the King James Version because they believe that all the other versions have been corrupted. The KJV is an extremely good translation, but it is not perfect. When we say that we believe in the inerrancy of the Bible, we mean that it is without error in the original transmission as it was given by God. It has been proven that the translating errors in the KJV are slight, and do not affect any major doctrinal teachings. But here is a case in point that is interesting. In Chapter 14, verse 1, the KJV omitted a phrase that is in the most ancient of manuscripts. Here is how the King James Version translates chapter 14:1, *"And I looked, and, lo, a Lamb stood on the mount Zion, and with Him an hundred forty and four thousand, having his Father's name written in their foreheads."* But here is the way the verse should read: *"Then I saw the Lamb standing on Mount Zion, and with Him were 144,000 who had His name and His Father's name written on their foreheads"* (Revelation 14:1 NLT).

All the later translations, including the Revised Version, the NIV, the New American Standard and the New Living Translation have corrected it. The Lamb, as we already know, is the Lord Jesus Christ. John the Baptist confirmed this in John 1:29b when he said of Christ, *"Behold the Lamb of God, which taketh away the sin of the world."*

We also know that the Apostle John in chapter 12 of Revelation sees the Tribulation saints overcoming Satan by the blood of the Lamb. So these 144,000 have the name of Christ and the name of God the Father written in their foreheads. This is the real mark, and shows up the counterfeit we saw in the last chapter where the unbelievers had the mark of the Antichrist written on their foreheads. I think this name on the forehead – whether it is for God or for the Antichrist – speaks your allegiance. It is very public. You can normally see the forehead under just about any condition so you are publicly declaring who has your allegiance.

Our first question in verse one is, "Who are these 144,000?" Commentator Matthew Henry of another generation says it is the Church.[1] I have a high regard for Matthew Henry, but bless his heart, he gets confused when it comes to prophecy. The 144,000 cannot be the Church. We will see shortly that the 24 elders are watching these 144,000, and we have shown conclusively in our discussion of Revelation chapter 4 that the 24 elders around the throne represent the Church. One writer said that these 144,000 are the very best Christians over the centuries – like Billy Graham, Charles Stanley, Jerry Falwell, W. A. Criswell, etc. As great humanly speaking as these men are, they owe all their abilities to God who endowed them. The Church is the Body of Christ. He would never split up His body in this manner.

Early in the history of the Jehovah's Witnesses, their doctrine proclaimed that these 144,000 are Jehovah's Witnesses and they represent "Christ's Church."[2] Their members went from door to door with the slogan, "Join now and be one of the 144,000 who will go to Heaven." Well, their sales began to slump when all of the 144,000 reservations were filled up. So, they cut it off in 1935 when their membership exceeded 144,000, saying that the others who become Jehovah's Witnesses will live on a renewed earth. It seems like they are sort of second class citizens.[3] This is so absurd, it needs no comment. We will see in a moment just who these 144,000 are.

Notice that both the Lamb and His followers are standing on Mount Zion. This is not Heaven. Mount Zion is a definite location in the city of Jerusalem in the nation of Israel. Zion always refers in Scripture either to the actual mountain on which Jerusalem was built, or to Jerusalem herself personified.

Did you know that Zion is the place God loves more than any other place on earth? Liberal churches had better take notice; I think they are upsetting God. Look at this news article from *World Net Daily* under the headline, "Presbyterians Host Anti-Israel Meeting." The article went on to say: "The Presbyterian Church USA hosted a three day meeting last week presenting what one church elder described as a panel of full-time, paid, anti-Israel propagandists." The

World Council of Churches in Geneva immediately praised the Presbyterian Church USA for its anti-Zionist stance.[4] The Catholic Church over the past several hundred years has been intensely anti-Semetic, but in the last 40 years great strides have been made to soften its stance against the Jews.[5]

All denominations need to understand that Israel plays an important part in God's end time plans. *"For the Lord hath chosen Zion; He hath desired it for His habitation. This is my rest for ever: here will I dwell; for I have desired it"* (Psalm 132:13-14). Psalm 48:2 (NASB) says: *"Beautiful for elevation, the joy of the whole earth, is mount Zion, on the sides of the north, the city of the great King."*

Psalm 110:2 pictures Christ reigning on earth, and states: *"The LORD shall send the rod of thy strength out of Zion: rule thou in the midst of thine enemies."* And again in Psalm 146:10: *"The LORD shall rein forever, even thy God, O Zion, unto all generations. Praise ye the LORD."* In Isaiah 2:3 (NLT), the prophet says: *"Many nations will come and say, 'Come, let us go up to the mountain of the LORD, to the Temple of the God of Israel. There He will teach us His ways, so that we may obey Him.' For in those days the LORD's teaching and His Word will go out from Jerusalem."*

Where are Christ's feet going to land when He comes back to planet earth? I have good news for you. It is not going to be in Salt Lake City or Rome or Geneva or New York City. We do not have to guess – the Bible tells us!

"Then the Lord will go out to fight against those nations, as He has fought in times past. On that day His feet will stand on the Mount of Olives, which faces Jerusalem on the east. And the Mount of Olives will split apart, making a wide valley running from east to west, for half the mountain will move toward the north and half toward the south …. Then the LORD my God will come, and all His holy ones with Him" (Zechariah 14:3-5b NLT).

He's coming back to Israel! He's coming back to Jerusalem! And if that doesn't pinpoint it, He is coming back to the top of the Mount of Olives! Hallelujah! You need to think twice – maybe 3, 4 or 5 times before you speak out against the nation and land that God says He loves and is coming back to.

Well, back to our question, who are these 144,000? Turn back to Revelation chapter 7:3-4. Here is what it says: *"Hurt not the earth, neither the sea, nor the trees, till we have sealed the servants of our God in their foreheads. And I heard the number of them which were sealed: and there were sealed a hundred and forty and four thousand of all the tribes of the children of Israel."* Before the Lord begins to pour out His judgments upon the earth, He says, "Hold on. The judgments cannot begin until I have sealed these special 144,000 Jewish evangelists." This sealing will protect them against the judgments throughout this awful period. And in the vision in chapter 14, John is permitted to look ahead – to experience a flash-forward to the end of the Tribulation. And what does he see? He sees the 144,000 standing with Christ on the Mount of Olives. John sees that they have finished their mission, they have been killed by the Antichrist, and now he sees them standing on Mount Zion with the Lord Himself where they are going to be honored.

Did you catch the fact that not one of them is missing? There are not 143,999 – there are not 139,000 – there are not 138,000 – there are still 144,000! When God seals His children, they are protected forever! Hal Lindsey said that this is a miracle of the first order since millions will be killed during the horrors of the Tribulation Period, yet not a single one of these 144,000 is killed until the mission is complete.[6] And you can be sure that the Antichrist will target them with every weapon and all the evil forces at his command. You can be assured that he will hate these evangelists with a passion, and will detest the message they will preach every day for 3½ years.

They remind me of what happened to Shadrach, Meshach, and Abednego, the three Hebrew children in Daniel that went through the fiery furnace, and the fire singed not so much as a hair on their heads. In their case, the fiery furnace was heated seven times hotter than normal (Daniel 3:19); and in the case of these 144,000, the seven years of tribulation will be far more intense than anything ever experienced before. In fact, Jesus said, *"For then shall be great tribulation, such as was not since the beginning of the world to this time, no, nor ever shall be"* (Matthew 24:21). But not to worry – God has the ultimate "seal of protection!" It is important to note that the same Greek word for sealed is used in Ephesians 1:13 when Paul tells us that as Christians we are sealed with the Holy Spirit. And just like these 144,000, if you are a true believer, you have been sealed by the Spirit of God and He will not lose a single one of you! Do you remember when the Good Shepherd had one hundred sheep? One was lost, but He did not rest until that one little sheep was safely home. And that is the way it is with you. He will not rest until you are safely home.

Let's see what awaits these witnesses. Revelation 14:2: *"And I heard a voice from Heaven, as the voice of many waters, and as the voice of a great thunder: and I heard the voice of harpers harping with their harps."* John hears a powerful voice like many waters. He has heard this voice before in chapter 1, verse 15b: *"and His voice as the sound of many waters."* Have you ever stood at the edge of Niagara Falls and listened to the sound of those mighty waters pouring over the side? You have to shout to be heard by the person next to you.

John goes on here in chapter 14, verse 2 to further describe this voice as the *"voice of a great thunder"*. We are instantly reminded of the scene around God's throne in chapter 4, verse 5: *"And out of the throne proceeded lightings and thunderings and voices"*. All of this symbolizes great power and great authority.

Then John hears music! It is evident that God loves music. Every time we see a scene around the throne it is always accompanied by glorious music. And this is no different as John hears the sound of many harps. I suppose this is where the rumor got started that all we have to do after we die is lie around on a cloud and play a harp. Folks, we will have plenty to do besides playing a harp, and we will see that as we get closer to the end of the Book.

After the harpers start to play, these 144,000 begin to sing a new song. Revelation 14:3: *"And they sung as it were a new song before the throne, and before the four beasts, and the elders: and no man could learn that song but the hundred and forty and four thousand, which were redeemed from the earth."* The harpers are harping, and the 144,000 are singing before the throne of God. And who else are they singing in front of? The King James Version says "four beasts," but we know that this is a faulty translation. Ten other translations render this as either "four living creatures" or "four living ones." Even the New King James Version which usually only corrects grammar, changes this to four living creatures.

We covered in chapter 5 the reasons we believe that these are four powerful angels. In fact, we said earlier that they are angels that are classified as seraphim because they devote their time to praise and worship. And here, they are singing before the elders. Again, in chapter 5, we saw very clearly that these 24 elders are a picture of the Church, the Bride of Christ. And there is no doubt the martyrs are the ones who were killed for the testimony of Christ during the Tribulation Period. Perhaps they are the ones playing the harps.

Scripture is clear that no one can learn this song except the 144,000. The KJV is a little confusing here. In the Greek, the word "learn" means "to understand through experience." In other words, as an illustration, you might sing along with Jewish holocaust survivors about how God protected them throughout that terrible ordeal with the Nazis. But you could not sing it out of experience. That is what these witnesses are doing. As the saying goes, "You had to have been there." These 144,000 are the only ones who know first hand what it was like to go all the way through the Great Tribulation for 3½ years with God's watch care.

This old world has seen lots of pain, heartache and bloodshed. Think of Attila the Hun and all his barbarians who swept across Europe leaving a trail of violence in their path. Think of Genghis Khan and his mighty forces which slew thousands. Think of Alexander the Great who conquered the then known world. And the wars in our day – World War II in the Pacific where on the little island of Iwo Jima 7,000 American Marines and 21,000 Japanese troops were killed in just a few weeks.[7] All of those awful, terrible times were just rehearsals for what the Antichrist is going to put the world through. And these 144,000 witnesses saw every bit of it and survived with the help of Almighty God. No wonder it is their song, and no one else can share in it. We can only listen, and praise God for His faithfulness. Don't you know these 144,000 evangelists will have some stories to tell, and some miracles to share?!

I cannot understand why some Christians never open their mouths during the singing in church. You don't have to sing on key. You are not trying to please those around you – you are singing from your heart to the Lord! When God saves us, He puts a song in our hearts, and we should praise Him in song with whatever natural abilities He has given us. I praise God that I have a pastor who sings along with the congregation instead of reading his sermon notes as many pastors do during the singing.

During the writing of this book, I was battling a tough case of non-Hodgkin's lymphoma. It was in remission for years, but then came back. My oncologist, Dr. Orr, said it is like an insect that has built up a resistance to an insecticide. This cancer had built up a resistance and had to be treated with a heavier formula of Chemo. As a result, I could not take the infusion of Chemo in a day and come back for another in a week. It would be too much for my body. Instead, I had to go into the hospital, and have it administered via a slow 24 hour drip over a five day period. This process had to be repeated each month for 6 months. The bright side of this is that Boone Pickens Cancer Hospital had free Wi-Fi and a nice desk by my bed. And on days when I felt like it, I made good progress writing this book. I have certainly prayed that the Lord would let me finish it, that it would advance His kingdom and that He would keep me from any gross misrepresentations. My, how can I ever repay the scores of people who told me they were praying for me every day? And I could feel those prayers!

One evening midway through my treatments I was home between hospital stays. It was 3 AM. I was in my den recliner with elevated fever, and not feeling well at all. I turned on "Pandora" on the TV and began listening to Gospel Music. It was not long until I heard one of the most powerful songs I have ever heard. I think God especially sent it to me that night. It was *"God Wants to Hear You Sing."* My spirit soared and I began to feel better. That song lifted me right to God's Throne of Grace. The words and music were written by Rodney Griffin. My friend, Kenny, sang it later in our church. I must share the words with you ....

"God wants to hear you sing when the waves are crashing 'round you, when the fiery darts surround you, when despair is all you see; God wants to hear your voice when the wisest man has spoken – and said your circumstance is as hopeless as can be – that's when God wants to hear you sing!" That song will encourage anyone who is having a tough time! Don't ever let anyone steal your song! God wants to hear you sing![8] The Book of Revelation is full of sorrow and sadness, but it is also filled with songs of redemption. When the Lamb comes into the picture, a song breaks forth.

Revelation 14:4-5: *"These are they which were not defiled with women; for they are virgins. These are they which follow the Lamb whithersoever He goeth. These were redeemed from among men, being the first fruits unto God and to the Lamb. And in their mouth was found no guile: for they are without fault before the throne of God."*

Scripture says that these are virgins. Commentators cannot agree on what this means. Some say the 144,000 will be celibate, while others believe this is talking about the fact that they did not commit spiritual fornication by worshipping the Antichrist or his image. It is difficult to say who is right, but we can be sure of some things: 1) during the Tribulation Period, it will be difficult for these witnesses to be married and be good spouses, and 2) they will remain pure in spite of living in a world filled with immorality and spiritual fornication.

Hal Lindsey says, "Most Bible commentators agree that the celibacy of these men refers not so much to sexual purity (although this is important), but to be separate from spiritual fornication and adultery."[9] And that old lovable commentator, Dr. J. Vernon McGee, said, "This is probably referring to chastity in both the literal and the spiritual sense. And this makes good sense, by the way."[10] I can just hear him saying that! This truth is also pictured in II Corinthians 11:2 concerning the Church, the Bride of Christ. God says: *"For I am jealous over you with godly jealousy: for I have espoused you to one husband, that I may present you as a chaste virgin to Christ."* God wants His people to be pure and holy, not entangled with Satan and his evil empire.

As we saw previously in verse 4, these witnesses were *"redeemed from among men."* This means they have been bought by the blood of Jesus Christ. In this verse, there is also a play on words relating to the harvest. During the time of reaping, there is always the "*first fruits*," then the "*general harvest*" and then the "*gleanings.*" We have seen previously that when the Bible speaks of the Rapture, it says that Christ is the first fruits; then they that are Christ's at His coming which is the general harvest (I Corinthians 15:23). But here in verse 3, it speaks of these saints being the "first fruits." I take it to mean that these are the first ones who are saved during the Tribulation with the greater harvest to follow.

Immediately after the Rapture, many Jewish scholars will know the Scriptures well enough that they will realize that Christ has taken His Bride to Heaven. When we were in Israel, we had a Jewish guide named "Shai Mater" – a burly mountain of a man. If we had found ourselves in a firefight, I would certainly want Shai on my side. Shai was very knowledgeable in all areas of the Bible which made him a proficient guide; however, his knowledge of the New Testament was head knowledge, not heart knowledge. They were just facts to him. He knew them, but did not accept them. There will be thousands of Jews like Shai who will realize that the Rapture has taken place, and what Scripture says the consequences will be. They will fall on their faces and ask God to forgive them and save them. And thus, they will be the first ones converted after the Rapture. Many no doubt will be part of the 144,000 who will become God's flaming evangelists.

Consider what the mission of these 144,000 witnesses will be. Their task will be to defy the Antichrist and expose his False Prophet. Their calling will be to preach the Gospel in a day when just to mention the name of Jesus will mean a trip to the guillotine. These witnesses will gloriously succeed in their mission as evidenced by the number of converts that no man can number. And so, they will stand with Christ on Mt. Zion when He comes back, and be given the honor of singing their new song to all the redeemed. What a day that will be!

Verse 5 tells us that no guile was found in their mouths. A guileless man is not a sinless man; he is one who has nothing to hide. He is not deceitful. One of the lesser known apostles was Nathaniel. In the 1ˢᵗ chapter of John, we read that Philip ran to Nathaniel and said, *"We have found the Messiah (which means the Christ)"* (John 1:41b ESV). And when Nathaniel learned that Jesus was from Nazareth, he asked, *"Nazareth! Can anything good come from there?"* And Philip said to him, *"Come and see"* (John 1:46 NIV). So Nathaniel decided he would go and check Him out. And when Jesus saw Nathaniel, He said, *"Behold an Israelite indeed, in whom is no guile!"* (John 1:47). Jesus did not mean that Nathaniel was sinless. He meant that what you see is what you get. Nathaniel had no deceit in him – he was a straight shooter.

This large company in Revelation 14:5 is not only described as having no guile in their mouths, but are also without fault before the throne of God. How can they be without fault? It is because they are not appearing there in any righteousness of their own, but they are saved by the same precious blood that today makes every believer faultless before the throne of God. Jude 24 tells us that God is *"able to keep you from falling, and to present you faultless before the presence of His glory with exceeding joy."*

We continue in the 14ᵗʰ chapter, but before we finish, we will see six different angels come upon the scene. The first one is in verse 6: *"And I saw another angel fly in the midst of Heaven, having the everlasting gospel to preach unto them that dwell on the earth, and to every nation, and kindred, and tongue, and people."* At least one respected commentator, Dr. Arno Gabelein, says, "The angel must not be taken as a literal angel. The preaching of any Gospel to those who dwell on earth is never committed to angels, but to men."[11] It is true that during the Age of Grace in which we now live the Gospel is presented to the world by Christian men and women – preachers, teachers and everyday laypersons. God has always used various means and messengers to present His message. In the Old Testament, He often used angels to bring a word from the Lord. In fact, the word angel means messenger; and Hebrews 2:2 tells us that the word spoken by God's angels is steadfast.

During the Tribulation, we have seen God use 144,000 Jewish evangelists. We have seen Him use the two faithful witnesses of chapter 11. And since the Bible says this is an angel, I choose to believe that it is an angel, and it probably is Gabriel since his job seems to be that of delivering important messages. He was sent to Daniel to deliver an important message; he was sent to Zechariah to tell him that Elizabeth would have a child named John.

Gabriel was sent to Mary to deliver the good news about the birth of Jesus. So, it seems fitting that Gabriel would be chosen to deliver this most important message. So what is this message? We are told it is the everlasting Gospel! "Everlasting" means it does not change – it is the same Gospel as in the beginning.

If someone asks you, "What is the Gospel?" could you tell them? You don't have to guess.

Paul defines the Gospel for us in his first letter to the Corinthians, chapter 15, beginning at verse 1: *"Moreover, brethren, I declare unto you the Gospel which I preached unto you, which also ye have received, and wherein ye stand; by which ye are also saved, if ye keep in memory what I preached unto you, unless ye have believed in vain. For I delivered unto you first of all that which I also received,* [NOW FOLKS, HERE IS THE GOSPEL] *how that Christ died for our sins according to the Scriptures; And that He was buried, and that He rose again the third day according to the Scriptures."*

The very first mention of the Gospel – the "Good News" – is found in Genesis 3:15 where God says, *"I will put enmity between thee and the woman, and between thy seed and her seed; it shall bruise thy head, and thou shalt bruise his heel."* In modern English, God is saying there will be a struggle – a conflict between good and evil –between the promised Seed of the woman (Jesus) and Satan. Satan will bruise Jesus' heel, that is, administer a hurtful, but non-lethal wound which Satan did at the cross. But Jesus will administer a lethal blow to Satan's head when Jesus casts Satan into Hell.

The Gospel is still the same – it hasn't changed – it is still the everlasting Gospel. In II Timothy 3:15, Paul is writing to Timothy: *"And that from a child thou hast known the Holy Scriptures, which are able to make thee wise unto salvation through faith which is in Christ Jesus."* The only Scriptures Timothy had at the time were the Old Testament scrolls, and Paul says they speak of Christ and how to be saved.

Do you remember that after Christ's resurrection, two men were on their way to a little village called Emmaus, a suburb of Jerusalem? This is recorded in Luke chapter 24. As they were walking, they were joined by a third man, but they did not know it was Jesus. Jesus said, "Why are you so sad?" And they said, "Oh, you must be a stranger here, and the only one in Jerusalem who doesn't know what has happened! This Jesus from Nazareth who did mighty works among us – we so hoped that He was the Messiah who would save Israel. But, the rulers crucified Him and now all is lost." After listening to them complain for a while, Jesus said to them, *"You are so thick-headed! So slow-hearted. Why can't you simply believe all that the prophets said? Don't you see that these things had to happen, that the Messiah had to suffer and only then enter into His glory?"* (Luke 24:25-26 The Message). In other words – the everlasting Gospel of Christ has not changed!

In the following references, the everlasting Gospel is called:

The Glorious Gospel in II Corinthians 4:4
The Gospel of peace in Ephesians 6:15
The Gospel of the kingdom in Mark 1:14
The Gospel of God in I Peter 4:17

The Gospel of Christ in Romans 15:19
The Gospel of the grace of God in Acts 20:24
The Gospel of salvation in Ephesians 1:13

The truth of the matter is that the everlasting gospel encompasses the complete work of Christ from eternity to eternity. And now in Revelation 14:6, we see that this angel is flying, as the KJV says, in the "midst of Heaven." The NIV says, "in mid-air" – it is the atmosphere that surrounds the earth. And notice that this message is preached to every nation, and kindred, and tongue and people. No one is left out. And since from a time frame, chapter 14 is a flash-forward almost to the end of the Tribulation Period. I am reminded of what Jesus said in Matthew 24:14: *"And this gospel of the kingdom shall be preached in all the world for a witness unto all nations; and then shall the end come."* God always gives adequate warning before He pours out His judgment. But it seems that every time God sends a messenger to offer mercy, the majority of the people blaspheme God that much more. One exception comes to mind – when Jonah preached "repent or be destroyed" to the inhabitants of Nineveh, the Ninevites repented and God kept His word and spared their city.

We find that this mighty angel is flying across the skies and by God's order, is giving those on earth one final chance to be saved. God is so merciful. He is not willing that any should perish. And so, in verse 7, this angel is speaking: *"Saying with a loud voice, 'Fear God, and give glory to Him; for the hour of His judgment is come; and worship Him that made Heaven, and earth, and the sea, and the fountains of waters.'"* The two things that the earth dwellers need to do is: *"fear God and give glory to Him."* The emphasis is on God as the Creator of Heaven and earth, the sea and the fountains of water. This is a starting point. God's right to judge men is based on the fact that He created them in the first place. If God is not Creator, He can hardly be their Savior. If we think that godless evolution is running rampant now, think what will be taught when the Holy Spirit and the Church are gone and the Antichrist is in control.

Men and women have to acknowledge God as their Creator, and then they will see their need for Christ as their Lord and Savior. No one during the Tribulation can ever accuse God of being unfair. Anyone who wants to find their way to Him will have the Gospel message available. The object of the angel's message – the everlasting Gospel – is to warn the inhabitants of the earth against the Antichrist and seek to turn them toward God. The critical point of the message is the word "worship." It is the same word used four times in the previous chapter and means "bow the knee to."[12] But what does it mean to "fear God?" Satan would have us believe it means to be afraid of Him, but this is incorrect. To fear God means to have a holy respect for Him, to believe He exists, and believe He reigns and that He will judge the world in righteousness. This kind of fear is the beginning of wisdom (Proverbs 1:7).

Verse 8: *"And there followed another angel, saying, 'Babylon is fallen, is fallen, that great city, because she made all nations drink of the wine of the wrath of her fornication.'"* Here is another angel on the heels of the first angel who was proclaiming the everlasting gospel, and the consequences of ignoring his warning. But this angel has an announcement instead of a warning. He announces that Babylon has fallen. Since this is a flash-forward for mortals, it is viewed in the eyes of God as though it has already happened. In actuality, it will happen at the end of the Tribulation.

The figure of speech used in this verse regarding Babylon making the nations drink of the wine of her fornication is very graphic and calls to mind Jeremiah 51:7: *"Babylon hath been a golden cup in the LORD's hand, that made all the earth drunken: the nations have drunken of her wine; therefore the nations are mad."* Think for a moment about the significance of Babylon. Of the thousands and thousands of cities around the globe, why does God single out Babylon to tell of its collapse? It is because Babylon was where evil, pagan religion originated. It represents all the anti-God philosophies and "isms" that have tried to blind the eyes of man since time began.

Going back into the early history of mankind in Genesis, we find in the sixth chapter of Genesis that man had degenerated about as far into depravity as he could go. Jesus said that same culture in Noah's time will exist in the last days. Matthew 24:37: *"But as the days of Noah were, so shall also the coming of the Son of Man be."*

What was running rampant in Noah's day? Violence and sexual immorality. We know this to be true because in Romans chapter 1 God describes such a culture that requires Him to pour out His judgment. What sins are most characteristic of our culture today? Violence and sexual immorality. No one can dispute that.

When God poured out His judgment in Noah's day, only eight humans survived to propagate the race. The folks who believe in the goodness of man had a perfect chance right there to prove it. Starting over with eight people in the family, the human race was headed up by a man named Noah that God in Ezekiel 14:14 said was one of the three most righteous men who ever lived. If man was going to get better and better morally and spiritually as our humanistic evolutionists teach, there was no better time in the history of mankind than right here. But, we see the opposite happening. And it did not take hundreds of years. It took only two generations!

One of the men on the Ark with Noah was his son, Ham. Later, Ham had a son, Cush. And Cush had a son, Nimrod. You can read all about Nimrod in the 10th and 11th chapters of Genesis. It says Nimrod was a mighty hunter – a powerful man – in today's world he would probably be called a superstar. He founded a city which he called Babel. It was there that man's pride reached its zenith. The people said, "Look who we are – look what we can do! Nothing can stop us from building a tower than can reach into the heavens itself" (Genesis 11:4).

In other words they said, "We don't need God. We can be gods ourselves. And God judged them for that pride. He scattered them across the globe and confused their language. But the city of Babel, later called Babylon, continued to be a hotbed of spiritual infidelity and idolatry. Babylon reached its zenith and earthly glory about 600 years before Christ during the reign of King Nebuchadnezzar.

Babylon was so noted for its idolatry that the very mention of its name conjured up visions of all the heathen gods made with wood and stone. It is equally bad in America today. It is called sin, but most want to give it some other name that does not sound so offensive. Prophetically in Scripture we find that when Babylon is mentioned, it could refer to three different entities. First, it is a literal city in Iraq on the banks of the Euphrates River. Saddam Hussein poured millions of dollars into the rebuilding of this city in hopes that it would prove to be a tourist mecca for the region. So far, it has flopped as a tourist attraction. It is pretty hard to attract tourists when your primary industry is building car bombs for suicide bombers.

I believe that the Antichrist will make Babylon into a showcase of beauty during his short tenure. There are some pretty good indications that there will be three primary cities that the Antichrist will use as a base of operations during the last days. These are: Babylon, Rome and Jerusalem. It seems that during the Tribulation Period, the Antichrist will make his headquarters in Rome; the False Prophet will make his headquarters in Jerusalem; and they will use Babylon as a trophy city to show the world what it can achieve under the leadership of the Antichrist.

When we get to the 18th chapter of Revelation, we will see that the city of Babylon will fall by God's judgment in one hour, much the same way that Sodom and Gomorrah did. Babylon is also used to refer to a religious system as we will find in Revelation 17 bearing in mind that it is the fountainhead of idolatry. "Spiritual Babylon" in the last days will be the culmination of what we see going on in the ecumenical movement of our day. "Ecumenical" is a big theological term which simply means the coming together of organized religion. It sounds good. As one liberal theologian said, "If all the churches could come together into one, it would erase the embarrassment of so many different denominations."

That is the goal of the World Council of Churches. That is the goal of the National Council of Churches. That is the goal of the Roman Catholic Church. It sounds so wonderful. But there is a greater danger than different denominations. It is all of the denominations giving up their respective doctrines in order to come together in a one-world religion that has no basis in sound doctrine. And it is going to happen! The Bible says that after the true Church has been called home at the Rapture, the false church headed up by the False Prophet will unite to give their allegiance to the Antichrist.

The word Babylon is also used to refer to a Satanic political system run by the Antichrist as described in Revelation 18. In this flash-forward in the 14th chapter, the fact that the angel says that Babylon "is fallen – "is fallen" – is making a double emphasis. Perhaps this refers to the fall of both the religious system and the political system as we approach the end of the Tribulation Period. We know both will fall, and we will see the actual details of the fall of Babylon when we get to chapters 17 and 18.

"And the third angel followed them, saying with a loud voice, 'If any man worship the Beast and his image, and receive his mark in his forehead, or in his hand, the same shall drink of the wine of the wrath of God, which is poured out without mixture into the cup of His indignation; and he shall be tormented with fire and brimstone in the presence of the holy angels, and in the presence of the Lamb: And the smoke of their torment ascendeth up for ever and ever: and they have no rest day nor night, who worship the Beast and his image, and whosoever receiveth the mark of his name'" (Revelation 14: 9-11).

First, note that this angel has a loud voice. Everyone on earth can hear him. The people cannot say they were not warned. The angel's message is to remind the earth dwellers of the eternal consequences of selling one's soul for a loaf of bread. This is sad to read, but God's patience has finally run out. We have seen previously in our study that if any person takes the Mark of the Beast, there is no turning back for them. It's the end of the line. It means they have forever turned their heart and soul over to the Devil.

As this verse 10 says, *"The same shall drink of the wine of the wrath of God, which is poured out without mixture into the cup of his indignation; and he shall be tormented with fire and brimstone in the presence of the holy angels, and in the presence of the Lamb."* Notice, it says this wine of the wrath of God is *"without mixture."* That means it is pure wrath. It was the custom to dilute strong wine with either water or some other softer liquid to quell its strength. But this wine of the wrath of God is without mixture. It is not diluted – there is no mercy or grace found in this cup of judgment. It is the dregs – the bottom of the cup as we would say.

The Jehovah's Witnesses go to great lengths to show that man's soul is not immortal, and, if he does not go to Heaven, he is annihilated – he ceases to exist. But they say, God does not do this until man is resurrected and after he sees the errors of his ways, i.e., that the teachings of Jehovah's Witnesses are true after all – and man is given a second chance to get it right. If he refuses to do so, then he is annihilated. The Mormon teachings are similar in that after death, man keeps spiritually evolving. It may take eons of years, but he will eventually be as God is now. But we will never catch God because He will be evolving into something greater. Nevertheless, they say there will be no such thing as eternal punishment. In fact, as far as I can tell, Judaism and Christianity are the only two major religions that teach eternal punishment – and the percentages of those believing that, have dissipated greatly in the past few decades.

Jesus had more to say about Hell than He did about Heaven. That is because He does not want anyone to go there. It was prepared for the Devil and his angels, but man will go there if he is persistent in rejecting Christ. We are also told in verse 10 that Hell is visible to the holy angels, and to the Lord Jesus Christ. It is not said that it is visible to the saints of God, and I doubt that it is.

Verse 11 says that the smoke of their torment goes up for ever and ever. They have no rest day or night. Isaiah 57:21 (NIV) says, *"There is no peace, says my God, for the wicked."* Not only will there be eternal suffering, there will be eternal fatigue. This does not make me gleeful. In fact, it makes me very sad. But imagine how God feels about this when He allowed His own Son to die on a cross at the hands of cruel individuals in order to provide a way of escape, and then, there are those who instead of joyfully accepting provision, blatantly say, "Aw….we don't care about You or Your Son!"

Why one person accepts Christ and another person, looking at the same evidence, rejects Him, I do not know. Billy Graham said that the same sun that melts the butter hardens the clay.[13] All we can do is be faithful in witnessing and presenting the Gospel and leave the rest to the Holy Spirit. The Bible says that the unbelievers will *"drink of the wine of the wrath of God"* (Revelation 14:10). But, that is not your destiny if you have put your trust in Christ. On the night of the Last Supper, Jesus uttered these words: *"But I say unto you, I will not drink henceforth of this fruit of the vine, until that day when I drink it new with you in my Father's Kingdom"* (Matthew 26:29). A very serious question that everyone should carefully consider is this: "Will you be drinking of the wine of the wrath of God, or will you be drinking that new wine with Christ in God's Kingdom?"

Let us look at another aspect of this one-world religion. First, keep in mind that the Holy Spirit has been removed from the earth at this point, making it more difficult for the average person to embrace TRUTH. And secondly, the false religions of the world will make it easier to embrace this one-world religion. Let me give you some prime examples. The Jehovah's Witnesses organization is a false religion. It has embraced the teachings of Charles Taze Russell and J. F. Rutherford whose views are diametrically opposed to what Scripture teaches. Since the KJV of the Bible does not support their outrageous doctrines, they had to come up with their own version of the Bible – *The New World Translation*. It was translated from the original Hebrew and Greek without having a single member of the translating team who were proficient in Hebrew or Greek. All of the world's top linguistic experts, whether they are Christians or atheists, say that *The New World Translation* is about the worst example of translating they have ever seen.[14]

Some have said that the Jehovah's Witnesses' translating team simply took the writings of Charles Russell and J.F. Rutherford, and translated the Scriptures to support the doctrines that those men had written down in the late 19th and early 20th Centuries instead of taking the earliest Biblical manuscripts available and translating what these documents said. If the Jehovah's Witnesses are willing to accept the doctrines of Russell and Rutherford as truth being handed down by God within the last 135 years, then they will have no problem accepting another smooth talking prophet when he comes upon the scene in the end times.

Consider the Church of the Latter Day Saints – the Mormons. If they accept that a man named Joseph Smith, less than 200 years ago, was given new doctrines that almost render the Bible useless, then they will have no problem accepting the message of a new slick talking messenger – the Antichrist. If Christian Scientists accept the visions and writings of Mary Baker Eddy from some 130 years ago as being more valuable than the Bible itself, they will have no problem accepting the message of this clever emissary – the Antichrist.

There is another group, maybe larger than those we have mentioned. It is that vast group of New Agers who are waiting for those Spirit Masters of the Universe who will tell us how we too can become gods. It includes those humanists who want to exalt man to the highest pedestal. I encourage you not to accept everything that is preached or taught, but do as the Bereans did. They *"searched the Scriptures daily, whether those things were so"* (Acts 17:11). Mohammed came on the scene 500 years after Christ. The Muslims listened to him rather than Jesus because Mohammed was the "most recent prophet from God." The tragic fact is that another prophet will arise. We know him as the Antichrist (the first Beast) and the unsuspecting will listen to him.[15]

All these various groups that are willing to listen to the most recent message purported to come from God will back the Antichrist to the hilt and pledge their loyalty to him. These are the ones – along with those indifferent souls who could not care less who is in charge as long as they get food to eat – who will readily deny Christ and accept the Mark of the Beast. All these new revelations from God have appeared in the last couple of hundred years even though God warned us, "[God] *in these last days has spoken to us in His Son, whom He appointed heir of all things, through whom also He made the world"* (Hebrews 1:2 NASB). You would have to close your eyes and ears to miss that one!

"Here is the patience of the saints: here are they that keep the commandments of God, and the faith of Jesus" (Revelation 14:12). These saints are facing the darkest time of the Tribulation. They will be pulling out their Bibles which have been secretly hidden away, and will be fervently reading what lies ahead. They will need this encouragement to stay strong!

Now we come to verse 13 of chapter 14. *"And I heard a voice from Heaven saying unto me, 'Write, Blessed are the dead which die in the Lord from henceforth: Yea, saith the Spirit, that they may rest from their labors and their works do follow them.'"* In our liberal seminaries across the country preachers are being taught that the Bible is full of myth, legend and superstition. One of my favorite commentators, Dr. J. Vernon McGee, calls them "liberal cemeteries." They say that the writers of the Bible, who were mostly uneducated men, had vivid imaginations, and they simply wrote down whatever came to mind. They even say that God never told them to write anything. They need to look at Exodus 34:27a, *"Write thou these words ...."*. And God proceeded to give Moses a list of rules and regulations for Israel.

Numbers 5:23a, God said, *"And the priest shall write these curses in a book."* And Numbers 33:2a says, *"And Moses wrote their goings out according to their journeys by the commandment of the LORD."* There are many, many such commands by God throughout the Bible. Then when you get to the Book of Revelation, you are overwhelmed with these writing commands. For example, in the first chapter, verse 11a John is told by Christ, *"What thou seest, write in a book ...."*. And in this very chapter we are studying, in verse 13, it says, *"And I heard a voice from Heaven saying unto me, Write ...."*. So you see the charge that the Bible was written by men who simply wrote down their fantasies has no merit. The Apostle Peter sums it up this way, *"For we have not followed cunningly devised fables, when we made known unto you the power and coming of our Lord Jesus Christ, but were eyewitnesses of His majesty"* (II Peter 1:16).

"Blessed are the dead which die in the Lord ...." (Revelation 14:13b). It would seem in death that every dream, every ambition, every hope is gone for good. Certainly for the non-Christian, death is a black hole. Others have described death as crossing a river and so, Thomas H. Ramsey wrote the song, *I Won't Have To Across Jordan Alone.* Here in verse 13, God says that when the Christians die, they will rest from their labors, and their works do follow them.

God says all those tasks, all those experiences and all those works will become an eternal reward for these dear saints. In fact, Scripture says in Psalm 56:8 that God collects all our tears in a bottle. That means He does not overlook a single one, but will comfort us as only He can.

God sees the tears that no one else sees. He hears the prayers that no one else hears. He sees that sacrificial gift that one can ill afford to give. But it is recorded in God's Book of Works, and those faithful folks will be eternally rewarded.

Death for the Christian is not a terrible experience. This world says, "Happy are the living." But the Bible says happy are the dead who die in the Lord. That is because it is changing this tired, worn out body for one that will never wear out. It is changing this corrupt world system of lying, cheating and sorrow into a glorious time of peace and joy. But, sadly this is not true for those who die and are not *"in the Lord."* They exchange the misery and suffering of this life for an even more hideous existence. Why would anyone want to do that? Why would anyone take such an awful gamble?

Scripture uses a beautiful expression for the death of a Christian. It is "resting." The Greek word is "koimeterion" and is where we get the English word cemetery – a sleeping place. The early Christians carefully laid their dead away. They believed, according to the Word and promise of God, that those who sleep in the dust of the ground will rise again. If you went to Rome today, you could visit the endless underground catacombs – places where the Christians laid to rest their beloved dead. The pagans and the heathen nations surrounding Israel burned their dead bodies. To them it was the end of all life; it was the end of the way; it was the end of every hope and dream without any future. But to the Christian, death was just falling asleep. With tender loving care, they laid their dead away, awaiting the final voice of the archangel and the sound of the trumpet when they will live again.

Expressing death as "sleep" for the Christian is used throughout the New Testament. In Luke, chapter 8, we read about a man named Jarius who was a ruler in the synagogue. He had heard of this healer – this miracle worker. And when he found Jesus, he fell down at His feet and pleaded with Jesus to come home with him. He had a problem. He only had one child, a little girl about 12 years of age, and she was desperately sick. Jarius said to Jesus, "Please come quickly. My daughter is dying." But as Jesus began to make His way to the man's house, He was besieged by throngs of people wanting to be healed of their infirmities. This slowed Jesus' pace, and shortly a servant came running and said, "Never mind. The daughter is dead." But with Jesus, death is not final. He has the last word!

Jesus proceeded to the house and took Peter, James and John inside with Him, along with the mother and the father of the little girl. All were weeping. But Jesus said, *"Why are you making a commotion and weeping? The child is not dead but sleeping"* (Mark 5:39 ESV). They knew she was dead, but to Jesus, there was not any difference between sleep and death because He is the Master of each. When Lazarus had been dead for four days, Jesus said to His disciples, *"Our friend Lazarus has fallen asleep, but now I will go and wake him up"* (John 11:11 NLT).

The Apostle Paul revealed to us that great mystery of the Rapture in I Thessalonians 4:13-14: *"But I would not have you to be ignorant, brethren, concerning them which are asleep, that ye sorrow not, even as others which have no hope. For if we believe that Jesus died and rose again, even so them also which sleep in Jesus will God bring with Him."* The Bible constantly depicts death for a Christian as the body falling asleep, but the spirit going directly to be with the Lord to await the resurrection.

The Bible does not prohibit nor condemn cremation. God can raise the dead, and put ashes back together the same as He can dust. In today's society, many have opted for cremation strictly because of cost considerations, and I do not begrudge anyone making that choice. But there is something to be said for the loving care that the early Christians gave to the body of one of their dead – coupled with the beautiful metaphors that our Lord used, comparing the death of one of His own with that of sleeping. The Greek word for rest does not carry the idea of inactivity. Instead, it means refreshment – it means revitalization. Our fatigue and weariness will be taken away, as Bro. Jim my pastor likes to say, "We will feel like we are 33 again."

I have heard this 13th verse used over and over at funerals: *"Blessed are the dead which die in the Lord,"* and they stop there. And that is certainly true as a principle – that when you die in the Lord, you are certainly blessed. But to be completely accurate in this passage, you must put it into context and add *"from henceforth."* What the Lord is saying here is that the Great Tribulation – the last 3½ years on earth – is SO AWFUL that the Lord is pronouncing a special blessing for those who die in the Lord HENCEFORTH – during the Great Tribulation. Why? Because it means that they are refusing to take the Mark of the Beast and, therefore, will be tortured, and put to death for not bowing their knee to the Antichrist. They become martyrs for Jesus Christ. As someone so aptly said, "Better to be killed by the Beast than to be tormented with him!"

To those enduring the suffering during the Tribulation, God's Word is patience. He says that the persecution will be intense during the Tribulation, but the time will be short in comparison to the glorious future for those who die in the Lord. He says that their works will follow them in the sense that these saints will be rewarded for their works and faithfulness to Christ. Describing the martyrs killed for their faithfulness to Christ, the writer of Hebrews in chapter 11, verse 38 says: *"Of whom the world was not worthy."* The Bible is consistent in this teaching: death is a blessing for those who die in the Lord. Psalm 116:15 says: *"Precious in the sight of the Lord is the death of His saints."* And Paul declared in Philippians 1:21: *"For to me to live is Christ, and to die is gain."*

In the great Rapture chapter, I Thessalonians chapter 4, the Apostle Paul tells us in verse 13, *"But I would not have you to be ignorant, brethren, concerning them which are asleep* – now listen to this – *that ye sorrow not, even as others which have no hope."* He is saying it is OK to weep when you lose a loved one. But you are crying because you will miss them, not because you will never see them again. I heard about a little 4 year old and his mother who went next door to comfort a man whose wife had just died. The little boy climbed up into the man's lap and laid his head on his shoulder. After the mother and son got back home, the mother asked her little boy, "Son, what did you say to him?" The boy said, "I didn't say anything – I just helped him cry." Sometimes when we do not know what to say to a grieving friend, maybe it is best that we just help them cry.

Maybe the following story will help illustrate what death is for a Christian. The doctor had just given his patient the bad news – the patient had only a few months to live. As the doctor was preparing to leave the examination room, the patient said to him, "Doctor, I'm afraid to die. Tell me what lies on the other side." Very quietly, the doctor said, "I am sorry, but I don't know." The patient said, "You don't know? I heard you are a Christian, and you don't know what is on the other side?" The doctor was holding the handle of the door. From the other side of the door came a sound of scratching and whining. As he opened the door, a dog sprang into the room and leaped on the doctor with an eager display of joy. Turning to the patient, the doctor said, "Did you notice my dog? He's never been in this room before. He didn't know what was inside. He knew nothing except that his master was here and when the door opened, he sprang in without fear. I know little of what is on the other side of death, but I know my Master is there, and when the door opens, I will leap through it with gladness and without fear."[16]

There is no scene more graphic and unsettling than the vision John records at the end of this chapter. Just the awesome description of the unfolding of God's judgment upon the earth should strike terror in the hearts of those who have not trusted Christ. *"And I looked, and behold a white cloud, and upon the cloud one sat like unto the Son of man, having on His head a golden crown, and in His hand a sharp sickle"* (Revelation 14:14).

We have a tendency to forget that the Apostle John is seeing history in advance – he is seeing the future as though it is happening now. He says, *"And I looked …."* and then he proceeds to write down what he saw. He sees a white cloud and sitting upon it was none other than the Lord Jesus Christ Himself. Our first observation is that the cloud is white signifying purity and righteousness.

Secondly, Christ has long been associated with the clouds. These clouds depict what is called the "Shekinah Glory" – the dazzling brightness of God. It was this cloud by day that guided the Hebrew children in their trek to the Promised Land (Exodus 13:21, 22). When Jesus ascended in the first chapter of Acts, this cloud received Him out of their sight (Acts 1:9). The same chapter says that Jesus will come again in like manner (Acts 1:11). And do not forget, at the Rapture you and I will be caught up together *"in the clouds"* (I Thessalonians 4:17).

Referring to the return of Christ at the end of the Tribulation, Matthew 24:30 says, *"And then shall appear the sign of the Son of man in Heaven: …. and they shall see the Son of man coming in the clouds of Heaven with power and great glory."* In the first chapter of Revelation, verse 7, John said, *"Behold, He cometh with the clouds."* And here in Revelation 14, John sees Christ sitting on a cloud. Judgment is about to be executed.

We have a preview of the Battle of Armageddon from verse 14 through the end of this chapter. This is actually a campaign between good and evil that comprises many battles. The battle referred to in these seven verses is the last battle of this campaign. And we will get a detailed look at the end of this battle when we come to Revelation 19, and Christ returns from Heaven to defeat the Beast and his Satan inspired armies. The crown in verse 14 identifies Christ as the King of kings, and the sickle signifies a coming harvest. Nowhere in this Book of wonders are there more remarkable visions than these two, closing the 14th chapter of the Apocalypse. It should strike terror in the hearts of all who do not know Christ as Savior. In Revelation 14:7, we had the announcement that the hour of His judgment had come.

There is a lot of confusion relating to this harvest. Many, such as our Churches of Christ and Catholic friends, believe that this pictures one general harvest. They are persuaded that these two visions – that of the harvest and that of the winepress – depict the same thing. They teach that there will be no Rapture, but that everything will continue the same until Christ comes back, and then sets up a general judgment dividing the sheep from the goats.

I can see how they might come to the conclusion that these two visions are the same. One is recorded in verses 15-16 and one in verses 17-20. There are similarities in the two. But, first I would ask, if these two visions depict the same event, why are there two visions? Let us look closer at what the Scripture says. We see there is a sharp sickle in both visions. And there is a reaping in both visions; but there the similarities end. We see vast differences that show the visions are not at all alike.

For the sake of distinction, I will call them the harvest and the vintage; the harvest being the gathering of the crop and the vintage being the crushing of the grapes to produce the wine or grape juice. The Son of God oversees the harvest because He is the One who separates the wheat from the chaff. The Lord said in Matthew 13 that the wheat and the tares will grow together until the time of the end, and then the tares will be bundled together to be burned while the wheat is gathered into the Lord's barn. It is a harvest of discrimination.

Today, discrimination is a bad word. But it should not be. It simply means to make an informed distinction between people or things. And here, the Lord is making a distinction between those that are lost and those that are saved. So, we see there is a discrimination in the first vision, but in the second, presided over by an angel of God, there is no discrimination. It is the harvest of the grapes of wickedness. In the vintage, they are not sorted out, but as a whole are cast into the winepress of the wrath of God.

Let us get back to the harvest for a moment. We find the description of the harvest in verses 15 and 16: *"And another angel came out of the Temple, crying with a loud voice to Him that sat on the cloud, 'Thrust in thy sickle and reap: for the time is come for Thee to reap; for the harvest of the earth is ripe.' And He that sat on the cloud thrust in His sickle on the earth; and the earth was reaped."*

Keep in mind that even at the end of this awful Tribulation Period, God has some of His own children on the earth. And in this reaping, there are both the saved and unsaved. There are God's children who are the wheat, and there are the children of the Evil One who are the tares. Look at Matthew 13:24-30: *"Another parable put He forth unto them, saying, 'The kingdom of Heaven is likened unto a man which sowed good seed in his field; But while men slept, his enemy came and sowed tares among the wheat, and went his way. But when the blade was sprung up, and brought forth fruit, then appeared the tares also.' So the servants of the householder came and said unto him, 'Sir, didst not thou sow good seed in thy field? From whence then hath it tares?' He said unto them, 'An enemy hath done this.' The servants said unto Him, 'Wilt thou then that we go and gather them up?' But He said, 'Nay; lest while ye gather up the tares, ye root up also the wheat with them. Let both grow together until the harvest': and in the time of harvest I will say to the reapers,*

'Gather ye together first the tares, and bind them in bundles to burn them: but gather the wheat into my barn.'"

Then, after the multitudes had dispersed, Jesus' disciples came to Him and asked the meaning of all this. So, He explained this parable to them as recorded in Matthew 13:37b-43: *"He that soweth the good seed is the Son of man; the field is the world; the good seed are the children of the kingdom; but the tares are the children of the wicked one; The enemy that sowed them is the devil; the harvest is the end of the world; and the reapers are the angels. As therefore the tares are gathered and burned in the fire; so shall it be in the end of this world. The Son of man shall send forth His angels, and they shall gather out of His kingdom all things that offend, and them which do iniquity; and shall cast them into a furnace of fire: there shall be wailing and gnashing of teeth. Then shall the righteous shine forth as the sun in the kingdom of their Father. Who hath ears to hear, let him hear."*

Notice the Lord oversees this harvest. No one who has placed their trust in Jesus will be lost to the fire. He carefully watches the entire process, and not one of His children will be forgotten or overlooked. You can be assured of that. *"For God is not unfair. He will not forget how hard you have worked for Him and how you have shown your love to Him by caring for other Christians, as you still do"* (Hebrews 6:10 NLT).

Jesus describes Himself as the Good Shepherd. He said, *"My sheep hear My voice, and I know them, and they follow Me"* (John 10:27). I would ask someone who believes that you can lose your salvation, "If you are His sheep, and He knows you, how can you ever be lost unless the Shepherd fails to do His job?" When a shepherd is tending his sheep, it is not the sheep's responsibility to stay close to the shepherd! No, if one is ever lost, it proves that person was not one of the sheep in the first place. The Bible calls them goats. So Christ is overseeing the harvest, but an angel is commissioned to tend to the vintage where God's wrath is poured out.

Scripture gives us a very telling insight into this that many people miss. It says they shall be cast *"into the furnace of fire: there shall be wailing and gnashing of teeth"* (Matthew 13:42). "Wailing" – that is worse than crying, worse than sobbing. It is a hopeless, haunting, howling from the depths of their soul. Gnashing of teeth means that the wicked are still unrepentant. They are still angry. They would strike out at God if they only could. This tells me that the residents of Hell will not go through eternity being sorrowful about their sins. They are going through eternity with a deep-seated hatred toward God, snarling and gnashing their teeth at the One on the throne.

Today, we see people unconcerned and uninterested about the things of God. Tomorrow, these same people will have a bitter hatred for Him. Oh, why don't they come to Him while there is still time and let Him change their hearts?! He is the ultimate heart doctor. He promises to replace that bad heart with one that will be pure and clean and filled with love! Don't miss an opportunity to tell your friends and relatives about this life-changing doctor.

Take a minute and look at the differences between the two crops being reaped. There is a harvest of wheat and a harvest of tares. Wheat is a beautiful picture and symbol of God's children. When it ripens, the full, rich heads are bowed to the earth. When the tares ripen, they stand up erect – full of pride and ego. But as the children of God mature and grow in grace, they humble themselves in the presence of God, and bow before Him. But a church member who is proud of himself, proud of his goodness, proud of his personal accomplishments, he is on dangerous ground if his motives are not pure. The more we grow in grace and in the knowledge of the Lord, the more we will be like the wheat. Our faces will bow toward the earth, humbled by the goodness and grace of God. We have an excellent example in Isaiah the prophet. When Isaiah saw the Lord, high and lifted up in all His glory, Isaiah cried out, *"Woe is me! For I am lost; for I am a man of unclean lips"* (Isaiah 6:5a ESV). His pride was not to be found.

The finer and nobler the children of God are, the more they resemble wheat. They bow in humility and thanksgiving. Wheat ripens upward, but dies downward. As the grain ripens unto God, the stalk and the roots that hold on to the earth die downward. As we grow Godward and heavenward toward the end of our journey, more and more there will be the relaxing of our hold upon this earth and this life, until finally, as the old song says, when we near the gates of Heaven, "The things of earth will grow strangely dim in the light of His glory and grace."[17]

Here is one final observation about the wheat as a picture of God's children. Wheat is an annual, and must be reaped in successive harvests. As the sun beats down upon it, it turns brown and ripens to death, and then to the harvest. So it is with God's children of the earth. In the trials of life, in the heat of the sun and the winds of the storm, we are helpless before it. In the dark hours of trial and anxiety, I have held the hands of many in my Sunday school class, and when I have asked what I can do, the answer is always the same. "Just pray for me."

God's children are not immune to the storms of life. If it were all sunshine and happiness, we would never experience the sweetness and blessedness of the presence and grace of God. It takes the sorrows to make us conscious of the joys. It takes old age and failing health to make us conscious of the glorious promises of Heaven with new resurrected bodies. This is God's way. This is the way He leads His dear children along. When life seems tough, just remember that we are the prize crop of wheat ripening toward God – we are His harvest!

So let us see how the vintage is described. We will find that it is total carnage. Verses 17-18: *"And another angel came out of the temple which is in Heaven, he also having a sharp sickle. And another angel came out from the altar, which had power over fire; and cried with a loud cry to Him that had the sharp sickle, saying, 'Thrust in thy sharp sickle, and gather the clusters of the vine of the earth; for her grapes are fully ripe.'"* This vision has reference to a very definite and horrible holocaust that is prophesied throughout the Word of God. First an angel comes out of the Temple in Heaven, and he has a sharp sickle. If any of you grew up on a farm, you are well acquainted with a sickle. It has a long handle and a curved blade used to cut down tall grass and stalks.

The angel is joined by another one who *"had power over fire"*. The parable is saying that the tares are going to be gathered into bundles and thrown into the fire. Notice this second angel comes out from the altar. This is the same altar in front of which the martyred souls in chapter 6 were crying out, *"O Sovereign Lord, holy and true, how long before you will judge and avenge our blood on those who dwell on the earth?"* (Revelation 6:10 ESV). And the angel with power over the fire comes to answer that prayer, and to deal with the injustice of mankind. And he says to the angel with the sickle, *"Gather the clusters of the vine of the earth; for her grapes are fully ripe"* (Revelation 14:18b).

This vine of the earth with these grapes representing wickedness is a counterfeit of the True Vine, the Lord Jesus Christ, of whom we are His branches, saved to bring forth acceptable fruit. But the vine of the earth represents unbelief and blasphemy. And so, we read: *"And the angel thrust in his sickle into the earth, and gathered the vine of the earth, and cast it into the great winepress of the wrath of God"* (Revelation 14:19).

The Bible says what you sow, you shall reap (Galatians 6:7). And the time has come for the reaping of all the earth's wickedness. In the fifth chapter of Isaiah, God gives the people a parable. He builds a beautiful vineyard, but it brings forth wild or bitter grapes. It is a picture of all He has done for Israel, and Israel turns her back on God and He brings judgment upon her. Listen to the first five verses of Isaiah, chapter 5: *"Now will I sing to my well-beloved a song of my beloved touching his vineyard. My well-beloved hath a vineyard in a very fruitful hill: And he fenced it, and gathered out the stones thereof, and planted it with the choicest vine, and built a tower in the midst of it, and also made a winepress therein: and he looked that it should bring forth grapes, and it brought forth wild grapes. And now, O inhabitants of Jerusalem, and men of Judah, judge, I pray you, betwixt me and my vineyard. What could have been done more to my vineyard, that I have not done in it? Wherefore, when I looked at it should bring forth grapes, brought it forth wild grapes? And now go to; I will tell you what I will do to my vineyard: I will take away the hedge thereof, and it shall be eaten up; and break down the wall thereof, and it shall be trodden down."*

Jeremiah the prophet said in Jeremiah 2:21, *"Yet I had planted thee a noble vine, wholly a right seed: how then art thou turned into the degenerate plant of a strange vine unto me?"* Compare that to what Jesus said in John 15:1-2: *"I am the true vine, and my Father is the husbandman. Every branch in Me that beareth not fruit He taketh away: and every branch that beareth fruit, He purgeth it, that it may bring forth more fruit."* And again in John 15:6, He says, *"If a man abide not in me, he is cast forth as a branch, and is withered; and men gather them, and cast them into the fire, and they are burned."* Remember, this is a flash-forward – showing what will take place when Christ comes back at the end of the Tribulation Period.

In verse 20, the last verse in this 14th chapter, we get a preview of the awful devastation that awaits mankind during the Battle of Armageddon, right before Jesus returns to the earth. *"And the winepress was trodden without the city, and blood came out of the winepress, even unto the horse bridles, by the space of a thousand and six hundred furlongs."* Walter Scott, a respected commentator of 150 years ago, wrote: "We do not, of course, hold that the actual Valley of Jehoshaphat and Armageddon are literally meant." And I say, why not? That is what the Scripture says. We will look at the details of this battle when we come to it in the 16th chapter of the Revelation, but it specifically says that it will occur in a place called Armageddon. A friend of mine told me recently that he knows exactly where the battle of Armageddon will be fought – near Babylon in Iraq. Why can't people just accept what the Bible says?

The Bible tells us over and over that the battle of Armageddon will be fought in the Valley of Jezreel at the base of Megiddo. "Ar" in Armageddon is short for "har" which means "hill" or "mountain." And "mageddon" is a derivative of the word "Megiddo". Putting those together in the Hebrew, you have the "hill of Megiddo" – "Har Megiddo" – "Armageddon." And it is not a secret where this place is located. Most tour groups that go to Israel stand on the top of Mt. Carmel near Haifi in Northern Israel, and look southeastward over this vast plain known as the Valley of Armageddon. And you can go to the southern part of the valley to the city of Megiddo where King Solomon built his fabulous horse stables, and look northwestward from the other end of the Valley of Armageddon. The view is breathtaking.

Looking out over this same valley some 200 years ago, Napoleon said, "This valley would be ideal for the world's final battle."[18] Folks, he was Biblically ignorant, but he knew battlefields, and he knew this one had all the ingredients for the greatest battle of all time. This battle will have devastating results, but notice three words in verse 20, *"without the city."* In old English, this means, "outside the city."

Here is a comparable example. If you were to go to Israel and visit the site of the crucifixion of our Lord, you would be directed to two different sites. One is the traditional site owned by the Catholic Church. It is in Jerusalem and the site is inside one of the gaudiest places you have ever seen. It is beyond imagination with all the brass hanging lamps and incense burning. But there is another site, discovered in the late 1800's by British archaeologists.

This is a large garden tomb and is surrounded by beautiful flowers and a garden. Archaeologists uncovered as a large underground winery storage nearby. This was obviously owned by a rich man. No one knows if it is the tomb owned by the rich man, Joseph of Arimathea, who donated the tomb for the burial of Jesus, but it certainly has all the necessary ingredients. It is just outside the city whereas the traditional site controlled by the Catholic Church is inside the city.[19] Why is this important? There is a verse in Hebrews that says Jesus was crucified outside the city gates – probably on the road to Damascus as a warning to others who would rebel against the Roman crown. *"So also Jesus suffered and died outside the city gates in order to make his people holy by shedding His own blood"* (Hebrews 13:12 NLT). This tomb was excavated at the turn of the last century, and the side of the cliff contains the features of a skull.

This is an interesting study in itself, but what I really want you to see is this old expression "without" which the KJV uses which means "outside of." And getting back to our verse 20 here in chapter 14, we find that this great battle is going to occur "without the city." That means that the great bulk of this destructive battle is going to occur outside the Holy City of Jerusalem. The city itself is going to be partially protected from this horrendous devastation because that is where Jesus is going to set up the throne for His earthly kingdom.

And just how much devastation and bloodshed is there going to be when this angel with the sickle reaps these clusters of bitter grapes and throws them into the winepress of the wrath of God? Verse 20b says *"and blood came out of the winepress, even unto the horse bridles, by the space of a thousand and six hundred furlongs."* "Sixteen hundred furlongs." A furlong is roughly 1/8th of a mile. Six hundred furlongs is about 190 miles – the approximate length of the land of Israel. What this is saying is that this land is going to be drenched with blood from one end of it to the other. So you might ask, "Just how many soldiers are going to be involved in this great battle?" Listen to Revelation 9, verse 16a: *"And the number of the army of the horsemen were two hundred thousand thousand ."* That is a "2" followed by eight zeros: 200,000,000! And from my study, it appears that this is only a description of the army opposing the Antichrist; it does not include the Antichrist's forces!

The Apostle John must have been bewildered because the total world population at that time was not much more than that.[20] Imagine, if you can, 200 million men, stretched out for 180 miles in length, and say perhaps a mile wide. This would allow each man an average of only 25 square feet in which to maneuver – that is only 5 feet x 5 feet. And that does not include all the war machines or horses.

The Antichrist and his forces will feel so smug as they face these invaders from the east. His sentiments were echoed by his followers in the previous chapter just after he had sustained what looked like a mortal wound, and yet recovered from it. "Who can make war against him? Look at the power he has. Look at his brilliancy. Look at his forces. He is invincible!" But the Antichrist will only leave behind a field of blood as he and his followers pay the supreme price for confronting Almighty God. Ezekiel 39:12 says the devastation will be so great it will take seven months to bury all the dead.

Do you weary of the wicked who seem to always triumph in this world? Weary not! God's promise is sure. He will harvest His own, and then, the Bible says after this great battle, *"they shall beat their swords into plowshares, and their spears into pruning hooks, when nation shall not lift up sword against nation, neither shall they learn war anymore"* (Isaiah 2:4b).

The Beast and his False Prophet were running down the believers, killing them with the sword, denying them food if they did not accept his mark, and beheading all who would not bow down to him. And so, God said, "Time Out!" and in this chapter He shows what will be the end of these God-haters. A great harvest will be conducted and the wheat will be separated from the tares.

The tares will be gathered into bundles and thrown into the fire. But first, God's angels will reap the clusters of wild grapes – depicting the unrepentant masses who have pledged their allegiance to the Antichrist. And God will oversee the greatest battle of all time, when blood will run from one end of the land of Israel to the other. But remember, God's children will be fully protected from this wrath.

In summary, this chapter has been a parenthesis. When God saw that the two beasts described in chapter 13 were literally "wearing out the saints," He saw these saints needed encouragement, and encouragement is what they got!

CHAPTER FIFTEEN

The Song of Moses and The Song of the Lamb

After the flash-forward that we studied in the last chapter, John is now shown some of the details regarding the Great Tribulation which is the last half of this seven year period of judgment. We are getting close to the end of the Tribulation Period – maybe six months before the end when Jesus comes back to set up His earthly Kingdom. But before that happens, God draws aside the curtain that we might see some of the details of that final consummation of the age. He wants us to know the end of this wicked world system, and that sin, unrighteousness and death will be purged from it. Instead of thorns and stickers and poison ivy, God will establish a Kingdom of righteousness where everything is in harmony with everything else.

We now come to the 15th chapter of Revelation which is by far the shortest chapter of the Book, serving more as an introduction to the bowl judgments of chapter 16. In this chapter and the next, we see God taking action against the spiritual gangsters and God-haters who have terrorized planet earth during the Tribulation. He acts swiftly and justly in carrying out His sentence against the guilty. And there is no appealing His decision because it is holy, fair and just in every way, and it comes in the form of seven judgments to be released upon the earth.

As we continue this study, bear in mind that chapters 15 and 16 go together. They are really one continuous vision, and they are the last things that happen on earth prior to Christ's Second Coming in Revelation 19:11. We will see that chapters 17 and 18 do not add anything to our timeline, but simply fill in for us more details of these events.

A lady told me, "I don't want to study or hear about the things in Revelation. They are dark and depressing." This is partially true. They are dark and depressing for the unbeliever, but they are comforting and refreshing as we see what awaits the believer. As we approach these judgments of God we must ask, "Are they consistent with the character of God?" The God of the Bible is not a bearded grandfather in a rocking chair. Too many people do not realize that God is a HOLY GOD and His holiness requires that justice be executed. If we have no confidence that God will deal justly with those unbelievers who deserve His wrath, how can we be sure He will deal justly with us who are saved?

This principle I am about to share with you is of utmost importance. God's judgments are not a function of anger or impetuousness. Rather they are an evidence of His holy justice. This principle is worth repeating. God's judgments are not a function of anger or impetuousness. Rather they are an evidence of His holy justice.

For all of recorded history, God has been stretching out His hand of grace and mercy to the human race with offers of compassion and forgiveness. Those who are judged with severe judgments during the Tribulation are judged because they have failed to respond to His Gospel of grace. Judgment is not a negative thing. It is a righteous thing – the right thing for God to do. And He has revealed these revelations to us for two reasons: first, out of kindness to us that we may be warned to avoid what lies ahead for this guilty world; and secondly, to shun every form of apostasy which He is soon coming to judge.

After Jesus Christ had suffered on the cross for the sins of the world, He cried out, *"It is finished."* What was finished? The wrath of God upon sin – poured out on God's own Son to pay the penalty for sinners – was finished. In Revelation 15:1, the Lord Jesus is again saying in effect the punishment for sin is completed.

This is a sobering reminder to all who reject His offer of salvation that there will come a time when the patience of God has been exhausted, and there will be no more opportunity to receive Christ as Savior. The only future for such persons is the Lake of Fire. Oh, friend of mine. Accept Christ today – don't delay – don't allow your memories to haunt you as you wonder why you didn't run to safety when you had the opportunity -- in the arms of Jesus!

Someone asked Mark Twain what he thought about the Bible. He replied, "It ain't the parts of the Bible that I can't understand that bother me, it's the parts that I do understand."[1] Our generation has lost sight of God's holiness. We have lost that "fear of God" – that healthy respect for who He is. We refer to Him flippantly as "the Good Lord" as though He lived next door; or the Man Upstairs. When we really see His awesome attributes such as His Righteousness, His Holiness and Majesty, we begin to understand the necessity of the judgments that will purge the earth of every kind of evil thing.

In Revelation chapter 11, verse 18, which we covered earlier, we find these words: *"And the nations were angry, and thy wrath is come, and the time of the dead, that they should be judged, and that thou shouldest give reward unto thy servants the prophets, and to the saints, and them that fear thy name, small and great: and shouldest destroy them which destroy the earth."* This verse declared that the end of the age had come. And now we are going to see the details of the events leading up to that very end. *"And I saw another sign in Heaven, great and marvelous, seven angels having the seven last plagues; for in them is filled up the wrath of God"* (Revelation 15:1). As Jack Van Impe says, "This is the completion of God's judgment when His wrath is unleashed against rebellious mankind."[2]

The word "sign" in Scripture bothers some people. To them, a sign is something that is a mystery, hidden and hard to understand. Since we were told in chapter 1 that this Book is written in signs, many conclude that the Book is obscure and difficult to discern. But if you examine the word "sign", you find that the very opposite is true. A mystery or "musterion" as the Greek says cannot be figured out by logic. God must show us the answer. The Rapture was a musterion. But God revealed it to Paul, and he recorded it so we would know what it is. But a sign is not a musterion. A sign is designed to help us understand more clearly, not to make the meaning more difficult. In John 12:32, Jesus told His listeners: *"And I, if I be lifted up from the earth, will draw all men unto Me."* This He said, signifying (or "sign-a-fying") what death He should die. Jesus was trying to explain His death, not obscure it.

The scribes and Pharisees approached Jesus to give them a sign. What they really wanted was for Him to perform a miracle for them. Instead, He told them the only sign He was going to give them was that of the prophet Jonah. And then He went on to tell them that as Jonah was in the belly of the great fish for three days and three nights, so He would be in the heart of the earth for three days and three nights (Matthew 12:39-40). Again, He was shedding light on His death, burial and resurrection. So when you see the word sign, it means God is trying to help you understand what will be taking place. Looking at it from another angle, a sign is a symbol or picture that conveys some great truth which God wants His people to understand.

After the sign, let's see what else John saw. *"And I saw as it were a sea of glass mingled with fire: and them that had gotten the victory over the Beast, and over his image, and over his mark, and over the number of his name, stand on the sea of glass, having the harps of God"* (Revelation 15:2). We have seen this sea of glass once before in this Book. In chapter 4, verse 6, it says: *"And before the throne there was a sea of glass like unto crystal."*

John saw a sea of glass like crystal. This reminds us of the basin in the Tabernacle. In the 30th chapter of Exodus, precise directions were given for the building of a laver or basin for the Tabernacle. This basin was for the purpose of the priests washing their hands and feet prior to performing their priestly duties. In Exodus 38:8, the Hebrew women contributed their mirrors to give it a glassy effect. This sea symbolized the Word of God for it contained the water used for priestly cleansing, and we are told in the New Testament that the Church is sanctified and cleansed by the *"washing of water by the Word"* (Ephesians 5:26).

I know some people who try to read baptism into it every time they come to a passage that mentions water. But Ephesians 5:26 has nothing to do with water baptism. It says we are cleansed and sanctified by the *"washing of water by the Word."* The Word of God is the cleansing agent. But this sea in chapter 15 is not for cleansing, therefore, it is firm like crystal. In fact, the NASB translation says the martyred tribulation saints are standing on it! It is still the Word of God, but it is no longer needed for cleansing. The sea of glass was needed for cleansing here on earth, but in Heaven it is crystallized.[3] The fact that these saints are in Heaven is evidence that they have been cleansed by His Word and by the blood of the Lamb, and there is no other cleansing necessary. Our cleansing does not have to be repeated, and so, the water is firm, solid and clear as crystal. So, this sea – the Word of God – abides forever, a glassy sea, yet solid like crystal. It is firm and glorious on which the people of God can stand eternally.

There is one big difference between the sea that is presented to us in chapter 4 and the one here in chapter 15. In chapter 4, the Church has just been raptured and is gathered around the throne. The sea is like crystal, not only pure, but also firm. The Church has been cleansed and is making herself ready as Christ's Bride. Listen to what Paul says in Ephesians 5:27 about the Church: *"That He [Christ] might present it to Himself a glorious Church, not having spot, or wrinkle, or any such thing; but that it should be holy and without blemish."* Do you long for a perfect Church? When we are raptured and arrive in Heaven and get our new white garments, we will be a perfect Church without spot or blemish – a perfect Bride because the garments we have put on are the righteousness of Christ.

This group in chapter 15 who are standing on this crystal sea is not the Church. It is the Tribulation saints who have been put to death by the Antichrist, and are now standing on this sea of glass before the throne. And notice there is another difference about this sea in chapter 15. It is mixed with fire. What a beautiful picture of these Tribulation saints standing firmly for Christ under the test of fire, having their feet planted solidly on the Word of God. Peter speaks in I Peter 1:7 of these very trials endured by these saints when he says: *"That the trial of your faith, being much more precious than of gold that perisheth, though it be tried with fire, might be found unto praise and honour and glory at the appearing of Jesus Christ."*

These Tribulation saints have gained the victory, not just in one area, but in four! First, it says they gained the victory over the Antichrist. And that is a big victory. They are standing up against the most powerful man in the whole world. And the Antichrist is not only going to use physical force and threats of violence, he is going to exercise mind control. Scripture says that God will send these unbelievers strong delusion so that they will believe a lie (II Thessalonians 2:11). What lie? The lie when the Antichrist claims that he is God. You can now see what a great accomplishment it is for these martyrs to have gained victory over the Antichrist and over his image. They did not allow his mark to be put on them or the number of his name: 666.

The Antichrist and his followers will think that they are overcoming the saints of God when they are killing them, but in reality, the Antichrist is sending them to their rewards before the throne of Grace! The Bible says they gained the VICTORY because they are now in Heaven, standing on the firm foundation of the Word of God and playing harps. These are not harps made by Stradivarius. These are harps made by God Himself. Can you imagine what melodious sounds will come from those strings? And they are singing! Look at verses 3-4: *"And they sing the song of Moses the servant of God, and the song of the Lamb, saying, 'GREAT AND MARVELOUS ARE THY WORKS, LORD GOD ALMIGHTY; JUST AND TRUE ARE THY WAYS, THOU KING OF SAINTS. WHO SHALL NOT FEAR THEE, O LORD, AND GLORIFY THY NAME? FOR THOU ONLY ART HOLY: FOR ALL NATIONS SHALL COME AND WORSHIP BEFORE THEE; for thy judgments are made manifest.'"*

Let me call to your attention the phrase, "Thou King of saints." This is a faulty translation. All the newer translations render this as "King of Nations," and even the NKJV has a footnote that says this should be "King of Nations." This is in harmony with Isaiah 2:2-3: *"And it shall come to pass in the last days, that the mountain of the LORD's house shall be established in the top of the mountains, and shall be exalted above the hills; and all the nations shall flow unto it. And many people shall go and say, 'Come ye, and let us go up to the mountain of the LORD, to the house of the God of Jacob; and He will teach us of His ways, and we will walk in His paths: for out of Zion shall go forth the law and the word of the LORD from Jerusalem.'"*

In Exodus 15, after Pharaoh's army had been destroyed as the Red Sea closed in on them, the Israelites stood on the far shore, and sang the song of Moses – a song of victory. And so do these Tribulation saints, but they also sing a song of redemption. John calls it *"the song of the Lamb"* (Revelation 15:3). Can you imagine the glorious sounds rolling through the halls of Heaven? What a chorus!

There are three groups to whom God gives harps. First, in chapter 5, the believers who have been raptured in the previous chapter receive harps from God. Second, in chapter 14, the 144,000 Jewish evangelists join us in song and are given harps by God. And the third group here in chapter 15 is the multitude of martyred saints who have gained victory over the Antichrist. These saints complete this heavenly choir and orchestra with their harps. They sing the song of the Lamb, praising Him for His works. The song also asks the question, *"WHO SHALL NOT FEAR THEE, O LORD?"* (Revelation 15:4). This refers to a reverential fear of God because He alone is holy. Have you ever just praised God for Who He is? In your quiet time, have you ever told Him that He is awesome and worthy to be praised? Do not neglect to do this!

All the nations and peoples of the earth will bow their knee and confess that He is truly Lord of all whether they want to or not. And finally, Jesus should be feared and glorified because His righteous acts will be revealed. Even His judgments will be righteous and holy because they are directed against those who hate Him and will not accept His authority.

The song of Moses is a song of earthly deliverance, but the song of the Lamb is about a spiritual deliverance.

Music is such a great part of worship. Oh, how my mother liked to sing, and I will get to hear her sing again! Several times in our study, the action of the Tribulation Period has gotten so intense that the Lord had to call a time-out, and show us the end of the Book that everything is going to turn out A-OK.

That musical genius, Johann Sebastian Bach, is said to have sometimes overslept. His children had a way of waking him up. They would go to the piano and play the scale: do-re-me-fa-so-la-ti …. and then they would stop. They would not hit the C note for "do." Bach would have to get up from his bed, go to the piano and hit the final note.[4] It seems that most of us are waiting for that last note on the final page of God's song of victory that He has given us from this chapter.

Look again at the song of Moses in verse 3. As Israel escaped out of Egypt and through the Red Sea, they rejoiced over the downfall of Pharaoh and his armies. In the same way, Christians rejoice over the downfall of the Antichrist at the close of the Great Tribulation. Read Moses' song in Exodus 15 and recognize that verses 1, 3 and 18 fit the overthrow of the Antichrist even better than they picture the overthrow of Pharaoh. The song was divinely inspired to fit both occasions. I was a teenager when Japan surrendered on what we called V-J Day. Christians are also looking for V-J Day – the one that proclaims Victory in Jesus!

Verses 5-6: *"And after that I looked, and, behold, the Temple of the tabernacle of the testimony in Heaven was opened: and the seven angels came out of the Temple, having seven plagues, clothed in pure and white linen, and having their breasts girded with golden girdles."* This is a frightening scene as the angels are about to execute judgment upon the earth.

Verses 7-8: *"And one of the four Beasts gave unto the seven angels seven golden vials full of the wrath of God, who liveth for ever and ever. And the Temple was filled with smoke from the glory of God, and from His power; and no man was able to enter into the Temple, till the seven plagues of the seven angels were fulfilled."* The angels left the Temple empty-handed, but the four living creatures give them bowls full of the wrath of God, and we will see them poured out in the next chapter.

When God's judgment has been completed, men may then enter the Temple, but until that time, all is dark and foreboding because of the smoke which fills the Temple. It seems the Lord is saying, "John, now that you have the big picture, I am going to go back and fill in the details." That is what we are seeing in our current study. In chapters 16-18 which we will study next, John is given a closer look at what these judgments are, and what the final days on this earth are going to be like.

CHAPTER SIXTEEN

The Seven Bowl Judgments

The final preparation for the establishment of God's Kingdom is detailed in the vision of the seven last plagues, also called the seven bowl judgments. Let me call to your attention again, Revelation 1:3: *"Blessed is he that readeth, and they that hear the words of this prophecy, and keep those things which are written therein: for the time is at hand."* Scripture says a blessing is pronounced upon me because I have read it and am passing it on, and upon you because you are reading it, and upon both of us if we take into our hearts the things that are written in it. Why? Because the time is short!

Jesus gave parable after parable picturing the same thing about what will happen when the master of the house, or the landholder, or the bridegroom goes away and then he comes back expectantly. Woe to those who are not ready nor looking for his return. We should get up every morning saying, "Maybe this will be the day!" We know this: it is one day closer than it was yesterday!

Do not be in the camp of the scoffers. And do not forget, though there have been signs of His return in every generation, there is one sign that was not there for my grandparents, and for the generations prior to May 14, 1948. And that sign is that Israel is back in their land! Israel has been regathered as a nation after being scattered for nearly 2,000 years to the four corners of the earth, and the Bible indicates that when Jesus comes back, Israel will be back in their land. Zechariah 12 begins with all the things that will happen to Israel in the last days after their regathering. The prophecies continue until two chapters later (Zechariah 14) when Christ returns to the Mount of Olives at His Second Coming.

The Day of Grace is fast slipping by. We need to share the Gospel as often as we can to as many people as we can. Is Jesus coming back? The scoffers do not think so. They think that assertion is laughable. Listen to II Peter 3:3-4 (NLT): *"First, I want to remind you that in the last days there will be scoffers who will laugh at the truth and do every evil thing they desire. This will be their argument: 'Jesus promised to come back, did He? Then where is He? Why, as far back as anyone can remember, everything has remained exactly the same since the world was first created.'"* Chapter 16 should cause everyone to examine their relationship carefully with Almighty God. The events we are about to study are both awesome and terrifying. The consolation for the believer is that he or she will not be present when these events actually take place. Before we finish this chapter, you will have a new appreciation of what Paul says in Titus 2:13: *"Looking for that blessed hope, and the glorious appearing of the great God and our Savior Jesus Christ.*" As believers in Christ, we are not looking for judgment. We are looking for that "*Blessed hope.*"

In chapter 16, we are going to find out just what is in those seven golden bowls of judgment, and what the angels do with them. So let us begin reading at chapter 16, verse 1: "*And I heard a great voice out of the Temple saying to the seven angels, 'Go your ways, and pour out the vials of the wrath of God upon the earth.'*" This great voice that is mentioned is none other than Jesus Christ. We have already seen in Scripture that God the Father has turned all judgment over to the Son (John 5:22). And also at the end of our last chapter, verse 8 tells us that the Temple in Heaven is filled with smoke from the glory of God, and that no man could enter it. So, this great voice has to be that of the Lord Jesus.

When we studied the seal judgments we got the impression that they were poured out over a period of time, probably during the first 3½ years of the Tribulation. Then we came to the trumpet judgments – they also occur over a period of time during the last half of the Tribulation. But these vial or bowl judgments occur rapidly one after another. If I had to speculate, I would say that they occur probably within a month of the end of the age. And another indication that these judgments occur rather quickly is that in the King James it says, "*And the first* [angel] *went .... and the second angel poured .... and the third angel poured ....*" (Revelation 16:2-4). The word "and" is not in the earliest manuscripts. It simply says, "*The first angel went.... the second angel poured ....the third angel poured....*" One after another, this earth is rocked with the wrath of God. He means business. The time to eradicate sin has come! And these seven angels take their orders directly from Christ Himself.

Each angel is given a portion of God's wrath. These judgments we are about to see are not man-made as we saw when the seals were opened. They are not instituted by Satan as we saw during the trumpet judgments. These bowl judgments are wholly the responsibility of a holy and righteous Judge. Because of the similarity between the judgments of the trumpets and these bowl judgments, some have been led to believe that they are the same thing. That is not true. They are similar, but they are not identical. For one thing, you will see that the bowl judgments are much more intense than their counterparts in the trumpet judgments.

Before proceeding any further, let me say that I believe these will be literal plagues. When it says that men will be infected with malignant sores, I believe they will be infected with malignant sores. Some commentators teach that all these judgments are just symbolic of what will be happening in society. I do not believe these sores simply mean that mankind is going to experience moral sores and be very uncomfortable with the breakdown of society. There is no reason to believe they will be anything other than literal. When we come to the plague of darkness in verse 10, it is really a plague of darkness and not just man's moral compass being thrown off. For one thing, losing their moral compass is not going to make men cry out in anguish. In fact, most of them will not even care. This is too graphic to be anything other than a literal fulfillment.

Another reason to believe these will be literal plagues is that four out of the seven of these plagues occurred during the 10 plagues in Egypt when Moses was confronting Pharaoh. And in each case, they were literal. These bowl judgments are very similar to the judgments we saw when the trumpets were sounded except for one distinguishing feature: the bowl judgments are much more intense. For example, the second trumpet affects the sea and kills one-third of all sea life. As we will see, the second bowl judgment also affects the sea, but it kills all of the sea life.

The bowl judgments are more intense than any of the other judgments we have seen thus far. In the next number of paragraphs, we will show how much more intense the bowl judgments are compared to the trumpet judgments which we studied earlier in Revelation chapters 8-9. With that in mind, let us read chapter 16, verse 2: *"And the first* [angel] *went and poured out his vial upon the earth: and there fell a noisome and grievous sore upon the men which had the mark of the beast, and upon them which worshipped the image."* This is similar but not identical to the plague that hit Egypt in the ninth chapter of Exodus when painful boils infected all the Egyptians. But that was nothing to compare with these horrible, malignant sores that break out on all those who have taken the Mark of the Beast. And just as in Egypt of old, these plagues do not bother the children of God – only those who are not followers of God.

No doubt the followers of the Antichrist are rising up in anger, demanding that the Antichrist do something to relieve them of their terrible pain. They need to call upon the Great Physician instead of the Fake Physician. And I am sure the Antichrist is broadcasting his message to the entire world on all channels each evening: "Be patient – our top scientists are working on this, and we will soon find a cure for this dreaded problem that has been dropped in our lap by that evil god, Jehovah!"

In today's society, doctors say they are losing the battle every day to new strains of microbes as they are constantly changing, and becoming immune to the antibiotics we have. Even my own oncologist said that he had to give me a stronger infusion of chemo because, when the same type of cancer reoccurs, it is more resistant to the previous chemo that was used.

Even though this plague is literal and is causing terrific pain and suffering, bear this in mind: A sore is an outward sign or evidence of some inward problem. And man's inward problem is sin! Jeremiah said, *"The heart is deceitful above all things, and desperately sick"* (Jeremiah 17:9 ESV). God has provided a cure for this problem and when men ignore the cure, they must pay the consequences. What a terrible price men pay for not believing God! In this case, these malignant sores are an outward sign of a depraved and wicked heart.

These earth dwellers have been masquerading as very religious people, and they have even been worshipping the Antichrist's image that he himself had erected. But now their bodies are beginning to mirror the sickness of their souls. Who in their right mind would choose to fight with the forces of evil against God? Yet hundreds are doing it every day in our community as they reject the salvation God has offered. This is the heart of what the Battle of Armageddon is all about. It is the world saying, "We will not bow our knee to God. We are too mighty. We are too important." But the Christian is saying, "Come, Lord Jesus – take us to your Marriage Supper – let's get on with the wedding!"

This brings us to chapter 16, verse 3: *"And the second angel poured out his vial upon the sea; and it became as the blood of a dead man: and every living soul died in the sea."* We see immediately that the second bowl judgment is worse than the second trumpet judgment which killed one-third of all sea creatures. This bowl judgment kills all sea life.

The poisoning of the waters by the second trumpet judgment (Revelation 8:8) was pictured as a burning mountain – possibly a large meteorite falling into the ocean. The bowl judgment poisons the waters by perhaps a bowl full of these meteorites blasting into the earth while the second angel pours out the contents of his bowl. Again this judgment is similar to one that God poured out on Egypt through his prophet, Moses. This is recorded in Exodus 7:17-19): *"Thus sayeth the LORD, in this thou shalt know that I am the LORD: behold, I will smite with the rod that is in mine hand upon the waters which are in the river, and they shall be turned to blood. And the fish that is in the river shall die, and the river shall stink; and the Egyptians shall loathe to drink of the water of the river. And the LORD spake unto Moses, 'Say unto Aaron, Take thy rod, and stretch out thine hand upon he waters of Egypt, upon their streams, upon their rivers, and upon their ponds, and upon all their pools of water, that they may become blood; and that there may be blood throughout all the land of Egypt, both in vessels of wood, and in vessels of stone.'"*

A scientist recently said that the composition of seawater is almost identical to the composition of blood. Only a relatively small modification is needed to change seawater into blood.[1] Blood is given its red color by the iron that is in the red corpuscles. In living flesh, these red corpuscles transmit oxygen to all the cells of the body so that Leviticus 17:11 is absolutely true. It says: *"the life of the flesh is in the blood."* Since Scripture says the life of the flesh is in the blood, I have never understood why the Jehovah's Witnesses refuse to have a blood transfusion. Their official teaching says, "Blood must not be eaten or transfused, even in the case of a medical emergency."[2]

If the life is in the blood, why wouldn't you want to preserve and restore life? It makes absolutely no sense to prohibit a transfusion. And if we take it a step further and look for the spiritual meaning of this, we can confidently say, "The life of the flesh is in the blood of Christ – for without Him, we are like dead men."

For Jehovah's Witnesses who break this rule regarding a blood transfusion, they have strict punishment: "A baptized Witness who unrepentantly accepts a blood transfusion is deemed to have disassociated himself from the group by abandoning its doctrines and is subsequently subject to organized shunning by other members."[3] Is that really brotherly love?! You disagree with them and they are ordered to have nothing to do with you anymore. This includes friends and relatives.

I had a sweet Christian lady in my Sunday school class several years ago. She had some serious health problems which resulted in extreme depression. About that same time, Jehovah's Witnesses came by her house. They were sympathetic and understanding, and she was temporarily brainwashed. She even went to several services at their Kingdom Hall with her teenage granddaughter. Fortunately, the granddaughter was well versed in the Bible and began to point out to grandmother some of the Witnesses' blasphemous teachings. When the Witnesses heard about this, they told her not to have anything more to do with her granddaughter. This was when her eyes began to see the devious teachings and doctrines behind this cult. When she told them not to bother her anymore, they came to her house, loudly knocking on the door and windows, throwing rocks against the house and demanding that she open the door so they could rescue her from the Devil. After they did this for several days, she had to call the police to get the Witnesses to leave. It all happened because she took her eyes off Jesus during her time of depression.

If you really want to know what goes on behind the scenes at the Jehovah's Witnesses organization (Watchtower Society), read the most informative book I have ever read on the subject. It is not primarily a book highlighting their false doctrines or teachings. It is a book written by two young married adults depicting the shocking events that they experienced firsthand in this blasphemous cult. For years, the Witnesses tried to keep this book out of the bookstores, but there are still copies that can be obtained. It is a small book of about 150 pages and is entitled, *Behind the Watchtower Curtain*, by David A. Reed.[4] It is a must read!

Returning to Revelation 16:4, when this bowl of wrath is poured out the waters become as the blood of a dead man. In other words, it contains iron and other chemicals which give it a blood red appearance but there is no life in it. In this toxic ocean, nothing can survive. And soon all the billions of fish and marine mammals and other sea creatures perish. Man has become so wicked that even creation turns against him, and the sea and its living creatures that once had been a giant food pantry has now become a sea of death. Apparently this food chain will not be necessary in the new earth because we are told in Revelation 21:1 that *"there was no more sea."*

No doubt the Beast had been telling his followers not to worry. "We still have springs and the fresh water outlets." Not so fast, Mr. Antichrist. Verse 4 (NLT): *"Then the third angel poured out his bowl on the rivers and springs, and they became blood."* At a party, a word association was played with a group of people. You could mention a word and ask them to say whatever word that first came to their mind. The word mentioned was water. The group's response was life. The word mentioned was wine. The group's response was joy. Isn't that just like what the world would think – associating wine with joy? The word mentioned was blood. And the group's response was death. But in reality, life is in the blood!

The third bowl judgment is worse than the third trumpet judgment. This plague will also be similar to the first plague in Egypt when God turned the waters of Egypt into blood. In Egypt, the fish died, the water stunk and the people could not drink it. However, it was confined to Egypt. The third bowl judgment affects the fresh waters all over the world.

Now just in case someone thinks that God is not acting in a just manner, an angel breaks in here and sets the record straight. Verse 5: *"And I heard the angel of the waters say, 'Thou art righteous, O LORD, which art, and wast, and shalt be, because Thou hast judged thus.'"* We have already encountered the four angels holding back the earth's winds. Now we learn that God has an angel in charge of earth's waters. And He declares that the judgment is deserved.

Verse 6: *"For they have shed the blood of saints and prophets, and Thou hast given them blood to drink; for they are worthy."* No doubt there will be a great and bitter outcry against their Creator, the God of Heaven, when men are forced to drink blood to survive. But complaining is not repenting, and so their complaints will gain them nothing.

The blood of the saints and prophets has been shed for thousands of years. And do you remember what happened in Revelation 11 when the Antichrist killed the two faithful witnesses that were preaching the Gospel? The people of the earth rejoiced. They were dancing in the streets just like the Muslims were doing in Bagdad right after 9-11.

Did you know there have been more people martyred for Christ in the last 100 years than the previous 2,000 years put together? God says, "My patience has come to an end. You have delighted in shedding the blood of my children. Well, you want blood? I will give you blood."

This reminds me of the time when that righteous servant Moses returned from his meeting with God on top of Mount Sinai. And what did he find the children of Israel doing when he returned? In direct violation of the first two commandments, and at the demand of the people, Aaron reluctantly made an image of a calf out of gold. When Moses returned, the people were dancing around and worshipping it.

The name "children" perfectly describes the Israelites. Most of the time they acted like immature children! Moses was beside himself (Exodus 32). So, he melted down the calf, ground it into powder, mixed it with water and made the people drink it. And they had to taste the vileness and bitterness of their apostasy. It is hard for some people to believe that a God of love can do this. But do not miss the point! God's love sent His Son to the cross. If anyone rejects that provision, they must contend with God's judgment.

One of the most contemptible acts I can think of is sexual child abuse. What if someone took your little children, and violently and sexually abused them? And you said, "I will forgive you – I am providing someone to take your penalty. All you will have to do is ask forgiveness, and repent of what you have done." And they say, "Forget that. I'm having too much fun. I'm going to continue to have my way with these kids." And again you offer them forgiveness. And they ignore you. They might even mock you. Will your patience finally run out? You know it would. I would not have near the patience that God does. I would zap them out of this world in nothing flat! But II Peter 3:9 says that God has unbelievable patience. He does not want any person to spend eternity with Satan. But His patience is not infinite. It eventually has an end.

Hebrews 10:28-29 (NLT) throws some light on this: *"Anyone who refused to obey the law of Moses was put to death without mercy on the testimony of two or three witnesses. Think how much more terrible the punishment will be for those who have trampled on the Son of God and have treated the blood of the covenant as if it were common and unholy. Such people have insulted and enraged the Holy Spirit who brings God's mercy to His people."*

Look at that last phrase *"Such people have insulted and enraged the Holy Spirit.."* Do you know what this is talking about? This is the unpardonable sin. The unpardonable sin is not lying; it is not stealing; it is not even murder! It is blasphemy against the Holy Spirit according to Mark 3:29-30 (NLT): *"But anyone who blasphemes against the Holy Spirit will never be forgiven. It is an eternal sin. He told them this because they were saying He had an evil spirit."* How do you blasphemy the Holy Spirit? Look at the last phrase of the verse we just read: *"because they were saying He had an evil spirit."* In other words, they said that the Spirit in Christ was from Hell itself. They were denying the deity of Christ and, if that denial continues until the death of that person, then there is no forgiveness available after the grave. Remember the sobering words we studied earlier in Revelation 13:10b, *".... he that killeth with the sword must be killed with the sword. Here is the patience and the faith of the saints."*

There is coming a time when God holds back His wrath no longer. In fact, Revelation 16:6 says that *"they are worthy"* – that means these apostates have fully earned their awful doom. Romans 6:23 says: *"For the wages of sin is death; but the gift of God is eternal life through Jesus Christ our Lord."* You do not earn a gift – that is why they call it a gift. That is what our salvation is – a gift. You cannot work for it. You cannot earn it. It is a gift. You work for wages. But this verse has just told us that we cannot work for our salvation. So what kind of wages will we get if we miss this gift? *"But the wages of sin is death."* Pretty clear, isn't it? *"And I heard another* [angel] *out of the altar say, 'Even so, Lord God Almighty, true and righteous are thy judgment'"* (Revelation 16:7).

There is a brief pause as the angel declares that God's judgments are true and righteous. Though God is certainly love, He is also every bit holy, and here we see that His holiness demands that true justice be carried out. Justice has always been a problem for mankind. In our own country which claims to have the highest judicial standards in the world, it seems that whoever can afford the best attorney gets the best verdict. This has been a problem throughout history. Unjust verdicts were so bad in Isaiah's day that he cried out in Isaiah 64:1a (NLT): *"Oh, that you would burst from the heavens and come down!"* Isaiah longed for true justice.

The prophet, Amos, said in 5:24: *"Let judgment run down as waters, and righteousness as a mighty stream."* Every person should hear this message loud and clear: God is a righteous God, and He will judge unrighteousness in a completely righteous way. That is why all of us are doomed as guilty men and women unless we accept the pardon God has provided through the blood of Jesus Christ. Isn't it ironic that, to the unbelievers, the rivers and streams become as the blood of a dead man, but to the saved the blood of Christ provides streams of living water that will never run dry? Dr. Henry Morris once said: "Saved men and women have always been judged in righteousness – and saved by grace."[5]

That brings us in our study to Revelation chapter 16, verses 8-9: *"And the fourth angel poured out his vial upon the sun; and power was given unto him to scorch men with fire. And men were scorched with great heat and blasphemed the name of God, which hath power over these plagues: and they repented not to give Him glory."* This will be the greatest heat wave in history! Just like the judgment of the first bowl that affected only the unbelievers, this scorching heat will only burn the defiant ones. To the believers, God says in Psalm 121:6: *"The sun shall not smite thee by day, nor the moon by night."* God will protect his children who are still alive on the earth from this scorching heat of the fourth bowl of wrath. Dear Reader: Take timeout to receive a blessing and read Psalm 121.

You will recall in the third chapter of Daniel, the three Hebrew children were ordered by King Nebuchadnezzar to bow down and worship him. That is exactly what the Antichrist commands when he takes control. And the Antichrist just like King Nebuchadnezzar says, "If you don't bow down and worship me, you will die." I love the answer that the three Hebrew children gave King Nebuchadnezzar – *"Our God whom we serve is able to deliver us from the burning fiery furnace, and He will deliver us out of thine hand, O king. But if not, be it known unto thee, O king, that we will not serve thy gods, nor worship the golden image which thou hast set up"* (Daniel 3:17-18). And there will be many who will give the Antichrist the same answer! And just like King Nebuchadnezzar, the Antichrist is also going to set up a giant image (probably of himself), and the people will be expected under penalty of death to bow down and worship it.

Here is the point I want to make. The three Hebrew children refused to worship the king or his image and so, they were thrown into the fiery furnace. But they were protected from the fire and scorching heat! They are a picture of God's children in the time of the fourth bowl judgment. When this scorching heat is burning men unmercifully, I have no doubt that the remnant of Israel – those who have trusted God – will be protected. While others are burning – they will be basking! You will note that the fourth bowl judgment is very similar to the fourth trumpet judgment in Revelation 8:12. There, a third of the sun was smitten so that light was drastically curtailed. Here, although the sun is also involved, the results are completely different and the judgment much more severe. Men are scorched with great heat.

For thousands of years, the sun has been a beneficial friend to mankind. It provides us with wonderful light. It provides us with warmth. Through evaporation, the sun pulls salt water from the sea, distills it and refreshingly pours it back on the earth. Without the sun, our seasons would not follow one after another and our food crops would not survive. But now, at the command of God, the sun brings its devastating heat to bear on mankind. Don't miss the fact that God has absolute power over His creation. The Beast, and Satan who is directing him, have no power to alleviate the suffering of their subjects.

Think of the worst sunburn you ever had and multiply it a hundred times over. And if humans are being scorched like this, think of the devastation to the food crops and vegetation. No doubt every night on the 10:00 o'clock news the Antichrist gives a blasphemous tirade against Jehovah, the God of Heaven, who is causing all this misery. Isaiah told of this time in Isaiah 24:6: *"Therefore hath the curse devoured the earth, and they that dwell therein are desolate: therefore the inhabitants of the earth are burned, and few men left."* The strong heat of the sun will bear down on them with a vengeance. They will sweat and thirst, and they have nothing to drink except blood.

Dr. William Pettingill says, "That great orb of the day which has been for the many centuries the source of all good for physical man – light, life and health – will become an unbearable plague, killing men with its intense heat. Just so, will the Son of God, the Light of the World, the Life of His people, and the Sun of Righteousness, become in that day a destroying, blazing flame, bringing awful vengeance to those who refuse to honor His Father. *'For our God is a consuming fire"* (Hebrews 12:29).[6]

These sufferings will cause them to finally admit that God exists and that He controls the plagues. We find that in Revelation 16:9, but do they repent? Do they cry out for mercy? No! They will not fall on their sore knees before God and ask for mercy. They had rather curse His name. The whole situation will be traumatic and maddening. It will be difficult to even think straight.

If God's love will not reach the hearts of these people, judgment will never do it. Verse 9 confirms this: *"and they repented not"*. In Romans 2, Paul tells us that it is the goodness of God that leads to repentance. People not won by grace will never be won. So, hard on the heels of the fourth angel's scorching heat, comes the fifth angel who empties his bowl of judgment. Verse 10: *"And the fifth angel poured out his vial upon the seat of the Beast; and his kingdom was full of darkness; and they gnawed their tongues for pain."* One minute they are burning up with fire from the sun, and the next they are plunged into total darkness. You just cannot imagine anything much worse.

Rome, Babylon and Jerusalem will be the prime cities during this time. The Antichrist will have operations in all three, but at any rate, he now finds them along with the rest of his kingdom in total darkness. How miserable is that? Maybe the Lord is preparing him and his followers for that time when the Bible says the unbelievers will be cast into outer darkness. After all, these God-haters have been living is spiritual darkness, but now they get to try out physical darkness.

Verse 11: *"And* [they] *blasphemed the God of Heaven because of their pains and their sores, and repented not of their deeds."* God is good. He deserves praise and exaltation, but these people curse and blame Him for all their misfortunes. They will not blame themselves for their sins, or even admit that they are getting justice for their wrongdoings. Though these people are given the opportunity to turn to God, they do not. No one but you are responsible for your actions. You cannot blame anyone else. I came across an insightful quote by Dr. Charles Swindoll. He said, "You are the gatekeeper of your life. Without discipline, you will be invaded." I love that. It fixes the responsibility where it must be – squarely on your own shoulders. Dr. Swindoll goes on to say, "There's an enemy on the loose. And whether or not we are aware of him, he is certainly aware of us. He despises whoever is carrying out God's work."[7] Scripture tells us to be strong, stable and self-controlled. To be on the alert is to be watchful and aware. Those are our commands because we are in a fierce battle with Satan.

This brings us to chapter 16, verse 12: *"And the sixth angel poured out his vial upon the great river Euphrates; and the water thereof was dried up, that the way of the kings of the east might be prepared."* This bowl judgment is preparatory to the final Battle of Armageddon that we will come to in chapter 19. That great expositor from the last century, Dr. Arno Gaebelein, says that this phrase "the kings of the east" literally means the kings "from the rising of the sun."[8]

The Euphrates River has long been regarded as a kind of barrier that separates the East from the West. The Euphrates is no ordinary river. The river is 1,780 miles long. It is first mentioned in Genesis chapter 2 just outside the Garden of Eden where sin was introduced. It is last mentioned here in Revelation 16:12 where sin reaches its utmost height. In other words, it was on the Euphrates River that civilization began, and it will be in this same area that civilization as we know it will end. Its birthplace was here, and its grave will be here.

Its flood plain was the site of the first human city, Babel, founded after Noah's great flood, and it was the site of Nebuchadnezzar's fabulous city, Babylon. It is the same area where the Antichrist will establish his magnificent city during the Tribulation Period. The Euphrates has long been a protection for Israel, both because of the difficulty of its passage, but also because God placed a wilderness between it and Canaan.

Twice before, God has dried up waters to accomplish His purposes. At the Red Sea, He parted the waters so that the Jews could escape from Pharaoh's army. And He stopped the waters of the Jordan River to allow a new generation of Israelites to enter the Promised Land.

This sixth angel pours his bowl of judgment onto the Euphrates and the river is dried up, allowing the hoards from the Far East to march across on their way to invade Israel. The West has invaded the East many times, but this will be the first time that the door will be opened for the East to invade the West. The East (China, Japan, India, Malaysia) is not about to accept the dictatorship of this great leader (Antichrist) from the West. But it is not just the armies from the East that will be marching into this area. The Euphrates is in the area of Iran, Iraq and Syria.

From Joel chapter 2, we learn that most of the nations of the earth will unite against Israel in an effort to wipe them out once and for all. *"Blow the trumpet in Jerusalem! Sound the alarm on my holy mountain! Let everyone tremble in fear because the Day of the LORD is upon us. It is a day of darkness and gloom, a day of thick clouds, and deep blackness. Suddenly, like dawn spreading across the mountains, a mighty army appears! How great and powerful they are! The likes of them have not been seen before and never will be seen again"* (Joel 2:1-2 NLT). And again: *"Fear grips all the people; every face grows pale with fright. The attackers march like warriors and scale city walls like trained soldiers. Straight forward they march, never breaking rank .... no weapon can stop them. They swarm over the city .... They enter all the houses .... The sun and moon grow dark, and the stars no longer shine .... the Day of the LORD is an awesome, terrible thing. Who can endure it?"* (Joel 2:6-11 NLT). But the Lord is always merciful. Here is His pleading in the next verse: *"That is why the LORD says, 'Turn to me now, while there is time!'"* (Joel 2:12 NLT).

It appears that every new judgment merely serves to harden man's unrepentant heart. It is as though men have become so possessed with hatred for God that they are eager for a final confrontation – a great battle that will determine for all time who will be the true King of the universe. Will it be the Creator or the devious Impostor? And if the nations on earth are eager for this final confrontation, the Beast wants it even more to show the world that Satan is king after all.

How do you suppose that all these great countries of the world with their fearsome military strategists and leaders – how did they decide to converge on this little out-of-the-way spot in the middle of nowhere that Mark Twain called the most godforsaken place on the planet? Why are they converging on this little area? We are about to find out that demon spirits are going to enter these godless leaders and supernaturally draw them to the Valley of Armageddon.

Verse 13: *"And I saw three unclean spirits like frogs come out of the mouth of the dragon, and out the mouth of the Beast, and out of the mouth of the False Prophet."* Before we discuss the three unclean spirits, let me say that the end times, as never before, will be characterized by evil spirits influencing mankind. That is why we need to constantly lean upon the Holy Spirit for our guidance. Did you notice that these unclean spirits came out of the unholy three – Satan, the

Antichrist and the False Prophet? Satan is orchestrating this great drama. He has assembled an army from the East comprised of 200 million soldiers. He has assembled tanks and weapons of mass destruction. This army from the East intends to wipe out Israel, and at the same time deal a mortal blow to the Antichrist – this arrogant Westerner whom they hate.

In the north, the Antichrist has organized and called down millions of his own military. He will have on his side the nations of Europe and the Arab countries who have assimilated into his one world government. He intends to wipe out Israel and at the same time deal a mortal blow to these rebellious Orientals whom he has always despised. These satanic spirits waste no time in influencing these wicked world leaders.

Verse 14: *"For they are the spirits of devils, working miracles, which go forth unto the kings of the earth and of the whole world, to gather them to the battle of that great day of God Almighty."* And what a day that will be! Satan, the Antichrist and the False Prophet are gleefully rubbing their hands together – goodbye Israel and goodbye to the Jews forever! No more chosen people – no more future Millennium where the Jews have been promised peace.

King David wrote prophetically of this very time in Psalm 83:4-5a (NLT), *"'Come,' they say, 'let us wipe out Israel as a nation. We will destroy the very memory of its existence.' This was their unanimous decision."* And Satan can hardly wait to see this happen! But wait! Sometimes you cannot see the forest for the trees. You are too close! Move back – away from Satan's little plans as he oversees these activities. Move back to the heavens for a bigger perspective of what is taking place.

These leaders think they are initiating a brilliant military strategy. Instead, it is all part of God's plan to utterly destroy all of them and execute justice throughout the earth. Look at Revelation 16, verse 15: *"Behold, I come as a thief. Blessed is he that watcheth, and keepeth his garments, lest he walk naked, and they see his shame."*

God is going to swoop down on them suddenly. He says, *"I will come as a thief."* You never expect a thief to come. You are not prepared for him. He comes as a complete surprise. I have had Christians tell me, "See, you cannot know anything about when He will come. He says He's going to come as a thief in the night" (I Thessalonians 5:2). I love it when people tell me that. I get a chance to turn to I Thessalonians chapter 5. In verse 2, it says very clearly that Christ is going to come as a *"thief in the night."* And that is where most people stop reading. But look at verses 4-6: *"But ye, brethren, are not in darkness, that that day should overtake you as a thief. Ye are all the children of light, and the children of the day: we are not of the night, nor of darkness. Therefore let us not sleep, as do others; but let us watch and be sober."*

God is coming for the world as a thief in the night as we are told in Revelation 16:15, but not for His children. He tells us to be watchful! How do we do that? In Revelation 7, we saw the saints of God clothed in white robes, and verse 14b of that chapter tells us how their robes got to be so white. They "*have washed their robes, and made them white in the blood of the Lamb.*" Our garments were cleaned in the first place by washing them in the blood of the Lamb. We keep them clean by holy living and being watchful, not by getting entangled with the garbage that the world wallows in.

I believe the ones mentioned in verse 15 that lose their garments and are naked are the hypocrites – those who profess to have "put on Christ," but who are not wearing His garments at all. Instead, they are pictured as they really are without Christ's righteousness – naked and shameful.

Now we come to that somber verse 16: "*And He gathered them together into a place called in the Hebrew tongue Armageddon.*" "Har" in the Hebrew means mountain. This is literally the "mountain of Megiddo" – "Armageddon." It says, "*He gathered them together.*" This is not speaking of the Antichrist who might have summoned his armies. Make no mistake about it. The "He" that is spoken of here, is God – He is calling the shots!

Verse 16: "*And He gathered them together into a place called in the Hebrew tongue, Armageddon.*" This verse has a chilling effect. As these multitudes gather in the Valley of Armageddon, I see no sign of revival. No sign of spiritual awakening. No outcry saying, "Oh, God have mercy on us." Nothing but defiance toward Almighty God and His chosen people, Israel.

Then, in verse 17, we see the seventh and last of these bowl judgments. "*And the seventh angel poured out his vial into the air; and there came a great voice out of the Temple of Heaven, from the throne, saying, 'It is done.'*"

This great voice is none other than God Himself. On the cross, Jesus declared "It is finished" when He completed the great debt He paid for the sins of the world. Now, as the plan of redemption for this earth and all that is therein draws to a close, God Himself declares, "*It is done.*"

Let me refer you back to that awesome verse in Revelation 10, verse 7a: "*But in the days of the voice of the seventh angel, when he shall begin to sound, the mystery of God should be finished.*" The mystery of God will be finished. He says with the blowing of the seventh angel's trumpet, "It is done!" We will learn the answers to these great mysteries of why God has waited so long in stamping out pain, heartache, evil and bringing in His eternal Kingdom. These things that seemingly work so tragically against us, things that we do not understand and have no control over, God says that for His people, in a mysterious way, these things are for the development of our souls and for the strengthening of our lives. In the battles and the losses that we do not understand, God says that one day He will show us how all these things worked together "*for good to them that love God, to them who are the called according to His purpose*" (Romans 8:28b).

What does John see next? Verse 18: "*And there were voices, and thunders, and lightnings; and there was a great earthquake, such as was not since men were upon the earth, so mighty an earthquake, and so great.*" These voices, thunders and lightnings emanate from the very throne of God as He begins to shake the earth. This earthquake is more powerful than anything that has hit the earth before. And there have been some huge ones. There were some gigantic ones hundreds of years ago.

In 1920, China had an earthquake that killed 200,000 people. In 1976, it was China again – this time it killed 242,000 people. Even though building codes have been upgraded to provide more protection, worldwide in the last ten years, earthquakes have killed nearly 350,000 people.[9] Scripture says those earthquakes are nothing compared to what lies ahead. It was left up to the prophet, Zechariah, to describe the final, terrible earthquake in the 14th chapter of his Book. The Mount of Olives will split down the middle, creating a great valley. All the mountains will be made flat, and Jerusalem will be lifted up to be the highest point on planet earth (Isaiah 2:2; 40:4, 9; Zechariah 14:10).

As Joel 3:16a says, *"The LORD also shall roar out of Zion, and utter His voice from Jerusalem; and the heavens and the earth shall shake."* What was the result of this earthquake? Verses 19-20 of Revelation 16: *"And the great city was divided into three parts, and the cities of the nations fell: and great Babylon came in remembrance before God, to give unto her the cup of the wine of the fierceness of His wrath. And every island fled away, and the mountains were not found."*

After this big earthquake and all the great cities are crushed, Jerusalem and Babylon are still standing. And this is not good news for the latter. The Bible says, *" and great Babylon came in remembrance before God."* Babylon is and always has been the very essence of sin and idolatry. It does not have a good record. It has always been a monument to humanism – man without God. From ages past when the tower of Babel was constructed to present day Babylon, it has consistently been at war with God. And God is going to execute judgment.

Jerusalem alone, of all the great cities of the earth, is thus to be spared destruction by the earthquake. It is the only city that will survive as long as the earth endures in its present form, finally being replaced by a new and refurbished city called, "The New Jerusalem." While other cities are being destroyed by a mighty earthquake, God's holy city is rendered more beautiful. As Psalm 48:2 (NLT) says of Jerusalem: *"It is magnificent in elevation – the whole earth rejoices to see it! Mount Zion, the holy mountain, is the city of the great King!"*

In verse 21 comes the final woe: *"And there fell upon men a great hail out of Heaven, every stone about the weight of a talent: and men blasphemed God because of the plague of the hail; for the plague thereof was exceeding great."* Can you imagine hailstones weighing close to 100 pounds each, slamming into the earth? This is the final woe that is poured out by the seventh angel. And Psalm 2:9 will be literally fulfilled: *"Thou shalt break them with a rod of iron; thou shalt dash them in pieces like a potter's vessel."* And yet, in spite of these traumatic events, men do not repent but instead blaspheme the God of Heaven.

John heard the message in chapter 14:8, *"Babylon is fallen – is fallen."* Now, we are going to be supplied with further details about the destruction of Babylon as we look at chapters 17 and 18. But first, we are reminded that Babylon is both a city and an evil system. As we learned earlier, there will be three major cities during the end times – Babylon, Rome and Jerusalem.

Let's look at each of these in detail. First of all, Babylon is a false religious system. You would be utterly amazed at how many commentators identify Babylon with the Roman Catholic Church. Are they the same? There are many inferences in Scripture that would lead in that direction, but I am hesitant to say outright that it is. It is much more extensive than that as we will see. But I believe you will agree, after we look at all the facts, it will make a fantastic launching pad for such a one-world religious system.

It appears to me that the Bible has some pretty harsh things to say about the Roman Catholic Church especially during the 17th chapter. So, whatever I say as we go through this, I want to emphasize that I am not demeaning individual Catholics, but I have a big problem with the teachings of the Catholic Church. Some Catholics have a burning desire to please Christ. Many others, unfortunately, are just like some in the Baptist Church; they are depending on their faith in the Church to save them. So, when I speak of Catholicism, I am referring to that false religious system that permeates salvation by works.

Pagan Rome was the literal successor of Babylon. Papal Rome absorbed all of the Babylonian mysteries, and Rome in the last days will be the seat of the revived satanic system that began with Nimrod and changed the truth of God into a lie. Nothing of this kind was known in the churches of God until the heathen mysteries of Babylon were grafted into Christianity around the 4th Century. The images of the mother and child that are enshrined in Rome's temples are only different in name to the images worshipped in the temples of Semiramis, Ashoreth, Isis and other "Queens of Heaven."

Look at the solemn warning in Jeremiah 51:6-9: "*Flee out of the midst of Babylon, and deliver every man his soul: be not cut off in her iniquity; for this is the time of the LORD's vengeance; He will render unto her a recompense .... the nations have drunken of her wine; therefore the nations are mad .... her judgment reacheth unto Heaven, and is lifted up even to the skies.*"

God is going to destroy Babylon and all that follow her example. Those of you who a want deeper study into this realm, I would highly recommend a book written 150 years ago by British author Alexander Hyslop entitled, *The Two Babylons*.[10]

CHAPTER SEVENTEEN

Mystery Babylon

So we begin chapter 17 with verses 1-2: *"And there came one of the seven angels which had the seven vials, and talked with me, saying unto me, 'Come hither; I will show unto thee the judgment of the great whore that sitteth upon many waters: With whom the kings of the earth have committeth fornication, and the inhabitants of the earth have been made drunk with the wine of her fornication.'"*

Who is this woman and why is God calling her *"the great whore?"* The Greek word used here is "porne" – from which we get our English word, "pornography." This woman represents all the false religions of the world that have united against God in the end times. She has committed spiritual adultery. God calls her *"Babylon – the great whore"* – because she is forsaking God, and embracing a false god, namely Satan, the Antichrist and all that is evil.

Everything in Christianity has a counterfeit. We have already seen the counterfeit Trinity: Satan, the counterfeit of God the Father; the Antichrist, the counterfeit of Jesus Christ; and the False Prophet, the counterfeit of the Holy Spirit. And now, we are going to be introduced to the counterfeit of the true Church of God. It is called *"Mystery Babylon."* To properly understand this, we must take a good look at the background of Babylon.

After Adam's son, Cain, killed his brother, Abel, he was driven out of the land where Adam and Eve dwelt. Genesis 4:16 says: *"Cain went out from the presence of the LORD, and dwelt in the land of Nod, on the east of Eden."* That would be east of the Mesopotamia in the general area of what is now known as northern Iran and Iraq. There Cain presided over a prosperous, but wicked society which eventually was swept away during the great flood of Noah's day. After Cain murdered his brother, God punished him by sending him away from his home and from God's presence forever.

The Bible says that Cain had a wife and that he eventually built a great city (Genesis 4:17-24). The infamous atheist, Robert Ingersoll, was fond of asking, "If no one except Adam, Eve and Cain were living at this time, where did Cain get his wife?" There is no question that Adam and Eve had to have daughters though the Bible does not enumerate them. According to the world renown scholar, the late Dr. Henry Morris, given the longevity of those early descendants of Adam and Eve, it can be mathematically shown that there could have been as many as 120,000 people living in the world long before Cain's death.[1]

Now at least one son and one daughter of Adam and Eve had to marry each other in the first generation in order for the race to survive. There was no danger in this since there were no mutant genes in the genetic systems of Adam and Eve as these had come directly from the creative hand of God Himself. In later generations, brother-sister marriages would come to be recognized as genetically dangerous for sexual relations and would be prohibited as incest (Deuteronomy 27:22). Thus the Bible is not only consistent with its own statements, but also with all known facts of science.

After the flood, a vast civilization sprang up under the leadership of a man named Nimrod. The Bible says in Genesis 10:9 that he was *"a mighty hunter,"* and he no doubt commanded the respect of all his peers. But the name Nimrod means rebel, and it was not long before he was leading his people to rebel against God and they began to worship false gods. By the time we get to chapter 11 of Genesis, the dominant religion was as it is today, humanism. We see man wanting to build the Tower of Babel – a monument reaching into the sky – a tribute to Man in all his glory.

Babylon was originally built by Nimrod for the purpose of defying God. Ancient Grecian writings tell us that Nimrod's wife was Semiramis, a woman more wicked than even Jezebel. She had a son named Tammuz. In Egypt, she was called Isis; her son was called Osiris. In Greece, she was Aphrodite; her son was Eros. In Rome, she was called Venus; her son was Cupid. There are many stories and legends about Semiramis. When one of her early husbands was king in Babylon, she convinced him to let her become "Queen for a Day," and when he did, she killed him and remained on the throne. Nice lady.

One of the more popular legends found in just about every culture of the day was that Semiramis' son, Tammuz, was killed by a wild boar. He was later resurrected to be hailed by the people as their great savior and a fulfillment of God's promise of a messiah that is recorded in Genesis 3:15. The false god, Baal, was identical with Tammuz. The religious system that grew out of this had many mysterious rites. These included the sprinkling of holy water, countless sacraments and the dedication of young girls as temple prostitutes.

When Tammuz was killed, there were 40 days of weeping by all the women. The current practice of 40 days of lent can be traced to this ancient practice.[2] In Ezekiel 8:14-15, Tammuz is mentioned by name and says this practice is an abomination before God. Later, Semiramis was pictured as Queen of Heaven, and with the babe in her arms, spread the worship of "mother and child". It was a common practice to give round cakes or wafers to this Queen of Heaven in order to win her favor. Since it is difficult to tell fact from fiction from those early stories, we will just leave it that she was undoubtedly a very wicked person.[3]

Let me give you an illustration of how Nimrod and his wife were throwing religion back into the face of God. The human race had to begin building itself again after the flood. Noah's son, Shem, lived 502 years; he outlived both Nimrod and Semiramis. Abraham was about 50 years old when Nimrod's wife died. Here's the point. This great pagan system of false worship, instituted by Nimrod and his wife, was introduced during the time these awesome patriarchs were still alive: Shem, Abraham, and of course, Job. Later, Abraham was called out of this very ungodly area to become the father of God's chosen nation of Israel.

This pagan religion that began in Babel became the mother of all the pagan religions of the world. Its full development is seen in the end times when all the false religions of the world unite into a one-world religion. Their leader is the second Beast to which we were introduced in chapter 13. He is also called the False Prophet, and he heads up this false religion called *"Mystery Babylon."*

We see in chapter 17, verse 1 where one of the angels, mentioned in chapter 16, came over to John to show him the destruction of *"the great whore that sitteth upon many waters."* What do you suppose are these *"many waters"* that are mentioned here? Well, we don't have to speculate what they represent. We are told in 17:15, they are *"peoples, and multitudes, and nations and tongues."* The picture is beginning to clear up for us! Here is the great one-world religion riding on the back of, or dominating you might say, all the earth dwellers during the Tribulation Period. Verse 2 says that the kings of the earth have committed fornication with her. This is talking about spiritual fornication – professed believers leaping out of the arms of God into the arms of a false lover and all the worldly associations that go with it.

God's Word instructs Christians to be separated from the world. We are not to fall in love with the world or anything that it contains (I John 2:15). Those who disregard these commands are spiritual adulterers or fornicators. That is why James 4:4b declares, *"Whosoever therefore will be a friend of the world* [meaning this godless world system] *is the enemy of God."*

Not so much in our day, but for a thousand years, the Roman Catholic Church was entangled, and intertwined with the political governments of the world. It dominated Europe and its kings until the 16th Century when the Reformation brought a measure of deliverance. So, in the end times, we find not only a revival of the Roman Empire, but also there will be a revival of Papal Rome in all of its former glory and power.

Many voices today are heard in Protestant churches suggesting that it would be great if we put aside all our differences and unite with the Roman Catholics making one unified church. But the fact is, the real body of Christ remains undivided in spite of Christendom's unhappy divisions for it is composed of all truly saved people who have by the Spirit's baptism been made one in Christ. While outward earthly unity is desirable, it would not be a blessing if it comes at the expense of truth. In the last days, this great false religious system will use Christian words and phrases to deceive millions; they will unite in the one world church.

Let us return to verses 1-2 of Revelation 17. *"And there came one of the seven angels which had the seven vials, and talked with me, saying unto me, 'Come hither; I will show unto thee the judgment of the great whore that sitteth upon many waters; With whom the kings of the earth have committed fornication, and the inhabitants of the earth have been made drunk with the wine of her fornication.'"* Many Bible scholars say this is a picture of the Roman Catholic Church during the end times, or that the Roman Church with all its organization and hierarchy simply paves the way for the formation of the one-world church that is coming. Certainly its history meshes with the description we just read, and so we will take this opportunity to look at the history of the Catholic Church.

Over the centuries, the Roman Church has been more than just entangled with the rulers of the world. Many popes have actually sought to control the politics throughout Europe. That is an established fact of history. So let us look at some of the false doctrines held by the Roman Church. To their credit, the Catholic Church has performed many human acts of kindness. It has built hospitals and orphanages around the world. It has sent medical missionaries into forgotten regions. It has stood firm in supporting human life and protesting abortion mills.

But just as with any denomination, you are going to find within its ranks many born again believers. They are the ones who found the true Light in spite of the stumbling blocks thrown up before them. And, unfortunately, you are going to find many others who trust in the Church for their salvation. I have heard people, including many movie stars say, "I give plenty of money to the Church. It's up to them to see that I get to Heaven." There is a tendency to say, "The Church can't be wrong; it's too big, and it has been around too long." And so they desperately try to trace the history and succession of the popes all the way back to whom they claim was the first pope, Simon Peter himself.

From time to time, the Roman Church sponsors "ecumenical councils" to explore unification with the Protestant churches. But to be clear, the Roman Church is not interested in changing any of its doctrines to satisfy other churches. It wants the Protestant churches of every denomination to compromise and come in under the Roman Church's authority. However, we have some major differences with Catholicism. We cannot sweep them under the rug as Pat Robertson did before the last ecumenical council. He has been in the forefront of being cozy with the Catholic Church. He said the time has come when Protestants should lay aside minor points of doctrinal differences and focus on the centralization of our faith in the Lord Jesus Christ.

Robertson went on to say this in an interview with Sean Hannity: "I had a wonderful meeting with Pope John Paul II. My friend, Cardinal O'Connor had a reception at his residence when the Pope came to New York and they had that wonderful mass in Central Park. I was in the consistory with him and the other officials of the church. It was a very moving thing. Just absolutely incredible."[4] But we not talking about red or blue carpet in the sanctuary; we are talking about life and death issues that count for eternity.

Let us look at a few of those differences. To anyone who bothers to research the Catholic position on salvation, the truth becomes apparent. The official position of the Church is that salvation comes through grace (so far, so good) – but grace is dispensed a little at a time by the priests serving the sacraments (the wine and the bread.) In the Church's official statement that was ratified at the Council of Trent, the Church declared that anyone who says that the sacraments are not necessary for salvation, and that salvation and justification can be obtained by faith alone in God, that person should be consigned to Hell.[5]

Then there is the issue of Mary. Unfortunately, most Protestants have not given Mary the honor and respect that she deserves. She is truly blessed among women. In her song to God, she sings, " .... *for behold, from henceforth all generations shall call me blessed"* (Luke 1:48b). This does not mean that Mary was sinless. Catholics would disagree. In fact, it was not until 1854, just 165 years ago, that Pope Pius IX declared that Mary was born without original sin, and that God kept her sinless throughout her life, at the end of which, she bodily ascended up to Heaven. This doctrine is called, "The Immaculate Conception."[6]

The Catholic Church teaches that the Immaculate Conception was believed all along through the ages, and Pope Pius IX in 1854 only formally defined this doctrine. But Scripture never even hints at such a thing. In fact, when Mary sings her song in Luke chapter 1, she sings, *"And my spirit hath rejoiced in God my Savior"* (Luke 1:47). Mary acknowledged she needed a Savior just like all of us. If she had never sinned, she would not have needed a Savior. This brings out something else in Catholic teaching that we could never embrace. When a pope makes a pronouncement, and declares what is called dogma in his official capacity as pope, he cannot err. Just like the Bible, his declarations are inerrant. How did this come about that the pope could declare something, and it would be on the same level and carry the same authority as the Bible? Has it always been like that? A resounding no!

There was a meeting called by the Roman Church on July 13, 1870. It was called "The 85th General Congregation of the Vatican Council." The main purpose of the convention was to debate the pros and cons of declaring this principle: that what the pope declares in his official capacity is without error and carries the same weight as Holy Scriptures. It was a lively debate! One of the most outspoken bishops who opposed this "Doctrine of Papal Infallibility" was Bishop Joseph Strossmayer of Croatia. He gave one of the most brilliant and impassioned speeches I have ever read on the subject. It was a long speech, running close to an hour.

Here are some edited excerpts from that speech: "Reading the sacred Scriptures – I do not find one single chapter or one little verse in which Jesus Christ gives to St. Peter the mastery over the apostles. It would have been wonderful if Jesus had said, 'When I have ascended to my Father, you should all obey Simon Peter as you obey me. I establish him as my representative here on earth.'"

Bishop Strossmayer continues, "An Ecumenical Council was assembled at Jerusalem to decide on questions which divided the faithful. This is recorded in Acts 15. If St. Peter had been pope, who would have called this meeting? If St. Peter had been pope, who would have presided at this meeting? If St. Peter had been pope, who would have summarized the findings of the Council? It is true that Peter had something to say in the debates, but so did all the other apostles. And when the meeting was coming to a close, it was James that summarized the findings that ended the discussion."

Then, Bishop Strossmayer saved his strongest argument until last. "Popes have reversed each other scores of times over the years. Were they infallible? Who was right? Pope Gregory I (785) declared that anyone taking the name of "Universal Bishop" was the same as the Antichrist; Pope Boniface III (607) took that title. Pope Hadrian II (867) declared civil marriages to be valid; Pope Pius VII (1800) condemned them. Pope Sixtus V (1585) published an edition of the Bible, and urged that it be read; the Council of Toulouse under the direction of Pope Gregory IX prohibited the laity from owning or reading the Bible or any translation thereof.

And then Bishop Strossmayer ended his speech with these words: "Save the Church from the shipwreck which threatens her, asking from the Holy Scriptures alone for the rule of faith which we all ought to believe and to profess. I have spoken. May God help me!" As he finished his speech, angry cries came from fellow bishops, "Out with the traitor. Let him be cursed to Hell!" At that point, a vote was called to determine the pope's infallibility. Approximately 667 bishops, archbishops and prelates cast votes; 76 sided with Bishop Strossmayer and opposed papal infallibility. The remaining votes were cast to approve it, and therefore it became official Catholic doctrine.[7]

Of course, the Vatican says that Bishop Strossmayer's speech never happened. Only the Vatican has access to the official minutes of that meeting. However, as a result of the decision by that Council, the pope can stand up after all these years, and declare that Mary was sinless, and that she later ascended into Heaven. They can assert this because the Council ruled that a pope cannot make an error in his official pronouncements.

It is ironic that truth was determined by a vote of Catholic priests. That is why at some future date we might even see a pope stand up and declare that Mary is co-redeemer with Christ. In theological terms, that is known as "Mariology" – the theology of Mary. There have been several movements underway in the Catholic Church to establish such a doctrine. In fact, one spokesman said, "Women might even feel more comfortable going to a female Savior." This even has a more disturbing aspect to it. God is the only one who can forgive sin. So, seemingly this doctrine would elevate Mary to be equal with God although Catholic scholars say this is a wrong interpretation – that it is simply an honorary title.[8] To date, the Church has not officially sanctioned the title, however a large number of bishops and cardinals are in favor of it. It could well be official Church dogma one day.

Pope John Paul II was a proponent of religious unity. However, he feared the unity he saw that was shaping up around him. He would not compromise on his stand against abortion, gay marriages, and women in the priesthood, but I am afraid that we will see the Roman Church softening considerably on these issues in the years ahead. In fact, Pope John Paul II, though he believed strongly in a number of basic Catholic beliefs, he would not bring these to an ecclesiastical vote to reaffirm them because he estimated about two-thirds of the bishops are extremely liberal, and probably would not support him.

Hundreds of bishops continue to push the following liberal agenda: They want priests to be able to marry; They want to elevate Mary to co-redeemer with Christ; And they want women to be ordained as priests. One of the reasons they want women to be ordained as priests is that they have had difficulty in getting new priests to fill their vacancies. The following story illustrates to what extent the Catholic Church will go to ordain new priests. One of my best friends at work several years ago was a lady whom we will call Carol. As unbelievable as this is, I saw it unfold first hand. She and her husband, Bill, were Catholics, but after a few years of marriage, she had two little ones and about this time her husband left her. To her credit, she never remarried, but raised those two kids by herself. They never got a divorce as Carol abided by her church's doctrine of no divorce.

Carol had many difficult times, but relied on the Lord to pull her through, and for strength she attended mass every Sunday. Carol and the kids had nominal contact with Bill over the years. The kids grew up, went to college and became exemplary citizens. The father in the meantime decided he wanted to try the homosexual lifestyle. After a couple of years, he bailed out, and you will not believe what came next.

One day Carol received a letter from her parish priest. It said that her husband, Bill, had come to see him and wanted to enter the priesthood. Carol was aghast and replied, "But we are married!" A week later, she got another letter. It was from the Archbishop. It stated that proceedings had begun to have her marriage with Bill annulled. Carol was beside herself. She wrote a hot letter to the Archbishop. "How can it be annulled? We have been married over 20 years. The marriage was consummated. We have two kids! If it is annulled, look what it will make my kids!!!"

In spite of all her protests, the annulment was accomplished. Bill entered a school for the training of priests, and now is a parish priest in another state. Unbelievable! It shows how desperate the Catholic Church is to fill the ranks of its ever dwindling priests, not to mention the integrity of the whole process. After getting over her anger, Carol started attending a Baptist church, but she never joined. She told me, "I was born a Catholic and I will die a Catholic."

There are other illustrations where our beliefs differ from the Roman Catholic Church. Some of you will remember Bishop Fulton Sheen, and his popular weekly television program from a number of years ago. He declared, "When I was ordained, I made a resolution to offer the Holy Eucharist every Saturday to the Blessed Mother." He urged his fellow priests to adopt a similar veneration for Mary, and to call upon her for intercession. Then, one day when they reach eternity, he said they would hear Christ say, "I've heard my Mother speak of you."[9]

I guess one of the biggest doctrinal differences has to do with the Lord's Supper – the bread and the wine. The Catholics call it the "Eucharist." Baptists and other Protestant denominations believe that the elements in the Lord's Supper represent the blood and body of Christ – that the bread is a picture of His body being broken for our sins, and the wine is a picture of His blood being poured out for us on Mount Calvary.

However, the Roman Catholic Church believes that, when the priest holds the bread and the cup of wine, and recites the almost magical words, elements in the bread and the wine miraculously change into the actual blood and body of Christ. This means according to their doctrine that every week when the sacrifice of the Mass is said around the world, Christ's body is being literally sacrificed again and again.

Roman Catholic priest Richard Chilson was interviewed on a video clip explaining the Church's position on this repeated offering of Christ at every Mass. When asked why the Church does not accept the finality of Christ's sacrifice, he was forced to say, "I don't know."[10] Rev. Chilson should read Hebrews 9:24-28 (NASB): "*For Christ did not enter a holy place made with hands, a mere copy of the true one, but into Heaven itself, now to appear in the presence of God for us; nor was it that He would offer Himself often, as the high priest* [when he] *enters the holy place year by year with blood that is not his own. Otherwise, He* [Christ] *would have needed to suffer often since the foundation of the world; but now once at the consummation of the ages He has been manifested to put away sin by the sacrifice of Himself. And inasmuch as it is appointed for men to die once and after this comes judgment, so Christ also, having been offered once to bear the sins of many, will appear a second time for salvation without reference to sin, to those who eagerly await Him.*"

After explaining what a superior high priest we have in Christ over human earthly priests, Scripture says, "*For it was fitting for us to have such a high priest, holy, innocent, undefiled, separated from sinners and exalted above the heavens; who does not need daily, like those* [former] *high priests, to offer up sacrifices, first for his own sins and then for the sins of the people, because this He did once for all when He offered up Himself*" (Hebrews 7:26-27 NASB). The most important phrase in this verse is "once for all!"

Even Peter (whom the Roman Church says was the first pope) acknowledges this: "*For Christ also died for sins once for all, the just for the unjust, so that He might bring us to God ....*" (I Peter 3:18a NASB). As to Christ's one-time sacrifice, how can Romans 6:9 (NASB) be any clearer? *"Knowing that Christ, having been raised from the dead, is never to die again; death no longer is master over Him."*

As we continue to track Babylon, we will see that she is a failure in all respects. As a woman, she is seen as the Mother of Prostitutes. A prostitute in this sense is a person who spiritually has stopped following the true God, and has turned to idols or false worship. Her daughters are followers of the New Age Movement, Satan worship, Hinduism, Islam and a host of other false religions.

In fact in our society today, the primary word we hear in the field of religion is "tolerance." There may come a time when everything will be tolerated except intolerance. If you claim your belief is superior to other beliefs, you will be intolerant and that will not be allowed. That clashes directly with Jesus' assertion, *"no man cometh unto the Father but by Me"* (John 14:6).

When Paul preached to the intellectuals on Mars Hill as recorded in the 17th chapter of Acts, they were ready to make an idol to honor Jesus Christ, and put it alongside the images to all their other gods. But Paul said, "What a minute. Jesus is not a god among many, but He is the one and ONLY true God." At that point, they began to jeer him, and if he had not left town, they probably would have plotted to kill him.

The new hate law bill in the U.S. is being pushed more strongly every day. Basically, it says you cannot say certain things or think certain things without violating the hate laws. And it will be a very short step to pass a law saying that it is hateful to say that homosexuality is wrong, or it is hateful to say that abortion is wrong. And certainly you will not be permitted to say that Jesus is the only way to Heaven; if you do, you will be subject to arrest.

If the Antichrist can get laws passed whereby your words or thoughts take precedent over your freedom of speech, he will have it made. Speaking of thoughts, I love the story about the fellow that appeared in court. He said, "Judge, if I call you a stupid idiot, would you put me in jail." The judge said, "You bet I would." The man said, "Judge, would you put me in jail if I were to just think that you are a stupid idiot?" The judge said, "No, I couldn't do that for just thinking it." The man said, "Well, judge, I think you are a stupid idiot!"

Babylon is not only a failure as a religious system, she is also a failure as a city as she will open her doors to the one-world government and the Antichrist. Chapter 17, verse 3: *"So he carried me away in the spirit into the wilderness; and I saw a woman sit upon a scarlet-colored Beast, full of names of blasphemy, having seven heads and ten horns."* This woman – this false religious system we have just been studying – is now sitting upon (or controlling) this red Beast that has seven heads and ten horns. We have seen this Beast before. Revelation 13:1 talks about this same Beast rising up out of the sea. Revelation 17:15 says the sea is a picture of the vast multitude of peoples, and this Beast has the same seven heads and ten horns seen previously. Why is the Beast pictured as red or scarlet? Because first of all, the Beast is empowered by Satan who in chapter 12:9 is called the red dragon. And secondly, by this time the Beast is red with the blood of a million saints.

This Beast is full of the names of blasphemy. That is no surprise! Babylon the Great has assembled all the false religions of the world and meshed them into one. And the Antichrist himself is about to enter the Temple in Jerusalem and declare himself to be God Almighty. After the Antichrist steps to the center of the world stage, most but not everyone, will welcome him with open arms. We saw that happen in chapter 6 when each of the seven seals was opened.

The rider on the white horse in chapter 6 is promising a false peace. But soon this peace evaporates and the Antichrist begins to take over. Whether a person is a Christian or not, once he has tasted freedom such as we have in the United States, that person will not be very excited about living under a dictatorship. The second, third and fourth seals in chapter 6 depict the bloodshed, violence and turmoil that will grip the world while the Antichrist is consolidating his power. Eventually, he will convince the nations of the world to accept his leadership. With some, he will do this by flattery and persuasion, but for others, it will be done through bloodshed and military power.

My best assessment is that soon after this, the Antichrist will then, in order to keep peace and show how gracious he is, divide the empire into 10 divisions or kingdoms. Each will have a king or potentate or whatever he might be called, who will be responsible for governing that particular division. Initially, the Antichrist will simply be one of the 10 kings and will have authority over one of the 10 kingdoms. I do not want to get ahead of myself, but I want to show you where we are heading.

We will see later in Scripture that the Antichrist will eventually make a bid to have the other nine kings turn over their authority to him. Three of them will refuse to do so. They are swiftly disposed of, and the other six quickly give in to everything the Antichrist demands. We will see this in detail before this chapter is over. Having said that, let us go back and look again at the statement in Scripture, "7 heads and 10 kings." We know what the 10 kings represent (10 divisions of the kingdom), but what do the 7 heads mean?

We do not have to guess. We are told clearly in Revelation 17:9-10a: *"And here is the mind which hath wisdom. The seven heads are seven mountains, on which the woman sitteth. And there are seven kings …."*. The Greek word translated mountains in the King James Version is "oros" which could be translated either mountains or hills. The NIV, the NLT, the Living Bible, and the Phillips' paraphrase – all translate oros as hills. This is how the New Living Translation puts 17:9: *"And now understand this: The seven heads of the Beast represent the seven hills of the city where this woman rules. They also represent seven kings."*

If you were a contestant on "Want to Be a Millionaire?" and they asked you, "What city has been known throughout history as 'the city built upon seven hills' – what would your answer be?" The Apostle John would not have had any trouble identifying it. The Encyclopedia Britannica does not have any trouble identifying it. It says that Rome is known as the city that was built on seven hills.[11] This woman, representing all the false religions coming together into a one-world religion, is controlling the one-world government headed up by the Antichrist. Their headquarters is in the city built on seven hills which the encyclopedia identifies as Rome! Is this a monumental coincidence? I think not!

Let us look at a further description of this woman. Verse 4: *"And the woman was arrayed in purple and scarlet color, and decked with gold and precious stones and pearls, having a golden cup in her hand full of abominations and filthiness of her fornication."* Purple and scarlet were the two chief colors of imperial Rome. Their banners and accessories were scarlet. The formal dress of their leaders and senators was purple. Is it a coincidence that scarlet and purple are the two primary colors of the attire of the pope and the cardinals?

The head of this false religious system is so enmeshed with the political power of Rome that she also is decked out in royal purple and scarlet. Dr. Jimmy Draper says, "Before we see the perfection of the Lamb and His Bride, we must see the Beast and his harlot. Final judgment must precede final blessing."[12] But the scarlet that this woman flaunts is not portraying the cleansing blood of the Lamb. She is portraying the shed blood of the millions of saints she has martyred.

In Matthew 15:9, we are told we cannot get to Heaven by following the commandments of man. In Mark 7:9, we are told we cannot get to Heaven by following the traditions of man. And in Titus 3:5, we are told that we cannot get to Heaven by doing the works of man.

It is only by trusting Christ, and being cleansed by His blood do we have the forgiveness of sin. This woman is decked out in beautiful jewelry and luxurious garments. She is irresistible to ungodly men. She seduces them and entraps them to partake of her pleasures. Her golden cup of sparkling wine in her extended hand deceives nation after nation, and multitudes are lost forever. Listen to this description of her given in Proverbs 5:3-5 so many years ago: *"For the lips of a strange woman drop as a honeycomb, and her mouth is smoother than oil: but her end is bitter as wormwood, sharp as a two-edged sword. Her feet go down to death; her steps take hold on Hell."*

Hal Lindsey said: "I have found this to be true of religion: the more false a religion is, usually the more wealth it has." The wealthiest religion in the world is Islam with all its oil. But the next wealthiest is the Roman Catholic Church, followed by the Church of Jesus Christ of Latter Day Saints (Mormons). It is unbelievable the amount of wealth that these three possess. It is hard to determine the exact worth of the Roman Catholic Church due to its financial secrecy. Financial experts say the Roman Church has gone to great lengths to obscure its financial holdings. One author says it was "dragged" into the 21st Century and is having a hard time dealing with the transparency that is required by federal regulators of most non-profits. Next is the Church of

Jesus Christ of Latter Day Saints (Mormons). In 2012, Reuters estimated that its real estate holdings totaled at least $35 billion.[13] Although not in the same league as large denominations, a number of individual preachers have accumulated giant nest eggs, such as – Kenneth Copeland ($760 million), Pat Robertson ($100 million) and Joel Osteen ($40 million).[14]

In this chapter, we have seen the ugly side of religion. It is reminiscent of the church in Thyatira (Revelation 2:20) where Jesus says about that church, *"thou sufferest that woman .... to teach and seduce my servants to commit fornication"*. Here is an insightful statement by prophecy teacher, Grant Jeffrey: *"Mystery Babylon,* the apostate church of the last days, will not develop overnight. Such an ecumenical organization, involving many diverse religious groups, will be created by negotiation and conferences over a number of years leading up to the beginning of the seven year Tribulation Period. It is therefore quite probable that we will witness the initial steps toward this one-world church of the last days before the Rapture takes the Christians home to Heaven."[15]

God hates idolatry. The first commandment says, *"Thou shalt have no other gods before Me"* (Exodus 20:3). God gives warning after warning against worshipping idols. Most people do not take these warnings seriously. They say, "Oh, I never bow down and worship statues nor idols." They are missing the point! An idol is anything that takes the place of God!

The very last word that John gives us in his first epistle is in I John 5:21. It says: *"Little children, keep yourselves from idols."* Let that sink in! Don't let the world and its attractions keep you from worshipping Him in His house each week. Well, back to the one-world church pictured by this seductive woman. After helping the Antichrist consolidate his one-world government, this woman will be cut to pieces by the very ones she helped rise to power. Sort of like what happened to Dr. Frankenstein. He was destroyed by the monster he created. We will see that before the end of this chapter.

Verse 5: *"And upon her forehead was a name written, MYSTERY BABYLON THE GREAT, THE MOTHER OF HARLOTS AND ABOMINATIONS OF THE EARTH."* Everything that opposes God had its organized beginning with the construction of the Tower of Babel. We find its culmination with the one-world religion orchestrated by its leader, the False Prophet.

Verse 6: *"And I saw the woman drunken with the blood of the saints, and with the blood of the martyrs of Jesus: and when I saw her, I wondered with great admiration."* John says, *"And I saw the woman drunken ...."*. In the Greek, the word "drunken or drunk" is in the present active participle, meaning continuously drunk with the blood of God's servants. She did not make a mistake one time, and get blood on her hands. She killed God's servants over and over and over. John was dumbfounded. He was confused. He was mystified. When it says he *"wondered with great admiration"* we get the wrong impression in our King James translation. It is not admiration at all! Actually, it is saying in the Greek, "He wondered with great amazement – he wondered with great bewilderment." The New Living Translation best describes how John felt in verse 6: *"I stared at her completely amazed."*

Why was John so amazed? John could not believe his eyes. In his day, it was pagan Rome under the Caesars that were persecuting the Christians. It was pagan Rome who was killing Christians with the sword, or crucifying them, or pitting them against the wild beasts in the arena. But now John sees the blood of the saints being shed by this rich and idolatrous church. No wonder John looks in amazement!

There is a dark blot in church history. It is called "the Inquisition" when millions of Christians were slaughtered by the Roman Catholic Church. Countless others were burned at the stake. Who would have ever dreamed that out of that humble, persecuted, outcast, little band of believers would arise a church so rich and powerful that it would martyr millions of Christians? Even the Roman Catholic Church acknowledges that this was one of the darkest periods of its history. One Roman Catholic historian said of that period in history: "The annals of the Church are the annals of Hell."[16] The book, *Foxes' Book of Martyrs,* is an accurate history of what happened to thousands of God's faithful saints during the time history calls the "dark ages."[17]

The following tells of two saints of God during the dark ages who remained faithful in spite of severe persecution. They were John Wycliffe and John (Jan) Huss. John Wycliffe lived from 1330-1384, and was a reformer in England who broke away from the Roman Church. He died a natural death, but the Roman Church was so angry at him that, 44 years later the Church ordered his bones to be exhumed and burned. Named after him is The Wycliffe Bible Translators who have their national headquarters in Duncanville, Texas. For years they have sent out teams of translators, most having earned PhDs. They go into the primitive areas of the world, translating Bibles into those languages that have no Bible.[18]

Many times, as with the Auca Indians in Ecuador, these translators have to build an alphabet and a written language for these people. These are the real heroes in our world, not the athletes who can throw or hit a little ball. Some of these translators have actually spent their entire lives so that others can read the Bible in their own language.

Then there was John Huss (sometimes called Jan Huss), a bishop in Prague who lived from 1373-1415. He carried on in the tradition of John Wycliffe. In 1411, Pope John XXIII issued what is called a "bull" in connection with the selling of indulgences. It is well named – that is exactly what I think of the practice. If you wanted to indulge in your favorite sin, you could buy an indulgence from the Roman priest, and you would be exempt from any sin or penalty connected with it. John Huss took this Papal order, and publicly burned it. Then he declared it to be what it is – a heresy and an abomination to God. The citizens of Prague protected Huss, and would not turn him over to the authorities, but the Church did seize three of his followers and beheaded them. Huss, himself, was lured out of the town some three years later to attend a church conference in Constance. There, Huss was arrested, tried for heresy and burned at the stake by the Roman Church on July 6, 1415.[19]

I could enumerate scores of other faithful servants who gave their lives for the testimony of the Lord Jesus Christ. No wonder verse 6 (NASB) says: *"And I saw the woman drunk with the blood of the saints, and with the blood of the witnesses of Jesus ."* That is why the Greek word for drunk means continuously intoxicated. The apostate Church has killed saints throughout history and here, during the Tribulation Period, John sees that she is still killing the saints. That is why John was amazed. He expected the imperial forces of Rome to kill Christians, but he never expected to see the Church killing them.

You will find this to be true: wherever Christianity has gone, the preaching of the Gospel and salvation by God's grace has been resisted, most of the time amidst bitter persecution. Why is there bitterness against a loving Creator? Why do people resist the offer of free salvation by the grace of God? The only answer is that the old dragon – Satan himself – has energized the forces of evil to oppose all that is good. We see this in the next verses.

Verses 7-8: *"And the angel said unto me, wherefore didst thou marvel? I will tell thee the mystery of the woman, and of the Beast that carrieth her, which hath the seven heads and ten horns. The Beast that thou sawest was, and is not; and shall ascend out of the Bottomless Pit, and go into perdition: and they that dwell on the earth shall wonder, whose names were not written in the Book of Life from the foundation of the world, when they behold the Beast that was, and is not, and yet is."*

We have seen this Beast before showing that it is without doubt, the Revived Roman Empire. The Bible is crystal clear that the old Roman Empire will come back into existence during the last days. But we also saw that this Beast refers to the Antichrist who heads up this godless empire. So, when Scripture talks about this Beast being mortally wounded and then comes back from the dead (which we saw in chapter 13), I believe it is in a general sense referring to the rise of the Roman Empire which had been dead for so many years.

But in a more specific sense, I think the Antichrist will personally sustain what looks like a mortal blow. It will appear that he dies, but is resurrected. That is when the people shout in Revelation 13:4, "nothing can stop him now." So, when we come to this phrase in the eighth verse of chapter 17 – that the Beast *"was, and is not, and yet is"* – let us first consider the Revived Roman Empire, and then the Antichrist.

If you know the history of the Roman Empire, you can certainly say it was and then it came to an end. And then, for 1500 years up to and including the present time, you could say it is not. And then, when it is revived during the seven years Tribulation Period, you could say and yet it is. You could also say this about the Antichrist. You could say "he was" when the Beast first came on the scene (Revelation 13:1). You could say "he is not" after the Beast is assassinated (Revelation 13:3). And you could say "and yet He is" after the Beast is revived (Revelation 13:3).

Verse 8 says that this Beast will come out of the abyss – the Bottomless Pit. You will remember that in chapter 9 we saw where Satan was given the key to the Bottomless Pit and all kinds of demon spirits poured forth. Just like a Christian can be filled with the Holy Spirit, the Antichrist will be completely indwelt by Satan and his demons which come out of the Bottomless Pit. Revelation 17:8 also tells what his fate will be – *"he shall go into perdition."* That means he will be cast into the Lake of Fire as we shall see in the 20th chapter of Revelation. Even worse news is that he takes a multitude of people with him. Who does he take? Look at the middle of verse 8. He takes those *"whose names were not written in the Book of Life from the foundation of the world"*.

Someone asked, "How can the world governments mesh into one in just a short period of time?" Sometimes, things happen faster than we could ever imagine. For example, in the mid-eighties if someone had told you, "If you will give me all of your money, I will guarantee three things will happen to you in the next 10 years:

1) You will have more money than the three largest banks in Dallas.
2) You will have better morals than two of the nation's leading preachers.
3) And you will have more girlfriends than Hollywood's leading actor.

Who wouldn't have jumped at that deal? Well, if you had, you would have lost every penny of your money.

1) "In 10 years, you will have more money than First National Bank in Dallas, Republic National Bank of Dallas, Mercantile National Bank at Dallas." In the late eighties, all three went bankrupt, and stockholders lost every dime they had invested.[20]

2) "You will have better morals than the two leading preachers in the country." In 1987, Jimmy Swaggart was convicted of soliciting a prostitute. And Jim Bakker was charged and sentenced to 45 years for defrauding people out of millions in a Christian resort scam.[21]

3) "You will have more girlfriends than the leading actor, Rock Hudson." It turned out that he was gay, and he died in 1985 of AIDS.[22]

That is how fast things can change! Now we come to chapter 17, verse 9: *"And here is the mind which hath wisdom. The seven heads are seven mountains, on which the woman sitteth."*

Knowledge comes from a person's own hard work and study. You go to school to get knowledge. I was always one to cram. You know what that means? Wait until the last minute to study for a big test, and then give it all you've got. But knowledge is not the same as wisdom. Proverbs 1:7 (NLT) says, *"But the fear of the LORD is the beginning of knowledge, but fools despise wisdom and instruction."* Twice in Revelation we are told: *"Here is wisdom."* We are told that in Revelation 13:18 in connection with the Antichrist's number 666; and again, we find it here in the 17th chapter in connection with the seven mountains mentioned in verse 9.

We were told in the first chapter of this Book that these end time mysteries are going to be revealed to us in signs and symbols. Some of the signs have double meanings. They mean more than one thing. We will see that with these seven heads. In verse 10 they represent seven kings; but here in verse 9, they represent seven mountains on which the woman sits. When John heard this description, he knew immediately it was referring to Rome. It was not too long before this that a decree from Rome had sent him as prisoner to the Isle of Patmos.

Nearly every city has a nickname – a name that reflects the character or the physical aspect of the city. Here is a few that I gleaned from the internet:

> Chicago - The Windy City
> Hollywood – Tinsel Town
> Dallas – Big D
> New York – The Big Apple
> Ft. Worth – Cowtown
> New Orleans – The Big Easy
> Philadelphia – The City of Brotherly Love
> Detroit – The Motor City
> Las Vegas – Sin City
> And then there is Rome – The City Built on Seven Hills!

When verse 9 refers to the city built on *"seven hills on which the woman sits"* – there is no question that it is referring to Rome.

Now we are to use wisdom in understanding this. History is available to the natural man, but prophecy can only be understood through the guidance of the Holy Spirit. British author William Wordsworth tells us that archaeologists have found imperial medals of Rome from the 200 to 500 A.D. era, and on them is imprinted a woman seated on seven hills.[23]

But in verse 10, we find that there are also seven kings. Let us read verse 10: *"And there are seven kings: five are fallen, and one is, and the other is not yet come; and when he cometh, he must continue a short space."* Who are these kings? There are two ways to interpret them. As I said before, many times prophetic Scriptures have a primary meaning and a secondary meaning. That is why we need to pray for wisdom. I believe that is the case here.

As we go through here, do not get bogged down with these mysterious descriptions. Just keep in mind that these kings can either be actual persons or their kingdoms or both. The information we are given fits them both, king and kingdom. The Greek word "basileus" (or plural "basileia") can mean either a king or a kingdom, however, at least 8 translations render this word as kings. These 7 heads or kings are also mentioned in Revelation 12:3.

Many scholars, including Dr. Jack Van Impe, believe this is referring to actual kings of the Roman Empire. He lists them as follows: 1) Julius Caesar; followed by 2) Tiberius Caesar; 3) Caligula; 4) Claudius; 5) Nero; and number 6, Domitian who was alive and ruling at the time John was writing this book on the Isle of Patmos; and number 7) is the Antichrist who will rise to power during the Tribulation Period.[24]

Prophecy teacher David Hocking says that these seven kings represent political empires or kingdoms as well as individual rulers.[25] Other Bible teachers, such as Hal Lindsey and Theodore Epp, say that the correct translation of this word in verse 10 should be "kingdoms" instead of kings. The fact that it says they have "fallen" seems to imply kingdoms.

Most historians tell us that there have been seven Gentile world kingdoms. Five have fallen, which are: the Egyptian, Assyrian, Babylonian, Medo-Persian and Grecian. These all existed before John's time, hence they have fallen. *"One is"* refers to the sixth kingdom that was in existence when John writes these words, which was, the Roman Empire or kingdom. And when it says *"the other has not yet come,"* it is referring to the Revived Roman Empire which will arise in the last days under the dictatorship of the Antichrist. This seventh kingdom will last a short space, that is, during the seven years of the Tribulation Period.

If that is not enough to fry our brains, we have another mystery in verse 11: *"And the Beast that was, and is not, even he is the eighth, and is of the seven, and goeth into perdition."* At first glance, this verse may seem like a puzzle. But it is easily understood when we look at it slowly and carefully. Who is king number eight if there are only seven kings in the first place? Think about this – king number seven is the Antichrist. But when he was (seemingly) assassinated, he *"was not."* And then when he was (seemingly) resurrected, he became king number eight.

Let me read verse 11 with some clarifying statements.
"And the beast that was" [before he was killed],
"and is not" [because of his mortal wound],

"even he is the eighth" [because of his resurrection],

"and is of the seven" [same guy as the seventh, only now he has been resurrected and filled with the power of Satan], *"and goeth into perdition"* [where he will eventually join Satan and the False Prophet]. So king number seven and king number eight are one and the same person. King seven is before he is assassinated, and king eight is after he has been resurrected and filled with the power of Satan.

As I mentioned, some scholars feel that these seven kings are really seven distinct kingdoms, with the seventh being the Revised Roman Empire, and with the eighth being a fully empowered Roman Empire controlled by Satan.

I can see valid points to this interpretation, but I tend to lean toward the interpretation that says these kings are individual leaders. Revelation 13:4 helps to shape my belief in this – the people marvel and flock after this Beast after he has been resurrected. I can picture this taking place in a much more realistic fashion if this is an individual who has been mortally wounded and then resurrected, as opposed to an Empire which has been mortally wounded and fades off the scene and then rises again to power.

I have great respect for Dr. C. I. Scofield, editor-in-chief of the Scofield Reference Bible. Here is his footnote in the Scofield Reference Bible as relates to Revelation 17:10-11: "Verses 10 and 11 are perhaps the most debated of all the passages in the Apocalypse. Since "fallen" is language more appropriate for kingdoms than for emperors, the best solution is probably to see the five fallen kings or kingdoms as Egypt, Assyria, Babylon, Medo-Persia and Greece. The sixth kingdom (*"one is"*) is the Rome of John's day. The last or seventh (*"the other is not yet come"*) is the revived form of the Roman Empire, first in its diversified form of ten kingdoms, eventually yielding to the eighth and final form of the Empire."[26]

You can almost see a progression here as this could easily be referring to seven kingdoms, but as time passes and end time events begin to accelerate, it seems to become more and more personal as the Antichrist moves to center stage. Aren't you thankful to God that He has promised to deliver us from these devastating times on the earth? As Christians, we are not going to suffer through the Tribulation Period, because we will have been raptured unto Him, and will be worshipping and praising the Lord around His throne.

Jesus told us that He is preparing a place for us. He has told us that we have not been appointed to wrath. And just like Noah who was lifted up above the floodwaters, and like Lot who was snatched out of Sodom before the brimstone fell, so we are to be caught up to meet the Lord in the air before the horrors of the Tribulation begin. This is described fully in the fourth chapter of I Thessalonians. It says this kingdom will only last a short time and then, as verse 11 tells us, it will descend into Hell itself.

Now we come to Verse 12: *"And the ten horns which thou sawest are ten kings, which have received no kingdom as yet; but receive power as kings one hour with the Beast."* These ten horns are ten kings – "co-kings" if you will, and are identical to what was presented in the Book of Daniel. In Daniel chapter 2, King Nebuchadnezzar saw a giant image representing the kingdoms of the world. The last kingdom had ten toes – the ten kings we see here. And Daniel looked until a stone out of Heaven smashed the image to bits, a perfect picture of when, as Revelation 11:15 says: *"The seventh angel sounded his trumpet, and there were loud voices in Heaven, which said: 'The kingdom of the world has become the kingdom of our Lord and of His Christ, and He will reign forever and ever'"* (NIV).

Although these ten kings start out as equals, they gradually come to acknowledge the superiority of the Beast, and will soon give all their sovereignty to him. So, if you had any doubts as to whether these rulers were operating under their own authority, then verse 13 will clear this up for you. *"These [ten kings] have one mind, and shall give their power and strength unto the Beast."* They hand over all authority to the Antichrist. He controls them and directs them even to the extent that he controls their wills! *"They have one mind"* – the mind of the Antichrist!

Satan is not omniscient – he does not know everything. Consequently, he must have a "potential" antichrist waiting in the wings. He must cultivate an individual in each generation who is so clever, so conniving, and willing to be possessed by the Devil, that he would make a perfect candidate to fill the shoes of the antichrist. Hitler could have been the Antichrist should the Rapture have occurred in 1940. Stalin could have been the Antichrist should the Rapture have occurred in 1950. The Devil has had an antichrist ready in every generation, and I think he has one picked out in our generation.

President Ahmadinejad of Iran seems to have lost a lot of his power in recent days, but he was a perfect picture of how the people will adore the Antichrist. He was addressing the assembly of the United Nations a few years ago. He recounts how he found himself bathed in light throughout the speech. But it was not a light from the building; he said it was a light from Heaven. He was not the only one who noticed this unearthly light. One of his delegation told him, "When you began with the words 'in the name of Allah', I saw a light coming, surrounding you, protecting you."

One delegate from the Iranian delegation said this: "On the last day when our President was speaking, a green light formed an aura around him, and for 28 minutes, all the leaders of the world did not blink. When I say they didn't move an eyelid, I am not exaggerating. They were looking as if a hand was holding them there in a trance – Praise Allah." President Ahmadinejad in his speech, said his main mission was to pave the way for the glorious appearing of a character in Islam who died over a thousand years ago – "Imam Mahdi." And the President continued, "When Imam Mahdi returns, he will reign on earth for seven years, before bringing about a final judgment and the end of the world."[27] This is unbelievable! Here is a devout Muslim talking about their coming Messiah reigning on the earth for seven years, not even realizing that the Christian Bible says that the Antichrist will reign for seven years during the Tribulation Period. Wow! Is this a coincidence?

Former U.S. Attorney General John Ashcroft said, "Islam is a religion of Muhammad whose god requires you to send your son to die for him. Christianity is a faith in which God sent His Son to die for you."[28] Muslim Holy Man Ali Lari said recently, "People are anxious to know when and how He will rise and what they must do to receive this worldwide salvation. There is a saying, when the students are ready, the teacher will come and they believe this will happen soon."[29] I believe I know what the Antichrist will tell them to do when he arrives: "Simply take my mark, number 666, on your wrist or on your forehead and acknowledge me as the one true God."

We mentioned that the ten kings turn all authority over to the Antichrist (who at this point is one of the ten kings). From Daniel 7:8, we find that at some point three of these ten kings decide to rebel against the Antichrist's rule and so he disposes of them. Remember by this time, Satan has taken full control of the Antichrist and, just as in demon possession, the Antichrist has surrendered his total will to this ruler of darkness. And do not forget, while all this intrigue is going on, the earth is being hammered by all the seal judgments, the trumpet judgments and the bowl judgments.

What do you suppose that Satan, the Antichrist and all their evil henchmen are focused upon? It is to conquer and destroy the Lord Jesus Christ. Verse 14: *"These shall make war with the Lamb, and the Lamb shall overcome them: for He is Lord of lords, and King of kings: and they that are with him are called, and chosen, and faithful."* There is so much wrapped up in this one verse. All creation has been waiting for this final battle on the plains of Jezreel in the Valley of Armageddon. This one phrase rings throughout the halls of Heaven, and bounces off a million stars throughout the universe: *"and the Lamb shall overcome them!"* Wow! No wonder we sing, *Victory in Jesus!* And all of us who have made that life-changing commitment to Jesus will be there with Him!

In verse 15 we have an explanation of a sign. *"And He said unto me, 'The waters which thou sawest, where the whore sitteth, are peoples, and multitudes, and nations, and tongues.'"* Remember verse 1 of this chapter? *"And there came one of the seven angels which had the seven vials, and talked with me, saying unto me, 'Come hither; I will show unto thee the judgment of the great whore that sitteth upon many waters'".* We have already been told that this great whore is the one-world religion that has absorbed all the false religions of the world. And she is sitting upon all the multitudes and nations and tongues. She has all of them under her control. But now we are going to see something simply amazing! This great false religion is headed up by the second Beast who is also known as the False Prophet.

During the first 3½ years of the Tribulation, this False Prophet uses his power and his influence in persuading the world to accept the Antichrist as their supreme leader. Without a doubt, this pompous, arrogant person grates on the nerves of the Antichrist as this second Beast struts around every day reminding the Antichrist, "You are in power because I put you in power!" The Antichrist can take it no longer. He has just entered the Temple in Jerusalem and declared himself to be God. He no longer needs the support of these underlings, including the False Prophet.

The Antichrist is fed up with this False Prophet's arrogance. Something must be done about it! So he stirs up the ten horns which are the ten regions we spoke of earlier, and they are eager to jump at the chance to destroy this despised despot, and the Beast gives them permission to do so. So they turn on the False Prophet, this second Beast heading up the false religious system, and they tear him and his system to pieces!

Verse 16: *"And the ten horns which thou sawest upon the Beast, these shall hate the whore, and shall make her desolate and naked, and shall eat her flesh, and burn her with fire."* Of course, the verse uses the feminine gender "her" because that is the way that a system or organization is always presented.

Dr. J. Dwight Pentecost, professor emeritus at Dallas Theological Seminary said, "The Beast, who was dominated by the one-world religious system (Revelation 17:3), rises against her and destroys her and her system completely. Without doubt the harlot system was in competition with the religious worship of the Beast, promoted by the False Prophet, and her destruction is brought about so that the Beast [Antichrist] may be the sole object of false worship as he claims to be God."[30]

Verses 17-18: *"For God hath put in their hearts to fulfill His will, and to agree, and give their kingdom unto the Beast, until the words of God shall be fulfilled. And the woman which thou sawest is that great city, which reigneth over the kings of the earth."* All of this crazy stuff – this fighting, this manipulation – is taking place all for the purpose of assembling the nations of the world under Satan's banner to bring war against the Lamb. And now we are told something we knew all along – that God is orchestrating all the events to His glory. He is ultimately behind the destruction of this one-world false religion, and He influences these satanic forces to carry out His will.

The Antichrist does not know it, but he is a puppet king just like the kings under him. God will plant the idea of destroying the false religious system into his heart and the hearts of his puppet kings. Without knowing it, they carry out God's will. What a marvelous thing: God accomplishes His purposes even by using His enemies. Even when we think that things are out of control, God uses our enemies to achieve His desired goals. When things get hectic, just remember: God is still in control!

Elizabeth Elliott and Rachel Saint and the other three widows had to remind themselves of this when their husbands were cut down in the prime of life by the vicious Auca Indians to whom they were bringing the Gospel in the jungles of Ecuador. As a result of the actions of these brave men, hundreds of savages accepted Jesus Christ as their Savior.[31]

Carrie McDonnall had to remind herself of this in Iraq when she and her young husband and three other missionaries were ambushed in broad daylight on the streets of Mosul and shot to pieces, with Carrie being the only survivor. Her resulting testimony and reliance upon God in times of heartache has blessed thousands.[32]

Just remember, God is in control, and He is moving history toward His desired conclusion. And it is great that He sometimes uses evil, godless men to accomplish His purposes. Babylon seems to be the very essence of sin itself, and in chapters 17 and 18, we see the details of her destruction. And here is where we need to really pray for the Holy Spirit's direction in our study. It appears to me that two aspects of Babylon are before us: *"Mystery Babylon"* and *"Babylon the Great."*

There is ample evidence that Mystery Babylon represents all the false religions of the world rolled into one, and is presided over by the False Prophet. But after the Antichrist rises to full power, and begins to really persecute the Jews, he gets weary of this false religious organization with their pompous leader. He and his cohorts then turn on it and destroy it completely. In the next chapter, we will learn the details of the Antichrist's enormous economic system – *Babylon the Great.*

CHAPTER EIGHTEEN

Babylon the Great

We now begin our study of Chapter 18 which deals with the commercial/political aspect of the city of Babylon. Babylon the Great appears to be a literal city and a one- world economic empire as opposed to Mystery Babylon in chapter 17 that represented the false one-world Church. As we mentioned earlier, there are three cities that will play a major role in the end times: Rome will be the political base, Babylon the commercial base and Jerusalem the religious base.

Throughout chapter 18, the emphasis is on the city of Babylon. *"Babylon the Great is fallen"* (verse 2); *"That great city Babylon"* (verse 10); *"That great city"* (verse 16); *"What city is like unto this great city"* (verse 18); *"That great city"* (verse 19); and *"That great city Babylon"* (verse 21). The city of Babylon is mentioned 260 times in Scripture – more times than any other city except Jerusalem.

Some commentators believe that the Babylon of chapter 17 and the Babylon of chapter 18 are one and the same. I believe they are two different entities. One reason is that in chapter 17 we see *"Mystery Babylon"* destroyed – picked to pieces and burned with fire. And then chapter 18 begins, " .... *after these things* ....". After what things? After what we have just seen: the destruction of Mystery Babylon – the one-world religious organization. Only Babylon the Great remains, and it recognizes the Antichrist as the true God and true political leader over the entire world. Secondly, an angel has been showing John what was going to happen to Mystery Babylon, and now "another" angel comes on the scene – one whose glory lights up the entire world.

There are levels of rank among the angelic hosts. Some have more authority than others and many have different duties. Scripture says that Michael, the archangel, is especially the defender of Israel. The angel Gabriel seems to be chosen when a special announcement needs to be made. In Revelation chapter 16 we were told that there is an angel in charge of the waters, and another angel has the power to burn men with fire. At any rate, we know from II Thessalonians 1:7 and II Peter 2:11 that all angels are characterized by might. They are powerful. They may have certain duties, but none has ever been given universal authority. That is a principle we find over and over in Scripture. God does not share His glory with another.

Christ's claim to universal dominion is not a conferred one, but is sovereign and independent, founded on the rights and glory of His Person as God and as Creator. (Colossians 1:16). The angel in chapter 18 does not have universal authority, but he has been given "great authority," and is probably the angel in charge of the judgment of Babylon.

When considering these two Babylons, keep this in mind: the false religious organization, *"Mystery Babylon,"* is destroyed prior to the end of the Tribulation Period by the Antichrist and his cohorts. The political and economic Babylon of chapter 18 is destroyed at the close of the Tribulation Period by the direct judgments of God. It is obvious then, that Revelation 17 and 18 are not speaking of the same entity when they refer to *"Mystery Babylon"* and to *"Babylon the Great."*

Babylon the Great appears to be the city of Babylon on the Euphrates which the Antichrist will rebuild as the commercial and economic capital of the world. Today, all eyes are on the Middle East. In this area of the world as you know there is a gigantic source of oil. There is an old story about a Jew and an Arab discussing Moses. The Jew said, "Moses was an idiot." And the Arab was greatly surprised and said, "Why do you say Moses was an idiot?" "Because, when he came out of Egypt, if he had turned right instead of left, we would have had the oil, and you would have had the sand!"

Israel is bordered on the west by the Mediterranean Sea. Being salt water, it is of course, not fit to drink. The only fresh water for the country, other than springs in various places, is the Sea of Galilee which is located in northern Israel. This was a problem 2,000 years ago in Israel. And so, Herod the Great solved the problem. He built a giant aqueduct which runs all the way from the Sea of Galilee in the north to Caesarea Maritime in the south. It is not too far from modern day Tel Aviv. Most of the aqueduct is still intact today.

At the southeast part of Israel, you will find the Dead Sea. Water from the Jordan flows all the way south, and empties into the Dead Sea. From there, it has no place to go. But it is not stagnant like we think of stagnant water. Bob in my Sunday school class, said he was so old that when he was born, the Dead Sea wasn't even sick!

The Dead Sea has so many heavy minerals it cannot sustain life. There is no plant life in it. There is no fish life in it. We went swimming in it. Correction – floating! It is 33% salt, so you have to struggle to go underwater. Our guide told us, "Nothing can live in the Dead Sea longer than seven minutes." I told him that he saved my life – I came out of the water after six minutes! But the Dead Sea is rich in minerals. Its healing power is in body lotions, mud packs and other cosmetics which are known far and wide. In fact some of the ladies' finest cosmetics such as "Ahava" lotion come directly from the Dead Sea. They can be purchased at Macy's and many other department stores. You are paying a fortune to rub mud on your face!

The Middle East occupies a strategic place geographically, and has even been called "the crossroads of the world." With our present-day construction abilities, it would be no problem to rebuild the city of Babylon into something magnificent in a relatively short time. Remember, the Tribulation Period does not start immediately after the Rapture, but it starts when the Antichrist negotiates a seven year peace agreement between the Jews and the Arabs. This could be several months or even a year after the Rapture, and could provide a jump start in rebuilding the city of Babylon.

Babylon was in its heyday during the reign of King Nebuchadnezzar 500 years before Christ. It was a magnificent city with walls around it so wide that two chariots could ride abreast. The city was beautiful and it was luxurious. So much so, that Greek historians have labeled the hanging gardens of Babylon that King Nebuchadnezzar built as one of the Seven Wonders of the ancient world although some have doubted its existence.[1]

But in 539 B.C., the city fell to King Cyrus of Persia, and from that time on, decay continued to set in and it soon became a desert. It remained that way until the last century.[2]

Babylon is located in modern day Iraq. Saddam Hussein decided that he would restore the city to its previous glory, and make it a profitable tourist attraction. He built several palaces there, but then came the Gulf War in the early 1990's and the city hasn't had much going for it since then.[3] There are a lot of Old Testament prophecies about Babylon. There are some prophecies that indicate Babylon will be destroyed, but it will not disappear. For instance, Isaiah 13:21 says: *"Wild beasts of the desert shall lie there; and their houses shall be full of doleful creatures; and owls shall dwell there"*. That was its condition for over 2,000 years.

But there are many Old Testament prophets who predicted that Babylon would be permanently destroyed. Isaiah 13:19 says the city will be burned completely, and will become as barren as Sodom and Gomorrah (Jeremiah 50:40). Isaiah says that Babylon will become desolate forever with neither man nor beast living there again. *"It shall never be inhabited* [again], *neither shall it be dwelt in from generation to generation; neither shall the Arabian pitch* [his] *tent there; neither shall the shepherds make their fold there"* (Isaiah 13:20). That is a pretty bleak prediction! Amillennalists say that all those prophecies were fulfilled long ago. But since there are remains in Babylon today, you cannot support the teaching that Babylon has been utterly destroyed so that no one will ever live there again. The fact of the matter is that some people are living there today! Therefore, its utter destruction is still in the future.

Unlike most of Iraq which is predominantly sandy, Babylon is located on the beautiful and fertile Tigris-Euphrates plain, and it is near some of the world's richest oil reserves. Furthermore, Babylon is very near the geographical center of the earth's land masses at the crossroads of the three continents of Europe, Asia and Africa. Dr. Henry Morris said that Babylon would be an ideal place in the world to build an international culture center for the nations and possibly, even the United Nations would build their headquarters there.[4] I do not doubt for a minute that the Antichrist will restore this city to its previous glory. As the Beast becomes more and more powerful, he will push this project ahead. It will become the center of education, communication and the hub of world trade and finance. He will want to show the world how prosperous it can be under his rule.

At the beginning of chapter 18, Babylon is a luxurious and opulent city. And we will see as we go forward, it will also be a city of unbelievable vice and wickedness, proudly flaunting its godlessness for all the world to see. But its inhabitants will soon begin to experience the awful plagues we saw in chapter 16 – the sores, the bloody waters, the intense heat and the battering hail. And before the Tribulation is over, we will see the city completely destroyed in "one hour."

We have seen storms roll in with their heavy winds, dark clouds and torrential rains. When the storm is over, the sun comes out and everything is so refreshed and clean and smells so good. That is what we will have with these final judgments. They roll in, cleansing and refreshing the earth. And when it is over, the sin and ugliness will have been swept away, and the earth is prepared for our wonderful habitation in the Millennial Kingdom. God will have removed from the earth all those who do not worship Him, and will throw open the windows of the world to allow justice and peace and joy to fill the air. The storms that the earth must experience will be severe just as the storms of life that each of us face sometimes seem insurmountable. But it will be worth it all to arrive at a place at last where no storm will ever bother us again.

Some teachers suggest that the great city described in this 18th chapter cannot be the literal Babylon in Iraq. They think the current city is too small, too remote, and more of a tourist attraction than anything else. But they overlook what the Antichrist will be able to do with the countries he rules. A hundred nations with unlimited financing, hundreds of engineers, modern equipment, and thousands of forced laborers can turn Babylon into a luxurious city virtually overnight. But first, let us look briefly at another intriguing theory – that this Babylon is really symbolic of one of the great countries of the world, possibly the U.S. Although I do not subscribe to it, nevertheless, it is an interesting scenario that some teachers embrace.

A question on the mind of everyone is, "Where is the U.S. in Bible prophecy?" It simply is not mentioned in end time prophecy …. or is it? Some people believe that the U.S. is mentioned in the Bible, but it is couched in secretive terms. Such as in Revelation 12:14a: "*And to the woman* [Israel], *was given two wings of a great eagle, that she might fly into the wilderness, into her place, where she is nourished*" and protected. They say that this great eagle is the U.S., and it will help Israel escape from the Antichrist in the end times. After much study, I have come to the conclusion that the U.S. is not directly mentioned in Bible prophecy, and I think the reason is that the U.S. will no longer be a super power when the Antichrist consolidates his empire using Europe as his super base.

Congress took the U.S. off the gold standard a number of years ago, and the fact that the U.S. simply prints paper money when it needs it could result in a financial disaster. If the U.S. ever gets to the point where its credit is not accepted in the world markets, its economy will collapse overnight because there are no gold reserves to back its assets. The U.S. has accumulated a staggering amount of debt both by the government and by individuals who have borrowed more than they can possibly repay. And it is increasing by the minute. A financial collapse is not out of the question. We even have a "financial debt clock" that shows how much the U.S. owes by the second. It is scary![5]

Another scenario is that either China or North Korea or some other rogue nation like Iran will use nuclear or biological weapons to devastate our country reducing the U.S. to a third world power. A third scenario which I tend to believe is this: We have more born again Christians per capita than any country in the world. What happens at the Rapture? These Christians will disappear in the twinkling of an eye to meet Christ in the air. That will devastate the country since many of our top leaders, businessmen and just good solid citizens will be gone.

Let us begin reading in Revelation 18:1, *"And after these things I saw another angel come down from Heaven, having great power; and the earth was lightened with his glory."* Some think that this angel is the Lord Jesus, and it might be. After all, we are told that He is the light of the world. Jesus is not an angel, but the word means messenger, and Jesus has been described as such before in this Book. But there are several distinct angels that appear in this chapter, and I believe this angel is just one among several. And we know that Jesus is not "one among anything" – He is THE One above all the rest. The fact that this angel is glowing, and lights up the world is simply an indication that he has come from the presence of God, and reflects God's divine glory.

This brightness is going to hurt their eyes. Remember, right before this, they have experienced total blackness when the fifth angel poured out his bowl judgment in Revelation 16:10. Just like when you awake from a deep sleep, and someone turns on a bright light, it hurts your eyes. But any momentary relief felt by the inhabitants will quickly turn to terror as they see the source of the illumination – an angel of mighty power coming down from Heaven. Perhaps this is the same angel that John heard earlier in Revelation 14:8 declaring the fall of Babylon.

Look at verse 2: *"And he cried mightily with a strong voice, saying, Babylon the great is fallen, is fallen, and is become the habitation of devils, and the hold of every foul spirit, and a cage of every unclean and hateful bird."* Wherever this Babylon is, you do not want to be there! The city has become the haven of every foul creature imaginable. As bad as these were under the false religious system of the False Prophet, a worse condition will ensue under the satanic filled Beast.

Sometimes it seems some of America's cities are almost this bad. A walk through downtown Detroit, Chicago, Los Angeles and a score of others reveal that they are filled with drugs, prostitutes and pornographic bookstores. Many of our communities have tried to fight these peddlers of smut, but our liberal courts have often thwarted such efforts.

The United States certainly has much in common with Babylon the Great. We are a nation that is in rebellion against God. Like Babylon the Great, we have become "the hideout of demons and evil spirits, a nest for filthy buzzards, and a den for dreadful beasts" (verse 2). In the present international context, it certainly sounds like an indictment of the United States.[6]

Is the United States a mirror of Babylon the Great where every unclean and hateful bird, controlled by foul spirits and demons, possesses the city? Many times I have cried out to the Lord that we would have a genuine spiritual revival in this country that would restore for us "the land of the free and the home of the brave." The Bible has a lot to say about justice. Human justice in America is pitiful. Oh, we get it right sometimes. Sometimes we convict the wrong party. Sometimes we have a chance to really execute justice and we blow it. Like the judge in Vermont did a few years ago. A man sexually abused a little girl for four years – four years – from the time she was six to the time she was ten! And the judge decided rehabilitation was what he needed, so the judge sentenced him to 60 days in jail and mandated that he go to counseling.[7]

While we are on this picture of injustice all around us, let me share with you an insight the Lord gave me. The Lord says in John 8:32: *"And ye shall know the truth and the truth shall make you free."* I had been taught all my life that when we come to Christ, we are liberated – we are free! But I did not know how to answer someone who said, "Free? A Christian is not free – he has the Ten Commandments. He has all the do's and don'ts and rules to go by. Now the lost person is the one who is free. He can do anything he wants to." That is how the world views it, so how do you answer that? The Lord showed me this is deceptive thinking. All of mankind is in bondage to sin because of the fact that all of mankind has sinned. *"For all have sinned, and come short of the glory of God"* (Romans 3:23).

Look at this verse closely as it has two important parts. *"For all have sinned"* – this is everyone; no exceptions. *"And come short of the glory of God."* How many people in their right mind would say they have never come short of the glory of God? That they are equal in purity and right up there alongside God with the glory and majesty that God possesses? Here is the point I want you to get. You are not only a sinner by nature which you inherited from Adam's race, but a sinner by choice and by practice. Does that sound like you are free to do anything you want? NO! You are a slave to sin! You can only be free when you come to Christ, and He breaks the bondage of sin that enslaves you. When you understand this, you will understand what Jesus meant when He said, *"And ye shall know the truth and the true shall make you free!"* It does not mean you will be sinless; but you will not habitually choose to sin.

This angel coming down from Heaven not only has a tremendous glow about him, but also has a booming voice. No one can say they didn't hear him. So this angel cries out with a loud voice making the announcement that *"Babylon is fallen – is fallen."* He says it twice, and I believe he is stressing that both Babylons have fallen – the false one-world religion and now political Babylon, the imperial city of economic greed.

Look at verse 3: *"For all nations have drunk of the wine of the wrath of her fornication, and the kings of the earth have committed fornication with her, and the merchants of the earth are waxed rich through the abundance of her delicacies."* It sounds to me like the nations and rulers of the world are going to be friends with the Antichrist and his regime. If the United States is still around, we would do well to continue to support Israel because Scripture says that those nations that bless Israel will be blessed, and those nations that curse Israel will be cursed (Genesis 12:3). But I am afraid that, with the Church having been raptured, it seems reasonable to conclude that the U.S. will be closely aligned with Europe and the Antichrist. It will hate Israel just as the United Nations does today. So it looks like at all levels – the nations – the kings – the merchants – all of them are a picture of greed gone to seed. They have cut deals, they have manipulated, they have cheated – all for the power that wealth can give them.

Wealth is a good thing if handled properly. The Bible cautions us over and over about the potential destructive forces of money. If you want to do yourself a favor, get out of debt as quickly as you can and stay out of debt.

Jesus said in Matthew 19:24: *"And again I say unto you, it is easier for a camel to go through the eye of a needle, than for a rich man to enter into the kingdom of God."* Having worked in the financial sector for nearly 40 years, I can attest to the fact that most rich people tend to place their faith in money rather than in God. And many take a cavalier attitude toward debt which often spells their downfall.

Jesus uses what is called "hyperbole," a form of literary expression to drive home the idea of how difficult it is for people to put money in its proper perspective. You know why? Because money makes us feel self-sufficient, and we think, "why do we need God?" Just like the end time church in Laodicea which said: *"I am rich …. and have need of nothing,"* when in reality Christ told them, *"and knoweth not that thou art wretched, and miserable, and poor, and blind, and naked"* (Revelation 3:17). Riches cloud our thinking. Most of us think, "I wish I would inherit a large sum of money. Think of all the good I could do." But God knows it tempts us in other directions, and that is why He has protected most of us from these heartaches.

As head of a large venture capital group for many years, I rubbed elbows with some very, very rich people. I am thinking of a fellow we will call "Ernie." He had a little company in California that was doing about $10 million of sales annually. That was peanuts in the industry in which he was operating. He wanted to expand his company, and so, he came to us and asked us to invest in his company. He had an innovative idea that would he believed would revolutionize the industry. We did invest a small amount in his company and his idea caught fire. Revenues increased rapidly, and stock prices accelerated. He was a millionaire overnight – heading to be a billionaire.

I had dinner with the gentleman one evening at the Mansion – Dallas' most exclusive restaurant. Knowing his net worth had increased dramatically, I wanted to see if he was interested in putting some of his money to work in godly causes. I hit his hot button. He nearly went ballistic in telling me he had no use for religion. He said his uncle was a preacher and a big time hypocrite. Also, he was proud that his son was publishing a new book – one of those large, artsy books that you put on your coffee table, except this one was very pornographic.

It was required to have a brown paper cover around it when it sold, and it was selling for upwards of $250.00. He was so proud that his son was publishing this disgusting book. I tried to steer the conversation toward the importance of the Gospel, but he was not in the least interested. Three years later, Ernie was lying on a cold slab in the morgue, and his relatives were fighting over his multimillion dollar estate that he left behind.

It underscores what Jesus said: riches cloud our thinking and entrap us so much, that it is very difficult for a rich man to get into Heaven. The following verse describes this perfectly: *"Go to now, ye rich men, weep and howl for your miseries that shall come upon you. Your riches are corrupted, and your garments are motheaten. Your gold and silver is cankered; and the rust of them shall be a witness against you, and shall eat your flesh as it were fire"* (James 5:1-3a).

Christ wants us to build our lives upon Him – the Solid Rock. When I hear of recession and job layoffs, my first thought is to wonder how many people affected by that have built their lives upon their job security instead of upon God Himself. Do you realize that, if you have given your heart and soul to the Lord Jesus Christ, you are now a child of the King, and that means you are now His responsibility?! Do not look to your possessions for security, look to the Lord.

Let us take a closer look at this end time city as we come to verse 4. *"And I heard another voice from Heaven, saying, 'Come out of her, my people, that ye be not partakers of her sins, and that ye receive not of her plagues.'"* This is *"another voice"* – not the same as the angel in verse 2 that had a strong voice. And what is the message? It is a call to be separate. God always calls His people be a separate people. The greatest tragedy in the world is Christian people who look and act just like worldly people – just like the earth dwellers.

I love the story that my pastor, Bro. Jim, tells about the young man who left home to work during the summer with a logging unit in the far north. His mother was so worried about him because he was a Christian, and he was going up there with all those rough loggers. At the end of the summer, when he returned home, his mother said, "Oh, son, did they give you a bad time because you are a Christian?" He said, "No, Mom. They didn't find out!"

You get the point. The Lord wants people to see a difference in our lives. Scripture says, *"Wherefore come out from among them* [the world], *and be ye separate saith the Lord"* (II Corinthians 6:17). He does not want His children to be caught up in the greed and avarice of this wicked city. By remaining in it, they would become partakers of her guilt and ultimately of her judgment. And the greatest illustration of them all – our generation has been given sign after sign that the Tribulation is coming. We are called to witness to our relatives, friends and neighbors to come to Christ and escape this awful time depicted here in Scripture.

It is important, therefore, that in these last days we do not compromise with present-day satanic systems. In II Corinthians 6:14, all believers are told: *"Be ye not unequally yoked together with unbelievers: for what fellowship hath righteousness with unrighteousness? And what communion hath light with darkness?"* And I John 2:15-17 says: *"Love not the world, neither the things that are in the world. If any man love the world* [that is, the world system], *the love of the Father is not in him. For all that is in the world, the lust of the flesh, and the lust of the eyes, and the pride of life, is not of the Father, but is of the world. And the world passeth away, and the lust thereof: but he that doeth the will of God abideth for ever."*

And the strongest verse I know along this line is James 4:4b which says: *"Know ye not that the friendship of the world is enmity with God? Whosoever therefore will be a friend of the world is the enemy of God."*

If we find that we are getting entangled with the world, we should remember 1 John 1:9: *"If we confess our sins, He is faithful and just to forgive us our sins, and to cleanse us from all unrighteousness."* Today, God is holding back His judgment, and some may think He does not notice the evil that is taking place. But that is not true as He says His eyes go to and fro across the globe (II Chronicles 16:9).

It pains me to say there will come a day when His wrath will be held back no longer. We sometimes wonder, "Has God ignored or forgotten these sins that are flaunted by these end time God-haters?" God answers this question: *"For her sins have reached unto Heaven, and God hath remembered her iniquities"* (Revelation 18:5). This is almost like an end time tower of Babel, only this time, it is not made with stones reaching unto the heavens; it is made with sins – one piled on top of another. The judgment of God may be delayed, but it is sure. It may seem to us that the world is getting by with sin, but God's judgment is coming. And what a judgment it will be!

Look at verse 6: *"Reward her even as she rewarded you, and double unto her double according to her works: in the cup which she hath filled fill to her double."* Babylon's rebellion has been long and deep and wide, and the time has come to drink the cup of wrath. Those who have meted out treachery to these Tribulation saints on earth are going to be punished double for all the pain they have caused.

Verses 7-8 give us a look at the inner being of this temptress – this Babylon the Great. Because of the stilted English language of 400 years ago, let us look at verses 7-8 in the New Living Translation and we will get a better feel as to what God is saying. *"She has lived in luxury and pleasure, so match it now with torments and sorrows. She boasts, 'I am queen on my throne. I am no helpless widow. I will not experience sorrow.' Therefore, the sorrows of death and mourning and famine will overtake her in a single day. She will be utterly consumed by fire, for the Lord God who judges her is mighty."*

She says, "I will live deliciously; I will never see sorrow." And suddenly, the seven bowls of wrath we saw in chapter16 begin to be poured out: terrible sores, the waters turning into blood and a scorching heat followed by impenetrable darkness. And then, this evil empire is brought down in one day at the final Battle of Armageddon.

We see a precursor – a picture of what is to come in the Book of Daniel. In the 5ᵗʰ chapter, we see drunken King Belshazzar, drinking out of the Temple cups that had been dedicated to God, living it up, no pain and no sorrow. What a fool! The Persian army dug under the great wall protecting Babylon, and the city fell that very night just as Babylon the Great in the end times will fall in a day.[8] Here God's law of sowing and reaping comes into effect. Job 4:8 (ESV) says: *"As I have seen, those who plow iniquity, and sow trouble reap the same."* Humanity cannot get away with sin forever. God hates sin because it is inconsistent with His holiness, and His patience eventually runs out.

Whether you live 25 years or 100 years, it is of short duration in the overall scheme of things. Do you want to know how to get the most out of your time here on earth? Gain an eternal perspective! Run your problems through the filter that says, "Will this make any difference 100 years from now?" Jim Elliott said it best. "He is no fool who gives up what he cannot keep to gain what he cannot lose."[9] I remember a little plaque that my mother had hanging in our living room when I was growing up. It was a poem attributed to a British missionary, C. T. Studd, which said: "Only one life – 'twill soon be passed, Only what's done for Christ will last."

Here in the 18ᵗʰ chapter we see that judgment is no longer held back. Babylon with all her sins comes crashing down in one hour! The beautiful new buildings and parks of the rebuilt Babylon, perhaps with the restored "hanging gardens of Nebuchadnezzar bathing in the sunlight like a proud peacock," will become a source of pain and sorrow in one day. The following verses in the Book of James fit the picture of the scene we have before us. Here is what it says: *"And a final word to you arrogant rich: Take some lessons in lament. You'll need buckets for the tears when the crash comes upon you. Your money is corrupt and your fine clothes stink. Your greedy luxuries are a cancer in your gut, destroying your life from within. You thought you were piling up wealth. What you've piled up is judgment"* (James 5:1-6 The Message).

The end of the age will not see communism enthroned; nor will it be socialism. Instead, capitalism will be the ruling power as ten regions of the Antichrist will bleed the world's inhabitants of their possessions. Do not misunderstand me. I hate the godless system called communism that has no place for God, and in the guise of helping the poor, it rewards laziness. Its cousin, socialism is not any better. But, within capitalism, we often find greed that is gone to seed. That is what this is talking about – exploiting the poor. I love the old story that says a politician was asked the question, "What do you think about the war on poverty?" He said, "Well, I think it is awful; it is deplorable. The government spends billions and billions of dollars in the war on poverty, and the poor people don't have anything to fight back with!"

I had lunch one day with a fellow named Rick. He had just purchased a division of a large Fortune 500 company. So here I am, dining with a fellow who is worth $300 million, a fellow who owns a $100,000 automobile and beautiful chalets all over Europe – and I am riding the bus to work! What do you talk about with a fellow like that? Certainly not where we vacationed last! And I was sure he did not want to hear about the glory days of Pleasant Grove where I grew up! The area is now the Southeast distributor of crime and drugs where a shooting happens almost every night.

Well, Rick did not want to hear about growing up in Pleasant Grove, and I did not want to hear about his zillion dollar home. But he was insistent to tell me all about his new home that he had purchased in Highland Park. He was going to spend several million dollars just renovating it. I saw him a couple of years later. He was in the midst of a big divorce, and his wife wanted to make sure that she got at least half of all his millions. The other half went to his creditors. He was greatly depressed, and was drinking heavily to drown his sorrows.

I have thought of that conversation many times, and that Jesus said it is easier for a camel to go through the eye of a needle than a rich man to make it to Heaven. I liked Rick very much, and I hope he straightened out his life. But praise God as He is building us a mansion that is far greater than anything in Highland Park. In fact, nothing on this old earth can compare with it.

Verses 9-11: *"And the kings of the earth, who have committed fornication and lived deliciously with her, shall bewail her, and lament for her, when they shall see the smoke of her burning, standing afar off for the fear of her torment, saying, 'Alas, alas, that great city Babylon, that mighty city! For in one hour is thy judgment come.' And the merchants of the earth shall weep and mourn over her; for no man buyeth their merchandise any more."* Out of fear, they are standing afar off. They can easily see the smoke of her burning, and they are aghast because it happens in one hour. Is this a nuclear blast? It could be, but whatever it is, it is a direct judgment from God. Just a short time before, in chapter 17, we saw the kings of the earth turn over their own kingdoms to the Beast (Revelation 17:17). They had enjoyed the luxuries and great prosperity that the Babylonian system had brought them.

It is true that these kings (rulers) become more and more concerned about all the plagues that were raining down on them, but they still had confidence in their leader, the Antichrist, to pull them through. But now, they see their dreams beginning to crumble. They see the enormity of the judgment that is being poured out upon their world, not only destroying its political capital, but also its financial and commercial centers as well.

A great and bitter lament is heard all around the world. We do not hear the terms "bewail" and "lament" much anymore. Bewail means uncontrollable sobbing, and lament means literally beating your breast in anguish. What a sight to see the leaders and kings of the earth doing this! These great kings of the earth, sobbing and shaking, are visibly terrified by what they see knowing that they have placed all their hopes for time and eternity on the Beast and the Devil.

Too late they realize that anyone who received the Mark of the Beast have no chance to repent or turn back. Maybe for the first time, they are aware judgment is coming and must soon stand before the Supreme Judge. However, there is one tiny glimmer of hope. If they can just amass all their armies maybe the Antichrist can lead them into battle, and overthrow God Himself. So you see, winning the Battle of Armageddon is the only hope they have left.

Verse 11 tells us that the merchants of the earth shall weep and mourn over Babylon. Their reaction is very similar to that of the kings of the earth. These merchants do not appear to be simple shopkeepers. They are kings in their own right – kings of banking, shipping, construction and communications. You might say, captains of industry and giants of commerce. We got a glimpse of them in Revelation 6:15-16: *"And the kings of the earth, and the great men, and the rich men, and the chief captains, and the mighty men, and every bondman, and every free man, hid themselves in the dens and in the rocks of the mountains; and said to the mountains and rocks, 'Fall on us, and hide us from the face of Him that sitteth on the throne, and from the wrath of the Lamb.'"* They sought to hide themselves from the One who sits on the throne, but now they realize there is no place to hide.

These are great leaders by human standards, but they are often kept in office by rich merchants who finance their undertakings and who, in turn, receive business contracts and favorable tax treatments from those they put in power. Christians should be satisfied with what God has given them. The Apostle Paul confirms this in I Timothy 6:8-10 (NLT) when he said, *"So if we have enough food and clothing, let us be content. But people who long to be rich fall into temptation and are trapped by many foolish and harmful desires that plunge them into ruin and destruction. For the love of money is at the root of all kinds of evil. And some people, craving money, have wandered from the faith and pierced themselves with many sorrows."*

These great merchants of the earth do not weep over their sins, nor do they mourn over the violent death of their colleagues in Babylon. Their crying and sorrowing is only for their own financial losses. No one will buy their merchandise anymore. Their profits will dry up. Their great financial empire is collapsing before their very eyes. Their main interest in life is being taken away. Just as Jesus said, *"For where your treasure is, there will your heart be also"* (Matthew 6:21).

We had a remarkable woman in our church who died a few years ago. Her name was Frances. In later life, she was a very frail lady whose steps were slow as she entered the church each week. She taught a women's Sunday school class. I did not know her well – our paths just did not cross. But I went to her memorial service. There was not a funeral as such because, even in death, she was giving – she gave her body to be used in research at Southwestern Medical

School. During her memorial service, I heard about the life of this dear lady and was moved to tears. In the course of reviewing her papers and documents, her relatives discovered something they were not even aware of. Quietly she had lived out her last few years, writing checks, not only to the church, but to other noble charities, and anyone who was in great need. She did not have a lot of assets, but she had a great heart.

How does Frances compare with those rich men we mentioned earlier? Jesus answers that in Luke 21:1-4 (The Message): *"Just then He looked up and saw the rich people dropping offerings in the collection plate. Then He saw a poor widow put in two pennies. He said, 'The plain truth is that this widow has given by far the largest offering today. All these others made offerings that they'll never miss; she gave extravagantly what she couldn't afford – she gave her all.'"*

The next few verses in Revelation 18 shine a spotlight on the merchandise that will no longer be bought. And notice, it is listed in descending order of importance – at least, in the eyes of these world traders and merchants. They see gold as the most important commodity and the souls of men as the least important. That is the diabolical thinking that started the awful practice of slave trading, placing gold ahead of men's souls.

Verses 12-13: *"The merchandise of gold, and silver, and precious stones, and of pearls,* [and other investments] *and fine linen, and purple, and silk, and scarlet,* [and fashionable clothes], *and all thyine wood, and all manner vessels of ivory, and all manner vessels of most precious wood, and of brass, and iron, and marble,* [and high class furniture], *and cinnamon, and odors, and ointments, and frankincense, and wine, and oil, and fine flour, and wheat, and beasts, and sheep, and horses,* [and satisfying entertainment], *and chariots, and slaves* [to increase their wealth], *and* [finally] *the souls of men* [for lust, slavery and other demeaning practices]."

The items listed are not essential, but they are items that have been valuable and costly in every age. The fact that 28 commodities are listed, that is, four groups of sevens, suggests that this list is representative and not exhaustive. Seven as you know is the number of completeness, and four as the number of the whole expanse of the earth (north, south, east and west), so theses combine to symbolize all the world's items of worth.

You will notice that the first four items listed have always served as the very measure of value and the basis of monetary systems. Throughout the ages men have tried to protect their savings by investing in items of intrinsic value, such as gold, silver, diamonds and pearls. All the endless variety of materialistic possessions which men and women have sought through the ages for which they have labored, and schemed, stolen and even killed, are symbolized here as the merchandise of Babylon, and it will all disappear suddenly in a great ball of fire.

Just think how vulnerable American merchants would be in this situation since our paper currency is backed by just that – paper. Next is listed the four kinds of valuable cloth for the apparel gurus of the world. The two most valuable materials: fine linen and silk; and the two most esteemed colors of royalty: purple and scarlet. I like what Dr. J. Vernon McGee says about this apparel. "You will not find a cotton dress or a pair of overalls anywhere in this list."[10] And I will add, nor blue jeans. Thyine wood is a very hard wood with a wonderful aroma. It would be comparable to our cherry wood today. And *"all manner vessels of brass and iron"* (verse 12) is comprehensive enough to cover metal structures and furnishings, musical instruments, machinery, weapons and a host of others.

The next group includes the luxury items: spices, perfumes and such – all in great demand as items of export. Wine is no doubt representative of all intoxicating beverages. We have seen earlier in Revelation 9:21 that sorcery comes from the Greek word "pharmakeia" which is the root word of our English word pharmacy, and implies rampant drug use in the end times. There are now at least 8 states (Washington, Oregon, California, Nevada, Colorado, Vermont, Rhode Island and Delaware) that have fully legalized marijuana and many others are soon to follow.

There is no question that the great demand for intoxicants and drugs in the coming days will be further stimulated by the ungodly and greedy merchants who greatly profit from them. I think it is prophetic that oil is mentioned in this list as it will probably dominate the economies of the world during the latter days just as it does today. I believe that Israel will be rich in oil in the last days, which is another reason that Israel's enemies will be so anxious to conquer her. There is active drilling going on currently in the northwest region of Israel.

In the 49th chapter of Genesis, Jacob knew he was about to die. He called his 12 sons ("the children of Israel") to gather around him for his final blessing and predictions for the future of their descendants. He addressed each of his 12 sons. Some of his predictions were dire, and some were good. For example, he said Reuben was firstborn but was unruly so he would no longer be first. Simeon and Levi were men of violence and their descendants would be scattered. Dan was compared to a poisonous snake by the road side. Since Dan was omitted from some of the later listing of the twelve (Numbers 1; Revelation 7), many have speculated that the False Prophet would be from the tribe of Dan.

One of the best prophecies was for Judah. *"Judah, your brothers will praise you. You will defeat your enemies. All your relatives will bow before you. Judah is a young lion that has finished eating its prey. Like a lion he crouches and lies down; like a lioness – who will dare to rouse him? The scepter will not depart from Judah, nor the ruler's staff from his descendants, until the coming of the one to whom it belongs, the one whom all nations will obey. He ties his foal to a grapevine, the colt of his donkey to a choice vine. He washes his clothes in wine because his harvest is so plentiful. His eyes are darker than wine, and his teeth are whiter than milk"* (Genesis 49:8-12 NLT). There is no question that this predicts that Jesus would be born from the lineage of Judah (Revelation 5:5 and Genesis 49:10).

Since we are talking about wealth, luxuries and riches here in the 18th chapter, the prediction for the descendants of Asher is very interesting. *"Asher will produce rich foods, food fit for kings"* (Genesis 49:20b NLT). The KJV says, *"He shall yield royal dainties."* In other words, look for Asher to be rich – rich – rich. Much of Israel's terrain is desert and rocks, but Asher was apportioned land in northwest Israel, the most fertile basin in all of Israel. Moses also had a prediction regarding Asher (Deuteronomy 33:24 ESV). *"And of Asher he said, 'Most blessed of sons be Asher; let him be the favorite of his brothers, and let him dip his foot in oil.'"* Think about it. Asher will be rich. Asher will dip his foot in oil. A light is beginning to come on. Every country that borders on Israel is rich in oil. Why doesn't Israel have any oil? Because there has not been very much exploration until now. Several years ago, a Texan by the name of John Brown read these verses, and strongly felt that God has given Israel this great natural resource for its blessing during the end times.[11]

John Brown founded Zion Oil and Gas and assembled an impressive team to find that oil. Recently, Zion Oil negotiated a lease on 99,000 acres from the Israeli government in the fertile basin in the Megiddo Valley – exactly where Asher's inheritance is located. As I write this, the drilling rig is in place and operations are proceeding. Whether Zion Oil is successful or not, we will continue to believe God's promise that He will bless those who bless Israel. Here in the 18th chapter, the great oil cartels must surely be included among these weeping merchants. Babylon itself is strategically located to control the oil production, and the exports of the oil-rich lands of the Middle East, but now it all collapses in an hour.

Fine wheat is listed, and represents only the finest of agricultural products reserved for the rich. Remember, in Revelation 6:6 when famine swept the earth? " .... *a measure of wheat for a penny, and three measures of barley for a penny ....*". Only the rich would eat wheat, the poor would be left with barley, a food generally reserved for animals. The animals listed could mean beasts of burden, but most likely referred to livestock for slaughtering. As we continue in Revelation 18:13, the inclusion of chariots is very interesting. The Greek word means a four-wheeled wagon for traveling, but could be interpreted to include modern day vehicles and the giant auto industry.

Finally, there is a sad reference to the slaves and souls of men. With the Antichrist firmly in control, and with all the effort it will take in rebuilding Babylon during the early days of the Tribulation, I tend to believe that he will institute again that malignancy on the human race – the sale of humans for slave labor. But, through the grace of God, we have eliminated forced labor; nonetheless, our society is still a picture of how material things are often placed far above the worth of the individual. When people lose the concept of God, no longer is man anything but an animal.

Where do we get the idea that man has worth? We did not get it from Lenin or Marx who embraced Communism which has long placed the rights of Government above individual rights. We did not get it from Hitler. He ordered the execution of millions. It got so expensive to use one bullet to blow the brains out of a person that Hitler commissioned a team to find cheaper ways to kill people. The Nazis began giving them lethal injections, but this was still too expensive. They loaded the Jews in trucks and ran an exhaust hose from the tailpipe into the back of the trucks to deliver a lethal dose of carbon monoxide. The cost of gasoline was too expensive to even do this. They settled on poison gas, but eventually incinerated them in large ovens.[12] If the Allies had not broken the back of Germany, who knows what cheap method for execution they would have come up with next? And the President of Iran said the holocaust never happened – that the U.S. and the Jews fabricated the entire story![13]

We learned the idea of our worth from the Lord Jesus Himself who told stories of the one lost sheep, the lost coin and the prodigal son. From our Lord we learned that the life of a person was of infinite worth because there is a dignity – there is a God-given quality because we are made in the image of God. Even our own constitution recognizes that. The constitution of the U.S., as great as it is, did not give us our right of freedom. The constitution simply recognizes that each of us is endowed with inalienable rights that come directly from God.

Our society just like the one described here in the 18th chapter puts more emphasis on material values, pleasure and entertainment. I am all for entertainment if it is the right kind and is not degrading. But something is wrong when the highest paid people in our society are athletes and entertainers. When you think about it, isn't it amazing that if you can hit a little ball into a hole in the ground, or if you can hit a ball the size of an orange over a fence, or if you throw a ball the size of a pumpkin through a hoop in the air, you can make a ton of money. These athletes are paid more than presidents, governors or legislators, more than doctors who minister to our bodies, more than preachers who chart our eternal destiny, and more than teachers who expand our minds. Our economic values are turned upside down. And here we see that under the rule of the Antichrist, gold and silver is more important than the souls of men.

The time is coming when the music will cease, industry will grind to a halt, and celebrations will no longer be heard in the great halls of state because God Himself will intervene and say enough is enough. That is what chapters 17 and 18 are all about. But it is not too late for folks right now to do something about it.

Look at verse 14: *"And the fruits that thy soul lusted after are departed from thee, and all things which were dainty and goodly are departed from thee, and thou shalt find them no more at all."* The Greek word for fruits actually means ripened fruits. They are still on the vine! God's judgment falls on these earth dwellers before their fruits can even be enjoyed. All these valuable things that they had lusted after are gone – never to return!

Verses 15-18: *"The merchants of these things, which were made rich by her, shall stand afar off for the fear of her torment, weeping and wailing, and saying, 'Alas, alas, that great city, that was clothed in fine linen, and purple, and scarlet, and decked with gold, and precious stones, and pearls. For in one hour so great riches is come to naught.' And every shipmaster, and all the company in ships, and sailors, and as many as trade by the sea, stood afar off, and cried when they saw the smoke of her burning, saying, 'What city is like unto this great city!'"*

All over the world, the news is broadcast – the great city of Babylon has fallen! In fact, it has not merely fallen, it has burned to ashes! Doesn't this sound like it might be some kind of nuclear explosion? People stand afar off – afraid to come near her. And her destruction is swift. She is brought down in an hour. It says the merchants were made rich by her. The "her" of course being the godless, commercial system that God is bringing down, and is portraying her as a woman. It is Babylon the Great – clothed in gold, fine linen, pearls, precious stones – all the things the world values highly.

Someone asked financier John D. Rockefeller when he was amassing his great fortune, "Just how much more money will quench your desire for riches?" He replied, "Just one more dollar."[14] But here, God is showing the world that all these so-called precious material things are, in the final analysis, worthless ashes! Men who spend a lifetime pouring over sales and profits should spend more time calculating what Jesus said: *"For what is a man profited, if he shall gain the whole world, and lose his own soul? Or what shall a man give for exchange for his soul?"* (Matthew 16:26).

I mentioned earlier about all the rich people I have met while I was in banking and finance for 40 years. Very, very few of them honored God with their money. I am thinking of one woman that I read about who did. She was born Selena Shirley in 1707, over 300 years ago. She later married into British aristocracy and was thereafter known as "Lady Huntington." She was saved during one of the great revivals sweeping England under the preaching of John and Charles Wesley. Her husband, Lord Huntington, died in 1746 and left his wife a large estate. The austere and formal Church of England, which today is as dead as a stump, was aghast at the Gospel being preached by these fiery Methodist preachers.

The Church of England which controlled the English pulpits, kept John and Charles Wesley from getting the needed ministerial licenses, thereby effectively cutting off any financial support they might need to carry on their work. But Lady Huntington knew they preached the true Gospel, and so, commissioned them as her "private chaplains," and provided them funds to carry out their revivals throughout England. Here is what one history book said of her: "Lady Huntington's unremitting generosity in support of the Methodist movement ushered in what has been called the revival that saved England."[15]

In my Bible class at Wheaton College, my dear old professor, Dr. Eugene Myers Harrison, told us about Selina Hastings, Countess of Huntington. It was so inspiring, so insightful, that I must share it with you. Lady Huntington quoted I Corinthians 1:26: *"For ye see your calling, brethren, how that not many wise men after the flesh, not many mighty, not many noble, are called."*

And then she said, "I am only going to Heaven by an m." Someone said, "Dear Madam – what do you mean?" And Lady Huntington replied, "I am so thankful that Scripture says, '.... *not MANY noble are called*' because if it had said, ' .... not ANY noble are called,' I would have been lost. I was able to get into Heaven by an m! Thank you, Lady Huntington, for that marvelous thought!

Dr. Harrison also told us about an evangelist by the name of Ebenezer Wooten. Rev. Wooten was pulling up the tent pegs at the close of one of his revivals. A young man approached him and said, "Now that the meetings are over, is there anything a person can do to be saved?" "Young man, you're too late," replied Wooten as he continued with his work. "You don't really mean that, do you, Mr. Wooten?" said the young man with a tone of alarm in his voice. "Yes, I do. You are entirely too late. There is nothing you can *do* to be saved. Everything that needed to be done was done by Christ 1900 years ago on the cross of Calvary. All you can do now is accept it and receive eternal life."[16]

It is so sad that the merchants of industry are not mourning the loss of life, but they are mourning the loss of property, their valuable materials, and their loss of future income. The city's whole system is gone. Retirement accounts are gone. Banks are broke. Money is worthless. Precious jewels are worthless. The stock market has collapsed. The beautiful structures the Antichrist erected are destroyed in one hour. Panic is everywhere.

When the people come to a realization of what has happened, look what they do! Verse 19: *"And they cast dust on their heads, and cried, weeping and wailing, saying, 'Alas, alas, that great city, wherein were made rich all that had ships in the sea by reason of her costliness! For in one hour is she made desolate.'"* Can you imagine being so distraught that you pour dirt on your head? This sounds strange to us today, but this was a common practice in ancient days when stressful situations arose. When Job's friends saw him in all his misery, here is what they did. Job 2:12: *"And when they lifted up their eyes afar off, and knew him not, they lifted up their voice, and wept; and they rent everyone his mantle, and sprinkled dust upon their heads toward Heaven."*

This is symbolic language here in Revelation 18:19 to proclaim their fear that all is lost, and that their bodies will soon die and turn to dust. It is not often you see grown men weeping and wailing, at least not in public. But there will be no macho pride left in any man. Everything they had is lost.

But now the scene changes! Look what is happening in Heaven! Verse 20: *"Rejoice over her, thou Heaven, and ye holy apostles and prophets; for God hath avenged you on her."* The saints in Heaven are rejoicing! This is what the Old Testament prophets prophesied. It is what the New Testament apostles predicted. And it is what the Tribulation saints prayed for. Justice at last! Heaven is not rejoicing at the calamities that are befalling these people; Heaven is rejoicing because God is finally exacting judgment upon sin. Neither saints nor heavenly angels delight when men suffer such judgment, but they must rejoice when people are constrained from causing others to turn away from God. God Himself has expressed this viewpoint over and over. Ezekiel 33:11a says: *"Say unto them, As I live, saith the Lord God, I have no pleasure in the death of the wicked."*

In Revelation 6:10, the martyred saints – millions who had been put to death by the godless government of the Antichrist – cried out, *"How long, O Lord, holy and true, dost thy not judge and avenge our blood on them that dwell on the earth?"* And remember God said in the next verse, "Be patient, my children – rest awhile – I will take care of this at the proper time." And now the proper time has come! The last part of verse 20 says, *"for God hath avenged you ...."*. All the apostles suffered great persecution, and all except John, were martyred by the enemies of Christ. They had preached faithfully against Babylon – that humanistic, greedy materialism characterized by the world system.

They had seen this evil empire apparently triumph over them as each had been beheaded. And so now they cannot hide their joy as they observe from the vantage point of Heaven the final and complete destruction of this corrupt system.

In the Book of James, it says: *"For whoever keeps the whole law and yet stumbles at just one point is guilty of breaking all of it"* (James 2:10 NIV). It is like a chain. You do not have to break every link in order for the chandelier to fall. Break one link and the whole chain falls. The same is true with our sins. When a man sins in one transgression, God sees the sin nature behind it. God knows that the man will do it again and again, and if he lives to be a thousand, he will still be doing it unless there is a change in his sin nature. So the Lord calls this city into judgment for all the blood of the prophets and saints. It is representative of the entire history of mankind, because the tendency of sin is to destroy all God's messengers. If there is lamenting on earth because of this judgment, there is rejoicing in Heaven.

On earth there are three groups of people who are mourning the destruction of this sinful city: the kings, the merchants and the seamen. And in Heaven there are three groups of people who are rejoicing over the destruction of this sinful city: the saints, the apostles and the prophets. And then in verse 21 it says: *"A mighty angel took up a stone like a great millstone, and cast it into the sea, saying, 'Thus with violence shall that great city Babylon be thrown down, and shall be found no more at all.'"* This symbolizes the sudden, violent and eternal destruction of the future city – Babylon the Great. It will disappear – never to be seen again.

Think of our major cities today. The Chamber of Commerce of each city would say their city is the greatest. You can go on the Internet and read their glorious reports. But when God's searchlight zeros in on them, how ugly they look. What seemed so glorious before was nothing but sham and corruption. The Dallas city council could not even have a Christian prayer to open their meeting without giving equal time to a Wiccan witch.[17]

Verse 22: *"And the voice of harpers, and musicians, and of pipers, and trumpeters, shall be heard no more at all in thee; and no craftsman, of whatsoever craft he be, shall be found any more in thee; and the sound of a millstone shall be heard no more at all in thee."* Everything from entertainment to manual labor will cease. There will be no more music in Babylon – no more going to work – no more craftsmen on the job. The city and all the sin it represents will be silenced forever!

Even before we get to these traumatic end time events, God tells us today to come out from the world's sinful system. Be careful of the books you read, the TV shows you watch, the movies you attend or rent. II Corinthians 6:14-15a, 17a says: *"Be not unequally yoked together with unbelievers: for what fellowship hath righteousness with unrighteousness? And what communion hath light with darkness? And what concord hath Christ with Belial* [Satan]? *…. Wherefore come out from among them, and be ye separate, saith the Lord."*

If anyone reading this is even considering being unequally yoked together in marriage – that is, one is a believer and one is not – before you do so, you owe it to yourself to go on the internet and listen to Dr. Jimmy Pritchard's message entitled *RSVP* preached July 10, 2017. It will save you a lifetime of heartaches, and it will build a marriage that is a dream come true! The internet link for the message is shown in the reference.[18] God leaves us here on earth to change society, not to condone it. Jesus said we are to be the salt of the earth, and if the salt loses its potency, God has no purpose in leaving us here (Matthew 5:13).

Revelation 18:23 says: *"And the light of a candle shall shine no more at all in thee; and the voice of the bridegroom and of the bride shall be heard no more at all in thee; for thy merchants were the great men of the earth; for by thy sorceries were all nations deceived."* The soft candlelight will someday go out. There will be no more sounds of the happy bride and the jubilant bridegroom. As Don Meredith used to say at the end of Monday night football, "Turn out the lights – the party's over."[19] Verse 24 says: *"And in her was found the blood of prophets, and of saints, and of all that were slain upon the earth."* Judgment has finally caught up with this wicked system which has shed so much innocent blood.

One of the most widely read books of all time is entitled *The Decline and Fall of the Roman Empire* by Edward Gibbon written over 240 years ago.[20] He lists five reasons that the Roman Empire fell. Here are the six reasons that Gibbon lists; and then we must ask what keeps America afloat.

1) The undermining of the sanctity of life and the home. (Think about legal abortions and homosexuality as an alternate lifestyle).
2) Higher and higher taxes – and free food and free education for the masses. (Think about the government's out-of-control spending in the welfare arena).
3) The mad craze for pleasure and entertainment.

(When a player gets $250 million to hit a little
ball, that is social values turned upside down).

4) U.S. citizens paid over $120 billion in the
entertainment industry in 2015. (Think how this
could help the underprivileged).

5) The building of greater and greater armaments.
(The U.S. defense budget is increasing every
year).

6) The decay of religion. (The ACLU with help from the government is trying to remove
God from public life).

There are three reasons that God's judgment is poured out on Babylon the Great:

1) Her love and obsession with money and riches (verse 3).

2) Her abusive use of drugs (the Greek word sorceries is pharmakeia – or pharmacy in
English (verse 23).

3) The hatred and persecution of God's people (verse 24).

The average age of the world's great nations throughout history is 200 years. America is
now over 240 years old. We are living on borrowed time.

CHAPTER NINETEEN

The Second Coming of Jesus Christ

We now come to the 19ᵗʰ chapter and, before it is over, we are going to see and hear some hallelujahs. I will say one right now – Hallelujah! The Tribulation Period is over; however, an all-out battle is waiting in the wings.

The destruction of the false church, Mystery Babylon, and the destruction of Babylon the Great, the evil empire set up and ruled by the Antichrist, marks the end of the most destructive seven years this planet has ever known. The seven seals of judgment have been opened by Jesus, the angels have blown their seven judgment trumpets, and the other seven angels have poured out their bowls of wrath upon the earth. During this time, thousands of faithful witnesses who would not bow their knee to the Antichrist have been killed. Babylon is gone forever, and the nations of the ungodly are retreating to make their final stand on the plains of Jezreel.

Satan and the Beast are in route to lead their followers into the last battle of the ages which will be between Heaven and Hell – the Battle of Armageddon. The enemy hordes are assembling in a tremendous column extending 200 miles from one end of Israel to the other – from Mount Carmel in the north to the Dead Sea in the south. Preparations for this battle are also underway in Heaven, but we will look at that in more detail later. With all of the dark and painful events taking place during the seven years of the Tribulation Period, especially during the last 3½ years, every believer has been longing for relief – a ray of sunshine in the midst of judgment. And it is getting ready to happen!

There is a drastic change in the tone of the Book of Revelation at this point. Darkness is giving way to light, and sobbing is giving way to song. The most anticipated event in all the history of mankind is about to take place – the Second Coming of Jesus Christ, which event actually forms a bridge between two important events in the Bible – the Tribulation Period that we are leaving, and the Millennial Kingdom we are about to experience. But before we get to the actual Second Coming, which is in verse 11 of this chapter, there are two other glorious and joyful events at which we need to look, both involving the Church.

This is covered in the first 10 verses of this chapter. The first event is the Marriage of the Lamb, and then immediately following is the wedding reception featuring the Marriage Supper of the Lamb. Whether you realize it or not, if you are a Christian, these are the most glorious events you have ever attended. As a believer in Christ, you will be a part of that wedding ceremony. In fact, you will be the Bride! As I mentioned previously, the Body of Christ, the Bride of Christ and the true Church – are all synonymous. In Matthew 16:18, Jesus said that He would build His Church, and the gates of Hell would not prevail against it.

Israel is God's chosen people as revealed to Abraham in the Book of Genesis. All the world was to be blessed by the Savior, who in His humanity, would be born a Jew – an Israelite. All of the great prophetic promises were given by God through the Jewish prophets promising that God's kingdom would someday be set up on earth. The prophet, Daniel, was even given a detailed timetable as to when all of this would take place, and that it would encompass 490 years involving Israel. But, due to sin and rebellion, this timetable was interrupted. Israel rejected its Messiah and then crucified Him. At this point, the great prophetic time clock that had been running while God was dealing with the nation of Israel came to an abrupt stop.

There are seven years yet to run of Daniel's original 490 years, and these seven years constitute the Tribulation Period. The details of these seven years are basically covered from chapters 6 through 18 of the Book of Revelation. Remember, these seven years are not running during the Church Age. They will start again when God begins to deal with Israel during the seven year Tribulation. Consequently, during this Church Age, God has temporarily set aside the Jewish nation of Israel, and He is calling out a people for Himself. They will be Gentiles and those Jews who accept Jesus as their Messiah.

The Church consists of all believers from the day of Pentecost to the Rapture. The Greek word for church is "ekklesia" which means "a called-out group."[1] When we were saved, we were called out of the world. We are now part of the true Church, the Body of Christ – soon to become the Bride of Christ. In this life, the greatest relationship that two people can experience is that of husband and wife. Throughout the Bible, this relationship is given the highest place of respect and honor by God Himself. The Marriage and the Marriage Supper of the Lamb are going to be the greatest events for the Church up to this time. We will look closely at this celebration when we get to it. But in the meantime, the most outstanding choral group ever assembled offer praises to God as their voices reverberate through the halls of Heaven.

Let us jump right into chapter 19, verse 1, as we look in on this glorious concert: *"And after these things I heard a great voice of much people in Heaven, saying, 'Alleluia; Salvation, and glory, and honor, and power, unto the Lord our God.'"* It says, *"After these things"* – after what things? Why of course, after the destruction of those two evil systems Mystery Babylon and Babylon the Great which we have just seen in the last two chapters. God is triumphant, and the host of Heaven is rejoicing! The multitude says, *"Alleluia"* in praise to the Lord for what has been revealed about Him throughout the Great Tribulation. Alleluia is the Greek version of the Hebrew word, Hallelujah, which means "praise to the Lord." "Hallelu" or "Hallal" means "praise to" and "Yah" is short for Jehovah.[2]

That great composer, George Frederick Handel, was inspired by the first six verses in this chapter to compose his masterpiece that is sung around the world each Easter – *The Messiah* containing the *Hallelujah Chorus.*

Hallelujah just like the word "Amen" means the same in any language. The Book of Revelation has more songs in it than any Book in the Bible except one. It is the Psalms, the Jewish songbook of the Old Testament. The Book of Psalms is divided into five major sections, each of which ends with a doxology of praise. Here are the endings of each of these sections:

Psalm 41:13: *"Blessed be the LORD God of Israel from everlasting, and to everlasting. Amen, and Amen."*

Psalm 72:19: *"Blessed be His glorious name for ever: and let the whole earth be filled with His glory. Amen, and Amen."*

Psalm 89:52: *"Blessed be the LORD forevermore. Amen, and Amen."*

Psalm 106:48: *"Blessed be the LORD God of Israel from everlasting to everlasting: and let all the people say, Amen. Praise ye the LORD."*

And finally, Psalm 145:2: *"Every day I will bless thee; and I will praise thy name forever and ever."*

Then the last six verses of the Book of Psalms provide a fitting praise to round out this Book of songs. Psalm 150:1-6: *"Praise ye the LORD. Praise God in His sanctuary: praise Him in the firmament of His power. Praise Him for His mighty acts: praise Him according to His excellent greatness. Praise Him with the sound of the trumpet: praise Him with the psaltery and harp. Praise Him with the timbrel and dance: praise Him with stringed instruments and organs. Praise Him upon the loud cymbals: praise Him upon the high-sounding cymbals. Let everything that hath breath praise the LORD. Praise ye the LORD."*

Our lives ought to always give praise to God. Someone said, "If there was more rejoicing and praise on the part of God's people rather than complaints, the world would have a lot better image of Christianity." I love it when I call someone on the phone, and get a recorded message from Psalm 118:24 praising the Lord – such as *"This is the day that the Lord hath made; let us rejoice and be glad in it.* We can't come to the phone right now but leave your name ....".

When we were in the 4th chapter of Revelation, Heaven was praising God for His creation. In the 5th chapter, they were praising Him for His redemption. And here in the 19th chapter, the heavenly host is praising God for His salvation, and are ascribing to Him glory, and honor and power. Though this chorus is made up of saints of all ages, it is probably being led by the Tribulation saints who have just come out of this terrible time.

They are rejoicing because of several reasons:

1) evil has run its course;
2) the Tribulation Period is virtually over;
3) Christ is preparing to return to earth with His saints;
4) the Antichrist and his armies are about to be crushed;
5) man is about to scrap his giant military budgets, and remake his swords into farm implements;
6) Christ is about to set up His Millennial Kingdom.

Such good news would make anyone shout, "Hallelujah!" Verses 2-3 appear to be a stanza of the song they are singing: *"FOR TRUE AND RIGHTEOUS ARE HIS JUDGMENTS: for He hath judged the great whore, which did corrupt the earth with her fornication, and HATH AVENGED THE BLOOD OF HIS SERVANTS AT HER HAND.' And again they said, 'ALLELUIA. AND HER SMOKE ROSE UP FOR EVER AND EVER.'"* Their songs of praises are lifted up because God's judgments are true and righteous. No crooked judge on the bench here! His justice is pure and just. And we will be seeing things through God's eyes as we have never seen them before. We will be praising the fact that He has destroyed this harlot – this false church which has led men's souls down the path to destruction. This false church has not only led men astray, but has killed millions of God's children as well. And God is avenging their blood.

In verse 3, the refrain of the song is repeated as God's people proclaim the fact that Babylon's doom is eternal. Never again will religious or political alliances send men into bondage. As a reminder of this, Babylon's smoke will ascend up forever and ever. In a secondary sense, this also pictures the inhabitants of Babylon – those unsaved souls who will be resurrected for the last judgment and will eventually be cast into the Lake of Fire.

I have read liberal commentators who would throw out this section of the Bible, declaring that God is love, and there is no place for vindictiveness such as this. But the Lord Jesus Himself said, and repeated it twice, that in that fearful destination to where they are headed, where *"THEIR WORM DIETH NOT, AND THE FIRE IS NOT QUENCHED* (Mark 9:44). From our earthly perspective, we do not fully understand what all this means because Paul tells us that in this life, we now see things darkly – we do not see the whole picture. But in verses 2 and 3, the saints see things as God sees them. They have experienced both Babylon's wickedness and God's love. They know that God has already been almost infinite in His longsuffering, and that His abundant mercy has been rejected and unwanted.

Once we are in Heaven and in the presence of the Lord, the scales will fall from our eyes and we will be in complete agreement with the judgments of God. The praise of these people in Heaven is manifold: first, for the destruction of the harlot who is the apostate church; second, because He will soon reign without someone attempting to take over His rightful throne; third, the blood of the martyred saints is about to be avenged; and fourth, the Marriage of the Lamb can take place because the false bride has been put away.

Verses 4-5: *"And the four and twenty elders and the four Beasts fell down and worshipped God that sat on the throne saying, 'Amen; Alleluia'. And a voice came out of the throne, saying, 'PRAISE OUR GOD, ALL YE HIS SERVANTS, AND YE THAT FEAR HIM, BOTH SMALL AND GREAT.'"* The 24 elders, you will recall from chapter 4, is a picture of the Church – the Bride of Christ. They fall down and worship God along with the four Beasts (living ones) which are special archangels around the throne. This is the last time the Church is referred to as the 24 elders. Do you know why? Because the Church is about to become "The Bride of Christ!" And then a voice from the throne says, *"Praise our God, all ye His servants …."*. I believe this is the Holy Spirit speaking – the third person of the Trinity whose mission is never to promote Himself, but always to direct praise and honor to the Father and the Son.

The day we have all been waiting for has arrived! It is our wedding day – the Marriage of the Lamb! The multitude of guests has taken their seats. The orchestra and harps are softly playing an introduction to the big event. The hour for the heavenly nuptials is at hand. The choir begins to sing and the processional begins. Everyone rises as the Father and the Son stand beside the throne looking expectantly toward the Bride. And there she is in all her radiant glory without spot or blemish!

Now we come to chapter 19, verse 6: *"And I heard as it were the voice of a great multitude, and as the voice of many waters, and as the voice of mighty thunderings, saying, 'Alleluia: for the Lord God omnipotent reigneth.'"*

This heavenly choir is an anthem of voices like you have never heard before. First, it sounds like the voice of a great multitude which it is. Second, it sounds like the voice of many waters. It makes the deafening noise of Niagara Falls sound like a little stream. Third, it sounds like the voice of mighty thunderings. This is an awesome choir as they echoed that great refrain captured by Handel's *Hallelujah Chorus* – "God omnipotent reigneth!"

Understanding the sequence of a Jewish wedding, will help us understand how the marriage of the Lamb is carried out. There are three major steps. Step one of the marriage is often accomplished by one or both of the parents of the bride and bridegroom by paying a dowry. This is called the "betrothal period" and it is legally binding.[3]

The father choosing a bride for his son is seen in the spiritual sense in Ephesians 1:3-4a: *"Blessed be the God and Father of our Lord Jesus Christ, who hath blessed us with all spiritual blessings in heavenly places in Christ: according as He hath chosen us in Him before the foundation of the world.*" The Father chose us to be the Bride of the Lord Jesus Christ even before we were born! Secondly, after the marriage was legal, the groom would depart to build a home for his bride. Often, this was a room to be built onto his father's house. During this time which generally lasted from 9 to 12 months, it would show everyone that the Bride had been faithful in all respects to her espoused husband.

The bride did not know exactly when her husband would come for her, and she had to be ready at all times. When he did come, it would be accompanied by a shout and it would be quite sudden. That is one reason why I believe in a pre-Tribulation Rapture. Our mid-Tribulation friends say that Christ cannot come back for at least

3½ years; our post-Tribulation friends say that Christ cannot come back for at least seven years. But Christ said for us to be ready because He can come at ANY time!

There is not a single prophecy that has to be fulfilled before Jesus comes for His Bride. Not one! That is why He said, *"Watch therefore: for ye know not what hour your Lord doth come"* (Matthew 24:42). Jesus gave a parable about this. The announcing party cried, *"Behold, the Bridegroom cometh"* (Matthew 25:6b). This is a tremendous picture of Christ coming for His Church at the Rapture. He has gone away to prepare a place for us, and at the Rapture, He will come for us. Paul says, *"For the Lord Himself shall descend from Heaven with a shout, with the voice of the archangel, and with the trump of God: and the dead in Christ shall rise first: then we which are alive and remain shall be caught up together with them in the clouds, to meet the Lord in the air: and so shall we ever be with the Lord"* (I Thessalonians 4:16-17).

Then an archangel with a strong voice will shout, *"Behold, the Bridegroom cometh."* Then the Bridegroom will shout, *"Come up here!"* (Revelation 4:1). No other love has the characteristic of marital love. Parents love their children because they are their children. Brothers and sisters have a love of natural relationship. Friendships are based on choice and on common interests. But the love of a bridegroom and bride is a special delight by forsaking all others and choosing each other. Think again of the words, *"Christ also loved the Church, and gave Himself for it"* (Ephesians 5:25b). He values His Bride as Himself. We will read in Revelation 21:2b, after a thousand years have passed, that she is still *"as a wife adorned for her husband."*

Is Jesus going to allow His future Bride to be beaten up by going through seven years of Hell on earth right before He comes back? No! He loves her, and He will keep her from being abused by the Antichrist! This is a marital love, a tenderness, a delight that will grow forever and ever. And what a joy for the Bride who realizes that Christ will never change in His affections!

The final stage of the wedding is the marriage feast which would often last for many days. From this picture, we see some clear parallels in our relationship with the Lord. First, the legal marriage takes place at the time of our conversion to Christ. We are "betrothed" to Him so to speak. In that sense, we are already united with Him by faith, but the actual ceremony has been delayed. But as His Bride, we are awaiting the time when the Groom will come to claim us for Himself and take us back to the mansion that He has been preparing for us.

Verse 7 says: *"Let us be glad and rejoice, and give honor to Him: for the marriage of the Lamb is come, and His wife hath made herself ready."* There is no one busier on a wedding day than the bride herself. The groom is lounging around, wishing the day would move on. The mother of the bride is fussing and fuming because her daughter is about to marry this idiot. But the bride, she has a thousand and one things to attend to, not the least of which is getting herself dressed and ready.

It was 104 degrees in Dallas the late afternoon of my wedding day, August 6, 1954 with the wind at 24 mph.[4] And this was before most homes and buildings had air conditioning. Arlene did not want to be sweaty for the ceremony so she asked the preacher if she could dress in his office which had a window air conditioner. He said, "Of course." So she went to the church a couple of hours early, planning to leisurely dress in the pastor's cool office. The custodian let her in and then left. She had the church to herself.

Just as she was getting dressed, the phone rang at the secretary's desk. How many women do you know that can let a phone ring without answering it? That's right: none. So she stepped into the outer office to answer the phone and then made a horrible discovery. The pastor's door had locked behind her. With time running out, she made a number of frantic calls trying to locate someone with a key to the office where her beautiful wedding gown awaited. Finally, the church custodian showed up with a key. Arlene was able to get dressed and the wedding went off without a hitch.

This Bride in verse 7 is prepared. Scripture says the Bride *"hath made herself ready."* And how did she make herself ready? She began a long time ago by trusting Christ as Lord and Savior. Jesus "imputes" His righteousness to us when we are saved. Therefore, His Bride is glorious not having spot or wrinkle (Ephesians 5:27). He will provide the Bride's beautiful gown.

We are not told the details of the wedding itself, only that the Bride has made herself ready. It will be magnificent, and that is all we need to know at this point; but I know it will be beyond our wildest imagination. In fact, regarding many of the things in Heaven, Scripture tells us that eye has not seen, ear has not heard, nor has it entered into our imagination just how grand and glorious this will be (I Corinthians 2:9).

As we mentioned previously, the Bride is composed of those believers from Pentecost to the Rapture – the Church Age. This is confirmed by John the Baptist who is not part of the Church. He was beheaded by Herod Antipas during Christ's public ministry before the Church was established. John knew he was soon to die. So he said, *"The Bride will go where the Bridegroom is. A Bridegroom's friend rejoices with him. I am the Bridegroom's friend, and I am filled with joy at His success"* (John 3:29 NLT).

Why was John the Baptist a friend of the Bridegroom and not a part of the Bride? Because John died before the day of Pentecost, and therefore he was not part of the Church Age which extends from the day of Pentecost to the Rapture. That does not diminish John the Baptist's role or importance in Heaven! Jesus said of him, *"Verily I say unto you, Among them that are born of women there hath not arisen a greater than John the Baptist."* (Matthew 11:11a). Though John is not part of the Bride, nevertheless, he is a friend of the Bridegroom and will be at the Marriage Supper of the Lamb as an honored guest (John 3:29).

Nor is Israel the Bride. How do we know this? Because Israel is already married. That is correct. Listen to Jeremiah 3:14 (NLT) with a message from God to Israel: *"'Return home, you wayward children,' says the Lord, 'for I am your husband.'"* And then God promised their return to the land He gave them. And on May 14, 1948 they again became a sovereign nation after nearly 2,000 years without a land of their own.

Jeremiah 3:18 (NLT) says: *"In those days the people of Judah and Israel will return together from exile in the north. They will return to the land I gave their ancestors as an inheritance forever."* Then the next verse (Jeremiah 3:19b NLT) says: *"I wanted nothing more than to give you this beautiful land – the finest inheritance in the world."* Jeremiah 3:20 (NLT) says: *"But you have betrayed Me, you people of Israel! You have been like a faithless wife who leaves her husband, says the LORD."*

Jesus' great discourse on marriage and divorce is found in Matthew 19. The Pharisees came to Jesus with a trick question asking Him, *"Is it lawful for a man to put away his wife for every cause?"* (Matthew 19:3b). That is when Jesus asked, *"Have ye not read .... FOR THIS CAUSE SHALL A MAN LEAVE FATHER AND MOTHER, AND SHALL CLEAVE TO HIS WIFE: AND THEY TWAIN SHALL BE ONE FLESH? Wherefore they are no more twain, but one flesh. What therefore God hath joined together, let not man put asunder"* (Matthew 19:5-6).

The Pharisees, still trying to trick Jesus, then asked why Moses approved a bill of divorcement. And Jesus replied because of the hardness of man's heart, and then he added these important words: *"but from the beginning it was not so"* (Matthew 19:8b). In other words, divorce is not in God's plan, but because of sin and the hardness of man's heart, sometimes it is necessary. But in the next verse, Jesus limits the acceptable reason for divorce: sexual impurity. Simply put: adultery.

That is exactly what Israel as God's wife did to Him in a spiritual sense. Listen to Jeremiah 3:6: *"The LORD said also unto me in the days of Josiah the king, 'Hast thou seen that which backsliding Israel hath done? She is gone up upon every high mountain and under every green tree, and there hath played the harlot.'"* Israel committed spiritual adultery against God as she continually chased after false gods and false lovers. So what did God do? He divorced her. Jeremiah 3:8a: *"And I saw, when for all the causes whereby backsliding Israel committed adultery*

I had put her away, and given her a bill of divorce." Israel is estranged from God during this present age. A blindness has settled over her as Paul says, and she does not recognize her Messiah (Romans 11:25). But she will be reconciled in the day of her national repentance when the Lord comes back. Israel will be the restored wife of Jehovah during the 1,000 year millennial reign.

Here is what Scripture says about Christ's Bride, the Church, *"For I am jealous over you with godly jealously: for I have espoused you to one husband, that I may present you as a chaste virgin to Christ"* (II Corinthians 11:2). Israel can be restored, but she can never be a virgin again. Only the Church fits this picture as she is clothed with Christ's righteousness. Would that every husband here on earth love their wife as Christ loves His Bride. Here is what Scripture says, *"Husbands, love your wives, even as Christ also loved the Church, and gave Himself for it; that He might sanctify and cleanse it with the washing of water by the Word, That He might present it to Himself a glorious Church, not having spot, or wrinkle, or any such thing; but that it should be holy and without blemish"* (Ephesians 5:25-27).

Christ's Bride – His Church – is going to be holy without spot and without blemish because she will have put on the righteousness of Christ. What a glorious Bride! I have heard of people searching for the perfect church. Folks, in this life, you will never find one. Our sin nature lives alongside our new nature, but when Christ comes for us, our old sin nature will die forever. Then we will belong to the perfect Church.

How much does Christ love His Bride? In Ephesians 5, it says Christ loved the Church and gave His life for her. It says a husband should have this same relationship with his wife. I would say to every husband, "Fellows, if you do not love your wives enough to lay down your life for her without hesitancy, your relationship is not what it should be." And I can safely say without fear of contradiction, if every husband in the country loved his wife as Christ loves the Church, there never would have been a women's lib movement.

Many people have asked, "Will we still live with our spouses in Heaven?" This is a difficult question to answer. We are not given a direct answer to this, but I love the comments made by the late Dr. Henry Morris. He states that Jesus said in Matthew 22:30, *"In the resurrection they will neither marry nor will they be given in marriage."* But then Dr. Morris continues: "It may be possible that husbands and wives will, in some cases, continue to live together in the same heavenly abode, but this is uncertain. Many people have been married more than once, and many have never been married at all. In some cases, one partner in marriage may have been a believer, while the other died without being saved. At various times in the past, some godly women have found themselves in polygamous households."

Dr. Morris adds: "It seems like an impossible paradox for God to solve." But here is the part I like as Dr. Morris continues: "On the other hand, it seems at least possible that, in those husband/wife unions which have been established and maintained on earth in accordance with

God's commandment, the Lord may well allow them to continue together in the same union and in the same mansion forever, serving Him in some capacity where such a relationship would be consistent with God's purposes for their future ministries."[5]

That may be wishful thinking, but remember, God said we could not imagine all the great things He has in store for us. In any case, all human relationships which have been spiritually fruitful in this life will surely be even more blessed in the life to come. Husbands and wives, parents and children, relatives and in-laws, friends and neighbors – all will love more and understand better than they could have ever imagined here on earth.

Jesus gave a parable illustrating how much He loves the Church. He says in Matthew 13:45-46: *"Again, the kingdom of Heaven is like unto a merchant man, seeking goodly pearls: Who, when he had found one pearl of great price, went and sold all that he had, and bought it."*

Some commentators say that the merchant man is a lost sinner, and the pearl of great price is Christ. This cannot be. Sinners are not looking for Christ. And if and when they find Him, they have nothing with which to pay given that they are dead in trespasses and sin. No, the merchant man is Christ seeking the lost which is the pearl of great price. And to obtain this pearl, Christ paid with His all – His very life – and bought salvation for everyone who will receive it. And those willing to receive this salvation become part of the Body of Christ, and eventually will participate in this great ceremony as a member of the Bride of Christ. I cannot speak for you, but I am going to be there for that ceremony and I can hardly wait!

In verses 8 and 9, Scripture quickly moves from the wedding ceremony to the Marriage Supper of the Lamb – the reception which follows the wedding. As you know, the Bride never wears the wedding gown to the Marriage Supper. These are different celebrations calling for different garments. At most of the weddings in the western world, the dinner comes before the wedding. In other words, the bride-to-be and the husband-to-be generally have a dinner in their honor a day or so prior to the wedding. That is not the case in eastern lands where the wedding always precedes the Marriage Supper. There is the wedding and then there is a feast – a fabulous food celebration that might go on for days.

We find in verse 8: *"And to her* [the Bride] *was granted that she should be arrayed in fine linen, clean and white: for the fine linen is the righteousness of saints."* Here we are not talking about the wedding gown, but a different garment – one that will be worn at the Marriage Supper of the Lamb. And I believe this garment will be one that we weave for ourselves. The phrase in verse 8b *"the fine linen is the righteousness of saints"* should really be *"the righteous deeds of the saints"* (ESV). We know that no believer will enter Heaven by virtue of his or her own righteous acts. In fact, Scripture says in Isaiah 64:6 that man's righteousness in his own power is like filthy rags before God.

So here is a paradox, yet one that is true. Our righteousness, if it is to be accepted by God, must be imparted to us by Christ. However, having been saved by grace through faith, every believer is enabled by the Holy Spirit to perform righteous acts for which he or she will be rewarded. Another way to put it is that there is a positional righteousness that a Christian has that is given to him by the Lord that puts him in good standing before God. But there is also a practical righteousness that the Christian earns when he does good works with the right motives in mind. Do not confuse the two. The righteousness that saves us comes from Christ. This is made clear in Titus 3:5a: *"Not by works of righteousness which we have done, but according to His mercy He saved us …."*.

Titus tells us that these works of righteousness that we do have nothing to do with our salvation. But the verse tells us something else. It tells us that we can do works of righteousness because Scripture says *"righteousness which we have done"*. How do we do that, and what do we gain from it? First, we are able to do works of righteousness because God, when He saved us, gave us the grace to do those works. Ephesians 2:10 (NLT) says: *"For we are God's masterpiece. He has created us anew in Christ Jesus, so that we can do the good things he planned for us long ago."* The NASB translates that same verse: *"For we are His workmanship, created in Christ Jesus for good works, which God prepared beforehand so that we would walk in them."*

We are weaving our own garments for the Marriage Supper by doing good works with the right motives. God has already told us in Ephesians 6:8a that He will reward us for good works: *"Knowing that whatsoever good thing any man doeth, the same shall he receive of the Lord"*. When will we receive these rewards? II Corinthians 5:10 (NLT) tells us: *"For we must all stand before Christ to be judged. We will each receive whatever we deserve for the good or evil we have done in our bodies."* This is written to Christians. This judgment is not to determine our eternal fate. The unsaved are already judged. The Bible says that all have sinned, and that the penalty of sin is death. The lost will have to appear at the official hearing or trial – at what is known as the Great White Throne Judgment. We will be covering that when we get to chapter 20. Only lost people will be at that judgment.

When a person accepts Christ as their Savior, the penalty for sin is immediately paid, and judgment for sin is over for them. Listen to the words of Jesus in John 5:24: *"Verily, verily I say unto you, He that heareth my word, and believeth on Him that sent me, hath everlasting life, and shall not come into condemnation* [or judgment]; *but is passed from death unto life."* So, what kind of judgment is it that Christians must go through as we stand before the judgment seat of Christ? As II Corinthians 5:10 says, we must account for our deeds whether they are good or bad in order to determine our rewards. We are told about this in detail in the third chapter of I Corinthians. This is the most complete description in the Bible about how rewards will be determined. *"For no one can lay any other foundation than the one we already have – Jesus Christ. Now anyone who builds on that foundation may use gold, silver, jewels, wood, hay, or straw. But there is going to come a time of testing at the judgment day to see what kind of work each builder has done. Everyone's work will be put through the fire to see whether or not it keeps its value. If the work survives the fire, that builder will receive a reward. But if the work is burned up, the builder will suffer great loss. The builders themselves will be saved, but like someone escaping through a wall of flames"* (I Corinthians 3:11-15 NLT).

Everyone's work is going to be tested by fire. If our work is built on the right foundation which is Christ, and if it is done with the right motives, it will survive the test. Otherwise, it will be burned up. For example, if it is a sacrifice for a person to contribute $100 to missionary causes to spread the gospel without making a big show of it, that person will receive a reward. But if that same person makes sure everyone knows he is giving $100 so he will be envied, Jesus says he already has his reward which is the admiration of the crowd (Matthew 6:2).

The presentation of rewards takes place in Heaven after the Rapture while the Tribulation is occurring on the earth. One writer said that the Rapture and the Second Coming form bookends. And in between them, the Tribulation is taking place on the earth while in Heaven the saints are receiving their rewards and are being fitted for their wedding garments.

There will be other rewards given out as well. The Bible mentions at least five different crowns: the crown of life, the crown of righteousness, the crown of rejoicing, the crown of gold and the crown of glory. These crowns were discussed in detail in chapter 4. But no doubt a good part of the rewards will be the garments that are to be worn at the Marriage Supper of the Lamb mentioned here in Revelation 19. A Bride fills her hope chest preparing beautiful and spotless articles of wearing apparel in view of her wedding day. We too have a spiritual hope chest to fill. Everything that is done for Christ adds something to that bridal chest.

Let us not be neglectful of this for the time is short and the night cometh when no man can work. All that is done for self, all that springs from pride and unholy motives, will disappear in that day. But that which is the result of His Spirit working within us will abide forever to His praise and glory. You may have forgotten all those little things you have done for the Lord or one of His children, but God has not forgotten. Hebrews 6:10 (NLT) says: *"For God is not unfair. He will not forget how hard you have worked for Him and how you have shown your love to Him by caring for other Christians, as you still do."* Have you forgotten to express gratitude to those who have helped you along life's path – school teachers, friends, special relatives? I challenge you to sit down and make a list of those people who have been a blessing to you. If they are still living, call them or write them a note of appreciation and tell them that you thank God for them!

When I was a freshman at Pleasant Grove High School, algebra did not make a lick of sense to me. Normally I made top grades, but I knew this was the first class that I was going to flunk. I was almost in tears. It seemed that today "x" was 15; tomorrow it might be 25. I just did not get it. My mom could not help me, but she remembered a teacher, Coach Virgil Mattingly, who taught algebra at the old Forest Avenue High School in Dallas. Coach Mattingly lived about a mile from us. She called him and he invited me over. I spent about two hours with him one evening, and once I understood the concept, I never had a problem with algebra after that!

I thought about Coach Mattingly a few years ago. I tracked down his son who told me that Coach was in a nursing home in Edgewood. I drove over there, and spent the afternoon with him. Coach was about 95, but his mind was still sharp as ever. He cried when I told him how much I loved him, and how much help he had been to me. He never knew about that and I am glad I told him. He died shortly thereafter.[6] I hope you will track down those who helped you along life's pathway while there is still time, and express your love to them.

Jesus said that a little cup of cool water given in His name will be remembered. In other words, when you try to meet the needs of a hurting person, God says He will remember that. Do you have a teacher who might still be alive that you need to contact? I wish you could just have a glimpse of the eternal rewards you will get for the work you are doing – a gift of charity here – a word of encouragement there – a card to a sick friend. It all adds up. Paul pleads with us to work diligently: *"My beloved brethren, be ye steadfast, unmovable, always abounding in the work of the Lord, forasmuch as ye know that your labor is not in vain in the Lord"* (I Corinthians 15:58). Our good deeds will provide material for the garments we will wear at the wedding reception. Will we be dressed shabbily or lavishly?

Let me give you a most encouraging verse that I came across recently. I Corinthians 4:5, written to believers, says: *"Therefore judge nothing before the time, until the Lord come, who both will bring to light the hidden things of darkness, and will make manifest the counsels of the hearts: and then shall every man have praise of God."* If you are a Christian, you are going to be rewarded for something you have done and maybe forgotten!

The two most important things in the Christian life are winning souls for Christ, and encouraging believers toward holy living in their daily walk with God. We can all encourage someone every day. We do not always have the chance to win souls, but we can always leave a witness. What we often forget is that it takes the efforts of many people to bring someone to Christ. Paul said, *"I have planted, Apollos watered; but God gave the increase. So then neither is he that planteth any thing, neither he that watereth; but God that giveth the increase. Now he that planteth and he that watereth are one: and every man shall receive his own reward according to his own labor"* (I Corinthians 3:6-8).

Often your prayers and your invitation to someone to attend church are just as important as the preacher who invites them to accept Christ as their Savior. I believe you are going to be overwhelmed when Jesus shows you the people in whom you have planted the seed of the Gospel, and the many prayers that you have said in their behalf.

It stands to reason that, after the Rapture but before the Marriage ceremony, there will be a time of fellowship and rejoicing with friends and relatives. We have already said that *"Christ loved the Church and gave Himself for it."* Why does He love us? We used to sing an old hymn that said, "Why did He love me so? Why did He love me so? Why did my Savior to Calvary go? Why did He love me so?"[7]

Do you know how much you are worth? In past generations it was estimated that the intrinsic value of our bodies is worth about $1.00, but if you include the skin add another $3.50. However, current research shows it is worth much more in today's use of organ transplants if you sell individual parts.[8] So, it is questionable whether it makes sense to spend ten thousand dollars to bury someone worth $4.50. But what you may not realize is that the one doing the loving creates the worth of that individual. Jesus loved the Church, and gave Himself for it. Our worth is incalculable, proven by Jesus' love for us. I have known husbands and wives in my Sunday school class whose love deepened as the years went by — whose satisfaction with each other was so genuine that outside forces could never separate them.

This is a picture of how Christ and the Church will enjoy more and more of each other throughout eternity. So, the Church – this beautiful Bride – will be adorned in a magnificent wedding gown of fine white linen, which is the righteousness provided by the Lord Himself. Notice that the Bride's beautiful white gown is in sharp contrast with the gaudy colors that the harlot wore in chapter 17.

Directly following the wedding ceremony is the reception; in this case, the Marriage Supper of the Lamb. It appears that the Bride will change clothes for this event as each individual believer will change into the celebratory garments they have weaved for themselves. This garment is to be worn only for the wedding feast and not for the wedding itself. After the wedding feast, it is laid aside for all eternity, and the Bride is again clothed in His righteousness. The Church is the Bride because of the righteousness of Christ, but the Bride is clothed for the wedding feast because of her righteous acts. Her righteous acts flow from a righteous character.

Why is this called the Marriage of the Lamb and the Marriage Supper of the Lamb instead of using one of the other 700 titles that Jesus is referred to in Scripture? It is because we fell in love with the Lamb. While we honor Him as King, and as Creator as well as the other 700 titles of which He deserves, we were saved by Him as the Lamb of God who taketh away the sins of the world! How we dearly love Him as the Lamb – slain for us from the foundation of the world!

Recall the time when Jesus changed the water into the most delicious drink that anyone could imagine at the marriage in Cana. When the guests ran out of wine, Jesus' mother pleaded with Jesus to do something about it. Outside on the porch were several water pots for the guests to wash their feet before entering the house. You can imagine the dust that was collected after walking some distance in their sandals. Jesus told the servants to fill the pots with water and then take a dipper full to the master of ceremonies. I am sure the servants were aghast, but they followed instructions. After tasting of the drink, the master of ceremonies said, *"Usually a host serves the best wine first. Then, when everyone is full and doesn't care, he brings out the less expensive wines. But you have kept the best until now!"* (John 2:10 NLT). They didn't even know they were drinking footbath!

The food and drink will be just that good when we gather around the table at the Marriage Supper of the Lamb. At the Last Supper, the Lord told His disciples in Matthew 26:29: *"But I say unto you, I will not drink henceforth of this fruit of the vine, until that day when I drink it new with you in my Father's kingdom."* That will be at the Marriage Supper of the Lamb!

I have a most exhaustive research book, *Wine in the Bible,* which discusses every instance that wine is mentioned in the Bible.[9] It proves that any time our Lord was involved with wine, whether at the marriage at Cana or the Lord's Supper, it was not the intoxicating kind. It was the fruit of the vine. Isaiah 65:8 clears this up when it says that *"new wine is in the cluster."* Proverbs 23:31-32 (NLT) confirms this as it adds: *"Don't let the sparkle and smooth taste of wine deceive you. For in the end it bites like a poisonous serpent; it stings like a viper."* In other words, when it is fermented, it bites like a poisonous snake.

The wedding ceremony is often pictured in the parables of Jesus. For example, Jesus said, *"The kingdom of Heaven is like unto a certain king, which made a marriage for his son, And* [he] *sent forth his servants to call them that were bidden to the wedding: and they would not come"* (Matthew 22:2-3). For the complete story, see Matthew 22:1-14 and Luke 14:16-24. The thrust of this parable is directed against those who refuse Christ's invitation. You see, everyone has been invited to His wedding, but most people decline His gracious invitation. Whatever excuses they came up with, they did not satisfy the king, and he sends his servant into the countryside to find those who will come. And so, Matthew 22:10 says, *"The wedding was furnished with guests."*

The host also provided all the guests with proper garments for the wedding, no matter how torn or filthy their own clothing might have been. When one man appeared at the feast without a garment, however, he was denied entry. He, like the others, had been invited, but he rejected the formal terms of the invitation preferring instead to come on his own terms rather than the terms of the host. It is like you put "black tie" on your formal wedding invitation and some fellow shows up in his blue jeans and a T-shirt. You can clearly see a picture of those unfortunate souls who preferred to say like Frank Sinatra, "I did it my way."

There is one other important parable we mentioned earlier. Jesus said, *"Then shall the kingdom of Heaven be likened unto ten virgins, which took their lamps, and went forth to meet the bridegroom. And five of them were wise, and five were foolish"* (Matthew 25:1-2). The foolish virgins were shortsighted, too busy, too concerned with their immediate comforts and pleasures to prepare for the great wedding. They had not declined the invitation; in fact, they expected to be a member of the wedding party. But for now, they had rather go to the lake – they had rather go to the ball game – they had rather watch a movie on TV. They were careless; they were not prepared. They did not have oil for their lamps. These foolish virgins were not saved. These foolish virgins had ample time to prepare, but their time ran out and the wedding was upon them. They ran out to find oil for their lamps (a symbol of the Holy Spirit), but it was too late. The wise virgins were ready, and they were invited into the wedding. And then, folks, we read one of the saddest verses in the Bible. *".... and the door was shut"* (Matthew 25:10). When the foolish virgins finally arrived and knocked on the door they said, *"'Lord, Lord, open to us.' But he answered and said, 'Verily I say unto you, I know you not'"* (Matthew 25:11-12). *"Therefore keep watch, because you do not know on what day your Lord will come"* (Matthew 24:42 NIV). That is why I teach Bible prophecy. It is not to impress anyone with the mysteries of God. It is to encourage you to be ready at all times!

In the first parable, many are excluded from the wedding by their own choice. In the second parable, the problem is their own negligence. They intended to get ready someday; but time ran out. Only true believers will be at this great wedding ceremony. The unbelievers will find that their way takes them to the Great White Throne Judgment, and that will not be a joyous event. For the unbeliever, prophecy says, "Don't be shut out of the wedding! Prepare yourself by accepting Christ's invitation!" For the believer, prophecy calls us to holy living because we want to be prepared when the Bridegroom comes.

It is so sad that many people in the world today, many of them our neighbors, ignore the simple instructions Jesus gave to be part of the wedding, and to avoid the Great White Throne Judgment. The friends of the Bridegroom will be all those saved people in Heaven who are not a part of the Church – such as the Old Testament saints and even John the Baptist who in John 3:29 declared that he was not part of the bridal party, but a friend of the Bridegroom. Look what verse 9 of Revelation 19 says: *"And he saith unto me, 'Write, Blessed are they which are called unto the Marriage Supper of the Lamb.' And he saith unto me, 'These are the true sayings of God.'"*

So here we have a class of saints who are certainly to be differentiated from the Bride. These are all the friends of the Bridegroom, who rejoice in His joy and share in His gladness. These are Old Testament saints, and those martyrs from the Tribulation Period who, though they form no part of the Church, share in this heavenly and glorious celebration. Their presence adds to the happiness and joy of the Bride and Groom.

Bible scholars are in agreement that the Marriage of the Lamb will take place in Heaven, but some think the Marriage Supper will take place in Heaven and others think it will take place on earth. I do not know that it will make a lot of difference. God the Father will be running the show, and that is good enough for me. But, for the record, I think that the Marriage will take place in Heaven and immediately thereafter, there will be the reception in Heaven called the Marriage Supper of the Lamb.

While that is going on in Heaven, the armies of the earth are assembling in the Valley of Decision (Joel 3:14) – the Valley of Armageddon. And when the Marriage Supper of the Lamb is concluded, Christ will break forth from the heavens with His saints, and with only a word from His mouth, the Battle will be over almost before it begins. He will then establish His Millennial Kingdom on earth, and if you want to look at it this way, He will begin His 1,000 year honeymoon with His new Bride in the New Jerusalem.

With the table spread with the best things God can serve, the Marriage Supper will be fantastic. But do you realize what the best part of it will be? It will be the fellowship! Sitting down and rejoicing with all our friends and loved ones – greeting our parents – our spouses – our kids – our friends from church. Why would anyone want to miss out on that?! Yet, there are those all around us who apparently do not care.

There are many characters and events in the Old Testament which we call types. They illustrate great events which are yet to come. For example, Jonah who was in the belly of the great fish was a picture or a type of Christ being in the heart of the earth for three days and three nights. In fact, Jesus Himself confirmed this in Matthew 12:40. The three Hebrew children that were in the fiery furnace were a type of Israel passing through the Tribulation. Lot and his family being taken out of Sodom before God's judgment rained down was a type of the Church being raptured before the judgments of the Tribulation Period.

The type I really want you to see is the story of Abraham's preparation of a bride for his son, Isaac, in Genesis 24. Abraham is a picture of God the Father, Isaac a picture of Christ, Abraham's servant Eleazar a picture of the Holy Spirit, and Rebekah is a picture of the Bride of Christ. Just as Abraham sent Eleazar to a foreign land to seek out a bride for Isaac, so the Holy Spirit has been moving throughout the earth seeking out the Bride of Christ. Every time someone is saved, the Bride's identity becomes more complete. Just as Isaac went to meet Rebekah, so Christ descends to meet His Bride as the Church leaves the earth at the Rapture. As Eleazar and Isaac took Rebekah to meet Abraham, so the Church will be taken before God the Father in order for the wedding ceremony to take place.

What a beautiful picture of this wondrous event that awaits all who put their trust in Christ, and claim Him as their personal Savior! And the angel emphasizes to John, write this down: these are the true sayings of God! Do not let another day go by without being sure you are part of the Bride of the Lamb because God said that these events really are going to take place.

Verse 10 says: *"And I fell at his feet to worship him, and he said unto me, 'See thou do it not: I am thy fellow servant, and of thy brethren that have the testimony of Jesus: worship God: for the testimony of Jesus is the spirit of prophecy.'"* What a great example of why this is the Word of God! If there was any portion of the Book of Revelation that John would like to omit, it is verse 10. He has just done a very foolish thing, and he was probably embarrassed by it. He allowed himself to become so caught up in this great scene about the wedding and the Marriage Supper that it overwhelmed him. And he fell down, and began to worship a created being instead of the Creator.

The recording of such human weakness proves that God wrote the Bible because John would not have recorded his mistakes. God, however, records them in order to show the world that all have sinned and come short of the glory of God. The angel quickly admonishes John: "Get up! I am only a servant of God, as you are!" Here we see an important lesson that is stressed over and over in Scripture. The angel tells John, "Do not worship me, worship God!" Think of all the statues that people bow down to and worship. The angel stressed, "Worship God!" John makes the same mistake in chapter 22 which we will see later, and again he is immediately corrected.

When Mary Magdalene and the other Mary saw Jesus on that first Easter morning, the Bible says, *"And they came and held Him by the feet and worshipped Him"* (Matthew 28:9b). We find throughout the New Testament, people worshipping Jesus Christ, and He never admonished them for this; that is because He is God.

The next time you run into someone who questions the deity of Jesus, tuck these two verses away in your mind. First, in Revelation 19:10, we are told that only God is worthy of worship. And then, in Hebrews 1:6, it says: *"And again, when He* [that is God the Father] *bringeth in the first begotten into the world* [that is Jesus], *He* [that is God the Father] *saith, 'AND LET ALL THE ANGELS OF GOD WORSHIP HIM* [that is Jesus].'" That is God the Father telling all the angels to worship Jesus! It is the same God who said, *"I will not give my glory to anyone else"* (Isaiah 42:8a NLT). If that does not prove deity, I do not know what does. To worship even the most exalted of God's creatures is idolatry. It is a sin that God Almighty calls an abomination. Oh, those poor creatures on earth who are bowing down and worshipping the Beast and his image.

We cannot imagine just how awesome this scene is that John is witnessing. Just think what he has already seen on the Mount of Transfiguration on the day of Pentecost. He saw the great vision in the 4th chapter of Revelation which included all the wonders of the seals, trumpets, bowl judgments and yet, when he sees the Church on its wedding day, he loses it. He falls at the feet of the angel. What an awesome event!

I have heard many people ask, "Why is it important to study prophecy anyway?" Listen to what the angel told John in Revelation 19, verse 10b: (NASB): *"The testimony of Jesus is the spirit of prophecy."* That is why we study prophecy because if taught correctly it is the study of Jesus! It points to Him – it magnifies Him. It calls the lost to escape the awful wrath that is to come, and it calls believers to live a holy life because our Lord could return at any time.

So now the wedding is over; the marriage supper is over; and it is time to go on a 1,000 year honeymoon. But first, the Groom has some business to take care of. He looks down and sees on earth the armies of the world led by the Antichrist and the False Prophet, assembling throughout Israel for the purpose of destroying God and His chosen people once and for all. And Jesus says, "Come, my Bride, you are going to see God's enemies destroyed." John says in verse 11: *"And I saw Heaven opened, and behold a white horse; and He that sat upon him was called Faithful and True, and in righteousness He doth judge and make war."*

For the second time in this Book, John saw Heaven opened. The first time, was in chapter 4 when the Church was called up (raptured) to Heaven. John said in chapter 4:1: *"After this I looked, and, behold, a door was opened in Heaven: and the first voice which I heard was as it were of a trumpet talking with me; which said, 'Come up hither ….'"*. At the Rapture, a door was opened in Heaven to receive the Church into the loving arms of Jesus. That door was then shut during the seven year Tribulation Period. Now, that door in Heaven is opened once more, only this time, it is not to receive the Church, it is for Christ together with the Church to come out of Heaven to confront the armies of the world.

Another way to put it is that Heaven opened the first time for the Rapture and the second time for the Revelation. The Old Testament prophets foretold of this second coming event. Jesus predicted it and the New Testament writers wrote about it – about 1,600 times. Yet the scoffers continued to mock. In II Peter 3:4a (NLT), *"This will be their argument: 'Jesus promised to come back, did He? Then where is He?'"* The answer is, He is right here in Revelation 19:11-16 ! *"And I saw Heaven opened, and behold a white horse; and He that sat upon him was called Faithful and True, and in righteousness He doth judge and make war. His eyes were as a flame of fire, and on His head were many crowns; and He had a name written, that no man knew, but He Himself. And He was clothed with a vesture dipped in blood: and His name is called The Word of God. And the armies which were in Heaven followed Him upon white horses, clothed in fine linen, white and clean. And out of His mouth goeth a sharp sword, that with it He should smite the nations: and He shall rule them with a rod of iron: and He treadeth the winepress of the fierceness and wrath of Almighty God. And He hath on His vesture and on His thigh a name written, KING OF KINGS, AND LORD OF LORDS."* The scoffers will wish they had never asked where He is!

If the Bible makes anything clear, it is this: the Second Coming of Christ will be a glorious event which the entire world will witness, both believers and unbelievers alike. Christ said that His coming would be like the lightning that begins in the east and shines all the way to the west illuminating the whole world (Matthew 24:27).

And riding on a white horse in the midst of that lightning will be the King of kings Himself, accompanied by His angels and all the saints. It is this scene that John saw in the 1st chapter of the Book of Revelation, verse 7a: *"Behold, He cometh with clouds; and every eye shall see Him"*.

Everything we have studied in Revelation has been building up to this. It will be a precious sight to the Tribulation saints who are still alive on the earth when this happens, but a terrifying sight to the Antichrist and his followers. The late Dr. Henry Morris wrote one of the better commentaries on this Book in 1983 entitled, *The Revelation Record.*[10] Imagine my dismay when I read the statement in his book regarding this eleventh verse. "This evidently is the same symbolic horse and rider that John had seen going forth "to conquer" at the very beginning of the Tribulation (chapter 6), and now he sees Him riding forth in this final conquest." No, no, no! These are not the same two riders! In chapter 6, the Lamb is in Heaven, and He has just opened the first seal of the seven-sealed scroll. And a rider comes forth on a white horse. That is where the similarity stops. In chapter 6, the rider comes from the earth, and he has a bow, and it appears he does not even have any arrows. It is a picture of "huff and bluff" bringing the world a false hope. It is the Antichrist saying, "Peace, peace ...." when the world is going to find out quickly that there is no peace. But now, will the REAL Prince of Peace stand up! It is Christ riding forth on His white horse. Up until this time, Christ has been directing everything from Heaven. Now He will intervene on earth directly. He will complete this distasteful task by destroying His enemies, and set up his earthly Kingdom just as He promised.

Verse 11 says that our Commander is called *"Faithful and True."* Nothing of that sort could be said about that fake leader riding a white horse in chapter 6! And what is the purpose of this Faithful and True Commander on the white horse? It is to judge and make war! I dare say in 95% of all the pictures I have ever seen of Jesus, He looks like He could not hurt a fly. He is holding a child, or He is healing a blind person, or just kneeling and weeping over Jerusalem. But now, His longsuffering patience has run its course. He is coming to judge and make war.

And notice, He is going to judge in righteousness. That means His judgments will be pure – His verdict will be right! Throughout the Bible, but especially in the Minor Prophets, we see that God hates injustice. He despises judges who take bribes and in other ways render unfair decisions. He will judge in perfect righteousness. I saw a bumper sticker which fits the Second Coming perfectly: "Jesus is coming soon, and boy is He mad!"

It is intriguing how many times the two aspects of Christ's return is depicted in the same passage. Sometimes, it is referring to Christ's First Coming, and sometimes His Second Coming. For example, in Isaiah 9:6a-7a it says, *"For unto us a child is born, unto us a Son is given"* [that is His First Coming]; *"and the government shall be upon His shoulder .... of the increase of His government and peace there shall be no end ...."* [that is His Second Coming]. Look at Philippians 2:8. You have probably read this a hundred times. *"And being found in fashion as a man, He humbled Himself, and became obedient unto death, even the death of the cross"* [that is His First Coming]. Then verses 9-10a, 11: *"Wherefore God also hath highly exalted Him, and given Him a name which is above every name: that at the name of Jesus every knee should bow ....*

and that every tongue should confess that Jesus Christ is Lord, to the glory of God the Father" [that is His Second Coming].

Let us go on to verse 12 which says: *"His eyes were as a flame of fire, and on His head were many crowns; and He had a name written, that no man knew, but He Himself."* John says His eyes are like a flame of fire. John recognized Him immediately as the same Lord he saw in chapter 1. The last phrase of Revelation 19:12 says, *" .... and He had a name written, that no man knew, but He Himself."* We have known Him in Scripture by many names, but this name is above our comprehension and so, only He knows it. We have known Him as the Lamb of God, the Savior, Master, Lord, Son of Man and on and on. But all of them together cannot express this name that only He knows. Maybe He will share it with us one day!

Verse 13 says: *"And He was clothed with a vesture dipped in blood: and His name is called The Word of God."* His garment dipped in blood speaks of the judgment which is about to be carried out. Isaiah was given a glimpse of this scene in Isaiah 63:1a (NLT) of his Book. He and the Lord have this dialogue. Isaiah asks: *"Who is this who comes from Edom, from the city of Bozrah, with His clothing stained red? Who is this in royal robes, marching in the greatness of His strength?"* And then the Lord answers: *"It is I, the LORD, announcing your salvation! It is I, the LORD, who is mighty to save!"* (Isaiah 63:1b NLT).

And then Isaiah asks in verse 2: *"Why are your clothes so red, as if you have been treading out grapes?"* And in verse 3 the Lord answers: *"I have trodden the winepress alone; no one was there to help me. In my anger I have trampled my enemies as if they were grapes. In my fury I have trampled my foes. It is their blood that has stained my clothes. For the time has come for me to avenge my people, to ransom them from their oppressors. I looked, but no one came to help my people. I was amazed and appalled at what I saw. So I executed vengeance alone; unaided, I passed down judgment. I crushed the nations in my anger and made them stagger and fall to the ground"* (Isaiah 63:3-6 NLT).

We are reminded of that somber scene in Revelation 14:20. The armies of the world are gathered in the Valley of Armageddon – over 200 million strong, and millions more throughout the land of Israel as we saw in chapter 9. Their judgment day has finally come – the culmination of the awful Day of the Lord. These Christ haters are pictured as grapes about to be run through the winepress. No wonder 19:13 depicts Christ's robe to be splattered with blood. He is coming to execute judgment on His enemies.

All creation is waiting for this glorious event when God cleanses this world of evil. Even the animal kingdom and the plant kingdom are waiting for the curse of sin to be removed so that creation can be put back like it was before the Fall of man. Listen to Romans 8:22-23: *"For we know that the whole creation groaneth and travaileth in pain together until now. And not only they, but ourselves also, which have the first fruits of the Spirit, even we ourselves groan within ourselves, waiting for the adoption, to wit, the redemption of our body."*

All of creation is groaning for the renewal of their bodies. *"So Christ was once offered to bear the sins of many; and unto them that look for Him shall He appear the second time without sin* [or apart from the sin question] *unto salvation"* (Hebrews 9:28). In other words, His Second Coming will be to squash sin and to complete our redemption. He is coming to execute judgment and establish divine authority over all the earth. John says His eyes are a flame of fire – nothing will be hidden from those eyes. John says His name is called "The Word of God" (Revelation 19:13). John has called Him that before. John 1:1 says: *"In the beginning was the Word, and the Word was with God, and the Word was God."*

How plain can this be? *"And the Word was God!"* No one can say this wasn't referring to Jesus because in John 1:14 says, *"And the Word was made flesh, and dwelt among us ….".* The Jehovah's Witnesses detest this verse. It completely destroys their doctrine that says Jesus was not God. So here in the 19th chapter, we find Jesus again being called *"The Word of God."* Interestingly enough, Psalm 33:6 says: *"By the word of the LORD were the heavens made; and all the host of them by the breath of His mouth."* And Hebrews 11:3 says: *"Through faith we understand that the worlds were framed by the word of God, so that things which are seen were not made of things which do appear."* In other words, the Word of God created what we see all around us out of nothing. What a Creator!

There is a story that is told of a group of scientists who were avowed skeptics. In a conversation with God, they said they now have the technology and brain power to create man just as God did. God told them to proceed. They said, "First you take a bucket of mud ….". God interrupted them and said, "Where did you get your mud?"

When the doors of Heaven are opened, and the Lord rides forth on a white horse, is He alone? Look at verse 14: *"And the armies which were in Heaven followed Him upon white horses, clothed in fine linen, white and clean."* Who makes up these armies? Are they angels? I am sure the angels are right there, too. They are not going to miss out on the action. Besides the angels, who else comprises these armies? Have you ever heard of *Onward Christian Soldiers*? Of course! The millions of Church Age believers will be coming back with the Lord to wreak havoc on the enemies of God. Does that mean we are going to fight? You might say we are the reserves, but God does not need us. You will soon see that a simple word from the mouth of the Lord slays His enemies.

The fact that Scripture goes out of its way to mention the army's dress – pure white linen – we are reminded that earlier in this same chapter, verse 8, we see the Bride of Christ dressed in fine linen, clean and white. Can you imagine the armies of the world there in the Valley of Armageddon, and the Antichrist and the False Prophet have loaded them with propaganda and great speeches saying, "We are going to kick God off the throne once and for all?!" And the people are so worked up in a frenzy they are yelling, "Right on! Bring on God! Yeah!" And then, can you imagine how they feel when they look up and see Heaven open, and this magnificent rider on a white horse comes forth leading an army that enormously outnumbers them?!

Notice where this godly army that is following Jesus comes from. It says, *"And the armies which were in Heaven …."* (Revelation 19:14). There is no doubt that these people are the saints of God dressed in their white clean robes. I would kindly ask my post-Tribulation friends, "When did these saints get into Heaven if they are supposed to be on earth waiting for the Lord's return? I'll tell you when: the Rapture in Revelation 4:1, that is when!"

Here is an army of saints which no man can number coming out of Heaven – riding on white horses! Have you ever ridden a horse? Get ready – you will! That tells me animals are in Heaven! Animals are also on earth during the Millennium. Listen to Isaiah 11:6: *"The wolf shall also dwell with the lamb, and the leopard shall lie down with the kid; and the calf and young lion and fatling together."* That tells me that God is not going to abandon the animal kingdom. He made them for companionship, and I personally believe that our pets in Heaven fall under that verse in I Corinthians 2:9: *"But as it is written, EYE HATH NOT SEEN, NOR EAR HEARD, NEITHER HAVE ENTERED INTO THE HEART OF MAN, THE THINGS WHICH GOD HATH PREPARED FOR THEM THAT LOVE HIM."*

Scripture says that John saw the armies in Heaven which followed Him. Besides the multitude of saints, there will also be the heavenly host of angels, no doubt led by that mighty warrior Michael whom the Bible says stands for Daniel's people, Israel (Daniel 12:1). It is not likely that the Old Testament saints and the Tribulation saints are included in these armies for the Scripture hints they will be resurrected after the Tribulation.

Here is what Jude had to say about it in verse 14 of his Book: *"And Enoch also, the seventh from Adam, prophesied of these, saying, 'Behold, the Lord cometh with ten thousand of His saints.'"* And then Jude 15 (NLT) tells the purpose of His coming: *"He will bring the people of the world to judgment. He will convict the ungodly of all the evil things they have done in rebellion, and of all the insults that godless sinners have spoken against Him."* In other words, this is exactly what is going to happen at the great supper of God's wrath. In Daniel chapter 12:1, it says that in the end times, Michael shall stand up for the nation of Israel. Then it describes the Tribulation period as being worse than anything that has ever happened or ever will happen to mankind.

Daniel 12:2 (NIV) says: *"Multitudes who sleep in the dust of the earth will awake: some to everlasting life, others to shame and everlasting contempt."* This has nothing to do with the Rapture. This involves those who have died during the Tribulation. And the context of this verse shows that this resurrection occurs immediately after the Tribulation Period. Those who are saved will be resurrected to everlasting life and will enter the Millennium, and those who are lost will be resurrected to stand at the Great White Throne Judgment. To the horror of the Antichrist and the False Prophet and their armies of 200 million soldiers gathered in the

Valley of Armageddon, they discover that Christ is coming to judge and make war. As the awful realization dawns on them that they have no place to hide, they realize too late that their leader, the Antichrist, cannot save them now.

When Jesus returns to earth, He will return to the Mount of Olives from where He left this earth. Remember, when He ascended to Heaven, He ascended from the Mount of Olives (Acts 1:10-11). *"And while they looked steadfastly toward Heaven as He went up, behold, two men stood by them in white apparel; which also said, 'Ye men of Galilee, why stand ye gazing up into Heaven? This same Jesus, which is taken up from you into Heaven, shall so come in like manner as ye have seen Him go into Heaven.'"* And where will Christ come back to? The same place from where He ascended – the Mount of Olives (Zechariah 14:4).

Let us quickly review the three views of the Millennium. They all have to do with timing. When will the Lord come back in relation to the Millennium? Pre-Millennialism teaches that the world will get worse and worse, and Christ will come back to set up His kingdom and restore order to the world. That is the teaching of most evangelical churches that take a literal interpretation of Scripture. Post-Millennialism teaches that the world will get better and better through the efforts of the church, until almost the entire world is converted. Then the Church will be instrumental in ushering in the Millennial Kingdom when Christ comes back. Amillennialism teaches that there will be no Millennium – that Christ will not set up a Millennial Kingdom on this earth or anywhere else.

"On that day His feet will stand on the Mount of Olives, which faces Jerusalem on the east. And the Mount of Olives will split apart, making a wide valley running from east to west, for half the mountain will move toward the north and half toward the south …. On that day the sources of light will no longer shine, yet there will be continuous day! Only the LORD knows how this could happen! There will be no normal day and night, for at evening time it will still be light. On that day life-giving waters will flow out from Jerusalem, half toward the Dead Sea and half toward the Mediterranean, flowing continuously both in summer and in winter. And the LORD will be king over all the earth. On that day there will be one LORD – His name alone will be worshipped" (Zechariah 14:4-9 NLT). The key verse is Zechariah 14:4: *"On that day His feet will stand on the Mount of Olives"*. Just like the angel said when Jesus ascended from the Mount of Olives 2,000 years ago: *"This same Jesus …. shall so come in like manner as ye have seen Him go into Heaven"* (Acts 1:11).

Let us continue with Revelation 19:15 where we have a detailed description of Christ as He rides out of Heaven on His white stallion. *"And out of His mouth goeth a sharp sword, that with it He should smite the nations: and He shall rule them with a rod of iron: and He treadeth the winepress of the fierceness and wrath of Almighty God."*

We are about to find out that Christ's armies, of which we are a part, do not fight here at all. We are spectators! Our Commander-in-Chief is the only weapon that is necessary. All the armies of the world are gathered to fight Him. It is the most one-sided battle that has ever been fought. Just a word from the Lord and the battle is over. In Genesis 1 during the account of creation, the phrase *"God said"* appears eight times. By the same power of His word the Lord Jesus Christ will execute judgment at His Second Coming. We have this clearly stated by the Apostle Paul in II Thessalonians 2:8: *"And then shall that Wicked* [one] *be revealed, whom the Lord shall consume with the spirit of His mouth, and shall destroy with the brightness of His coming."* Yes, there is awesome power in just the voice of Jesus.

In the 18th chapter of John verse 6, when the Romans came to arrest Jesus the night He was betrayed, they said they were looking for Jesus of Nazareth. And Jesus answered them, *"I am He!"* And the Bible says that they fell backwards on the ground. That is how powerful His spoken word is. In Revelation 19:15, it says that out of the Lord's mouth goes a sharp sword and with it He will smite the nations.

I have some liberal friends who deride our literal interpretation of this Book. They say, "Hey, why don't you teach that Christ literally has a sword hanging out of His mouth?" Keep this in mind. There are both literal and symbolic descriptions throughout this Book. Sometimes you have to use common sense. When Jesus said, *"I am the Bread of Life,"* He did not mean that He was packaged in a loaf that you get at the store. And we know that when Jesus said in John the 10th chapter, *"I am the Door,"* He did not mean that He had a knob on His side that you turned and walked through Him. These statements are obviously used symbolically to picture a greater truth. John saw this sharp sword before in Revelation 1:16 describing the fierceness of Christ's judgment. But in the seventh chapter of Revelation when God's servants are sealed – 12,000 from each tribe of the children of Israel – it means 12,000 from each tribe of the children of Israel! The Book of Revelation is to be taken literally unless common sense tells you otherwise.

It is good to be reminded of another principle that we mentioned earlier. Almost every sign or symbol used in the Book of Revelation is referred to or alluded to somewhere else in the Bible. That is why a blessing is promised to those who keep the things in this Book because to keep them and understand them, you are going to need a working knowledge of the entire Bible. This is another reason it is so important to get into your Bible daily!

This verse 15 says that Christ is going to rule the nations with a rod of iron. That does not mean that He is going to beat the people into submission. It means that there will be no bending of the rules – the world will experience His perfect will being carried out at all times. The time will have come for this prayer to be answered: *"Thy will be done in earth as it is in Heaven"* (Matthew 6:10).

Have you ever thought about how this world would be if everyone respected his neighbor – no killings – no robberies – no thefts – no dope-dealing. No reptiles that bite – no insects that sting – no weeds to choke out the beautiful flowers and delicious fruits. Just everyone enjoying all the benefits of this wonderful world as it was intended to be. That is what the Millennium is all about! I have had Amillennialists ask me, "What is the purpose of the Millennium?" The purpose of the Millennium is to show how great that life would be on this planet if everyone obeyed God and followed the manual (Bible) He gave us for living here.

I often get peeved with the way things go in Washington. It would take a dictator to come along with hard and fast rules to sweep away the thousands and thousands of conflicting laws. Unfortunately, that dictator will probably be the Antichrist, and millions of people will look to him to clean up all the governmental messes.

But they will find out too late that it is like jumping from the frying pan into the fire. But praise the Lord – the dictator that follows him will be what is called a "Benevolent Dictator." He will be the Lord Jesus Christ, and He will govern with His rules in a way that is best for all people.

Notice also, that this verse 15 says, *"He treadeth the winepress of the fierceness and wrath of Almighty God."* We saw that spelled out in detail in chapter 14 of this Book. The world and all its wickedness was pictured as a cluster of over-ripened grapes. There was a mighty angel who thrust his sharp sickle into earth and harvested the grapes, and threw them into the great winepress of the wrath of God. Then the following verse says that this action caused blood to flow up to the bridles of the horses for 1600 furlongs which happens to be the length of Israel from one end to the other.

I was talking to a fellow a few months ago who told me, "I think that many preachers today present a wrong picture of Jesus to us. I believe that if we lived back then and were around Him, we would find that He was a regular guy – one who laughed and cut up with us – one who never got angry over anything – and was never judgmental about the things we choose to do – just one of the boys." Sounds to me like a big old teddy bear instead of a holy God – one who would say, "I know you get drunk, I know you lie and cheat on your spouse, I know you live a rotten life, but I am going to overlook all of that because I'm such a nice guy." Folks, such a God does not exist! The God of the Bible is a God of love, but He also hates sin. The Bible says that what a man sows, he also reaps. The Bible says that God's patience will someday run out, and He will deal with sin. And verse 11 of this 19th chapter of Revelation says He is coming back to judge and make war! Joel 3:13 speaks of this time: *"Put ye in the sickle, for the harvest is ripe …. their wickedness is great."*

No more can He be pictured as a namby-pamby weakling. He is not coming as the meek Lamb to be slain on a cross. NO! He is coming not as a Lamb, but as a Lion – the conquering Lion of the tribe of Judah. The whole earth is going to feel the sting of His judgment as His rules and His laws are set in place. Truly it will be a time when His will is done in earth as it is in Heaven.

In the days of His flesh, those sorry soldiers cast lots for His vesture. Now His vesture drips with the blood of all such blasphemers. The soldiers had mocked Him – "Hey, did you say you are a king? Ha....ha....ha!" There is no mocking now – nothing but trembling as the mighty angel's voice booms out *"King of kings and Lord of lords."* Every earthly king will submit to Him. Every individual will bow and call Him Lord. No doubt with great pomp and splendor the Antichrist will march at the head of his army, assembling themselves in the Valley of Armageddon. He will have all the latest weapons at his disposal. He will have taken over those vast underground hangers of the Israeli Air Force there in the Valley. But none of this will stand a chance against just a word spoken by the Lord. As suddenly as it all started, it will be over.

Chapter 19, verse 16: *"And He hath on His vesture and on His thigh a name written, KING OF KINGS AND LORD OF LORDS."* You just cannot get any more majestic than that. It says it all. This is His official title as far as the world is concerned. Earth would not recognize His claims when He came here the first time. They gave Him a crown of thorns, but God is soon going to reverse that, and we are going to be witnesses to it! Scripture tells us that Jesus has had many names. And we are reminded of that in this same chapter, verse 13. It says that Jesus' name is *"The Word of God."* And in verse 12, it says He had a name written that no man knows, save He Himself. It must be such a glorious name that it is beyond our understanding.

Instead of bowing to Christ in the present, the world would rather perpetrate such frauds on the people such as *The DiVinci Code* that says Jesus was just a man, nothing more.[11] Or the movies that make Judas look brilliant and portrays Jesus as less than God such as *The Last Temptation of Christ*[12] and the movie *Judas.*[13] I am reminded of Paul's admonition in II Timothy 4:3-4: *"For the time will come when they will not endure sound doctrine; but after their own lusts shall they heap to themselves teachers, having itching ears; And they shall turn away their ears from the truth, and shall be turned unto fables."*

On the heels of this wonderful proclamation about Jesus' return as King of kings and Lord of lords, we have another mighty announcement! Verse 17: *"And I saw an angel standing in the sun; and he cried with a loud voice, saying to all the fowls that fly in the midst of Heaven, 'Come and gather yourselves together unto the supper of the great God.'"* The Book of Revelation is the unveiling of Jesus Christ at the end of the age. And prophecy, in the Old Testament and in the New Testament, without exception, says that the end of the world comes at the end of an awful and indescribable conflict. World history ends in war and desolation.

This angel in verse 17 is *"standing in the sun."* He stands where all can see him, and where he can survey the whole situation. The supper to which he invites the fowls comes after the battle. I wonder if he is the same angel who is responsible for the sun to heat up so severely during the latter days of the tribulation as recorded in Revelation 16:8-9. Do you remember what is going on in the earth at this time? The demonic spirits have convinced the kings and armies of the earth to gather in a place called Armageddon to make a final attempt at throwing God off His throne.

Look at these verses from the third chapter, verse 2 of Joel: *"I will gather all nations, and will bring them down into the valley of Jehoshaphat, and will plead with them there for my people and for my heritage Israel, whom they have scattered among the nations, and parted my land."* God says to the nations of the world: "You have parted my land, and I am angry!" What has been happening in the news in Israel for the last several years? It was President Bush the first, then it was President Clinton, then President Bush the second and then Obama – they all have put pressure on Israel to give up land to the Palestinians to appease them, to try to get the terrorists to quit bombing.

You can never appease your enemy who has sworn to wipe you off the face of the earth. You would think that we would have learned this lesson with Hitler in WWII. In the early days of his power, the Allies approved the giving up of Czechoslovakia and Poland and the other Baltic states to Hitler because Hitler said, "This is all I want." Too late, we learned that when Hitler said he wanted peace – he really did! He wanted a piece of France, a piece of Denmark, a piece of Belgium. Prime Minister Neville Chamberlain of England said later, "We would have gotten peace if only Hitler hadn't lied."[14] Good grief! This prophecy in Joel 3 is as fresh as tomorrow's newspaper! God says He is angry because the nations of the world are dividing the land He gave to Israel. And that is exactly what is taking place in Israel today as the United Nations continues to put pressure on Israel to give land to the Palestinians.

God has gathered the armies of the world together in the Valley of Jehoshaphat – the Valley of Armageddon – and there He will deal with them, these enemies of God and enemies of Israel. The king of the north, Russia, will be coming down. The king of the West, that is the confederation of the old Roman Empire of Europe, will be there. And I believe that the U.S. will be a part of this European Union. The United States has always belonged to the federation of the West, and this will be even more evident after the Rapture, and the Christians have been taken from the earth. And the kings of the East shall come – those hoards from China, Japan, and the other oriental powers. And the king of the South will come up – Egypt and all those nations comprising the vast continent of Africa.

All of these will converge on Israel to wipe out God in the land He has called "Holy." These evil forces are led by the Antichrist and the False Prophet both of whom are possessed by and empowered by Satan himself. And the angel sees them gathered there and invites the fowls of the air (carrion is the correct term) – buzzards, vultures and other meat-eating fowl to feast on what to us will be a most disgusting meal. This is the second supper described in this chapter.

We just finished studying about the Marriage Supper of the Lamb and it was glorious. But the Supper of God is entirely different. An angel will stand in the sun, and beckon for all the scavengers of the air to gather together for a great feast prepared by God. It is pretty gross, but the best description is one of "blood and guts."

John does not see the actual battle. Maybe it is over too quickly. He simply sees the aftermath of it. In contrast to this, in Revelation 19:9b, an angel told John to write, *"Blessed are they which are called unto the marriage supper of the Lamb."* So it is very important which supper you are going to attend! Friend, let me ask a serious question: do you want to be AT the supper – or do you want to BE the supper?!

These armies who have opposed God are destroyed physically at this time. But 1,000 years later, after the Millennium, they will be resurrected to stand before the Great White Throne to be judged and punished spiritually for their rejection of the King of kings. As we think of all these godless nations bent on throwing God off the throne, I cannot help but be reminded of that great Psalm 2:1-9 (NLT) that paints a picture of this very scene. *"Why do the nations rage? Why do the people waste their time with futile plans? The kings of the earth prepare for battle; the rulers plot together against the LORD and against His anointed One. 'Let us break their chains,' they cry, 'and free ourselves from this slavery.' But the One who rules in Heaven laughs. The LORD scoffs at them. Then in anger He rebukes them, terrifying them with His fierce fury. For the LORD declares, 'I have placed my chosen king on the throne in Jerusalem, my holy city.' The King proclaims the LORD'S decree: The LORD said to me, 'You are my Son. Today I have become your Father. Only ask, and I will give you the nations as your inheritance, the ends of the earth as your possession. You will break them with an iron rod and smash them like clay pots.'"* Yes, Jesus is coming back and He has a name written on His vesture – "King of kings and Lord of lords."

We are fast approaching the end of the Tribulation Period, and the last gasp of the Antichrist to rule the world. Men have been trying to rule the world since time began. A few years ago, I received one of the most unique Christmas cards I have ever seen. On the front of it, it has the picture of various men – Alexander the Great – Caesar – Lenin – Hitler – Napoleon. Above their pictures, the card says, "History is crowded with men who would be gods" – and then you open the card and it says " …. but only one God who would be man." I love it!

The godless armies of the world have gathered in the Valley of Armageddon for the final battle against God and His chosen people, Israel. More than 200 million strong have come from the East (China) and millions more from the North (Russia), the South (Egypt and Africa) and the West (Europe). Their first objective is to annihilate Israel, and then to defeat God Himself.

The Bible hints that there are many who are chaffing about the Antichrist. They resent his high-handed methods and, although they do not have any love for God, they also do not have any love for the Antichrist. I believe that this organized rebellion will occur in Russia and in

China. Neither country has ever been a real member of the Roman Empire. They will have a deep resentment against the Antichrist and his bullish methods until it finally boils over. We get a hint of this in Daniel chapter 11. The Antichrist is away plundering Egypt, Libya and Ethiopia when he gets a startling message.

Listen to Daniel 11:44a: *"But tidings out of the east and out of the north shall trouble him."* The Antichrist gets this disturbing message. Directions in the Bible are always given with Israel being the focal point. So bad news is coming out of the east, that is China; and bad news is coming out of the north, that is Russia. On earth, these massive armies that are coming together in the Valley of Armageddon will have all the latest weapons – mechanized vehicles, missiles and nuclear warheads. The ground itself will seem to shake with the hundreds of millions of soldiers' feet marching into that valley. The skies overhead will darken with aircraft, and up and down the Mediterranean Sea near the Gulf of Suez and the Persian Gulf, warships and vessels will crowd the waters. And little Israel is caught squarely in the middle.

However, God says He will protect Israel. Listen to Jeremiah 15:20-21 (NLT): *"They will fight against you like an attacking army, but I will make you as secure as a fortified wall. They will not conquer you, for I will protect and deliver you. I, the LORD, have spoken! Yes, I will certainly keep you safe from these wicked men. I will rescue you from their cruel hands!"*

It could be that all these earthly armies decide that they will take care of Israel first and then they will throw God off the throne. Then they will fight it out among themselves. I am reminded of a good example of this. When I was a teenager growing up, I loved wrestling. In 1949, I went over to a friend's house to watch Saturday night wrestling in black and white on his 7" TV screen. If you'd have told me it was all a fake, I'd have argued with you. We didn't call it wrestling; we called it "rassling."

It was a real treat when I would go to the old Sportatorium on Industrial Boulevard. Promoter Ed McLemore brought some of the biggest names to Dallas – Duke Keomuka, Gorgeous George, Wild Bill Longson and world champion, Lou Thesz. I remember Eric Holmbeck from the Klondike who had a 68 inch chest which he loved to show off before his match. But my favorite was Andre the Giant. A HUGE MAN! Baylor Hospital has a section on the first floor of more than 100 bronze casts of famous people's hands.[15] They have on display the hands of Roger Staubach, Tom Landry, Van Cliburn, Billy Graham, Mickey Mantle and dozens of others. They also have the bronze-cast hands of Andre the Giant. You will not believe how big they are! You see, he suffered from a disease called "acromegaly".[16] He was born with an over-abundance of growth hormones.

For a coming attraction, the Sportatorium advertised a fantastic match – 10 wrestlers in the ring at once. If you were thrown out of the ring, you were eliminated. The last one standing in the ring would win $25,000. All the wrestlers were there, including Andre the Giant. And

I was there too. I was going to see Andre walk away with the prize money. Who could defeat him? He stood nearly 7½ feet tall and weighed in at more than 520 lbs. He was dubbed the "eighth wonder of the world."[17] He was a cinch to be the last one standing, and he would have no problem winning the $25,000. Boy was I wrong. The other nine wrestlers knew they didn't stand a chance against him, so as soon as the opening bell rang, they teamed up with each other, and all nine tossed Andre out of the ring.

That is what the armies in the Valley of Armageddon thought they would do. The armies from the north, south, east and west – millions of them who do not like each other, teaming up to toss God off His throne. They do not realize it, but they do not stand a chance!

I saw a cartoon that first appeared several years ago in a Russian newspaper. At the bottom of the cartoon were pictures of a number of churches all smashed to bits. Beyond the rubble of the ruined churches was a tall ladder leaning against the clouds. There was a workman with a big hammer climbing the ladder toward Heaven. In Heaven was pictured God the Father, the Son and the Holy Spirit. The Russian workman was taking his hammer, and was getting ready to smash them with it. The caption below the cartoon said, "Having destroyed this God business down here on earth, we are going to destroy it in Heaven." Will he be in for a surprise!

As the armies of the earth march toward Israel, the Lord Jesus Christ bursts from the heavens with an army of His saints to slay these godless enemies who have marched into the Valley of Armageddon. We hear frequently about the Battle of Armageddon, but it really isn't a battle. It is over almost before it begins. Christ speaks a word, and the enemy falls dead in their tracks. It will be the most staggering defeat a vast army has ever suffered in the history of the world. There are only two prisoners taken as we will see in a moment. The rest of the forces are decimated.

The Apostle Paul gives us the outcome of this great "battle" in II Thessalonians 2:8: *"And then shall that Wicked* [one] *be revealed, whom the Lord shall consume with the spirit of His mouth, and shall destroy with the brightness of His coming."* Then, the ominous cry of the angel, summoning all the buzzards and carnivorous fowls of the air to what is termed the great Supper of God. It is clean up time for the millions of dead bodies that will lie in the Valley of Armageddon – a gruesome picture of what happens to those who side with Satan and the Antichrist and oppose the living God!

That brings us to verse 18 where the angel has a message for these carnivorous fowls who have been summoned: *"That ye may eat the flesh of kings, and the flesh of captains, and the flesh of mighty men, and the flesh of horses, and of them that sit on them, and the flesh of all men, both free and bond, both small and great."* All will die: kings, generals, admirals, colonels – down to the least recruit. None will escape. Their day of opportunity has past. Some of these mighty men are the same ones mentioned in chapter 18 who cried over the destruction of Babylon.

Nothing like this has ever happened in the history of the world. How can the Amillennialists say that this has already been fulfilled in the 1st Century? You would have to have a PhD in imagination to claim that all this has been fulfilled!

There are only two survivors of this great battle. Verse 20 (NASB) tells us who they are: *"And the beast was seized, and with him the false prophet who performed the signs in his presence, by which he deceived those who had received the mark of the beast and those who worshiped his image; these two were thrown alive into the Lake of Fire which burns with brimstone."* This would make a good trivia question: "Who are the four men in the Bible who never experienced physical death?" Probably most Bible scholars could not name all four. Most everyone is familiar with Enoch and Elijah. In Genesis 5:23-24 (NLT) it says, *"Enoch lived 365 years in all. He enjoyed a close relationship with God throughout his life. Then suddenly, he disappeared because God took him."* I like the little boy's version of it. He said, "Enoch walked with God. One day, God said, 'Enoch, we're closer to my house than yours, so come on home with me.'"

The second person who never experienced physical death was Elijah. He and Elisha, soon-to-be his successor, were walking along talking. Elijah had just revealed to Elisha that God was soon going to take him home. And then we find this in II Kings 2:11 (NLT): *"As they were walking along and talking, suddenly a chariot of fire appeared, drawn by horses of fire. It drove between them, separating them, and Elijah was carried by a whirlwind into Heaven."*

Elijah and Enoch are the two men who normally are mentioned as not experiencing physical death. And as such, they are a perfect picture of those dear saints who are alive at the time of the Rapture – they are caught up to meet the Lord, never having to experience physical death – Enoch representing the Gentiles, and Elijah representing those Jews who have accepted Jesus as their Messiah. Here in chapter 19, we are told of two more men who never experience physical death. They are captured alive after the Battle of Armageddon, and are cast into the Lake of Fire. So that makes four men in the Bible who never taste physical death: Enoch, Elijah, the Antichrist and the False Prophet.

Some folks believe that Hell means annihilation, that if you are cast into the Lake of Fire, you cease to exist. If you believe this, I have some bad news for you. We will cover it again when we get to the next chapter, but I want to nail it down here. It is clear from Scripture that the Antichrist and the False Prophet are cast alive into the Lake of Fire. At least those two are not annihilated. When we get to chapter 20, we will see that Satan is bound, and cast into the Bottomless Pit for a thousand years. When the Millennium is over, Satan is judged; and in verse 10 of chapter 20, we see that Satan is cast into the Lake of Fire *"where the Beast and the False Prophet are."*

The Beast and the False Prophet have been in the Lake of Fire for a thousand years, and they are still alive! Otherwise, the verse would have said, "And Satan was cast into the Lake of

Fire where the Beast and the False Prophet had been thrown." This also disproves purgatory. If they are supposed to be rehabilitated, they sure haven't made much progress. After a thousand years the Beast and the False Prophet are still suffering. And did you notice that the Beast and the False Prophet have the distinction of being the first two cast into Hell? They even made it in there before the Devil did! And here is another important point. Some teach that Hell is not real – when the Bible says you go to Hell it simply means that you are separated from God. You can see clearly from this account that Hell is a place and not a condition. You cannot be taken and cast into a condition!

Regarding the Antichrist, author J. R. Church had this to say: "The Antichrist will perhaps be the greatest intellectual, the greatest politician, the greatest statesman and the greatest economist who ever lived, but when he gives his allegiance to Satan, he will become the greatest fool who ever lived."[18]

Verse 21: *"And the remnant were slain with the sword of him that sat upon the horse, which sword proceedeth out of His mouth; and all the fowls were filled with their flesh."* Right to the very end, with the vultures circling above, with the memories of the recent earthquake, and the fall of Babylon, this remnant still hoped against hope that they will gain the victory. Just think how devastated they will be when they see their seemingly invincible leaders, the Beast and the False Prophet, suddenly snatched from their midst. We do not know if Christ sent angels to get them, or simply by His word transports them to their destination. But whatever the method, these two most feared men on the face of the earth are brought low – never to be feared again. It reminds me of Adolph Hitler, once the most feared man on the face of the earth. One of the last men to see him alive, and speak with him in his bunker beneath the city of Berlin, noted that he was shaking so badly that he could not hold a pen. That is what happens when you meet the God of the Universe, and you are not on the winning side.

Jesus described the scene for us in Luke 21:26-27: *"Men's hearts failing them for fear, and for looking after those things which are coming on the earth: for the powers of Heaven shall be shaken. And then shall they see THE SON OF MAN COMING IN A CLOUD with power and great glory."* Then a great flock of ravenous birds will swoop down from the heavens, gorging themselves on the flesh and blood of these once high-and-mighty rebels. Gradually the earth will be cleansed of its pollution, and Christ will stand on the Mount of Olives with His 144,000 faithful evangelists as we saw pictured in chapter 14. When man refuses the salvation offered by Almighty God, denying His word and blaspheming His name, there must one day come a time of reckoning. Ecclesiastes says: *"To everything there is a season, and a time to every purpose under the heavens* (Ecclesiastes 3:1). God's great purpose for His creation is to completely purge it of sin and restore it to its original perfection. That will be accomplished when He comes back.

We have finished our study in chapter 19, and chronologically at this point we are at the end of the seven year Tribulation Period. The Antichrist, the False Prophet and all the godless armies of the world will have poured into the Valley of Armageddon to do battle with God's chosen people, Israel. And at this climactic point in history, the sky splits open – and there for all to see – comes Jesus Christ riding on a white horse, and declaring Himself to be KING of kings and LORD of lords! All the heavenly saints are with Him. And with just a word from His mouth, the Battle of Armageddon is over.

Blood runs from one end of the valley to the other, as God's wrath is poured out on all those who would love to overthrow God. This awful event is referred to in the Bible as "the great Supper of God," and the scavenger fowls swoop down to take their fill. In fact, the Bible says, it will take seven months to bury the dead and clean up the carnage (Ezekiel 39:12). All these enemy soldiers are killed except the Beast and the False Prophet who are cast alive into the Lake of Fire.

CHAPTER TWENTY

Satan Bound, White Throne Judgment, Final Rebellion

Chapter 20 introduces us to the most beautiful, peaceful and rewarding age this world will ever know – the Millennium. It is the 1,000 year reign of Jesus Christ as King of kings and Lord of lords. Isaiah the prophet spoke of this in Isaiah 9:6-7. We are all familiar with the first part – we read it at Christmas, but maybe not so familiar with the last part.

"For unto us a child is born, unto us a son is given: and the government shall be upon His shoulder; and His name shall be called Wonderful, Counselor, The mighty God, The everlasting Father, The Prince of Peace. Of the increase of His government and peace there shall be no end, upon the throne of David, and upon His kingdom, to order it, and to establish it with judgment and with justice from henceforth even forever. The zeal of the LORD of hosts will perform this" (Isaiah 9:6-7). The first part of the verse has to do with His birth; the last part has to do with the Millennium.

The 20th chapter of Revelation has been the major battleground of the various systems of Biblical eschatology (end time events). The way in which this chapter is interpreted to a large extent determines how the entire Book of Revelation is interpreted. It is in this chapter that we find the 1,000 year millennial reign of Jesus Christ. It is in this chapter we find that Satan is bound for a thousand years, and the world is ruled in righteousness by Christ and His followers.

The major question that confronts us is this: should this 20th chapter be taken literally? Is this thousand year period really 1,000 years, or is it a symbolic number meaning a long period of time and there is really no Millennium? Is Satan literally imprisoned during this time, or is this only a figure of speech referring to the eventual conversion of the world through the preaching of the Church, and thereby in a sense, Satan is bound?

There are 3 major approaches to eschatology: 1) pre-Millennialism, 2) post-Millennialism and 3) Amillennialism. We discussed this earlier, but since this chapter directly deals with this issue, it is good for us to review it.

The first position is pre-Millennialism. This is the position from which we will be studying. It is basically a literal interpretation of Scripture whenever possible. "Pre" means before, so this means that Christ will come back before the Millennium begins. This position says that the Church through its preaching will never convert the entire world, and so it is essential that Christ come back to establish the 1,000 years of peace.

Pre-Millennialism also teaches that Christ's personal return to the earth in glory, as described in chapter 19, is followed by the literal binding of Satan in Hades. This is followed by a literal thousand year reign of Christ and the resurrected saints on the earth. This will fulfill dozens of Old Testament prophecies to Israel.

The second position is post-Millennialism. "Post" means after, so this means that Christ comes back after the Church has converted the world to Christ through missions and evangelism. In other words, after the Church has converted the world, and it has experienced 1,000 years of peace, Christ comes back to establish the New Heaven and the New Earth. Somewhere, this view must address Satan being bound, and so they spiritualize it and say Satan was bound by Christ's death on the cross.

If the Church is going to convert the world, this presupposes that at some point, everything will be getting better and better. There is no other conclusion – everything has to get better and better if you are going to end up with the whole world converted to Christianity.

This teaching of post-Millennialism was the darling of the seminary professors a hundred years ago. Even the renowned, Dr. George W. Truett, of the First Baptist Church, Dallas, subscribed to this teaching at the turn of the last century. Missions were expanding – the Gospel was being preached around the globe – and it was easy to imagine (or at least dream) that one day, everyone would become a Christian.

Then something happened to shatter this hope. It was called World War I. And before the world could recover from this traumatic war, it was followed closely by World War II which was even more traumatic than the previous war. It reached the very bottom of the depravity of man. After viewing the horrors of the holocaust, the medical experiments and ultimate killing of 6 million Jews, and then looking at the vicious war in the Pacific, and learning about the barbaric treatment of our prisoners by the Japanese – could anyone in their right mind say that the heart of man was getting better and better? And today, we can go on the internet and view terrorists chopping off the heads of innocent people! Is the human heart nearing perfection? NO! Jeremiah hit the nail squarely on the head when he said, "*The heart is more deceitful than all else, and is desperately sick*" (Jeremiah 17:9 NASB).

Though George W. Truett embraced post-Millennialism, strong theologian voices laid a great foundation for the pre-Millennial viewpoint including Charles H. Spurgeon, Dwight L. Moody, H. A. Ironside and W. A. Criswell.[1]

After viewing the utter inhuman acts of the human race during the last 100 years, it is safe to say that post-Millennialism has been all but abandoned. It has very few adherents today. But sadly enough, all these liberal seminary professors who abandoned post-Millennialism did not run over to the camp of the pre-Millennialists. They still were not ready to accept a literal interpretation of the Bible. And so they embraced the Amillennial position, meaning no Millennium at all.

The basic tenets of Amillennialism were originally developed by the Roman Catholic

Church. They were forced into this position because of the 17th and 18th chapters of Revelation. The Roman Church had to explain that these chapters had nothing to do with the Roman Church. Although these two chapters clearly picture the false church (and possibly the Roman Church) in the end times, it behooved them to say these descriptions were fulfilled in the 1st Century. Over the years, the mainline denominations generally adopted the Roman Catholic position of Amillennialism on this issue.

Amillennialism is a simple system. I call it the "Lazyman's Guide to the End Times" because it requires little study. It simply says, "There will be no Millennium; there will be no Rapture. There is just one general resurrection when Christ returns. He will separate the sheep from the goats, and you either go to Heaven or Hell and that is the end of it." Those who oppose the teaching of a literal 1,000 year reign of Christ upon the earth claim that this doctrine of Millennialism is built on a single chapter of the Bible. First of all, if one chapter teaches it, and it is not contradicted by another section of the Bible, it must be the truth. And in this 20th chapter alone, the 1,000 years is mentioned no less than six times. How many times must God say it for it to be true? It seems to me that God wants us to know that there will be a Millennium.

These churches who teach there will be no Millennium – such as the Roman Catholics, the Churches of Christ, the Reformed Churches – I wish they would be intellectually honest and simply say, "We do not believe that the 20th chapter of Revelation belongs in the Bible." They should stop with chapter 19, instead of trying to make chapter 20 say something that it does not say. The truth of the matter is that events of chapter 19 and 20 are sequential. They build upon one another. What begins in chapter 19, such as the capture of the Beast and False Prophet, continues in chapter 20.

If there is no Millennium in Israel's future, then dozens of Old Testament prophecies immediately go down the drain and God's unconditional promises are proved worthless. Consider the following verses. They could never depict Heaven because they occur on earth.

Isaiah 11:6a: *"The wolf also shall dwell with the lamb."*
Micah 4:4: *"But they shall sit every man under his vine and under his fig tree; and none shall make them afraid."*
Isaiah 32:1a: *"Behold, a king shall reign in righteousness."*
Daniel 2:44: *"And in the days of these kings shall the God of Heaven set up a kingdom, which shall never be destroyed …. it shall stand forever."*

The center of all this kingdom activity is Jerusalem, not Heaven's golden shores. Here is the proof:

Psalm 2:6: *"Yet I have set my King upon my holy hill of Zion."*

Isaiah 2:3b: *"Out of Zion shall go forth the law, and the word of the LORD from Jerusalem."*

Joel 3:16a: *"The LORD also shall roar out of Zion, and utter His voice from Jerusalem."*

Zechariah 8:3a: *"Thus sayest the LORD; I am returned unto Zion, and will dwell in the midst of Jerusalem."*

A millennium is simply a time period. It is a thousand years just as century is a hundred years and a decade is ten years. In Latin, "mille" means "thousand" and "annum" means "years." Put them together and you have "millennium" – 1,000 years. This will be the fulfillment of all prophecy in Scripture about God's Kingdom. He told us to pray, *"Thy Kingdom come, Thy will be done in earth as it is in Heaven"* (Matthew 6:10). Finally, that day will have arrived when the Millennium bursts on the scene.

Joel 3:10 speaks of a time right before the Millennium at the beginning of the Battle of Armageddon. The nations are in an uproar. Joel says that they will *"beat their plowshares into swords."* In other words, men will even turn peaceful tools into weapons. But when the Battle of Armageddon is over, and the peaceful, Millennial Kingdom comes on the scene, Micah describes it this way: *"And He shall judge among many people, and rebuke strong nations afar off; and they shall beat their swords in plowshares, and their spears into pruning hooks: nation shall not lift up a sword against nation, neither shall they learn war any more"* (Micah 4:3).

During the Millennium, prosperity and peace will reign over all the earth. Poverty will be unknown. There will be no prisons, no hospitals, no mental institutions, no bars, no homes for the aged. Such things will be a distant memory. Cemeteries will be crumbling relics of the past. Jesus will be King over all the earth, and He will rule the nations with a rod of iron. This does not mean He will have a whip beating everyone into submission, but it does mean that everyone will know what His rules are and there will be swift punishment when the rules are broken. Justice will be perfect because it will be administered by the Judge who is perfect. It will be wonderful to stand there at the beginning of the Millennium and realize that we are going to experience 1,000 years of peace on the earth. We will be living on this planet with all the elements of nature and the animal life working in perfect harmony as God intended. Then we will cry out, "It has been worth it all!"

That great preacher, the late Dr. W. A. Criswell who was my pastor for 20 years said, "To my amazement, I have listened to interpreters who tell me that we are in the Millennium now. My soul, my soul! If this is the Millennium with all of the death and misery and heartache and tears and sufferings and war and fear and terror that we know in this present world, and if Satan is currently bound, then words do not mean what they say, and God doesn't know how to communicate."[2]

In verse 2, God says Satan will be bound for 1,000 years, and the next verse says after the 1,000 years Satan will be loosed for a short time. In verse 4, He says that the saints will reign with Christ for a thousand years, and the next verse says the unsaved dead will not be brought up for judgment until after the 1,000 years. In verse 6, He says that all who have part in the first resurrection will reign with Christ for 1,000 years, and in verse 7, we are told that Satan will be loosed out of prison for a short time when the 1,000 years are over. Six times God mentions specifically that a 1,000 year period is very important in His end time plans. Yet, I am astounded by how many teachers say, "Oh, God didn't really mean 1,000 years. He just meant a long period of time." Then I would say to them, "Then make up whatever you want this to mean because you can make the Bible say anything to fit your beliefs."

That brings us to the view which I think is the correct one: the pre-Millennial view. It will stand the test of Scripture! Let us begin reading at verse 1 of chapter 20: *"And I saw an angel come down from Heaven, having the key of the Bottomless Pit and a great chain in his hand."* Some commentators think this is Jesus simply because we know from Revelation 1:18, it is He who holds the key to the underground prisons – Hades and Hell. But I am not so sure verse 1 is referring to Jesus. First of all, I think John's description would have been vastly different. He did not hesitate to describe Jesus in all His glory when John saw Him in chapter 1. But here, John simply describes him as "an angel."

Secondly, we have seen all through the Book that Jesus does not hesitate to delegate authority. He could have easily handed off this key to the Bottomless Pit to one of His angels. Christ used angels to open the seals of judgment that fell upon the earth. He used angels to separate the wheat from the tares, and then to bundle the tares and cast them into the fire. He used Michael and his angels to fight Satan and his evil forces and to kick them out of the outer limits of Heaven as described in Revelation chapter 12. Christ probably used Michael again here, because after all, Michael and Satan know each other well – they are old enemies. They had many run-ins before (Jude 9; Revelation 12:7). But, maybe – just maybe – it would be like God to simply use just an ordinary angel. An ordinary angel to further humiliate Satan, and show to the world that with God's power even an ordinary angel can render Satan helpless!

Look what this unusual verse says: the angel has a *"great chain in his hand"* (Revelation 20:1). There have been many scoffers who have said, "Ha-Ha-Ha – does this angel think he can control Satan simply with a great chain?" Let me give you an illustration that will clear this up for you. Around the middle of the 1800's, Spiritists and other mediums were gaining popularity throughout the United States with their séances, and claims of speaking to departed loved ones. Maggie and Catherine Fox, known as the Fox Sisters, are given credit for popularizing the Spiritist movement. They were a sensation as they traveled across the country, allowing themselves to be tied up. While they operated in the darkness all kinds of strange phenomena occurred like popping noises, lights floating around the room, strange voices, etc. It gave them a pretty lucrative living.

One of their favorite tricks at a séance was to have the guests seated around a table. One of the guests would securely tie the arms of the medium with heavy rope to his or her chair. Then the lights were turned out and all sorts of mysterious things would happen. Dead relatives were asked to answer questions by knocking on the table or a tiny light would be floating over the table. All sorts of weird and mysterious things took place. But when the lights were turned on, there were the Fox sisters with arms securely tied in place. But after years of fleecing the public, in 1888 they finally admitted it was all a hoax. The strange popping was the result of their unusual ability to loudly crack their toes. They never really contacted dead relatives, but they made a good living pretending they did.[3]

One of the famous people who swallowed this Spiritism business hook, line and sinker was Sir Arthur Conan Doyle, the author who created Sherlock Holmes mysteries. Doyle's wife of many years died, and he grieved greatly. He just could not get over it. He so wanted to believe that he could contact his beloved wife. His best friend at the time was Erik Weisz better known as the great Houdini, one of my all-time heroes. Harry Houdini was probably the greatest escape artist who ever lived. Doyle wanted to contact his departed wife, so he had discussions with Houdini as to whether it was possible to contact the dead. Doyle wanted to believe it was possible, while Houdini tried to convince him it was not. The discussions turned into heated arguments. Eventually, Doyle and Houdini parted ways over the Spiritism issue, but continued to converse by letter. Though they were civil to each other, their relationship was definitely strained during their remaining years.[4]

Doyle, whose fictitious character Sherlock Holmes could match wits with the most devious minds in the world, was completely hoodwinked by the Spiritist charlatans. They bilked him out of thousands of dollars as they claimed to receive messages from his dead wife. Doyle continued to be deceived in trying to contact his wife at various séances until he finally died a grief-stricken and broken old man. Houdini was so distraught over what happened to his friend, he dedicated his life from that time on to exposing Spiritists whenever he encountered them. He was totally upset at them, who in Houdini's words were nothing but frauds, preying on bereaved families and relieving them of large sums of money.

Houdini campaigned tirelessly, often visiting séances in disguise to expose their ringleader as frauds. In 1926 he testified in Congress in support of a bill to outlaw the practice of "pretending to tell fortunes for reward or compensation." *The Denver Express* published an article that said Houdini offered a $5,000 reward if he could not duplicate any "physical phenomena" that could not be explained rationally (no one ever collected).[5] One medium took him up on it. I will call him Professor Brown. The event was covered by all the big newspapers. When it came time to tie Professor Brown in his chair, there was a big argument. The Professor wanted one of the other guests to tie him, not Houdini. The guests shouted down the Professor, saying if he could really do supernatural acts, then it did not matter who did the tying. Finally, the Professor gave in to the pressure and let Houdini tie him. The next day, a reporter wrote in the newspaper, "Last night, at Professor Brown's séance – there were no usual manifestations – no floating objects – no trumpets – nothing unusual happened at all." Then the reporter added these insightful words which were very prophetic: "I guess, when the Master does the tying – you are permanently tied."

I love Houdini – his heart was in the right place, humanly speaking. He was a man of integrity. Once he was performing in Paris, and a lady came to see him after the show. She has been described as the "greatest actress the world has ever known," but now she was in her final years. It was none other than the French actress, Sarah Bernhardt. Ms. Bernhardt suffered from diabetes, and eventually her leg had to be amputated. She was a great fan of Houdini's. She visited him after his show, and told him she had a very important favor to ask of him. Gentleman, that he was, Houdini responded, "Anything within my power, I will certainly do to help you." She said, "Then, please, restore my leg to me." Houdini thought she was joking. He was dumbfounded that she thought he could perform such a miracle. He said, "Madame Bernhardt, you cannot be serious. You are asking me to do the impossible." She leaned closer and said, "Yes – but you can do the impossible!"[6] From that time on, Houdini never failed to tell his audience before each show that the feats he did were not supernatural, that anyone could do them if they only knew how the tricks were accomplished. I have always admired Houdini for being honest.

The rest of the story is that his death was tragic. Houdini was a muscle builder. He had a stomach like iron when he tightened his abdominal muscles. One evening, he was showing some college kids how solid his muscles were. He invited them to punch him in the stomach. Pow! Pow!

It was like hitting steel. But as they talked, one of the young people decided to play a prank on him. He hit Houdini in the stomach unexpectantly, hard, without warning. Houdini did not have time to prepare by tightening his stomach muscles. The blow hurt him severely, but he did not let it show. He was hit several more times in the stomach. He went home and later that night his stomach began to hurt. The pain got so bad that he finally called for help and was rushed to the hospital. But it was too late. His appendix had ruptured and he died of peritonitis.[7]

On what day did Houdini die? It was Halloween – October 31, 1926. He had told his wife, Bess, on several occasions that, should anything ever happen to him, she was to hold a candlelight vigil every year on the anniversary of his death. He said, "I don't know what is on the other side, but I have never found a lock I couldn't open or a prison that I couldn't break out of." So, in accordance with his wishes, she held a candlelight vigil on October 31, 1927. And she did this for nine consecutive years thereafter. On the 10th year of the anniversary of his death, she finally said, "Goodbye, my sweet, you are not coming back."[8] As far as I can tell, Houdini, a Jew, never accepted Christ. I can only hope that he did; he was an honorable and trustworthy man.

When scoffers laughed at the fact that a chain could hold Satan, I always thought of that reporter's comment when Professor Brown was tied to his chair by Houdini: "When the Master does the tying – you are permanently tied!" Let us see what this angel did with his chain. Verses 2-3: *"And he laid hold on the dragon, that old serpent, which is the Devil, and Satan, and bound him a thousand years, And cast him into the Bottomless Pit, and shut him up, and set a seal upon him, that he should deceive the nations no more, till the thousand years should be fulfilled: and after that he must be loosed a little season."* Although all of Satan's evil demons are not mentioned specifically in this passage, the binding of Satan necessarily assures that all those under his command will be locked up as well so there will be no deceiving of the nations.

Before we leave this verse, notice who is being bound. First, he is referred to as the dragon because of his horrible cruelty. Then he is called the old serpent because of his deception. Then he is called the Devil because he is the tempter of man. And finally, he is called Satan because he is the accuser of the brethren. So Satan is bound in order to set the stage for the Millennium. Everyone initially going into the Millennium will be saved people. There will be several different groups. There will be the Old Testament saints in their glorified bodies. There will be the New Testament saints in their glorified bodies. There will be the martyred saints who were killed during the Tribulation Period. They will be in their glorified bodies.

There will also be a number of saved believers who made it through the Tribulation Period without taking the Mark of the Beast, and without losing their lives. Jesus said regarding the Tribulation, *"But he that shall endure unto the end, the same shall be saved"* (Matthew 24:13). And since they have never died physically, they will not yet have their glorified bodies, but will be in their natural physical bodies. From this group, there will be, through natural childbirth, millions and millions of people born during these 1,000 years. They will need to be educated, and consequently, many of us will be teachers and administrators during this period.

These people born during the Millennium will inherit the fallen sin nature of Adam. Each one of them will need to be born again spiritually and accept Christ as their personal Savior just like in today's world. Population will increase exponentially as there will be plenty of food because the land will be abundantly productive just as God intended it to be before man polluted the planet. There will neither be wars nor disease to reduce the population. The Bible indicates that life spans will be greatly expanded as they were before the flood.

I want you to underline a phrase in verse 3 that totally destroys the arguments of the

Amillenialists and others who say that we are in the Millennium now. It is the phrase in the middle of verse 3 that says "*that he should deceive the nations no more, till the thousand years should be fulfilled ….*". If you read verse 3 in its entirety, you will see that this is the reason that Satan is bound for these 1,000 years – so he cannot deceive the nations! If you say we are in the Millennium now, as some teachers do, you must conclude that Satan is bound right now, and the nations of the world are not being deceived by him. I do not know how anyone can say that Russia, Syria, Iran, China and dozens of other countries are not being deceived at this time by Satan! This verse more than any other shows conclusively that the Millennium is still in the future because God has not yet bound Satan and put him in the Bottomless Pit so the nations cannot be deceived.

Two things must come to pass before the Millennium can occur. Jesus must return in power and glory, and Satan's rule over this earth must come to an end. Chapter 19 covers Christ coming back in glory and now in chapter 20 we are going to see the demise of Satan. The pre-Millennial position fits with Scripture perfectly – Christ comes back at the end of the Tribulation – and He binds Satan for 1,000 years during which time the earth enjoys peace as Christ rules with a rod of iron over His kingdom.

We said earlier that there will be many born during the Millennium, and they will inherit Adam's sin nature. As such, many will not like the rules set down by the Master Rule Maker. And because of that sin nature, Scripture says that Jesus will reign with a rod of iron during the Millennium. People will be constrained to live according to His rules. Consider this: in this present age in which we live, righteousness *suffers* (Matthew 5:10). The world puts righteousness down at every opportunity. During the Millennium, Scripture says that righteousness *reigns*, as Christ rules with a rod of iron (Revelation 2:27). But after the Millennium, when we enter the eternal state, righteousness *dwells* (II Peter 3:13).[9] Righteousness will be at home as every adverse thing will have been abolished. Praise the Lord!

We must address one final phrase in verse 3 before we move on. Scripture says that at the end of the Millennium, Satan must be loosed from his prison for a short span (Revelation 20:7). What is this all about? God has Satan locked away in the Bottomless Pit where he has been for 1,000 years, but now he is going to be released. Why in the world is God going to turn him loose again? First, it will prove that Satan's evil nature will not change simply because he is confined for a thousand years. This also proves God's justice is perfect when He pronounces eternal judgment upon Satan. But there is a lesson here for us as well. Man's old nature, which we inherited from Adam, does not change over time even though Christians try to keep it in subjection by the power of the Holy Spirit.

We have not covered this yet – we will when we get to verse 8 – but millions of unsaved people will be ready to unite under Satan's banner and again attempt to dethrone God. This clearly shows for all time that if people's hearts are not changed, their sin nature bubbles to the top every time. And many unsaved people during the Millennium will decide that everything is going great, and they do not even need God. They will have an outward appearance, but not an inward change.

The philosophy in our current society is that if you can give a man an ideal environment, he will continue to improve ethically and morally. Psychologists advance this argument all the time, even though, it has been proven wrong time and time again. Take a bank robber for instance who has just been sentenced for robbing a bank. Clean him up, give him a great education, and when he comes out of prison give him a white collar job. He will no longer be using a pistol to steal thousands; he will get a job as an accountant, and will use his pencil to steal millions! If his heart is not changed by Christ, his sin nature will not change either. The Millennium will prove this. When Satan is loosed from his chains, he will find many disgruntled misfits that will rally around him at one last effort to dispose of God and His Christ.

What does John see in verse 4? *"And I saw thrones, and they sat upon them, and judgment was given unto them: and I saw the souls of them that were beheaded for the witness of Jesus, and for the word of God, and which had not worshiped the beast, neither his image, neither had received his mark upon their foreheads, or in their hands; and they lived and reigned with Christ a thousand years"* (Revelation 20:4). There is that thousand years showing up again. I wish the Bible would quit mentioning a thousand years if it does not mean a thousand years! This age of unspeakable blessing and glory for all the earth is revealed throughout the entire Bible. The Old Testament contains hundreds of unfilled promises of blessings for Israel, the nations of the earth, and even for all creation which have never seen even a partial fulfillment.

Isaiah is full of such promises. Take Isaiah 2:2-4 for example. *"And it shall come to pass in the last days, that the mountain of the LORD'S house shall be established in the top of the mountains, and shall be exalted above the hills; and all nations shall flow unto it. And many people shall go and say, 'Come ye, and let us go up to the mountain of the LORD, to the house of the God of Jacob; and He will teach us of His ways, and we will walk in His paths: for out of Zion shall go forth the law, and the word of the LORD from Jerusalem. And He shall judge among the nations, and shall rebuke many people: and they shall beat their swords into plowshares, and their spears into pruninghooks: nation shall not lift up sword against nation, neither shall they learn war anymore.'"*

Mankind has longed for this kind of peace since time began, but it will never happen until the Prince of Peace reigns over His Kingdom. Daniel mentions this in his second chapter. *"And in the days of these kings shall the God of Heaven set up a kingdom, which shall never be destroyed ...."* (Daniel 2:44a). The New Testament also clearly points to such an age of glory for this earth –passages such as Matthew 19:28, Acts 3:19-21, Romans 8:19-23, Ephesians 1:10, Philippians 2:9-11, Colossians 1:20.

John sees thrones, and sitting on them are judges. Who are these people? I don't want to scare you, but those judges are God's children. The prophet Daniel saw these same thrones which he described in chapter 7 of Daniel. There are at least three groups of people that comprise this assembly of judges. First, the redeemed saints of the Old Testament and the New Testament. Paul says in I Corinthians 6:2a, *"Do ye not know that the saints shall judge the world?"* And then verse 3a says, *"Know ye not that we shall judge angels?"* You will have the perfect mind of Christ and your judgment will be perfect in every respect.

Verse 4 specifically points out another group. *".... and I saw the souls of them that were beheaded for the witness of Jesus ...."*. Those dear souls were martyred for Christ and they are now judges. They are resurrected after the marriage and the marriage supper (Revelation 19:7-9), just on the eve of the Millennium. That is because they are neither part of the Bride nor among the guests at the bridal supper. There is still a third group who are judges: *".... and which had not worshiped the Beast, neither his image, neither had received his mark upon their foreheads, or in their hands"* Revelation 20:4b). These dear saints were able to hide out and avoid the execution squads of the Antichrist, and they are part of a small group who come out of the Tribulation alive and enter into the Millennium – and they will be judges! (Matthew 24:13).

Notice what it says of all these redeemed of all ages: *".... and they lived and reigned with Christ a thousand years"* (Revelation 20:4b). I guess John was mistaken again when he said a thousand years. No! I believe he said a thousand years six times in this chapter because he meant a thousand years! Christ's kingdom was announced in chapter 11:15, and a description of the details followed in the next few chapters. But here it actually unfolds.

Here is a short summary of the Millennium. How long will it last? 1,000 years. When will it occur? It will occur between the end of the Tribulation and the beginning of the eternal state covered in Revelation 21 and 22. What is its purpose? First, to fulfill all of the promises God made to Israel and to restore the earth to its intended harmony. And second, to prove that man, without God giving him a new nature, can never aspire to righteous living. What is the nature of the kingdom? God's righteous rules will be in effect, and His saints along with Christ will judge in all matters. What will the physical condition of the earth be like? The curse on nature will be lifted. The wolf will lie down with the lamb. Poisonous plants will not be poisonous anymore. The cow and the bear will eat straw together.

What will the environment be like? Isaiah 35:1-2 describes it: *"The wilderness and the solitary place shall be glad for them; and the desert shall rejoice, and blossom as the rose. It shall blossom abundantly, and rejoice even with joy and singing .... they shall see the glory of the LORD, and the excellency of our God."* Who will inherit the Kingdom? The short answer is the saints of God. Another way to put it is this: everyone who has part in the first resurrection. Will public safety be a problem? Micah 4:4-5: *"They shall sit every man under his [own] vine and under his fig tree; and none shall make them afraid."* When I was reading Micah 4:4-5, I could not help but think of all those poor Israeli farmers simply wanting to get along and raise their crops and *"sit under their own tree and not be afraid."* Not long ago, Katusha rockets were sailing in and crashing onto their land from Hezbollah in southern Lebanon. That is why the Millennium is necessary in order to bring peace on earth at last.

Almost 300 years ago, a man by the name of Isaac Watts wrote a hymn based on Psalm 98 called *Joy to the World*.[10] We sing it every Christmas to celebrate Christ's birth. But did you know that His first coming is not what the song is really all about? Isaac Watts wrote this hymn to celebrate Christ's glorious appearing at His Second Coming when He comes back to rule over all the earth!

Look at the words:

Joy to the World! The Lord is come! Let earth receive her King! (This is referring to the Millennium – the world did not receive her King the first time He came).

Let every heart prepare Him room. (Has every heart prepared Him room now? Of course not, but in the Millennium, things will be different.)

And Heaven and nature sing. (Yes, all Heaven and nature will join in this celebration. This is when the lamb will lie down with the wolf.)

Joy to the earth, the Savior reigns! (He is not reigning now, but He will during the Millennium.)

Let men their songs employ, While fields and floods, rocks, hills and plains repeat the sounding joy! (That is all of nature rejoicing together as confirmed in Romans 8:19-21.)

Listen to the next verse:

No more let sins and sorrows grow. (In our day, sin is still increasing – as the news reports show.)

Nor thorns infest the ground. (It is easier now to grow weeds than a crop.)

He comes to make His blessings flow. (They flow now, but not like they will when Satan is out of the way.)

Far as the curse is found. (That is from one end of the globe to the other.)

He rules the world with truth and grace. (He begins to rule in earnest during the Millennium.)

And makes the nations prove the glories of His righteousness and wonders of his love. (The nations will certainly prove His righteousness during the Millennium.)

Truly a great Second Coming song!

Now we come to Revelation 20, verse 5 where we see a startling statement: *"But the rest of the dead lived not again until the thousand years were finished. This is the first resurrection."* The Greek phrase here is most emphatic: *"he anastasis he prote"* meaning, "This is the resurrection – the first. The Greek word "anastasia" is used more than 40 times in the New Testament and it always means "standing again" – a dead body rising from the dead.

The last sentence of verse 5 is one of the most important sentences in this chapter: *"This is the first resurrection."* Saying it another way, "This completes the first resurrection." Why is it important to be included in the first resurrection? Because those included in the second resurrection will have their part in the Lake of Fire.

Let us clarify just who is in the first resurrection. Verse 4 tells us it is composed of 3 groups: 1) those who sat upon thrones, 2) those who were beheaded for the sake of the Gospel, 3) those who survived the Tribulation without taking the Mark of the Beast. Revelation 20:15 expands this to anyone whose name is written in the Lamb's Book of Life. Now, the Bible does not specifically say when, but at some point this third group of Tribulation survivors must receive their resurrected, glorified bodies which they will have throughout eternity. In other words, all true believers of every age will be part of that first resurrection.

This word "but" in verse 5 is going to show us what happens to those who are not included in the first resurrection. *"But the rest of the dead"* – that is, the lost – did not live again until after the Millennium when they will be resurrected to be judged and cast into the Lake of Fire. Verse 6 confirms this: *"Blessed and holy is he that hath part in the first resurrection: on such the second death hath no power, but they shall be priests of God and of Christ, and shall reign with Him a thousand years."* In other words, those who take part in the first resurrection will reign with Christ during the Millennium. The unsaved remain in their graves to be raised from the dead after the Millennium to be judged at the Great White Throne Judgment.

This verse tells us that there are six things about those who will have a part in the first resurrection. Look at the specific words:

1) Blessed – they will be happy in their eternal state.
2) Holy – they will be identified as God's special people.
3) Priests – they will serve in the presence of God.
4) Reign – they will share with Christ in governing the kingdom.
5) A thousand years – the length of their earthly reign with Christ.
6) The second death – they will never be cast into the Lake of Fire.

We discussed the different resurrections earlier in our study, but chapter 20 places such grave importance on it, we need to clearly understand it. There is enormous confusion about this in Christendom. There are two resurrections in type, but not in number. We find a good illustration of this in chapter 5 of this Book of Revelation. It says there is a seven-sealed scroll. As each seal is broken (i.e., opened by Christ), it produces a specific judgment on the earth. Without studying the Scriptures further, one might conclude that there are only seven judgments (i.e., seven seals) before the end of the world. On the surface, it seems there are seven seals, each with a specific judgment – and when the seals are opened, the judgments are completed. But you must look further! When the seventh seal is opened, out of it comes seven trumpets, each with its own judgment. When the seventh trumpet sounded, out of it comes the seven bowl judgments.

Before you make up your mind on a particular belief in Scripture, you must bring every related Scripture to bear on it. So, a superficial look at the resurrections might cause you to think there are only two in number.

For example, a cursory look at Daniel 12:2 appears to indicate only two resurrections. *"And many of them that sleep in the dust of the earth shall awake, some to everlasting life, and some to shame and everlasting contempt."* That sounds like two resurrections in number. One is to LIFE and one is to DESTRUCTION, or you might say, one is to HEAVEN and one is to HELL.

Jesus reiterated this truth in John 5:29 when He said there is a resurrection of life and a resurrection of judgment. But Scripture confirms there are actually multiple resurrections. Listen carefully: there are two resurrections in TYPE. One, as Jesus said, is a resurrection of LIFE and one is a resurrection of JUDGMENT. Another way to say this, is how this 20th chapter of Revelation says it: the FIRST resurrection and the SECOND resurrection. Or, the FIRST death and the SECOND death.

Let us look at the second death first since it is the easiest to understand. It is one resurrection in type, and it is also one resurrection in number. When a lost person dies, his spirit goes to Hades to await his final judgment. His body goes into the grave to return to the dust of the earth. At the Great White Throne Judgment, his body is supernaturally resurrected and reunited with his spirit to stand in judgment before Almighty God. That is all there is to it for the unbeliever – one resurrection in type which is also one resurrection in number. Daniel calls this the resurrection of contempt; Jesus calls it the resurrection of judgment. Revelation 20:15 calls it the second death.

The resurrection of LIFE for the believer is a different story. It is ONE in type (that is, a resurrection to life), but it is multiple in number – four to be exact. In other words, the resurrection of life occurs in four stages. You already know this if you have absorbed what I have been teaching. There is the resurrection of Church Age believers at the Rapture when the dead in Christ arise. This is not referring to spirits (spirits of the saved are already in Heaven) – it is talking about bodies coming out of the grave at the Rapture. The Rapture is a specific promise to the Church so what about all the Old Testament saints? They have to be resurrected at some point. And then we have all those martyrs whom the Antichrist beheads. When are they going to be resurrected? So you see, the resurrection of life has multiple stages.

The verse that really clarifies it for us is I Corinthians 15:20-24. *"But now is Christ risen from the dead, and become the first fruits of them that slept. For since by man came death, by man came also the resurrection of the dead. For as in Adam all die, even so in Christ shall all be made* alive. *But every man in his own order: Christ the first fruits; afterward they that are Christ's at His coming. Then cometh the end, when He shall have delivered up the kingdom to God even the Father; when He shall have put down all rule and all authority and power."* Verse 23 is key since Scripture gives the order of the first resurrection. Christ is the first fruits, and then those that are resurrected at the Rapture. And finally, in verse 24, those that are resurrected (Old Testament saints and Tribulation martyrs) at the beginning of the Millennium.

Paul has been using the imagery of the harvest. In Bible times, the harvest was conducted in three stages. It began with the gathering of the first fruits which were offered as a sacrifice of thanksgiving to God. The first fruits were followed by the general harvest. But not everything was taken. Some of the crops were purposely left to benefit the needy. This was called the "gleanings." You will this described in Leviticus 19:9-10. Using this imagery, the Bible presents the resurrection of Jesus as the first fruits of the resurrection. The Rapture, which is the gathering of the Church Age saints, is the general harvest. This is pictured in John 14:1-3 and I Thessalonians 4:13-18. But there is a third and final stage to this resurrection of the just. It is the gleanings, and it occurs at the end of the Tribulation when the Lord's Glorious Appearing takes place. This resurrection will include two groups: the Tribulation martyrs who had been put to death during the Tribulation, and the Old Testament saints.

A few teachers teach that ALL believers, including Old Testament believers, will be resurrected at the Rapture, but this cannot be. The Rapture is a specific promise to the Church. On the other hand, the Old Testaments saints, we are told in Daniel 12:1-2, will be resurrected at the end of the "time of distress." In other words, as promised to Israel, the Old Testament saints will be resurrected at the end of the Tribulation just in time to enter the Millennial Kingdom. In summary, the first resurrection, which is the resurrection of the just (the righteous), occurs in three stages beginning with Christ; then His believers at the Rapture, and concluding with the Old Testament saints and Tribulation saints at Christ's Second Coming.

Someone asked, "What about those who die during the 1,000 year Millennium?" There will be no need for a resurrection of the righteous at the end of the Millennium because all those born during the Millennium who accept Christ as Savior will live to the end of the Millennium. We get an indication from Isaiah in the 66th chapter that those who outwardly defy the King's reign during the Millennium will be dealt with swiftly (Isaiah 66:17) and many will die. They will be resurrected at the end of the Millennium with the rest of the unsaved dead to be judged at the Great White Throne Judgment.

The longevity of the believers will be quite a different story. We are told this in Isaiah 65:19-20 (NLT): *"I will rejoice in Jerusalem and delight in my people. And the sound of weeping and crying will be heard no more. No longer will babies die when only a few days old. No longer will adults die before they have lived a full life. No longer will people be considered old at one hundred!*

Only sinners will die that young!" In verse 22b (Holman) it says: *"For My people's lives will be like the lifetime of a tree."*

In other words, life spans during the Millennium will return to what they were before the great flood of Noah's time – about 1,000 years. This is understandable, since there will not be any injuries or diseases and everyone will return to a vegetarian diet of fresh fruits, vegetables and nuts. There will be no wars – no earthquakes – no tornados – nor tsunamis to decimate the population.

Let me reiterate why the Millennium is necessary. First, it is to reward the people of God. Believers will reign with Christ over all the earth, fulfilling numerous Old Testament prophecies. And this is one of my favorites: the Millennium is necessary to redeem creation. Listen to Romans 8:19-22 (NLT): *"For all creation is waiting eagerly for that future day when God will reveal who His children really are. Against its will, everything on earth was subjected to God's curse. All creation anticipates the day when it will join God's children in glorious freedom from death and decay. For we know that all creation has been groaning as in the pains of childbirth right up to the present time."*

I Corinthians 2:9 tells us that we cannot imagine what God has in store for us for our enjoyment. The Millennium is necessary to re-emphasize man's total depravity. It will demonstrate that after 1,000 years of peace, a wonderful environment with nature working with man at every turn and a government run by a benevolent King who has man's interest at heart – yet at the end of the Millennium there will be a vast number of people who want to overthrow God and put Satan on the throne (Revelation 20:7-9). If anyone ever had a doubt about the inherited sin nature of man, this final act of rebellion will prove it.

Let me summarize the characteristics of the Millennium. It will be a time of peace. Man has dreamed of this since time began, but this old world has been wracked by war after war. There will be no wars during the Millennium. It will also be a time of prosperity as never before known. Everyone will have their needs met by God from His bountiful warehouse. It will be a time of purity. There will be no lack of people worshipping God and pursuing righteousness. There will be no sickness, no disease, no birth defects, no retardation of any type. The superficial happiness that covers the world today will be replaced by true joy that only God can give. And who will be the beneficiaries of all these blessings? It is those who take part in the first resurrection. In spite of all these blessings, there will be a number of people who will be chaffing under Christ's rules and will be hoping He will be overthrown by Satan. We know this because when Satan is turned loose for a short period at the end of the Millennium, many will immediately join forces with him.

The religious leaders of Jesus' day had always been blind to God's true plan for mankind. They confronted Jesus demanding a sign to prove He was the Messiah (Matthew 12:38). On another occasion, Jesus was again asked for a sign to prove He was from God. Jesus asked them, "You mean that you can discern the signs of the weather, but you cannot even discern the signs of the times?" (Matthew 16:3).

We now come to Revelation 20:7-8 and things are going to quickly get very dark. We will see Satan unchained and immediately he stirs up trouble. *"And when the thousand years are expired, Satan shall be loosed out of his prison, And shall go out to deceive the nations which are in the four quarters of the earth, Gog and Magog, to gather them together to battle: the number of whom is as the sand of the sea."* Satan has been locked away in the Bottomless Pit during the Millennium for the expressed purpose of keeping him from deceiving the nations. Now, as we were told earlier in verse 3, he must be loosed for a little while at the close of the Millennium.

I can remember reading a book when I was in high school that made quite an impression on me. Some of you may have read it. It was entitled, *I Escaped From Devil's Island.*[11] Devil's Island was a penal colony located off the coast of French Guiana. It was opened in 1852 by Napoleon III, President of France and nephew of Napoleon Bonaparte. It housed its most hardened criminals from France and its colonies. It was operated for nearly 100 years until it was permanently shut down in 1946 from pressure by various human rights organizations. It had over 80,000 prisoners in captivity during its period of operation. Most of those who were sent there, were never heard from again. The prison itself was surrounded by dense jungles, home to a variety of ferocious animals and poisonous snakes. The small island itself was surrounded by shark infested waters brimming with crocodiles. There were a number of escape attempts, but only a handful of prisoners ever claimed they had escaped from there. The French government says that no one ever escaped and lived to tell about it.[12]

If you think Devil's Island was bad, then the Bottomless Pit where Satan is imprisoned with all its hideous demons must be worse than can be imagined. And make no mistake about this, Satan does not escape! He doesn't break his chains and overpower the guards. He was turned loose by God. Why does God turn him loose? It is so the Devil can assemble those unbelievers from the Millennium and prove for all time that, unless man is born again and given a new heart, he will forever be at enmity with God. Man has been tried and tested under every possible condition, and has failed in every age. He failed under the law; he failed under the age of grace, and now under the most idyllic conditions during the Millennium man fails again.

Only the touch of God in salvation can change a person's heart and life. Some people in our society just cannot understand this. The ACLU works hard to get all the Bibles removed from prisons and to eliminate prison chaplains or any religious teachings in prison. They actively do this even though statistics overwhelmingly show that inmates who are exposed to such a religious environment have a much lower percentage of recidivism. The liberal do-gooders think that giving these prisoners an education or improving their social status will straighten out their lives. But only Jesus Christ can change a heart, and give them a new purpose in life.

After Satan is loosed, it does not take long for him to cover the four quarters of the earth, and whip up support for his plan of dethroning God. Gog and Magog are not to be confused with the same terms used in a battle described in Ezekiel 38 and 39 which occurs prior to or early on in the Tribulation. The Revelation 20 battle occurs at the end of the Millennium. The invasion of Israel as described in Ezekiel 38 is simply a prototype of the full scale invasion that will occur in Revelation 20.

Some teachers have gone to great lengths to show that Gog and Magog refer to a northern power synonymous with Russia. And I think it does in Ezekiel 38, but its practical usage has expanded to mean all diabolical forces who oppose Almighty God. Most scholars agree that the people of Gog represent the warlike Slavic nations of whom Russia is foremost. They are the descendants of Japheth, the oldest son of Noah. Magog is specifically mentioned in Genesis 10:2 as being the grandson of Noah.

Here in Revelation 20:8 it says that the number of these rebellious hoards are as plentiful as the sands of the sea. In other words, too numerous to count. You might ask, "How could such a large number be ready to join forces with Satan? After all, they have lived through the glorious Millennium, had their every need met, and lived in peace by the rules set down by the King of kings. What more could they want?" But then, I discovered that many will feign obedience. They will only be pretending. It is not the obedience that comes through faith and love, but a compelled submission out of fear of this all-powerful, benevolent Dictator, Jesus Christ. It is interesting to note there are at least two references having to do with submission to the Lord, but in each case, it is feigned obedience as many marginal notes say. They are obeying only because they fear to do otherwise (Psalm 66:3; 81:15).

After Satan assembles this mighty force from around the world, he makes his final attempt to overthrow God. Verse 9: *"And they went up on the breadth of the earth, and compassed the camp of the saints about, and the beloved city."* They tromp around the earth causing havoc. They surround and harass Christians, and they also surround the city of Jerusalem where Christ has His earthly throne. To put it in today's context we see on the nightly news, the forces of evil are burning the Christian flag, stomping on it and carrying posters that say, "Death to Jesus Christ and death to Israel." Such hate is prevalent in our current society as shown by an internet posting by this avowed atheist who was protesting in California and carrying a sign which read: "I'm Darwin Bedford. If that self-made (expletive), Jesus, returns again I think we should really nail him to a cross and let Him hang suffering until he dies."[13] Unless Mr. Bedford comes to his senses, what a fate awaits that poor fellow. We need to pray for him. One day he will bow and confess that Jesus Christ is Lord!

It enables me to picture these evil forces surrounding God's people in all directions energized by the great adversary himself, Satan. So once again, Satan orchestrates a plan to overthrow God, and eliminate Israel as well as Christ's followers. I heard the President of Iran say on television: "I have the solution to the Middle East crisis between Israel and the Palestinians." That got my attention. Then he said: "The way to solve the Israeli-Palestinian problem is – to eliminate Israel!"

Satan hates Israel – the nation that gave us the Bible as well as the Savior. And Satan has put this anti-Semitic feeling against the Jews in the hearts of non-believers around the globe. It is strange, but most believers will tell you they have a love toward Israel and the Jewish people. God has put this love in their hearts. We have two wonderful Christian (non-Jewish) friends, Gene and Shelley, in our church who have gone to Israel several times and voluntarily served short periods with the Israeli Defense Forces in order to witness to and serve these dear people.

Just when things look the darkest for Israel – the Cavalry arrives! Look at the last part of Revelation 20:9b: *".... and fire came down from God out of Heaven, and devoured them."* Malachi 4:1 is even more graphic: *"For behold, the day cometh, that shall burn as an oven; and all the proud, yea, and all that do wickedly, shall be stubble: and the day that cometh shall burn them up, saith the LORD of hosts, that it shall leave them neither root nor branch."*

Was Satan destroyed with them? No. Jesus said in Matthew 25:41 that Hell was prepared for the Devil and his angels. And he is about to go there. His doom was predicted a long time ago. We find that fact in the third chapter of Genesis which contains the very first prophecy of the Bible. God said in Genesis 3:15 (NLT) referring to Christ's clash with Satan, *"He will crush your head, and you will strike His heel."* In other words, Satan will strike a non-lethal blow (which he did at Calvary), but Christ will administer a lethal blow (which He is doing here in the 20th chapter of Revelation).

In verse 10 we find the last mention of God's arch enemy: *"And the Devil that deceived them was cast into the Lake of Fire and brimstone, where the Beast and the False Prophet are, and shall be tormented day and night for ever and ever."* Notice the word "are." Satan is cast into the Lake of Fire where the Beast and False Prophet are – and they are still there after 1,000 years! And Scripture says they will be there *"forever and ever."*

Look at the last verse in this chapter again, and you will see some good news in it. *"And whosoever was not found written in the Book of Life, was cast into the Lake of Fire."* You say, "I do not see any good news." Look at that second word in the verse: "Whosoever." God says that everyone still has a choice. We are ALL "whosoevers!" "Whosoever will" may come to Christ, and have their name written in the Book of Life! (Revelation 22:17b). And whosoever that wills not to come, will be cast into the Lake of Fire. God is not discriminatory, He gives us the choice! I pray that our choice will be to have our names written in the Book of Life, and to take as many folks with us as we can get on board.

We now come to verse 11. This section of Scripture has to be the most gripping and somber passage in all the Bible. It is the end of the road – the final destination – a journey of no return. The Great White Throne Judgment! Its very sound is ominous. Verse 11: *"And I saw a great white throne, and Him that sat on it, from whose face the earth and the Heaven fled away; and there was found no place for them."* John says the words "I saw" 34 times in this Book of the Apocalypse. Remember the Greek word Apocalypse? It means "unveiling." This Book has many mysteries, but its primary theme is the unveiling of Jesus Christ – a clear picture of the glorious Lamb of God! But this time when John writes "I saw," he views the darkest hour in all of history – the judgment of the wicked. He sees a White Throne. The word "white" throughout the Bible is symbolic of purity and holiness. Isaiah 1:18b says, *"Though your sins be as scarlet, they shall be white as snow."*

In the 19ᵗʰ chapter of Revelation, it says that Christ's Bride *".... was granted that she should be arrayed in fine linen, clean and white ...."* (Revelation 19:8a). White indicates faithfulness and purity and is the color chosen by most brides.

Do not confuse this white throne with the one in chapter 4. Compare the differences: in chapter 4 we saw a throne set in Heaven with a rainbow around it. The rainbow is a sign that God keeps His promises to those who trust in Him. But here in chapter 20, the throne has no rainbow. The only promise to those before the Great White Throne is justice and retribution. In chapter 4, the throne had rumblings and warnings coming from it like a red flashing light at a railroad crossing. But here in chapter 20, there is nothing but the silence. The warnings have come to an end. In chapter 4, there were prayers and pleadings before the throne, but here in chapter 20, the lamp of mercy has gone out and the time for prayers has ended. And finally in chapter 4, John heard songs of praise being lifted unto God. But at this final Great White Throne scene set at the end of history, there are no longer voices of praise – no songs to sing – nothing but the silence of the damned.

It is a judicial throne because judgment is executed from it. But it is a temporary throne because it is needed only for this one time when the unbelievers of all ages will be judged. The One sitting on the throne is so awesome – so brilliant – that even Heaven and earth just melt away. Peter had this in mind in his second letter, chapter 3, verse 10b, when he says, *".... the heavens shall pass away with a great noise, and the elements shall melt with fervent heat, the earth also and the works that are therein shall be burned up."*

Just who is this that is sitting on the Great White Throne of judgment? Some might say, "God the Father." Some might say, "Michael, the archangel." But it is none other than the Lord Jesus Christ Himself! The One with the nail prints in His hands, scars on His back and side.

How do I know that this Judge sitting on the Great White Throne is the Lord Jesus Christ? John 5:22: *"For the Father judgeth no man, but hath committed all judgment unto the Son."* And a few verses later, it says: *"And* [the Father] *hath given Him authority to execute judgment also, because He is the Son of man"* (John 5:27).

In Acts 10:42, Peter declared that Christ was ordained by God to be the Judge of the living and the dead. II Timothy 4:1 says that Jesus Christ will judge the *"quick and the dead."* The "quick" or living He has already judged at the beginning of the Millennium (Matthew 25:31). Now He is about to judge the dead. The term "dead" here has a two-fold significance. First, it refers to those unsaved ones whose bodies had physically died and so, are called up to be united with their spirits for this judicial occasion. Secondly, the term dead here has a deeper meaning. All those who are at this judgment are spiritually dead. There was a movie entitled, *Dead Man Walking.*[14] It referred to a man who was sentenced to death, but the sentence had not yet been carried out. That is the case here. All that appear at the Great White Throne are, in effect, dead men walking.

I want you to notice something else. Go back to verse 6 of this 20th chapter. It says that death has no power or authority over those who are involved in the first resurrection. That is the believers, the children of God. But it states by implication, that death DOES have power or authority over those involved in the second resurrection.

Turn to Acts 17:31. The KJV is a little confusing with all the pronouns – so I am going to supply the proper names. We are told, *"Because He* [the Father] *hath appointed a day, in the which He* [the Father] *will judge the world in righteousness by that Man* [Jesus Christ] *whom He* [the Father] *hath ordained; whereof He* [the Father] *hath given assurance unto all men, in that He* [the Father] *hath raised Him* [Jesus] *from the dead."*

So there is no question that the Father has delegated all judgment into the hands of the Son. And it is the Son we see seated on the Great White Throne. There will be a Judge, but no jury. There will be a prosecutor, but no defender. There will be a sentence, but no appeal because the sentence is just. It is the place where sinners stand before a holy God to give an account of their lives. There is no more awesome scene in the history of mankind than the one that is depicted here.

Robert Ingersoll, the infamous atheist, 150 years ago visited the People's Church in Kalamazoo, Michigan. It was a beautiful church, and he was given a guided tour by its pastor, Patricia Bennett. Later, he said, "I was most impressed with the People's Church. If it were near my home, I think I would join." The wire services carried this news across the country, and the rumor quickly spread, "The great atheist is nearly converted." And then Ingersoll clarified the story. People's Church was Unitarian. It had no creed. It had no stated beliefs. It accepted everyone for membership whatever their beliefs, convictions, or lack thereof. No wonder he would have liked to join it![15]

Robert Ingersoll was dead and gone when someone picked up one of his books, and it had a profound impact on setting the course for that person's life. Remember, we said a man does not completely die when he dies. Let me explain: his influence lives on. Well, he influenced a young lady whose life has turned hundreds, maybe thousands away from Christ. Her name? Madalyn Murray O'Hair. At the Great White Throne Judgment, Robert Green Ingersoll must share his load of responsibility for how this bitter and deluded woman turned out. I have heard of fathers teaching their little sons to curse or drink beer, and then laugh about how funny it is. There will be a payday – someday.

In another vein, one might ask, "Where does this judgment take place?" It cannot take place on earth because, at the Judge's appearing, earth and Heaven fled away. They were not destroyed – they were just moved out of the way. It appears that this judgment undoubtedly takes place somewhere in the vast reaches of outer space. The name of the throne is more important than the location.

Verse 12: *"And I saw the dead, small and great, stand before God; and the books were opened: and another book was opened, which is the book of life: and the dead were judged out of those things which were written in the books, according to their works."* This group includes every Christ-rejecter of every age. The small and the great are all there. No one will be too important to get out of his appointment, and no one will be too insignificant to be overlooked. And they " …. *stand before God."* There are no caves, crevices or caverns to hide in. There is no shelter or escape. The sinner must stand face to face with this awesome, but Holy Judge.

During college, I had a general idea of the big picture of prophecy, but had not seriously devoted much time to it. But in the mid-1960's, I had to wait at least 30 minutes on a ride to work every morning. Trying to make the best use of my time, I began to read. I happened to read a commentary on Revelation by Dr. H. A. Ironside, long time pastor of Moody Memorial Church in Chicago. I was so moved by the Spirit of God that for the next several years I read everything I could get my hands on by Dr. Ironside – over 40 books. I learned that the Bible teaches that one day a trumpet is going to sound, and there is going to be the shout of an archangel and the dead in Christ are going to rise up to meet Him in the air. Those believers living on earth at the time will be caught up in the air, and all will receive new bodies on the way up – designed for eternal life (I Thessalonians 4:16-17; I Corinthians 15:52-53).

I decided my first act if I have time will be to take my glasses and smash them into the ground because I am so tired of not being able to see details. Where I am going my eyesight will be 20/20. If I have time, I will take my watch, and throw it to the earth because where I am going time will not be important. I will not worry about Arlene being late anymore! Bro. Jim can preach and preach and preach, and no one will complain about his sermon being too long. And if I have time, I will reach into my medicine cabinet and throw away my Scope because there will be no sickness in Heaven. And bad breath is sick! You heard it here first – "there ain't no bad breath in Heaven!"

In my studies of eschatology, I made a startling discovery. "Every body talkin' 'bout Heav'n ain't goin' there." In fact, the Bible tells us that not only is there a resurrection for the saved person, there is a resurrection for the lost person as well; but they are very different. The resurrection of the saved is accompanied by shouts of praise and joy. But for the unsaved, there are no happy shouts by the angels – no joyous sounds coming from the trumpet – no white robes being passed around. For this scene is an awesome and tragic one. Everyone resurrected in this second resurrection is destined for eternal judgment.

Turn to Revelation 20:11. Keep your place there. When you read this scene, you cannot help but think of a drowning man. I saw a drowning man once. A drowning man clutches for anything he can grab. He goes down and comes up. He goes down again and comes up. But if he goes down the third time probably he will not come up. Going – going – gone! This is what happens to a man who decides to live his life apart from Jesus Christ.

"And I saw a great white throne, and Him that sat upon it, from whose face the earth and the Heaven fled away; and there was found no place for them. And I saw the dead, small and great, stand before God; and the books were opened: and another book was opened, which is the book of life: and the dead were judged out of those things which were written in the books, according to their works" (Revelation 20:11-12).

He says the books were opened. God's books will be totally accurate because He sees every move humans make. *"The eyes of the Lord run to and fro throughout the whole earth"* (II Chronicles 16:9). And again, *"And no creature is hidden from his sight, but all are naked and exposed to the eyes of Him to whom we must give account"* (Hebrews 4:13 ESV). One cannot hide from God. The Lord knows the thoughts, the deeds and the motives of every one of His creatures. Even though sin of any kind is an abomination to God, nonetheless, some sins are more grievous as far as human relationships are concerned than others. Consequently, the Lord tells us there will be degrees of punishment in Hell (Luke 12:47-48). The books that are opened will be used to determine the severity of the punishment.

The "other book" in verse 12 – the Book of Life – will determine the final destiny of that individual. Unfortunately, every person who is being judged at the Great White Throne will not find their name in the Book of Life. God keeps meticulous records. He knows a person's thoughts, deeds and actions. He even knows what motivates one to do certain things. And He does not misplace a file.

A number of verses that support this teaching of degrees of punishment are: Luke 12:47-48; Romans 2:5; Matthew 11:24; Matthew 23:14. All these actions, whether good or bad, will determine the degree of punishment. Hitler will be punished much more severely than a lost man whose major sin was stealing automobiles. But, sin is sin, and requires separation from God. But God is just. He dispenses perfect judgment. Consequently, a Madalyn Murray O'Hair will receive more severe punishment than say, a man who never had time for God. But don't get me wrong. The lightest punishment in Hell will be worse than we can imagine because it will last eternally.

We mentioned some books previously. Here is a few more: the Book of Conscience. Romans 2:15 (ESV): *"They show that the work of the law is written on their hearts, while their conscience also bears witness, and their conflicting thoughts accuse or even excuse them."* Did we violate our own conscience in the things we did? Our conscience is not an infallible guide to right or wrong, but when it is openly violated, it shows a cavalier attitude toward sin.

The Book of Memories will reveal the many times the unsaved felt the tug of the Holy Spirit to accept Christ. Listen to what the psalmist said in Psalm 139:1-4 (ESV): *"O LORD, you have searched me and known me. You know when I sit down and when I rise up; you discern my thoughts from afar. You search out my path and my lying down and are acquainted with all my ways. Even before a word is on my tongue, behold, O LORD, you know it altogether."*

Here is one we will all understand: The Book of Words. Jesus said, *"But I say unto you, That every idle word that men shall speak, they shall give account thereof in the day of judgment"* (Matthew 12:36). All of us are so guilty of idle words. We should ask forgiveness for them every day! And why is it important to publicly confess Christ as Savior? I love to see churches that allow new members to publicly tell the congregation how they feel about Christ. He says in Matthew 12:37: *"For by thy words thou shalt be justified, and by thy words thou shalt be condemned."*

Did you know that scientists tell us that no word that is ever spoken out loud is ever lost? The sound waves continue on indefinitely, only waiting to be recaptured someday. Wouldn't the police like to have a machine that could capture the words that a suspect said yesterday – or last week – or at the very crime scene itself? God has that ability, and in His Book of Words, He will allow every person at this judgment to hear themselves incriminated by their own voice – or justified by their own voice as they accept Christ.

What about the Book of Secret Works? None of us likes this! That is why, if you are a follower of Christ, you will not have to go through this with the world watching. The Apostle Paul said that: *"God will judge the secrets of men by Jesus Christ"* (Romans 2:16). King Solomon in Ecclesiastes 12:14 said: *"For God will bring every work into judgment, including every secret thing, whether good or evil."* But this will not be at the White Throne Judgment if you are a believer. It will be at the Bema Seat of Christ. And it will not be to embarrass you. In fact, Jesus concludes this section by saying in I Corinthians 4:5, that every man will have praise of Christ. But for the unbelievers, there is a different scenario. There will be no secrets before the

Great White Throne and the Judge who will sit thereon. Those things which men thought would never be used against them because they were hidden for all time – they will be revealed as testimonies against them.

There was a series of articles in the *Dallas News* a few years ago about a woman by the name of Mary Ellen Bendtsen. Mrs. Bendtsen was quite elderly. She was always living in the past when she used to be known as the "queen of the ball" and the talk of every party. Nearing 90, she still kept that dream alive, yearning to hear people tell her how beautiful she was. Her treasure in life was 4949 Swiss Avenue, once a sprawling, elegant mansion in Dallas, but now, a run-down, sagging relic of the past. She had no other love in life except her home, and just like her, it was under the curse of rot and decay and years of neglect. Two unscrupulous young men gained her friendship, told her how beautiful she still was, and convinced her that she should have nothing to do with her daughter. These two young men convinced her on her deathbed to change her will over to them, which she did. But after her death, the new will was bitterly contested by the daughter. After a lengthy court battle, the daughter won.[16]

All such detestable actions, done in secret, will be made manifest at the Great White Throne Judgment. Another book will be opened: the Book of the Law. It details what God requires for a sinless life – the 10 commandments – lived out perfectly for every second of every day of one's entire life. Few will argue that they have lived a perfect life. There may be some other books that are opened, but the most important one opened that day will be the Lamb's Book of Life In John's day, the cities had a register which listed the names of every citizen of that town. If that person committed a crime or otherwise defiled his standing in the city, he would be called before a tribunal and his name removed from the registry – in other words, blotted out!

There are several other things I want you to see in Revelation 20:11-12. First are the conditions of the Great White Throne Judgment. John writes this: *"And I saw a Great White Throne, and Him that sat on it, from whose face the earth and the heaven fled away and there was found no place for them."* All that is left is nothing but darkness and blackness. And suddenly, John writes, "I saw a White Throne appear." And there was One on the Throne whose countenance is awesome. Who is this One on the Throne? It is Jesus because the Bible says that God has committed all judgment to the Son (John 5:22). And John further says, *"I saw the dead …."* (Revelation 20:12). All the dead through the ages? No! The saved people have already been whisked away. This is the lost people of all ages and generations.

In this life we are famous for making distinctions among people. We constantly classify them into different groups. We look at a woman and say, "She is classy." Or a man and we say, "He is cool." That is the way we look at things in this life, but in the next life, there are no distinctions. "I saw the dead – small and great – rich and poor – black and white – all of them lined up before Jesus. The only thing that matters in this life is what you do with Jesus Christ.

Can you say you are saved? *"And I saw the dead, small and great, stand before God; and the books were opened: and another book was opened, which is the book of life: and the dead were judged out of those things which were written in the books, according to their works"* (Revelation 20:12). That is a mind-boggling thought: somewhere in Heaven today, your name is written down. You are not lost in a computer. Your file has not been misplaced. Somewhere in Heaven today, your name and your deeds are written down.

Your name is recorded in either the Library of Works or the Lamb's Book of Life. If your name is in the Lamb's Book of Life it means you have given your life to Christ. It means that you have accepted His righteousness instead of your own. It means that you will never have to stand before the Judge at the Great White Throne. If your name is in the Library of Works, it means that you have not made that commitment to Christ, and you will have to account for every idle deed, every idle thought, and every action recorded as evidence against you.

Someone said, "Good grief, there is not enough room in Heaven to have every sin of every person who ever lived written down." I do not know if God has it on a microchip or on a video disc for instant replay, but you can be assured He has it recorded. I heard Evangelist Gary Holder say this: "A fellow told me 'God said it, I believe it and that settles it.' But I have a better one. God said it, and that settles it; whether you believe it or not is immaterial."

Look at verse 13: *"And the sea gave up the dead which were in it; and death and hell delivered up the dead which were in them: and they were judged every man according to their works."* What does it mean that the sea gave up its dead? Think of the thousands of people through the ages that have lost their lives at sea. Every unbeliever of every age will be there. Whether they have been buried at sea – whether they have been buried in the ground – whether they have been cremated or whether they have been blown to pieces by a bomb – God will supernaturally bring together the very elements of their body, to be reunited with their soul, and they will stand before the judgment bar of God to await their sentencing to Hell.

The Lake of Fire is synonymous with Hell. No wonder that our Lord said to avoid Hell at any cost. That is why He said, *"And if thy right eye offend thee, pluck it out, and cast it from thee …. And if thy right hand offend thee, cut it off and cast it from thee: for it is profitable for thee that one of thy members should perish, and not that thy whole body should be cast into Hell"* (Matthew 5:29a-30).

Jesus was reciting the most outlandish examples He could think of – pluck out your eye – cut off your hand – that would be no sacrifice at all compared to the eternal fires of Hell.

After a terrible bombing of London by the German Luftwaffe during WW II, the fires were raging out of control and the anguish cries of victims could be heard at a distance. An evangelist was standing in the midst of this turmoil preaching to anyone who would listen. While he was preaching, a skeptic interrupted him and said, "Listen, preacher, I'll tell you what

Hell is. The bombing of London is Hell." And the preacher replied, "Sir, I'll give you three reasons why this is not Hell. One, I am a Christian, and there are no Christians in Hell. Two, there is a church right around that corner. There will be no churches in Hell. And three, I am preaching the Gospel of the Good News of the Son of Man – and there will be no Gospel of Good News in Hell!"[17]

The little town of Forney seems to be overrun with real estate agents. Every time the mail comes, there is another agent wanting to sell my house. They should keep an eye on Hillcrest Cemetery because one of these days, it will have a sign that says, "Vacancy." First the Christians are gone at the Rapture, and then the lost are called up to stand before the Judge. The cemetery is empty! The truth of the Scripture is this: you do not have to bow your knee to Jesus right now. Your tongue does not have to confess right now that Jesus is Lord. But mark it down friend, there is coming a day when your knee WILL bow and your tongue WILL make that confession in the presence of Almighty God. Make that decision now!

Get the picture of the lost: from the sea – from the graveyard – their bodies are coughed up, their souls are joined with their bodies in one miraculous event, and they are judged according to their works! Someone said, "I don't understand why God would choose to do it like that. Why doesn't God just judge people one by one instead of waiting until the end of time? It seems it would be much easier to judge them all together instead of one at a time." We answered that earlier. It is because "a man does not completely die when he dies." Our influence lives on whether good or bad. Only an omnipotent and omniscient God can check out a man at the end of time – to see where he has been – to see what he has done – to what his influence has been – and judge him fairly. Revelation 20: 14-15 says: *"And death and Hell were cast into the Lake of Fire. This is the second death. And whosoever was not found written in the book of life was cast into the Lake of Fire."*

Christ mentioned Hades or Hell eleven times (Mathew 11:23; 16:18; Luke 10:15; 16:23; Acts 2:27; 2:31; I Corinthians 15:55; Revelation 1:18; 6:8; 20:13; 20:14). He mentioned Gehenna or Hell twelve times (Matthew 5:22; 5:29; 5:30; 10:28; 18:9; 23:15; 23:33; Mark.9:43; 9:45; 9:47; Luke 12:5; James 3:6).

After studying all 23 of these references, you will see that the verses we are studying today – Revelation 20, verses 13-14, make perfect sense. Death (or the grave) and Hell delivered up the dead which were in them. The grave and Hell are two separate places. Jesus spoke three words about Hell for every one word He spoke about Heaven. Hell is not a popular doctrine, but its existence is clear in Scripture. We seldom hear sermons about it. Someone asked, "Will Christians be there to witness what takes place at the Great White Throne Judgment?" I doubt it because we would not be able to bear listening to our unsaved loved ones when they say, "Why didn't you tell me?"

If you know someone who, as far as you can tell, will not be found in the Book of Life, won't you tell them soon about how they can have their names listed there? Whether they choose Jesus is their responsibility, but whether they have the choice may be yours! *"And whosoever was not found written in the book of life was cast into the lake of fire"* (Revelation 20:15.) The judgment just discussed is only for those whose names are not found inscribed in the Book of Life. If one is saved, he does not need to be concerned about Hell as his eternal destiny, because *"He that believeth on Him is not condemned: but He that believeth not is condemned already, because he has not believed in the name of the only begotten Son of God"* (John 3:18).

You can be wrong about a lot of doctrines – you can be confused about a lot of religious teachings – you may not understand prophecy – but if your name is not recorded in the Lamb's Book of Life, you are in big trouble. Why would a man refuse to be counted among the children of the saved? I cannot understand it. It is just as if an angel entered into Sodom and Gomorrah and stood in the gate and shouted, "All who will turn to God, I will write their names in this Book of Life, and they will be saved." But the citizens cry out: "No, we had rather be damned and burn with eternal fire." That is what men say today. I cannot understand such a stupendous decision – or is it a stupid decision? Most people do not literally say, "I reject Christ." They just do not have time for Him.

Here is one of the saddest poems I ever read: "I knelt to pray, but not for long, I had too much to do. I had to hurry and get to work. I had bills that soon were due. So I knelt and said a hurried prayer, and jumped up off my knees. No time, no time, too much to do. That was my constant cry. No time to give to souls in need, but at last I had time to die. I came before the Lord that day, and stood with downcast eyes. For in His hands God held a book. It was the Book of Life. God looked into the Book and said, "Your name I cannot find." I once was going to write it down – but never found the time."[18]

When a man dies outside the grace of God, he dies forever. There is nothing you can say. There is nothing you can read. All you can do is weep. Why would a family choose to be like that? I cannot understand it, except that Satan tries to place a veil over our message to cloud it, to say, "There is all the time in the world for God – later – but for now, let's grab the gusto." And when that final day comes, either at death or at the Second Coming, it will come quite suddenly like a thief in the night. There will be no time for decisions.

We have looked at the conditions; now we will look at the consequences. The Lake of Fire – translated in the Hebrew, Gehenna – was once a beautiful spot outside the gates of Jerusalem. Years ago, King Solomon began to collect a number of beautiful wives. And in the process of doing so one of his wives brought her own god with her – the god of Molech. There in the Valley of Hinnon, they erected temples to this god, Molech, and practiced child sacrifice. God's chosen people in order to please this false god murdered and burned their own babies there in the Valley of Hinnon. Then good King Josiah came on the throne and cleaned up the whole mess (II Kings 22:1-30). This place then became known as Gehenna. There they dumped and burned the bodies of dead criminals – the bodies of dead animals – and finally, the garbage from the city.

Jesus likened Hell unto Gehenna – a stinking, rotten place of eternal fires! He called it "outer darkness" (Matthew 8:12). Scripture calls it a place of everlasting destruction (II Thessalonians 1:9). Those Jews listening to Jesus could instantly visualize that rotten trash heap where the fires smoldered constantly. And when Jesus said there would be gnashing of teeth, they remembered the jackals and wild dogs that slipped in at night to bite and tear at the carcasses. And when Jesus warned of a place where *"the worm never dies"* (Mark 9:44), they could see in their minds' eye the maggots that crawled through the stench and filth of that garbage dump outside the gates of Jerusalem. Jesus warned as clearly as any warning could ever be given: "You ignore Me, and you will have a one-way ticket to Gehenna – this is the second death!" How many times have we heard, *"The wages of sin is death?"* (Romans 6:23).

The Bible says, *"And as it is appointed unto men once to die, but after this the judgment"* (Hebrews 9:27). We are all going to die a physical death unless, as believers, we are alive at the time of the Rapture. That is the only way we will beat the grim reaper. But the payment of sin is not physical death. It is not getting your brains blown out by a carjacker. It is not getting mowed down on Central Expressway. It is not even being laid low by cancer. All of that is a consequence of sin, not the payment. The payment is eternal separation from God in Hell which is spiritual death. It is called the second death which leads to the Lake of Fire. Who will experience this? Verse 15 says that *"Whosoever was not written the book of life was cast into the Lake of Fire."*

A person told me, "I know you are sincere, and I know you mean what you say, but I don't believe a word you are saying. I was not brought up that way, and my god would never do that." I said, "You are right. Your god would never do that, but your god only exists in your mind. Because the Bible says the God of this Book is a holy God, and because He is holy, the penalty of sin must be paid." You can either accept Christ's payment for your sins or you can pay for them yourself – in the Lake of Fire. If God would not spare His own Son, what makes you think He would spare you? The greatest proof you have that Hell is real is this very thing – that Jesus paid the supreme price – His life – for the penalty of sin. If God was just going to let down the gates of Heaven at the end of time and say, "Everyone come on in," then Jesus' death on the cross was a travesty and a waste of time.

If there is one thing that stands out in the entire history of man, it is Jesus, and what He did on the cross to save mankind. And friend, it is the only thing that will keep you from the fires of Hell, and take you to Heaven. I often wonder, "Why is the Book of Life there anyway? If all these folks are lost, and God knows their names are not in the Book of Life, why is the

Book there?" Well, it occurred to me one day that there will be a lot of folks there – some Baptists – some from other denominations – who never dreamed of showing up at the Great White Throne. They are going to say: "Lord, didn't I do many works in your name? Lord, I'm a church member. I've been baptized. I turned in my tithe card." And Jesus is going to point to the Lamb's Book of Life and say, "Your name is not here." He will then say, *"I never knew you: depart from Me, ye that work iniquity"* (Matthew 7:23b). And they will finally realize that there is a big difference in trying to be good in their own power and in trusting Christ as their Savior.

The Lord is long-suffering and patient toward anyone really seeking the truth, but He has little patience for those who adamantly rejected His message. Read Matthew 23 for His response to them. We have been looking in-depth at the Great White Throne Judgment. The self-righteous will be there: the ones who did not feel the need of salvation. I have known plenty of these folks in my life – educated, cultured and had everything materially they would ever want. No concern for the hereafter. Most self-righteous people have a problem accepting Christ's free gift of salvation. They want to earn it by works. One good approach is to agree with them, at least partly. Agree that salvation is by works – but not their works! Titus 3:5a makes this clear: *"Not by works of righteousness which we have done, but according to His mercy He saved us."* These self-righteous people think they live pretty good moral lives. And humanly speaking, they probably do. But if someone is about 50 years old, and if they only committed one sin a day (and that is a big IF), then they have committed over 18,000 sins. And if you have committed an average of one an hour –wow – they do add up fast, don't they?

The procrastinators will be there. I once heard about a man who was going to make a decision to quit procrastinating, but he put it off until tomorrow. Probably this is the largest group. They know they are lost, but they intend to do something about it someday. A friend of mine said his motto is, "Don't put off till tomorrow what you can put off until day after tomorrow." Paul witnessed before King Agrippa in Acts 26:28a. The King said, " …. *almost thou hast persuadest me to be a Christian."* But then he put off any decision for another time and, as far as we know, his opportunity was gone forever.

Unfortunately, there will be many church members that will procrastinate as well. They have met the pastor, but not the Master! In most churches across the country, about one-third of the membership attends regularly. That is a disgrace. I shudder to think of Christ's reaction to that in the light of what He said about commitment.

Here is just a few of His comments:

"For where your treasure is, there your heart will be also" (Matthew 6:21 ESV).
"Jesus said unto him, 'No one who puts his hand to the plow and looks back is fit for the kingdom of God'" (Luke 9:62 ESV).

"They went out from us, but they were not of us; for if they had been of us, they would have continued with us" (I John 2:19 ESV).

And what about this powerful verse: *"And let us not neglect our meeting together, as some people do, but encourage and warn each another, especially now that the day of His coming back again is drawing near"* (Hebrews 10:25 NLT). Church members at this awesome judgment will be those who professed Christ but did not possess Christ. Some churches teach that you can be saved and then fall away (becoming unsaved). No, Christ said, *"I never knew you"* (Matthew 7:23). But to the true believers, He said: *"And I give eternal life to them, and they will never perish; and no one will snatch them out of My hand"* (John 10:28 NASB).

How long is eternal life? Is it 10 years – is it 10,000 years? Is it till you become weak and fall away? No – eternal life is eternal life! God knows how to communicate and if He says, "I give you eternal life," then you have eternal life. What do Christ's sheep do? Jesus says that they know His voice (John 10:4). Oh, there are a lot of pretenders within the Christian ranks. Christ illustrated this by the parable of the sower. So we know that there will be no one at this Great Judgment bar except lost people, and they must stand alone, without anything or anybody to help.

Time is short. The Lord says the harvest will soon be over when no man can work. If you have loved ones and friends that you want to join you in Heaven, now is the time to talk to them about it. Death awaits all of us.

It is amazing how different "last words" were for some people. P.T. Barnum, the circus millionaire, asked right before he died, "How were the circus receipts today in Madison Square Gardens?" How sad![19] But there are no more poignant last words than those spoken by evangelist Dwight L. Moody. His relatives gathered around him in the waning minutes. He closed his eyes – then he opened them and said excitedly: "Earth recedes. Heaven opens before me. If this is death, it is sweet! There is no valley here. God is calling me, and I must go …. this is my coronation day!"[20]

What a difference between the fate of believer who will spend eternity in Heaven and an unbeliever who must appear before the Great White Throne. Here is a summary of what will happen at the Great White Throne Judgment: Christ is on the throne as Judge; the unsaved, great and small, stand before Him; the books are opened and searched; a person's works are noted whether good or bad; the Law is read showing that everyone comes up short; the Book of Life is searched and shows no entry for that person; eternal judgment is rendered and the sentence is carried out.

Everyone who ever lived will meet Jesus Christ one day. We have an appointment with Him. I pray it will be as Savior and not as Judge!

CHAPTER TWENTY-ONE

The New Heaven, The New Earth, The New Jerusalem

When you plan to go on a vacation, there are two questions that will consume your thoughts. Where will we go, and what will the place be like? As you plan a great trip, you first visualize the journey to where you are going and all that awaits you when you get there. And then as you come back, you can hardly wait to get home.

I am thinking of a magnificent trip we had early in our marriage to the beautiful coastal beach of Puerto Vallarta, Mexico. What really impressed us about this trip was this – here we were flying into Mexico, and a flight attendant came down the aisle and sprayed us with disinfectant! I guess they can't be too careful.

Today, we are going to begin an incredible journey – one that will take us to that place we have looked forward to for so long. And if you have not looked forward to it, you will by the time we finish these lessons! I am speaking about Heaven. I am planning to go there, and I hope you are too. What do we know about Heaven? Well, the bookstores are filled with books that tell of people dying, going to Heaven, and then coming back to earth to tell us about it. One of the more popular ones is *90 Minutes in Heaven*.[1] Some of my friends have really gotten excited about it. The book is written by a Baptist pastor, Don Piper. I am not saying it happened – I know it was real to Don Piper. I just have not read any place in Scripture where God allowed a person to come back to earth to tell about it. Of course, Christ came back, and Moses and Elijah were allowed to appear with Him on the Mount of Transfiguration, but they all had glorified bodies by then.

A number of years ago, I read a book that was on everyone's lips, *Embraced by the Light* by Betty Eadie, a member of the Church of Latter Day Saints. It tells of her fantastic experiences during her stay in Heaven after she "died."[2] Here is what she says on her website: "When I was 31, I died in a hospital after undergoing surgery. What happened next has been called by some, the most profound near-death experience ever. I journeyed to a beautiful world beyond this life. There I met Jesus. Jesus gave me a message to give to others when I returned. In my book, I share that message." Millions of people have purchased her book over the years. It was on the New York bestseller list for over twelve months. And folks, you too can find out what Jesus wants her to tell you by sending her only $16.95 plus postage. I am wondering if Jesus told her when she got back, to sell His important message to the world for $16.95 (it has been recently lowered from $18.95 and if you want a used copy, Barnes & Noble has it for $1.99 plus postage). After all, she could have put it on the internet so everyone could read what Jesus had to say to everyone free of charge.

I came across a critique of Mrs. Eadie's book by Probe Ministries, a conservative evangelical group. The review is eight pages long, and it is entitled *Embraced by the Light – of Deception.*[3] It really highlights her deficiencies. Here is what Jesus supposedly told Mrs. Eadie: "All of us were with God in the beginning, helping Him to create the earth – we just don't remember it. We are all God's children, and are put on earth to learn the lessons we need for our spiritual evolution. Eventually, everyone will learn that lesson and all of us will be saved." Apparently, Eve did not sin. Her "initiative" made it possible for the human race to have children. She says there is no such thing as judgment day. Mrs. Eadie met whom she calls the "real" Jesus during her death experience. He told her not to bother with the Bible because it has been corrupted over the years by too many translations. Mrs. Eadie is a very confused lady, and her ramblings are pretty close to what the Mormon Church teaches.

Does the name "Bridey Murphy" mean anything to you? In 1952, a New England psychologist by the name of Morey Bernstein wrote a book entitled, *The Search for Bridey Murphy*. I was in my first year in college when I read the book. It seems that Bernstein hypnotized a housewife who told of her past life – 200 years ago in Ireland. While under hypnosis, and with the tape recorder running, she sang Irish songs and recalled details of her childhood in Ireland that, according to experts, she would have known only if she had actually lived back then in Ireland.[4] After a number of exhaustive investigations by experts, the conclusion was there that was no evidence Bridey Murphy had lived an earlier life. Most believed that the whole thing was a hoax – but not before the book had sold millions of copies and was number one on the New York bestseller list.[5]

It seems that people are always anxious to buy into the idea of reincarnation. I do not mean to be overly critical of these accounts – well, some of them I do since they have been proven to be hoaxes – but some of them are probably very real to the people involved in them. A few of these accounts may have authentic components, but most are unbiblical and misleading. The fact of the matter is the Bible tells us everything we need to know about Heaven – much more than you possibly realize. But why are there so many books about Heaven and the afterlife? Because the human heart cries out for answers to life beyond the grave. For the most part people in all walks of life, from the aristocrat to the wildest savage, want to believe in life after death. Australian aborigines pictured Heaven as a place just over the horizon. Early tribes in South America thought they went to the moon after death. American Indians looked forward to going to their "happy hunting grounds" and were often buried with their bows and arrows.

A study of anthropology will tell you that every culture – be it ancient or modern – has an inborn sense of life after death. Everyone wants to believe that this world is not all there is in spite of the beer commercial that says, "Go for the gusto because you only go around once." A number of years ago, archaeologists discovered a document that was written in 125 A.D. by a philosopher by the name of Aristides. Here is what he said about this strange new religion called Christianity. "If any righteous man among the Christians dies, they rejoice and offer thanks to God, and sing songs as if he were going to another place nearby."[6] It reminds me of what Paul said in the first chapter of Philippians: *"To me, to live is Christ, and to die, is gain .... I desire to depart and be with Christ ...."* (Philippians 1:21, 23b). And in II Corinthians 5:8b (NIV), Paul said: *"I would prefer to be away from the body and at home with the Lord."*

When Jesus told His disciples, *"In My Father's house are many mansions"* (John 14:2), He deliberately chose common, physical terms – house, rooms, a place – to describe where He was going, and what He was preparing for us. He wanted to give His disciples something tangible to look forward to, an actual place where they would be with Him. It was not going to be the twilight zone. It was not going to be a never-never land of disembodied spirits, floating around because human beings are not suited for such a place. A "place" by its very nature and definition is physical, just like human beings by nature are physical. What we are suited for, what we have been specifically designed for, is a place like the one God has planned for us – a New Earth!

As we go through this study, we will find that God has never given up on His original plan for human beings to dwell on the earth. In fact, the climax of history will be the creation of a New Heaven and a New Earth inhabited by resurrected people living with the resurrected Jesus (Revelation 21:1-4). Only a small group of atheists choose to believe otherwise – that death ends it all. And even then, one of their foremost spokesman, atheist Robert Ingersoll, gave a hint that he was not so sure. He purportedly said on his deathbed, "I am taking a fearful leap into the dark," however, some of his relatives questioned this.[7]

Jim was a terrific guy on the Board of Trustees of Lamb & Lion Ministries for over 20 years. He was my dear friend and a shining testimony for the Lord and a blessing to all who knew him. He was diagnosed with Parkinson's disease, and put up a valiant struggle but eventually succumbed to the illness. Here is what his son, Jimmie, said about Jim's last day on earth. "Dad was never in any great pain. He mainly suffered from weakness to the point he could hardly get out of bed. On his last day, Dad became very nervous and highly agitated. No matter what they did for him, it did not help. Mom said it was his very worst day. About four in the afternoon he settled down, but then suddenly looked up at the ceiling, smiled, raised his right arm up as if to grasp something, and said, 'WOW!' That was his last word as he died moments later."[8]

What a contrast between a child of God and one that does not know Him! But sadly, our seminaries, our families and even most churches have given us very little information about this place where we will live forever with Christ and His people – The New Heaven and the New Earth. I have prayed earnestly that the Lord will lead me down the right paths in this study.

We will rely on Scripture to form the foundation for everything we have to say; however, to a smaller degree we will use logic and the common sense God gave us to arrive at our conclusions. Speculation will be held to a minimum.

We will make I Thessalonians 5:21 one of our guiding verses: *"Prove all things; hold fast that which is good."* It is up to you to test everything by God's word while holding on to what is scriptural and rejecting what is not. There will be some things presented as we go through here that may be new to many of you. All I ask is that you keep an open mind, listen patiently and search the Scriptures to see if these things be so. We will be considering the difference between the present Heaven where Christians go today if they die, and the New Heaven where God will dwell forever with His resurrected people on the New Earth.

In our study, we will cover such questions as, "Is Heaven a real, material place?" "Can loved ones see what is happening on earth?" "Will there be a difference between the New Heaven and the New Earth?" "What will it mean to rule with Christ?" "Will there be animals on the New Earth?" "Will we eat and drink?" "Will we work and play?" "Will we remember things from this world?"

It is always sad when we hear of someone who has a terminal disease; however, the fact is, we all have a terminal disease. It is called sin, and it will cause us to die. We start dying the day we are born. The current death rate for humans is 100%. It is an equal opportunity employer showing no bias. It just takes some of us longer than others to achieve it, but given enough time (and barring the Rapture occurring in the meantime), we will all eventually get there. I heard about a man who was being sentenced for murder. The judge read the sentence – 75 years in prison. The man said, "Judge, I'm 35 years old. I can't serve 75 years." The judge replied, "Well, son, go on down there and give it your best shot!"

We do not like to think about death, yet worldwide about 2 people die every second, 120 every minute and 7,200 during a typical church service. That means there are about 173,000 people departing this earth every day with their ticket punched that says either Heaven or Hell.

David said in Psalm 39:5 (NLT): *"My life is no longer than the width of my hand. An entire lifetime is just a moment to you; human existence is but a breath."* Picture a single breath from your mouth on a chilly day. That is the brevity of life. God uses sickness and suffering to get our minds off of this glitzy world and say, "Wait a minute, slow down, and make sure you are ready for the next world." Some people in accidents are gone before they even get such a warning. I am trying to get out of the habit of saying, "I lost my mother several years ago." I did not lose her. I know where she is – around the throne singing praises to our Lord. Rather, I should say, "My mother went home to Jesus several years ago."

Most people are unprepared to die. But it is reported that Philip II of Macedon, father of Alexander the Great, ordered one of his servants to come before him every day and say the words, "Philip, you are going to die." Philip never wanted to forget his mortality![9] In direct contrast, France's Louis the 14th decreed that death should never be mentioned in his presence. Many of us are like that. We live under the fear of death. It grips us and we cannot shake it.

You have probably thrilled to many Perry Mason episodes as did I. But when Perry Mason, whose real name was Raymond Burr, was terminally ill, he fought death to the last because of his fear. Someone asked him what he had learned from his struggle. He said that "death is ugly and messy and not one whit romantic."[10]

Thinking that death could not come so long as he was awake, he propped himself up in bed and took no-doze pills, and drank coffee around the clock. Unfortunately, after about 40 hours, he lapsed into unconsciousness and death soon followed. Perry Mason almost never lost a case on television – but he lost this one to the grim reaper.[11]

Alfred Hitchcock also had a dread of death. He spent his life producing films that scared the wits out of the public. Who will ever forget the shower scene in *Psycho*? All of his movies were preoccupied with death and murder. But despite this, when it came time for him to face death, he was petrified with fear, and reportedly cried like a baby.[12]

Jesus came to deliver us from the fear of death as we are told in Hebrews: *"Since the children have flesh and blood, he too shared in their humanity so that by his death he might destroy him who holds the power of death – that is, the Devil – and free those who all their lives were held in slavery by their fear of death"* (Hebrews 2:14-15 NIV). Are you held in slavery by the fear of death? You should not be, unless you do not have a personal relationship with Jesus Christ. In that case, you should fear death!

But for the Christian, there is no need to fear death because Jesus tells us in Revelation 1:18: *"I have the keys of Hell and death."* In light of the coming resurrection of the dead, the Apostle Paul asks, *"O death, where is thy sting? O grave, where is thy victory?"* (I Corinthians 15:55). The Christian life is one of perseverance. We are admonished over and over in Scripture to keep pushing onward, not to give up, but trust in the Lord as we *"press toward the mark for the prize of the high calling of God in Christ Jesus"* (Philippians 3:14).

In 1952, young Florence Chadwick slid into the chilly waters of the Pacific Ocean off the coast of Catalina Island, intending to be the first woman to swim the 22 miles to the mainland of California. She was already the first woman to swim the English Channel. It was foggy and the water was cold. She had been swimming for 15 hours, and she was bone tired and emotionally spent. Her mother was in a nearby boat encouraging her on. Finally, she pleaded with those in the boat, "I can't go on – help me," and they pulled her into the boat. What she and the others did not know because of the dense fog, she swam 21½ miles. She was only one-half mile from the California coastline! Later she told reporters, "If only I could have seen the shore, I would have made it."[13]

Sometimes, we go through tough times – we get sick – we get bone tired – friends let us down. We go to the cemetery, and say goodbye to dear friends and loved ones and we think we cannot go on. But, if we can just see the shoreline, we can make it! And that is what chapter 21 seeks to do – show us the shoreline!

Now we are going to turn our attention to what lies beyond. It is called the Eternal State or the New Heaven. We are nearing the end of our long journey – we will soon be home! In some ways, it has been a long and sometimes dark journey through Book of Revelation. And now it is good to emerge into the brightness and beauty of God's new day. I rejoice in what I see as the inheritance of every child of God in eternity with Jesus Christ. But I also feel a twinge of sadness, for we sense something of the great heart of God. There are many who will not be in the New Heaven and the New Earth, and so, there is a sort of reluctance on the part of God to bring down the curtain, to say, "Mercy is now over."

We are now going to explore the dwelling place of the saved. And we have some important questions to consider. Is Heaven a real place? By that, I mean is it a material place that you can touch and feel, or is it a kind of hazy, non-physical place for spirits? Is the New Earth a real place? Does a better life await the human race? What is eternity all about?

As we move into the last two chapters of this Book of Revelation, we will be trying to answer these questions. If you were going to move to Australia, and live there the rest of your life, I am sure you would want to know as much about it as possible. What is the climate? What clothes will I need? What are the customs? It would be very strange indeed if you said, "Oh, I don't care to know. I will find out when I get there." Yet that is what the average Christian says about Heaven. We are told extensively "how" to get to Heaven by placing our trust in Christ, but very little is said about what it is like and why we should want to go there.

Oh, one could always say, "I want to go there to escape Hell." Well, that is a good reason. But a better reason is that we want to go there because we can see the benefits that await us. So, before we go to our eternal home, we should try to learn as much about it as we can. When in his early twenties, the famous preacher, Jonathan Edwards, wrote out a list of life's resolutions for himself. One of them read: "Resolved, to try to obtain for myself as much happiness in the other world as I possibly can."[14]

The French philosopher, Pascal, concluded: "All men seek happiness. This is without exception."[15] Men use various ways and means to maneuver through life, but Pascal concluded that happiness is their bottom line. The problem with that goal is that happiness is superficial. It depends on your current set of circumstances. What people really need and want is JOY.

Joy is much more important than happiness because it is deep in your being irrespective of outward circumstances. When I was in high school, our youth group sang a song: "If you want joy – real joy – wonderful joy – let Jesus come into your heart."[16]

You see, happiness does not produce joy, but joy produces happiness. It is not shallow; it goes all the way to the bone. Real joy comes from knowing Christ and fellowshipping with Him and His believers no matter what might be going on around us. I heard about a fellow who said, "Whenever I think about Heaven, it makes me depressed. I'd rather just cease to exist when I die. I can't stand the thought of that endless boredom." He pictured it as a church service that goes on and on forever. Nothing could be further from the truth.

My pastor, Jimmy Pritchard, said, "During seminary days a friend of mine had tremendous joy and enthusiasm about knowing Jesus Christ. It was pure joy being around him. One day another seminarian visited with us. After my joyful friend left, the other seminarian commented, 'I can remember when I had that kind of joy. It won't last. He will get over it.' I replied, 'I pray to God that I never get over it!'"[17] And he hasn't!

A teacher once told a little girl, "When you get to Heaven, you won't know anyone there, and they won't know you." It scared the poor little girl out of her wits and made her afraid of Heaven. Well, let me set the record straight. You are going to love Heaven, and by the time we get through with our study, you are not going to fear it. Instead, you are going to be squinting your eyes to see if you can get a better look at the shoreline!

Some people do not like to read, but there is a whole world of exciting things that you miss out on if you do not read. I have always loved to read. One of my favorite books growing up was about Huckleberry Finn. That is a classic. I could not believe my eyes a few years ago when I saw that some group was trying to get it banned from the public school library due to a charge of racism. In one section of the book Huck said all the people in the Bible were dead and he tried not have anything to do with dead people. He did not understand Heaven. Here is what Huck said about his teacher, Miss Watson. "She told me all about the good place. She said all a body would have to do there was go around all day long with a harp and sing, forever and ever. So I didn't think much of it. But I never said so. I asked her if she reckoned Tom Sawyer would go there and she said, 'Not by a considerable sight.' I was glad about that, because I wanted him and me to be together."[18]

If Huck's teacher had studied what the Bible really says about Heaven, she would have told him about living in a perfect body and being with people we love on a beautiful New Earth with gardens and rivers and mountains and untold adventures. That would have gotten his attention, and it would have been absolutely true. Gary Larson captured a common misconception of Heaven in one of his *Far Side* cartoons. In it a man with angel wings and a halo was sitting on a cloud, doing nothing, with no one nearby. He had the expression of someone marooned on a desert island with absolutely nothing to do. A caption revealed his inner thoughts: "Wish I'd brought a magazine."[19]

Where do folks get these crazy ideas about Heaven? Certainly not from the Bible. Paul said to go and be with Christ is far better than anything this world has to offer (Philippians 1:21). Satan loves for us to have a stilted conception of Heaven. He constantly wants the world to believe that Heaven is vague, dull and boring. Listen to Revelation 13:6 (NLT): *"And he* [the Antichrist] *spoke terrible words of blasphemy against God, slandering his name and all who live in heaven, who are his temple."* So here we see Satan's spokesman, the Beast, bad-mouthing three things: God, God's people and God's home. We learned when we went through Revelation chapter 12, that Satan was forcibly booted out of Heaven. The King James says that Satan was beside himself with anger. What is the most exclusive luxury hotel you can think of? The Gaylord Texan? The Hyatt Regency? If you were literally kicked out of there, and barred from coming back, you probably would say, "That place is not worth going to anyway." That is what Satan did when he was kicked out of Heaven.

When you go home for dinner today, why don't you get your plate and fill it full of gravel from the driveway? Do you know why you won't? It's very simple. God did not design your body to digest gravel. No matter how sincere we are, and no matter how hard we try, it is not going to work. What will work is the way God designed us. You see, resurrected people living on a resurrected Earth is not our idea, it is God's.

J. C. Ryle, a 19th Century theologian said, "I pity the man who never thinks about Heaven."[20] I have a better statement: "I pity the man who never accurately thinks about Heaven." It is our inaccurate view of Heaven that makes us not think about it very much. Some of our greatest theologians of the past had little to say about Heaven, and that is a shame. That great Presbyterian preacher, John Calvin, wrote scores of books and many commentaries on the Bible, but he never wrote one on the Book of Revelation, and he never had much to say about our eternal home.[21]

When I was in college, I remember the darling of the liberal theological world was a great thinker from Germany – Reinhold Niebuhr. He wrote a huge two volume set called *The Nature and Destiny of Man,* but he had nothing to say about Heaven.[22] If you take any seminary course on theology, you will discover the writings of William Shedd. His three volume work entitled, *Dogmatic Theology* is highly acclaimed, but guess what? He devotes 87 pages on Hell and eternal punishment – and two pages on Heaven.[23] Theologian Martyn Lloyd-Jones, wrote a massive 900 page book entitled, *Great Doctrines of the Bible,* and devoted less than two pages on Heaven and the New Earth.[24] This is amazing! The place where we are going to spend eternity and most Christians do not know a thing about it. But if you were to ask, most of them are interested in finding out!

The popularity of Southern Gospel music has really come to the forefront in the last 25 years. Why? Listen carefully to the words. I would guess about 75% of the Southern Gospel songs relate to Heaven, and our going to that wonderful home. Most Americans believe in

Heaven and Hell, but their conception varies greatly. That is because they get their conception for the most part, not from the Bible, but from television, movies or fiction books. Satan does not have to convince people that Heaven does not exist. He just needs to convince them that it is boring. We live in a secular world whose motto seems to be: if we can't see it, if we can't smell it, if we can't touch it – it doesn't exist. And if it does exist, it is boring!

When Marco Polo came home from his trip around the world, he described a world no one could fathom – a world that could not be understood without an imagination.[25] That is why God has given us glimpses of Heaven, to fire up our imagination and kindle a desire for Heaven in our hearts. If God did not want us to imagine what Heaven will be like, He would not have told us as much about it as He has. We have a wonderful friend who visited with us not long ago. In the course of our conversation, old radio programs came up – The Lone Ranger, Jack Armstrong, etc. Our friend said he could never get anything out of them because he just did not have an imagination. That is sad.

Through Gates of Splendor is an incredible book that was later made into a movie, *Eye of the Spear*.[26] It is the true story of five brave missionaries who carried the gospel to the Auca Indians (now called the Waodani) in Ecuador in 1956. Those savages had never seen a white man before. They had no conception of what we take for granted – airplanes, television, movies, cars or streets. We are like the Aucas when it comes to Heaven. The writers of Scripture present Heaven in many ways – as a garden, a city, a kingdom. Because we are familiar with these things, they act as a bridge to understanding the real thing. Some people make the mistake of assuming that these are just symbols, but Scripture makes it clear that Jesus is preparing a place for us, and a physical as well as a spiritual, resurrection awaits us.

Here is one of the most important concepts I want you to grasp in this study. We are not, as Plato taught, merely spiritual beings temporarily encased in bodies. Our bodies are a very real part of us. It is true that when we die, we leave this shell behind. But God has promised that one day, He will resurrect this shell, and transform it into a glorified, perfected body that will never wear out, and miraculously put it together with our spirit (I Corinthians 15:52-54). A fellow told me one time, "I think we will be raised with spiritual bodies, but they will not be physical." In other words, you will not be able to touch them. But Jesus was resurrected with a physical body. And in the 20th chapter of John, verse 17 (NIV), Jesus told Mary, *"Don't cling to me .... for I haven't yet ascended to the Father"* – indicating that it was possible for her to have touched Him. Later, He ate fish with His disciples and told Thomas to touch His side where the spear print was.

Just like Jesus, our resurrected bodies will also be physical. They will never wear out. They will not be susceptible to illness or disease. The Bible calls them glorified bodies. In Genesis 2:7, we see that Adam did not become "a living being" until he was both body and spirit. We are physical beings as much as we are spiritual beings. That is why our bodily resurrection is absolutely essential to complete our entire person; otherwise, there is no need for a resurrection. We need to ask for God's help to remove the blinders and our preconceived ideas about Heaven so we can begin to get a picture of what it will really be like.

I read a book about Heaven a few years ago and the author said, "We cannot know what Heaven is like, but it will be more wonderful and beautiful than we can imagine." I used to say that, too. But in a sense, when we say that, we are dumping cold water on everything the Lord has told us about it. If we cannot envision it, we probably won't look forward to seeing it. I have heard people trying to put down Christians by saying, "You are so heavenly minded, you are no earthly good." But the opposite is true. C. S. Lewis said: "If you read history, you will find that the people who did the most for the present world were those who thought most about the next. Aim at Heaven and you will get the earth thrown in; aim at Earth and you will get neither."[27]

Nearly every time I discuss Heaven, someone will quote one of my favorites verses, I Corinthians 2:9: *"But as it is written, EYE HATH NOT SEEN, NOR EAR HEARD, NEITHER HAVE ENTERED INTO THE HEART OF MAN, THE THINGS WHICH GOD HATH PREPARED FOR THEM THAT LOVE HIM."* But, they do not complete the passage! Read the next verse: *"But God hath revealed them unto us by His Spirit: for the Spirit searcheth all things, yea, the deep things of God."* It is true that we will not know everything about Heaven until we get there, but that verse just told us that the Holy Spirit has revealed much of this to us. How has He done this? Not through dreams and visions, but through God's Holy Word. Deuteronomy 29:29b says that the secret things belong to the Lord. But again, most people do not finish the verse. The rest of it says: *"But those things which are revealed belong to us and our children".* Aren't you glad that God has chosen to reveal some of these things to us?

You do not need to look up into the clouds and try to picture what Heaven will be like. Look around you and imagine what this world would be like without sin and death and pain and decay. Take a walk – smell the roses – imagine everything in its original condition. The dog with the wagging tail, not a snarling beast. The beautiful flowers with no leaves wilting, no dying petunias in front of my house, no weeds choking out the flower bed, a beautiful lawn with no chinch bugs and no water restrictions. Picture the most beautiful place you have ever seen, complete with palm trees, waterfalls, and mountains in the distance. And picture that you are there with the Person you were made for, in the place that was made for you.

You say, "What is that ahead – there in the distance? Is it a feast? A party? Yes! It is a celebration for YOU! If you have had your share of pain and sorrow, Jesus says, *"Be of good cheer; I have overcome the world"* (John 16:33b). Your new house is nearing completion. Moving day is almost here! But sadly, some will not be there. A recent survey indicates that for every American who believes he is going to Hell, there are 120 who believe they are going to Heaven.[28] 120 to

1! Something is wrong with this picture because Jesus said, *"Enter through the narrow gate. For wide is the gate and broad is the road that leads to destruction, and many enter through it. But small is the gate and narrow the road that leads to life, and only a few find it"* (Matthew 7:13-14 NIV). C. S. Lewis sums this up eloquently when he said, "The safest road to Hell is the gradual one – the gentle slope, soft underfoot, without sudden turnings, without signposts."[29]

Sin separates us from a relationship with God because He cannot allow sin in His presence. We cannot enter Heaven with our fallen nature. That is why we need a new birth. Those of you with computers will like the way one writer put it: "Heaven is not our default destination." I am sorry to tell you that unless your sin problem is resolved, you will go to your true default destination – a place called Hell.

I have been to a lot of funerals during my lifetime. You probably have, too. I wish I had kept track of how many. Judging by what is said at most funerals, you would think that everyone is going to Heaven. But we cannot just cross our fingers, and hope we make it. Jesus was very clear about who is going. Revelation 20:15 says you must have your name written in the Lamb's Book of Life.

How do you get your name in the Lamb's Book of Life? *"He that believeth on the Son hath everlasting life …."* (John 3:36a). That is how you get your name written in the Lamb's Book of Life!

I read that in an Indiana cemetery there is a tombstone, more than a hundred years old, with the following inscription:

"Pause, stranger, when you pass me by,
As you are now, so once was I.
As I am now, so you will be,
So prepare for death and follow me."
But then someone came along later, and scratched these words under the existing inscription:
"To follow you, I'm not content, Until I know which way you went."[30]

The Apostle John told us specifically, in his first epistle, I John 5:13 (NIV): *"I write these things to you who believe in the name of the Son of God so that you may know that you have eternal life."* There are very few denominations which teach that you can know you are going to Heaven. It is a cardinal doctrine of the Baptists. Most groups say, "We hope so – we might – you will if you attend church – if you partake of the Lord's Supper each week – if you live a good life," and on and on. They say it is presumptuous to say we can know we are saved. It is not being presumptuous – it is taking God at His word. At least these liberals ought to be honest and pray, "Our Father …. if you are our Father ….".

Scripture says we can know we have eternal life, and we can know we are going to those two great events – the Marriage of the Lamb and the Marriage Supper of the Lamb because our names are written in the Lamb's Book of Life! And the good news is that it is free! The price for our ticket into the Marriage Supper of the Lamb has already been paid. Many Christians do not realize this.

If you have trusted Christ as your Savior, your place at the Marriage Supper of the Lamb has been paid for and you have a reserved seat! But, like any other gift, forgiveness of our sins can be offered, but it is not ours until we choose to receive it. A convicted criminal can be offered a pardon by the Governor, but the courts have ruled that if he or she rejects it, it is not valid. To benefit from it, you must choose to accept it!

Many years ago, it is said that there was a man in Europe who saved up all his money to come to America. After months and months, he finally had just enough money to purchase the ticket on a passenger ship. It was going to take two months to cross the Atlantic, so he brought a suitcase filled with the only food that he could afford – cheese and crackers. When the other passengers on the ship went to the beautiful dining room to have their fancy meals, he would go over into a corner and eat his cheese and crackers.

Week after week, he could smell the delicious foods and wanted to join the other passengers so badly. The last day on the trip, another passenger came over and said, "I see you always over here eating cheese and crackers. Why didn't you come over and have dinner with us?" The man was embarrassed and replied, "I only had enough money to buy my ticket. I didn't have enough to purchase the meals." The other passenger shook his head and said, "Didn't you realize the meals were included in the price of the ticket? You could have eaten with us the whole time."[31]

There are countless groups, religious and secular, that will assure you Heaven is your automatic destination. Or that it can be attained by your hard work and living a good life and joining the right church. This is simply not true. Jesus said, "*Take heed that no man deceive you*" (Matthew 24:4b NIV). Author Randy Alcorn said, "A Christ-centered church is not a showcase for saints – it is a hospital for sinners."[32] The people you are joining with at church are human, imperfect and needy. Most church members are not self-righteous. Those who are should be pitied because they do not understand God's marvelous grace.

Contrary to how cartoons picture it, Hell will be a wretched place – a place of eternal torment and suffering. Is it unloving to speak of Hell? If your friends were going to visit a beautiful cliff in Big Bend National Park, and you know that the road to it is forked, you would alert them of the danger – one fork is a wide, well paved road, but halfway up, there is a sudden drop-off of thousands of feet. The other fork is a gravel road. It does not look all that inviting, but it is straight and safe all the way to the top. Would you tell them only about the paved road? No, hopefully, you would tell them about the safe, gravel road, but you would also warn them about the other road to be avoided. Satan's big lie is that it is unloving to speak to people about Hell. But the truth is there are only two destinations after death: Heaven or Hell. And each is just as real and just as eternal as the other.

I recently was diagnosed with an aggressive form of non-Hodgkin's Lymphoma. Was it unloving when the doctor told me I had a potentially fatal cancer? And shouldn't the doctor have told me what to do about it? Then why don't we tell people about the cancer of sin that leads to physical and spiritual death, and what can be done about it?

You were made for a Person and a place. Jesus is the Person. Heaven is the place. They are a package. You cannot get Heaven without Jesus or Jesus without Heaven. I am looking forward to going there. I am looking forward to long walks with good friends, and endless laughter at no one's expense. I am looking forward to meaningful service with plenty of time for reading and fishing and praising God. For occasional entertainment, I do not rule out stadiums and ballparks. I think competition between friends will be healthy in Heaven. There might even be ice hockey without fights, baseball without brawls, and basketball playoffs where losing is valued just as much as winning. Plus many other enjoyable acts that we have not even thought of. God has given us these things for our enjoyment.

I discovered Psalm 37:4 one day and now it is one of my favorite verses. *"Delight thyself in the LORD; and He shall give thee the desires of thine heart."* God loves nothing more than to make His children happy. And what is the secret to obtaining this happiness? *"Delight thyself in the LORD."* Put the Lord first – delight yourself in Him in everything you do. In the books you read – in the movies you watch – delight yourself in Him and, so long as it is not harmful or hurtful to you or others, He will give you the desires of your heart.

That great preacher, Dr. David Jeremiah, illustrates this perfectly. When he was in college, his goal was to someday be on the radio. It was his lifelong dream. He even got a part time job as a radio disc jockey in his college town. When the Lord started leading him in another direction, he was disappointed, but said, "OK, Lord, I don't know where You are taking me, and I really want to be on the radio, but I am following You wherever you lead me." The Lord led him to seminary where he eventually earned his doctor's degree, and became a pastor of a church in California.

Dr. Jeremiah continued to delight himself in the Lord. Did the Lord keep His promise of giving Dr. Jeremiah the desires of his heart to be on the radio? I will let you judge. He is not a disc jockey in some little backwater town. He is not spinning the latest rap music on some popular radio station. He is broadcasting on the radio everyday on more than 2,200 stations nationwide and around the world, proclaiming the Gospel of Jesus Christ to a potential listening audience of more than 2.7 billion people, not to mention the scores of TV stations he is seen on. The Lord truly gave Dr. Jeremiah the desires of his heart![33]

I am trying to imagine a Heaven that builds on the good we know, while leaving behind the evil. As a ten year old, I thought Heaven might be boring. The streets of gold and gates of pearl did not impress me. What I really like was playing baseball, collecting rocks and tromping in the woods with my favorite hound dog. But after many years, and after many funerals, I have changed the way I think about Heaven. I still have questions. I still have imaginations. But what I really like is the idea of TRUSTING God to make everything great and exciting.

Paul seems to imply this when he talked about his "out-of-body" experience in II Corinthians 12. Apparently, whatever Paul heard and saw was so exhilarating that if he had dwelt on it, it would have distracted him from an ongoing dependence upon the grace of God. I am convinced that the God who taught Paul to depend on Him one day at a time is now teaching us to rely on Him for an eternity that is beyond our ability to understand.

I am convinced that God is planning one surprise after another, and that Heaven will be far more than we have ever dreamed. It will also bring us new friends as well as being with old friends. We have a lot of loved ones just waiting for us to get there! Is there anyone there that you have unfinished business with here? They left here before you could hug them and say, "I am sorry." Or, telling them, "What a blessing you are." We will have ample opportunities to get it right.

Plato, the Greek philosopher, taught that all material things including the human body and the earth, are evil, while immaterial things, like the soul and Heaven are good. This view is called Platonism.[34] It is incredible how Plato has affected the average Christian into thinking that everything in Heaven is without material substance.

Eden was never destroyed! What was destroyed was mankind's ability to live there. There is no indication that Eden was stripped of its physicality, and transformed into a spiritual entity with no physical qualities. Paradise was simply removed to a realm that we, in our sinful bodies, do not have access to. More likely it is in Heaven since we see in Revelation 2:7 that the Tree of Life grows there.

There is a passage we covered earlier that throws a lot of light on Heaven. Turn there for a minute. Revelation 6:9-11: *"And when he had opened the fifth seal, I saw under the altar the souls of them that were slain for the word of God, and for the testimony which they held: And they cried with a loud voice, saying, 'How long, O Lord, holy and true, dost thou not judge and avenge our blood on them that dwell on the earth?' And white robes were given unto every one of them; and it was said unto them, that they should rest yet for a little season, until their fellow servants also and their brethren, that should be killed as they were, should be fulfilled."*

Pretend you are Columbo, the detective, for a minute and you will be surprised how much these little verses tell us about Heaven.

1) When these people died, they immediately went to Heaven (vs. 9). These people in Heaven are the same ones who were killed for Christ while on earth (vs. 9). Our personal history follows us. The martyrs personal history extends directly back to their lives on Earth. "They called out" – (vs. 10) – they expressed their feelings. They raised their voices – they are passionate – they have emotions.

2) They asked God a question, in other words, we do not know everything in Heaven, but we are always learning.

3) They have limited knowledge about what is happening on earth, and they ask God to intervene. They know that their enemies have not yet been destroyed.

4) They remember their lives on earth. Does God wipe away our bad memories? Probably sometimes, but not always. These folks even remember that they were murdered.

5) They see what is happening to their fellow saints, and are praying for them.

6) Though it seems like saints in Heaven are praying for us, there is no indication anywhere in the Bible that we should pray to them. We should pray only to God.

7) Verse 11 says that " …. each of them is given a white robe." We are individuals, and our robes have been made specifically to fit us. It might even be made by a Jewish tailor!

Did you hear about the Jewish fellow who made a robe for Jesus? It was so beautiful that Jesus said, "Let's go into business together." The Jewish man liked the idea, but he wanted his name to be printed on the sign first. But Jesus said "No," and Jesus won the argument – and so, their business became known as …. "Lord and Tailor".

Before we move on, let me address one more question about Heaven that I hear all the time. "How can those in Heaven be aware of people and events on earth because that would make them unhappy because of all the suffering and pain here?" That is a fallacious argument. Christ knows what is taking place on earth, yet His happiness is not diminished in the least. Likewise for the angels. And we have been promised that we will be like Him (I John 3:2).

So let us begin this incredible journey of what Heaven will be like as we look at what the Scriptures tell us. Revelation chapter 21, verse 1 (NASB): *"Then I saw a new heaven and a new earth: for the first heaven and the first earth passed away; and there is no longer any sea."*

One of my former pastors, Dr. L. D. Ball, made this statement which I love so much that I wrote it in my Bible: "Heaven will be a place where we will not struggle to do right – nor fear to do wrong." There will be no possibility for rebellion against God in the New Heaven and the New Earth. One writer asked, "If Adam sinned in his perfect environment of Eden, why can't some man in Heaven someday repeat that sinful act of rebellion?" I will tell you why: because we will have a new heart and mind – the heart and mind of Christ. That is what the new birth is all about.

God is not only holding back His judgment against mankind in our day, He is also holding back His judgment against the earth. We are told in II Peter 3:7: *"But the heavens and the earth, which are now, by the same word are kept in store, reserved unto fire against the day of judgment and perdition of ungodly men."* Why is God waiting? Why is He holding back His judgment of the world? II Peter 3:9 tells us it is so that more people can be saved. This is the day of grace. God has a reluctance to bring it to an end because further opportunities for the lost will be gone. But one day, it will happen, and His patience will have run out. *"A partial hardening has come upon Israel, until the full number of the Gentiles has come in"* (Romans 11:25b ESV). In other words, when the last person accepts Christ as their Savior, then the curtain will come down. But for now, we are left here to preach the Good News of Jesus Christ, offering men and women everywhere their chance to be saved, and to go to this wonderful Heaven that we are exploring.

Verse one tells us *"there is no more sea."* Let me say that one of the most difficult tasks in going through this Book is discerning whether a statement should be taken literally or whether it is symbolic. One of the confusing, and to some people disappointing, statements of Scripture is the verse we just read that says on the New Earth *"there will be no more sea."* When we read this, we might jump to the conclusion that there will be no more swimming, no more surfing, no more fishing and no more fun on the beach. But put this into context. What did the sea mean to John? First, it meant separation. He was on a lonely island, cut off by the sea from his loved ones and friends. To the early believers, no more sea meant no more of the cold, treacherous waters that separate nations, destroy ships and drown loved ones. There will be no more sharks or piranhas or stingrays to unleash their havoc against mankind. If there are, they will have been defanged. To the ancient peoples, the sea was frightful and fearsome – a watery grave.

These early seamen had no compass to guide them in the open waters. On a cloudy day, their ships were absolutely lost without the sun to guide them. Besides that, their ships were frail, and were at the mercy of the treacherous storms. The loss of human life in the sea is beyond calculation. Some theologians believe that the sea was part of the judgment of God. There was some type of sea or water in Genesis 1 because God made the fish and the underwater creatures. But it was probably not to the extent of the vast oceans we see now. I say that, because in Noah's flood, the Bible says the bottoms of the deep were opened up, allowing the release of great bodies of water along with the rain (Genesis 7:11). The oceans covered great land masses, and became a barrier separating what we now call continents, further dividing the human race.

A case can be made that, given the fallen state of nature, the salt in the oceans function as a great antiseptic to cleanse the earth and make life possible here. Dr. Chris Smith, medical consultant at Cambridge University, tells us that the salt in the ocean actually absorbs and cleanses pollution and filth poured into them.[35] On the New Earth, such cleansing will no longer be necessary because there will be no pollution. At my home, we have an underground water filtration system to take out the impurities and make the water pure and soft. Do you know what is poured into the purification tank each month to cleanse the water? Salt crystals!

Even if *"no more sea"* means no more oceans or large bodies of water, we still know from other verses that there will be water in Heaven. Trees and plants will be growing and will need water, and also we are told there will be the River of Life flowing from the throne of God through the main arteries of the city. Rivers must flow somewhere, so I would expect there to be lakes or bodies of water with all the fun and pleasure that goes with them without the dangers of the sea. Someone asked me, "Will there be fishing?" Well, Romans chapter 8:22 says that "the whole creation" is groaning, waiting for its redemption – waiting to be restored to its original beauty and purpose as in the Garden of Eden. The whole creation means all the plant and animal life which includes fish. Is there anything sinful about fishing? I would say no – just as there is nothing sinful about baseball or knitting. Besides, fishing was one of the favorite past times of the Apostles. We are not told, but they may have "painless hooks," and we might have to "throw 'em back."

It is people who inject selfishness and greed into the way man acts that makes these activities sometimes sinful. In and of themselves, they are not sinful – they are neutral. Let me tackle a harder question. Will there be seasons or weather patterns? Most people would be quick to say, "No" because they do not think of Heaven as a physical place. But the New Earth where we will live is a physical place. Now there is a passage that relates to this in Ezekiel 34:26-27: *"And I will make them and the places round about my hill a blessing; and I will cause the shower to come down in his season; there shall be showers of blessing. And the tree of the field shall yield her fruit, and the earth shall yield her increase …."*. This primarily relates to the Millennium, but probably to the New Earth as well.

Is rain a bad thing? Floods are, but rain, per se, is not; it is refreshing. There are fruit bearing trees on the New Earth. We presume that they will be rained on. Will there be snow in some areas? God created snow, and He said that everything He created was good. I believe that just as resurrected people will still have eyes, ears, arms and feet, a resurrected earth will still have rain, snow and wind. Job 37:3-6 says that lightning, thunder, rain and snow all declare the greatness of God. Is there any reason to conclude such things will not be part of the New Earth? None. Of course, no one will die or be injured by such weather just as no one will drown in the River of Life.

There will be no earthquakes or other violent acts of nature that were the result of sin entering the world. In 1985, the late Dr. Richard DeHaan was watching on TV the devastating results of the great earthquake that had just hit Mexico. As he was watching the horrendous scenes of death and destruction, he noticed an inscription at the bottom of the program. It said, "These pictures are brought to you by SIN." Of course, it was referring to the Spanish International Network, but in reality, it was pointing to the culprit in this disaster.

When a tornado comes through and people are killed, I am always amazed that the newscasters and the insurance companies call it an "act of God." They called the tsunami "an act of God." Look at your insurance policy. Most of them exclude major disasters which they call an act of God. So, in one breath they call it an act of God, yet when Dr. Reagan suggested that "Katrina might be a judgment from God" – these same people went ballistic. They cannot have it both ways! I believe that nature in Heaven, including variations in climate and weather, will be a source of joy and pleasure; they will not be destructive.

I love each of the seasons. They each have their own individual beauty and purpose. In Genesis, we find that God created the seasons before the fall of man. The seasons are not, of and by themselves, sinful. Since there will be no more death or dying, God can certainly create a cycle of seasonable beauty apart from death.

One writer asks, "Is the New Earth like our old earth?" and then he answers his own question by saying, "probably not." But I say, if not, then why does God call it a New Earth? Why doesn't He call it something else – like a "New non-earth." The reason is because He wants to convey to us a picture – though it might be incomplete – of where we will live. The primary thing that is new about the New Earth is this: God has eliminated from it: sin, sickness, death, decay, pain, sorrow and anything that would take away from its beauty and wholesomeness.

We would not expect a non-earth to have rivers and mountains and trees and flowers, but God did not promise us a non-earth. He promised us a New Earth. We are told that Abraham *"looked for a city which hath foundations, whose builder and maker is God"* (Hebrews 11:10). If he was looking for that city, don't you think he was imaging what it would be like? In II Peter 3:13 (ESV) we are told, *"But according to his promise we are waiting for new heavens and a new earth in which righteousness dwells."* Are we looking forward to and longing for an unearthly realm? No! We are longing for a New Heaven and a New Earth just as God has promised us!

One commentator put the word "place" in quotations whenever he used the word to denote Heaven or Hell. But Jesus did not say it was a condition – or state of being – or state of mind. He spoke of a house with many rooms – a place that He is preparing for us! And He said He would "come back" and "take" us there (John 14:3). It sounds like an actual place to me.

When 3 year old Lisa's granddaddy suffered heart failure, he was taken to the local hospital where he was pronounced dead. A few weeks later, Lisa and her parents were driving by the hospital when Lisa pointed to it and said, "There's Heaven." She knew her granddaddy was in Heaven – she knew he went to the hospital on the day he died, so she thought the hospital was Heaven. Her mother later wrote, "Lisa's comment made me realize that Heaven is truly a real place and it comforted me greatly."

We have all lost loved ones. Have you ever thought about this – each day we live, brings us one day closer to seeing and talking with that precious one. Wow! What a day that will be – talking again with parents, with children and spouses who have gone on before us. The years of heartache we have experienced will be forever erased. No more having to say goodbye. We will have forever to love and be loved. Like the first heaven and the first earth, all these former things that are painful will have passed away. But make no mistake about it: death will only be glorious to those who have truly accepted Christ as their Savior. Ecclesiastes 11:3 (NLT) says, *"When the clouds are heavy, the rains come down. When a tree falls, whether south or north, there it lies."* That is just a poetic way of saying, when you die, your destiny is fixed. It cannot then be changed. There is a destiny for you and it is decided in your lifetime. It may be a fabulous destiny; it may be a fateful destiny. But this is certain: it will be a final destiny. There is no chance after death to change it. When the tree falls, it lies there. *"Today is the day of salvation"* (II Corinthians 6:2).

When I have witnessed to people over the years, the question always comes up, "What about the heathen in the darkest part of Africa who has never heard the Gospel?" That is simply their way of changing the subject. I usually say, "We are talking about you, and you have heard the Gospel. What are you going to do with it?" The Bible says, *"He that believeth on the Son hath everlasting life: and he that believeth not the Son shall not see life; but the wrath of God abideth on him"* (John 3:36).

Some people tend to make light of death so it will take away the scary part of it. I was surfing the internet recently when I came across this quote by Hunter S. Thompson expressing his view of life. "Life should not be a journey to the grave with the intention of arriving safely in an attractive and well-preserved body, but rather to skid in sideways, chocolate in one hand, martini in the other, body thoroughly used up, totally worn out and screaming, Wooo haa…. What a ride!"[36] All this sounds cute for the moment, but I wonder if he is saying that now. Thompson committed suicide at age 67 in 2005.

Someone asked me, "Do you think that in Heaven we will have the same abilities we had on earth? Will we have the same occupations we have had on earth?" I do not know for sure, but I can tell you a number of occupations that will not exist in Heaven. There will be no more porn actors – no more doctors or nurses. There will be no more lawyers because justice will be dispensed through the authority of the perfect Judge whose rulings are always correct. And thank God! There will be no funeral directors – no undertakers – no life insurance salesmen – no morticians – no gravestone cutters – no obituary writers – because there will be no more death! Death is our last enemy to be defeated and the Bible says that it will be cast into the Lake of Fire along with Satan.

Dr. Albert Einstein was once traveling from Princeton on a train when the conductor came down the aisle, punching the tickets of every passenger. When he came to Dr. Einstein, this great physicist reached in his vest pockets. He could not find his ticket, so he reached in his trouser pockets. It was not there either, so he looked in his briefcase. No ticket. He searched the seat beside him. Finally, the conductor said, "Dr. Einstein, I know who you are. I am sure you bought a ticket. Don't worry about it." The conductor proceeded down the aisle, but when he returned a few moments later, there he saw the Dr. Einstein down on his hands and knees looking under the seat. The conductor rushed up and said, "Dr. Einstein – Dr. Einstein. Don't worry, you don't need a ticket. I know who you are." Dr. Einstein replied, "Young man, I know who I am, too. I just don't know where I'm going."[37] Folks, you know who you are, but do you know where you are going?

Billy Graham lived to be 99 years of age. What a life lived for Christ! A few years ago, he was diagnosed with Parkinson's disease. His beloved wife, Ruth, of nearly 64 years of marriage died a few years before. At the time, he said he could not imagine her not walking by his side after all those years. A reporter was interviewing Dr. Graham later, and asked him, "You have met with kings, presidents, and world renowned ministers. Who was the most dedicated Christian you have ever known?" And without hesitation Dr. Graham said, "My wife, Ruth." What a man – what a wife – and what a marriage![38]

God says Heaven is a place where there are no more tears. What would that mean to someone who had never cried? God says there will be no more death. What would that mean to someone who has never stood beside the grave and never said goodbye to someone they loved more than life itself? God says there will be no more sorrow. What would that mean to someone who has never bowed under the weight of this world's heartaches?

Jan St. Michael said this about Robin, her beautiful daughter: "When Robin was growing up and was afraid of something, I promised her I would never let anything happen to her. But there was nothing I could do for her on that fateful night. At 20 years of age, my beautiful and sweet daughter was hit and killed by a drunk driver." Death is just such a separation – but praise God it is not permanent!

Many of you who are reading this have lost spouses and loved ones, and you look forward to that great Reunion Day. In the Believers Sunday school class which I taught for nearly 20 years, we had 34 of our class members pass away. We faithfully pledged to each other to have a reunion near the Eastern Gate. I can hardly wait! It is because we have experienced such painful things as this that Heaven will be sweeter.

Our grandson, Taylor, asked me my age a number of years ago. I said, "Taylor, I'm 74." He said, "No way …. you mean 64." I said, "No – I am a lot farther down the trail than that." He teared up and hugged me and said, "Granddaddy, I don't know if I can stand it when you die." I immediately said a silent prayer – "Lord, keep me faithful to You and don't ever let me disappoint this boy because I want to share Heaven with him someday." God said He will wipe away our tears (Revelation 21:4), and he will have to – because when we get to Heaven and see our loved ones, it will be hard not to cry – but it will be tears of joy!

Look at verse 2: *"And I John saw the holy city, new Jerusalem, coming down from God out of Heaven, prepared as a bride adorned for her husband."* There is not a more beautiful sight in this earth than a beaming bride looking at her husband as she comes down the aisle! And God compares the New Jerusalem with this incredible sight.

There are three cities that are called Jerusalem that are prominent in Scripture. One is the earthly city which is the home of the Jews today. The second is the rebuilt earthly city which is the home of the Jews during the Millennium. And the other is the heavenly, New Jerusalem which Jesus has been preparing for His Bride for the last 2,000 years.

Jesus said, *"I go and prepare a place for you"* (John 14:3a). A place has substance; it is not a condition, it is a location. And He has prepared it for His Bride. Notice, it does not say that this city IS the bride. It says that the New Jerusalem is prepared *"as a bride adorned for her husband"* (Revelation 21:2b). You will never see a woman any more beautiful than she is on her wedding day. She is adorned for that special occasion. And in the same way, this city is elegant, it is wonderful, it is beautiful and it has been built by the Lord Himself for His precious Bride whom He loves and for whom He gave Himself (Ephesians 5:25). We will learn more about the New Jerusalem and all that it means when we come to the last half of this chapter.

I grew up on a small farm east of Dallas. My Dad always had some pigs, a cow or two and some small calves. Have you ever seen a new calf when it has been let out of a stall for the first time? He is so happy! He will jump and kick his legs in the air! He cannot contain himself. Did you know the Bible says that is exactly the way we will act when we see Heaven for the first time? Listen to Malachi 4:2 (NASB): *"But for you who fear My name, the Sun of Righteousness will rise with healing in its wings; and you will go forth and skip about like calves from the stall."* Wow! Our first day in Heaven and we are jumping around like a calf coming out of a stall. Just think how our friends in the nursing home are going to love that!

Revelation 21:3: *"And I heard a great voice out of heaven saying, Behold, the tabernacle of God is with men, and He will dwell with them, and they shall be His people, and God Himself shall be with them and be their God."* Up to now, God's Tabernacle – where God lives – has been located in Heaven. But in this verse, we discover a change of address for God. He is going to dwell with us, but where? In Heaven? On earth? It is my belief that this earth will be our home forever and ever for all eternity. I think the heavens and the earth are everlasting. They were here before sin entered in. We can learn a lot about Biblical things, just by examining the Greek words that are used.

Jesus said at the end of Matthew, *"Lo, I am with you alway, even unto the end of the world. Amen"* (Matthew 28:20b. What does this phrase mean, *"the end of the world?"* In Scripture, there are three Greek words translated as "world". The first is "ge". It means earth – ground – this terrestrial globe on which we live. It is the first syllable of our word geography. A second

Greek word translated world is "kosmos." Its primary meaning is adornment – embellishment. It is where we get our word cosmetics. When the early Greeks looked at the beautiful and well-ordered universe, they began to call it the kosmos. It eventually became to mean the cultured civilization of mankind – our world. The third Greek word that is translated world is "aion." From it, we get our word "eo" referring to an indefinite period of time. We say that dinosaurs were here eons ago. This is the word that is used whenever the end of the age or end of the world is stated.

Now, we must look at one more Greek word. It is important to nail down the fact that this world – this "ge" – is the same earth that we are going to be living on. Revelation 21:1 says: *"And I saw a new heaven and a new earth: for the first heaven and the first earth were passed away* ("parechomai"). Our Lord used this same expression in Mark 13:31: *"Heaven and earth shall "parechomai", but My words shall not "parechomai".* What did our Lord mean by that statement? This word does not mean annihilation or extinction. Rather, it refers to a change from one place to another, or a change from one condition to another.

For example, a ship would "parechomai" through the sea. It passes through the sea over the horizon. It is gone from sight, but it does not mean that the ship is destroyed; it does not mean that it is annihilated. If I said David got up and "parechomai" through the door, he has not passed out of existence. He has changed from one location or condition to another. That is what John means when he says that the heavens and the earth "parechomai" – passed away. He means they underwent a change – a renovation. They are still here, but are renovated and renewed under the mighty hand of God.

One other quick example. In II Peter chapter 3, Peter is talking about the Lord coming back. The scoffers are saying, *"Where is the promise of his coming? For ever since the fathers fell asleep, all things are continuing as they were from the beginning of creation"* (II Peter 3:4 ESV). And the next verse says, *"For this they* [scoffers] *willingly are ignorant"* – that is dumb on purpose. And verse 6 says that the world in Noah's time was overflowed with water. It says the world perished. The word he used for world is kosmos – the civilized order of man perished, the cities were destroyed and the villages were wiped out, but the earth we live on did not cease to exist.

Then in verse 7 of II Peter 3 (NASB), there is a further word regarding the destiny of this earth we live on. *"But by His word the present heavens and earth are being reserved for fire, kept for the day of judgment and destruction of ungodly men."* He says the earth is being kept by the word of God – waiting for it to be purged by fire, when the ungodly men are judged.

In the words of the Apostle Peter, in Noah's time the world was judged and perished, but did not cease to exist. This judgment of the earth by fire will be a purging, a renewing, rejuvenation, not annihilation. These two passages, in II Peter 3 and one in Revelation 21, speak of the same event – the redemption or cleansing of the planet earth. Why is this cleaning necessary? Because when sin entered the world, all of God's creation was marred and ruined. The earth is contaminated with all its pollution. The animal kingdom for the most part lives off blood and the tearing of flesh. The plant kingdom is almost overrun with all its weeds, thorns and poison ivy.

Even in humanity as we look around we see that cute, adorable child at play. If that child lives to maturity, he or she will eventually turn into an old feeble man or old woman with aches and pains. The curse of sin touches every part of the universe.

Scientists argue over the fate of the human race. Will global warming eventually burn us up? Or will, as some scientists claim, the sun finally burns out, leaving us to die on a frozen planet? We are told that even the stars are burning out! God's creation needs to be renewed! In chapter 22, we will see just what all this means when the curse of sin is finally removed from the earth.

I like the prospect of our home being here on this earth forever. I like almost everything here, but there are some things I do not like and neither does God. How do you feel about this world? Do you feel comfortable in this world? Are you in love with this world, or do you yearn for something better? There are some things in this world that I hate with a passion, and I hope you do, too. Let me hasten to say, I do not hate God's marvelous and beautiful creation. I am not a big traveler, but I have had the privilege of traveling to a few places. I have camped out in the deep, almost jungle-like woods of East Texas. It was so refreshing! Once I slept all night in the woods with my hunting pal, Mike Hyden, pistol at my side, dozing against a tree while a light drizzle fell till daylight. And I loved every minute of it.

I have hiked through the swamp lands of the Everglades, and it seemed that they breathed life from every pore. I have been awed by the beauty of the Rocky Mountains. In fact, I have climbed to the top of Cheyenne Mountain in Colorado, and signed my name to a scroll which I placed in an iron pipe and put under a large boulder. I wonder if it is still there after 70 years.

I have enjoyed a sport called "rock sliding" on a mountain near Colorado Springs, till I fell and had to have several stitches in my head. Cheyenne Mountain is a triple-peaked mountain in El Paso County, Colorado, southwest of downtown Colorado Springs. Its elevation is 9,570 feet. The mountain serves as a host for military, communications, recreational and residential functions. The underground operations center for the North American Aerospace Defense Command (NORAD) was built during the Cold War to monitor North American airspace for missile launches and Soviet military aircraft. Built deep within granite, it was designed to withstand bombing and fallout from a nuclear bomb. Its function broadened with the end of the Cold War, and then many of its functions were transferred to Peterson Air Force Base in 2006.[39]

I never cease to be amazed at the unique beauty of the Southwest and the beautiful hill country of South Texas. I have seen the indescribable Canadian snow peaks and witnessed the awesome power of Niagara Falls. I have seen the sunset at the edge of the Judean wilderness and breathed in the stark beauty of the land of Israel. I have sat breathless in the middle of the Sea of Galilee, and watched those blue waves, bluer than blue itself, lap gently against the side of the sail boat.

When I say, "There are some things I hate in the world," I am not speaking of God's wonderful creation. I am speaking instead of the kosmos – the evil world system. I hate it with a passion. Let me give you some examples of what I am taking about. I hate a world in which thousands of babies are murdered each day in their mothers' wombs. I detest a world where young people in their prime have their lives destroyed by drugs and alcohol. I hate a world that makes a mockery of justice; the rich are protected while the poor are given long prison sentences. I abhor a world that applauds vulgar entertainers such as Madonna and Howard Stern.

Something is wrong with the picture when professional athletes are paid tens of millions of dollars while thousands of homeless people have no place to sleep at night. Or a world where governments have tried to remove God from public life. I detest a world where thousands of people starve to death every day. Or a world system that calls good evil, and evil good by demanding that homosexuality be recognized as an alternative lifestyle – a lifestyle that God calls an abomination. Pastor Robert Jeffress summed it up this way: "Gay is not OK. What homosexuals do is filthy. It is so degrading that it is beyond description. And it is their filthy behavior that explains why they are so much more prone to disease."[40] I hate a world where people's lives are cut short by cancer, diabetes, and heart attacks. I loathe a world that uses the name of my wonderful Lord as a filthy curse word.

I hope you now understand what I mean when I say there are things in this world I would change in a heartbeat if I could. Let us see if God shares this same feeling about the things of this world. Let us look at what James, the brother of Jesus, had to say about this in James 4:4 (NASB): *"You adulteresses, do you not know that friendship with the world is hostility toward God? Therefore whoever wishes to be a friend of the world makes himself an enemy of God."* That is strong language folks. He says those who are friends of this world, who are comfortable with this world, are spiritual adulterers because they have forsaken their Lord for this world. *"Friendship with the world is hostility toward God."*

Turn to I John chapter 2, verse 15. Here is the Apostle John writing in his old age. He must be over 90 at this time, and he says: *"Love not the world, neither the things that are in the world. If any man love the world, the love of the Father is not in him."* I do not know how anything could be clearer than that. How do you constantly remind yourself that you are not to be a friend of this world? Here is one suggestion. I have a little card I carry in my billfold at all times. It is not American Express, but I never leave home without it. Every now and then I just pull it out and read it. I must if I am to keep my sanity in this crazy world. It says: "Lord – keep me looking upward." That is all it says. Folks, this attitude is essential if you are going to grow in spiritual maturity, and get to the point where you are not in bondage to the things of the world. "Lord – keep me looking upward."

Year after year, we make New Year's resolutions, not only in our personal life, but the country does it in its national life as well. But things just seem to get worse and worse. Fires gut our forests. Pollution contaminates our air. Droughts dry up our water sources. Did you know that 71% of the earth's surface is covered by water?[41] Our blood is made up primarily of plasma which is 90% water.[42] Our flesh is made up of 65% water. But mankind is utilizing only about 10% of all water available. Granted, much of this unutilized water contains salt, and it is very expensive to purify it. Nevertheless, it can be done.[43] And here is a surprising fact. We cannot actually waste the total volume of water; we can waste the water that has been processed for our use. But, scientists tell us, that not one drop of water has been lost. The same amount of water here on earth now was here when Joshua entered the Promised Land. However, water changes form. It goes from liquid to vapor to solid and back to liquid. But the total amount of $H2O$ remains the same.[44]

How we look forward to the time when the curse is removed from this globe and we experience life on earth as it was during the days of Eden! What a life that will be! The Almighty God descends to earth with His heavenly host, to begin global operations from the New Jerusalem. Why would anyone want to miss that? In the present Church Age, God is with us through the indwelling of the Holy Spirit, but in the Eternal State, He will actually dwell with us and we will commune directly with Him. This simply fulfills a promise made to the children of Israel long ago in Leviticus 26:11a-12: *"I will set My tabernacle among you .... And I will walk among you, and will be your God, and ye shall be My people."* This is echoed again in Zechariah 2:11 which says: *"And many nations shall be joined to the LORD in that day, and shall be My people; and I will dwell in the midst of thee."*

Heaven is so glorious, so wonderful that I cannot get my arms around it. The vast difficulty in describing Heaven is illustrated by the various writers of Scripture. For example, the Apostle Paul was caught up in the third Heaven where God dwells. He writes about it in II Corinthians 12:1-4. Does Paul give us real insight into the features of Heaven? Does he say what he saw and what he heard? No! All the Apostle says is this: he heard words that are unspeakable and that are not lawful for a man to utter. We are reminded of our human frailties by I Corinthians 2:9: *"EYE HATH NOT SEEN, NOR EAR HEARD, NEITHER HAVE ENTERED INTO THE HEART OF MAN, THE THINGS WHICH GOD HATH PREPARED FOR THEM THAT LOVE HIM."* Our mind cannot even imagine it. But the next verse, I Corinthians 2:10 says, *"But God hath revealed them unto us by His Spirit: for the Spirit searcheth all things, yea, the deep things of God."* Paul is saying there is a language of the soul and with our eyes of faith we can feel these things – we can sense them even though we cannot fully describe them.

Now look at verse 4 of this 21ˢᵗ chapter of Revelation which brings us some wonderful news. *"And God shall wipe away all tears from their eyes; and there shall be no more death, neither sorrow, nor crying, neither shall there be any more pain: for the former things are passed away."* You could not improve on the beauty of this passage. It would be like trying to paint a rose. The painting could never do justice to the rose itself. From the moment sin entered the Garden of Eden, sorrow has been multiplied to the human race. Job puts it best in Job 5:7: " *.... man is born into trouble, as the sparks fly upward ....".*

In Eden, God announced that mankind would universally experience sorrow, pain, sweat and death. Now God announces that these things will come to an end. However, getting rid of it came at a great price. Jesus Himself had to experience sorrow, pain and death. Is it any wonder that He was described in Isaiah 53:4a as having *".... borne our griefs, and carried our sorrows."*

This truth we read in Revelation 21, verse 4, was first revealed in Isaiah 25:8a: *"He will swallow up death in victory; and the Lord God will wipe away tears from off all faces."* I know that as long as we are in this earthly body, tears will be a part of us. Until we arrive in Heaven itself, God's people will know how to cry. We may forget how to laugh, but we will never forget how to cry.

Not until we enter the New Jerusalem will God wipe away the tears from our eyes (Revelation 21:4). All humanity shares in suffering. It does not matter your station in life nor how much or how little money you have, tears and suffering are the common denominator of the human race. Sometimes we feel we cannot bear such sorrow. When my faithful dog, Hanna, who had been my loyal friend for 14 years, passed away, I seriously wondered if I would ever laugh again. But Paul reminded us that one day we will look back on all our sorrows and they will seem quite small because we will be looking at the big picture then.

We will understand clearly the words in II Corinthians 4:17-18: *"For our light affliction which is but for a moment, worketh for us a far more exceeding and eternal weight of glory; While we look not at the things which are seen, but at the things which are not seen: for the things which are seen are temporal; but the things which are not seen are eternal."* Here is how Dr. Eugene Peterson paraphrases this verse: *"These hard times are like small potatoes compared to the coming good times .... the things we see now are here today, and gone tomorrow. But the things we can't see now will last forever!"*[45] Small potatoes! This is so grand and elegant, how do we put this in crude earthly language? I have thought many times, "Oh, how I would like for the Rapture to come – what joy it would be if it came today." But another part of me says give the unbelievers another chance.

Charles Spurgeon, that great Baptist preacher of a century ago, said a most unusual thing. I have never heard it from anyone else. "If I had my choice between being raptured at the coming of the Lord, and taken up into glory and changed in a moment, in the twinkling of an eye, at the last trump; if I had my choice between [that] and dying and being resurrected, I would choose to die the agonies of death ….". Spurgeon continued: "I [had rather] experience the suffering of my Lord, the pangs of death, to die and be buried that I might experience the power of the resurrection of God as He raises me up into glory."[46] Such a marvelous insight into death brings tears to our eyes!

The years of heartache we have experienced will be forever erased. No more having to say goodbye. We will have forever to love and be loved. Like the first heaven and the first earth, all these former things that are painful will have passed away. But make no mistake about it: death will only be glorious to those who have accepted Christ as their Savior. Ecclesiastes 11:3 (NLT) says, "*When the clouds are heavy, the rains come down. When a tree falls, whether north or south, there it lies.*" That is just a poetic way of saying, when you die, your destiny is fixed. It cannot then be changed. There is a destiny for you, and it is decided by you in your lifetime. It may be a fabulous destiny. It may be a fateful destiny. But listen: it will be a final destiny. There is no chance after death to change it. Now is the day of salvation!

When I was 8, I had a friend by the name of William Jennings McClain who was a year older than me. We were great friends at Forney Avenue Baptist Church in Dallas and I looked forward to seeing him every Sunday. On January 20, 1942, William and two of his friends, Billie Allen and James Good, both 8 years old, were playing close to his house at a nearby creek. It was a few weeks after Christmas, and the water in the drainage ditch had frozen over.

William walked out on the ice and it broke through, sending him plunging into the 5 foot freezing water. The two friends ran and got his mother who raced to the scene and jumped into the water. She found William and was trying to pull him out of the water when two men heard the commotion. They had been cutting wood in the area. They ran to the creek and pulled both Mrs. McClain and William out of the water. An ambulance arrived on the scene and the driver used a "pullmotor"– a resuscitation device for drowning victims to try to revive William, but without success. The funeral was held at Forney Avenue Baptist Church with Bro. George McGuire officiating.

The boys in his Sunday school class were chosen as pallbearers. It was my first time to be a pallbearer. I remember the special music at the service, *Footsteps of Jesus.*" And while I was riding to the burial site at Laurel Land in Oak Cliff, I vividly remember praying fervently as only an 8 year old could pray that William would be resurrected before he was put into the ground. I was miffed at the other boys in the car with me. They were laughing and joking with each other, and seemingly had no concern or respect for the loss of our friend. A couple of weeks after the funeral, his mother, Mrs. McClain, called my mother. She said that she wanted me to have William's Marx electric train that he had just gotten for Christmas. I have faithfully kept it for over 75 years, and it still runs! Often over the years, we have had the train circling our Christmas tree amid the presents. A short time ago, I went to Laurel Land Memorial Park, and viewed William's burial place. I look forward with eager anticipation to resurrection morning when God will wipe away all our tears, and I will see my buddy, William, again – around the Throne of Grace. Some of you reading this have lost spouses, parents and friends, and you cannot wait for that great Reunion Day!

It was sad times like this that reminds me of the time we lived outside the city on a couple of acres on Old Military Trail. This was before old age and mowing forced us to move into town. Our mailbox was near the road which was a couple of hundred feet from our house. One morning in the dead of winter, I saw Carla in her trusty mail truck stop at our mailbox. We looked forward to seeing the mail truck each day as we had few cars driving down Old Military Trail. I was expecting a special package so without thinking, I ran out of the house without a coat and down the long driveway to our mailbox. It was bitterly cold – the temperature was in the single digits. There was an open field behind us, so there was nothing to break that brisk wind that blew out of the north. To make things worse, the ground was covered with several inches of snow. I retrieved my key and opened the mailbox, pulled out the mail, and was about to make a dash for the house when a shiny magazine with bright colors caught my attention. On a closer look, it was a catalogue advertising beautiful plants and vegetables. I usually didn't buy anything from them, but I always enjoyed looking at their colorful pictures.

A variety of beautiful flowers graced the front cover. On the back were huge Big Boy tomatoes that you could almost taste. As I stared looking at the colorful pictures, I was completely unaware of how cold it really was. Suddenly, I was in the world of sweet corn, okra, bright orange carrots and green beans. I turned a page and there was purple and I thought, "My, it's been a long time since I have seen rhubarb in the stores, and Arlene's rhubarb cobbler is out of this world!" We had a small garden, but nothing like this. The smell of roses and gardenias hung in the air as I flipped through the pages. For a few moments, it was spring! Winter was past with its freezing temperatures, its ice and snow. I could almost feel the warmth of the sun as it seemingly penetrated my body. But then the biting gusts of wind brought me back to reality. As the cold hit my bones I began to shiver. I ran back to the house as fast as my legs would carry me. When inside and I was beginning to thaw, I thought how my moments at the mailbox mirrored our Christian walk. Christians are not immune to the cold. Jesus never promised us a rose garden in this life. Just like the discomforts of winter, we live through disappointments and sorrows as friends let us down, illnesses wrack our body, and we gather at the cemetery to say our goodbyes to our loved ones.

It is during our journey through life that we feel the heartaches and the hurts just like unbelievers who do not share our hope of the resurrection. The storms of life batter us along with those who have no hope. But here is the big difference. In our hard times, in our times of intense hurting, we have a seed catalogue picturing better times ahead. It is called the

Bible. We can leaf through it and find that it tells us not *"to grieve as those who have no hope"* (I Thessalonians 4:13). Why? Because spring is on the way! Our faith catalogue tells us that resurrection and harvest is just around the corner. It says that Christ is the first fruits; then we who are His will be resurrected at His coming.

Jesus told us that in this world, we are going to suffer persecution, pain and sorrow. Even Jesus was not immune to suffering. He went through everything that we go through and much more. But thank you Jesus for your great and precious promises that you will be with us in the good times and the bad. You told us that you will never leave us nor forsake us. And like the seed catalogue that comes in the dead of winter, you give us hope for springtime because we know – we know – that roses WILL bloom again!

Look at verse 5. The One on the throne begins to speak. *"And He that sat upon the throne said, 'Behold, I make all things new.' And He said unto me, 'Write: for these words are true and faithful.'"* Sometimes, it is difficult to determine exactly who is speaking because the descriptions of Christ and God the Father are many times indistinguishable one from another. That is because, *"Whoever has seen me has seen the Father"* (John 14:9b ESV). Notice that this is not a frivolous promise in verse 5. Instead, it is a fact: *"I [will] make all things new."*

Have you ever heard of the law of entropy, also called the second law of thermodynamics? In layman's terms, it describes things that progress from order to disorder. This is so apparent, how can there be any question about it? It disproves evolution in every area of life you observe. I do not know about you, but my experience at home is that everything is wearing out. Dr. Jobe Martin clearly explains this in his book.[47] We have to replace the dishwasher. The Venetian blinds break. We have to re-paint. We have to repair the roof. We have not observed any instances where we have come home and said, "Gee – the paint on this house just renewed itself." But when Christ says, *"Behold, I make all things new"* (Revelation 21:5) – they will stay new. We can throw away our computer button that says "refresh"!

You may have different responsibilities in Heaven, but I know one thing you will not be doing. You will not be cleaning the rust off the gates of Heaven. And you ladies will not have to dust the walls of Jasper or sweep the streets of gold! All things will remain eternally young and fresh and new, just as they were in the week of creation itself. The curse of decay will have been removed. The second law of thermodynamics will have been erased.

Even our bodies will be renewed. I do not know about you, but I am looking forward to a new body – one that is like what we had at age 33 according to my pastor, Bro. Jim. I suspect that those who die in old age here on earth will find themselves young again, and those who die in infancy will grow to full maturity. At any rate, we will be in our prime because when Christ appears, the Bible says we will be like Him (I John 3:2b).

Jesus says in Revelation 21:5, "Write this down – these words are faithful and true because

I cannot lie." I was reading an article by a liberal theologian who was trying to say that the Apostles took the words of Jesus and twisted them, and in writing the New Testament, turned them into a theology that even Jesus would not recognize.

He went on to say, "Jesus never wrote a word in the Bible nor did He ever tell His disciples what to write down." I say, "Sir, in all due respect, did you ever read the last Book of the Bible?" In the first chapter of Revelation, Jesus tells John: *"Write the things which thou hast seen, and the things which are, and the things which shall be hereafter"* (Revelation 1:19). Sure sounds to me like a command to write! And then, here in chapter 21, verse 5 Jesus says: *"Write: for these words are true and faithful."* Sounds like another command to write. His words are true and faithful – no wonder He is called our Solid Rock!

Now look at verse 6: *"And He said unto me, 'It is done. I am the Alpha and Omega, the beginning and the end. I will give unto him that is athirst of the fountain of the water of life freely.'"* Jesus told the Samaritan woman at the well that if she drank the water He provided, she would never thirst again. I think the water of life is both symbolic and literal. It is symbolic of the Holy Spirit who gives us living water, and it is literal as we see a sparkling, pure river flowing through the Holy City to be enjoyed throughout the ages (Revelation 22:1). Alpha and Omega – the First and the Last. Christ loves this name for Himself. He also calls Himself by this name in Revelation 1:8. Alpha and Omega are the first and last letters of the Greek alphabet.

The first time I went to Israel was in 1994. We had with us an American Indian from Oklahoma. His name is Richard Pickup. He is a powerful and fiery evangelist, and is a full-blood American Indian. He was honored recently by the Cherokee Nation.[48] Richard was asked to bring a message while we were sitting on the side of the Mount of Beatitudes where Jesus delivered His famous "Sermon on the Mount." Richard said that God took a dirty old Indian, laying in a filthy ditch in Oklahoma, drunk as a skunk, and changed him into a faithful preacher of the Gospel of Grace. Richard forcibly drove home the fact that Jesus is "Alpha and Omega – He is our A to Z and all points in between." I will never forget his powerful message there on the hill of the Beatitudes. Toward the end of his sermon, when he had shown that Jesus is every letter of the alphabet, someone said, "You left out the letter X". Richard thought for a minute and then answered, "The Bible 'say-z' (the pronunciation he always used) in Philippians 2:9, *'Wherefore God also hath highly X-HALTED Jesus, and given him a name which is above every name!'"* What a great preacher!

Today, we will learn even more good news. Chapter 21, verse 7 says: *"He that overcometh shall inherit all things: and I will be His God, and he shall be My Son."* You will remember that we read some promises in chapters 2 and 3 of Revelation regarding overcomers. In Revelation 2:26, Jesus promises to give power over the nations to those who are overcomers. In chapter 3, verse 5, Jesus makes a promise to the overcomers that He will not blot their names out of the Book of Life. And in verse 7, He says that those who overcome will inherit all things. Wow! These overcomers sound like a special group. Do you remember how to get in that group so that you will inherit all things? The same person that is penning these words, the Apostle John, defines these overcomers for us. In I John 5:4 (NIV), he says: *"For everyone born of God has overcome the world. This is the victory that has overcome the world, even our faith."* And then he nails it down in the next verse by asking, *"Who is he that overcomes the world?"* And then he answers, *"Only he who believes that Jesus is the Son of God."*

Christ has made the provision of a full inheritance for us. This is because we have a son/daughter relationship. Romans 8:16-17a says: *"The Spirit Himself beareth witness with our spirit, that we are the children of God. And if children, then heirs; heirs of God, and joint-heirs with Christ …. ".* The overcomer becomes both a child and an heir of the mighty God of creation.

We are reminded of the words of Job as he contemplated the greatness of God, *"What is man, that thou shouldest magnify him? And that that thou shouldest set thine heart upon him?"* Job 7:17). It is hard to believe that the God of Creation who made all the wonderful things we see around us – loves and cares about us. Until Jesus came, the Jews saw God as the One who thundered from Mount Zion, and who frightened the people. But when Jesus came, God revealed Himself in a whole new way. Scripture says that when we see Jesus, we see the Father (John 14:9). God is showing us that He counts us as sons and daughters and, as such, we will inherit with Christ all things.

A story is told by Rev. Woodrow W. Kroll illustrating our inheritance. It was about a wealthy man who lived in a large mansion in the Midwest. He lived there with his only son since his wife had died a few years before. He loved to collect rare works of art from Picasso to Rembrandt. When the Viet Nam conflict broke out, the son went to war. He died in battle while rescuing another soldier. When his father was notified, he grieved deeply for his only son. Just before Christmas of that year, there was a knock at the old man's door. He opened the door and saw a young man holding a large package. "May I help you?" the old gentleman asked. "Sir, you don't know me, but I am the soldier for whom your son gave his life. He was carrying me to safety when he was killed. He often talked about you, and your love for art."

The young man held out his package. "I know this isn't much. I'm not really a great artist, but I think your son would have wanted you to have this." The father opened the package and discovered it was a portrait of his son painted by the young man standing before him. The father stared in awe at the way the soldier had captured the personality of his son in the painting. The father was so moved that tears welled up in his eyes and he offered to pay the young man for the picture. "Oh, no sir. I could never repay your son for what he did – this is a gift from me." The father hung the portrait over his mantle. Every time visitors came to his home to see his rare art collection, he always took them to see the painting of his son.

A few months later, the father died. It was announced in the paper that a great auction would be held to sell the man's famous art collection. Art enthusiasts were beside themselves as they showed up at the auction, anxious to bid on such rare works of art. On the platform sat the painting of the old man's son. The auctioneer pounded his gavel. "We will start the biding with this picture of the owner's son. Who will make the first bid?" There was silence. They could tell this was not a famous painting. It was simply a portrait of the man's son, painted by a fellow soldier. Then a voice in the back of the room shouted, "We came to see the famous paintings – skip this one." But the auctioneer persisted. "Will someone start the bidding for this picture? Who will bid $200? Or even $100?"

Another voice shouted angrily, "We didn't come to see this painting. We came to see the Van Goghs and the Rembrandts. Get on with the real bids." But the auctioneer continued, "The son, the son. Who will bid on the son?" Finally, a voice came from the very back of the gallery. It was the longtime gardener of the man and his son. "I will give $10 for the painting. I would give you more, but I'm poor, and that is all I have." The auctioneer continued: "We have a $10 bid – $10 – who will bid $20?" The crowd murmured and became restless. They did not want the picture of the son; they wanted the more famous paintings for their collections. The auctioneer pounded the gavel. "Going once – going twice – sold for $10 to the gentleman in the back."

A man sitting on the second row shouted, "Now let's get on with the real bidding." The auctioneer laid down his gavel. "I'm sorry, but according to the will of the deceased, the auction is over – the bidding is now closed." The angry crowd shouted, "Over? What do you mean over? What about the rest of the paintings?" The auctioneer said, "I'm sorry, but the will of the deceased is very clear – whoever gets the son, gets everything."[49] God gave His Son to die on a cruel cross to insure our inheritance. And it is true today, just as in this illustration, whoever gets the Son, gets everything!

But unfortunately, everyone will not share in this inheritance. False teachers and false churches have led the unsuspecting to enter the wide gate that leads to destruction. Brooksy was a member of my Sunday school class for many years. One day he showed me an advertisement in *Time Magazine*. It was by the Unitarian Church which teaches that everyone will eventually be saved. The ad said, "Is God keeping you from church? Then join us – you can make God to be anything you want to."

I have only been to one Unitarian funeral in my life. My co-worker and friend, Jack, stayed home on Labor Day where "it was safe." It was a hot day and he was trimming bushes when a swarm of wasps stung him multiple times and he had a bad reaction. His wife called an ambulance, but he was brain dead when he reached the hospital. At the Unitarian funeral, Jesus was not mentioned, and there was no Scripture reading. There were two readings, one from Shakespeare and one from Ralph Waldo Emerson. As their ad said, "You can make God to be anything you want to." My goodness – how they will be held accountable for leading people down the path to destruction!

Verse 8 tells us some of the other folks who will not be in Heaven: *"But the fearful, and unbelieving, and the abominable, and murderers, and whoremongers, and sorcerers, and idolaters, and all liars, shall have their part in the lake which burneth with fire and brimstone: which is the second death."* It is crystal clear – not everyone is going to be saved. They will not get to enjoy God's new creation. There was an article published in the *Los Angeles Times* by staff writer, Connie Kang, in which she asks, "Is your next stop the Pearly Gates or Hell?"[50] The article published their survey results: 119 out of every 120 Americans believe they will go to Heaven when they die. That is not what Jesus said. He said that the gate into Heaven is narrow and that very few are going to find it (Matthew 7:14). For the same reason, we must not believe Satan's lie that it is unloving to speak to people about Hell. There are only two possible destinations: Heaven or Hell, and each is just as real and eternal as the other. This verse tells us that the Lake of Fire is also called the second death. The first death is when you die physically and the second death is when you die spiritually.

Let's look at this list for a moment at some of those who will not be found in Heaven. The fearful – those who reject Christ because someone might make fun of them. In II Timothy 1:7a-8a, we are told: *"For God hath not given us the spirit of fear"* ....". And then verse 8 says: *"Be not thou therefore ashamed of the testimony of our Lord ...."*. Do you get embarrassed in a secular crowd if someone brings up the topic of Christ? Are you ashamed to admit you are a follower of Him? If so, you may be one of the fearful that is mentioned here. Then it lists the unbelieving – those who reject Christ as the only way to salvation. They just do not believe what the Bible says.

The abominable – those who engage in vile practices that God despises. The murderers – those who willfully take people's lives as well as those who carry hatred in their hearts for other people. Speaking of the words murder and abominable, there is another word that encompasses both of them. It is called abortion. God calls it an abomination, and I would be held accountable if I did not tell you what the Scriptures have to say about it. President Franklin Delano Roosevelt called December 7, 1941, "a day that will live in infamy." We could say the same thing about January 22, 1973 in the case of Roe vs. Wade. Let me put this in perspective. A little over 400,000 Americans lost their lives as a result of the action taken on December 7, 1941. But close to 60 million Americans lost their lives as a result of the action taken on January 22, 1973 …. 400,000 compared to 60 million!

In the last few chapters of Deuteronomy, that great Jewish patriarch, Moses, was coming to the end of his days. He thought back over everything that God had enabled him to do for the Jewish people. Moses had led them out of the clutches of Pharaoh in Egypt and he had brought them to the edge of the Promised Land. A lot had transpired during his lifetime and now, he is telling his people "goodbye." As a father's parting words to his children, this great man of God is giving final instructions to those he considered his spiritual children.

He called them all together, and this was what he said in Deuteronomy 30:19 (NLT): *"Today I have given you the choice between life and death, between blessings and curses. I call on Heaven and earth to witness the choice you make. Oh, that you would choose life, that you and your descendants might live."* Choose life!

I want to tell you about a cancer that is eating at the very soul of America. Some call it abortion. God calls it an abomination. Liberals call it "freedom of choice." Freedom of choice to do what? Why don't they finish the sentence? Freedom of choice to commit murder. This whole controversy could be cleared up if people would admit what the Bible proclaims – that life begins at conception!

Consider these four cases:

Case #1. There is a traveling preacher and his wife who are living in poverty. They already have fourteen children. Now she finds out she is pregnant with the fifteenth child. They are very poor and probably will be unable to afford a doctor's care. Considering their poverty, the excessive world population and the number of children they already have, would you recommend she get an abortion?

Case #2. The grandmother is an alcoholic and the father spends his evenings drinking in the taverns. His mother has tuberculosis. She has already given birth to four children. The first child is blind, the second child died, the third child is deaf, and the fourth child has tuberculosis. Now the mother is pregnant again. Given the extreme situation, would you recommend an abortion?

Case #3. A white man raped a thirteen year old black girl and now she is pregnant. Her family lives in extreme poverty; in fact, to survive, they often have to steal food. If you were her parents, would you recommend or require her to have an abortion?

Case #4. A fifteen year old girl is pregnant. She is not married and lives in a cave in an outback area with very little money or resources. The man she hopes to marry is not the father of the baby. There is no hospital or doctor available. Most people would recommend an abortion in each of these cases. Would you?

Let us consider that you recommended an abortion in each of these cases. Now look at the facts.

Case #1: You would have just killed the world famous Methodist preacher John Wesley.
Case #2: You would have just killed the great composer Ludwig van Beethoven.
Case #3: You would have just killed Ethel Waters, the marvelous black Gospel singer.
Case #4: You would have just killed Jesus Christ, the savior of the world![51]

I will be honest with you; abortion is a tough subject. I get very emotional about it because I see no gray areas. When God tells me something, I believe it. There is no wiggle room – not even in our Constitution. According to the Constitution of the United States, the Supreme Court is only supposed to interpret laws, not make them. When Iraq was struggling to write a constitution, someone said, "Let's send them ours – we don't use it anymore."

After the uprisings in Egypt and the overthrow of President Mubarak, Egypt wanted to write a constitution for their new government. Supreme Court Justice Ruth Bader Ginsberg suggested that Egyptian revolutionaries not use the U.S. Constitution as a model after the Arab Spring uprising. "I would not look to the U.S. Constitution if I were drafting a constitution," Ginsberg said in an interview. However, she was basing that on her belief that the Constitution should have more clearly addressed the rights of women and minorities. "I might look to the constitution of South Africa …. it really is a great piece of work."[52]

On January 22, 1973, nine black-robed individuals rendered an unbelievable decision – that it was legal to kill an unborn baby. They were very appropriately dressed in black because they have never made a darker, more ominous decision. They ruled that all you need are 3 things. 1) An unborn child; 2) a willing mother; and 3) a willing doctor to perform that grizzly task. First, it goes against the original Hippocratic Oath that doctors swear to uphold – and then some do not follow it. It says, "I will neither give a deadly drug to anybody who asked for it, nor will I make a suggestion to this effect." Similarly, the original Oath prohibits giving a woman an abortive remedy. In other words, the Oath clearly precludes euthanasia and abortion. But many doctors get around that by saying that the Oath is outdated for modern times, and the swearing to abide by it is simply a formality.[53]

Secondly, an abortion goes against a mother's natural inclinations. She should be willing to give her life for her baby – not kill the baby for selfish reasons. I am not a lawyer, praise the Lord, but I do have enough common sense to read and understand the Constitution of the United States. I read it regularly. In the 14th Amendment, the Supreme Court found a woman's right to privacy! There is nothing that even remotely suggests this so-called right in the entire Constitution, let alone the 14th Amendment!

Here is the 14th Amendment to the U.S. Constitution in its entirety: "All persons born or naturalized in the United States and subject to the jurisdiction thereof, are citizens of the United States and of the State wherein they reside. No State shall make or enforce any law which shall abridge the privileges or immunities of citizens of the United States; nor shall any State deprive any person of life, liberty, or property, without due process of law; nor deny to any person, within its jurisdiction the equal protection of the laws."[54] Did you find a woman's right to privacy in this Amendment? The Supreme Court did! Look at this section: "No state shall make or enforce any law …. [depriving] any person of life, liberty, or property ….". The Constitution is very clear. It states that every person is entitled to protection under the law. These unborn babies are executed without trial and without legal representation – which is a basic right under the Constitution.

To get around the Constitution, the Supreme Court had to come to the conclusion that an unborn child is not a person; otherwise they would have no case. I have a question to ask those men and women in black robes that sanctimoniously sit on the High Court taking the place of God in matters of life and death. If you are pronounced dead when your heart stops beating, why aren't you pronounced alive when your heart starts beating? A baby's heart starts beating 18 days after conception!! Is this an elephant? A donkey? Or a baby human? If it is a baby human, then it is a person and is protected under the Constitution of the United States! God crafted the womb to provide the best care and protection possible for the unborn – it is warm – it is cushioned – but in today's society, a womb is sometimes the most dangerous place for a baby to be.

We hear from the pulpits across the country that we need spiritual revival in our country. Let me ask you point blank – how can we expect God to send spiritual revival when we continue to murder babies in the womb? Abortions in the U.S. in 1995 were over 1,200,000, but have decreased every year since then to the latest number of just over 600,000.[55] That is an improvement, but we need to do much more. Pro-life churches and organizations have faithfully continued to educate people to the fact that life begins at conception.

It is hard to believe but, since Roe vs. Wade, we have murdered more unborn babies than the combined population of the states of Texas, Louisiana, Arkansas, New Mexico, Oklahoma, Kansas, Nebraska, Missouri, Iowa, South Dakota, North Dakota, Minnesota, and West Virginia. Don't you wish all those babies could have grown up to help pay for Social Security?! And what are the chances that one of those 60 million aborted babies would have found a cure for cancer or Alzheimer's or even Arthritis?

Yet our government says, "We are not killing the babies fast enough." And so, doctors who refuse to do this grizzly task on the grounds of religious objections, risk having their medical licenses revoked. And if they can kill babies, it is a short step to kill the elderly. After all, many are now saying that old people are a drag on society. Why should the young people have to pay to support them? A sobering statement to consider is this one: "If parents can pay doctors to kill their children, the time will come when those same children will pay doctors to kill their parents."[56] It is not coming – it is here. It is legal for the doctor with your consent to kill your parents that are terminally ill in the states of California, Colorado, Oregon, Vermont, Washington and Washington, D. C. In Oregon they have even given it a soothing name – "Death with Dignity."[57] All you have to show in court is that they do not have a quality of life. But who defines that? Quality of life is so subjective. It can mean anything such as, "I can outrun Mimi." "I can swim farther than Jack." Does that mean that I have a better quality of life than they do? No, that is no test for quality of life.

Here is what one reviewer said about Supreme Court Justice Neil Gorsuch's new book on euthanasia:

"In clear terms accessible to the general reader, Neil Gorsuch thoroughly assesses the strengths and weaknesses of leading contemporary ethical arguments for assisted suicide and euthanasia. He explores evidence and case histories from the Netherlands and Oregon, where the practices have been legalized. He analyzes libertarian and autonomy-based arguments for legalization as well as the impact of key U.S. Supreme Court decisions on the debate. And he examines the history and evolution of laws and attitudes regarding assisted suicide and euthanasia in American society. After assessing the strengths and weaknesses of arguments for assisted suicide and euthanasia, Gorsuch builds a nuanced, novel, and powerful moral and legal argument against legalization, one based on a principle that, surprisingly, has largely been overlooked in the debate–the idea that human life is intrinsically valuable and that intentional killing is always wrong."[58]

I do not know everything that the new healthcare law will provide, but I can assure you it will not be long until, at a certain age, a person's condition will be too expensive to be treated. It is coming folks! And while we are at it, they will include the crippled, the Down syndrome kids, the mentally challenged, the blind, the ALS patients, the paraplegic, etc. Hitler did. He said they were a "drain on society." Iceland has already starting touting that it has eliminated the Down syndrome problem. How? They are able to determine if an unborn is a Down syndrome baby – and they simply abort it. That's their solution![59]

Abortion is so emotionally charged, I do not think we have ever had a real debate on the subject. Let us look at the abortion question from two different viewpoints – what the Bible says, and for those who reject the Bible. The basic question in the argument is, "When does life begin?" If an unborn child is a person, then that child is protected by the United States Constitution! The abortionist cannot stand to refer to the unborn as a baby. They had to coin a new word not known in centuries past – a fetus. "I've got a fetus growing in me." It sounds like a disease.

Anti-abortionists go to great lengths to de-humanize the unborn. Here are some of the atrocious terms used by them to describe babies growing in the womb: "a gobbet of meat protruding from a human womb" (Philip Wylie); "a child-to-be" (Glanville Williams); "the fetal-placental unit" (A. I. Csapo); "fallopian and uterine cell matter" (Joseph Fletcher); "a part of the mother" (Oliver Wendell Holmes); "a part of the mother's body" (Thomas Szasz); "unwanted fetal tissue" (Ellen Frankfort); "sub-human non-personhood" (F. Raymond Marks); "the child who-might-have-been" (James Kidd); "so much garbage" (Peter Stanley); "a collection of cells" (Malcolm Potts); "potential life" (Supreme Court Justice Blackmun) and "a non-viable fetus ex utero" by the National Commission for the Protection of Human Subjects of Biomedical and Behavioral Research (p. 196,197).[60]

According to Sarah Weddington, the lawyer who brought this issue to the Supreme Court in 1973, the unborn child is a "chunk of meat." Then why doesn't someone ask her, "Why don't we remove it and sell it to Kroger? There's nothing wrong with it – it's just a chuck of meat." Weddington argued before the court that an unborn child is not a "person" protected by the U.S. Constitution until it has developed to the point of viability, defined as "potentially able to live outside the mother's womb, albeit with artificial aid."[61] I would like to see if Sarah Weddington is 'viable' at the North Pole, naked and without any help from anyone.

The number one dufus award goes to Supreme Court Justice Harry Blackmun, who wrote the majority decision in Roe vs. Wade, and said that the unborn child is "potential life."[62] Potential life?! Duh! Sounds like it is dead and might come to life some day! Carol Tobias, president of the National Right to Life Committee, called January 22, 1973, "the saddest day in American history."[63]

In 1856, the Supreme Court of the United States ruled that black babies born of slave parents were "non-persons" much in the same way that our modern Court has ruled that unborn babies are "non-persons." But our all-knowing Supreme Court cannot tell us what exactly they are – except maybe "chucks of meat" or "potential life." The 1856 vote in the Supreme Court ruled that Negroes could never be American citizens. The vote was 7-2. And a little over a hundred years later, in 1973, our Supreme Court ruled that unborn babies were – non-persons. And the vote was also 7-2! Two awful decisions that are a blight on our judicial system. In 1857, the Supreme Court heard arguments in the "Dred-Scott Case" which involved a Negro slave. In their historic decision which the Supreme Court got wrong, it ruled that all Negroes were not and could never be citizens of the United States.[64]

Did you know you can be charged up to $250,000 for destroying an eagle egg, but you can destroy babies in the womb without any penalty?[65] Because everyone knows an eagle is in that egg!! It does not take a rocket scientist to know there is a baby in the womb! I confess I have not always been pro-life. When I was in college, I was not sure what to think about the issue.

I went on a long journey – research – reading – digging – and studying to find out what God thinks about this practice called "choice." The first question I had to answer was this: "Is an unborn baby a human or is it a non-person as Hitler claimed. I turned to science. I discovered that medical science is forced to admit that when the egg and sperm come together at conception that egg has EVERYTHING that determines that baby's characteristics, even its own DNA![66] THERE IS NOTHING FURTHER THAT THE BABY ACQUIRES OR REQUIRES TO MAKE IT A HUMAN BEING! From that moment on, the baby receives nothing but food and water and oxygen from the mother. If it is a non-human at that point, it is going to grow into a big non-human. Because all it is doing is growing! There is only an argument about this when politics and money clash with morality and science.

Psalm 139:13-16 (NLT) says: *"You made all the delicate inner parts of my body and knit me together in my mother's womb. Thank You for making me so wonderfully complex! Your workmanship is marvelous – and how well I know it. You watched me as I was being formed in utter seclusion, as I was woven together in the dark of the womb. You saw me before I was born. Every day of my life was recorded in Your book. Every moment was laid out before a single day had passed."* Scientists now have to admit these statements are true! Your DNA which you received at conception determines all of your characteristics. It says every moment was laid out before a single day had passed!! Does this sound like just a chunk of meat?

Look at Jeremiah 1:5 (NLT): *"I knew you before I formed you in your mother's womb. Before you were born I set you apart and appointed you as My spokesman to the world."*

We are told that after Mary the mother of Jesus became pregnant she visited her relative, Elizabeth, who was pregnant with John the Baptist. And the Bible says when Mary entered the house and said, "Hello Elizabeth" – at the sound of Mary's voice, the unborn John the Baptist in the womb of Elizabeth leaped within her and she was filled with the Holy Spirit. John the Baptist as an unborn child in the womb, supernaturally leaped with joy in the presence of His Savior. So who is right about the nature of the unborn, God or the U. S. Supreme Court? I know who I am sticking with!

God told Isaiah in Isaiah 44:24a (NIV): *"This is what the LORD says – Your Redeemer, who formed you in the womb …."*. Job said in 10:8a, 10 (NLT): *"You formed me with Your hands …. you guided my conception and formed me in the womb."* It is clear that the Bible is not talking about "so much garbage" – it is talking about a person!

So, the real question is not about choice! The real question is, "Is it murder to kill an innocent person?" What do you think? Let us start with Exodus 20:13: *"Thou shalt not kill."* The liberals love this verse when it comes to capital punishment. But I wish they would read the whole Bible. They say the Ten Commandments were done away with by the cross. However, a commandment was given to man regarding how to apply justice long before the Ten Commandments were given to Moses. Genesis 9:6: *"If anyone takes a human life, that person's life will also be taken by human hands. For God made human beings in His own image."* Clear enough.

But let us look closer at the commandment, *"Thou shalt not kill"* (Exodus 20:13). The Jews had ten different words for killing. There was a word for murder. There was a different word for killing in war; there was a different word for killing in self-defense. There was another word for accidental killing. There was another word for capital punishment by the authorities, etc. The Hebrew word used here in Exodus 20:13 is "ratsach" and means cold-blooded murder. The verse actually says, "Thou shalt not commit cold-blooded murder!" The Bible says in Proverbs 6:17, that God hates *"hands that shed innocent blood."* Tell me one human being who is more innocent than an unborn child. You cannot do it!

Here is the clincher that settled it for me. Exodus 21:22. (NLT): *"Now suppose two people are fighting, and in the process, they hurt a pregnant woman so her child is born prematurely. If no further harm results, then the person responsible must pay damages in the amount the woman's husband demands and the judges approve."* Two men are fighting. In the process a pregnant woman is hit, and it causes her to deliver prematurely. But the child is unhurt. So the offender must pay the doctor bill and any other charges the judges require; but read verse 23. *"But if harm results, then the offender must be punished according to the injury. If the result is death, the offender must be executed."*

This injury is referring to either the woman or the unborn – otherwise the fact that she is pregnant would not have been mentioned in the first place. It does not get any plainer than that! If injury results in the death of either the mother or the baby in the womb, then the death penalty is required. That proves beyond the shadow of a doubt that the Bible considers the unborn baby a person, and the killing of an unborn person as murder! And to rule otherwise as the Supreme Court did in Roe vs. Wade calls into play the condemnation of Isaiah in 5:20 (ESV): *"Woe to those who call evil good and good evil, who put darkness for light and light for darkness, who put bitter for sweet and sweet for bitter!"* There will be a payday someday because God said He *"never lets the guilty go unpunished"* (Nahum 1:3a).

Congresswoman Nancy Pelosi, a Roman Catholic, flew to Rome for a private meeting with Pope Benedict XVI in 2009. I usually do not praise the pope, but in this case, insiders say that the pope gave Mrs. Pelosi a grand dressing down over abortion. He should have ex-communicated her on the spot. The official report of the meeting said he stressed to her that everyone, especially our lawmakers, should pass laws protecting the unborn.[67]

When I was in the business world a number of years ago, I worked with a lot of liberals who did not see a thing wrong with abortion – no more than clipping an unwanted hangnail. One of my friends, Gloria, was a staunch Episcopalian – and she strongly supported abortion, and she happened to be pregnant. I remember discussing the issue with her one day, and things began to heat up. She said indignantly, "I should have a choice as to what I do with MY body." I said, "I agree with you, Gloria. If you want to abort your body, go right ahead. But we are not talking about your body. We are talking about another person's body – a guest whom you invited to live inside you for nine months, and God has not given you the right to terminate that agreement!

I have a great question to ask abortionists. Why limit the mother's right of abortion up to the time of birth? It is a fact that when President Obama was a senator in Illinois, a bill was introduced called the "Induced Infant Liability Act." It simply said that, if an abortion was botched by the doctor and the baby was born alive, that baby would be protected and given the right to live. Illinois Senator Obama, along with other liberal Senators, voted that in such cases it was OK to allow the doctor to go ahead and kill the baby because that was the mother's original intent. The public should have decided right then that those liberal politicians forfeited their right to hold any future public office. But, that shows you how far off the trail our society has wandered. May God have mercy![68]

So I ask, "Why limit the age of the baby?" There are probably several mothers who would like to extend their option to kill the baby through the terrible twos. What about extending abortion rights to age 16? "I told you, Junior, to clean up your room." Blam! Blam! I know one thing: kids would behave better and their grades would come up if they knew this was an option. And you would not have to remind them of the fifth commandment: honor thy Father and Mother.

I have assembled the arguments that the Abortionists have put forth and I have taken the six best ones. Let us look at them.

1) The fetus is not human. Evolution has proved this. Over 100 years ago, an evolutionist by the name of Ernst Haeckel compared a human embryo with that of various animals, and drew sketches to show that the human fetus goes from being a fish to a reptile to a mammal.

   Answer: Thirty years after Hegel published his findings, he admitted under oath that he outright lied – that he doctored the sketches to make them look like humans. We have known that for over 85 years, but some of our textbooks that are in use today still contain his lying sketches. Dr. Jonathan Wells, who holds a PhD. in Molecular and Cell Biology from the University of California at Berkley, wrote: "As it happens, all of these examples [such as Haeckel's drawings], as well as many others, purportedly standing as evidence of evolution, turn out to be incorrect. Not just slightly off. Not just slightly mistaken. On the subject of Darwinian evolution, the texts contained massive distortions and even faked evidence."[69]

2) The fetus is not viable. The Supreme Court ruled that an unborn baby cannot live on its own, but is dependent upon its mother for nourishment.

Answer: Take a newborn which everyone agrees is a baby. Lay it on the sidewalk – it cannot survive without someone giving it food and help. Neither could you survive if you were lying naked at the North Pole without any help. That is no test for whether the unborn is human or not! Good grief; we expect the Supreme Court to use common sense. Besides, I know some 35 year olds that cannot survive on their own without help from Mother and Dad.

3) The baby may be unwanted.

Answer: We have many children ages 3-15 that are unwanted. Child Protection Services has scores of them. Shall should it be legal to kill them?

4) The baby may be a financial burden.

Answer: Tell me one that isn't. If that was the criterion, parents could kill a lot of children that are a drain on their finances.

5) The baby may have been conceived as a result of a rape.

Answer: A study in Minneapolis showed that out of 3,500 rapes in the city, only one pregnancy resulted. It happens, but it is rare. But there is no reason to kill the innocent baby! If you have to kill someone, kill the rapist! And if the mother does not want the child, there are scores of takers waiting in line to adopt the baby. In the early 1900s, a young black woman was raped. The doctors wanted her to have an abortion. The woman said no, and eventually her young child was born. And as a result of that mother's decision, literally thousands upon thousands were blessed when that child – born out of rape – grew up and sang, "His Eye is On the Sparrow." That baby turned out to be none other than the great Ethel Waters! Other celebrities born out of rape are: Eartha Kitt, Jesse Jackson and the Fox News anchor, Kelly Wright.[70]

6) Abortion is not a crime – it is legal.

Answer: That is the same argument Hitler used to kill the Jews. He said, "Jews are not human, and besides, it is legal to kill them." That argument did not hold up at the Nuremberg Trials, and it will not hold up at God's Great White Throne Judgment either.

Rebecca Kiessling confronted Gov. Rick Perry regarding rape being a legal reason for abortion. Here is what she said to Gov. Perry: "When you make rape a legal reason for abortion, it is like you are saying to me that I deserved the death penalty for the crimes of my father. According to the U.S. Supreme Court, my father didn't even deserve the death penalty. The

Supreme Court has said there is no death penalty for rapists. But you say that I, as the innocent child of rape, deserved the death penalty." And Perry said, "No, no, I don't believe that." Her confrontation with him made a difference. Perry now insists that the life of the mother should be the only consideration when it comes to abortion. If the mother's life is not at jeopardy, then there should be no abortion.[71]

We all see the problem but what can we do about it? More violence is certainly not the solution. We can pray. We can let God know we do not stand with those murderers. God knows whether your soul is vexed every day – just like Lot when he was surrounded by the evils of Sodom. And for goodness sake – vote like God would vote – vote for those candidates who put LIFE above politics and money! I have known people who have voted for pro-choice candidates because they thought their union retirement funds might be at risk. What will God think about that when He said, *"For where your treasure is, there your heart will be also"*? (Matthew 6:21 ESV).

We need to show compassion to those young mothers-to-be who are confused and do not know what to do. A lady in our church, Barbara stands ready to help and encourage young mothers in making the right decision.

I want to end on a note of encouragement. Share it with anyone who has ever had an abortion – and it is this: God loves you. He wants to forgive you and heal you and put His arms around you. Trust Him and ask Him to show you what to do to keep others from going through this terrible experience. May God have mercy on America – may we confess our sin of killing the innocent and of being complacent in allowing this to happen on our watch. Pray that God will heal our land, that our Supreme Court will reverse Roe vs. Wade and that God bring spiritual revival to America!

Back to our list of those who will be barred from Heaven. The whoremongers – those who engage in sexual immorality either through fornication (pre-marital sex) or adultery (extra-marital sex) or perverted sex. The sorcerers – those who engage in illicit drugs. The word sorcerer in Greek is pharmakeus from which we get our word pharmacy. The sorcerers often used these drugs to induce occult experiences, to get a high and escape the realities of life. The Idolaters are those who worship or embrace anything that takes the place of God. All liars. How many of us do not fall into that category? Satan himself is called the father of liars (John 8:44).

God says these people will not be in the Kingdom of God. Oh my goodness – we have done our share of sinning in our life and we are guilty as charged. How can we ever get to Heaven? When we trusted Christ as our Savior, He gave us a new nature. It lives alongside our old nature which is not dead yet. Consequently, there is a difference between a person who slips and lies occasionally, and one who is an habitual liar.

Let me share an insight with you that proves beyond a shadow of a doubt that everyone reading this is a liar. It is because one time you lived in this realm of lying. Listen to I John

2:22a: *"Who is a liar, but he that denieth that Jesus is the Christ?"* You have not always believed in Christ. There was a point in time when you were not saved, and therefore, you did not believe God. In refusing to believe God, you were calling Him a liar – and since God cannot lie, it makes you a liar. God said, *"He that believeth on the Son of God hath the witness in himself: he that believeth not God hath made Him a liar; because he believeth not the record that God gave of His Son"* (I John 5:10). Scripture is plain and simple. Those in whom sinning is a way of life will not be in God's new creation. And in the midst of telling about the New Heaven and New Earth, God warns of the necessity to commit our lives to Jesus Christ.

This terrible list of those who will not be in the new Kingdom is mentioned again in I Corinthians 6:9-10 (NLT). But I do not want you to miss an important distinction here. Remember, this is written to Christians: *"Don't you know that those who do wrong will have no share in the Kingdom of God? Don't fool yourselves. Those who indulge in sexual sin, who are idol worshipers, adulterers, male prostitutes, homosexuals, thieves, greedy people, drunkards, abusers, and swindlers – none of these will have a share in the kingdom of God."* And now listen to the next verse (verse 11) which is a blockbuster: *"There was a time when some of you were just like that, but now your sins have been washed away, and you have been set apart for God. You have been made right with God because of what the Lord Jesus Christ and the Spirit of our God have done for you."* Did you find yourself on that list? I found myself there. But here is the distinction. I am so grateful that it said, though we were once like that, now our sins have been washed away. And now we can look forward to joy beyond what we can imagine.

A little later, we will get a description of the city – the New Jerusalem. It is inlaid with precious stones. These jewels are some of the hardest substances known. They indicate the New Earth is solid. It is physical. It is not a misty vapor. There will be lots of duties in our heavenly home. Will these new bodies get tired? Probably not in the same way they do now, but I think they will require times of refreshing and this is always enjoyable. In Revelation 14:13, it says that we will rest. And Hebrews 4:10-11 says we will enjoy that rest. So you see, the problem is not that the Bible does not tell us much about Heaven. It is that we do not pay attention to what it tells us.

When God created the heavens and the earth, He declared them to be "very good." At no time did He renounce His creation. He is not going to abandon it. He is going to restore it. And then, the goal of Ephesians 1:10 (NLT) will be fulfilled: *"And this is the plan: At the right time He will bring everything together under the authority of Christ – everything in Heaven and on earth."*

God has not given up on His original creation. Somehow, we have ignored a whole vocabulary of Biblical terms that start with the letters "re." The words are: reconcile, redeem, restore, recover, return, renew, regenerate, resurrect." Each of these "re" terms as I like to call them, means going back to a condition that was ruined or lost by Adam and restoring it to its perfect condition. For example, "redemption" means to buy back that which was originally owned. "Reconciliation" means the restoring of a prior friendship or relationship that had been severed. "Renewal" means restoring something to its original state. "Resurrection" means becoming alive again, not creating a new entity, but resurrecting the old, and giving it new life, new properties and a new meaning.

Professor Albert Wolters writes, "[God] refuses to abandon the work of His hands; in fact, He sacrificed His own Son to save His original project. [Mankind] which has botched its original mandate is given another chance in Christ ....".[72] God could have scrapped the whole thing, and sent us to Hell and started over. But that would have defeated God's original plan and purpose. So instead, God has planned to redeem and restore His original creation. He is the ultimate salvage artist – redeeming what has become junk and restoring its value.

If I was trying to express this as our modern advertisers such as Master Card does, here is what I would say: "Collecting a bag of old aluminum cans and turning them in for recycling, $4; brushing the dust off an old Babe Ruth baseball card and selling it on eBay, $500; trading in your old hip for new hip, $28,000; cleaning this filthy, rotten world of all its pain, sorrow and death, and turning it into the most incredible Garden of Eden imaginable along with its residents who are made pure and holy and who have bodies that are eternally perfect, priceless! Peter preached in Acts 3:21 (NLT): "[Christ] *must remain in Heaven until the time for the final restoration of all things, as God promised long ago through His prophets.*"

When a friend or relative dies, we say that he or she "passed away." That sounds final. Did they cease to exist? No! And just as we will be raised and given new resurrected bodies, so shall the earth be resurrected to a New Earth. The Greek word used here for new is "kainos." Paul uses the same word "kainos" when he speaks of a believer becoming a new creation (II Corinthians 5:17). The New Earth will be the same as old earth in the same sense that you became a new creation when you were saved, yet you are still the same person. Different, yes, but also the same you. The earth will be different, but it will be the same earth yet "new and improved."

We have an interesting conversation between Peter and our Lord in Matthew 19:27 (NIV). Peter had asked, "*We have left everything to follow you! What then will there be for us?*" Here is the Lord's reply in Matthew 19:28 (NIV): "*I tell you the truth, at the renewal of all things, when the Son of Man sits on His glorious throne, you who have followed Me will also sit on twelve thrones ....*".

The point I want to emphasize is this: Jesus said, "*at the renewal of all things*" – He did not say "after the destruction of all things" nor "after the abandonment of all things" but at the "*renewal of all things.*"

This is not a small point of semantics. It draws an important distinction between two schools of theology. One school says there will be a complete destruction of physical things, and

Heaven will consist of only non-physical, mystical stuff. And the other school says that there will be a complete cleansing and renewal of God's original work, restoring all of creation to even greater heights than in the beginning. That is exactly what Christ's incarnation, death and resurrection secured – a renewed humanity living upon a renewed earth. If God annihilates the present cosmos, Satan will have won a great victory. He will have succeeded in botching God's creation to such an extent that God would have had to start over. But Satan has not won such a victory. On the contrary, Satan has been decisively defeated. God will reveal the full impact of that defeat when He renews this very earth on which Satan deceived mankind.

Dr. John Piper, noted commentator, writes this: "When Scripture says that the present earth and heavens will pass away, it does not mean that they will go out of existence, but that there will be such a change in them that their present condition passes away."[73] We might say, "The caterpillar passes away and then the beautiful butterfly emerges." There is a real passing away, but there is also, a real connection with the past. Hundreds of years ago, Isaiah was given an insight into this New Heaven and New Earth. He describes it in Isaiah chapters 60, 65 and 66.

Most of us are unaccustomed to thinking of nations, rulers, civilizations, cultures in Heaven, but Isaiah chapter 60 clearly depicts that the New Earth will be just that – earthly! Isaiah was an incredible prophet that God used mightily. And for those who want to spiritualize all of this, let me point out something that is not easily dismissed. All of Isaiah's prophecies regarding Christ's first coming, and they are numerous, were fulfilled literally. Born of a virgin; born in the city of Bethlehem; betrayed by a friend; silent before His accusers – and on and on. All of these First Coming prophecies were literally fulfilled, so it is reasonable to expect that all the Second Coming prophecies will also be literally fulfilled, including the New Heaven and the New Earth.

Theologian Anthony Hoekema correctly sums it up this way: "Since one of the results of sin had been death, the promised victory must somehow involve the removal of death. Further, since another result of sin was the banishment of mankind from the Garden of Eden, from which mankind was supposed to rule the world for God, it would seem that the victory should also mean man's restoration to some kind of restored Paradise from which he could once again properly and perfectly rule the earth."[74]

When Adam sinned, God did not sit idly by, nor did He relinquish His claim on mankind and the earth. Instead, He immediately revealed His plan in Genesis 3:15 to defeat Satan and restore all things to their original perfection. Without realizing it, you have probably sung this very plan in the hymn, *This is My Father's World*. A line in the third verse says, "Jesus who died shall be satisfied, and earth and Heaven be one."[75] Look at it this way. Heaven is where God lives. Earth is where we live. Jesus Christ, the God-Man, forever links God to mankind and thereby forever links Heaven and earth.

As you know, Satan successfully tempted Adam in the Garden of Eden causing all of mankind's problems. Satan tried to tempt Jesus and defeat Him just as he did with Adam. But Jesus resisted Satan with the Word of God and successfully rebuffed him (Matthew 4). But then Jesus was crucified and three days later was resurrected, thus assuring Satan's final defeat. Satan's grip on this world was loosened by the cross. It is still strong, but once he is cast into the Lake of Fire, and God re-fashions the old earth into the New Earth, mankind and earth will forever slip from Satan's grimy hands never to be touched by him again.

Christ has already defeated Satan. This happened at the cross, but the full scope of this victory is yet to be realized. Satan is like a condemned man, but his sentence has not yet been carried out. Some judgments have been delayed as have some benefits. For example, our bodies are wearing out. They are subject to illness and pain. But if our physical healing is included in the verse *"by His stripes we are healed"* (Isaiah 53:5) – how do we explain this when we get sick again? Here is the truth of the matter. Sometimes in God's will we are temporarily healed. But we will get sick again. Some of the benefits of the cross are deferred – such as our permanent healing. But when our redemption is fully realized, we will have bodies that will never get sick, never wear out and never die – they are incorruptible (I Corinthians 15:52-53).

Let us explore this more fully since this 53rd chapter of Isaiah has sometimes caused confusion in the Body of Christ by well-meaning teachers. Beginning at verse 4 through verse 5: *"Surely He hath borne our griefs"* – the Hebrew is "nasa" – literally, our sicknesses. *"Surely He hath borne our griefs* [sicknesses], *and carried our sorrows: yet we did esteem Him stricken, smitten of God, and afflicted. But He was wounded for our transgressions, He was bruised for our iniquities: the chastisement of our peace was upon Him; and with His stripes we are healed."*

There has been a lot of confusion about these verses. Did Jesus heal us of our sicknesses or did He not? Some go as far as to say that it is ALWAYS God's will for you to be healed of all your ailments, and they say, "If you are ill, it is your own fault because you do not have enough faith." We know that is not true because the Apostle Paul prayed three times without success for his ailment to be removed. So we reiterate, some benefits of the cross are delayed including our permanent healing when we receive our glorified bodies.

Are we healed spiritually? Are we saved from our sins? The answer is yes – but in phases. We have been saved from sin; we are being saved from sin; and we will be saved from sin. Let me explain. We HAVE been saved from the penalty of sin when we accepted Christ; we ARE being saved every day from the power of sin as we rely upon the Holy Spirit; and we WILL be saved from the presence of sin when we go to our home in Heaven.

Let me throw more light on Isaiah 53. Satan's power and influence has always been limited by God. We see this as far back as Job. When Satan was dealing with Job, it was within the boundaries that God had laid down for him.

There is no question that Satan was further limited by the cross. After Jesus' ascension, He sent the Holy Spirit to reside in the Believers. And His word tells us that *"He that is in you is greater than he that is in the world"* (I John 4:4). Satan is further limited during the Millennium. He is bound and chained and thrown into the Bottomless Pit, and the Bible gives us the reason: *" …. that he should deceive the nations no more"* (Revelation 20:3b). So, he is further limited. Satan's ultimate limitation will be after the Millennium when he is taken and thrown into the Lake of Fire, to be forever banned from interfering with God or His people. However, currently, the Bible says he marches to and fro upon the earth seeking whom he may devour.

Mary Baker Eddy and Christian Science followers claim that there is no such thing as sin, sickness or death. It is all an illusion; it is all in your mind. Mrs. Eddy says Jesus did not really die. He was alive the whole time, hiding in the tomb, and then He came out to show everyone there is no such thing as death.[76]

I must relate to you one of my favorite stories involving pain which Christian Science says is an illusion. It is in a rare book entitled *Christian Science* that is in my library written by Mark Twain. Mark Twain was a contemporary of Mary Baker Eddy. He followed her antics and teachings regularly in the newspapers. Twain even talked with a Christian Science lecturer to learn more about this strange religion. The teacher had spent about thirty minutes explaining to him that there is no such thing as pain – that we only imagine we have pain. Pain does not really exist, it is just our imagination. At that moment, the teacher stepped backward onto the tail of a large Siamese cat who was sleeping on the floor. "Yeohhhh……!!!!!" The cat screamed and let out some cat profanities. Mark Twain couldn't resist: "Ma'am, you say that pain is simply your imagination?" "That's right." "Well, Ma'am, that cat sure has a good imagination!"[77]

Verse 9: *"And there came unto me one of the seven angels which had the seven vials full of the seven last plagues, and talked with me, saying, 'Come hither. I will show thee the Bride, the Lamb's wife.'"* Jesus is proud of His Bride. When I attend a wedding, the highlight for me is watching the groom's face as his bride comes down the aisle. And here, the angel is anxious to show off the Lamb's Bride. He says, "Come on – let me show you her dazzling beauty."

John's head is probably spinning by now. In chapter 17, an angel told John to "Come over here" in order to show him the judgment of the great harlot, the false church. Here in chapter 21, an angel tells him to "Come over here" to see the Bride, the Lamb's wife. In both cases, John was shown a great city – Babylon in the first instance, and the New Jerusalem in the second.

In the case of Babylon, John saw the great city of the last days brought down to destruction to disappear forever. (Revelation 18:21). In the case of the New Jerusalem, he saw it coming down from Heaven with glory to endure forever.

The Lamb's wife, the Bride, is the Church. As you know, she has already been raptured (by this time in Scripture) to meet her Groom in the sky – she has already been given her rewards based on her faithfulness - she has already been clothed in fine white linen, evidencing her righteousness – she has attended the Marriage ceremony – and celebrated joyously at the Marriage Supper of the Lamb – and has enjoyed her 1,000 year honeymoon in the Millennial Kingdom. And now John sees her in her new home, the New Jerusalem.

Let me ask you this: why did Magellan and Columbus and other explorers head out seeking a "new world?" It is because we have an inbred desire to explore new things. That is the way we are made! We were made to be seekers of knowledge. We are curious by our very nature.

In high school, I remember studying the Bathysphere that William Beebe invented about the time I was born. Its purpose was to take man to the floor of the ocean. It was a round steel bubble with windows, crude by today's standards, but it enabled man to go farther under the sea than he had ever been – over 3,000 feet down, off the coast of Bermuda.[78]

Decades later, in the other direction, we were all astounded when we witnessed a space flight that traveled all the way to the moon, and we heard the voice of the first man to ever walk on the moon, Commander Neil Armstrong, saying "That's one small step for man, one giant leap for mankind."[79] We are born with an innate desire for knowledge. As we seek and explore God's beautiful creation, we will become increasingly motivated to explore all the wonders that He has made. Probably the first place we will want to explore is our new home and capital of the New Earth, the New Jerusalem. There will be other cities on the New Earth, but none to compare with the capital. The King of kings Himself will call the New Earth home!

A city is composed of people. That is why it is called a city. Sometimes we say that a city is wicked; or we might say, the city is very generous. When we do that, we are referring to the people, not the buildings or streets. The physical identity of the Holy City will include rivers, trees, streets and mansions. But the real identity of the city will be the Lamb and His Bride – that is what truly makes it the Holy City. A perfect union will exist between Jesus and His Church, similar to the union that exists between a bridegroom and his bride.

Just as we are made unique and different from our neighbors right now, it is likely that our cultural tastes will differ in Heaven so that some of us will prefer to gather in auditoriums for great cultural events, while others will want to withdraw to quietly feed the ducks on a nearby lake. So, John views New Jerusalem not only as an actual dwelling place, but also the home of the Bride. He is immediately impressed by the brilliance, the size and beauty of the city.

Verse 10: *"And he carried me away in the spirit to a great and high mountain, and showed me that great city, the holy Jerusalem, descending out of Heaven from God."*

Right now, the Holy City is being built along with its many mansions. It has been under construction for 2,000 years. And if God created this beautiful earth in just 6 days, just think what the Holy City will look like after 2,000 years! Verse 10 says that the Holy City will descend out of Heaven. There is a lot of debate among theologians as to how far it will descend. Some think it will descend until it touches the earth. Others think it will be suspended above the earth. We are not told specifically. One thing is for sure. What goes on in the Holy City will be more important than what takes place in the New Earth because the Holy City will be the headquarters of God's new creation.

Jesus went away to do two things. One is to pray for us. He intercedes for us as our High Priest because we need His prayers and His power to withstand the wiles of the Devil. Hebrew 7:25 confirms this: *"Wherefore He is able also to save them to the uttermost that come unto God by Him, seeing He ever liveth to make intercession for them."* Quicker than you can blink your eye, Satan would destroy us were it not for the never-ending intercession by our Lord and Savior. But there is a second reason Jesus went away, and this was to prepare a place for us, to build a home and a city worthy of His Bride. It will be wonderful to behold, planned down to the finest detail by the Master Architect.

Scripture describes Heaven as both a country (Luke 19:12; Hebrews 11:14-16) and a city (Hebrews 12:22; 13:14; Revelation 21:2). Fifteen times in Revelation 21 and 22 we are told that we will live with God in a city. The detailed description of the architecture all suggest that the term "city" is not just a figure of speech. It is an actual location. After all, where do we expect physically resurrected people to live if not in a physical environment?

Everyone knows what a city is – a place with buildings, streets and residences occupied by people, and subject to a common government with common rules. Cities have inhabitants, visitors, cultural events, religious activities, education, entertainment and athletics. If the capital city of the New Earth does not have these defining characteristics of a city, it would seem misleading for Scripture to repeatedly call it a city.

We will see a more detailed description of the city with its walls, its gates, its streets and its dimensions later in this chapter. But let's go on to verse 11: *"Having the glory of God: and her light was like unto a stone most precious, even like a jasper stone, clear as crystal."* The presence of God in the Holy City will cause it to shine with His glory. His pure light will burst forth like the brilliance of an expensive jewel. We are told it is crystal clear and is like a jasper. The diamond seems to fit the description of a jasper closer than any other precious stone known to man. The jasper was clear and is a symbol of purity and holiness. It was one of the twelve stones in the breastplate of the High Priest (Exodus 28:20).

I am fortunate that the Lord gave me a spouse that is not extravagant, and is not overly desirous of precious stones. When I went to Israel several years ago, all Arlene asked me to bring back for her was a Star of David necklace. While we were in Tel Aviv, we had an opportunity to visit the Diamond Factory. It is the largest diamond cutter facility in the world where they cut and polish raw diamonds to be shipped all over the globe. We were told that 90% of all raw diamonds, whether they come from the mines in Africa or whether they are owned by DeBeers and come from elsewhere, are sent to Israel to be cut, polished and graded. It is an occupation that requires 25 years or more to become an expert. It runs in the family, and usually the diamond craftsman can point to the fact that his father and grandfather were in the same business before him.[80]

Bro. Jim, my pastor, was my roommate and when we visited the Diamond Factory, he volunteered to sweep it out every night for free. They did not take him up on it. At any rate, he said, "Wayne, while we are at the Diamond Factory, let's buy something and surprise our wives with it when we get home." I agreed it was a great idea. So we did. I picked out a gold Star of David, and then I picked out a small diamond to be set in the center of it. They said it would take about 15 minutes. In the meantime, I charged it on Master Card.

Bro. Jim was doing the same thing for his wife, Jeanette, and he charged his purchase on Master Card as well. The salesperson came back in a few minutes and said to me, "We are sorry, but the Star of David you picked out was too delicate for the fire in setting the diamond and it melted. You will need to pick out another medallion that is a little heavier." So, I did. They cancelled the first charge and ran through the charge on the second one. This time, Master Card denied the credit. I could not believe it. My credit was impeccable, and I was not near my credit limit. What I did not know was that the eagle eyes at Master Card saw two charges come through from the Middle East within moments of one another. They did not see that one of them was cancelled.

Suspecting fraud, they called my house, and Arlene answered. "Have you authorized a couple of charges from the Middle East on your credit card?" Without thinking, Arlene said, "No, we have not made any purchases like that." Bingo! They cut off my credit. The exact same thing happened to Bro. Jim. They called Jeanette, and they cut off his credit too! Bro. Jim said later, "Here we are, half way around the world, and our wives are still controlling our pocketbooks!"

Back to the precious stones here in chapter 21. The Church is to be the vessel for the display of the glory of God throughout the ages to come, just as we are told in Ephesians 5:27: *"That He might present it to Himself, a glorious Church, not having spot or wrinkle, or any such thing; but that it should be holy and without blemish."* The church on earth today is not without blemish. Think of all those who are on the church rolls that do not care whether the church survives or not. They seldom attend; they do not invite people to come to worship; they do not contribute money. They could not care less about the health of the church.

But the Church that God honors in Revelation 21 is composed of members that have been washed clean by His blood, and who love the Church with all their heart and soul, and they "love the brethren" – those are the other believers. Those are the ones whom Jesus will honor! And the Bride's new home, the Holy City, will be like no other city. Remember, the

Antichrist's city, Babylon, was arrayed in purple and scarlet, decked with gold and precious stones (Revelation 17:4). The New Jerusalem is arrayed in radiant light, shining with the very glory of God.

It is good to note that the Holy City does not generate its own light. The illumination comes from the Son of God. Later in this chapter, we are told that the city has no need of light because the Lamb is the light. You see, the believer does not produce or generate the light of Christ, but only reflects His glory. Christians are the light of the world in the sense that they are light reflectors – Jesus Himself is the light. We are told in Matthew 5:16: *"Let your light so shine before men, that they may see your good works – WHY? – so that they will glorify your Father which is in Heaven."*

The earthly beauty we now see in the world will not be lost in the world to come. We will not trade earth's beauty for the beauty of Heaven, but we will retain earth's beauty and gain even more beauty. It will have all the advantages we associate with earth, but none of the disadvantages. The city will be filled with natural wonders and magnificent buildings, but it will have no crime, pollution, garbage nor traffic fatalities. It will truly be "Heaven on earth."

I like the way Randy Alcorn describes the New Jerusalem: "The Artist's fingerprints will be seen everywhere in the great city. Every feature speaks of His attributes. The priceless stones speak of His beauty and grandeur. The open gates speak of His accessibility. All who wish to come to Him at His throne may do so at any time. We can learn a lot about people by walking through their houses. The whole universe will be God's house, and the New Jerusalem will be His living room. God will delight to share with us the glories of His capital city – and ours."[81]

On the New Earth, we will not have to leave the city to find natural beauty. Just as our resurrected bodies will be better than our current ones, the New Earth's natural wonders will be more spectacular than those we see on earth. Everything God tells us about the New Earth suggests that we will look back at the present earth and conclude, "God was just practicing!" We will also see a river, pure as crystal, with refreshing water, that is flowing right down the middle of Main Street. I am sure it will have countless streamlets flowing throughout the rest of the city. You can just imagine people talking and laughing beside this river, sticking their hands and faces into the water and drinking. This will give new meaning to the song, *Shall We Gather at the River.*[82] We will see a little later that we will need only to follow the river upstream to its source to arrive at the city's centerpiece, the Lamb's Throne. But, wherever we go or whatever we choose to do, we will not leave the presence of the King. For although He dwells especially in the New Jerusalem, because of His mighty attribute of being omnipresent, He will be fully present with us no matter where we go in the New Universe.

Verse 12: *"And had a great wall and high, and had twelve gates, and at the gates twelve angels and names were written thereon, which are the names of the twelve tribes of the children of Israel."*

Each gate has the name of one of the tribes of Israel written on it. We have seen that Satan likes to copy or counterfeit everything God does. That is why that horrendous city of sin that the Antichrist re-built, Babylon, had the names of blasphemy written on it according to Revelation 17:3. But these names of the twelve tribes are a constant reminder that our Bible and our Savior came to us through God's chosen nation, Israel. Throughout the history of mankind, walls have always been erected for security and for protection. The walls in Heaven speak of strength and security, but they are not needed because nothing is allowed that would defile.

In Bible times, giant walls were built around the cities as a means of protection for the citizens who lived within the walls. Some countries throughout history have even erected walls or fences to insure their safety. Do you remember studying in school one of the most fantastic building feats in the history of mankind? It was the Great Wall of China. Stretching nearly 4,000 miles, it kept China from being invaded by enemies for many centuries.

Today in Israel a concrete wall or barrier has been erected by the Israelis to keep out the terrorists who seek to destroy them and terrorism has been drastically reduced. The wall is about 8 feet high, with sophisticated electronic alarms, listening devices and frequent guard stations which can direct troops immediately to areas of the wall that have been breached. The U.S. is considering a controversial wall between the U.S. and Mexico to try to stop the influx of illegal aliens and reduce drug trafficking. Only time will tell whether this will prove to be effective. I can think of one wall that was not built to keep out intruders – it was built to keep in its citizens! It was, of course, the Berlin Wall, which President Reagan set his sights on, by declaring, "Mr. Gorbachev – tear down that wall!"[83]

Let me ask you this: if there are no murderers and thieves and scoundrels in Heaven, why is it necessary to have a wall around the city? Here is the answer. The walls are NOT necessary for security. They are there as an eternal reminder that the God of love eternally protects His people. The walls are a memorial to the fact that our lives are hidden, secure and protected in Christ (Colossians 3:3). The walls are also a source of incredible beauty as we will see shortly.

Verse 13: *"On the east three gates; on the north three gates; on the south three gates; and on the west three gates."* So these walls have three gates on each side of the city – a total of 12 gates in all. I am sorry to disappoint you, but contrary to popular belief, St. Peter will not be standing at the Pearly Gates to check your I.D. We are told that these gates are staffed with angels who welcome those possessing the privilege of entering the city, in other words, the children of God.

I will have to admit, however, some pretty funny stories have come out of the idea that St. Peter is guarding the Pearly Gates. Such as the woman who was killed in an auto accident, and suddenly found herself at the Pearly Gates in front of St. Peter. She started to go in when he said, "Hold it! To enter, you must spell one word." She said, "Which word?" He said, "It does not make any difference. But one must correctly spell one word in order to enter Heaven." She said, "How about the word love: L-O-V-E." St. Peter said, "That is correct – come right on in." Before she could get settled, St. Peter said, "I have an errand to run. Please watch the gate for me." She said, "But what am I supposed to do if someone comes up?" St. Peter said, "Just ask them to spell a word, and if they spell it correctly, they can come in." So she is standing at the gate when she looks up and sees a man walking toward her. As he gets closer, she realizes, "Oh, no! It is my first husband who deserted me." He starts to come in and she says, "Wait. You must spell a word correctly or you cannot come in." He said, "What word?" She said, "Czechoslovakia!"

You will recall the wilderness tabernacle that Israel constructed. Three tribes were camped outside each of the walls. On the east were: Judah, Issachar and Zebulun (Numbers 2:1-9). On the south were: Reuben, Simeon and Gad (Numbers 2:10-16). On the west were: Ephraim, Manasseh and Benjamin (Numbers 2:18-24). And on the north were: Dan, Asher and Naphtali (Numbers 2:25-31).

I do not see any significance to the order in which they are presented here in Revelation, but I will point out that east is mentioned first, and it seems that the east has always played a significant role in Scripture. Let me highlight this. In the third chapter of Genesis, we find the story of man being driven out of the Garden of Eden, and an angel was placed on the east side of it to prevent re-entry. Each Christmas we hear of the wise men who saw the star, and came from the east to worship the Christ child. In the seventh chapter of Revelation, John saw an angel ascending out of the east to put the seal of God on the 144,000 Israelites. And most importantly, there are hints that Christ will return out of the east (Matthew 24:27) to enter Jerusalem through the Eastern Gate (Ezekiel 44:2-3). But the east will not be kind to the Antichrist. In Daniel 11, he hears rumblings and bad news out of the east, and he hurries his army to confront the problem and this results in his downfall.

We find that throughout the Bible, God delights in giving particular angels certain assignments. It appears that Michael was the angel charged with the responsibility of watching over the children of Israel. And, knowing how organized God is, He undoubtedly had an angel assigned to guard each of the 12 tribes of Israel, probably reporting to Michael as their Commander. If that is the case, then each of these 12 angels who stand at the 12 gates, are most likely the same 12 angels who were assigned to each of the 12 tribes of Israel, just as Michael was assigned to protect the Jews in general.

Let me just say a brief word about numbers in the Bible. This is a whole study in itself, and some scholars have spent a lifetime interpreting the meaning of Biblical numbers. There is no question that God has ordained certain numbers to signify different things.

Let me give you a few examples:

> Number 1 – Stands for Unity
> Number 2 – Union or witnessing
> Number 3 – Resurrection and renewal
> Number 4 – Relates to the world
> Number 5 – Grace or God's goodness
> Number 6 – Weakness of man; the manifestation of sin
> Number 7 – Divine perfection
> Number 8 – New birth; new beginning
> Number 9 – Fruit of the Spirit
> Number 10 – Law and responsibility
> Number 11 – Judgment and disorder
> Number 12 – Governmental perfection

We could go on, but I want to zero in on Number 12, governmental perfection. This number 12 is used 187 times in the Bible – 22 times in the Book of Revelation. Twelve is the number for Government by Divine Appointment. Jesus said in Matthew 19:28: *"Verily, I say unto you, That ye which have followed Me, in the regeneration* [or renewing of all things] *when the Son of Man shall sit in the throne of His glory, ye also shall sit upon 12 thrones, judging the 12 tribes of Israel."*

So, there were 12 tribes to make up the nation of Israel. There were 12 stones in the High Priest's breastplate (Exodus 28:17-21). There were 12 cakes of shew bread placed in the Holy Place (I Samuel 21:4-6), a loaf for each of the 12 tribes. There were 12 spies sent out by Moses to check out the land of Canaan (Numbers 13). Elijah built an altar of 12 stones when he had his confrontation with the prophets of Baal on Mt. Carmel (I Kings 18:31). Jesus chose 12 disciples to follow Him (Luke 6:12-16). Jesus was 12 years old when He first visited the Temple (Luke 2:42). And in Revelation 12:1, there was a woman with a crown of 12 stars. And here in Revelation 21, we have 12 gates, 12 angels guarding them, 12 foundations, 12 names on the gates, 12 pearls, the measurements of the wall and city in Chapter 22 are multiples of 12 and the trees in the Holy City bear 12 manner of fruits. So you see, 12 is an important number in God's eyes, and He frequently uses numbers throughout Scripture to signify certain things.

Verse 14: *"And the wall of the city had twelve foundations, and in them the names of the twelve apostles of the Lamb."* When I go into an important building, maybe it is beautiful, or maybe it is very historic like the State Capitol. Maybe it is providing a great service to mankind like Baylor Hospital. I like to study the building's plaque that shows its history. It shows the name of its architect, when it was built and who the benefactors are. If it is a public building, it will show who was in office that approved its construction.

As we look upon the New Jerusalem, we see the names of those who made it possible: Matthew, John, James, Peter and the others. Just think, they will be there with us. You might be looking at the plaque when someone says, "Hey, here comes Andrew. Let's go talk to him a while." Won't that be great?! So, we see that the city has twelve foundations, and each one is emblazoned with the name of each of Jesus' apostles.

A foundation is one of the most important features of a building. If you go to sell your home, people might "oohh and aahh" over the beautiful carpet or the lovely crown molding in the dining room. But the really smart buyer will walk around the outside of the house, and study the foundation. Is the concrete separated? Are there any cracks in the bricks? No one wants to buy a house with a faulty foundation because big trouble lies ahead.

After we were married, we lived in a suburb of Dallas – Pleasant Grove for 27 years. I was just out of the Army and had very little money. We wanted a new house, but like all newlyweds, we had very limited funds. Fortunately, one of the deacons in our church who was a home builder, overwhelmed us. He came to us and said, "I'd like to build you a new house at cost plus $100. All you have to do is buy a lot, and when it is free and clear, use it as collateral, and I will build the house for you." What a deacon sent to us by God! We purchased a lot about 3 blocks from W. W. Samuell High School. We moved in with my parents and I put every spare dime on the lot, and we had it paid for in about a year. The builder, W. O. Laminack, who later founded Laminack Tire Company, built for us a beautiful 1,700 square foot home complete with hardwood floors and a cedar lined closet – all for $12,500! The Lord was so gracious to us, and we praised God for this wonderful Christian man.

After about twenty years, I woke up one day and discovered a crack in the sheet rock above a door. I patched it, and painted over it. A few weeks later, there was another crack. I painted over it. It happened again. I called a repairman. He said, "Mr. Gaylord, your problem is in the foundation." I said, "You don't understand. The problem is up there in the sheetrock." He said, "No, you don't understand. The problem in the foundation is causing the sheetrock up there to crack." That is when I first learned that the foundation is the most important part of a house.

Jesus knew this when he told the story in the seventh chapter of Matthew of the two men who built their houses on different foundations. One was built on sand, the other on bedrock. And you will remember, that the rains came and the wind blew and the house on the sand did not survive. The one built on the solid rock stood firm.

The analogy is clear. If you build your faith on the solid rock of Jesus Christ, you will endure. That is where we get our beloved song, *Rock of Ages.*[84] The New Jerusalem has 12 foundations, each bearing the name of one of the 12 apostles. Someone asked me, "Will Judas' name be on one of the foundations?" Well, we do not have to speculate on that one. Notice the words of scripture: " *…. and in them* [are] *the names of the twelve apostles OF THE LAMB."* Not just 12 apostles, but 12 apostles of the Lamb! Was Judas a true apostle of the Lamb? Jesus said in John 6:70, *"Have I not chosen you twelve, and one of you is a devil?"* Scripture is even more telling in Luke 22:3a: *"Then entered Satan into Judas …."*. Folks, Satan can put stumbling blocks before us; he can even tempt us; but as a believer, he can never possess us! Why? Because our bodies are the temple that the Holy Spirit resides in, and we are told that *"greater is He that is in you, than he that is in the world"* (I John 4:4).

So, who are the 12 apostles whose names are on the foundations? Well, we know 11 of them right away: Simon Peter, Andrew, John, Philip, James, Bartholomew, Thomas, Matthew, Simon the Zealot, Jude and James the Lesser (younger) who was the brother of Jesus. But who is the twelfth? We know it is not Judas Iscariot, so who is it? In the first chapter of the Book of Acts, the apostles had come together in the upper room. Peter stood up and said, "We need to replace Judas." The eleven apostles were so anxious to fill Judas' shoes that they did not even wait as the Lord had instructed them to do. So they chose two godly men, Joseph Justus and Matthias, and they voted on them (Acts 1:23). I think they were hasty. They did not wait on the Lord to see who His choice would be. Instead they cast lots and Matthias became the twelfth apostle (Acts 1:26). We do not ever hear of him again! No doubt he was a good man, but I do not think he was God's choice for the job. It seems clear to me that God's real choice was Saul who met God on the road to Damascus, and God changed his name to Paul (Acts 13:9).

Paul is called an apostle twice in Romans, five times in I Corinthians, and also called an apostle in II Corinthians, Galatians, Ephesians, Colossians, I and II Timothy and in Titus. Who called him to be an apostle? The other 11 apostles did not vote on him. Listen to I Corinthians 1:1: *"Paul, called to be an apostle of Jesus Christ, through the will of God …."*. I think one of the foundations will bear the name of Paul, an Apostle of the Lamb. It might have an asterisk by his name like Barry Bonds has on his homerun record; it might say in smaller print, "And also Matthias."

As the wall has 12 gates, so it also has 12 strong foundations, extending down to the solid bedrock of the New Earth – one foundation pier at each corner. I am reminded of Hebrews 11:10 which talks about this city, a city *"which hath foundations whose builder and maker is God."* This city will be a joy to behold, designed and built by the Master Architect of the Universe!

We now come to verses 15-17: *"And he that talked with me had a golden reed to measure the city, and the gates thereof, and the wall thereof. And the city lieth foursquare, and the length is as large as the breadth: and he measured the city with the reed, twelve thousand furlongs. The length and the breadth and the height of it are equal. And he measured the wall thereof, a hundred and forty and four cubits, according to the measure of a man, that is, of the angel."* The angel measures the city with a golden rod. That is appropriate since the streets are pure gold as well as the city. It is a good thing thieves are not in Heaven or the gold freeways would soon disappear.

My pastor, Bro. Jim, tells about a fellow who accumulated quite a bit of gold here on earth and when he died, he was determined to take it with him. He was clutching his bag of gold so tightly that when he arrived at the Pearly Gates, he still was squeezing his bag of gold. He sort of pushed by the angel at the gate when another angel said, "Wait just a minute fellow. What do you have in your bag that you are trying to sneak in here with?" The man thought, "Oh, no. I've been caught." But the other angel took a peek in the bag and said, "It's OK. You can go in – it's only paving material."

So the angel takes his golden measuring rod, and measures the city for the benefit of John right before his eyes. Though the angel is using a golden measuring reed, John is told that the measurement is in man's terms so he can understand it. I want to point out that when God takes a measurement in Scripture, He is always evaluating something against God's perfect standard and if it falls short it comes under judgment. In Revelation chapter 11 we saw an angel measuring the Temple during the Tribulation Period. It was the Temple in which the Antichrist proclaimed himself to be God. In that case, the Temple was unholy. It did not measure up to God's standards, and so it was marked for destruction. But here in Revelation 21, every measurement of the city is carefully made and recorded, satisfying fully God's perfect standard.

The dimensions of the city are found to be 12,000 furlongs wide, 12,000 furlongs long, and 12,000 furlongs high. Most scholars say that this is a distance of 1,500 miles in each direction. This makes the city's surface area two million square miles and would have enough room for 20 billion residents – 75 acres for each resident![85] For comparative purposes, if this were placed over the United States it would extend from the northern most point of Maine to the southernmost part of Florida and from the East coast all the way to Colorado. That is just ground surface – we have not even gone straight up yet.

The major cities we know around the globe – London, New York, Los Angeles and Paris would just be small villages in comparison. This will give you an idea about how big the New Jerusalem is. The United States has always had the tallest skyscrapers in the world. That is, until 2004 when a building was completed in Taiwan that was 1,667 feet tall.[86] The Sears Tower in Chicago is a mere 1,450 feet tall. The Twin Towers were ranked fifth and sixth in the world until they were destroyed on 9-11.

We have been talking about the height of our skyscrapers which we think are gigantic, and they are around 500 yards high. That is equal to the length of five football fields. The New Jerusalem is 1,500 miles high. It is beyond our ability to visualize it. And since we will not be bound by the laws of gravity, this city can contain every person who has ever been born plus billions more. However, Jesus said that every person who has ever been born will not go there.

As a result, none of its residents will feel cramped in the least – no one will have a lack of space. No one will be singing *Don't Fence Me In*.[87]

The late Dr. Henry Morris, founder of The Institute for Creation Research (ICR), made this calculation. Since the time of Adam to the present time, approximately 40 billion people have been born. Then, assuming that a similar number will be born during the Millennium, and allowing for another 20 billion for those who died from abortions or soon after birth, it can be reasonably assumed that 100 billion men, women and children will be members of the human race – past, present and future.

Dr. Morris assumed that 20% of these 100 billion will be saved including those who died before the age of accountability. This is just a guess, but the Lord did make it plain (Matthew 7:13, 14) that the great majority of mankind will never be saved. If this figure is in the ballpark, then that means the New Jerusalem will have to accommodate 20 billon residents. As a side note, not all of these will be living in the New Jerusalem; some will be on the New Earth and will only visit the New Jerusalem as they see fit.

Suppose that Dr. Morris is correct and that 20 billion will be living in the New Jerusalem. Also, he said for us to assume that 25% of the city is used for mansions while the rest is allocated to streets, parks, public meeting places, etc. Therefore, after applying a mathematical formula, he concludes that each person's space would be a little over one-third of a mile in each direction – some might have more, some less, but that would be about the average size.[88]

That is pretty big, folks! The Holy City is 2,250,000 square miles, but wait a minute! It is a cube – it is also 1,500 miles high. That means it is 3,375,000,000 cubic miles. We know from what Scripture tells us that the Holy City will be laid out like a square. Its length will be the same as its width, and its height will equal its length.

Putting it another way, the New Jerusalem is about 1,500 miles wide, 1,500 miles long and 1,500 miles high. Some believe this city is a sphere similar to our earth which rests in space like one of our planets. Others believe that it is a perfect cube. Still others think it will be a pyramid. We really do not have enough information to prove either view as each has some good points.

Those thinking that it will be a pyramid, visualize Christ appearing at the top where the throne of God is located and out of which will flow the river of pure water. Sounds good! But those who think it will be a cube, cite the instructions that God carefully gave to the children of Israel in building the Holy Place. He gave them precise instructions with exact dimensions and it was a perfect cube (I Kings 6:20). Both the language and the symbolism seem to favor the cubical shape, and would certainly provide much more available space than would a pyramid. But who knows? God does! Maybe we will not need the space.

Unfortunately, most commentators will spiritualize every bit of this. They say that this is not a literal city, that these dimensions simply mean that Heaven is vast, and that there are no real streets or real buildings. They are always seeking to make such descriptions into allegories or illustrations of some kind. They always assume that God does not know how to communicate with us. But John said, "I was there – I saw it!" And Jesus told him to write down what he saw. And I for one have no problem believing that these are literal descriptions and measurements of a literal city that we are going to live in.

The Apostle Paul told us we are going to have a literal, physical body just like Christ had after His resurrection. That is the purpose of our resurrection. Our spirits have already gone to be with the Lord around God's throne. So, if we are going to just remain spirits, why is the resurrection necessary at all? It is necessary to unite our spirits with our new, literal, perfected bodies, to live in our new, literal perfected mansion, located in our new, literal, perfected city!

I just finished reading an article by my friend, Evangelist Nathan Jones. With tongue in cheek, he puts a fantastic spin on this business of always spiritualizing prophecy when the context shows it to be literal. I will share an excerpt with you – it is great.

"I'm Eschatologist Nathan Jones, and here at Maranatha Labs, we research day and night to fight the deadly disease known as "Symbolically." Those infected with this inhibitive condition are at first difficult to spot, for they look like any other Christian. Show them a symbol out of everyday life, and they can identify it with ease. But, show them a symbol taken from Bible prophecy, and their brains are quickly overcome by Symbolically. In nine out of ten cases, those afflicted with Symbolically will intentionally spiritualize the Scriptures, choosing whatever interpretation that suits their fancy, and then argue automatically that the plain sense meanings found in the Bible are not their true meanings. If you are suffering from Symbolically, there is hope. Ask your local Eschatologist about the fast acting Golden Rule of Interpretation. Yes, the Golden Rule of Interpretation is the cure that will guide you to a literal interpretation of the Bible. Just generously apply this motto every single time you read the Bible – 'If the plain sense makes sense, don't look for any other sense, lest you end up with nonsense' – And you, too, will be cured from spiritualizing Scriptures!"[89]

Recently I read the seven book series, *The Chronicles of Narnia* by C.S. Lewis. It was wonderful. C. S. Lewis is probably the most profound Christian thinker of the last 100 years. I am convinced that God gave that great man a special insight into the next world. I am going to read a passage from his final book in this series entitled *The Last Battle*. You need to read the entire series! There are several main characters. You will live with their struggles throughout the six books, experience all the hardships they encounter, all the treachery they endure, all the pain and suffering that comes their way – and then they arrive on the other side. They arrive in Heaven!

Their feelings are summed up by one of the characters, a Unicorn named Jewel. "He stamped his right hoof on the ground, and neighed, and then cried, 'I have come home at last! This is my real country! I belong here. This is the land I have been looking for all my life, though I never knew it until now …. '. He shook his mane and sprang forward into a great gallop, a Unicorn's gallop, which in our world would have carried him out of sight in a few moments. But now a strange thing happens. Everyone else began to run, and they found to their astonishment that they could keep up with the Unicorn; not only could the dogs and the humans keep up, but also Puzzle, the fat little donkey. The air flew in their faces as if they were seeing it from the windows of an express train. Faster and faster they raced, but no one got hot or tired or out of breath."[90]

What a marvelous description; though fiction, it captures the essence of the wonderful things that God has waiting for us. Why would anyone choose to miss it? There is only ONE gate into Heaven, and that is through Christ. But after we get inside, there are 12 dazzling gates to the beautiful New Jerusalem, the city whose builder and maker is God. I can hardly wait to see that magnificent city in all its glory with its 12 breathtaking entrances.

Verse 18: *"And the building of the wall of it was of jasper: and the city was pure gold, like unto clear glass."* John is describing the wall, but he is probably at a loss for words. I can remember as a kid when I first saw the movie, *The Wizard of Oz.*[91] I was a little disappointed at first when the movie began in black and white. But then when we traveled to the Land of Oz with its Emerald City, suddenly the movie burst into full color. I thought it was about the most beautiful thing that I had ever seen! Now, I realize that the Emerald City cannot hold a candle to this city of gold which is like unto clear glass. And then John, as best as he can, begins to tell us the magnificent things he sees as he gazes upon this glorious city.

Verses 19-20: *"And the foundations of the wall of the city were garnished with all manner of precious stones. The first foundation was jasper; the second, sapphire; the third, a chalcedony; the fourth, an emerald; the fifth, a sardonyx; the sixth, a sardius; the seventh, Chrysolite; the eighth, beryl; the ninth, a topaz; the tenth, a chrysoprasus; the eleventh, a jacinth; the twelfth, an amethyst."* It is evident that God loves beautiful colors. In the New Jerusalem, the foundations of the walls are garnished with all manner of precious stones, corresponding to the stones seen in the breastplate of the high priest. The first foundation is jasper. That is the closest thing to our diamond, utterly breathtaking, and it pictures the glory of God. What gold is to metals, jasper is to precious stones. The second is the sapphire, similar to the diamond in hardness, but is a clear blue gem picturing peace and serenity. Then there is the Chalcedony, a combination of gray, blue and yellow. Next, the Emerald, a brilliant green stone the color of life. The Sardonyx, a reddish white onyx similar to the color of healthy fingernails. The Chrysolite, a transparent golden yellow stone. The Beryl, a beautiful sea green gem. The Topaz, a transparent greenish golden stone. The Chrysoprasus, a mixture of blue, green and yellow. The Jacinth, a mixture of red, violet and yellow. And the Amethyst which is a deep lavender.

A brilliant rainbow would be just a pale glimmer compared to what these foundation stones look like. Remember God is light and His light passing through these many different jewels will be awesome. It will make a kaleidoscope look dreary in comparison. There is considerable uncertainty among commentators as to what these stones and colors symbolize. And that is probably intentional on the part of God. The purpose of John's description is to impress upon us the indescribable glory and beauty of the Holy City, reflecting its heavenly light in the translucent and rainbow hues passing through its mighty jasper walls.

We would love to know the Spirit's mind as to the deeper meanings of all these colors, but we will just have to wait and ask Him when we get there. We can tell that everything in the city is in order. Every column is perfectly straight. Can you imagine a crooked column? Would it not violate something inside you to see a column leaning? Arlene can spot a picture hanging crooked a mile away. She is always straightening pictures. Where does that come from? It comes from God. He likes things in order. And He made us that way.

Everything about Jesus' life was symmetrical and perfect, without flaw or blemish. His life, His personality, His mind, His heart, His soul, His affections, His will, His desires, His physical manhood – all is perfect. So our home in Heaven is like our Lord, beautiful, symmetrical and perfect. We shall live in a great city where there is harmony, not monotony; variety, not sameness.

Verse 21 (ESV): *"And the twelve gates were twelve pearls, each of the gates made of a single pearl, and the street of the city was pure gold, transparent as glass."* The gates of pearl remind us at every entrance of that one pearl of great price for which our Lord, the heavenly Merchantman, traded all that he had to buy the Church, His Body of believers. For though He was rich, yet He became poor, that He might make us His forever. In the second chapter of Ephesians, Paul is discussing the unity of all believers. In Heaven, we will have Baptists, Methodists, Churches of Christ, Presbyterians, Catholics, Nazarenes and other denominations – all who have truly trusted Christ as their Lord and Savior. Paul says that we are *"built upon the foundation of the apostles and prophets, Jesus Christ Himself being the chief cornerstone"* (Ephesians 2:20). That is exactly what we have pictured here in the New Jerusalem.

People have used the common expression "pearly gates" without even realizing the deep meaning it has. The pearl is different from all other precious stones. All the other stones come from the earth, and are mined from rock and ore that are not alive. They are taken and cut and polished to uncover their real beauty. But the pearl comes from the sea. A little grain of sand or particle works as an irritant and begins to cut into the side of a living cell, usually an oyster. In order to protect itself from pain, the oyster manufactures and excretes a fluid to coat the grain of sand and to mitigate its painful effect. As the grain continues to cut and irritate, the oyster coats it with layer upon layer of the protective fluid, almost like shedding tears to form in the final analysis, a beautiful pearl.[92]

The gates of pearl are there to remind us throughout eternity that we were the grain of sharp, dirty sand that was a continual hurt to God. We were not attractive. We were in rebellion, walking according to the course of this world. But God took that ugly thing, which was you and me, and covered it with His tears, and made something beautiful out of it. The beauty is not in the grain of sand. The beauty is not in us, but in what the Lord puts around us – His righteousness. We have no value in ourselves, yet we are the pearl of great price. The price the Lord paid is what gives us our value.

The great reformer Martin Luther said, "God does not love us because we are valuable; we are valuable because God loves us."[93] Here is a perfect story that illustrates this. It comes from my friend, Evangelist Dennis Pollock. Consider two very different teddy bears. One is made of solid gold, through and through. It is worth millions. The other is a cloth teddy bear. It was beautiful in its day, gorgeously designed, but it is now a far cry from its earlier beauty. One of the eyes is missing, the stuffing is coming out of its back, and it has a number of stains and large gashes from top to bottom.

Suppose you go on a worldwide tour and take the teddy bears with you. Everywhere you travel you ask people what they would be willing to pay for them. By the time your trip is over, it is quite clear which bear has the greater value. Great numbers of people from every country have offered you millions for the bear made of gold. But no one will even bid on the cloth bear. It seems absolutely valueless. As you arrive home you set the golden bear on its golden stand and say to yourself, "Now, there is something with real value."

Looking at the cloth bear that no one cared for, you pick it up and start to throw it into the trash when suddenly your four year old daughter, Janie, comes running up to you. 'Please, please don't throw away my teddy bear! That's my bear and I love him!' Now let me ask you. Does the cloth bear have value or not? In a certain sense it has almost none. It is but a shadow of its former glory and no one wants it. Well, almost no one. But there is a little four year old in whose eyes it has incredible value. You see, the cloth bear has been given great value because of the one who loves it.[94]

That is exactly the way Christ feels toward us. We are not worth much, but the price He paid – His very life –and the love He has for us – that is what gives us value! As a result of sin, we have a penalty of death and Hell laid on each one of us. Yet in the midst of all of that, a Savior has come along and has said, "Don't throw that one away. I love him, and I am ready to adopt him into the family of God." So, do we have value? We have incredible value! Jesus gives us a new nature – sews up the gashes, cleans off our stains and before long we began to look a whole lot better.

Every gate bearing its beautiful pearl, silently preaches this message every time someone passes through it because we can only enter into the New Jerusalem by going through one of the twelve gates, made of solid pearl. We are there only through suffering and travail of Jesus, through His redemption and blood and through the agony of the cross. What a great picture we have in these gates of pearl – a pearl made from a wound. Without the wound, the pearl is never formed. We enter into the New Jerusalem through the gates of pearl – a constant reminder that He was wounded for our transgressions!

Now you can see why some commentators do not think we should take these descriptions literally. They say, "Where would a pearl the size of a city gate come from?" The answer is from God, not from an oyster. They should not forget God is building this city. He can build it any way He wants to! Even a beautiful jewel must have a beautiful setting in which to be encased. And these beautiful gates of pearl are encased in the magnificent wall of pure jasper. The streets of pure gold remind us that our feet shall stand on the righteousness of God forever. The gold is unstained and unclouded. We just cannot imagine it. The gold we see here on earth is opaque. Light does not pass through it. But this gold in Heaven is so pure, so perfect that it is transparent. Light shines right through it like gold passes through a clear diamond.

I am convinced that this is a literal city because of its literal description. If gold does not mean gold, if pearls do not mean pearls, if precious stones do not mean precious stones, if exact measurements and real dimensions mean something else, then the Bible gives us nothing that is accurate or reliable. The stones described in the breastplate of the High Priest may have been symbolic, but they were literal stones in a literal breastplate of a literal High Priest.

These stones picture something else, just as the stones in the foundation and the pearls in the gates signify something deeper. But that does not mean they are not real stones! I have a picture of Arlene in my billfold. It is a real picture, but that does not mean it does not stand for something else – her real likeness. A second reason for believing this is describing a literal city is that there is nothing in the verses to indicate that it should not be taken literally. John did not say he saw something "like unto a city", he said he saw a city. Thirdly, I believe that this is a real city because Abraham and the patriarchs *"looked for a city which hath foundations, whose builder and maker is God"* (Hebrews 11:10). They were not looking for a state of mind nor a condition.

I am reminded of a little girl who was in church with her mother. The preacher came to John 14:3 in his sermon where Jesus said, *"I will come again …."*. The preacher said, "Of course, Jesus did not mean that He would actually come again in person." The little girl looked at her mother and said, "Momma, if Jesus did not mean what He said, why didn't He say what He meant?" Great question! She was more perceptive than the liberal preacher.

You know, even those of us blessed with eyesight, who have seen the beautiful landscapes, the sunsets, all this natural world has to offer – we still cannot fathom the glorious beauty of this Holy City. But what about those who have been blind from birth? How can they understand? We were blessed when sweet little Mary blind from birth, who came to speak to our class several years ago and sang so beautifully for us. She never saw a color in her life. Never saw a rainbow.

Never saw a cardinal. Never saw a sunset. We also have a wonderful lady, Netta, in our church. She has been blind since a young child. Though sightless, God has gifted each of these ladies in a special way. Mary is a host on a local radio station[95] while Netta served for many years helping blind veterans adjust to everyday life. I believe God has blessed each of them with an imagination that none of us will ever know. What joy it will be for them to view Heaven and its array of colors; to view the Jasper walls and the gates of pearl!

I am reminded of sightless Terri Gibbs who song that beautiful song, *The First Thing I Will See* on the Bill Gaither Homecoming video entitled, *Sunday Meetin' Time*.

"I have never seen a flower or a tree
Or the sky alive and blue on a summer afternoon.
Never seen a sunrise or ocean waves at midnight
But one day I'll have my sight
In a place where there's no night.
And the first thing I'll see will be Jesus.
The first thing I'll see will be my Lord.
Oh, He'll look at me and then
He'll say, 'Well done my faithful friend'
The first thing I'll see will be Jesus!

I can hardly wait to see those pearly gates
And I know those streets of gold
They'll be something to behold.
And all around the crystal sea,
I'll sing praises to my King.
Oh, I'll stand before the throne
Where I'll worship Him alone.
And the first thing I'll see will be Jesus."

I think of all the people who have told me, "Oh, I don't read the Book of Revelation – it's too scary." Then I realize they do not have a clue as to what this Book is all about. What will be their excuse when they stand before God? "Oh, I didn't read your Book because I didn't have time." "Oh, I didn't read Revelation because it was too scary." And God says, "The main theme of the Revelation is the unveiling of Jesus Christ in all His Glory. Do you find that scary?" So we should tell people, "Sure, there are some frightening parts in here, but not for the Christian." How can we get excited if we do not know what is in store for us? God could have

The New Heaven, The New Earth, The New Jerusalem

waited to reveal all of this to us after we have been called home and are about to enter the city. But I am sure there will be many details that we will not know until then, but He wants us to be excited about it now!

As I reflect on our journey through Revelation, I have come to the conclusion that God has in mind two purposes for the Book in addition to the primary purpose of unveiling Jesus Christ. First, it is to impress upon us that our time here on earth is short, that there is judgment coming, and that we should share the good news of the Gospel of salvation with as many of our relatives, friends and neighbors as we can. Secondly, the Book is written so that we may be encouraged. God knows the difficult times we will have as we journey through this life. We cannot go very far without falling down, experiencing pain, losing loved ones, being overcome with grief, coping with loneliness and ultimately facing death ourselves. But through all of this, God wants to show us that our journey will end in joy and peace and all our tears will be gently wiped away forever. He wants to show us as the beloved song says, *It Will Be Worth It All When We See Jesus.*[96]

Verse 22: *"And I saw no temple therein: for the Lord God Almighty and the Lamb are the temple of it."* In religious life on earth, a temple or tabernacle or even a church has always been where God's presence is felt the strongest. Because of sin, God had Moses build a Tabernacle where the people would go to worship. Even then, God separated Himself from the people by residing in the Holy of Holies within the Tabernacle. And the High Priest could only go in there once a year. Later, God directed Solomon to build a Temple to give a more permanent place to worship. This was destroyed, rebuilt and later refurbished by Herod, only to be completely destroyed by the Romans in 70 A.D.

The Jews have not had a Temple in Jerusalem for 2,000 years. They would love to build one now on its designated spot, the Temple Mount in Jerusalem, but it is currently controlled by the Muslims. But the Jewish Temple will be rebuilt on that location – God will see to it.

We know that, at the beginning of the Tribulation Period, the Antichrist will negotiate a seven year peace treaty between the Arabs and the Jews, enabling the Jews to proceed with their building of the Temple on the top of the Temple Mount. The Antichrist will eventually break his peace agreement, take over the new Temple, and declare himself to be the true God (Daniel 9:27; Matthew 24:15). After the Tribulation Period runs its course, the Millennial Kingdom will be launched and Christ will govern along with His believers during these 1,000 years of peace on earth (Revelation 20:6).

When the Millennial is over, we are ushered into the eternal state where we are told there will no longer be a Temple (Revelation 21:22) . You might look at it this way: the Old Testament Temple was prophetic, pointing to the coming Messiah. The Temple in the Christian era in which we now live, is our bodies, inhabited by the Holy Spirit. The Temple in the Millennium will be a memorial pointing backward to Christ's finished work. But in the ages of eternity, all prophecies will have been fulfilled, and the presence of the Lamb with us will render any memorial unnecessary.

Verse 23: *"And the city had no need of the sun, neither of the moon, to shine in it: for the glory of God did lighten it, and the Lamb is the light thereof."* There will be no need of the sun or moon anymore because the glory of God will provide the light. After the entrance of sin into the old creation, we find in Genesis 1:2b that God withdrew His continued presence, and Scripture says, " .... *darkness was upon the face of the deep*".

Someone asked me if "dark" is inherently evil. I was not sure, so I did an in-depth study of dark and darkness in the Bible. God stated in Genesis after revealing the morning and the evening, that it was good. That sounds to me like darkness is not inherently evil. But, I will say this: when darkness is mentioned, it is usually associated with evil. Dark itself is simply an absence of light. Since Jesus is the Light of the world; and since men love darkness rather than light because their deeds are evil; and since there will be no night in Heaven; and since the unsaved will be cast out into outer darkness; and since God is light and in Him there is no darkness (I John 1:5), I would conclude that darkness has a lot in common with evil.

It does not say that the sun and moon are going to be destroyed. It simply says that in the New Earth, light is not needed. It will not be needed because of the light from the glory of God. Paul got a glimpse of that glory on the road to Damascus, and it left him blind for 3 days.

We will have new resurrected bodies that will include new resurrected eyes. We will be able to see and enjoy everything in our new heavenly home including the glory of God.

Verse 24: *"And the nations of them which are saved shall walk in the light of it: and the kings of the earth do bring their glory and honor into it."* This is probably one of the most difficult passages to understand in the whole Book of Revelation. One item that all translators agree upon in this verse is this: it should read, *"they bring their glory and honor unto it"* – not into it. So if the Jews and the Christians are living in the Holy City with the Lamb of God, who are these nations and kings that bring their glory unto it? Most commentators skip right over this verse. It appears that there are still "nations" even in the eternal ages to come, and they have their kings that apparently come from places in the New Earth that are outside the Holy City.

One of the best explanations comes from Dr. Arno Gaebelein, famed scholar of another generation. He says these are neither Jews nor are they part of the Church, but are undoubtedly, the throngs that were born during the Millennial Period who were converted to Christ.[97] Dr. Jack Van Impe adds that they also include the millions of Gentiles who were saved during the Tribulation Period, and did not follow the Antichrist into the Battle of Armageddon.[98] That is about as good an explanation as I have heard. So, it appears to me that the New Jerusalem which is suspended above the New Earth will be the home of the Church. The New Earth will be the home of the Jews and the Gentiles saved during the Tribulation and the Millennium. Also, there will be a lot of residents as well as visitors going back and forth between the Holy City and the New Earth. As we will see in the next verse, the gates will always be open.

Verse 25: *"And the gates of it* [that is, the New Jerusalem] *shall not be shut at all by day; for there shall be no night there."* There are places on this earth where you are constantly shut out, barred from entry, but locks will be a vague memory to all of us in that land. The gates will never be closed nor locked. New Jerusalem will have no enemies; they have already been dispensed with. All residents of the New Earth are welcomed. The gates act as gracious invitations, not forbidding deterrents. The city will be one great body of light and glory. It will be perpetual high noon. No cloud will ever darken the sky. We can sing *The Unclouded Day* because that will be what it is.[99] The long dark nights of fear, terror and loneliness will be a thing of the past. We will have entered our eternal day which knows no setting sun, no gloomy forecast.

Verses 26-27: *"And they shall bring the glory and honor of the nations into it. And there shall in no wise enter into it anything that defileth, neither whatsoever worketh abomination, or maketh a lie; but they which are written in the Lamb's Book of Life."* Ancient cities kept rolls of their citizens, and guards were posted at the city gates to keep out enemies and criminals by checking their names against the list. All enemies of the Kingdom will have no chance to enter the New Earth, so the gates will remain open, with no need for searches or metal detectors. Any citizen of the New Earth (those with their names written in the Lamb's Book of Life) is always welcome to come and go as they please.[100]

Let me illustrate how important it is to have your name written in the Lamb's Book of Life. This is a true story. Ruthanna Metzgar is a world famous soprano and teacher at Seattle Pacific University. I spoke to her recently and she gave me permission to use her story in this book. She has a beautiful voice. She was asked to sing at the wedding of a multimillionaire on the west coast. According to the invitation, the reception following the wedding was to be held on the top two floors of Seattle's Columbia Tower, the tallest and most elegant skyscraper in the entire Northwestern United States.

Ruthanna and her husband, Roy, were so excited they could hardly stand it. The wedding took place and Ruthanna Metzgar sang beautifully. After the wedding, as is the custom, people made their way to the place of the reception, there in the luxurious Columbia Tower. As waiters in tuxedos offered luscious hors d'oeuvres and expensive beverages, the crowd gathered near a beautiful glass staircase that led to the top floor where the reception was to be held. Someone cut a satin ribbon draped across the bottom of the stairs, and the announcement was made that the wedding feast was about to begin. Bride and groom ascended the stairs to the applause of everyone present. Then they were followed up the crystal stairs by their guests.

At the top of the stairs, a maitre d' with a gold bound book greeted each guest outside the big double doors to the ballroom. "May I have your name please?" "I am Ruthanna Metzgar and this is my husband, Roy." The attendant searched the M's. "I am not finding it. Would you spell it please?" Ruthanna spelled her name slowly, M-e-t-z-g-a-r. After searching again, the maitre d' looked up and said, "I'm sorry, but your name isn't here." Ruthanna said, "There must be some mistake. I'm the singer. I just sang at their wedding." The gentleman smiled and said, "I'm so sorry, Madam. It doesn't matter who you are or what you did. Without your name in the book, you cannot attend the marriage banquet."

He motioned to a security guard and said politely, "Please show these people to the service elevator." The Metzgars followed the man past the beautifully decorated tables laden with fresh shrimp, smoked salmon and all the trimmings. All the musicians were decked out in white tuxedos and they began to play softly. The security guard ushered the Metzgars into the elevator, pushed "G" for the parking garage and said, "Have a pleasant evening."

The Metzgars drove home in almost total silence. Finally, Roy reached over, put his hand on Ruthanna, and said, "Sweetheart, what happened?" Ruthanna began to sob softly. "When the invitation arrived, I was busy. I never bothered to RSVP. Besides, I was the singer. Surely I could go to the reception without returning my reservation card." Ruthanna, a devout Christian, said later, "I not only missed the most lavish banquet of my life, but also, I had a taste of what it will be like someday for people as they stand before God and find that their names are not written in the Lamb's Book of Life."

They were too busy to respond to Christ's invitation to His wedding banquet. They will say, "But we attended church, we were baptized, we sang in the choir, we gave money to the building fund and our names were on the church roll." But that is not enough, for you see, their names were not written in the Lamb's Book of Life. The saddest part, however, is this. It will not just mean going down the service elevator to the garage. It will mean going down to Hell itself – forever![101]

Here we are 2,000 years later, and you can ask ten people on the street how to get to Heaven, and invariably you will get the same answer – "try to do good." It is what we call "works salvation." It is hoping that our good deeds will outweigh our bad deeds. But that has nothing to do with it. We have a sin nature! Verse 27 reminds us that since we have sin baggage, we cannot get into Heaven. We do not need a teacher; we do not need a philosopher. We need a Savior who will cleanse us, give us a new nature and write our names in the Lamb's Book of Life so that we can enter this beautiful land.

I John 3:3 (NASB) tells us, "*And everyone who has this hope fixed on Him* [Christ] *purifies himself, just as He is pure.*" When Arlene and I fixed our wedding date in 1954, I put it in large letters on the calendar. Thoughts of her consumed my waking hours. I would check the calendar several times a day to make sure nothing had changed. I had no time to look at other girls or other distractions. And that is what this verse says about Christ. When we have our hope fixed on HIM, we purify ourselves and we have no time to be entangled with the cares of this world.

When we meditate on Heaven, sin is very dull and unattractive. Heaven should affect our activities and ambitions, our recreations, our friendships and the way we spend our time and money. What will last forever? God – His Word – and His people! Spending time in God's word and investing in people will pay off in eternity and bring us joy in the present. Heaven should be our North Star reminding us where we are and in which direction we are going. The Bible compares our life to a race. And Heaven is the finish line! Paul says, *"Forgetting what is behind and straining toward what is ahead, I press on toward the goal to win the prize for which God has called me heavenward in Christ Jesus"* (Philippians 3:13b-14 NIV). We must endure a lot of things in this life, but do not ever think that God is not aware of what we go through. We will learn later that all these irritants and obstacles are for our growth and maturity.

Chief Justice John Roberts of the U.S. Supreme Court gave a most unusual commencement speech to the 2017 ninth grade graduating class at Cardigan Mountain School in New Hampshire where his son was graduating. Chief Justice Roberts began by wishing them bad luck which raised a lot of eyebrows. But then, what he said made a lot of sense.

Here is an excerpt from his speech. "Now commencement speakers will typically wish you good luck, and extend good wishes to you. I will not do that and I'll tell you why. From time to time in the years to come, I hope you will be treated unfairly so that you will come to know the value of justice. I hope that you will suffer betrayal because that will teach you the importance of loyalty. Sorry to say, but I hope you will be lonely from time to time so that you will not take friends for granted. I wish you bad luck from time to time so that you will be conscious of the role of chance in life. And that you will understand that your success is not completely deserved, and that the failure of others is not completely deserved either. And when you lose, as you will from time to time, I hope every now and then your opponent will gloat over your failure. It is a way for you to understand the importance of sportsmanship. I hope you'll be ignored so you know the importance of listening to others. And I hope you will have just enough pain to learn compassion."[102]

Good advice from Chief Justice Roberts, but it would have been great advice had he concluded it with: *"God is our refuge and strength, a very present help in trouble"* (Psalm 46:1).

CHAPTER TWENTY-TWO

The Eternal State

When we began studying the Book of Revelation, some of you thought we would never make it through, but we have finally arrived at the last chapter. It has been quite a journey. In our last lesson, we saw some of the features of Heaven – its beauty – its nature – its tranquility.

When we finish Revelation, you will see that it terminates God's written Word to man. All we need to know about God, about Jesus Christ, and about His plan for mankind has been revealed and recorded. Now we must simply live by the manual and await its fulfillment.

The last chapter of the Revelation is one of the most exciting and meaningful chapters anywhere in Scripture. It is wonderful to see what inheritance awaits every child of God through Jesus Christ. But I also feel a twinge of sadness for the many who will not be present in the New Heaven and New Earth. God in His infinite intelligence has worked out a plan that would not compromise His holiness, while at the same time, provide an escape for the human race. All we have to do is accept the sacrifice made by God's Son. That is what we plead for people to do, but sadly, many choose their own agenda and it breaks God's great heart. We have been left on the earth to help our Heavenly Father achieve His goals by telling others of the Good News of the Gospel.

This New Heaven and New Earth we have been discussing have never before been seen by human eyes, except as John saw it in a vision. Let us begin our final countdown by reading chapter 22, verse 1: *"And he showed me a pure river of water of life, clear as crystal, proceeding out of the throne of God and of the Lamb."*

Some commentators spiritualize this river, but I tend to view it literally. There is nothing as refreshing as pure, crystal clear water, especially when its source is the very throne of God. You will not have to distill this water or add chlorine. You will not have to go up to St. Peter and ask for a bottle of Deja Blue. I can hardly wait to drink from that clear stream coming out of the throne of God; it is going to taste good like heavenly water should! Pollution will be non-existent in the Holy City. There will be an abundance of luxurious grasses and trees everywhere just as there were in the Garden of Eden.

Verse 2: *"In the midst of the street of it, and on either side of the river, was there the tree of life, which bare twelve manner of fruits, and yielded her fruit every month: and the leaves of the tree were for the healing of the nations."* These first two verses establish the fact that in our new glorified bodies we, as inhabitants of the Holy City, will continue to enjoy the pleasure of eating. Why not? Jesus in His glorified body ate with His disciples as recorded in Luke 24:43, and the Bible says that we shall be like Him!

If you can, picture a beautiful street of pure gold with mansions of gold on either side and a river of pure water flowing down the middle of it. On each side of the river is the Tree of Life bearing twelve different kinds of fruits – a different one each month. We first saw the Tree of Life in Genesis. After the fall, in their sinful state, Adam and Eve were banished from the Garden to keep them from eating of the Tree of Life lest they would live forever in their miserable condition (Genesis 3:24). Notice that there is no mention of the Tree of Knowledge of Good and Evil in which Adam and Eve brought shame upon themselves. That great Bible teacher, Dr. A. C. Gaebelein of another generation said, "The tree whose taste brought death, was withered by the cross."[1]

Scripture says that the leaves of the tree are for healing. This immediately raises a question. Does this mean we will be sick in Heaven? Absolutely not! A better translation for the Greek word, "therapeia," would be that the leaves are for "health" instead of for healing.

The word translated in the King James, "healing", is the word from which we derive our English word "therapy." Therefore, the leaves of the Tree of Life are not for the purpose of healing, but for the purpose of yielding continuous health to the occupants of the New Jerusalem.

On earth, an apple a day keeps the doctor away. In Heaven, fruit from the Tree of Life insures that we are always 100% healthy in mind, soul and spirit. Some of the health nuts today might get pretty excited if they learn we are going to eat leaves in Heaven.

There are numerous references to fruit trees in Scripture; however, it is surprising how few different kinds of fruit are actually mentioned. There are grapes, figs, apples, pomegranates, melons and olives and probably dates since palm trees are mentioned so frequently. Since this food comes directly from God, you can well imagine how nourishing and nutritious it will be. My pastor, Bro. Jim, thinks that manna is really deep-dish pizza. And he might be right!

Verse 3: *"And there shall be no more curse: but the throne of God and of the Lamb shall be in it; and His servants shall serve Him."* The curse that the earth was placed under in Genesis as a result of sin, is partially removed during the Millennium. Now it is gone forever – no more curse – no more sin – no more sickness – no more death. No one will ever age, and our work will be productive and enduring. In the New Earth, the law of entropy (resulting in decay) will have been revoked by God. And verse 3 says that His servants will serve Him. There can be no higher privilege than to serve the King of creation, exercising dominion for Him and conveying knowledge about Him throughout His creation.

Life in the future will not be merely a life of rest and worship and singing, although there will be time for that; it will also be a life of productivity, teaching, learning and just plain having fun with our friends and relatives. Dr. Reagan says it has always been his belief that God will somehow show us, either through super HDTV or an advanced time machine, historic scenes from the past. Maybe there will be a library in Heaven like a Blockbuster store or Netflix. You can go in and tell the Librarian (who will be Arlene, of course), "I would like to see the confrontation between Elijah and the prophets of Baal on Mt. Carmel" and she will say, "No problem."

I would like to see Daniel witnessing to King Belshazzar as the mysterious hand begins to write on the wall. What a thrill it will be to listen to Noah describe his experiences on the Ark. A little boy asked his preacher, "What did Noah do all day on the Ark?" The preacher said, "Well, he probably went fishing." And the little boy said, "I'll bet he didn't fish very long." The preacher said, "Why do you say that?" The boy said, "Because he didn't have but two worms."

Did you ever stop to think that each of us will have our own story to tell? Our defeats, our struggles, our victories as we describe how God was faithful through it all. But we might be hesitant to speak after hearing from the martyrs as well as the survivors from the Tribulation. What a story they will have! David Jeremiah says that in Heaven we will enjoy the three "s's" – "Singing, Serving and Sharing."

Verse 4: *"And they shall see His face; and His name shall be in their foreheads."* Our greatest thrill in Heaven will be to see Jesus face to face. His name will be in our foreheads. A name stands for much, or little, depending on whose name it is. In World War II, the name "Hitler" was anathema. In all my years since, I have never run across anyone named Hitler – or Jezebel for that matter.

Chapter 13 tells us of the ones who took the name or Mark of the Beast. They are linked forever with the Antichrist; his destiny is their destiny. In this life, you carry your family name. For good or for bad, your actions reflect upon your family's reputation. But when God puts His name on us, it is the greatest name of all. It stands for His character and His faithfulness. It is His seal of ownership and He is staking His very reputation on us. Every believer in eternity will bear the likeness of God. John says in I John 3:2: *"Beloved, now are we the sons of God, and it doth not yet appear what we shall be: but we know that, when He shall appear, we shall be like Him; for we shall see Him as He is."* Yes, we shall see Him and we shall reign with Him forever and ever!

This brings us to verse 5. *"And there shall be no night there; and they need no candle, neither light of the sun; for the Lord God giveth them light: and they shall reign for ever and ever."* Lamps, light bulbs and flashlights will be a thing of the past. Those in the city will enjoy perpetual [Son] Light. Never will there be clouds or storms or darkness because Jesus will be our light. There will be no night. Many dear souls sometimes lay in bed in the dark, dreading the demons that are trying to get in, wondering if tomorrow will bring more pain and suffering.

Sometimes the dark can be scary. My pastor, Bro. Jim, tells of a little boy who went to bed but was afraid of the dark. I suspect it might have been one of Jim's own young sons. The boy called out, "Daddy, will you come sleep with me?" "No, son, go to sleep." A little while later, "Daddy, will you come sleep with me?" "I said to hush and go to sleep." Finally, the little boy said, "Daddy, is your face turned toward me?" "Yes, it is." "Then I can go to sleep." No more night. No more nightmares. God's face will be turned toward us.

With our new bodies, we will never get tired, and rest as mentioned in Scripture will take on a whole new meaning for us. Hebrews 4:9-10 says, *"There remaineth therefore a rest to the people of God. For he that is entered into his rest, he also hath ceased from his own works, as God did from His."* This is in stark contrast from those in the Lake of Fire of which Scripture says, *"They have no rest day nor night"* (Revelation 14:11a).

Verse 6: *"And he said unto me, These sayings are faithful and true: and the Lord God of the holy prophets sent His angel to show unto His servants the things which must shortly be done."* Where have we heard those words before? It is in chapter 1, verse 1, and it tells us how John received this revelation. The English word translated "shortly" comes from two Greek words "en tachos" which means "in haste." It does not carry the meaning that it will be necessarily tomorrow or next week although it could be. It carries the meaning that, when these things begin to unfold, they will swiftly be carried to a conclusion and consummated in a short period of time. In this verse, God emphasizes that these writings are faithful and true. These prophecies certainly do not tickle your ears. Many are not what you want to hear. With so much doom and gloom predicted, most people choose to ignore the dire predictions in this Book and maybe they will go away. However, God says these sayings are faithful and true and whether you like it or not, these things will come to pass and they will come about swiftly.

As mentioned previously, the Book of Revelation quotes from the Old Testament more than any other New Testament book. God designed it that way. It is easier to understand this last Book if you have a working knowledge of the rest of the Bible. Virtually every sign or symbol mentioned in the Revelation is either quoted or alluded to somewhere else in the Bible. These Old Testament prophets prophesied over and over about the events leading up to Christ's First and Second Coming as well as the events subsequent to them.

Verse 7: *"Behold, I come quickly: blessed is he that keepeth the sayings of the prophecy of this book."* We are reminded again of chapter 1, verse 3, where God pronounces a blessing on all those who read and keep the words of this Book. He would not mock us by promising a blessing on those who read it and keep its sayings unless He intends for us to understand it. A friend told me he was a member of another denomination for nearly 30 years. He said on one occasion his pastor preached through the New Testament, and when he finally arrived at the Book of Revelation, he told his audience, "No one has ever understood it, and no one ever will." It is no wonder that the audience let out a groan, and the subsequent studies in Revelation were sparsely attended.

The Holy Spirit is the official interpreter of Revelation, and if we pray and lean on Him, He will show us great gems, uncut diamonds, from this rich field. I am not saying we will understand every detail in the Book. There are verses throughout the Bible that we do not understand completely, but God will give us what He wants us to absorb in direct proportion to our desire to learn it. I mentioned previously in chapter 15, even that crusty old fellow, Mark Twain, who was not noted for being very religious, was being honest when he said, "It is not the parts of the Bible that I don't understand that bothers me – it's the parts I do understand."[2]

Also, notice that the blessing is on those who *"keep those things which are written therein,"* (Revelation 1:3). The reader is urged to keep, that is, to guard or hold fast what Revelation teaches. The purpose of studying Revelation is not simply to keep these teachings to ourselves, nor to try to impress anyone with how much we know about the Scriptures. If we study prophecy in the right way, it will do two things in our lives: it will motivate us to holy living, and it will motivate us to witness to our friends and neighbors as never before so that they might escape the wrath that is to come.

Finally, this passage says it is very serious business to take the words of this Book and twist them to make them mean anything you want them to mean. My best example is from an article in a newspaper I read by a theological professor. He preached an Easter message a number of years ago that was subsequently published in a local newspaper. He asked the question, "Did Jesus bodily resurrect from the dead?" And then he surprised everyone by saying, "Jesus did not rise physically, but He came alive in the disciples' hearts. It is like Dr. Martin Luther King's followers. After his death, they were sitting around a campfire remembering and retelling stories of Dr. King. Suddenly, he became so real that Dr. King became alive in their hearts!" The professor said this is what the disciples experienced. They talked about Jesus so much that pretty soon, He came alive in their hearts and in their imaginations. His obvious conclusion is this: if Jesus did not rise from the dead, He surely will not come back. Folks, this is NOT guarding the words of this Book. It is twisting Scripture to make it say whatever you want it to say!

Our society loves to ridicule Revelation as the incoherent ramblings of a lonely old man named John, exiled on a remote island. God knew this ridicule would come, so 2,000 years ago, He commissioned Peter to write about it in II Peter 3:3: *"Know this first, that there shall come in the last days scoffers, walking after their own lusts. And saying, 'Where is the promise of His coming? For since the father fell asleep, all things continue as they were from the beginning of the creation.'"* God says that scoffers will come in the last days, and He nails down why they are scoffers – because they are "walking after their own lusts." They do not want God putting any restrictions on them! They want to do their own thing, so they ridicule God and His promises.

Revelation 22:7 says, *"Behold, I come quickly."* He repeats this idea in verse 20. The Greek word translated here as "quickly" does not carry the connotation that He is coming tomorrow or the next day though He might! "Quickly" here means that once the sequence of events has started, they follow rapidly on the heels of one another. He can come very soon. There is not one prophecy that must be fulfilled before He comes in the air for His Church. But to be precise, we should say, as does this verse 7, when He comes, it will happen very suddenly, in the twinkling of an eye.

What God is saying is that there is an appointed day on which He will come regardless of anything else. And when these events begin to unfold, they will unfold rapidly. Regarding His First Coming, Scripture says, *"When the fullness of time was come, God sent forth His Son …."* (Galatians 4:4). He came at exactly the right time. The same is true when God sent His Holy Spirit to be our Comforter until Jesus comes back. Acts 2:1 says, *"When the day of Pentecost was fully come, they were all with one accord in one place. And suddenly there came a sound from heaven as of a rushing mighty wind, and it filled the house where they were sitting. And there appeared unto them cloven tongues like as of fire, and it sat upon each of them. And they were all filled with the Holy Ghost, and began to speak with other tongues, as the Spirit gave them utterance"* (Acts 2:1-4). The Holy Spirit came at exactly at the right time. God appointed these days, and He is always right on time – never too soon and never too late. There is no cataclysmic event caused by man that makes Jesus' return sooner or later than God wants Him to return. All the "date setters" over the years should heed what Jesus said: *"Only My Father knows the exact date"* (Matthew 26:36).

People are not in control of the Second Coming, God is. We cannot regulate when God will send Christ back to the earth. Instead, we are part of what one writer calls, "The drama of Grace and the drama of Redemption" that is now taking place. And we are to be ready! In Luke 21:28, Jesus tells His disciples that when these end time signs BEGIN to take place, God's plan for mankind will fall into place rapidly. Jesus said that when you see the fig tree begin to sprout, take notice for the time is near (Matthew 24:32). The fig tree has long been a symbol for Israel, and she began to sprout and blossom on May 14, 1948 when Israel became a nation again after nearly 2,000 years. It is time for us to look expectantly toward the eastern sky. As one old faithful prophecy teacher, the late Charles Pack said, "I don't look for signs anymore – they're too numerous – instead, I am listening for sounds." Amen! We yearn earnestly for the sound of Gabriel blowing his trumpet, and the voice from Heaven shouting, *"Behold, the Bridegroom cometh."* May this be the day!

In 1967, a little over 50 years ago, a beautiful young girl of seventeen dove into the Chesapeake Bay, not realizing there was a huge rock just below the surface. She suffered a broken neck, leaving her a quadriplegic, not able to use her arms and legs and being confined to a wheelchair the rest of her life.[3] But this courageous lady did not give up. She learned to paint, holding the brush in her mouth. Since then, with the help and encouragement from folks like Billy Graham, she has blessed thousands with her paintings, especially on Christmas cards. When I think of Jesus saying, *"Behold I come quickly,"* I immediately think of that lovely lady, Joni Eareckson Tada, who is longing to see Jesus, and at the same time receive her new body. Joni who has been confirmed to a wheelchair all these years and after reading this verse said, "I can't wait!"

In the summer of 2018, we seemed to have rain every day or so. The middle of July it was barely 90 degrees. Then the big thunderstorms hit, and we prayed, "Lord, if you will get me through these storms, I will not complain about summer again." Then, summer was over almost before it began. The rain slackened to a drizzle, and the outside air felt like it was 15 degrees cooler. We picked up the fallen branches, and my friend, Ray, even had a 40 foot tree fall across his driveway. The sweet smell of rain and clean air came floating into our nostrils.

You think, "It takes a good storm to refresh everything." That is what the Book of Revelation is all about. A storm called the Great Tribulation is brewing just over the horizon. It is going to shake and thrash planet earth with a fury never seen before in order to wash the foul smell of rebellion out of the air. And only after that storm has subsided, will the planet experience the refreshing of which the Old Testament prophets spoke about so often. Isaiah 55:12 says that the mountains and hills will burst into song, and the trees of the field will clap their hands. The curse that has weighed so heavy upon nature will be removed.

Chapters 1 and 22 of this Book serves as bookends to these enormous truths we have been studying. Chapters 1 and 22 are so diverse, yet strangely enough, they have a number of things in common. Let me mention a few of them:

1) In both chapters we are told that these prophecies are from God: Revelation 1:1 and Revelation 22:6.
2) In both chapters the message is validated by an angel: Revelation 1:1 and Revelation 22:6.
3) In both chapters John is mentioned as the human agent used in writing the book: Revelation 1:1 and Revelation 22:8.
4) In both chapters there is a blessing promised upon those who heed and keep this prophecy: Revelation 1:3 and Revelation 22:7.
5) In both chapters there is a tone of urgency and our time for response is short: Revelation 1:1 and Revelation 22:6.
6) In both chapters we are given titles for Jesus Christ that we are to remember: Revelation 1:5, 8 and Revelation 22:13, 16.

Throughout this great Book, the recurring message to the Church is: "How shall we live while awaiting the King's return?" In a nutshell, it teaches us to walk submissively and obediently to the Word of God. We are to discover God's will and then obey it. Many times this will put you out of step with today's culture, today's society, but this is OK. In fact, usually that is a good sign that you are walking in step with God.

Verse 8: "*And I John saw these things and heard them. And when I had heard and seen, I fell down to worship before the feet of the angel which showed me these things.*" John has been overcome before in chapter 19 when he bowed down to the angel who was showing him the marvelous Marriage Supper of the Lamb. And the angel had to rebuke John at that time, and tell him we should only worship God. And here in chapter 22 John does the same thing. Scripture does not say that he worshipped the angel, only that he worshipped before the feet of the angel. Nevertheless, this was inappropriate and must be corrected.[4]

In verse 8, John tells us these prophecies were not hearsay. He says he heard and saw these things and he has faithfully reported them. Thirty six times in this Book, John said, "I saw." John has told us much about what he saw and heard there on the Isle of Patmos. You have to remember that John did not dream these things; he actually saw them. What did he see that overwhelmed him? He saw a river, pure as crystal flowing out of the throne of God. He saw trees on each side of the river bearing 12 varieties of fruit. He saw that the fruit of these trees were therapeutic; they do better than heal you, they keep you from getting sick!

Then John was told that every believer would see God face to face. And John saw that there was no darkness there for the Lord God is the light of the city. And then when he heard the words about Jesus coming back, he could not control himself. Is it any wonder that John was so overcome with emotion that he fell down at the feet of the angel that was with him and began to worship?

Verse 9: "*Then saith he unto me 'See thou do it not; for I am thy fellow servant, and of thy brethren the prophets, and of them which keep the sayings of this book: worship God.'*" I am indebted to all the Christian scholars who have spent years and years learning the Greek language, not the Classical Greek, not the colloquial Greek spoken today, but the Koine Greek that was spoken in the time of Jesus. This is the language in which the New Testament was written. And if we do not go back to the original manuscript, we often miss the full meaning of a particular word. This is easily illustrated by the King James Version of the Bible. Though it is one of the best translations ever produced, it is not infallible. When it was translated about 1611, it was translated into the language that the common people spoke. That is the way God intended it to be. He wants people to understand what He is saying. And so, the Old Testament was written in Hebrew, the language that the Jews spoke in everyday conversations.

When John bowed to the angel in Revelation 22:9, the angel told him, "*Worship God.*" In the Greek, we are told that the tense is in the "aorist-imperative," and literally means "*Worship God only!*" There are many passages in Scripture that tell us that Jesus is God, equal with the Father. And here is one in Revelation 22:9, "*Worship God only.*" We find over and over in

Scripture people worshipping Jesus. And Jesus never admonished them about this, but always accepted their praise and worship because He IS God!"

Some people accuse Christians of worshipping the Bible. Christians should not worship the Bible, but worship the God of the Bible. The Book of Romans tells us that even the heathen can see God in nature, yet it is the Bible that tells us about His Person and character, and His plan for mankind. If your view of Scripture does not lead you to fall down at the feet of Jesus, and declare the Bible to be His infallible Word, then you are worshipping at the feet of human rationalism and reason. Notice this angel does not have the pride that brought the Devil down. He does not say, "I want to be like the Most High." Instead, he tells John in effect, "Worship God only – only God is worthy of worship."

The largest religious group in the world that names the name of Christ whose headquarters is in Rome will forever be plagued with the sin of idolatry. How many people have they taught to bow down and worship at the feet of images and statues? They say, "When we bow down at the feet of a statue, we are not worshipping the statue, we are worshipping God." But they are commanded not to do this. Look at the Second Commandment in Exodus 20:3-5a: "*Thou shalt have no other gods before me. Thou shalt not make unto thee any graven image, or any likeness of any thing that is in heaven above, or that is in the earth beneath, or that is in the water under the earth: Thou shalt not bow down thyself to them, nor serve them.*"

Look closely at Revelation 22, verse 8b. John says, "*I fell down to worship before the feet of the angel ….*". Whether John was worshipping the angel or whether he was falling at the feet of the angel to worship God, he was told not to do this. John should have known not to worship angels. He no doubt was familiar with the writings of Paul from Colossians 2:18 that clearly instructs us that we are not to worship angels. In the 4th chapter of the Book of Daniel, we saw King Nebuchadnezzar strutting around and accepting the worship and adoration that belonged to God. And so, God struck him with insanity with which he suffered for seven years. In the 12th chapter of Acts we find the people worshipping King Herod like he was a god, and he was drinking it all in, accepting praise and adoration due only to God. And do you know what happened? God struck him dead that very night (Acts 12:23). Do not take these words lightly: worship God only!

Now we come to verse 10: "*And he saith unto me, Seal not the sayings of the prophecy of this book: for the time is at hand.*" The time is at hand – the word is "kairos" in Greek. It means the correct season. God says the time for the revealing of the prophetic truth has come. He is saying that people are to be made aware of what is coming, so they can prepare accordingly. So therefore, do not seal up this Book. This calls to mind that powerful message that was given to Daniel in his Book, "*Go thy way, Daniel: for the words are closed up and sealed till the time of the end*" (12:9). It is implying that these words will be understood in the end times.

During Daniel's time, there were many prophecies that had to be fulfilled before the time of the end. But we are now living in the last days; that is why John was told in Revelation 22:10, *"Seal not the sayings of the prophecy of this book for the time is at hand."* The Book of Revelation in Greek is called the Apocalypse, "the unveiling." It is meant to be revealed and understood. I am amazed at pastors who say they never preach on prophecy. They consider it a waste of time. But in reality, it is one of the greatest evangelistic tools we have for reaching people for Christ. The Apostle Paul said in II Corinthians 5:11: *"Knowing therefore the terror of the Lord, we persuade men."* Paul is saying, "I know what is coming down the pike, and that is why we plead with people to accept Christ."

Anyone who can read about the coming wrath of God during the Tribulation Period, and not be motivated to tell others how to escape this terrible time, has not been touched by its prophetic message. There will be a great number of people who are saved during the Tribulation Period, but there will be a greater number who will stiffen their necks and resist God's calling. That is the same as it is today. There will be many who will be greatly blessed and keep the words of this prophecy, but there will be many more who will hold them up to ridicule and mockery.

This brings us to chapter 22, verse 11: *"He that is unjust, let him be unjust still: and he which is filthy, let him be filthy still: and he that is righteous, let him be righteous still: and he that is holy, let him be holy still."* This verse sets forth a divine principle. It is almost like the old saying, "a leopard doesn't change its spots." In this life, sin has man in captivity. Without God's help, you cannot change yourself. You cannot "turn over a new leaf." It will not last. This verse is talking about your condition when Christ comes back. This is a solemn truth: however you are found when Christ comes back as far as your salvation is concerned, that is the way you will be for all eternity. The choices you make today, determines your future tomorrow and all the days thereafter.

That is why we plead with people; today is the accepted time; today is the day of opportunity. But in the world to come, it is too late for any power to make the unjust righteous or make the filthy clean. *"He that is unjust, let him remain unjust still"* (Revelation 22:11a). Sad words. The implication of this verse is that the unjust will become more unjust, and the filthy will become filthier. The condition of a lost person gets worse and worse as the monster of sin gains more and more control.

Those who make choices in this life that produce a wicked character will find that a change for the better in eternity will be impossible. Listen to this sentence: present choices will become permanent choices. Exceptions to this are rare. If you look closely at Matthew 8:12, you will see that there is no thought of repentance for the unsaved. Jesus says they will be cast into outer darkness where there will be wailing and gnashing of teeth. This sentence tells us a lot. There will be wailing – that is worse than crying. But the last part of the sentence says there will be gnashing of teeth. That is a sign of anger and hatred toward God. On the other hand, all believers will be accepted and given entrance to the Holy City where they will continue to grow in grace. *"And he that is righteous, let him be righteous still"* (Revelation 22:11b). Hope and holiness will always be ours.

This is a solemn warning regarding the separation of the lost and the saved. The lost will be in the Lake of Fire where the unjust will continue to be unjust. The saved will be in the Holy City where the righteous will continue to be righteous. Charles Spurgeon once said: "Morality may keep you out of jail, but it takes the blood of Jesus Christ to keep you out of Hell."[5]

Now we come to verse 12: *"And, behold, I come quickly; and my reward is with Me, to give every man according as his work shall be."* Earlier we covered rewards, but let me refresh your memory. Do not confuse rewards, gifts and wages. They are not the same. Let's discuss them in reverse order. First, wages. As you all know, wages are payments earned by working. Theoretically, salvation can be earned. I said theoretically. All you have to do is keep all Ten Commandments every second of your entire life, and be as holy as God is holy. You know that is impossible. In fact, I John 1:8 clears this up for us real fast: *"If we say we have no sin, we deceive ourselves, and the truth is not in us."* So it is easy to see that we can never earn our salvation.

That brings us to gifts. Gifts are something that you cannot earn. They are given to you from a heart of love. This is how we get our salvation – the gift of eternal life. Ephesians 2:8-9 says this: *"For by grace are ye saved through faith; and that not of yourselves: it is the gift of God: Not of works, lest any man should boast."* Throughout the ages of eternity, no one will ever be able to stand up and say, "Hey! I am here because I earned it with my good works." There will be no room for boasting. So you see there is a clear difference between a wage and a gift.

Once you have become a child of God by accepting His free gift of salvation then you will be rewarded for good works done in His name with the right motives. I Corinthians chapter 3 tells us all about this awards ceremony. At that ceremony, called "The Bema Seat of Christ," our works will be put under God's searchlight to determine if rewards are justified. As Baptists, we stress that a born again believer cannot lose his or her salvation. And this is true. But we often fail to remind folks that they can lose their rewards. We are cautioned to be on guard – " .... *hold that fast which thou hast, that no man take thy crown* (Revelation 3:11). Do not let the Devil steal your reward by enticing you into unsavory situations! Jesus is coming to reward those who have faithfully served Him. Most have served Him out of the limelight, faithfully caring for others. I think of many in my Bible class who in later life have been caregivers for their spouses or children and/or aging parents. This service will not be forgotten by God. He says in I Timothy 5:8 (NIV), *"If anyone does not provide for his relatives, especially for his immediate family, he has denied the faith and is worse than an unbeliever."*

We have a very dear friend by the name of Ann. She is in her 70's now. Her younger sister was a Down Syndrome child from birth. Although the younger sister lived until she was over 50, her mind never expanded more than that of 10 year old. Her parents took care of their daughter until they passed away. Ann never married. It was her mission in life to care for her younger sister – day in and day out. For years, Ann fed her, tucked her into bed, and made life as comfortable for her as she knew how. God sees this unselfish love. He sees this heartfelt devotion, and He will not forget it.

Jesus says here in Revelation 22:12 that He is coming back, and He says He is bringing our rewards with Him. We are all going to get our rewards on the same day at this reward ceremony (II Timothy 4:8). There will be no envy or jealousy on our part; we will be cheering all our friends and fellow believers as they receive their rewards. I came across a little story that beautifully illustrates how doing things with the right motives is all about.

A successful Christian businessman was growing old and knew it was time to choose a successor to take over his business. Instead of choosing one of his directors or one of his grown children, he decided to do something altogether different. He called a meeting of all his young executives. Mr. Marshall said, "It is time for me to step down, and choose the next CEO of the company, so I have decided to choose one of you. I am going to give each of you a seed today – one very special seed. I want you to plant the seed, water it, and come back here one year from today with what you have grown from the seed that I have given you. I will then judge the plants that you bring in, and then I will know who will be the next CEO."

One man, named Jim, was there and, like the others, received a seed. He went home and excitedly told his wife about his big opportunity. She helped him get a pot, the soil, the compost and he planted the seed. Every day he would water it and watch to see if it was growing. He heard other executives in the office tell about how their plants were beginning to flourish. Jim kept checking his seed, but nothing grew. Three months went by, four months, eight months, still no plant. The others kept telling how well their plants were doing. Jim did not say anything, but deep inside he knew he was a failure. He knew, somehow, he had killed his seed because the others were telling how tall their plants had become. Jim kept watering and fertilizing. Oh, how he wanted his seed to grow!

A year finally went by and the CEO told all the young executives to bring in their plants for inspection. Jim told his wife that he just could not take in an empty pot. For a fleeting second, he thought about stopping by the nursery and buying a plant, but he quickly dismissed the idea. He and his wife prayed, and they both knew that he would have to tell the truth. Jim felt sick at his stomach. It was going to be the most embarrassing moment of his life. When he carried his empty pot into the board room, he was amazed at the variety of plants grown by the other executives. They were beautiful in all shapes and sizes. Jim placed his empty pot on the floor beside him and many of his associates laughed while a few felt sorry for him.

When Mr. Marshall arrived, he surveyed the room and greeted his young executives. Jim looked at the floor, not wanting to make eye contact with his boss. "My, what great plants, trees and bushes you have grown," said the CEO. "Today, one of you will be appointed the next Chief Executive Officer to run this fine company for years to come." All of a sudden, Mr. Marshall spotted Jim at the back of the room standing beside his empty pot. He ordered his financial officer to escort Jim to the front of the room. Jim was terrified. He thought, "Not only am I a failure, but now I'm going to get fired in front of everyone."

When Jim got to the front, the CEO asked him what had happened to his seed. Jim told him the whole story – that he had diligently watered it, fertilized it, but all to no avail. His seed did not germinate. Everyone snickered. Mr. Marshall asked everyone to sit down except for Jim, whom he asked to remain standing next to him. Mr. Marshall announced, "Gentlemen, meet your next Chief Executive Officer" as he smiled and motioned toward Jim. Jim thought there must be some mistake. Why, he had not even been able to get the plant to poke through the dirt! How could he possibly be chosen to lead this company?

Then Mr. Marshall said, "One year ago today, I gave everyone in this room a seed. I told you to take the seed, plant it, water it and bring it back to me in one year. What you did not know is that I gave all of you seeds that I had boiled on the stove – seeds that were as dead as doorknobs – impossible for them to sprout. All of you, except Jim, have brought me trees and plants and bushes. When you found your seeds would not grow, you substituted another seed for the one I gave you. Jim was the only one with the courage and honesty to bring me a pot with the dead seed still in it. Therefore, he is the one who will be the new Chief Executive of the company." When Jim got home, his wife reminded him, "God says when you trust in Him, He will direct your paths."[6]

Jesus says in verse 13: "*I am Alpha and Omega, the beginning and the end, the first and the last.*" He used these same words in chapter 1 of this Book and, in case anyone was confused as to who is speaking, in chapter 1, verse 18, He adds, "*I am He that liveth, and was dead; and, behold, I am alive for evermore, Amen; and have the keys of Hell and of death.*" That clears up who is speaking. It is none other than the Lord Jesus Christ. How can anyone, including the various cults such as the Mormons, Moonies, Jehovah's Witnesses, Christian Scientists, Scientologists – how can they say that Jesus is just another angel? Why, this is a description of GOD!

Verse 14: "*Blessed are they that do His commandments that they may have right to the tree of life, and may enter in through the gates into the city.*" The NASB relied on older manuscripts and here is the way it translated the verse. "*Blessed are those who wash their robes, so that they may have the right to the Tree of Life, and may enter by the gates into the city.*" In the King James, it appears that our right to the city rests on our doing His commandments. Works salvation!

But, oh, how different the true rendering is. Washing our robes (in the blood of Christ) gives us the right to the city.

Of course, if we truly trust Christ, we will seek to do what He has commanded us to do. I John 3:23 says: *"And this is His commandment, That we should believe on the name of His Son Jesus Christ, and love one another, as He gave us commandment."* But the important point to see here is that our right to Heaven does not rest on legalistic grounds. It is not doing that gives one title to his home in Heaven. It is Jesus' blood that has washed us and our robes white as snow and gives us entrance into our heavenly home. We find this statement again in an earlier reference to the Tribulation saints who *" …. washed their robes, and made them white in the blood of the Lamb"* (Revelation 7:14b). Scripture is very plain: salvation is by God's grace. Those who choose to wash their robes in Christ's blood will be granted two essential privileges: 1) access to the Tree of Life, and 2) permission to pass through the gates of the Holy City. Those who leave their robes dirty by refusing to accept Christ will not be allowed into the city.

Revelation 21:27 which we studied in the previous chapter says this about Heaven: *"And there shall no wise enter into it any thing that defileth, neither whatsoever worketh abomination, or maketh a lie: but they which are written in the Lamb's Book of Life."* Nothing shall be allowed into the City that defiles it or makes it unclean in any way.

We have discovered as we have gone through here, an important lesson. For the believer, the Book of Revelation tells us some awesome and beautiful times are ahead. You are probably familiar with the Sermon on the Mount found in Matthew, chapter 5, with all the Beatitudes – all the "blessed" verses. But few are familiar with the Beatitudes found in this Book of Revelation. And to many people, they are missing a host of blessings because they ignore this Book. Let us look at some of the blessings that are in this last Book of the Bible.

Revelation 1:3: *"Blessed is he that readeth, and they that hear the words of this prophecy, and keep those things which are written therein …."*.

Revelation 14:13b: *"Blessed are the dead who die in the Lord from henceforth …."*.

Revelation 16:15: *"Blessed is he that watcheth, and keepeth his garments* [pure]*…."*.

Revelation 19:9: *"Blessed are they which are called unto the marriage supper of the Lamb."*

Revelation 20:6a: *"Blessed and holy is he that hath part in the first resurrection: on such the second death hath no power …."*.

Revelation 22:7: *"Behold, I come quickly: blessed is he that keepeth the sayings of the prophecy of this book."*

Revelation 22:15 tells us who will not be allowed into the Holy City: *"For without* [without is the old English word for outside] *are dogs, and sorcerers, and whoremongers, and murderers, and idolaters, and whosoever loveth and maketh a lie."* The first ones mentioned that are barred from entrance are "dogs." Jesus is using a play on words here. He is not talking about our wonderful pets. He is talking about those people who exhibit the nature of a lower animal and go back to their sinful habits.

Paul uses this same analogy in Philippians 3:2 when he says "beware of dogs," and he is talking about a particularly obnoxious group of people. This is evident from II Peter 2:22: *"But it happened unto them according to the true proverb, the dog is turned to his own vomit again; and the sow that was washed to her wallowing in the mire."* Isaiah speaks of the unfaithful teachers in Israel and calls them "dumb dogs" (Isaiah 56:10). God knows the lower nature of animals.

We always had one or two pigs when I was growing up. And we all know that you can take a pig, scrub it as clean as can be, tie a ribbon around its neck, and the pig is miserable until it can go roll in the mud again. And God is saying that this is a picture of human nature. If we have not experienced the new birth and been given a new nature, then no matter how much we try to clean up, we will return to our old filthy habits. Of course those who are liars will not be admitted entrance. That includes all atheists who in effect call God a liar by saying there is no God. I am reminded of the 19th Century novelist Gustave Elaubert who used to laugh about the archaeologist who was an atheist. He discovered a stone tablet from a million years ago that said, "I do not exist. Signed: God." And the atheist exclaimed, "See! I told you so!"[7]

Verse 16: *"I Jesus have sent mine angel to testify unto you these things in the churches. I am the root and offspring of David, and the bright and morning star."* Jesus says "testify" – tell these things in the churches. Now that the Book of Revelation is almost complete, the Lord again calls attention to the fact that it is intended primarily for instruction of the true Church during our present age. Notice something very, very important in this verse. It is the first time that the Church is specifically mentioned since the end of chapter 3 when we read the letter to the church at Laodicea. This is because the universal Church was called up to Heaven in Revelation 4:1 at the Rapture and is not mentioned again during the Tribulation Period.

In chapter 22, verses 16-17, Jesus says: *"I, Jesus have sent mine angel to testify unto you these things in the churches. I am the root and offspring of David, and the bright and morning star.* Now wait a minute. This is a paradox – a mystery. How can He be the root David and also the offspring of David?

In college, my roommate, Dave Johnson and I used to entertain at class parties. I played the banjo and Dave played the "bucketar" which I had made from a metal garbage can turned upside down with a 4 ft. slat attached to the side of it. It had a real bass string extending from the top of the slat to the bottom of the garbage can. I kid you not, when strummed, it sounded like a real bass fiddle! We were joined by Don on the guitar and Doug on the fiddle. The four of us were known as the Sons of the Corncobs and we played at many of the class socials.

One of the songs we sang was *I'm My Own Grandpa,* a humorous song written by Ray Stevens. He must have gotten the idea from this verse. How can Jesus be the "root" (the beginning – the spark that first gave life to David), and at the same time, be the offspring (the descendent) who sprang from the loins of David? A simple explanation is that He was the root of David because He was with the Father in the beginning and created all things, and He was the offspring of David because when He was born in Bethlehem from the lineage of David. Let us explore this more fully. And let us answer the second question first. How can Jesus be the offspring of David? Well, what an intriguing Book is the Bible! We cannot plumb its depths. We cannot get our arms around all its riches.

We know about the sin of Adam in the Garden and the awful consequences that followed. But then, in Genesis 3:15, we have the very first prophecy in the Bible – God promised a Redeemer. The Bible says that Satan would deliver a blow to the Redeemer's heel, but the Redeemer would deliver a blow to Satan's head. In other words, Satan would deliver a non-lethal blow which he did at Calvary, and Christ would deliver a lethal blow which He will do when He casts Satan into the Lake of Fire (Revelation 20:10).

Satan is like a condemned man on death row. He has been sentenced but his penalty has not yet been carried out. Go back to Genesis 3:15. Of the millions of people who would be born into the world, how was anyone to know which one would be the Redeemer? Well, God narrowed it down in Genesis 12 to the lineage of a man named Abraham. This is an intriguing story and we do not have time to go into it in detail. I will just hit the highlights. Abraham had two sons, Isaac and Ishmael. Isaac fathered the nation which is known as Israel. Ishmael fathered the peoples who are known as the Arabs. God made it clear that the Redeemer would come from the lineage of Isaac (Genesis chapters 12-17; 26:1-5) and from the lineage of David (Matthew 1:6).

Jesus could say He was the root of David because He was in the beginning with the Father. He is the root of David because Jesus is David's creator – David sprang from Him. John tells us in his gospel, *"In the beginning was the Word, and the Word was with God, and the Word was God"* (John 1:1). A few verses later, we find that the Word was " .... *made flesh and dwelt among us"* (John 1:14a). This is a description of Jesus, and we are told that He was with the Father from the beginning. He was in the Godhead with the Father and the Holy Spirit, and was part of the "us" when the words were recorded *"Let us make man in our image"* (Genesis 1:26).

Jesus Himself said, *"Before Abraham was, I AM"* (John 8:58b). He did not say "I was" because no matter how far you go back in time – no matter how far you go ahead in time – Jesus IS there! He is the great "I AM." The deity of Christ drips from every page in this Holy Book. At Christmas, from Isaiah 7:14, we read the promise of the coming Redeemer. *"Therefore the Lord himself shall give you a sign; Behold, a virgin shall conceive, and bear a son, and shall call his name Immanuel* [meaning God with us]. And He shall also be called *"Wonderful, Counselor, The mighty God, The everlasting Father!"* (Isaiah 9:6). The child that was born in the cattle stall in Bethlehem is the eternal Word of God. The prophet Micah says the Redeemer will be born in Bethlehem, and then he says of this ruler of Israel *" .... whose goings forth have been from of old, from everlasting"* (Micah 5:2b). In other words, He has always been with God the Father.

How can anyone miss the deity of Christ? Yet nearly every month a new book comes out proclaiming that Jesus was just an ordinary man teaching us how to live by the highest standards mankind has ever known. C. S. Lewis, maybe the greatest religious thinker of our time, exploded that myth in a hurry. He said that Jesus claimed He was God, and Jesus claimed He was the ONLY way to get to Heaven. If Jesus was lying, He was the greatest liar of all time, and therefore could not be the greatest moral teacher of all time. You cannot have it both ways. Either Jesus was who He said He was, or He was a fraud and a liar. There is no other option.[8] No, Jesus was not a liar nor was He just another man sent here to teach us a new moral ethic. He was not another Plato or Socrates and He sure was not another Mohammed. He was God in the flesh, and mankind has never been the same.

The Bible teaches that only God can forgive sin. Yet in Matthew 9:2b, Jesus said to a crippled man, *"Thy sins be forgiven thee."* John was told twice in the Book of Revelation by an angel, "Stand up! Do not worship me. Worship only God!" Yet, Jesus accepted divine worship time after time after time (Matthew 2:11; 8:2; 9:18; 14:33; 15:25; 28:9; Luke 24:52; John 9:38).

Remember back in the 5th chapter of Revelation? We read about a seven-sealed scroll that was being held by a strong angel, and John and the others were weeping because no one was worthy to open the scroll. At that point, one of the elders told John, *"Weep not: behold, the Lion of the tribe of Judah, the Root of David hath prevailed to open the book, and loose the seven seals thereof"* (Revelation 5:5). We learned that it was the title deed to the earth that God originally gave to Adam, but Adam was cheated out of it by Satan. Only the Root of David, the Lord Jesus Christ, was worthy to break the seals and redeem the title deed. As each seal was broken, a specific judgment was unleashed upon the earth. This was God's plan to cleanse and redeem the earth. At the conclusion of the seven seals, the Bible proclaims, *"The kingdoms of this world have become the Kingdom of our Lord"* (Revelation 11:15 NIV). And that folks is why Jesus can truthfully say, *"I am the root and offspring of David ...."* (Revelation 22:16).

Jesus said to His detractors, *"Your father Abraham rejoiced to see my day: and he saw it and was glad."* When they questioned how Jesus could have associated with Abraham since Jesus was not yet 50 years old, He replied, *"Before Abraham was, I AM"* (John 8:56-58), indicating He had eternally existed (as confirmed by Micah 5:2). Over and over the Bible stands the test of scoffers, and repeatedly shows their ignorance! Finally, in the last part of verse 16, Jesus declares Himself to be the bright and morning star. Have you ever gotten up just before dawn and seen the morning star in the southeastern sky? It is actually Venus and it is the brightest light in the sky just before the sun rises. Satan at one time was called Lucifer, the son of the morning (Isaiah 14:12). But here in Revelation, Jesus is pointing to the fact that He Himself is the Bright and Morning Star, not Satan, the counterfeit.

Satan intended that his rising star would continue to rise until he exalted himself above the very God of Heaven. But his ambitions collapsed like a falling star, and he will be entombed forever in the Lake of Fire. The Lord Jesus Christ on the other hand is the true Morning Star, and His brightness will illumine the entire Holy City, so much so that John could write, *"And the city had no need of the sun, neither of the moon, to shine in it: for the glory of God did lighten it, and the Lamb is the light thereof"* (Revelation 21:23). The correlation to this is that Jesus will come back in one of the darkest moments of world history as the Morning Star for His Bride at the beginning of the Tribulation Period, and He will come back with His Bride after the Tribulation Period for a 1,000 year honeymoon called the Millennium. Praise God! May it be today as we continue to look for Jesus our Bright and Morning Star!

Now we come to Chapter 22, verse 17: *"And the Spirit and the Bride say, 'Come.' And let him that heareth say, 'Come.' And let him that is athirst come. And whosoever will, let him take the water of life freely."* There are so many jewels in this one little verse! Take for instance the first phrase: *"And the Spirit and the Bride say come."* The Holy Spirit continually beckons to unbelievers to come to Christ, and then, the Church – the Bride of Christ – is crying out to lost people, "Come and be saved."

However, I believe the primary thrust of this verse is a yearning for Christ to return to earth. He has just been revealed as the Bright and Morning Star and immediately, the cry goes out "Come!" "Don't delay any longer!" So we see the Holy Spirit and the Church invite Christ to return. All who really know the Lord are yearning for His return. But I am afraid that by and large, the Church is not yearning – it is yawning. Visit any number of churches that you wish, and see how many messages you hear on the return of Jesus Christ. There will be very few. It should be on our lips every day – Come, Lord Jesus!

Let me give you a great example of what I am talking about. We kid about getting some peace and quiet when our spouses go away, but we know that is not true. When your wife or husband goes away on a long trip, don't you just yearn for the day when they will come back? I do! You can take out your billfold or purse, and look at their picture, just as you can read Scripture, and visualize a picture of Christ. Or you can pick up the phone and talk to them, just like you can talk to Jesus in prayer. But there is nothing that can compare to that face-to-face meeting. Oh, Come Lord Jesus!

Then the last part of this verse turns the invitation completely around. It is the other side of the coin. It is not us inviting Christ, but it is Christ inviting all others to come to Him. And it is a three-fold invitation. First, *"Let him that heareth come"* (Revelation 22:17b). The Bible says that *"Faith cometh by hearing"* (Romans 10:17). People have to hear; they do not absorb the Gospel by osmosis. Therefore, it is important that we invite people to come to church. They need to hear the Gospel. Jesus sums up the Gospel message in John 5:24: *"Verily, verily I say unto you. He that hearth my word, and believeth on Him that sent me, hath everlasting life, and shall not come into condemnation* [judgment]; *but is passed from death unto life."*

The second part of the invitation to the lost is: *" …. And let him that is athirst come"* (Revelation 22:17b). When you are really thirsty on a hot day and you have been working outside, you might settle for a glass of Gatorade. But what you really want is a cool, clear glass of water.

I saw a special on the Discovery Channel recently. It was about the U.S.S. Indianapolis during WW II. The ship was cruising off the coast of Leyte in the South Pacific when it took a direct hit from a Japanese torpedo. The ship was mortally wounded and was going down fast. A frantic message was sent – "SOS, SOS, we are sinking and we need help immediately." The result was so sad it will make you cry. The Navy received the message alright, but thought it was a trap, a ploy by the Japanese. So the Navy ignored the message. When I saw that, I was crushed. Twelve hundred of the Navy's finest found themselves floating in the cold waters of the Pacific. Most had life jackets – a few had rafts to climb in or at least cling to.

The men faced shark infested waters over the next few days. Oceanographers tell that sharks are not vicious per se; they generally attack people only when they are hungry. The men were in the water four days and five nights without food and water. Toward the end of their ordeal, their thirst was unbearable. Though they were cautioned not to drink the seawater, many could not resist as their thirst was so great. Drinking seawater, even in small amounts results in diarrhea, dehydration and death.[9]

When the stranded sailors of the Indianapolis were finally spotted by a passing U.S. airplane, and they were eventually rescued by a Navy ship, there were only about 300 survivors out of the nearly 1,200 that went into the water a few days before.[10] Our young people need to be aware of such heroic exploits that guarantee the freedoms they enjoy every day. However, with less and less American history being taught to them in the classrooms, this is not the case.

All that water and none of it to drink. It reminds me of a poem we had to learn when I was in high school. It was called, *The Rime of the Ancient Mariner.* It was about a ship that was stranded in the middle of the ocean. Men were dying of thirst. I used to be able to quote the entire poem which was quite lengthy, but after 70 years, I only remember one stanza: "Water, water everywhere and all the boards did shrink. Water, water everywhere and not a drop to drink."[11]

Water can sometimes be scary as it was for these sailors. But at other times, it can be refreshing. If you had to describe one word for the wonderful taste of water, what would it be? Refreshing? Satisfying? That is the living water that Jesus offers.

During WWII, one of the most famous survivals at sea involved Captain Eddie Rickenbacker. He was an ace fighter pilot during WWI, shooting down more than 25 enemy aircraft. In later life, he was a senior executive of Eastern Airlines for many years. During WWII, he came out of retirement at the request of Henry Stimson, Secretary of the Navy, to deliver a secret message from President Roosevelt to General MacArthur. He was flying a B-17 bomber known as the Flying Fortress, when the plane ran out of fuel and crashed in a remote part of the South Pacific. Even though the Japanese controlled nearby islands, Rickenbacker and his six man crew were never spotted.

The men inflated their life raft and floated to parts unknown. They ran out of food in three days. On the eighth day after praying hard, a seagull landed on Rickenbacker's head. Slowly – slowly – he moved his hand upward and fortunately grabbed the seagull by a leg. They divided it and ate most of it; the rest of the organs they used for fishing bait. Occasionally, it would rain and they would catch the water in any container they could find. They also, after a light rain, wrung out their clothes to trap this precious drinking water. Rickenbacker assumed leadership, encouraging and browbeating the others to trust in God and keep up their spirits. But one airman died and was buried at sea.

The Navy's patrol planes planned to abandon their search after several weeks, but Rickenbacker's wife persuaded them to persevere a while longer even though newspapers were reporting that the Captain died at sea. Then on November 13th a search plane spotted and rescued them. They had been adrift in the Pacific Ocean for 24 days. His co-pilot later wrote a bestseller about their ordeal at sea entitled, *We Thought We Heard the Angels Sing.*[12]

Max Lucado wrote that Captain Rickenbacker traveled extensively during his later years speaking publicly about his traumatic experience. He always remembered to thank God for His protection. And he never forgot to thank the seagulls. Here is what Max Lucado wrote about him: "For 30 years, every Friday evening about sunset on a lonely stretch along the eastern Florida seacoast, you could see an old man walking – white-haired, bushy-eyed, slightly bent. His bucket was filled with shrimp and his heart was full of thanks, to remember that one bird, on a day long past, gave itself up without a struggle – so he could live."[13] He was asked what was the biggest lesson he had learned from that experience. He replied, "The biggest lesson I learned was this: if you have all the fresh water you want to drink and all the food you want to eat – you ought never to complain about anything!"[14] What a great perspective!

Now we come to chapter 22, verse 18 in our study. *"For I testify unto every man that heareth the words of the prophecy of this book, If any man shall add unto these things, God shall add unto him the plagues that are written in this book."* This is serious business. We have seen some pretty horrible things taking place during the Tribulation Period: war, disease, famine, water turning into blood – I do not think you would want to experience any of these plagues, do you? And yet, these plagues are promised upon anyone who adds to God's Holy Word. It is beyond me in the face of these clear and stern warnings, why would anyone add anything alongside of or in place of God's Holy Word?

But that is what every one of the groups we call "cults" have done, including the Mormons, the Jehovah's Witnesses, the Moonies, the Christian Scientists and a thousand more according to Watchman Fellowship, a conservative cult-watching-group.[15] They have either replaced the Bible with their own book or they have elevated their own book, saying you cannot understand the Bible without their written enlightenment. Some have thrown out the Bible, and replaced it with their own personality as they build a following around themselves. It is surprising how many fall in the latter category and more are being added every day.

Some false teachers try to water this down by saying these warnings about adding or changing only relate to the words in the Book of the Revelation since it says, "this prophecy." This is technically true, but there is a principle here relating to the entire Bible. This principle applies to anyone who seeks to intentionally distort God's Word. Moses gave a similar warning in Deuteronomy 4:1-2, where he cautioned the Israelites that they must listen to and obey the commandments of the Lord, neither adding to nor taking away from His revealed Word. Proverbs 30:5-6 contains a similar command to anyone who would add to God's words: he will be rebuked and proven to be a liar. We must be careful to handle the Bible with care and reverence so as to not distort its message and incur horrendous judgments.

Changing God's Word is dangerous! We can tell by Revelation 22:18 just how serious God is about this matter. How would anyone dare come along with another so-called inspired book from God or false teachings contrary to God's Word when we are told flatly the following?

1) If anyone adds to this Book, they will inherit the awful plagues that are spelled therein (Revelation 22:18-19).
2) Paul said if anyone, including an angel, comes to you with teachings opposite to or adding to the pure Gospel, let him be cursed (Galatians 1:8).
3) In Hebrews 1:1, Scripture says that in times past God spoke to us by His prophets, but in these last days (since the cross) He has spoken to us through His Son (a clear indication that God's Holy message to us is complete; we do not need any further revelations or additions from so-called "latter day prophets").

Let us look at a few of these groups who have "added to or taken away from God's Word." First, there is Islam. Muslims believe in the same Bible we use, however they add the Koran.

Here is their main argument: Mohammed came on the scene 600 years after Christ. Therefore, Islam says Mohammed has the latest message from God and so we should listen to him. So Islam is a perfect example of "adding to" God's word. And since all these groups are accepting the latest word from God from these Johnny-come-lately prophets instead of relying on the Bible which was *once delivered to the saints* (Jude 1:3), I have bad news for them. There IS coming a man who will claim he has the latest word from God. In fact, he will claim he IS God. That man is Antichrist, and all these groups will fall in line behind him!

Another example of adding to God's Word is the Church of Jesus Christ of Latter Day Saints, commonly called "the Mormons." This strange religion began in the 1830's when a fellow named Joseph Smith was digging for gold in upstate New York when he purportedly uncovered some mysterious golden plates (no person ever saw them other than Smith). These plates had weird carvings on them – characters and pictures almost like Egyptian hieroglyphics. Smith could not make heads or tails of these writings until he was confronted by an angel who said his name was Moroni.

Angel Moroni gave Smith some magic reading glasses. When Smith put them on – bingo! He could read and understand clearly the strange carvings. But what was amazing is that he could read them in King James English which was not even the language that the people spoke at that time! Throughout the Bible, God always transmitted His messages in the current language that the common people spoke. If Mormons could clearly grasp the import of this truth, they would clearly see through the charlatan, Joseph Smith. He began to translate these strange figures and characters into stilted old English which was not spoken in the 1830's. Obviously, Joseph Smith had done extensive copying from the King James Bible to make his writings sound "biblical." That is why his book has "he sayeth " and "he heareth" and "straightway they went up" even though no one talked that way at the time. And so, if the Mormons would go solely by God's Holy Word as we have it without their treasured *Book of Mormon*, their doctrines would collapse immediately. They had to add to the Word of God to justify their beliefs.

Many of these beliefs came from Joseph Smith's dark side, such as having multiple wives contrary to what Jesus taught. Most people are aware that Joseph Smith was the leader of the Mormons, but few people realize that his best friend, Sidney Rigdon, was the brains behind their teachings and the structuring of their doctrines. The complete story of Joseph Smith's rise to power – warts and all – is recorded by a respected Mormon historian who faithfully documented these events.[16]

Another good example is the group called *Christian Scientists.* What a strange bunch of beliefs! It was founded by Mary Baker Eddy in 1866, after she had a bad fall on her icy sidewalk. Her doctor told her she had a mortal wound, and would die in two or three days. She miraculously rose from her deathbed in three days (she said just like Jesus did) and discovered the principles of Christian Science.[17]

Sometime afterward, she wrote, *Science and Health with Key to the Scriptures* in which she says that you cannot understand the Bible without her book. She even stated that if someone had to choose between the Bible and her book, they would be far better off if they chose her book. Her basic premise is that everything material is an illusion such as death, pain and suffering. She says, "Even Jesus did not die, but was hiding in the tomb, to come out and show everyone that there was no such thing as death."[18] But Mary Baker Eddy "thought" she died on December 3, 1910. Unfortunately she was not able to convince her friends that she was not really dead, so eventually they buried her.

Minister and researcher Jan Karel van Baalen, Princeton Seminary, wrote: "Mary Baker Eddy lived long enough to spend her last years in utter loneliness and in mortal fear of the malicious animal magnetism which her enemies were said to direct against her to kill her mentally. She died at eighty-nine, worn out and silent, yet leaving behind a host of followers ready to defend the legend of her supernaturalism. Bronson Alcott, early teacher and father of Louisa May Alcott, upon reading *Science and Health* said that no one but a woman or a fool could have written it.[19]

How about the Jehovah's Witnesses? This is the most tenacious group of all. If you make the mistake of letting them in your house, there is big trouble ahead. I know of two such incidences with elderly widows, members of our church. In each case, the person was feeling sorry for themselves, feeling neglected and feeling that no one cared for them. At that opportune time, the Jehovah's Witnesses came by and offered an encouraging word.

They comforted these poor widows, and their trap was set, convincing these ladies that "after all, we both worship the same Jesus." Really? They did not tell the ladies what the JWs really believe: that Jesus was a created being; that when He died on the cross, His body stayed dead. Only His Spirit was resurrected. His physical body was snatched away forever by Satan. Jesus gave His body to Satan as a ransom (down payment) on the curse that Adam put on the human race.

JWs teach that Jesus' death on the cross, in and by itself, was insufficient to effect man's salvation. Instead, several additional requirements must be added. According to the Watchtower Organization, there are four requirements to complete man's salvation.[20]

1. Taking in knowledge of the only true God, and of the one whom God sent forth, Jesus Christ. 2. Obey God's laws. 3. Be associated with God's organization. God is using only one organization today to accomplish his will (JWs). 4. God requires that prospective subjects of his Kingdom support His government by loyally advocating His Kingdom rule to others.

The only way for Jehovah's Witnesses to defend their weird doctrines is to have their "own

Bible." The King James Version, which they used for years, was giving them too much trouble defending their strange beliefs. So in 1950, they came up with their own translation called, *The New World Translation of the Bible.* There is not a single renowned Greek or Hebrew scholar in the world that will tell you that this is an accurate or trustworthy translation. Former Jehovah's Witness David R. Reed wrote: "When asked for the credentials of the men on *The New World Bible* translating committee to verify whether they possessed the expertise that would qualify them to overrule traditional authorities on biblical languages, JWs reply that the identity of the translators remains confidential. Why? They say so that all credit will go to God rather than to men. But the real reason for their anonymity was exposed in recent years when defectors who resigned from the Watchtower headquarters identified the members of the committee, revealing that none of them had any expertise in biblical Hebrew, Greek or Aramaic – the original languages from which the Bible must be translated."[21]

Any verse in God's Word that contradicts their teachings, has been translated to conform and support their diabolical doctrines. It is pitiful! I will give you one example among many. In John 1:1, it says: *"In the beginning was the Word, and the Word was with God, and the Word was God."* A little later in this same chapter (verse 14), we are told that *"the Word became flesh and dwelt among us",* so we know *"the Word"* is referring to Jesus.

The Jehovah's Witnesses teach that there is no such thing as the Trinity; that Jesus was not God after all – He was a created being just like the angels. So, they had to do something to change John 1:1 as it would completely destroy their teaching on this subject. So they decided to come up with their own translation that supported their doctrines. Here is the way they translated John 1:1 in their *New World Translation*: "In the beginning was the Word and the Word was with God and the Word was a god." "A god" – little "g." You will not win an argument with them because they are trained extensively to twist the scriptures using the *New World Translation* to support their weird doctrines.

Leading Greek scholar Dr. Julius Mantey said: "I have never read any New Testament so badly translated as *The Kingdom Interlinear Translation* of the Greek Scriptures (i.e., their *New World Translation of the Bible).* In fact, it is not their translation at all. Rather, it is a distortion of the New Testament."[22]

British scholar H. H. Rowley calls this translation "a shining example of how the Bible should not be translated," classifying the text as "an insult to the Word of God."[23] As the late professor, Dr. Charles L. Feinberg noted, "I can assure you that the rendering which the Jehovah's Witnesses give John 1:1 is not held by any reputable Greek scholar."[24]

Dr. Bruce M. Metzger, professor of New Testament at Princeton University, calls the *New World Translation* "a frightful mistranslation."[25] And Dr. William Barclay wrote: "The deliberate distortion of truth by this sect is seen in their New Testament translation – and it is abundantly clear that a sect which can translate the New Testament like that is intellectually dishonest."[26]

One of the best arguments I have found with Jehovah's Witnesses is to point out that their founder, Charles Taze Russell, was well known in various courts as having lied under oath. He was sued for false claims of his "miracle wheat" that he was selling at inflated prices. His wife sued him for "indecencies" with a young woman named Rose Ball that lived in their house and worked at the Watchtower office. He claimed under oath in court that he was proficient in "Koine Greek" in which the Bible was written, but he perjured himself a few minutes later as he was handed a Greek New Testament and had to admit that he did not know a word of Greek. If you want to verify this you can read the actual transcript of the trial which is available in official court archives via the internet which proves that he was a liar and a fraud.[27]

The best advice I can give you is this: if the Jehovah's Witnesses come to your door, follow the instructions given in II John 1:10 (NIV): *"If anyone comes to you and does not bring this teaching, do not take him into your house or welcome him."* As they were leaving, I would sometimes say, "Have a nice day." I do not say this anymore because of the next verse which says, *"Anyone who welcomes him shares in his wicked work"* (II John 1:11 NIV).

Verse 19 of Revelation 22 addresses the "other side of the coin." It says: *"And if any man shall take away from the words of the book of this prophecy, God shall take away his part out of the book of life, and out of the Holy City, and from the things which are written in this book."* So, we have seen how serious it is for anyone to add to God's Word, and this verse shows us it is just as serious to take away from God's Word. How do you take away from God's Word? One way is to deny its validity – to deny its truth. And these attacks for the most part are not coming from the skeptics and the unbelievers who are always there attacking. Much of the time, these attacks are coming from so-called Christians. This saddens God's great heart and makes Him angry at the same time. If He were in earth's court of law, He could sue them for libel and slander. How would you like someone telling lies in your name, saying things that you did not say and attributing them to you?

I am sorry I have to say this, but if I were an Episcopalian, I would be embarrassed because of some of my leaders. I have heard of some Episcopal churches which are conservative and very sound, but many are not. One of the top Episcopal leaders, retired Bishop John Spong of New Jersey, has written some of the most blasphemous books in which he denies the virgin birth, denies the miracles of Jesus, denies the resurrection, denies the Second Coming and claims that Paul and Timothy were homosexual lovers.[28] In spite of those ridiculous assertions, Spong is still respected as one of the top leaders of the Episcopal Church and a frequent spokesmen for them in national venues.

The late popular TV Pastor Robert Schuller said that, "It is not necessary to be born again."[29] But Jesus said, *"Truly, truly, I say to you, unless one is born again he cannot see the kingdom of God"* (John 3:3 ESV). I think I will stick with what Jesus said. Rev. Schuller also had a warped view of what the cross of Jesus was all about. He said in his book, "The cross sanctifies the ego trip. For the cross protected our Lord's perfect self-esteem from turning into sinful pride."[30] The New Testament clearly shows that without the shedding of blood by Jesus on the cross there is no forgiveness of sin (Hebrews 9:22).

I am thinking about one more group called the Jesus Seminar which has committed blasphemy when it comes to God's Word. It was founded in 1985 by liberal scholars, headed up by the late Rev. Robert Funk, a top leader in the Disciples of Christ denomination. The Jesus Seminar was composed of 74 members – Protestants, Catholics, atheists, professors at universities and seminaries, one pastor, one filmmaker and three members of the Westar Institute in California which sponsored the project. Of the 74, there were three women and two Jews. Thirty-six, almost half, have a degree from or currently teach at one of three schools – Harvard, Claremont or Vanderbilt. These universities have some of the most liberal departments of New Testament studies anywhere. Only a handful come from outside North America; European scholarship is almost entirely unrepresented.

As many as 200 scholars participated in the Jesus Seminar over the years, but toward the end of its life, the final group had dwindled to 74. People dropped out for various reasons. Some expressed discomfort with how the most radical fringes of New Testament scholarship were disproportionately represented on the Jesus Seminar. Others voiced disagreement with Funk's purposes of promoting liberalism over conservative Christian credibility. Liberal to the core, the Jesus Seminar said their objective was to find out what Jesus actually said in the Bible. They did not use the Bible as their authority, but rather relied strictly on outside documents. One of the main documents they relied on is called, "The Gospel of Thomas." It was discovered in Egypt in 1945. We do not know when it was written, but Bible scholars estimate it was written at least 200 years after Christ walked the earth.

The Jesus Seminar, for unexplained reasons, said the Gospel of Thomas is more reliable than the Gospel of John, even though the Gospel of Thomas is not a narrative or a story, but rather a collection of sayings and proverbs. In fact, the gospel of Thomas starts off in its first verse by saying: "These are the secret sayings of Jesus as written down by Thomas."[31] This document was written two hundred years after Christ walked the earth and yet liberal scholars say it is more reliable than John's writings which were written much earlier. Let me ask you this. Let's say that George Washington made certain remarks relating to the U.S. Constitution. Would you believe Benjamin Franklin's recording of Washington's remarks, or would you believe Jimmy Carter's recording of what Washington said 200 years after the fact? I think you have to go with the writer who was on the scene!

These Jesus Seminar scholars (I call them skeptics) came to this conclusion: Jesus was a wandering sage, a local holy man who did not establish a new religion. He did not rise from the dead, but His followers made a god out of Him. When the Jesus Seminar finished its two year study, the members were given different colored beads with which to vote on Jesus' sayings.

A red bead meant Jesus actually said it.
A pink bead meant Jesus probably said it.
A gray bead meant Jesus probably did not say it.
A black bead meant Jesus definitely did not say it.

When they tallied the votes, here is what they found. In the Lord's Prayer recorded in Matthew 6:9-13, the only words that got a red bead was, *"Our Father."* That is all! In the whole Gospel of Mark, the only thing Jesus definitely said (according to their red marbles) was in Mark 12:17b: *"Render unto Caesar things that are Caesar's, and unto God the things that are God's."* And the Gospel of John had only one verse they said was authentic. It was John 4:44: *"A prophet has no honor in his own country."* According to the Jesus Seminar, all the other sayings by Jesus are legends, myths or superstitions.[32]

Since this august group says we are ignorant for believing the Bible, I have a word for them. It comes directly from God's Word. It is in Romans 1:22: *"Professing themselves to be wise, they became fools."* Robert Funk, who founded this blasphemous seminar, has gone on to meet his maker. I shudder to think about that meeting when God asks, "Why did you call me a liar by taking away what I said?" Jesus not only said the words in the Bible, He meant every word of what He said.

We have just seen that as we approach the end of God's Word to mankind, and before He puts His final stamp of approval on the Bible, God pronounces a solemn judgment upon anyone who would *"add to or take away the words"* from this Holy Book (Revelation 22:19). If anyone comes forward with some supposed new "revelation," and claims it to be from God though it might contradict Scripture, that very fact will demonstrate that he or she does not really know the Lord. Otherwise, how else would God ever be able to tell us when His revelation was complete? It would have to be open-ended to new revelations, and you would never be able to tell the true from the false. This includes those people who would add extra writings and give them the same weight of authority as God's Word. It also includes those who spiritualize and liberalize the plain teaching of the Bible so that it robs us of God's blessings for us.

Church history is lined with people who have stepped forward with the same message: "God told me all the denominations in Christendom are wrong, and He gave me the only true Gospel." Some of the worst offenders are: Joseph Smith, Charles Taze Russell, Mary Baker Eddy, Herbert W. Armstrong and Rev. Sun Moon.

As we approach the end of the "unveiling of Jesus Christ" one thing is certain – He is coming back! And as the incredible song, *The Midnight Cry* says, "It's closer now than it's ever been ….!"[33] Every time I have been in Israel, I have taken a boat to the middle of the Sea of Galilee where Peter and James did their fishing and where Jesus calmed the stormy waters. Each time, our boat stopped in the middle of the waters and shut off its engines, Dr. Reagan brought us a message about Jesus walking on the water. And before we started back to shore, he would read a poem to us by Carl Sandburg.

Epistle

"Jesus loved the sunsets on Galilee,
Jesus loved the fishing boats forming silhouettes
against the sunsets on Galilee,
Jesus loved the fishermen on the fishing boats
forming the silhouettes against the sunsets on Galilee,
And when Jesus said, "Goodbye, goodbye,
I will come again" –
Jesus meant the goodbye for the
sunsets, the fishing boats, the fishermen,
and the silhouettes against the sunsets of Galilee
And that goodbye, and that promise meant
all or nothing at all."[34]

Jesus meant all – He IS coming back!

Now we turn our attention to the last two verses of chapter 22, verses 20 and 21. *"He which testifieth these things saith, 'Surely I come quickly. Amen.' Even so, come, Lord Jesus."* And then John ends the entire panorama of Holy writ by penning, *"The Grace of our Lord Jesus Christ be with you all. Amen."*

We know from chapter 1 that *"He which testifies these things"* is none other than the Lord Jesus Christ. And "these things" of which He spoke includes all the events, the promises and warnings of this great Book, culminating in His solemn promise to deal swiftly with those who tamper with His Word.

And then Jesus says, *"Surely I come quickly."* Surely means absolutely – without a doubt. The word quickly is like a two-edged sword. Its primary meaning is that when these things begin to unfold, they will happen – bang – bang – no delay – right on course.

Jesus wants every generation to look for Him as though they are the terminal generation.

The secondary meaning of "quickly" is soon, maybe today, maybe next week. We were driving down Broad Street one day in downtown Forney when Arlene pointed to a sign on the old Sonic drive-in. It said, "Doe Belly Catfish Coming Soon." The sign was there for months and months, and we soon learned that "soon" is a relative term in the mind of the one coming.

This concept has been put into words by Gloria Gaither better than anything I have ever heard. It was written by Gloria more than twenty years ago to her soon-to-be-born grandson, Will Garrison Jennings.

"Dear Little One: It is a Spring-like day in Indiana. The crocuses are blooming, and there are big buds forming on the daffodils. As I write, this is the year of my 50th birthday. How appropriate that you are being formed in your mother's womb as your grandmother is beginning another half century. We once thought it wild to imagine the year 2000, but it will be a reality for you. And this anniversary will be celebrated on your eighth year of life. If Jesus has not returned for His Family by then, you will be told, as I was, as your parents were, that Jesus is coming soon. 'Soon' is a relative term, as you will 'soon' learn. When you are tired on a long trip, you will say, 'When will we get there, Daddy?' And your daddy will answer, 'Soon.' When you are toddling about the house, someone who loves you will be sure to say, 'That baby will be in kindergarten before we know it – all too soon.' And at some family reunion, one of the more mature relatives is sure to say to your mother, 'You better enjoy that child while you can. Pretty soon he will be pulling out to head for college.' This will seem strange to you that all these far-off things will be considered 'soon.' But you must trust what a very short lifetime and a little wisdom has taught: childhood rushes by, babies are leaving for college before you know it, and Jesus is coming 'soon' – in the twinkling of an eye!"[35]

I hope I have convinced you that Jesus could come at any time. John tells us in I John 3:3 that whosoever has this hope in them, that Jesus could come at any time, purifieth himself. In other words, you will clean up your act on a daily basis because this could be the day! And in response to Jesus' declaration that He is coming back, John cries out, *"Amen. Even so, come, Lord Jesus!"* (Revelation 22:20b). And it is the cry from the heart of all true believers: *"Come, Lord Jesus!"*

When the Rapture occurs, and God's children are called to meet Him in the air, the seven year Tribulation follows closely behind. And when the Tribulation has run its course, then the Great White Throne Judgment follows. After that, the Millennium unfolds in all its beauty ushering in the eternal state.

At the turn of the 20th Century in the early 1900's, missionaries Henry Clay Morrison and his wife were on a ship coming back to America. They had spent 40 years ministering to the poor in Africa. Over the years, they had faced poverty, disease and hardship in order to take the Gospel to a group of forgotten natives halfway around the world. They sailed from Africa for the last time, and coming home, as their ship approached the New York Harbor a band began to play, and the crowd on the dock began to cheer. Everyone on the ship came to the deck to join in the celebration. For you see, President Theodore Roosevelt was on the same ship coming home from Africa from one of his famous hunting trips.

The crowd and the band were on hand to welcome home the arrival of their President as he waved and marched down the gangplank amid the celebration. Minutes later, Henry Clay Morrison and his wife slowly shuffled down the same gangplank. There were no bands, no cheering crowds, no welcoming committee for these two precious saints that had spent their lives preaching the Gospel in a lonely and desolate place. Realizing this, a tear began to run down his cheek when an almost audible voice seemed to whisper, *"But Henry Clay – you're not Home yet!"*[36]

Have you ever been with family and friends, maybe at Christmas or after a delicious Thanksgiving dinner, and wondered if it can get any better. Well, the greatest moment on earth will be ordinary in Heaven by comparison. It will be like sitting in front of a warm fireplace with the ones we love, enjoying memories, laughing uncontrollably, dreaming of adventures to come, and then going out and living those adventures together.

How do we know this? Because in Revelation 21:5, Jesus said, *"Write these words for they are trustworthy and true."* And we can believe Him! We were all made for a Person and a Place. That Person is Jesus. The Place is Heaven – our real Home! And just when we think it can't get any better than this – it will!

God bless every one of you – and I'll look for you just inside the Eastern Gate in God's own time!

REFERENCES

Chapter 1

1   LaHaye, Tim, *Prophecy Study Bible,* (AMG Publishers 2001), p. 9

2   Reagan, David R., *God's Plan For the Ages,* (Lamb & Lion Ministries 2005), pp. 194-201

3   http://robertagrimes.com/jesus/apocalyptic-nonsense

4   Reagan, David R., *The Master Plan,* (Harvest House Publishers 1993), p. 43

5   Morris, Henry M., *The Revelation Record,* (Tyndale House Publishers, Inc. and Creation-Life Publishers, 1987), p. 25

6   Criswell, W. A., *For the Time is at Hand,* 8:15 am service FBC, Dallas, 1/15/61; the W. A. Criswell Sermon Library

7   Reagan, *The Master Plan,* op. cit., pp. 41-42

8   Chalfant, William B., *Aspects of Preterism: A Study of an Aberrant View of Prophecy*

9   Price, Frederick K. C., *Praise the Lord* broadcast on TBN, 9/21/90, as quoted by Hank Hanegraaf in *Christianity in Crisis,* (Harvest House Publishers 1993), p. 95

10   Price, Frederick K. C., *Ever Increasing Faith,* broadcast on TBN, 12/9/90, as quoted by Hank Hanegraff, ibid., p. 187

11   Young's Analytical Concordance to the Bible With Hebrew/Greek Lexicon, *(Funk & Wagnalls, 1936)*

12   *Stefanovic Ranko,* Revelation of Jesus Christ: Commentary on the Book of Revelation, *(Andrews University Press 2009), p. 18*

13   *Ironside, Harry A.,* Revelation, *(Loizeaux* Brothers, Inc. 1920), pp. 13-14 14)

14   https://www.latimes.com/archives/la-xpm-1985-06-24-me-851-story.html

15   Moulton, W. F., Moulton, H. K., Geden, A., *Concordance to the Greek Testament,* (Edinburgh: T&T Clark, 1980), 5th edition, p. 107

16   Walvoord, John F., *The Bible Knowledge Commentary,* (Victor Books 1983), p. 925

17   http://www.astrovera.com/bible-religion/176-bible-number-7.html

18   Lightner, Robert, *Angels, Satan and Demons,* (Thomas Nelson Publishers 1998), p. 63

19   https://www.britannica.com/topic/transitive-law

20   Kurian, George T. (Editor), *Nelson's New Christian Dictionary,* (Thomas Nelson Publishers 2001), p. 127

21   Ibid., p. 444

22   https://www.amnesty.org/en/what-we-do/discrimination/lgbt-rights/

23   Van Impe, Jack, *Revelation Revealed,* (Jack Van Impe Ministries 1982), pp. 19-20

24   Ironside, *Revelation,* op. cit., p. 22

25   Thompson, Jacob M., *The Romans 10 Controversy,* (Sinners to Repentance, Publisher 4/20/19), p. 99

26   Criswell, W. A., *Expository Sermons on Revelation,* (Zondervan Publishing House 1962), Vol. 1, p. 177

Chapter 2

1   Young, op. cit., p. 37

2   Birthday card from Bill Gothard in the author's personal file

3   Radio Station KRLD, Dallas, debate between Dr. W. A. Criswell and Madalyn Murray O'Hair, February 8, 1975 (author has recording)

4   Foxe, John, *Foxes's Christian Martyrs of the World,* (originally published in 1563, republished by Barbour Publishing 1994)

5   ten Boom, Corrie, *The Hiding Place,* (G. K. Hall & Co. 1973), pp. 54-55

6   *The Martyrdom of Polycarp,* originally compiled in the 2nd Century by several church fathers including Eusebius. (Translated by J.B. Lightfoot, Athena Data Products 1990)

7   Duck, Daymond R., *Revelation for the Biblically Inept,* (Starburst Publishers 1998), pp.33-34

8   Ironside, *Revelation,* op. cit., pp. 44-46

9   Ibid., p.47

10 Stam, C. R., *The Epistle to the Hebrews,* (Worzalla Publishing Co. 1991)

11 Ironside, H. A., *Letters to a Roman Catholic Priest,* (Loizeaux Brothers, Inc. undated booklet acquired by the author 8/2/58

12 Ironside, *Revelation,* op. cit., p. 51

13 Calloway, Donald H., *Immaculate Conception in the Life of the Church: Essays from the International Mariological Symposium in Honor of the 150th Anniversary of the Proclamation of the Dogma of the Immaculate Conception,* (Marian Press 8/25/2004

14 https://www.catholic.com/tract/immaculate-conception-and-assumption

15 http://www.newadvent.org/cathen/10673b.htm

16 https://www.britannica.com/topic/papal-infallibility

17 https://www.catholicnewsagency.com/news/could-mary-be-getting-a-new-title-this-year-44675

18 https://www.npr.org/2018/08/18/639698062/the-clergy-abuse-crisis-has-cost-the-catholic-church-3-billion

Chapter 3

1   Criswell, Revelation, op. cit., Vol. 2, p. 150

2   Schaff, Philip, *Creeds of Christendom,* (Scribner, New York, 3 Vols., 6th ed., 1890), pp. 3:356-82

3   Cairns, Earle E., *Christianity Through the Centuries: A History of the Christian Church,* (Zondervan Publishing House 1954), pp. 278-283

4   https://www.mayoclinic.org/diseases-conditions/hypothermia/symptoms-causes/syc-20352682

5   Lindsey, Hal, *There's a New World Coming,* (Harvest House Publishers 1983), p. 265

6   Cairns, op. cit., p. 419

7   White, Kathleen, *John and Betty Stam: Men and Women of Faith* (Bethany House Publishers 1990)

8   Criswell, W. A., *The Scarlet Thread Through the Bible,* (Broadman Press 1970), p. 2

9   http://www.sbc.net/resolutions/1146/on-the-%20disney-boycott

10 https://www.orlandoweekly.com/orlando/how-%20gay-day-pushed-disney-out-of-the-%20closet/Content?oid=2262655

11 https://afajournal.org/past-issues/1997/june/why-american-families-should-boycott-disney/

12 http://www.sbclife.net/article/349/eisner-lashes-out-again

13 https://www.thewaltdisneycompany.com/wp-content/uploads/2015/10/1999-Annual-Report.pdf

14 Ironside, *Revelation,* op. cit., p. 74

15 https://www.politico.com/story/2016/07/full-text-hillary-clintons-dnc-speech-226410

16 Email to the author dated 8/31/17 from Mike Mike Gendron, founder and CEO of Proclaiming the Gospel.org

17 Epp, Theodore H., *Practical Studies in Revelation*, (Back to the Bible Broadcast 1970), p. 176

18 Ibid., p.81

19 www.bpnews.net/43362/2nd-view-freddie-gage-6-decades-an-evangelist-dies

20 Draper, James T., Jr., *The Unveiling*, (Broadman Press 1984), pp. 98-99

21 McGee, J. Vernon, *Thru the Bible*, (Thomas Nelson Publishers 1983), Vol. V, p. 925

22 Soulen, Richard N., Soulen, R. Kendall, *Handbook of Biblical Criticism*, (Westminster John Knox Press 2001), 3rd Edition, p. 78

Chapter 4

1   Ankerberg, John and Weldon, John, The Facts *on Jehovah's Witnesses* (Harvest House Publishers 1998). pp. 57-59

2   LaHaye, Tim, *The Rapture,* (Harvest House Publishers 2002)

3   Scofield, C. I., *The Scofield Reference Bible,* (Oxford University Press 1945)

4   Duck, *Revelation,* op. cit., p. 67

5   Josephus, *Antiquities of the Jews*, Book 3, Chapter 7, Verse 5

6   Ironside, Revelation, op. cit., p. 82

7   Hamilton, Floyd E., *Basis of Christian Faith*, (Harper & Row 1946)

8   Ironside, *Revelation,* op. cit., p. 83.

9   Reagan, David R., *The Beginning and the Ending,* (The Lamplighter September/October 2011), Vol. XXXII, No. 5, p. 4

10 McGee, J. Vernon, *Thru the Bible,* (Thomas Nelson, Inc. 1983) Vol. V, p. 931

Chapter 5

1   Miller, Stephen M.; Huber, Robert V., The Bible: A History, (Good Books Publisher 2004), p. 173

2   Hendricks, Howard & Jeanne, *Footprints: Walking Through the Passages of Life,* Multnomah Press 1981, p.27

3   https://www.snopes.com/fact-check/all-dogs-go-to-heaven/

4   Paine, Albert Bigelow, *Mark Twain: A Biography,* (Harper & Brothers 1912)

5   Moser, Don, *All the Presidents Pooches,* (Smithsonian Magazine June, 1997)

6   Reagan, *God's Plan,* op. cit., (Lamb & Lion Ministries 2005), pp. 230-236

7   Ibid., pp. 128-134

8   Author unknown. The story is based loosely on a previous story written by Earl Hamner, Jr. for the Twilight Zone, entitled "The Hunt;" broadcast January 26, 1962.

9   Malgo, Wim, *The Rulership of Heaven,* (Midnight Call 1984), p. 30

10 Criswell, *Revelation,* op. cit., Vol. 3, p. 73

11 Ibid., pp. 82-83

12 Reagan, David R., *The Lamplighter,* (Lamb & Lion Ministries, vol. XXXIII, number 4, July/August 2012, pp. 3-8.

13 Jones, Col. Robert E., *History of the 101st Airborne Division: Screaming Eagles* (Turner Publishing 2010)

Chapter 6

1   Sadler, Paul M., The Triumph of His Grace, (Berean Bible Society 1995), pp.40-41
2   *English, E. Schuyler,* Re-Thinking the Rapture, *(Southern Bible Book House 1954), p. 69*
3   *Fountain, Charles,* Sportswriter: The Life and Times of Grantland Rice, *(Oxford University Press 1993)*
4   Reagan, David R., *The Jewish People: Rejected or Beloved?* (Lamb & Lion Ministries 2014) pp. 93-124
5   https://www.unicef.org/press-releases/global-hunger-continues-rise-new-un-report-says
6   https://www.britannica.com/event/Black-Death
7   https://www.sabin.org/updates/news/10-most-important-diseases-no-licensed-vaccine
8   http://penelope.uchicago.edu/josephus/ant-11.html
9   Anderson, Sir Robert, *The Coming Prince,* (originally published in 1895 and reprinted by Kregel Publications in 1982), pp. 51-66
10 https://www.britannica.com/event/Siege-of-Jerusalem-70
11 *Did Many People Disappear,* DVD produced by Nathan Jones and Lamblion.com
12 Author unknown
13 Reagan, David R., *Living on Borrowed Time* (Lamb & Lion Ministries 2013) p. 39
14 https://www.foxnews.com › story › church-attendance-back-to-normal
15 Daniel, Carey, *The Bible's Seeming Contradictions,* (Zondervan Publishing House 1941), pp. 46-47
16 https://abcnews.go.com/Technology/US/crooks-%20erase-past-erasing-fingerprints/story?id=11236512 17) Ironside, *Revelation,* op. cit., p. 169

Chapter 7

1   www.tfes.org
2   Thiessen, Henry Clarence, *Lectures in Systematic Theology,* (William B. Eerdmans Publishing Company 1952) p. 198
3   Goldman, Karen, *The Angel Book: A Handbook for Aspiring Angels,* (Simon & Schuster 1-4-93), p. 33
4   Swanson, Sandi L., *The Authorized Left Behind Handbook,* (Tyndale House Publishers 1/24/05) pp. 11-12
5   *Look to Jehovah for Comfort,* (The Watchtower: November 1, 1996) p. 10
6   Ironside, *Revelation,* op. cit., p. 125
7   Reagan, David R., *God's Plan for the Ages,* op. cit., p. 39
8   www.christinprophecy.org/article/the-mysterious-144,000/
9   Criswell, *Revelation,* op. cit., Vol. 3, p. 146
10 https://www.theaquilareport.com/hate-god-hates/
11 Draper, *The Unveling, op. cit.,* p.135
12 DeHaan, M. R., *Revelation: 35 Simple Studies on the Major Themes in Revelation,* (Zondervan Publishing House 1946), p. 136

Chapter 8

13 Lindsey, New World Coming, op. cit., p.118
14 Epp, op. cit., p. 103

15 https://www.nbcnews.com/mach/science/nasa-reveals-new-plan-stop-asteroids-they-hit-earth-ncna885316

16 http://curious.astro.cornell.edu/disclaimer/38-our-%20solar-system/the-earth/impacts/51-what-would%20 happen-if-an-asteroid-10-kilometers-across-hit-the-earth-beginner

17 https://www.nytimes.com/1998/01/08/us/what-if-huge-asteroid-hits-atlantic-you-don-t-want-to-know.html

18 https://www.rxlist.com/wormwood/supplements.htm

19 Lindsey, Hal, *The Terminal Generation* (Fleming H. Revell 1976), pp. 92-93

20 Ironside, *Revelation,* op. cit., p. 151

21 Melton, J. H., *52 Lessons in Revelation,* (Crescendo Publications undated), p.102)

22 Van Impe, Jack, *Revelation,* op. cit., p. 115

Chapter 9

1   Alighieri, Dante, The Divine Comedy (Alfred A. Knopf, publisher 1908) canto II

2   https://www.express.co.uk/news/world/675140/Locusts-Russia-Dagestan-plague

3   https://www.nationalgeographic.com/animals/invertebrates/group/locusts/

4   Newell, William R. Newell, *The Book of Revelation,* (Moody Press 1935), p. 130

5   Duck, op. cit., p. 130

6   McGee, op. cit., p. 968

7   https://www.independent.co.uk/news/science/dna-clues-could-predict-when-people-will-die-10014400.html

8   Hanegraff, op. cit., p. 163

9   https://www.preteristarchive.com/2009_reckart_catholic-deception6

10 Cantor, Norman F., *In the Wake of the Plague: The Black Death and the World It Made,* (Simon & Schuster 10/14/2014

11 https://www.statista.com/topics/1750/violent-crime-in-the-us/

12 Woodward, Bob, *The Choice,* (Simon & Shuster 1996) pp. 129-134

13 https://fdrfoundation.org/blog/page/23/

14 Ironside, *Revelation,* op. cit., *p. 169*

Chapter 10

1   Lightner, Robert, op. cit., p.63

2   https://www.christianscience.com/

3   Mary Baker Eddy, *Miscellaneous Writings,* 1883-1896, (originally published by Christian Science Publishing Society, Boston, c.1896), p. 170 Republished in June, 2005 by Kessinger Publishing, LLC

4   Martin, Walter, *Kingdom of the Cults,* (Bethany House Publishers 1985) p. 141

5   Eddy, Mary, *Science and Health with Key to the Scriptures,* (The First Church of Christ, Scientist 1994), p. 42

6   Martin, op. cit., pp. 413-414

7   *The Lamplighter,* (Lamb & Lion Ministries, Vol. XXVII, No. 4, July-August 2006), p. 8

8   Greene, Oliver B., *The Revelation,* (The Gospel Hour, Inc. 1963) p. 273

9   Beamer, Lisa, *Let's Roll,* (Tyndale House 2002) p. 187

10 Scott, Walter, *Exposition of the Revelation of Jesus Christ,* (Kregel Publishers 1979), pp. 223-224

11 *My Way,* written by Paul Anka and sung by Frank Sinatra, 1969

12 https://www.thebereancall.org/content/july-2005-extra
13 https://dbts.edu/2014/09/22/john-macarthur-on-joel-osteen/
14 http://texanonline.net/archives/5071/

Chapter 11

1 Criswell, Revelation, op. cit., Zondervan Publishing House 1965), Vol. 4, p.13
2 https://www.britannica.com/event/Siege-of-Jerusalem-70
3 https://www.aljazeera.com/indepth/features/ 2017/07/al-aqsa-170719122538219.html
4 http://www.danielpipes.org/84/the-muslim-claim-to-jerusalem
5 Reagan, David R., *The End Time Prophecies of Daniel,* (The Lamplighter November/December 2009), Vol. XXX, No. 6, p. 7
6 Church, J. R., *Daniel Reveals the Bloodline of the Antichrist,* (Prophecy Publications 2010)
7 Reagan, David R., *America the Beautiful?* (Lamb & Lion Ministries 2009), p. 82
8 Ruebner, Josh, *Shattered Hopes: Obama's Failure to Broker Israeli-Palestinian Peace,* (Verso Publishing 2014)
9 http://www.thesanhedrin.org/en/index.php/Historical_Overview
10 Kaufman, Asher, *Biblical Archeology Review,* Vol. IX, No. 2, Mar/Apr 83
11 Britannica, *Seige of Jerusalem*
12 https://www.bible-history.com/jewishtemple/JEWISH_TEMPLEThe_Court_of_the_Gentiles.htm
13 www.historynet.com/assyrian-march-against-judah.htm
14 Cline, Eric H. and Graham, Mark W., *Ancient Empires from Mesopotamia to the Rise of Islam,* (Cambridge University Press 2011)
15 Akin, Daniel L., *Exalting Jesus in Mark,* Holman Reference, Publisher 6-1-2014) p. 99
16 *Then Came the Morning,* song written by Bill and Gloria Gaither, and Chris Christian, 1982
17 *I Wish I Could Have Been There,* song written by Joel Lindsey and Wayne Haun, 2002
18 Kushner, Rabbi Harold, *When Bad Things Happen to Good People,* (Harper Perennial 12/1/83)

Chapter 12

1 Sermon by Paige Patterson, former President of the Southern Baptist Convention, at 11:00 a. m., January 25, 2004 at First Baptist Church, Forney, Texas entitled, "What On Earth is Going On?"
2 Epp, op. cit., p. 164
3 Pentecost, J. Dwight, *Things to Come,* (Zondervan Publishing House 1958) p. 287
4 St. Jerome, *The Perpetual Virginity of Blessed Mary,* (Independently published, June 24, 2019)
5 Reagan, David R., *Jewish People,* op. cit., pp. 39-40
6 Eddy, *Miscellaneous Writings,* op. cit., p. 170
7 https://endtime.org/public/library/hanna/prophetic_vision.html
8 Lindsey, Hal, *New World,* op. cit. pp. 222-223
9 Yurchak, Alexei, *Everything Was Forever, Until It Was No More,* (Princeton University Press 10-23-2005)
10 Dr. V. Raymond Edman's funeral service at Wheaton College, Wheaton, Illinois, 9/25/67, recording is in the author's library
11 Wiersbe, Warren W., *Wiersbe Bible Commentary NT,* (David C. Cooke, publisher 2007), p. 379

12 *Van Impe, op. cit., pp. 164-167*

13 Jeremiah, David, *Escape the Coming Night,* (Word Publishing 1997) p. 173

14 Richards, Jim, *Revelation: The Best Is Yet To Come,* (Aneko Press 2014), p. 80

15 DeHaan, *Revelation,* op. cit., pp. 165,169,170

16 Ironside, *Revelation,* op. cit., pp. 213-216

17 Hagee, John, *Beginning of the End*, (Thomas Nelson Publishers 1996), p. 171

18 Email to the author from Daymond R. Duck dated 9/27/17.

19 Duck, *Revelation,* op. cit., p. 175

20 Rogers, Adrian, *Unveiling the End Times in Our Time: The Triumph of the Lamb in Revelation,* (Broadman & Holman Publishers 2004) pp. 146-147

21 Ham, Mordecai F., *The Book of Revelation,* from the manuscript of Rev. W. A. Hamlett, (1933), Louisville, Ky., publisher un-named, p.62

22 Criswell, *Revelation,* op. cit., pp. 85, 93

23 Epp, op. cit., pp. 179-180

24 *Gaebelein, Arno C.* The Revelation: An Analysis and Exposition of the Last Book of the Bible, *(Loizeaux Brothers, Inc. 1982), p. 76*

25 Morris, *Revelation,* op. cit., p. 225

26 Draper, James T. Jr., op. cit., pp. 181-182

27 Larkin, Clarence, *The Book of Revelation: A Study of the Last Prophetic Book of Holy Scripture,* (Erwin W. Moyer 1919), p. 96

28 www.walvoord.com/article/270

29 Reagan, David R., *The Lamplighter,* (Lamb & Lion Ministries 2011), Vol. XXXII, No. 1, pp. 3-8

30 www.preteristarchive.com/StudyArchive/c/church-of-christ.html

31 Sandy Gist, wife of evangelist Al Gist, stated this in the Believers Sunday School Class on July 9, 2017

32 https://www.ncbi.nlm.nih.gov/pmc/articles/PMC1199634/

33 https://www.cbsnews.com/news/tsunami-survivor-raped-by-rescuer/

34 Ramsland, Katherine, *Confession of a Serial Killer: The Untold Story of Dennis Rader,* (Fore-Edge Publisher 8/8/2017)

35 Pink, Arthur W., *The Total Depravity of Man,* (Prisbrary Publishing 6/18/2012)

36 Matthew, Colin, and Harrison, Brian (Editors), *The Oxford Dictionary of National Biography,*(The Oxford University Press 12/3/2007), p. 159

37 *The Writings of Rev. John Bradford: Prebendary of St. Paul's and Martyr,* (Presbyterian Board of Publication 1842) p. XXI; held in the Pennsylvania State University Library

38 David Jeremiah, *Escape,* op. cit., p. 173

39 https://www.jewishvirtuallibrary.org/latest-population-statistics-for-israel

40 https://www.heraldofhope.org.au/great-eagle-of-revelation/

41 https://www.pharmaceutical-journal.com/opinion/blogs/nebuchadnezzar-and-boanthropy/11123165.blog

42 Email from Dr. Reagan to the author 1/2/19

Chapter 13

1 Scott, Walter, Expositon of the Revelation of Jesus *Christ,* Revell Company, publisher January, 1968), pages unnumbered but under first page of section entitled "*The First Beast: Historical Revival of the Roman Empire*"

2   Blackstone, William E., *Jesus is Coming,* (Fleming H. Revell Company 1875), p. 108

3   https://www.britannica.com/event/Treaty-of-Rome

4   https://www.britannica.com/event/Maastricht-Treaty

5   https://scholarship.law.berkeley.edu/cgi/viewcontent.cgi?article=1286&context=bjil

6   O'Toole, Finton, *Historic Failure: Brexit and the Politics of Pain,* (Apollo Publishers 11/22-/2018)

7   Sloss, David L.; Ramsey, Michael D.; Dodge, William S., *International Law in the U.S. Supreme Court* (Cambridge University Press 4/25/11)

8   Hymn written by Cleavant Derricks in 1934

9   Keating, Karl, *Catholicism and Fundamentalism: The Attack on "Romanism" by "Bible Christians",* (Ignatius Press 1988) p. 200

10 https://www.britannica.com/place/Seven-Hills-of-Rome

11 Ironside, H. A., *Daniel,* (Loizeaux Brothers Publishers 1911), p. 167

12 Campbell, Donald K., *Daniel: God's Man in a Secular Society* (Discovery House Publishers 1988), pp. 143-144

13 Gibbon, Edward, *The Decline and Fall of the Roman Empire,* (published in six volumes 1776-1789 and reprinted by AMS Press 1974)

14 https://millercenter.org/the-presidency/presidential-speeches/september-11-1990-address-joint-session-congress

15 *The Lamplighter* (Lamb and Lion Ministries May- June 2001), vol. XXII, No. 3, p. 7

16 www.dennisprager.com/explaining-the-arab-israeli-conflict-through-numbers/

17 https://fas.org/irp/world/para/docs/880818a.htm

18 https://winstonchurchill.hillsdale.edu/churchill-on-islam/

19 Carroll, Lewis, *Through the Looking Glass,* (Random House 1946) p. 76

20 https://www.foxnews.com/politics/rep-keith-ellison-says-kim-jong-un-acting-more-responsible-than-trump

21 http:www.pewresearch.org/fact-tank/2017/08/09/muslims-and-islam-key-findings-in-the-u-s-and-around-the-world/

22 http://www.pewforum.org/2017/11/29/europes-growing-muslim-population/

23 https://www.cnn.com/2018/01/10/politics/muslim-population-growth-second-religious-group-trnd/index.html

24 Rice, Allen Thorndike, *Reminiscences of Abraham Lincoln by Distinguished Men of His Time,* (Harper & Brothers Publishers 1909), p. 242

25 Duck, op. cit., 195

26 Turner, Ted and Burke, Bill, *Call Me Ted,* (Business Plus, publisher 11/02/2009

27 https://www.newyorker.com/magazine/1948/06/26/the-lottery

28 http://bookhaven.stanford.edu/tag/kay-haugaard/

29 Gaebelein, Arno C., op. cit., pp. 78-84

30 Goodman, Phillip, *The Assyrian Connection,* (Land Publishing & Design, Prophecy Watch Books 2003)

31 Ironside, *Revelation,* op. cit., p. 247

32 Ibid

33 https://disneyworld.disney.go.com/attractions/magic-kingdom/hall-of-presidents/

34 Myers, David G., *Psychology* (Worth Publishers, 6th edition 2001), p. 370

35 https://www.experian.com/blogs/ask-experian/cash-vs-credit-cards-which-do-american-use-most/

36 LaHaye, Tim, and Jenkins, Jerry, *The Mark of the Beast,* (Tyndale House Publishers 2000), Book #8, Chapter 20

37 Jones, Nigel, Countdown to Valkyrie: The July Plot to *Assassinate Hitler* (Frontline Books, publisher 3/09/2009)

Chapter 14

1   Kurian, Nelson's Dictionary, op. cit., p. 360

2   Rutherford, J. F., *The Harp of God,* (Peoples Pulpit Association 1922), p. 187

3   https://www.jw.org/en/bible-teachings/questions/go-to-heaven/

4   http://www.wnd.com/2005/02/28918/

5   https://www.jewishvirtuallibrary.org/the-catholic-church

6   Lindsey, *New World,* op. cit., p. 186

7   https://www.nationalww2museum.org/sites/default/files/2017-07/iwo-jima-fact-sheet.pdf

8   Words and music written by Rodney Griffin 1999

9   Lindsey, *New World,* op. cit., p. 187

10 McGee, op. cit., Vol. 5, p. 1008

11 Gaebelein, op. cit., p. 87

12 Ham, op. cit., p. 72

13 Sermon preached by Billy Graham in his New York Crusade 5/23/57; printed in Decision Magazine 2/6/18

14 Martin, op. cit., pp. 71-83

15 Conversations by the author in 1955 with Captain Jahangir Kamkar in the Iraq army, an expert on Islam

16 http://epistle.us/inspiration/iknowmymaster.html

17 *Turn Your Eyes Upon Jesus,* hymn written by Helen Howarth Lemmel (1918)

18 Ironside, *Revelation,* op. cit., p. 279

19 White, Bill, *A Special Place: Story of the Garden Tomb,* (Stanborough Press 1990)

20 https://www.census.gov/data/tables/time-series/demo/international-programs/historical-est-worldpop.html

Chapter 15

1   Frank, Leonard Roy (Editor), Random House *Webster's Quotationary,* (Random House Reference 2001), p. 62

2   Van Impe, op. cit., p. 207

3   Ironside, *Revelation,* op. cit., p. 271

4   Adrian Rogers, op. cit., p. 181

Chapter 16

1   Morris, Revelation, op. cit., p. 298

2   *The Watchtower,* (Published by the Watchtower Bible and Tract Society of Pennsylvania September 1, 1986), p. 25

3   Jehovah's Witness Public Affairs Office's press release, June 14, 2000

4   Reed, David A., *Behind the Watchtower Curtain,* (Crowne Publications, Inc. 1989)

5   Morris, *Revelation,* op. cit., p. 300

6   Pettingill, William L., *Simple Studies in the Revelation,* (Fred Kelker, publisher l906), p. 65

7   Swindoll, Charles R., *Dropping Your Guard,* (Word Books 1983) p. 199

8   Gaebelein, *Revelation,* op. cit., p. 94

9   https://www.reuters.com/article/us-iran-quake-global/timeline-worlds-14-deadliest-earthquakes-of-last-decade-idUSKBN1DD257

10 Hyslop, Alexander, *The Two Babylons,* (Forgotten Books, publisher 2016

Chapter 17

1   Morris, Henry M., The Genesis Record, (Baker Book House 1976) pp. 143-144

2   Criswell, *Revelation,* op. cit., Vol. 4, p. 183

3   Ironside, *Revelation,* op. cit., pp. 290-292

4   https://www.foxnews.com/story/rev-pat-robertson-shares-his-memories-of-meeting-pope-john-paul-ii

5   http://www.vatican.va/archive/ccc_css/archive/catechism/p123a9p3.htm

6   https://www.catholic.com/tract/immaculate-conception-and-assumption

7   Strossmayer, Bishop Jose, *Bishop Strossmayer's Speech In the Vatican Council of 1870,* (Loizeaux Brothers 1872)

8   https://www.catholicnewsagency.com/news/could-mary-be-getting-a-new-title-this-year-44675

9   https://hannemanarchive.com/catholic-page/lovely-lady-dressed-in-blue-teach-me-how-to-pray/

10 Catholicism: Crisis of Faith, *DVD, interview with Roman Catholic Priest Richard Chilson, directed by former Roman Catholic priest, James G. McCarthy 3/01/1991*

11 https://www.britannica.com/place/Seven-Hills-of-Rome

12 Draper, *Unveiling,* p. 228

13 https://www.businessinsider.com/fancy-mormon-temples-2014-8

14 https://www.beliefnet.com/faiths/christianity/8-richest-pastors-in-america.aspx?p=2

15 Jeffrey, Grant, *Final Warning: Economic Collapse and the Coming World Government,* (Harvest House 1996), p. 153

16 Ironside, *Revelation,* op. cit., p. 305

17 Foxe, *Martyrs,* op. cit., (originally published in 1563, republished by Barbour Publishing 1994)

18 Kurian, *Nelson's Dictionary,* op. cit., pp. 212-213

19 Ibid., pp. 378-379

20 Grant, Joseph M., *The Great Texas Banking Crash: An Insider's Account,* (The University of Texas Press 1996)

21 https://people.com/archive/cover-story-the-fall-of-jimmy-swaggart-vol-29-no-9/

22 https://www.smithsonianmag.com/smart-news/hollywood-star-who-confronted-aids-silent-epidemic-180965059/

23 https://coinweek.com/ancient-coins/ngc-ancient-coins-roman-coin-designs-and-origins-of-the-roman-republic/

24 Van Impe, *Revelation,* op. cit., p. 238

25 Hocking, David, *The Coming World Leader,* (Multnomah Publishing 1988), p. 249

26 Scofield, *Reference Bible,* op. cit.

27 https://www.rferl.org/a/1063353.html

28 *The Lamplighter,* (Lamb & Lion Ministries March-*April), Vol. XXII, No. 2), p. 4*

29 https://www.csmonitor.com/2006/0104/p07s02-wome.html

30 Pentecost, *Things,* p. 368

31 Elliott, Elizabeth, *Through Gates of Splendor,* (Harper & Brothers 1957)

32 McDonnall, Carrie, *Facing Terror,* (Thomas Nelson & Co. 2008)

Chapter 18

1 https://www.britannica.com/place/Hanging-Gardens-of-Babylon

2 https://www.britannica.com/place/Babylon-ancient-city-Mesopotamia-Asia

3 Ibid.

4 Morris, *Revelation,* op. cit., p. 115

5 www.usdebtclock.org/

6 Reagan, *America,* op. cit., pp. 74-75

7 https://www.foxnews.com/story/light-sentence-for-child-molester-leaves-vermont-judge-under-fire

8 Ironside, H.A., *Daniel,* (Loizeaux Brothers 1911), pp. 82-86

9 Elliott, Elizabeth, *Shadow of the Almighty: The Life and Testament of Jim Elliott,* (HarperCollins, publisher 1979) p. 15

10 McGee, op. cit., vol. 5, p. 1040

11 https://www.zionoil.com

12 Hansen, Horace, *Witness to Barbarism,* (Thousand Pine Tree Press 2002). Hansen was chief prosecutor for war crimes committed at the Dachau Concentration Camp, Dachau, Germany

13 "Iran's Ayatollah Khamenei Posts Holocaust Denial Video on Remembrance Day", Newsweek Magazine 8/16/19

14 Upshall, M., *New York Encyclopedia,* (Colour Library Book, publisher 1-1-1988)

15 Cook, Faith, *Selina: Countess of Huntington – Her Pivotal Role in the 18th Century Evangelical Awaking,* (Banner of Truth, publisher 11/1/2001

16 Harrison, Eugene Myers, *How to Win Souls,* (Van Kampen Press 1952), p. 59

17 Smith, Suzy (aka Rain Dove), *The Tangled Web of Wicca,* (Author House Publisher 10/23/2014), p. 40

18 https://vimeo.com/224981158 or contact FBC, Forney for the DVD

19 https://www.britannica.com/biography/Don-Meredith

20 Gibbon, *Roman Empire,* op. cit.

Chapter 19

1 Evans, William, The Great Doctrines of the Bible, (Moody Press 1949) p. 182

2 https://www.crosswalk.com/faith/bible-study/what-is-the-meaning-of-the-word-hallelujah.html

3 Walvoord, John F. and Zuck, Roy B., *The Bible Knowledge Commentary,* (Victor Books 1983, New Testament Edition), pp. 18, 20

4 https://www.wunderground.com/history/daily/us/tx/dallas/KDAL/date/1954-8-6

5 Morris, *Revelation,* op. cit., p. 470

6 https://www.legacy.com/obituaries/name/virgil- Mattingly-obituary?pid=86456666

7 *Why Should Me Love Me So?* (song written by Robert Harkness, 1924)

8   https://www.thoughtco.com/worth-of-your-elements-3976054

9   Bacchiocchi, Samuele, *Wine in the Bible: A Biblical Study on the Use of Alcoholic Beverages,* (Biblical Perspectives 2001)

10   Morris, op. cit., *Revelation,* p. 391

11   Brown, Dan, *The Da Vinci Code,* (Anchor Publishing 2003)

12   *The Last Temptation of Christ,* a movie directed by Martin Scorsese, (Universal Pictures 1988)

13   *Judas,* a movie directed by Charles Robert Carner, (Fatima Productions 2004)

14   https://christinprophecy.org/articles/the-iraq-study-report/

15   http://www.juliatexas.com/historichands.htm

16   https://www.merriam-webster.com/dictionary/acromegaly

17   www.andrethegiant.com/

18   Church, J. R., *Guardians of the Grail,* (Prophecy Publications 1989) p. 312

Chapter 20

1   Akin, Daniel L., A Theology for the Church, (B & H Publishing 6-1-2014) p. 695

2   Sermon by W. A. Criswell entitled "For the Time is at Hand," delivered at FBC, Dallas at 8:15 a.m., 1/15/61

3   Houdini, Harry, *Houdini: A Magician Among the Spirits,* (Harper Brothers Publishers 1924, pp. 1-16

4   ibid., pp. 138-165

5   ibid., pp. 279-280

6   https://www.nytimes.com/2009/01/22/opinion/22iht-edjohnson.3.19600014.html

7   Weaver, Janice, *Harry Houdini: The Legend of the World's Greatest Escape Artist,* (Harry N. Adams, publisher 10-1-11)

8   Kelly, Victoria, *Mrs. Houdini,* (Atria Books 3/1/2016)

9   ronside, H. A., *Expository Notes on the Epistles of James and Peter,* (Loizeaux Brothers 1947) 2 Peter 3, p. 99

10   Words written by Isaac Watts in 1719 based on Psalm 98:4

11   Belbenoit, Rene, *I Escaped From Devil's Island,* (Bantam Books 1949)

12   https://www.news.com.au/travel/world-travel/south-america/70000-came-to-this-island-archipelago-few-made-it-out-alive/news-story/eadd237e79e5641c67576c66b82a19c6

13   If-Jesus-returns-kill-Him-again.com

14   *Dead Man Walking,* movie directed by Tim Robbins 1995, produced by PolyGram Filmed Entertainment (which merged with Universal Pictures in 1999)

15   peopleschurch.net/who-we-are/about-peoples/ peoples-church-history/

16   https://www.dallasnews.com/news/2012/07/28/seven-years-later-mary-ellen-bendtsens-swindling-suitor-gets-justice/

17   W. A. Criswell, *Revelation,* op. cit., Vol. 5, pp. 97-98

18   Author unknown

19   https://www.biography.com/business-figure/pt-barnum

20   https://christianhistoryinstitute.org/it-happened-today/12/22

Chapter 21

1   Piper, Don, 90 Minutes in Heaven, (Fleming H. Revell 2004)

2   Eadie, Betty, *Embraced by the Light,* (Bantam Publishers 1994)

3   https://probe.org/embraced-by-the-light-of-deception/

4   Bernstein, Morey, *The Search for Bridey Murphy,* (Doubleday Publishing 1956)

5   http://skepdic.com/bridey.html

6   *The Apology of Aristides,* 125 AD, translated from the Syriac Version into English in 1891)

7   Graham, Billy, *Facing Death and the Life Thereafter,* (Word Publishing 1987), p. 36

8   Email dated 9/5/15 to author from Jim's son, Jimmie

9   Leland, Thomas, *The History of the Life and Reign of Phillip, King of Macedon,* (Gale ECCO Print Edition 6/10/2010) as quoted by Diarmid, Matthew P. (ed.), *Poems of Robert Ferguson: A Critical Biography,* (Scottish Text Society, Edinburgh1954) Vol. II, p. 314

10 Starr, Michael Seth, *Hiding in Plain Sight: The Secret Life of Raymond Burr,* (Applause Theater and Cinema Books, publisher 9/1/2009) p. 210

11 *The Lamplighter,* (Lamb & Lion Ministries May- June 2003), Vol. XXIV, No. 3, p. 8

12 Ibid.

13 Alcorn, Randy, *Heaven,* (Tyndale House Publishers 2004), p. xxii

14 www.desiringgod.org/articles/the-resolutions-of-jonathan-edwards (resolution #22)

15 Pascal, Blaise, *Pensees,* (Penguin Classics 12/1/1995)

16 *If You Want Joy, Real Joy,* song written by Joseph D. Carlson, former director of the Toronto Youth for Christ in 1939 shortly after his conversion

17 Pritchard, Jimmy D., *Calling Down the Fire,* CrossHouse Publishing 2005, p. 122

18 Twain, Mark, *Adventures of Huckleberry Finn,* (Dover Publications, Inc. 1994) p. 2

19 Lucado, Max, *3:16: The Numbers of Hope,* (Thomas Nelson, Inc. 9-11-2007), 85

20 Alcorn, op. cit., p. 8

21 Ibid.

22 Ibid.

23 Ibid.

24 Ibid.

25 Rugoff, Milton (editor), *The Travels of Marco Polo,* (Signet Publishing 2004)

26 Elliott, Elizabeth, *Through Gates of Splendor,* (Harper & Brothers 1957)

27 Lewis, C. S., *Mere Christianity,* (Simon & Schuster 1996) p. 119

28 Alcorn, op. cit., p. 23

29 Lewis, C. S., *The Screwtape Letters,* (Macmillan Publishing Co. 1982) p. 56

30 Rhodes, Ron, *The Undiscovered Country: Exploring the Wonder of Heaven and the Afterlife* (Harvest House 1960), pp. 39-40

31 https://www.joelosteen.com/Pages/Blog.aspx?blogid=13546

32 Alcorn, Ibid., p. 35

33 https://www.jesuscalling.com/blog/dr-david-jeremiah/

34 Alcorn, op. cit., p. 52

35 https://www.thenakedscientists.com/articles/science-features/oceans-cleaners

36   Thompson, Hunter S., *The Proud Highway: The Saga of a Desperate Southern Gentleman,* (Villard Books: division of Random House 5-6-1997)

37   http://www.bpnews.net/4742/billy-graham-and-daughter-challenge-un-to-consider-jesus

38   https://billygraham.org/gallery/billy-and-ruth-graham-through-the-years

39   https://www.peterson.af.mil/

40   Reagan, David, *God's Prophetic Voices to America,* (Lamb & Lion Ministries 2017), p. 207

41   Lawrence, Ellen, *Covered in Water,* (Bearport Publishing Co. 1-1-2016)

42   https://www.texasheart.org/heart-health/heart-information-center/topics/blood/

43   Williams, Joe; Swyngedouw, Erik, *Tapping the Oceans: Desalination and the Political Ecology of Water,* (Edward Elgar Publishing 11/30/2018

44   https://www.lenntech.com/water-trivia-facts.htm

45   Peterson, Eugene, *The Message,* (Navpress 1993), p. 328

46   Criswell, *Revelation,* op. cit., Vol. 5, p. 119

47   Martin, Jobe, *The Evolution of a Creationist,* (Biblical Discipleship Publishers 2008) p. 65

48   Fixico, Donald L., *That's What They Used to Say: Reflections on American Indian Oral Traditions,* (University of Oklahoma Press 2017)

49   https://www.crossroad.to/Victory/stories/TheSon.html

50   https://www.latimes.com/archives/la-xpm-2003-oct-24-na-heaven24-story.html

51   https://christinprophecy.org/articles/a-thought-about-abortion/

52   https://www.dailysignal.com/2012/02/08/justice-ginsburg-i-would-not-look-to-the-u-s-constitution/

53   Miles, Steven H., *The Hippocratic Oath and the Ethics of Medicine,* (Oxford University Press 6/2/2005)

54   *The Constitution of the United States*, 14th Amendment, ratified July 9, 1868

55   https://www.cnn.com/2013/09/18/health/abortion-fast-facts/index.html

56   Reagan, David R., *The Lamplighter* (Lamb & Lion Ministries September/October 2012) Vol. XXXIII, No. 5, p. 4

57   https://www.oregon.gov/oha/PH/PROVIDERPARTNERRESOURCES/EVALUATIONRESEARCH/DEATHWITHDIGNITYACT/Pages/faqs.aspx

58   https://press.princeton.edu/titles/8317.html

59   https://www.americamagazine.org/politics-society/2017/12/04/patricia-heaton-iceland-isnt-eliminating-down-syndrome-they-are-just

60   https://www.theaquilareport.com/parallels-between-abortion-and-the-holocaust-part-1/

61   https://www.britannica.com/event/Roe-v-Wade

62   https://www.law.cornell.edu/wex/roe_v_wade_%281973%29

63   https://www.dallasnews.com/news/news/2013/04/19/for-sarah-weddington-the-lawyer-who-won-roe-vs-wade-celebrity-or-notoriety-came-early (Author's note: When I because writing this book in 2015, this quote by Carol Tobias was a factual reference. Since that time, the *Dallas News* has scrapped all reference to this quote).

64   https://www.britannica.com/biography/Roger-B-Taney

65   https://www.fws.gov/midwest/eagle/history/protections.html

66   Moore, Keith L., T.V.N. Persaud, Mark G. Torchia, *The Developing Human: Clinically Oriented Embryology,* (Saunders College Publishing 2015)

67   https://www.archbalt.org/catholic-legislators-must-protect-life-pope-tells-speaker-pelosi/

68   https://www.cnn.com/2012/02/24/politics/fact-checking-gingrich-infanticide-charge/index.html

69 Wells, Jonathan, *Survival of the Fakest,* (The American Spectator December 2000/January 2001), pp.19-20

70 https://www.theatlantic.com/politics/archive/2014/01/inside-world-anti-abortion-activists-who-were-conceived-rape/357314/

71 http://rebeccakiessling.com/gov-rick-perrys-change-of-heart/

72 Wolters, Albert M., *Creation Regained: Biblical Basis for a Reformational Worldview,* (William B. Eerdmans 1985), p. 41

73 https://www.desiringgod.org/messages/what-happens-when-you-die-glorified-and-free-on-the-new-earth

74 Hoekema, Anthony *The Bible and the Future,* (William B. Eerdmans Publishing 1994) p. 277

75 https://library.timelesstruths.org/music/This_Is_My_Fathers_World/

76 Eddy, *Science,* op. cit., p.44

77 Twain, Mark, *Christian Science,* (Harper & Bros. 1907), pp. 8-11

78 Beebe, William, *Half Mile Down,* (Harcourt, Brace & Co. 1934)

79 Hansen, James R., *First Man: The Life of Neil A. Armstrong,* (Simon & Schuster 11-27-2012)

80 https://en.israelidiamond.co.il/about-the-israeli-diamond-industry/

81 Alcorn, op. cit., p. 245

82 Song was written by Robert Lowery in 1864

83 Ratnear, Romesh, *Tear Down This Wall: A City, a President, and the Speech that Ended the Cold War,* (Simon & Schuster 11/23/2010)

84 *Rock of Ages,* written by Augustus M. Toplady in 1776

85 Rhodes, Ron, *What Happens After Life: 21 Amazing Revelations About Heaven and Hell,* (Harvest House Publishers 2014) p. 69

86 Lee, C. Y., *Taipei 101: The Tallest of the Tall,* (Images Publishing Group, Australia 2/15/2012)

87 Song was written by Cole Porter and Robert Fletcher, 1934

88 Morris, op. cit., *Revelation,* pp. 449-452

89 Go to lamblion.com and enter into the search box, "Symbolically." It will show this article: Inbox #14: Should Bible prophecy be interpreted literally or symbolically?"

90 Lewis, C. S., *The Chronicles of Narnia: The Last Battle,* (Harper-Collins 1956), p.760

91 Baum, L. Frank, *The Wonderful Wizard of Oz,* (Dover Publications 5/20/1996)

92 Criswell, *Revelation,* op. cit., Vol. 5, p. 130

93 Tinker, Melvin, *Wisdom to Live By: Living Biblically in a Complex World,* (Christian Focus Publications 1998), p. 115

94 Dennis Pollock, *Making Room for Jesus,* (Lamb & Lion Ministries 2001), pp. 41-43

95 www.wrr101.com/mary-sefzik/

96 http://www.hymnpod.com/2009/06/15/when-we-see-christ/

97 Gaebelein, op. cit., pp. 166-167

98 Van Impe, op. cit., p. 300

99 The song was written in 1879 by Josiah K. Atwood

100 Alcorn, *Heaven,* op. cit., p. 243

101 Correspondence with the author by Ruthanna Metzgar dated 9/15/17

102 time.com/4845150/chief-justice-john-roberts-commencement-speech-transcript/

Chapter 22

1   Gaebelein, Revelation, op. cit., p. 169

2   *Lamplighter*, (Lamb & Lion Ministries May/June 2000) Vol. XXI, No. 3, p. 13

3   Graham, Billy, *Joni: An Unforgettable Story*, (Zondervan Publishing House 8/1/2001)

4   Morris, *Revelation*, op. cit., p.473

5   Cole, Neil and Helfer, Phil, *Church Transfusion: Changing Organically from the Inside Out*, (Jossey-Bass, publisher 2012)

6   https://www.linkedin.com/pulse/20140817172015-254040822-how-one-ceo-taught-his-employees-a-lesson-in-integrity

7   https://world.wng.org/2007/06/backward_atheist_soldiers

8   Lewis, C. S., *Mere Christianity*, (Simon & Schuster Publishers 1996), Book 2, Chapter 3, p. 56

9   https://oceanservice.noaa.gov/facts/drinksw.html

10 Kurzman, Dan, *Fatal Voyage: The Sinking of the USS Indianapolis*, (Broadway Books 8/14/2001)

11 Coleridge, Samuel Taylor, *The Rime of the Ancient Mariner and Other Poems*, (Dover Publications 9/18/1992)

12 Whittaker, James C., *We Thought We Heard the Angels Sing*, (E. P. Dutton & Co. 1943)

13 Lucado, Max, *In the Eye of the Storm*, (Word Publishing 1991) pp. 221, 225-226

14 Dean, Amy E., *Peace of Mind: Daily Meditations for Easing Stress*, (Bantam Books, March 1995)

15 https://www.watchman.org/

16 Van Wagoner, Richard S., *Sidney Rigdon: A Portrait of Religious Excess*, (Signature Books 1994)

17 Martin, op. cit., p. 134

18 Eddy, *Science*, op. cit., p.44

19 Van Baalen, Jan Karel, *The Chaos of the Cults*, (Wm. B. Eerdmans Publishing Co. 1951), p. 98

20 https://carm.org/salvation-according-watchtower-organization-part-1

21 Reed, David A., *Answering Jehovah's Witnesses: Subject by Subject*, (Baker Books, a division of Baker Book House, publishers 1996), pp. 170-171

22 http://www.bible.ca/trinity/trinity-Mantey.htm

23 https://mbcpathway.com/2015/12/21/four-examples-of-where-the-new-world-translation-gets-it-wrong/

24 https://www.jehovahs-witness.com/topic/53827/new-world-translation-errors?page=7

25 http://www.bible.ca/Jw-NWT.htm

26 Rhodes, Ron, *The Complete Guide to Bible Translations*, (Harvest House Publishers 2009), p. 250

27 Van Baalen, *Chaos*, *op. cit., pp. 39-44*

28 Reagan, David R., *Living for Christ in the End Times*, (Lamb and Lion Ministries 2000), p. 42

29 Ibid.

30 Schuller Robert, *Self Esteem: New Reformation* (W Pub Group, June 1, 1982), p.75

31 https://www.pbs.org/wgbh/pages/frontline/shows/religion/maps/primary/gthomas.html

32 Reagan, *Living*, op. cit., pp. 46-47

33 *The Midnight Cry* is a song written by Chuck and Greg Day in 1986

34 https://christinprophecy.org/?s=Carl+Sandburg+ Epistle

35 *Lamplighter*, Vol. XVI, No.7, September 1995, p.3, reprinted from a book entitled *365 Meditations for Grandmothers*, (Dimensions for Living September 1, 2006)

36 https://timothytennent.com/2009/11/13/for-such-a-time-as-this/

CPSIA information can be obtained
at www.ICGtesting.com
Printed in the USA
BVHW050113231120
593941BV00008B/289